QUALITATIVE
RESEARCH

SAGE was founded in 1965 by Sara Miller McCune to support the dissemination of usable knowledge by publishing innovative and high-quality research and teaching content. Today, we publish over 900 journals, including those of more than 400 learned societies, more than 800 new books per year, and a growing range of library products including archives, data, case studies, reports, and video. SAGE remains majority-owned by our founder, and after Sara's lifetime will become owned by a charitable trust that secures our continued independence.

Los Angeles | London | New Delhi | Singapore | Washington DC | Melbourne

QUALITATIVE RESEARCH

Edited by

DAVID SILVERMAN

BUSINESS LIBRARY

Los Angeles | London | New Delhi
Singapore | Washington DC | Melbourne

Los Angeles | London | New Delhi
Singapore | Washington DC | Melbourne

SAGE Publications Ltd
1 Oliver's Yard
55 City Road
London EC1Y 1SP

SAGE Publications Inc.
2455 Teller Road
Thousand Oaks, California 91320

SAGE Publications India Pvt Ltd
B 1/I 1 Mohan Cooperative Industrial Area
Mathura Road
New Delhi 110 044

SAGE Publications Asia-Pacific Pte Ltd
3 Church Street
#10-04 Samsung Hub
Singapore 049483

Editor: Mila Steele
Editorial assistant: Alysha Owen
Production editor: Tom Bedford
Copyeditor: Gemma Marren
Proofreader: Audrey Scriven
Marketing manager: Ben Griffin-Sherwood
Cover design: Shaun Mercier
Typeset by: C&M Digitals (P) Ltd, Chennai, India
Printed and bound by CPI Group (UK) Ltd,
Croydon, CR0 4YY

Chapter 1 and Editorial Arrangement © David Silverman 2016
Chapter 2 © Michael Bloor 2016
Chapter 3 © Anne Ryen 2016
Chapter 4 © Jody Miller and Barry Glassner 2016
Chapter 5 © James A. Holstein and Jaber F. Gubrium 2016
Chapter 6 © Sue Wilkinson 2016
Chapter 7 © Giampietro Gobo and Lukas Marciniak 2016
Chapter 8 © Thomas S. Eberle and Christoph Maeder 2016
Chapter 9 © Marie Buscatto 2016
Chapter 10 © Katarina Jacobsson 2016
Chapter 11 © Lindsay Prior 2016
Chapter 12 © Jonathan Potter 2016
Chapter 13 © John Heritage 2016
Chapter 14 © Annette Markham
and Simona Stavrova 2016
Chapter 15 © Nalita James and Hugh Busher 2016
Chapter 16 © Joanne Meredith 2016
Chapter 17 © Johann W. Unger, Ruth Wodak and Majid KhosraviNik 2016
Chapter 18 © Michael Emmison 2016
Chapter 19 © Christian Heath 2016
Chapter 20 © Tim Rapley 2016
Chapter 21 © Kathy Charmaz and Antony Bryant 2016
Chapter 22 © Catherine Riessman 2016
Chapter 23 © Mary Dixon-Woods 2016
Chapter 24 © Libby Bishop 2016
Chapter 25 © Anssi Peräkylä 2016
Chapter 26 © Amir Marvasti 2016

First edition published 1997. Reprinted 2003
Second edition published 2004. Reprinted 2006 (twice), 2008, 2009
Third edition published 2011. Reprinted 2011 (twice)

Library of Congress Control Number: 2015955183

British Library Cataloguing in Publication data

A catalogue record for this book is available from the British Library

ISBN 978-1-4739-1656-2
ISBN 978-1-4739-1657-9 (pbk)

At SAGE we take sustainability seriously. Most of our products are printed in the UK using FSC papers and boards. When we print overseas we ensure sustainable papers are used as measured by the PREPS grading system. We undertake an annual audit to monitor our sustainability.

For Helen, Renee, Louise, Laurence, Sam, Alan, Jacob and Ashley and all my other friends on the first floor, Lady Sarah Cohen Home, Friern Barnet, London

Contents

The Editor and Contributors

David Silverman is Emeritus Professor of Sociology at Goldsmiths' College, London, Visiting Professor at the Management Department, King's College, London, UK, and the Business School, University of Technology, Sydney, and Adjunct Professor, Education Faculty, Queensland University of Technology, Australia. His research interests focus on medical encounters. He is the author of many textbooks on qualitative research and runs workshops in qualitative research for PhD students and faculty in several European and Australian universities.

Libby Bishop (PhD) is a Manager for Producer Relations at the UK Data Archive, University of Essex, UK. She provides support and training on data management to researchers and data producers, with specialization in consent, confidentiality, anonymization and secure access to data. She also teaches workshops on secondary analysis of qualitative data. Individually and with others, she has published on data management and qualitative secondary analysis, including a book, *Managing and Sharing Research Data* (Sage, 2014), and has a forthcoming article on ethical issues in using big data.

Michael Bloor was until recently a Professorial Fellow at the Seafarers International Research Centre in Cardiff University's School of Social Sciences, UK. His books include *Keywords in Qualitative Methods* (with Fiona Wood, Sage, 2006) and *Focus Groups in Social Research* (with Jane Frankland, Michelle Thomas and Kate Robson, Sage, 2001). He retired in 2013.

Antony Bryant is currently Professor of Informatics at Leeds Beckett University, UK. His research includes investigation of the ways in which the Open Source model might be used more widely, and in particular how it can be developed as a contributory feature for the reconstructed financial sector in the wake of the economic meltdown; coining the term *Mutuality 2.0* and developing the concept in various contexts. He has written extensively on research methods, being Senior Editor of *The SAGE Handbook of Grounded Theory* (co-edited with Kathy Charmaz, Sage, 2007). A new, companion edition is currently in the early stages of preparation. His book *Grounded Theory and Grounded Theorizing* is due to be published in 2016 by Oxford University Press.

Marie Buscatto is a Professor of Sociology at the University of Paris 1 Pantheon Sorbonne, France. She is a sociologist of work, of gender and of arts. She also develops epistemological reflections related to the uses of ethnography. Her recent publications in English include the special edition of *Qualitative Sociology Review*, 3 (3), 'Ethnographies of artistic work' (co-edited with Howard S. Becker, 2007); the chapters 'Artistic practices as gendered practices: ways and reasons' (in T. Zembylas (ed.) *Artistic Practices*, London, Routledge, 2014, 44–55) and 'Trying to get in, getting in, staying in: the three challenges for women jazz musicians' (in J. Halley and D. Sonolet (dir.) *Bourdieu in Question: Recent Developments in French Sociology of Art*, forthcoming).

Hugh Busher (PhD) is a Senior Lecturer in Education in the School of Education, University of Leicester, UK. He has published extensively in areas of qualitative research that includes critical perspectives on people, power and culture in education-based communities, representations of students' and teachers' voices and identities, and hybrid learning communities. His books include *Online Interviewing* (co-authored with Nalita James, Sage, 2009).

Kathy Charmaz is Professor of Sociology and Director of the Faculty Writing Program at Sonoma State University, USA. She has written, co-authored or co-edited 14 books including two award-winning works, *Good Days, Bad Days: The Self in Chronic Illness and Time* (Rutgers University Press, 1991) and *Constructing Grounded Theory* (Sage, 2006), which has been translated into Chinese, Japanese, Korean, Polish and Portuguese. The much-expanded second edition of *Constructing Grounded Theory* came out in 2014, as did a co-edited Sage Benchmarks in Social Research Methods *Grounded Theory and Situational Analysis* (four-volume set) with Adele Clarke. Professor Charmaz lectures and leads workshops around the globe on grounded theory, qualitative methods, writing for publication, medical sociology and symbolic interactionism.

Mary Dixon-Woods (DPhil) is Professor of Medical Sociology at the University of Leicester, UK, and Deputy Editor of *BMJ Quality & Safety*. She holds visiting or honorary appointments at Johns Hopkins University, Imperial College London, and Dartmouth College. A fellow of both the Academy of Social Sciences and the Academy of Medical Sciences, she has interests in social science research methods, ethics, and quality and safety in healthcare.

Thomas S. Eberle is Professor Emeritus of Sociology and former director of the Institute of Sociology at the University of St Gallen, Switzerland. His research areas are the sociology of culture and of organization, phenomenology and ethnomethodology, methodology and qualitative methods. Recent publications include 'Phenomenology as a research method' (*The Sage Handbook of Qualitative Data Analysis*, 2014); 'Exploring another's subjective life-world: a phenomenological approach' (*Journal of Contemporary of Contemporary*

Ethnography, 2015); 'Qualitative cultural sociology' (*The Sage Handbook of Cultural Sociology*, 2016); 'Organizational memories – a phenomenological analysis' (*The Routledge International Handbook of Memory Studies*, 2016); *Fotografie und Gesellschaft* (transcript, 2016).

Michael Emmison is an Honorary Research Fellow and formerly Reader in Sociology in the School of Social Sciences, University of Queensland, Australia. His interests are primarily in the area of visual research methods and language and social interaction, and his current research deals with advice seeking on a number of helplines. His previous books include *Accounting for Tastes: Australian Everyday Cultures* (with Tony Bennett and John Frow, Cambridge, 1999), *Researching the Visual* (2nd edn) (with Philip Smith and Margery Mayall, Sage, 2013), and the co-edited collection *Calling for Help: Language and Social Interaction in Telephone Helplines* (John Benjamins, 2005).

Barry Glassner is Professor of Sociology and President of Lewis & Clark College in Portland Oregon, USA. His books include *The Culture of Fear* (Basic Books, 1999), *The Gospel of Food* (HarperCollins, 2007) and *Bodies* (Lowell House, 1992). He has published scholarly articles and commentaries in publications including *American Sociological Review*, *Contemporary Sociology*, the *New York Times* and the *Wall Street Journal*.

Giampietro Gobo is Professor of Methodology of Social Research and Evaluation Methods, and former Director of the centre ICONA (Innovation and Organizational Change in Public Administration), at the University of Milan, Italy. He has published extensively in the areas of qualitative and quantitative methods. His books include *Doing Ethnography* (Sage, 2008), *Qualitative Research Practice* (co-edited with C. Seale, J. F. Gubrium and D. Silverman, Sage, 2004) and *Constructing Survey Data: An Interactional Approach* (with S. Mauceri, Sage, 2014).

Jaber F. Gubrium is Professor and Chair of Sociology at the University of Missouri, USA. He is an ethnographer and conducts research on the narrative organization of service and care in people-processing institutions. Interest in discursive practice and intertextuality has been applied in representing the everyday contours of professional work in nursing homes, physical rehabilitation, mental health, dementia and residential treatment for emotionally disturbed children. He is currently collaborating with Norwegian colleagues in a project that aims to reimagine the service relationship as a social form.

Christian Heath is Professor of Work & Organisation at King's College, London, UK, and Co-Director of the Work, Interaction and Technology Research Group. Drawing on ethnomethodology and conversation analysis, he is currently undertaking video-based studies of operating theatres, markets, and museums and galleries. His publications include *Body Movement and Speech in Medical Interaction* (Cambridge 1986), *Technology in Action* (with Paul Luff, Cambridge, 2000), *Video and Qualitative Research* (with Jon Hindmarsh and Paul Luff, Sage, 2010) and *The Dynamics of Auction: Social Interaction and the Sale of Fine Art and Antiques* (Cambridge, 2013).

John Heritage is Distinguished Professor of Sociology at UCLA, USA. His research focuses on social interaction and its interface with social institutions, with particular reference to medicine and mass communication. His publications include *Garfinkel and Ethnomethodology* (Polity Press, 1984), *Structures of Social Action* (co-edited with Max Atkinson, Cambridge University Press, 1984), *Talk at Work* (co-edited with Paul Drew, Cambridge University Press,1992), *The News Interview: Journalists and Public Figures on the Air* (with Steven Clayman, Cambridge University Press, 2002), *Communication in Medical Care* (co-edited with Douglas Maynard, Cambridge University Press, 2006), and *Talk in Action: Interactions, Identities, and Institutions* (with Steven Clayman, Wiley Blackwell, 2010).

James A. Holstein is Professor of Sociology in the Department of Social and Cultural Sciences at Marquette University, USA. He has written extensively on various aspects of qualitative inquiry. Collaborating with Jaber F. Gubrium, he has published *Varieties of Narrative Analysis* (Sage, 2012), *Analyzing Narrative Reality* (Sage, 2009), *The New Language of Qualitative Method* (Oxford University Press, 1997), *The Active Interview* (Sage, 1995), *Handbook of Constructionist Research* (Guildford, 2008), and *Handbook of Interview Research* (Sage, 2012). His most recent book (with Richard Jones and George Koonce) is *Is There Life After Football? Surviving the NFL* (New York University Press, 2015).

Katarina Jacobsson is Professor at the School of Social Work, Lund University, Sweden. Her current project deals with documenting practices among human service workers. A selection of previous work include studies of bribery ('Accounts of honesty' in *Deviant Behavior*, 2012) and medical staff's categorization work ('Categories by heart' in *Professions and Professionalism*, 2014). A methodological text, 'Interviewees with an agenda' (with M. Åkerström), is published in *Qualitative Research* (2013).

Nalita James (EdD) is a Senior Lecturer in Lifelong Learning in the Vaughan Centre for Lifelong Learning, University of Leicester, UK. She specialises in qualitative research on access and participation in higher education and learning communities and identity. She has published extensively in the area of qualitative online research and co-authored *Online Interviewing* (with Hugh Busher, Sage, 2009).

Majid KhosraviNik is a Lecturer in Media and Discourse Studies and Director of MA programmes in Media at Newcastle University, UK. He is interested in the theory, methods and application of critical discourse studies in a range of topics and media discourses including the intersection of discourse and (national/ethnic/group) identity. He has previously published widely on immigration identity discourses in mass media. Within the past few years, he has been working on the theory and application of CDA on digital media, e.g. social media. He sits on the boards of a number of international journals, including *Critical Discourse Studies* and *Journal of Language and Politics*, and is a co-founder of the Newcastle Discourse Group. Publications include *Right-Wing Populism in Europe: Politics and Discourse* (co-edited with Ruth Wodak and Brigitte Mral, Bloomsbury Academic, 2013) and his new book *Discourse, Identity and Legitimacy* (John Benjamins DAPSAC series, forthcoming).

Christoph Maeder is Professor of Sociology at the University of Education Zurich, Switzerland. He specialises in ethnographic research on 'people-processing organizations' such as schools, welfare bureaucracies, prisons and hospitals. His most recent publication in English is on the use of computer technology in the classroom in a primary school.

Lukas Marciniak is Associate Professor at Lodz University, Poland, and Director of the Research & Development Laboratory (PRK). He specialises in field research and the study of social interaction and his interests focus mostly on professional identity, economic phenomena and tacit knowledge-sharing practices. He has recently published studies of street vendors' activity, market competition, and coaching and counselling encounters. He is in favour of applied social sciences based on qualitative approaches.

Annette Markham is Associate Professor of Information Studies at Aarhus University, Denmark and Affiliate Professor of Digital Ethics in the School of Communication at Loyola University, Chicago, USA. She is internationally recognized for her research on innovative qualitative methodologies for studying digital sociality and ethics of social research and interaction design. Her work can be found in a range of international journals, handbooks and edited collections. Her books include *Life Online: Researching Real Experience in Virtual Space* (Altamira, 1998) and *Internet Inquiry: Conversations about Method* (co-edited with Nancy Baym, Sage, 2009).

Amir Marvasti is Associate Professor of Sociology at Penn State University, Altoona, USA. His research focuses on the social construction of identity in everyday encounters and institutional settings. He also has an active publication record on the pedagogy of qualitative research. His books in this area include *Qualitative Research in Sociology* (Sage, 2004) and *Doing Qualitative Research: A Comprehensive Guide* (with David Silverman, Sage, 2008).

Joanne Meredith is a Lecturer in Psychology at the University of Salford, Manchester, UK. She specialises in using interactional methods, including conversation analysis and discursive psychology, for online communication. Her research has focused predominantly on studies of instant messaging communication, and comparing these interactions to other forms of interaction. She is also interested in developing new and innovative methods for collecting qualitative data from online sources.

Jody Miller is a professor in the School of Criminal Justice at Rutgers University, USA. Her research utilises qualitative methods to investigate how inequalities of gender, race, sexuality and place shape participation in crime and risks for victimization. Her books include the award-winning *Getting Played: African American Girls, Urban Inequality, and Gendered*

Violence (NYU Press, 2008) and *One of the Guys: Girls, Gangs, and Gender* (Oxford University Press, 2001). Miller is a Fellow of the American Society of Criminology.

Anssi Peräkylä is Professor of Sociology at the University of Helsinki, Finland, and Vice-Director of the Finnish Centre of Excellence in Research on Intersubjectivity. His publications include *Conversation Analysis and Psychotherapy* (co-edited with C. Antaki, S. Vehviläinen and I. Leudar, Cambridge University Press, 2008) and *Emotion in Interaction* (co-edited with M.-L. Sorjonen, Oxford University Press, 2012).

Jonathan Potter is Distinguished Professor and Dean of the School of Communication and Information at Rutgers University, USA. He has developed the field of discursive psychology through a number of books and articles and is known for his contributions to the rigorous analysis of qualitative data.

Lindsay Prior is a Professor Emeritus in the Centre of Excellence for Public Health at Queen's University, Belfast, UK. Previous publications include a four-volume edited collection, *Using Documents and Records in Social Research* (Sage, 2011) and *Using Documents in Social Research* (Sage, 2003). He is currently writing a book on exploratory methods in social research.

Tim Rapley is a Senior Lecturer at the Institute of Health and Society, Newcastle University, UK. He has written a book, *Doing Conversation, Discourse and Document Analysis* (Sage, 2007), and keeps contemplating writing another one on qualitative data analysis.

Catherine Kohler Riessman is a medical sociologist and Emerita Professor at Boston University, USA. She has also served as Research Professor in the Sociology Department at Boston College. Her most recent book is *Narrative Methods for the Human Sciences* (Sage, 2008). Throughout a long career she has studied and compared the narratives women and men develop to account for biographical disruptions, including divorce, infertility and chronic illness in mid-life. The author of many journal articles and book chapters in recent years, her early books include *Divorce Talk* (Rutgers University Press, 1990) and *Narrative Analysis* (Sage, 1993). She has been awarded Leverhulme, British Academy and Fulbright fellowships and has served as a visiting professor at the University of London, Victoria University in Melbourne, and the University of Western Sydney in Australia.

Anne Ryen is Professor of Sociology at University of Agder, Norway. She has been doing research in East Africa for more than two decades and was leader of a research programme with Mzumbe University, Tanzania. She is now a member of the Management Committee of the pan-European COST Action on Femicide across Europe and active in the working group on culture. She has published extensively in books and journals in Africa, Europe and the US, in particular on qualitative methodology and research ethics in cross-cultural contexts.

Simona Stavrova is a researcher of information studies and digital culture at Aarhus University, Denmark. Her research focuses on how identity practices are constrained and enabled by digital platforms, algorithms and other structural aspects of the internet. She received her MA in international business communication and is completing a second MA in digital living/information studies.

Johann W. Unger is a lecturer and Academic Director of Summer Programmes in the Department of Linguistics and English Language at Lancaster University, UK. He researches mainly in the areas of language policy and digitally mediated politics from a critical discourse studies perspective. His recent publications include 'Rebranding the Scottish Executive' in the *Journal of Language and Politics* (2013), the book *The Discursive Construction of Scots: Education, Politics and Everyday Life* (John Benjamins, 2013), the co-edited book *Multilingual Encounters in Europe's Institutional Spaces* (Bloomsbury, 2014), and the co-authored textbook *Researching Language and Social Media: A Student Guide* (Routledge, 2014). He is an editor of the book series Discourse Approaches to Politics, Society and Culture.

Sue Wilkinson is Professor of Feminist and Health Research in the Department of Social Sciences at Loughborough University, UK. She has published widely in the areas of gender, sexuality, health and qualitative methods. Her current research uses conversation analysis to examine helpline interactions, and she is particularly interested in the practices and actions of conversational 'repair'.

Ruth Wodak is Distinguished Professor of Discourse Studies at Lancaster University, UK. Her research interests focus on discourse studies, identity politics, language and/ in politics, prejudice and discrimination. She is co-editor of the journals *Discourse & Society*, *Critical Discourse Studies* and *Language and Politics*. Recent book publications include *The Politics of Fear: What Right-Wing Populist Discourses Mean* (Sage, 2015), *Analysing Fascist Discourse: European Fascism in Talk and Text* (with John Richardson, Routledge, 2013), *Right-Wing Populism in Europe: Politics and Discourse* (with Majid KhosraviNik and Brigitte Mral, Bloomsbury Academic, 2013) and *The Discourse of Politics in Action: Politics as Usual* (Palgrave, 2011).

PART I
SETTING THE SCENE

This introductory section seeks to provide the context for the topics discussed in this book. It asks: why does qualitative research matter and by whom should it be judged?

In the six years since the third edition of this book appeared, qualitative researchers have increasingly acknowledged that we live in an electronic, digitally mediated age. This new edition, therefore, now devotes a vastly expanded section to the new technologies emerging from the internet. Chapter 1 outlines these and other changes to this book. It also argues that qualitative research is not simply a set of techniques but a theoretically driven enterprise, different from but complementary to quantitative research.

Michael Bloor's chapter locates qualitative research within the wider community. It asks whether we should or can influence how society works. Bloor's concern with the responsibility of researchers is taken up by Anne Ryen's chapter on research ethics. She shows that working in the field involves emergent ethical dilemmas which are different from survey research and cannot be sorted out at the outset. This means that the underlying biomedical model of most guidelines with their 'audit culture' may unduly simplify the social world as understood by qualitative researchers.

ONE
Introducing Qualitative Research
David Silverman

This book provides a guide to the latest developments in qualitative research written by internationally recognized authors in their field. It sets out to overcome several erroneous assumptions about our field that may confuse the beginning researcher:

- that doing research is purely a matter of learning a few techniques and hence that research methods are atheoretical
- that qualitative research (QR) is in competition with quantitative research
- that QR is just about understanding people's 'experiences'
- that anything goes in QR (i.e. QR is not rigorous).

I have selected authors who disagree with many of these assumptions. Most of them agree with me that:

- QR is a theoretically driven enterprise
- QR complements quantitative research in particular by entering into the 'black box' of how social phenomena are constituted in real time
- QR is as much about social practices as about experience
- QR is, or should be, a credible, rigorous enterprise.

This edition offers a newly updated introduction to such cutting edge issues, written by leading scholars in our field. Chapters from the third edition have been revised and updated by their distinguished authors. In addition, reflecting the changing face of qualitative research, the book has been transformed in the following ways:

- New technologies and new sources of data have emerged in the past few years, particularly in relation to electronic data. To reflect this, three new chapters on analysing internet data have been written by recognized authorities in this field (Chapters 15-17).
- Eight new authors, outstanding scholars in their field, have written brilliant original chapters (Chapters 10, 15-17 and 24).
- An exciting new chapter has been written to reflect the important issue of how ethnographers engage in the 'field' (Chapter 9 on 'reflexivity').
- Chapter 25 now discusses the validity of all kinds of qualitative research.
- Chapter 26 on 'writing' now includes a discussion of online publishing.
- To ensure even greater reader-friendliness, each chapter now includes summary boxes throughout. Each chapter ends with a discussion of future prospects, study questions and an annotated list of recommended reading and internet links.
- In recognition of their importance, chapters on ethics and the practical application of qualitative research are now placed immediately after this Introduction.

Like earlier editions, this text is supported by a number of assumptions set out below:

1. The centrality of the relationship between analytic perspectives and methodological issues and the consequent requirement to go beyond a purely 'cookbook' version of research methods.
2. The need to broaden our conception of qualitative research beyond issues of subjective 'meaning' and towards issues of language, representation and social organization.
3. The desire to search for ways of building links between social science traditions rather than dwelling in 'armed camps' fighting internal battles.
4. The belief that a social science, which takes seriously the attempt to sort fact from fancy, remains a valid enterprise.
5. The assumption that we no longer need to regard qualitative research as provisional or never based on initial hypotheses. This is because qualitative studies have already assembled a usable, cumulative body of knowledge.
6. The commitment to a dialogue between social science and the community based on a recognition of their different starting points rather than upon a facile acceptance of topics defined by what are taken to be 'social problems'.

Each of these assumptions is, implicitly or explicitly, highly contested within contemporary qualitative research. This is largely, I believe, because such research has become a terrain on which diverse schools of social theory have fought their mock battles. Ultimately, the assumptions set out here try to move the terrain of our field towards an analysis of the everyday resources which we use in making our observations. This point, which is implicit in many of these contributions, is set out in detail in *A Very Short, Fairly Interesting, Reasonably Cheap Book about Qualitative Research* (Silverman, 2011).

Of course, avoiding such battles, while being committed to a cumulative social science, is far more likely to make our trade appear relevant to the wider community. As we look outwards rather than inwards, with confidence rather than despair, the way is open for a fruitful dialogue between social scientists, organizations, professionals and community groups.

Moreover, it is worth noting that we present ourselves not only to the wider community but also to the students we teach. Like my two other books, *Doing Qualitative Research*

(2013) and *Interpreting Qualitative Data* (2015), *Qualitative Research* derives from 30 years of teaching methodology courses and supervising research projects at both undergraduate and graduate levels. That experience has reinforced the wisdom of the old maxim that true learning is based upon doing. In practice, this means that I approach taught courses as workshops in which students are given skills to analyse data and so to learn the craft of our trade. Like many contemporary teachers, I believe that assessments of students' progress are properly done through data exercises rather than the conventional essay in which students are invited to offer wooden accounts of what other people have written.

It follows that I have little time for the conventional trajectory of the PhD in which students spend their first year 'reviewing the literature', gather data in year two and then panic in year three about how they can analyse their data. Instead, my students begin their data analysis in year one – sometimes in week one. In that way, they may well have 'cracked' the basic problem in their research in that first year and so can spend their remaining years pursuing the worthy but relatively non-problematic tasks of ploughing through their data following an already established method.

My hope is that this book will be used by students who are not yet familiar with the approaches involved, their theoretical underpinnings and their research practice. Worked through examples of research studies and study questions make the arguments accessible. Moreover, the chapters are not written in standard edited collection style as chapters addressed to the contributors' peers but inaccessible to a student audience. This means that the presentation is didactic but not 'cookbook' in style.

The particular contribution of this reader lies in its assembly of a very well-known, international team of researchers who share my commitment to rigorous, analytically derived but non-polarized qualitative research. Nine US-based researchers join 15 from the UK, two from Switzerland and Denmark, and one each from France, Sweden, Poland, Italy, Norway, Finland and Australia. While the majority of the contributors are sociologists, psychology, feminist studies, health, education, communication, social work, media studies, socio-legal studies and linguistics are also represented. In any event, I believe that all contributors have succeeded in making their presentations accessible to a multidisciplinary audience.

Each author has written a chapter which reflects on the analysis of each of the kinds of data discussed in *Interpreting Qualitative Data*: observations, texts, talk, visual and digital data, focus groups and interviews. Each uses particular examples of data analysis to advance analytic arguments. Rather than denying their own analytic position in favour of some woolly centre ground, my authors have clearly set out the assumptions from which they proceed while remaining open to the diverse interests of their diverse audiences.

One audience for our research may be policy-makers, practitioners, clients or research subjects. The first section of this book positions qualitative research within the wider community. Michael Bloor's chapter deals with a topic that concerns most qualitative researchers: the ability of our research to contribute to addressing social problems. Bloor argues that our focus on everyday activities makes it particularly relevant in helping practitioners to think about their working practices. He demonstrates his argument by detailed discussions of case studies which he conducted of male prostitutes in Glasgow and of the health of sailors. Both sets of studies illustrate Bloor's point about the ways in which rigorous qualitative research can have relevance for service provision, even if, at least in Britain, it is unlikely to have much impact upon policy debates at the governmental level. Finally, Bloor reviews (and rejects) the argument that social scientists should not be practitioners' helpers.

The next chapter by Anne Ryen addresses how ethical issues arise within qualitative research. As she shows, ethics involves many more interesting matters than the tedious business of form-filling in order to satisfy ethical review committees about 'informed consent', 'confidentiality' and 'trust'. Our search for 'rich' data can mean that we organize long stays in the 'field'. Ryen uses her data from research on Asian businesses in East Africa to illustrate and discuss the complexity of research ethics in ethnography. Working in the field involves emergent ethical dilemmas which are different from survey research and cannot be sorted out at the outset. This means that the underlying biomedical model of most guidelines with their 'audit culture' may unduly simplify the social world as understood by qualitative researchers. Instead, we must unpick difficult issues involved in the ethics and politics of matters like rapport, intrusion and harm. As she concludes: 'Qualitative research calls for moral responsibility in a field scattered with dilemmas not for quick pre-fixed answers'.

Following Ryen's reminder of the importance of the researcher–researched relationship, the three chapters in Part II on interviews and focus groups show us that both respondents and social scientists actively construct meaning in each other's talk. Jody Miller and Barry Glassner address the issue of finding 'reality' in interview accounts. I argue in *Interpreting Qualitative Data* that the desire of many researchers to treat interview data as more or less straightforward 'pictures' of an external reality can fail to understand how that 'reality' is being represented in words. Miller and Glassner set out a position which seeks to move beyond this argument about the 'inside' and the 'outside' of interview accounts. They draw upon their research on gender inequality in youth gangs and on violence against African American young women in urban neighbourhoods. Based upon this research, they argue that interview accounts may fruitfully be treated as situated elements in adolescents' social worlds, drawing upon and revising and reframing the cultural stories available in those worlds. For Miller and Glassner, the focus of interview research should be fixed upon what stories are told and how and where they are produced.

In their chapter, James Holstein and Jaber Gubrium show us how a focus on story and narrative structure demands that we recognize that both interview data and interview analysis are active occasions in which meanings are produced. This means that we ought to view research 'subjects' not as stable entities but as actively constructed through their answers. Indeed, in Holstein and Gubrium's telling phrase, both interviewee and interviewer are 'practitioners of everyday life' who 'animate' the interview. As they put it: '*all* interviews are active, despite attempts to regiment, standardize, and neutralize the interview process'. Thus the issue that should confront qualitative researchers is not whether interview accounts are 'distorted' but the interpretive practices present within each interview.

They then invite us to locate the interpretive practices which generate the 'hows' and the 'whats' of experience as aspects of reality that are constructed in collaboration with the interviewer to produce a 'narrative drama'.

Sue Wilkinson's chapter on focus groups carries forward Holstein and Gubrium's concern with how we construct the social world with our respondents. Using illuminating extracts from her own data on breast cancer patients, Wilkinson reveals the complicated interpretive activities between members of focus groups as they try to make sense of each other (and the researcher). This close attention to the details of data is contrasted with how most focus group (and interview) research is usually conducted. Wilkinson's concern with theoretically driven, detailed data analysis stands apart from the dominant tendency to treat focus group talk as a straightforward means of accessing some independent 'reality'. Above all, Wilkinson shows us that content analysis and a concentration on the mechanics of how to run a focus group are no substitute for theoretically informed and detailed data analysis of talk-in-action. Like all the contributors to this volume, Wilkinson underlines the fact that we must never overlook the active interpretive skills of our research subjects.

The three chapters on ethnography seek to rescue observational work from the pitfalls of mere 'description' and lazy coding and move towards exciting methodological and analytic directions for observational research. In Chapter 7, Giampietro Gobo and Lukas Marciniak show how observation is the basic tool of ethnographers. They provide a useful history of ethnographic studies brought up to date by contemporary participative and critical ethnographies. They demonstrate why, if we want to understand behaviour and interaction, it is not enough to ask questions. We must also observe the routines and practices of social actors. And we can do this reliably and consistently. Moreover, as they note, ethnography, like any other methodology, is not simply an instrument of data collection. It is born at a particular moment in the history of society and embodies certain of its cultural features. Gobo's concept of the 'observation society' focuses upon why ethnography has come into fashion.

Thomas Eberle and Christoph Maeder's chapter gives us more specific insights into how ethnographers go about studying organizations. As they argue, abstract organization theory is not a necessary starting point for research and there is a continuum between theory- and data-guided ethnographic studies. Their chapter contains some illuminating case studies which demonstrate the methodological strengths of observing routine practices within organizations. They conclude with a helpful account of practical considerations in doing organizational ethnography such as field access and participation, data collection and data analysis, informant and field relations, reporting back, ethical questions and finally writing up.

If ethnography is not merely a timeless technique but positioned in time and place, how can it be credible? As Marie Buscatto asks: 'how can we guarantee that researchers do not become travellers, journalists or autobiographical novelists while at the same time ensuring that they are not constrained to practise ill-adapted procedures and investigation methods following an inept positive method?'. She shows that a recognition of the observer's involvement in the field she studies is (or should be) a commonplace of all research. Her chapter on reflexivity calls for a balance between 'involvement' and 'detachment'. She helpfully sets out three principles of ethnographic detachment using cogent examples from her research on female jazz singers and musicians and an insurance company.

Part IV on 'texts' shows how the analysis of texts and documents can fruitfully work within a diverse set of analytic traditions. Both chapters in Part IV contest the majority view of documentary data in sociology and qualitative research that documents are detached from social action As Katarina Jacobsson remarks: 'ethnographic methods can advance our knowledge of a setting through its documents as well as help the researcher to grasp a document in its setting'. Her chapter shows how observing what people do with documents is just as important as analysing document content. She uses several fascinating case studies to demonstrate how we can study the ways in which documents are produced and used in particular social and economic contexts.

Unlike the stultifying theoretical level of some introductions to this topic, Prior has written a delightful, accessible chapter which develops Jacobsson's arguments about what happens when people 'do things with documents'. Avoiding references to a knowing 'subject', Prior shows us how we can instead focus on the ways in which a text instructs us to see the world. Using examples as diverse as a statistical summary of prevalence rates of mental illness and airline pilots' pre-take-off check lists, he reveals a thought-provoking toolbox that we can use when working with textual material.

Part V is concerned with audio data. Jonathan Potter discusses 'discursive psychology', more commonly known as discourse analysis (DA), as a way of analysing naturally occurring talk. Potter shows the manner in which DA allows us to address how versions of reality are produced to seem objective and separate from the speaker. Using examples drawn from television interviews with Princess Diana and Salman Rushdie and talk from a relationship counselling session, he demonstrates how we can analyse the ways in which speakers disavow a 'stake' in their actions.

For Potter, DA focuses on rhetorical organization in the context of sequential organization. Conversation analysis (CA) is concerned squarely with sequential organization. John Heritage's chapter presents an accessible introduction to how conversation analytic methods can be used in the analysis of everyday interaction. He clearly presents the assumptions and basic principles of CA. From a methodological point of view, Heritage then helpfully sets out the nuts and bolts of doing CA. Using extracts of talk, he shows us how he goes about deciding whether a conversational practice is distinctive, how to locate it in a sequence and then how to determine its role or function. He concludes with a powerful reply to critics who maintain that CA cannot deal with the social context of talk.

In the twenty-first century, however, the internet is as much a place for interaction as face-to-face talk. As the chapters in Part VI reveal, the internet is now perhaps the prime site where words and pictures circulate. Annette Markham and Simona Stavrova's chapter develops this insight and, in so doing, offers readers an invaluable guide to interpreting such data. They point out that the internet not only collapses distance, it also can disrupt the way in which time is relevant to interaction since it can accommodate both asynchronous and synchronous communication between individuals and groups. In this way, social and physical presence are not necessarily connected, and time is a malleable variable of interactions. Markham and Stavrova show the importance of distinguishing research studies which simply use the internet as a tool to gather data (e.g. online interviews) from studies of internet practices and social media networks as phenomena in their own right (e.g. the mechanics of online dating or chatrooms). Following this latter option, we learn, as in the other chapters on texts, how participants actively construct meaning.

Nalita James and Hugh Busher next provide a helpful account of the mechanics of online interviews. They unpick the differences between such interviews which can be textual or visual, asynchronous or synchronous, one-to-one or group. Particularly useful to beginners is their discussion of how to build research relationships to facilitate online interviewing and how researchers can address the particular ethical considerations that can arise when we interview online.

Of course, understanding the mechanics and ethics of gathering data is only half the battle. In some senses, it is much more important to know how to *analyse* your data. Joanne Meredith's chapter addresses this very issue, exploring how to use the specific analytic frames of conversation analysis and discursive psychology (DP) for the analysis of online data. Her chapter begins with a lively address of one data extract and later uses many examples from online forum and instant messaging data to demonstrate the power of these frames to illuminate how participants construct meaning in the context of the opportunities and limits of particular online technologies.

But CA and DP are not the only analytic frames available for analysing online data. The next chapter by Johann W. Unger, Ruth Wodak and Majid KhosraviNik outlines the approach of critical discourse studies (CDS) and suggests how it may be applied to social media data. They helpfully explain what makes digitally mediated data different and interesting for researchers who adopt a critical perspective to social phenomena. Students will also find useful their description of how eight methodological steps from one approach to CDS (the discourse-historical approach) can be applied to social media data. Their case study analysing protest movements (Arab Spring, Occupy) illuminates their discussion.

Unger, Wodak and KhosraviNik's case study nicely leads into Part VII on visual data. Michael Emmison begins by analysing the shift towards involving participants in the generation and analysis of visual data. This leads on to his argument that visual researchers have worked with inadequate theories. For instance, most tend to identify visual data with such artefacts as photographs and, to a lesser extent, cartoons and advertisements. Although such work can be interesting, it is, in a sense, two-dimensional. If we recognize that the visual is also spatial, a whole new set of three-dimensional objects emerge. By looking at how people use objects in the world around them (from streetmaps to the layout of a room or urban street to the design of a hospital), we can study the material embodiment of culture.

Emmison cites Christian Heath's use of video technology to capture interactional conduct as one way of looking at three-dimensional data in fine detail. Like Emmison, Heath differentiates the wide-ranging interest in the 'visual' in sociology and cognate disciplines, from research that uses video recordings to analyse conduct and interaction in everyday, naturalistic settings. Beginning with a clear account of CA's focus on sequential organization, Heath shows how CA can be used to study visual conduct and how the physical properties of human environments are made relevant within the course of social interaction. He argues that the most significant contribution of video-based research has been to our understanding of work and organization through what has become known as 'workplace studies'. Heath uses fascinating audio-visual data from an auction to analyse its unfolding interactional order. Heath also provides highly practical information for students about field relations when using video and how best to record and transcribe such data. He concludes by showing the relevance of these insights to studies of the workplace, including human–computer interaction.

The next section on qualitative data analysis deals with the more 'nuts and bolts' issues of doing qualitative research. Tim Rapley clearly and informally reveals what he calls the 'pragmatics' of qualitative data analysis. As Rapley shows, the hard work begins when we try to explore and explain 'what is "underlying" or "broader" (in our data) or to "distil" essence, meaning, norms, orders, patterns, rules, structures, etc. (the level of concepts and themes)'. Rapley goes on to offer invaluable advice about how to do good qualitative data analysis, emphasizing the importance of detailed readings, reviewing and refining your categories and using your provisional analysis to inform how you collect, transcribe and analyse data when you return to the field. As Rapley argues, good qualitative research is about 'living in the detail'. However, like any good research, we must not rush to offer generalizations but actively seek out contrary cases.

Like Rapley, Kathy Charmaz and Antony Bryant seek to remove the veil from what they call 'the almost magical emergence of theories and concepts from data'. They elucidate the elements of grounded theory (GT) and show what, in their view, has been right and wrong about criticisms of the GT approach. They then go on to demonstrate how grounded theory already contains underused strategies that increase both its methodological power and the credibility of its data analysis. They focus on how GT's key basic strategies engage researchers with their data and emerging analyses. They show how GT can be used to enhance methodological rigour, theoretical promise and the power of the subsequent analysis. Like Rapley, they helpfully explain the nitty-gritty of data analysis from doing line-by-line initial coding, writing memos and conducting theoretical sampling. Using illustrations from their own data analysis, they demonstrate what a 'constructivist' GT methodology can look like in practice, showing how we can achieve analytic and theoretical credibility.

In her chapter on narrative inquiry (NI), Catherine Riessman continues this hands-on, student-friendly approach to the pragmatics of data analysis. Her aim is to distinguish such work from GT and from other methods of analysing interview data. For Riessman, NI, like oral history, is concerned with case-centred research. Hence the leap to broader theories or generalizations is slowed down or even avoided in favour of the interrogation of particular instances, sequences of action, the way participants negotiate language and narrative genres in conversations, and other unique aspects of a 'case'. For Riessman, NI involves resisting what she calls the 'seductive power' of stories. Instead, it asks: why was the story told *that* way? How do narrators position themselves in their stories? What other readings are possible, beyond what the narrator may have intended? Using a long interview, Riessman shows how we can answer these questions by examining the way a segment of data is organized and the local context, including the questioner/listener, setting and position of an utterance in the broader stream of the conversation. Her argument that the research interview is a collaborative conversation ties in nicely with Holstein and Gubrium's earlier chapter on interview data.

As every student is taught, elegant data analysis presupposes a well-defined research topic, based on a review of earlier studies. Mary Dixon-Woods asks how we can make our literature reviews more robust. She distinguishes *aggregative syntheses* which focus on summarizing data from *interpretive syntheses* which involve processes similar to primary qualitative research, in which the concern is with *generating* concepts that have maximum explanatory value. Dixon-Woods clearly evaluates the extent to which the conventional systematic review template is appropriate to the synthesis of qualitative research studies. As she argues, a key question concerns the extent to which conventional systematic review methodology, with its frequent focus on estimating the effectiveness of a particular intervention on average, can be consistent with the aspirations of those aiming to produce more interpretive forms of overview of bodies of research evidence.

From the point of view of the research student, there remains the problem that we can spend so much time on literature reviews that we have too little time to gather and analyse our data. As I suggest in *Doing Qualitative Research*, one quick solution to this problem is to work with secondary data. Libby Bishop helpfully discusses the ethics of using such data and distinguishes the different ways these can be used in research design and methodological development, through re-analysis and re-purposing, to learning and teaching. She shows that the chief reservation expressed about secondary analysis of qualitative data is that secondary analysts will not have the kind of detailed contextual knowledge about the circumstances of data collection possessed by the primary researcher. Bishop argues that this rests in part on an unexamined stereotype of the way analysis of quantitative data sets proceeds. Deriving insights from data does not depend solely on being close to the data, but on judiciously balancing close observation with analytical distance. Moreover, for some research questions, archived data may be analysed with methods and for purposes that do not require in-depth knowledge of context. She supports her argument with case studies of school leavers' essays, migration and parenting, and oral history interviews which show the degree to which general methodological debates are relevant to this form of research practice. Once one gets involved with a data set it is often possible to show the value of secondary analysis without falling into the pitfalls imagined by the critics. She concludes that she used 'to have to search hard to find high quality examples of reuse; now there are so many I cannot keep up with all the new publications'.

Like Bishop and Dixon-Woods, Anssi Peräkylä is concerned with the credibility of qualitative research. He is particularly interested in how qualitative research can offer reliable and valid descriptions of its data. Following Heritage's chapter, Peräkylä illustrates his argument with CA research. As I argue in Chapter 3 of *A Very Short, Fairly Interesting, Reasonably Cheap Book about Qualitative Research*, paying attention to sequences of data, rather than apparently striking instances, is a hallmark of all good qualitative research rather than something confined to CA. Recognizing that CA is a specialist field, in this newly revised chapter, Peräkylä extends his argument to qualitative research as a whole. Validity questions are discussed in terms of the comparative method and conventional 'deviant case analysis' as well as specifically CA methods, such as validation through 'next turn'. He also demonstrates one way of generalizing from case studies and discusses the uses and limits of quantitative techniques in qualitative research.

Ultimately, good qualitative data analysis is expressed in how well we write. Amir Marvasti argues that novice researchers need to learn the basic skills or craft of writing. In qualitative research, there is no such thing as a format for 'the standard scientific paper'. Marvasti shows that different genres are available to us and describes the stylistic choices available and their advantages and limitations. He also comments upon the strategic choices authors have to consider as they try to publish their work and make it accessible to various audiences. He suggests that a 'perfect paper' is one that strikes a balance between craft skills, genre and intended audience. In this new version of his chapter, Marvasti helpfully outlines the possibilities of online publishing.

Not all of the contributors to this volume are in agreement about every issue. Nonetheless, I believe that my authors share enough in common to make this a coherent volume. Many, I suspect, would agree with most of the six points listed earlier in this chapter. With more certainty, I would claim that we share a fairly common sense of what constitutes 'good' qualitative research. For instance, even though we come from different intellectual traditions, I would be surprised if we were to have any fundamental disagreement about, say, the assessment of an article submitted to us for refereeing. This common sense of what we are 'looking for' derives, I believe, from our common commitment to qualitative research as a theoretically based and rigorous methodology, responsive to ethical considerations and to our various audiences.

I would like to express my gratitude to my contributors for tolerating my schoolmasterly messages about deadlines and for the brilliant work they did in offering suggestions on each other's draft chapters. I thank my Sage Editor, Mila Steele, for her helpful suggestions about this volume. As always, my thanks are also due to Gillian for putting up with me, to Sara Cordell for keeping my back in working order, and to my friends at the Nursery End, Lord's, and at the SCG for giving me northern and Antipodean summers to which I can look forward.

YOUR GUIDE TO *QUALITATIVE RESEARCH*

Textbooks work best when their authors aim at the needs of particular groups of students. This guide explains the audience that *Qualitative Research* is aimed at and distinguishes it from my other three textbooks.

I recognize that academic books are not usually read in the same way as novels. For instance, although you may want to resist the temptation to skip to the final chapter of a whodunnit, no such prohibitions are sensible when using a textbook. So, for example, if you are currently having troubles with your data analysis, in this book you may want to begin by reading Tim Rapley's chapter. Each chapter is more or less self-contained and so there should be no problems in zig-zagging through the book in this way.

Zig-zagging also makes sense because qualitative research rarely follows a smooth trajectory from hypothesis to findings. Consequently, most readers will want to move backwards and forwards through the book as the occasion arises. Alternatively, you may find it useful to skim read the book in advance and then work through certain chapters in greater detail to correspond with different stages of your research.

As already noted, all the chapters found here have helpful student-oriented features. However, in my view, certain chapters stand out as particularly relevant to a student audience. So, if you are a novice, you might want to begin by reading Ryen's chapter on research ethics, Gobo's chapter on ethnography, Holstein and Gubrium on interviews, Emmison on visual data, Markham and Stavrova on internet research, Rapley on data analysis and Marvasti on writing.

As an edited book, this is ideal for bright final year students, as well as people beginning masters and doctoral programmes. The most comprehensive qualitative research book available, it is the perfect all-in-one companion for any student embarking on a qualitative research course or project. It introduces students to the big picture of qualitative research, teaching both the 'why' and the 'how to' of getting started, selecting a method and conducting research and data analysis. It is written by world experts of the highest calibre, upfront about their analytic positions, but distilled into an accessible language and format for beginning researchers who will soon be tackling their own research study, whether at an undergraduate or postgraduate level. The particular added value of *Qualitative Research* is that it gives you an entrée into qualitative methods from leading experts in the field who address the needs of students who need to brush up their research skills prior to their own research projects.

By contrast, *Interpreting Qualitative Data* is aimed squarely at undergraduate students, teaching the basic nuts and bolts of different qualitative methods. It offers practical ways to analyse different kinds of qualitative data and shows how to make that analysis credible, ethical and relevant to the outside world.

Doing Qualitative Research is an essential step-by-step guide to carrying out a research study and writing it up effectively, aimed particularly at MA and PhD students. Its unique appeal is that it is based upon multiple examples of actual student projects with helpful advice in each case. It is organized around the steps you will take to complete your research project, starting with research design and leading you through how to collect and analyse your data to writing it all up. This is the book that will guide you from start to finish on your own research project.

By contrast with my other three books, my *A Very Short, Fairly Interesting, Reasonably Cheap Book about Qualitative Research* is aimed at students with enquiring minds at every stage of their studies. Unlike the balanced arguments of a textbook, it is a polemic which, depending upon your position, may stimulate or enrage you.

References

Silverman, D. (2011) *A Very Short, Fairly Interesting, Reasonably Cheap Book about Qualitative Research* (2nd edn). London: Sage.

Silverman, D. (2013) *Doing Qualitative Research* (4th edn). London: Sage

Silverman, D. (2015) *Interpreting Qualitative Data: Methods for Analysing Talk, Text and Interaction* (5th edn). London: Sage.

TWO

Addressing Social Problems through Qualitative Research

Michael Bloor

About this chapter

This chapter explores two case studies which provide illustrative details of different approaches for researchers who wish to address social problems and who are also sceptical of the possibilities of extensive influence among the policy-making community. One case study addresses the attempt to influence practitioners rather than policy-makers and links particularly well with qualitative research methods. An ethnographic research project is viewed as an analogue or partial paradigm of successful practitioner work, in this case outreach work among male prostitutes: in effect, the ethnography may be viewed as a demonstration or pilot outreach project. The second case study is concerned with attempts to address social problems through a direct appeal to the public and illustrates some of the challenges for sociologists in achieving public engagement.

Keywords

ethnography, social problems, practice-relevant research, policy-relevant research, public sociology

SOCIAL RESEARCHERS AS SOCIAL ENGINEERS?

In Carey's (1975) social history of the 'Chicago School' of sociology, he writes that in the 1920s the foremost practitioners of the foremost school of sociology were divided about how sociological knowledge should be applied. Should it be used to influence policy-makers? Or (and here lies a surprise) should sociologists intervene in social problems directly as consulting professionals, like clinicians or architects? Some hundred years earlier Auguste Comte had proposed a similar priestly cadre of sociologists to direct society along enlightened (and Enlightenment) paths. It was the absence of power, rather than humility, which thwarted the would-be social engineers of the 1920s: in Carey's analysis (1975: 71–94), it was the lack of the kind of institutionalized authority which medicine exercises over a lay clientele, rather than any acknowledged deficiency in knowledge or in technical competence, which determined the path along which sociology would develop. Sociologists eventually opted to set out their stalls as scientists rather than professionals, and the West was largely spared the directive intervention of social experts (the peoples of the Soviet Union were less fortunate).

SOCIAL RESEARCHERS AS 'ENLIGHTENERS' OF POLICY-MAKERS?

Since the 1960s, the more limited aspiration of sociologists to influence policy-makers has also been under attack. Various critics pointed out that the policy community rarely sought *policies* from researchers: instead, research would be commissioned to confirm a preferred policy option, or perhaps to delay a necessary but inconvenient intervention. Bulmer (1982), in *The Uses of Social Research*, was one of those who sought to redefine an influential role for social science in the face of these criticisms. Bulmer argued that research cannot directly engineer changes of policy, but it can have an important indirect impact on the policy climate through processes of intellectual association and influence. Silverman (2006) has termed this the 'state counsellor' role and has gently ridiculed how Bulmer's book on 'the uses of social research' turns out to be solely about the uses of social research for policy-makers.

Both the 'enlightenment' and 'engineering' models have been under sustained attack. Becker (1967), for example, posed the rhetorical question 'whose side are we on?' and argued for a partisan sociology that spoke up for the underdogs against the elites, elites which would include policy-makers in their number. And Burawoy's Presidential Address to the American Sociological Association called for a 'public sociology' that addressed a concerned public over the heads of policy-makers (Burawoy, 2005).

Both the followers of the enlightenment and engineering models and their critics have been subject to postmodernist attack. In late-modern society it is no longer universally accepted that planned intervention is capable of bringing about desirable social change, or that scientific knowledge can facilitate this, or that social research can produce such knowledge. Hammersley's (1995) review of these postmodernist criticisms leads him to the assessment that they serve to qualify, rather than demolish, the possibility of an impact for social research: the scope for, and feasibility of, successful policy intervention has been overestimated, and the role of research in bringing change about has been exaggerated and misunderstood, but this does not mean that social improvement is impossible or that knowledge lacks all authority.

A PRACTITIONER AUDIENCE FOR SOCIAL RESEARCH?

The policy community is not the sole audience for qualitative social research. Silverman (2010) has written about the needs of lay audiences for qualitative social research: the general public wants ideas for reform, suggestions on how to manage better and get better services, and assurances that others have shared similar experiences and problems to their own. In addition, sociologists who have conducted research on sociological aspects of health and medicine have long been aware that there are also audiences of practitioners (clinicians and other health professionals) for social research.

Practitioner-oriented social research can take different forms. One possible approach relates to the rich descriptions of practitioner practice that can be found in ethnographic research: through reading reports of ethnographic research on practitioners' everyday working practices, other practitioners can make evaluative judgements of their own practices, experimenting with the adoption of new practices where this seems appropriate. For example, a comparative ethnography of eight different therapeutic communities concluded with a detailed list of seven aspects of successful practice found in one or more of those communities which might be successfully adopted elsewhere (Bloor et al., 1988: 173–85). Relatedly, the close relationships that may occur between ethnographers and practitioner research participants in the course of ethnographic fieldwork may encourage practitioners to 'invest' in the research study and be receptive to suggested possible changes in practice.

This chapter reports in detail on a different approach to practitioner-oriented social research, namely a case study of how street ethnography could act as a possible pilot study for a social work outreach project. The case study in question was a street ethnography of HIV-related risk behaviour among Glasgow male prostitutes. Safer and unsafe commercial sexual encounters were compared: unsafe encounters were found to be associated with control of the sexual encounter by the clients of prostitutes; safer sex was associated with particular techniques of power exercised by prostitutes. These findings indicate possible lines of successful intervention for those engaged in sexual health promotion, while the fieldwork methods and experience offered lessons for the design of outreach work in this area.

Case A: Male prostitutes' HIV-related risk behaviour

The need for services

Prior to the HIV epidemic, targeted services for male prostitutes hardly existed in the UK and did not exist at all in Glasgow. Not all male prostitutes have much need of services, but others have multiple and complex problems (legal problems, health problems, housing problems, financial problems) which are sometimes unnoticed, or inadequately addressed by, service providers. The illegality of male prostitution made specialist service development difficult: most Glasgow male prostitutes contacted in our study were below the then age of consent for homosexual acts and many of those acts did not occur in private; although the police adopted a stance of qualified toleration to female street prostitution, whereby female street prostitution was 'policed' rather than suppressed, that toleration was never extended to male street prostitution.

The HIV epidemic, along with its toll on lives and health, represented an opportunity to change the policy climate in respect of male prostitution. The situation was analogous to that in the drugs services, where a range of services (most notably syringe exchanges) was put in place for existing drug injectors who were not motivated to abstain from drugs. This new drugs policy, which became known as that of 'harm reduction', argued that 'the spread of HIV is a greater danger to individual and public health than drug misuse ... [and that] services that aim to minimize HIV risk behaviour by all available means, should take precedence in development plans' (Advisory Council on the Misuse of Drugs, 1988). In similar fashion, it became possible to argue the case for services targeted at male prostitutes which had as their priority not the elimination of prostitution, but the minimization of individual and public health risks.

Study methods and service provision

The findings and the methodology of the study have been described elsewhere (Bloor, 1995; Bloor et al., 1993). After pilot work, six different sites – two parks, two pubs and two public lavatories – were selected for time-sampling; non-streetworking prostitutes (escorts, masseurs and call men) were contacted through their advertisements and the study's own advertisement in the gay press. The ethnographic fieldwork was conducted in pairs for security purposes. Participants were contacted by a combination of cold-contacting and snowballing. It was recognized from the outset that the fieldwork also offered opportunities for health promotion: relations between fieldworkers and research participants can never be scientifically neutral and an attempt to preserve a fictional neutrality should never be used as an excuse for failing to attempt to save lives. The Greater Glasgow Health Board provided condoms suitable for oral and for anal sex for the researchers to distribute (when the fieldwork started condoms suitable for anal sex were not freely commercially available); an advice leaflet was also handed out which gave advice on HIV prevention and also gave contact numbers for HIV/AIDS counselling and for other relevant services such as welfare rights and homelessness.

Study findings

If the handing-out of condoms and advice leaflets could be thought to generate a 'reporting bias', discouraging the reporting of unsafe commercial sex, then such discouragement can only have been marginal because at least a third of those prostitutes contacted reported unsafe sex with at least some of their current commercial partners (unsafe sex was defined, following the Terrence Higgins Trust, as anal sex with or without a condom, because of the greater risk of condom failure in anal sex). Unsafe commercial sex was associated with client control. In contrast to female street prostitution, where safer commercial sex was almost always practised and the women assumed directive control of the encounter (McKeganey and Barnard, 1992), in many male prostitute–client encounters it was the client who assumed control and decided on matters such as the type of sex and its location. Safer commercial sex among male prostitutes was associated with particular strategies of power to wrest the initiative away from clients. Seeking payment up-front (universally practised by female prostitutes) was one such successful strategy. Getting payment up-front was not popular with the clients, who feared (with some justification) that the prostitute might 'do a runner', but the minority of male prostitutes in the sample who *did* insist on prior payment were all currently practising safer commercial sex.

However, getting the money up-front was not the only successful countervailing strategy of power used by male prostitutes to insist on safer sex. Male prostitution was often a highly covert and ambiguous activity, few words were exchanged and it was not even always clear to both parties that the encounter was a commercial one. Safer sex was likely to be associated with any techniques that served to dispel the ambiguity that surrounded the encounter and made type of sex (and prices) a matter for overt discussion, as in the following field note:

> His procedure was to stand at the urinal. The client would come and stand beside him. When the coast was clear, the client would put out a hand and he would immediately say 'I'm sorry but I charge'. Some would leave at that point. With the remainder he'd negotiate a rate. He would accept 10 pounds but sometimes got 20 pounds ... He always did hand jobs or oral sex ... If clients asked him for anal sex he told them to eff off.

The substitution of overt negotiations between prostitutes and clients for the furtive and largely non-verbal exchanges characteristic of many encounters also had other advantages, including an attendant reduction in the levels of violence surrounding male prostitution. Rapes, muggings and assaults (of clients by prostitutes, of prostitutes by clients and of both prostitutes and clients by 'queer bashing' third parties) were commonplace; during the 16-month fieldwork period, three of our 32 research subjects were charged with assault and a fourth was imprisoned. Many (but not all) of these violent altercations were disputes about money. There were no 'going rates' for the various sexual services on offer: prostitutes took what money they could and, without prior agreement on charges (sometimes without even prior agreement that a charge was to be levied), the scope for violent disputes was considerable, as is illustrated in the following field note:

['Sammy' said he'd] never been cheated out of his money: he'd make sure he always got his money (this was said with a sudden hard emphasis ...). He and 'Kenny' laughingly recalled an altercation with one of 'Colin's' punters [i.e. clients]. Colin was demanding twenty-five pounds and the punter swore he was only due fifteen pounds, refusing to hand over the extra ten pounds. Kenny, in his cynical way, was disinclined to believe Colin, but Sammy said he'd rather believe a mate than some dirty old punter. Sammy had intervened, whipped a knife out and held it in front of his face (this was mimed for our benefit). The punter instantly pulled out the extra cash, shot off and had never been seen at the toilets since.

Implications for service provision

This project had two possible policy pay-offs. First, it indicated how both unsafe commercial sex and violence could be reduced, namely through encouraging male prostitutes to engage in overt negotiations with clients. And, secondly, it indicated a possible medium for that encouragement, namely outreach work associated with condom distribution at regular prostitution sites.

Outreach work, taking services to clients rather than waiting for clients to attend at agencies, is the only means of delivering services to clients who are unable or unwilling to attend agencies. Glasgow had no outreach project targeted at male prostitutes. Ethnographic fieldwork, in its protracted and regular contacts with research subjects, has much in common with services outreach work and it was therefore possible for the ethnographic study to take on the character of a local feasibility study for a male prostitute outreach service, demonstrating to the sceptical that appreciable numbers of male prostitutes were working in Glasgow, that levels of HIV-related risk behaviour were high and that outreach contact could be established. Moreover, the nature of the fieldwork contact that was established augured well for a future outreach service: large quantities of condoms were distributed (to clients as well as prostitutes); even highly socially isolated individuals with no contact with other prostitutes proved contactable; working relationships were established with important local individuals such as bar-owners and managers, toilet attendants and (at an appropriate distance) the police.

Throughout the fieldwork period I had briefed public health personnel, social work staff and AIDS charity workers about project developments and provisional findings. When the fieldwork finished I arranged, with the permission of my research participants, to introduce them to a local social worker who was to be employed as an outreach worker. The introductions were accomplished but the planned outreach post was 'frozen' (along with other local authority posts) owing to a local authority budgetary crisis associated with non-payment of the 'poll tax' (i.e. 'the community charge', a form of local authority taxation that was abandoned soon after its introduction because of widespread unpopularity and widespread non-payment). Nevertheless, the commitment to a male prostitution outreach service had been made and the establishment of such a service was merely postponed, taking place at a later date.

Case B: Public sociology and seafarers' work and training

Not all sociologists conduct research in topic-areas where there are practitioner communities able to implement research findings in their own practices. There is thus a seemingly strong case for researchers to attempt to draw their findings to public attention through newspapers and magazines, broadcast and social media. However, as Silverman has pointed out: 'nearly all social science goes unreported by such media' (Silverman, 2006: 269). Specialist magazines which used to report sociological findings have disappeared. But, in their place, the internet offers an alternative channel of communication between the academy and the public which has great potential. For example, Michael Burawoy (who has made great efforts to promote a 'public sociology' as an antidote to policy-maker disinterest in sociological research) had a 57-minute lecture entitled 'What is public sociology?' uploaded on YouTube in 2012, with 25,000 views 32 months later (Burawoy, 2012).

My second case study is an account of the use of special techniques (and considerable additional effort) to attempt to reach a public audience, with only limited success. The case study concerns an article that was published online in 2012 and in print in January 2013. The article was in the form of a poem, 'The rime of the globalised mariner' (Bloor, 2013), written as a pastiche of Coleridge's famous poem *The Rime of the Ancient Mariner*. Sociological poems are not unknown (see the discussion in Denzin, 1996), but are rare enough to occasion interest and generate publicity. As the 'Rime' ran to 404 lines, it was too long to be published in a poetry magazine. And being from an unpublished poet, it would be most unlikely to attract interest from a book publisher. Fortunately, it was accepted for publication by *Sociology*, the journal of the British Sociological Association (the *American Sociological Review* had turned it down without sending it out to referees).

Study methods

Over a 12-year period I had conducted a series of research projects on seafaring and the shipping industry. Findings from three projects in particular formed the sociological background to 'The rime of the globalised mariner'. Firstly, a comparative study of ship inspections carried out by Port-State Control inspectors in India, Russia and the UK: this involved the observation of 104 ship inspections and 37 semi-structured interviews with inspectors and a range of industry stakeholders (for more details see Bloor et al., 2006). A second study was part of a larger qualitative and quantitative study of training capacity in six major seafarer supply countries. The methods used varied in part between the different countries and depended in part on the size of the maritime education and training field in each of the visited countries. Fuller details are available elsewhere (Bloor and Sampson, 2009) but, in illustration, in one of the major supply countries I visited 18 maritime education and training institutions, conducted nine focus groups with local seafarers, observed two examinations, and interviewed six employers, two staff of national regulatory bodies and one senior examiner. In the third relevant study, I conducted 37 semi-structured interviews with seafarers on the relationship between their work and their health; most of the interviews were conducted in two port missions (which perform an important welfare function and cater for seafarers of all religions and none), while the remainder were conducted while accompanying a port chaplain on ship visits (see Bloor, 2011).

Dissemination of the study findings

The results had been presented by my co-researchers and myself at shipping industry and academic conferences as well as being published in journals; free research reports were available on the website of Cardiff University's Seafarers International Research Centre; policy-makers had been contacted – I had served as a delegate to the International Labour Organisation's Joint Maritime Commission, and I had submitted evidence to the House of Commons Transport Committee. Nevertheless, if I had been asked what the impact of all these reporting efforts had been on seafarers' living and working conditions, I would have had to admit that the impact seemed to be negligible. So I decided to try and publish, as a would-be piece of public sociology, 'The rime of the globalised mariner', which would rework some of those sociological research findings in a novel way.

The poem used Coleridge's ballad format and narrative approach to outline a political economy of the shipping industry: it described the outsourcing of seafarer labour, and the associated threats to the quality of seafarer training, made worse by defective local enforcement of international training standards; it described the defective local regulation by flag-states of seafarers' hours of work and rest and the accompanying fatigue occasioned by the inhuman excessive hours that many seafarers routinely worked; and it suggested that a possible remedy may lie in public pressure on charterers to require ship operators to demonstrate adequate labour standards in the transportation of their goods. The poem used the voices of a Filipino mariner, a late-modern consumer, an inspector and a chorus of Greek shippers; it was in six parts and had 404 lines, a gloss and an afterword. The popular ballad form (rhyming only the even-numbered lines) arguably allows the tackling of even socio-economic issues in readily accessible terms, as when the chorus of Greek shippers speak in their own defence:

> Pay for training? Better wages??
> Remember shipping's quite anarchic:
> We'd love to be more generous
> But you cannot buck the market. (Bloor, 2013: 37)

Articles in the journal *Sociology* can only be freely accessed by subscribers (largely, those with access to university libraries). However, I was able to increase public access by getting the poem published (using my own pdf, not that of the journal) on the website of a seafarers' trade union newspaper, the *Nautilus Telegraph*, which also carried a story about the 'Rime' on its front page. I contacted my university's Media Centre and staff there considered that having a poem published in a respected sociology journal was sufficiently newsworthy for the university's website to carry the story as its lead news item at the time of the online publication. The university's Media Centre put out a press release jointly with the British Sociological Association and the Media Centre also arranged for the production of a five-minute video of the 'Rime' to appear on YouTube. A posting on Facebook also gave a link to the YouTube clip.

I narrate all these details to bring home the point that real efforts were made through various media to generate public interest in the living and working conditions of the million-or-so seafarers working in the international fleet. Two years on, as I write, it is perhaps still premature to make a final judgement on the fruits of those labours, but some interim results can be stated. The press release led to stories on the BBC Wales website and in the international shipping industry's daily newspaper *Lloyds List*. These in turn generated more stories, especially in shipping industry magazines and on shipping industry websites. Several people tweeted about the 'Rime', including a trade union leader. It was also discussed in several blogs. Media coverage of the 'Rime' led to my being invited to take part in a *Dispatches* TV programme on UK's Channel 4 on working conditions in the cruise ship industry. And the print (as opposed to online) publication of the 'Rime' in 2013 led to it being discussed in a five-minute slot on a BBC Radio 4 programme. So there was a reasonable amount of media coverage.

But what about the hoped-for public response? Members of the public rarely contact academic sociologists about their research, so perhaps I should have been satisfied with the trickle of emails (and even a couple of letters) I received. Certainly they were all very positive, but they were all from seafarers and retired seafarers, rather than concerned consumers unhappy with how their goods were being shipped on the high seas. The YouTube clip, to date, has received just 870 views. It rather looks as if the 'Rime', as an exercise in public sociology, has not been a great success. The objective of the 'Rime' was not to show solidarity with over-worked seafarers, but to encourage consumers to put public pressure on the industry to improve labour conditions and training:

> So come all you kind consumers,
> Who the honey'd wine have sipped,
> Take pity on the mariner,
> Beware how your goods are shipped. (Bloor, 2013: 41)

Possibly the mobilization of public opinion is a larger and more difficult task than the average academic is equipped to undertake. Burawoy (2005) makes a distinction between 'traditional public sociology', where the researcher seeks to instigate public debate among an invisible public, and (Burawoy's preferred alternative) an 'organic public sociology' in which the researcher works closely with a counter-public such as neighbourhood groups or human rights organizations. In this instance, the 'Rime' had the goodwill of at least some in the labour movement, but there was (and still is) no consumer movement intimately concerned with the labour conditions under which their consumer goods are shipped, as opposed to a concern with the greenhouse gas emissions associated with the shipments. This lack of a counter-public partner for the would-be public sociologist may not be an uncommon state of affairs.

CONCLUSION

Policy influence for social researchers is quite possibly a chimera, which is glimpsed tantalizingly from time to time but always eludes us. Some might say that policy-makers themselves are a chimera: a distinguished epidemiologist of my acquaintance claims never to have met one – for reasons perhaps of protective colouration, everyone is convinced that they are mere policy-implementors, simply interpreting and elaborating edicts passed down from some more august authority. Analogous, if less colourful, arguments have been constructed by some empirical researchers of policy processes (e.g. Rock, 1987), namely that policy is a situated discourse, a set of tacit assumptions and implicit meanings found within particular offices and occupational groupings.

It is this policy discourse, this amalgam of committee asides, gossip and unspoken assumptions, that Bulmer would seek to influence through the gentle diffusion of ideas and research findings. But social researchers are rare visitors to these corridors and committee rooms: their capacity for cultural diffusion is minimal. The argument in this chapter has been that the real opportunities for social research influence lie closer to the coalface than they do to head office, that the real opportunities for influence lie in relations with practitioners, not with the managers of practice.

This role for qualitative researchers as practitioner helpmeets will not be found by some to be wholly satisfactory. All practitioner–client relationships are power relationships. In a Foucauldian analysis (see, for example, Foucault, 1980), power cannot be wished or legislated away, it is inherent in all relationships. Therapeutic advance has as its corollary the extension of the controlling therapeutic gaze: the growth of public health medicine since the nineteenth century, for example, has brought great health benefits, but it has also subjected populations to increasing surveillance and regulation (Armstrong, 1983). Surveillance as a technique of power is increasingly complemented by other techniques, most notably that of 'pastoral care' (Foucault, 1981), whereby clients of agencies find themselves 'shepherded' into disciplinary relationships with practitioners whose avowed goals are merely those of care and advice. Assisting in the extension of outreach work to new populations, or suggesting ways to increase the effectiveness of therapeutic interventions, are each alike analysable as endeavours which tighten the disciplinary grip of experts on citizens. In a new twist on Becker's old 'whose side are we on?' question, it may be argued that researchers should be assisting not in the extension of power, but in the extension of resistance – resistance to meddlesome interference in prostitutes' street dealings, and resistance to expert orchestration of patients' private lives. The opposite of power is not its absence, but the resistance it provokes; researchers, so the argument goes, should be laying the groundwork for citizen resistance rather than fostering the extension and effectiveness of expert power. Foucault himself did not follow up his celebrated analysis of prisoner surveillance, *Discipline and Punish* (Foucault, 1977), with attempts to influence prison staff, but with work for prisoners' groups such as the CAP, the Prisoners' Action Committee (Major-Poetzl, 1983: 46–54).

However, this critical view of sociological influence on practitioners is a new version of an old song, the song of the Leninist vanguard party which always knows best, having learned the Lessons of History. It matters not, in this critical view, that male prostitutes may welcome the provision of a service where there was none before. What matters is resistance to experts' disciplinary power. Yet if the critical analysts are themselves experts, what kind of disciplinary relationship do they have with their audience? Should not they too be resisted? It follows that we can skirt these sophistries: where citizens themselves commend the work of practitioners, then it is not the place of researchers to murmur of false consciousness and demand resistance to pastoral care.

This issue (of whether or not social research should seek to assist the resistance of clients and patients) is part of a broader debate about the epistemological status of social research, about whether value neutrality can and should remain a constitutive principle of social research. The claim that social research can and should be value neutral is under attack from two sides. On one side, battle has been joined by those who argue that research should be explicitly politically participatory, embracing particular political aims, such as combating racism or patriarchy. On the other side are those who argue that *no* practice or policy prescriptions can be offered by researchers under any circumstances,

Table 2.1 Researcher roles and associated problems

Suggested roles for researchers	Problems
Researchers as 'social engineers'	• Low technical competence • Lack of institutional authority
Researchers as policy formulators/evaluators	• Policy-makers rarely seek policies from researchers • Policy-makers may commission research on policies in order to delay implementation
Researchers as emancipators	• Involves a prior commitment to an objective reality revealed to the researcher, but not to policy-makers, practitioners or laity
Researchers as 'public sociologists'	• Media interest may be difficult to generate • Victims may be more readily mobilized than ordinary consumers/citizens

since all knowledge is socially constructed and there are no grounds for the researcher to claim superior knowledge.

The argument about participatory research is perhaps seen most clearly in the responses which greeted the publication of Foster's (1990) findings on the lack of evidence for racist practices in British schools. Foster found little evidence that black pupils were treated unfairly in lessons or that they were misallocated to ability groups. The study generated a considerable critical response from those committed to some version of anti-racism. Hammersley's (1995) review of the controversy firmly supports Foster's position against various implicit and explicit charges, notably that as a middle-class white male he was experientially disabled from collecting and understanding evidence of institutional racism, and that the primary objective of research is not the production of knowledge but the changing of society.

The argument of the 'strict constructivists' (the term is Best's, 1989) that researchers should be silent on social problems (having no basis for claiming superior knowledge or 'reality claims') was stated succinctly by Woolgar and Pawluch (1985). Best argues the case for a 'contextual constructivist' position in distinction to the 'strict constructivist' position. Best is doubtful about whether it is practically possible to achieve the strict constructivists' goal of analyses wholly free of assumptions about objective reality; he cites various examples of how such assumptions may creep in at the backdoor of such analyses – all our writing and thinking is saturated in reality claims. Contextual constructivists, in contrast, may collaborate with collectivity members in examining and debating competing policy claims.

It seems, therefore, that qualitative researchers *may* address social problems and that they *may* address them most effectively by influencing practitioner practice. Qualitative researchers have several advantages in achieving such influence. Where specialist services (such as male prostitute outreach services) do not currently exist, qualitative research can provide detailed descriptions of the circumstances and behaviour of potential service-users such that material assistance is given with the design of targeted services. Another advantage relates to influencing practitioners who are the researcher's research participants, and to influencing practitioners who are the wider audience for the research findings. In respect of practitioners who are research participants, qualitative researchers can call upon their pre-existing research relationships with their research subjects as a resource for ensuring an attentive and even sympathetic response to their research findings. In respect of other practitioners (who are not research participants), the qualitative researcher is able to provide rich descriptions of everyday practice which enable practitioner audiences imaginatively to juxtapose their own everyday practices with the research description. There is therefore an opportunity for practitioners to make evaluative judgements about their own practices and experiment with the adoption of new approaches described in the research findings. Shaw (1996) has developed at length the argument that qualitative methods can provide a paradigm or exemplar for practitioners seeking to reflect upon and modify their work practices.

Future Prospects

Practitioners may not always have the local autonomy to develop new services to target new populations of clients, but all practitioners have the autonomy to modify their everyday work practices. In seeking the chimera of policy influence, sociologists rather neglected how research findings can address social problems through the encouragement of modifications and developments in practitioners' everyday practices. In researching topic-areas such as the shipping industry, where there is no powerful practitioner community to influence, researchers may try to reach the public directly, but successful contact is by no means certain.

CHAPTER SUMMARY

Table 2.2 Qualitative researchers addressing social problems through influence on practitioners' practices

Advantages	Alleged Disadvantages
• Qualitative researchers can capitalize on fieldwork relationships with practitioners to stimulate interest in their findings	• Assisting practitioners in improving service delivery may be viewed as conspiring with experts against the laity
• The rich descriptions of everyday practice found in qualitative research allow practitioners to compare their own practices with those reported in the research	• Researchers should be silent on social problems having no basis for superior knowledge
• New practices can be adopted from research descriptions	• The scope for successful changes in practice is frequently over-estimated
• Ethnographies may even provide a partial model for new outreach services	• Practitioner autonomy is limited, especially in the creation of new services

ACKNOWLEDGEMENTS

I wish to thank Ian Shaw, Anssi Peräkylä, Clive Seale and David Silverman for their helpful comments on an earlier draft of this chapter. Nearly all the research reported on here was conducted with co-workers whose help was invaluable. Those co-workers were Marina Barnard, Ramesh Datta, Andrew Finlay, Victor Gekara, Yakov Gilinskiy, Neil McKeganey and Helen Sampson.

Study questions

1.   What is meant by the 'enlightenment model' of social policy research and what are the main problems with it?

2. What kinds of sociological research might attract a 'practitioner' audience? Why might they be attractive to practitioners? Illustrate your answer with examples.
3. 'For whom and for what do we pursue sociology?' (Burawoy, 2005).

Recommended reading

The section on 'generalizability' in Anssi Peräkylä's chapter in this volume addresses cognate issues.

Hammersley, M. (1995) *The Politics of Social Research*. London: Sage.
A comprehensive guide to the inevitable limitations researchers face in influencing policy.

Heath, C. and Luff, P. (1992) 'Collaboration and control: crisis management and multimedia technology in London Underground line control rooms', *Journal of Computer Supported Cooperative Work*, 1: 69-94.
A good early example of 'workplace studies', analysing workplace interaction and claimed by conversation analysts and video analysts to have high practical utility for practitioners and managers.

Shaw, I. (1996) *Evaluating in Practice*. Aldershot: Ashgate.
Offers suggestions on a closer relationship between research and practice.

Silverman, D. (2010) *Doing Qualitative Research: A Practical Handbook*. London: Sage.
Chapter 27 considers the different audiences for social research.

References

Advisory Council on the Misuse of Drugs (1988) *AIDS and Drug Misuse: Part One*. London: Department of Health and Social Security.

Armstrong, D. (1983) *Political Anatomy of the Body: Medical Knowledge in Britain in the Twentieth Century*. Cambridge: Cambridge University Press.

Becker, H. (1967) 'Whose side are we on?' *Social Problems*, 14: 239–48.

Best, J. (ed.) (1989) *Images of Issues: Typifying Contemporary Social Problems*. Hawthorne, NY: Aldine de Gruyter.

Bloor, M. (1995) *The Sociology of HIV Transmission*. London: Sage.

Bloor, M. (2011) 'An essay on health capital and the Faustian bargains struck by workers in the globalised shipping industry', *Sociology of Health & Illness*, 33: 973–86.

Bloor, M. (2012) 'The rime of the globalised mariner'. www.youtube.com/watch?v=vVAw W1cFuwg, uploaded 2 August 2012 (accessed 3 October 2014).

Bloor, M. (2013) 'The rime of the globalised mariner', *Sociology*, 47: 30–50.

Bloor, M., Barnard, M., Finlay, A. and McKeganey, N. (1993) 'HIV-related risk practices among Glasgow male prostitutes: reframing concepts of risk behaviour', *Medical Anthropology Quarterly*, 7: 1–19.

Bloor, M., Datta, R., Gilinskiy, Y. and Horlick-Jones, T. (2006) 'Unicorn among the cedars: on the possibility of effective smart regulation of the globalised shipping industry', *Social & Legal Studies*, 15: 537–54.

Bloor, M., McKeganey, N. and Fonkert, D. (1988) *One Foot in Eden: A Sociological Study of a Range of Therapeutic Community Practice*. London: Routledge.

Bloor, M. and Sampson, H. (2009) 'Regulatory enforcement of labour standards in an outsourcing globalised industry: the case of the shipping industry', *Work, Employment & Society*, 23: 711–26.

Bulmer, M. (1982) *The Uses of Social Research*. London: Allen and Unwin.

Burawoy, M. (2005) 'For public sociology: 2004 presidential address', *American Sociological Review*, 70: 4–28.

Burawoy, M. (2012) 'Lecture 1 – what is public sociology?'. www.youtube.com/watch?v=d29t1 Tshc9M (accessed 3 October 2014).

Carey, J. (1975) *Sociology and Public Affairs: The Chicago School*. London: Sage.

Denzin, N. (1996) 'Punishing poets', *Qualitative Sociology*, 19: 525–8.

Foster, P. (1990) *Policy and Practice in Multicultural and Antiracist Education*. London: Routledge.

Foucault, M. (1977) *Discipline and Punish*. London: Allen Lane.

Foucault, M. (1980) 'The eye of power', in *Power/Knowledge: Selected Interviews and Other Writings 1972–1977*, ed. C. Gordon. Brighton: Harvester, pp. 146–65.

Foucault, M. (1981) 'Omnes et singulatim: towards a criticism of political reason', in S. McMurrin (ed.), *The Tanner Lectures on Human Values II*. Salt Lake City: University of Utah Press, pp. 223–54.

Hammersley, M. (1995) *The Politics of Social Research*. London: Sage.

Major-Poetzl, P. (1983) *Michel Foucault's Archaeology of Western Culture*. Chapel Hill: University of North Carolina Press.

McKeganey, N. and Barnard, M. (1992) *AIDS, Drugs and Sexual Risk: Lives in the Balance*. Milton Keynes: Open University Press.

Rock, P. (1987) *A View From the Shadows: Policy Making in the Solicitor General's Office*. Oxford: Oxford University Press.

Shaw, I. (1996) *Evaluating in Practice*. Aldershot: Ashgate.

Silverman, D. (2006) *Interpreting Qualitative Data: Methods of Analysing Talk, Text and Interaction* (3rd edn). London: Sage.

Silverman, D. (2010) *Doing Qualitative Research: A Practical Handbook* (3rd edn). London: Sage.

Woolgar, S. and Pawluch, D. (1985) 'Ontological gerrymandering: the anatomy of social problems explanations', *Social Problems*, 32: 214–27.

THREE

Research Ethics and Qualitative Research

Anne Ryen

About this chapter

This chapter offers a brief review of some major contemporary ethical issues in qualitative research. In contrast to quantitative research, the long lasting relations typical of much qualitative research make dilemmas unfold in the field. Since these dilemmas are emergent and contextual they call for situational responses which are different from the assumptions in the underlying biomedical model of most guidelines. This makes research ethics itself a socially constituted and situated field (Ryen, 2004). The chapter is written from a constructionist position.

Keywords

qualitative research, research ethics, field relations, epistemology, cross-cultural contexts

---

RESEARCH ETHICS: AN EVER INCREASING FIELD

'To comprehend some meanings of life, one must get close to that life', as Stake and Jegatheesan (2008) remind us. This is a good description of much qualitative research, and ethnography, in particular. Searching for rich data invites emergent challenges with which qualitative researchers must deal. They are integral to our work and most of them cannot be sorted out and solved in the office prior to fieldwork unlike survey research.[1] Interestingly, to some qualitative research tends to invoke an image of risks and threats for the researched and calls for external control and reaction. Sometimes, this has been needed. Most times not. Others argue that getting close also invites attending to the researched or co-researcher with respect and protection, and some remind us that qualitative researchers' potential to do harm is rather moderate. However, the public discourse about research ethics has itself played an active part in constructing the troublesome image of qualitative research and of the relationships among members in it as one between potential victims and their assailants. This is why we also need to look beyond research relations.

To respond to these issues, I now consider the classic research ethical issues as we find them in most guidelines. These are illustrated by data from my own research. Then I ask the bigger question: why do universities devote so much attention to control their[2] active research staff?

Now a brief look at the more traditional issues in research ethics.

CLASSIC AND FREQUENTLY RAISED CONCERNS

The three most frequently raised questions in the Western research ethical guidelines formulated by the professional associations deal with:

- codes and consent
- confidentiality
- trust.

For different reasons each topic raises more questions than answers.

Codes and consent refer in particular to 'informed consent'. This means that research subjects have the right to know that they are being researched, the right to be informed about the nature of the research and the right to withdraw at any time. In some countries this means that it is mandatory that research participants sign an informed consent form. Other places accept oral consent unless you are working with certain groups like children, pupils, clients, patients, etc. In many cases, the researcher will need to follow special and long procedures for approval of the theoretical sample and for approval to contact potential research participants (for dilemmas with informed consent in oral communities, see Ryen, 2007).

---

[1]And as opposed to so-called externalities like volcanic eruptions, flooding and civil wars often excluded from economic models – with devastating results.

[2]'Their', not 'our', reflects the critics' argument about organizational transformation.

The relationship between informed consent and covert research serves as the ultimate illustration of ethical dilemmas in data collection. On the one hand, the distinction between overt and covert research is often unclear, as pointed out by Robert Dingwall (1980). On the other hand, as argued by Punch (1994), to make written informed consent mandatory would mean the end of much 'street-style' ethnography. Another dilemma refers to informed consent or rather asking for 'process consent' when data will be archived because no one knows what and how data will be used for secondary analyses. This makes it difficult for research participants to know to what they are consenting. Based on my own research from East Africa, I refer to 'layers of consent' where the major gatekeeper in rural areas most often is a local government representative who actually provides the researcher with a sample of people who always tend to consent. In small communities with overlapping relations the person asked may depend on the official representative's decision in other matters which makes the invitation to consent a more intricate matter (Ryen, 2004 and 2007). This links gatekeeping, access and 'informed' consent with power (Miller and Bell, 2012: 62; and Mellick and Fleming, 2010, on revealing the identity of persons in the social network). Finally, consent in our multiple places and spaces in virtual and non-virtual realities from chatting and blogs to Google Maps[3] adds to the complexity.

A good piece of advice is always to invite experienced researchers with particular knowledge in research ethics and in your field to discuss these issues with you. You could invite your supervisor or your project colleagues for a meeting or a department seminar before you proceed. Also, certain issues are fit for discussions in the field.

Confidentiality means we are obliged to protect each participant's identity, places and the location of the research. However, we cannot always assume that participants want to be treated anonymously (which often is the case in Tanzania). Again, we need to talk to experienced researchers in the culture where our research takes place. However, we also need to be aware that Western research ethical guidelines are not necessarily universal (Riessman, 2005; Liamputtong, 2010; Mertens et al., 2013). The recommended order if you do research in another country than your own is to identify the relevant guidelines in your home country and in the country in which you do your research (you are governed by both), then compare and discuss with colleagues before you act.

Trust, the third classic concern, refers to the relationship between the researcher and the participants, and to the researcher's responsibility not to 'spoil' the field for others in the sense that potential research subjects get reluctant to be studied (Ryen, 2004). In this way trust also applies to the report or the discursive practices defining the standards for presenting both the researcher and the work as trustworthy (Fine, 1993). Trust is the classic key to good field relations and is a challenge constantly unfolding during the research process, though more so in ethnographic studies than in other kinds of fieldwork.

---

[3]Research ethics in online research goes beyond the limits of this chapter. See Markham in this volume.

At times we come across delicate situations that involve hidden or problematic information where someone may be harmed or put at risk (like crimes being planned), or where
certain findings may be discomforting (like job evaluations or health information) or even
dangerous to some subjects (like some kinds of illegal activities). This calls for decisions
on whether or not we should do such projects (alone or with someone), if there are data
we do not want to get (we may turn off the tape recorder or the smartphone, or move the
conversation onto another track or be more explicit), or if we simply need to shut down
the whole project.

Undoubtedly the three ethical issues of consent, confidentiality and trust are closely
linked. If you intervene by calling in an external person, you show the participant that he
or she is no longer being treated anonymously and can no longer trust you. Probably the
participant will be very hesitant to accept other researchers later. The general advice is not
to make such dilemmas your own individual load but to invite others to discuss how to be
prepared and ways to react before (make an informed decision), during (discuss possible
challenges, worst case included, and in the particular contextual and cultural setting of
your fieldwork) or after fieldwork (communicating your research).

However, such recommendations often tend to reflect a rather simplistic approach to
qualitative research practice. Let us therefore look at the more fundamental assumptions
on which the institutional management of such issues is based.

OUR MORAL RESPONSIBILITY
IN COMPLEX REALITIES

In this section we will look at some of the main arguments in the contemporary discussion
of research ethics. Later this feeds into a discussion on concerns regarded as specific to
qualitative research. These also constitute the background to claims that ethical guidelines
and much institutional governance are problematic particularly in ethnographic research.

Any model based on a pre-fixed, rather naive, ideal research subject (or rather, object),
fails to capture what is special about qualitative research. With reference to the classic concern 'Can we trust them?', questions of validity and research ethics such as confidence and
trust become closely entangled especially in the data collection phase.

The response in positivism is based on the assumption that language refers to an external reality 'out there' that makes access to the assumed reservoir of stocked information
crucial. In the constructionist model, social reality is a more complex phenomenon where
we examine how members produce recognizable forms that are treated as real or 'worlding'
to cite Gubrium and Holstein (1997: 42, also see Silverman, 2006), or simply how they
do this. The stories we get, are produced *with* rather than *by* someone; they are contextually produced, designed for a particular audience, serve purposes locally produced and
embedded in wider cultural contexts. As researchers we have a responsibility for producing

rigorous research. However, just as research which some see as dubious may provide us with data otherwise difficult to get (such as in covert research, or the fine balance in our information when recruiting informants etc. – Fine, 1993), naive simplified assumptions about field relations pose another dilemma.

For qualitative research informed by constructionist epistemologies and other than utilitarian ideas, social reality is a much more complex, multi-dimensional and contextual phenomenon. This makes research ethics more, not less, complex. This calls for a debate about moral responsibility grounded on a critical meeting between philosophy, epistemology and research practice. The absence of pre-fixed answers adds to the researcher's continuous moral responsibility.

Key points

- The bureaucratic procedures of research ethics governance bodies are based on an epistemology that is incompatible with most qualitative research.
- Constructionists argue that the social world is accomplished. This makes codes and consent, confidentiality and trust, more complex phenomena and also informed by methods and epistemology.
- Guidelines, courses and literature, experience, and discussions with colleagues, supervisors and respondents/co-researchers, may prepare us for moral practice.

AN ILLUSTRATION: RESEARCHING ACROSS CULTURES

I now want to illustrate the complex issues so far discussed using data extracts from my own research in East Africa. In research practice ethnographers often find themselves squeezed between definitions of the ethical and the acceptable as well as the workable. As you will see, I position myself within the non-universalist research ethical position, and we all need to make our statements credible. I will do so in two steps. First, I will show a few data extracts to illustrate what is emergent and flexible in research relations. Second, I will discuss the implications for research ethics in qualitative research and how these differ from what follows from the underlying assumptions of the structured positivist-informed perception of such relations and challenges.

Transcending the geographically bound

New technology has enabled a more flexible perception of the place–space issue. This makes the geographically bound 'field' more complex and decentred with no 'clear-cut distinction between *the here* and *the elsewhere*' as put by Stake and Rizvi (2009: 525).

My data on Asian business in East Africa consist of mobile talk, text messages, taped talk and notes from casual talk across contexts. As I have been accepted into my informant Mahid's network of regular contacts, we never lose complete track of each other despite months between our meetings. In a more classic perspective, it is this connectedness so prominent in qualitative research and so crucial to successful ethnographic fieldwork that paradoxically also poses its own moral concerns as relations evolve and fluctuate.

The emergent and contextual side of ethnographic field relations

According to the classic model, fieldwork is an activity between the ethnographer and the respondent or the key informant. It is these pre-fixed, structural field roles that are the main target of most textbook protocols and research ethics governance. However, the claim that the social world can be discovered by being 'there', as in traditional ethnography, has long been disputed by those who argue that social reality is accomplished rather than experienced. It follows from this that the more formal relationship of 'researcher–informant' is but one of several relationships that develop such as 'friend–friend', and that this brings with it additional ethical and moral issues as the fieldwork unfolds.

According to Harvey Sacks the central research question is how societal members 'see' or 'hear' particular activities and therefore offers a way of describing 'methods persons use for doing social life' (Sacks, 1984; Silverman, 1998). This makes language into more than a passive medium for transferring external meanings or experiences. Members collaboratively make social order happen in their unfolding sequences of talk and the researcher's job is to describe how this reality is created. By using Sacks's membership categorization device (MCD) (Silverman, 1998: Chapter 5), we can describe how people come to hear things the way they do in everyday life based on assumptions about what people are doing. This is possible because each of the pairs (of MCDs) or paired identities as shown in the extracts below, implies commonsense expectations about what sort of activity is appropriate. However, as clearly stated by Carolyn Baker, attributions may be explicitly pronounced or just hinted at 'indicating the subtlety and delicacy of much implicit categorization membership work' (Baker, 2004: 174).

Let me present a couple of the paired identities invoked by Mahid and myself. Altering the way we see field relations has, as I shall shortly make clear, crucial implications for research ethics in qualitative research. Let us start with the classic image.

Emergent relational identities

The classic researcher–key informant

Mahid is my key informant. This implies much everyday talk about his business activities and unstructured interviews about his business life history. Here is a sequence about employing a professional hotelier in one of his businesses:

Extract 1

1 A: so why did you hire the person?
2 M: I hired the person because I needed a professional hotelier here
3 A: ehe
4 M.   Ok, none of us were professional hoteliers, ok. And hotel is a job where the kitchen has to be looked
5   after which is very important, the bar has to be looked after, the clients' interests have to be looked
6   after ...

(Taped talk, Kenya 2002) (Ryen, 2008c: 90)

In the classic way, the researcher here (line 1) asks a question and the key informant responds (line 2) followed by the researcher's cues (line 3) to prompt further elaborations (4–6). This is how we jointly *invoke* the standard pair of researcher–key informant traditionally portrayed as the only legitimate roles in the field (Ryen, 2004 and 2008a). Because constructionism as in feminism, poststructuralism, postmodernism and ethnomethodology focuses on the constitutive side of field relations we are invited to see the active and emergent character of field relations as they unfold (see Holstein and Gubrium in this volume). Careful analysis of my tapes also offers more paired identities. Here is one example:

Friend-friend

After a few years, we now and then shared events in our lives associated with health and illness and also to account for not responding to calls. One morning I found this message on my mobile sent by Mahid in the middle of the night after his son had died from cancer:

Extract 2

Hi got a bad news [my son] passd away i am in shock wil talk 2morow

(Text message 2005, his son's name made anonymous) (Ryen, 2008c: 238)

When I called him the next morning he said he appreciated my emotional support.

Despite the protocol on emphatic and smooth relations, long-lasting field relations also invite unforeseen eruptions. Here is Mahid's rather humorous response to my efforts to repair relations after a disagreement, by sending a text message saying he probably was right:

Extract 3

I am glad. I must kneel down. I told u to listen to the great man.

(Text message 26 January 2006) (Ryen, 2008c: 94)

Let us now look into how this relates to what is claimed to be the particulars of research ethics in qualitative research.

RESEARCH ETHICS IN RESEARCH PRACTICE: COMPLEX FIELDS

According to the professional guidelines, the researcher is responsible for informed consent, for trust and protection, and for protecting their privacy by confidentiality (Ryen, 2004: 231–6). A signed consent form then becomes a guarantee that participants are informed about the research and consent to participate. Unfortunately, this procedure misleads us to perceive moral responsibility as something to get done with initially, something to be ticked off as 'done', a symbol of goodness. This undermines the qualitative side of qualitative research (see Ryen, 2004 and 2007 for illustrations from East Africa). This external policing also tends to make research ethics into an either/or issue: participants either consent or they do not consent, things are good or bad, harmless or not. And, it presupposes a clear, static research problem typical of a positivist-informed epistemology.

If we accept the constitutive nature of qualitative research or knowledge production as a meaning-making process, inevitably there are issues unfamiliar or problematic to positivist-informed notions of correct or acceptable research relations and whatever they might bring about. The idea of the professional–private divide works well to pinpoint the particulars of qualitative inquiry and moral responsibility. Prominent examples of dilemmas associated with good rapport are friendship/deception, privacy/intrusion and emotional stress. Despite their interconnectedness, I will discuss them in separate sub-sections. They refer to the whole process from negotiating access to the field to data gathering and analysis, and they all in different ways relate to the classic issues of consent, confidentiality and trust of research ethics.

The professional-private divide: is good rapport a problem?

Interviews and ethnographic studies are dependent on building up rather long-lasting relations in the field to get access to 'there'. To do this we draw on mundane practices; we link up with people, spend time together and build up a stock of joint experiences. Friends do the same. This invites us to reflect on intricate issues such as nuances in friendship, niceness and instrumentality. When I some years ago called Mahid, I found him alone in the middle of a malaria attack that I rightly came to see as different from the ordinary ones and called for help. This illustrates how long-term fieldwork informs us and guides action, though in retrospect it may appear as instrumental.[4]

Duncombe and Jessop (2012) discuss the parallel between interviewing skills and 'doing rapport' and refer to Hochschild on 'emotion work' and her argument concerning the commercialization of human feelings. She argues that those who do such jobs may feel and even

---

[4]He was diagnosed with brain malaria.

become 'inauthentic', like women employees in service jobs when simulating empathy to make people feel well. If textbook prescriptions for successful interviews encourage good rapport, they see such friendships as detached and opposed to Ann Oakley's advocacy of minimal social distance between feminist researchers and research subjects in order to offer 'an emotionally emphatic, egalitarian and reciprocal rapport' (1981: 108). Despite a somewhat naive assumption of authenticism, there is a good resonance with research ethics.

The commercialization of interviewer skills on 'doing rapport' into 'management of consent' implies a more personalized approach to building trust. However, if power inequalities in 'faking friendship' are ignored, the interviewer will 'run the risk of breaching the interviewee's right *not* to know or to reflect on their own innermost thoughts' (Duncombe and Jessop, 2012: 112). Qualitative interviewers even adopt counselling skills and language to increase the interviewee's personal insight to improve introspection. Rightly Duncombe and Jessop critically ask if this is the kind of disclosure to which the interviewee consented. Also, they are quite right that the danger is present that such talk could escalate into a quasi-therapeutic interview and create severe problems in drawing boundaries around the 'friendship' or 'intimacy'. So, we could argue that it is as important to know the boundaries around one's skills as it is to know one's skills. Ethnographers are trained in ethnography not in therapy.

Fieldwork is a delicate balance between the interesting, the workable and the acceptable ingredients in our search for knowledge. The alternatives are neither stricter rules, nor to call in a committee. I do share Kant's ethical concern with the individual over the group (deontology as opposed to utilitarianism, Ryen, 2004) – and with research participants over committees. However, for analytic purposes we need to explore across occasions and contexts but we do not need to go 'deep' for 'authentic' experiences. I will come back later to the emotional and private.

This accentuates the qualitative dimension to qualitative research, so let us explore further how such issues relate to knowledge.

Interpersonal distance and comprehensibility: are qualitative researchers intruders?

Stake and Jegatheesan (2008: 1–13) have shown that the road to understanding participation is assumed to go via reduced interpersonal distance – hence the importance of rapport, but at some point we may intrude into that person's zone of privacy. 'The points that bound these zones are not points at all. They are shadings, passages … Through empathy, intuition, experience, something, we need to rely on ourselves to back off' (2008: 8), and quite rightly they emphasize that 'Privacy is not defined only by the content of disclosure, but also in terms of audiences and circumstances involved' (2008: 2).

Prescriptions or external control mechanisms cannot solve this dilemma though the tilt towards revelation is more prominent in some qualitative paradigms (like emotionalism and postmodernism) than in others (see Table 15.1 in Ryen, 2004: 244, for an overview of values and ethics in some contemporary paradigms). However, a positivist-informed belief in an external reality is no guarantee that you will avoid undue introspection or intruding into the private lives of participants. External control is not necessarily the answer to emergent challenges.

Cross-cultural contexts make some challenges more visible with long narratives (I have some of more than three hours) assumingly depicting 'authentic' experiences. Also participants are active and may in different ways exercise power in relations with the researcher from withholding information to over-enthusiasm (Bourne-Day and Lee-Treweek, 2008). What then about the informants? Did Mahid text-message me in the hospital because he feared he might lose his free 'counsellor'? Was it convenient to have me around when he was broke so I could pay for lunches at times even with his contacts? Why do informants volunteer (Ryen, 2008c)? Exploring the meaning-making process will better enable us to recognize problematic zones. They are not standardized.

My conclusion has been that I, with Mahid, must listen to so-called private stories because I have been sanctioned for not listening and spent days managing eruptions. Interestingly, this has been very informing about our Western notions of 'privacy', how narratives change, etc. It reminds us of our obligation to reflect on our own position from which we see because the categories and the tags put in are anchored in alternative epistemologies such as ethnomethodology, feminism and indigenous research. It has also taught me to recognize local shades or passages in gendered ethnographies of third world organizations (see Ryen on flirtation, 2008d).

Emotional stress: do qualitative researchers cause harm?

It is common knowledge that good rapport in long-lasting relations may invite participants to disclose emotional experiences, as Mahid did to me. The question is whether or not this is harmful to our participants and thus ethically problematic (despite participants' efforts at times also to intrude into the ethnographer's privacy).

McIntosh and Morse (2009: 91) argue that 'emotional distress motivates purposive participation, creates relational connections, facilitates self-knowledge of participants and their experiences, and expresses its voice in the emotional space afforded by the interview'. This makes it an integral part, not a by-product, of unstructured interview research and reflects how emotions in the West are associated with valence and polarity. But this is too simplistic to account for the complexity, multi-dimensional and contextual nature of pain and pleasure.

Mahid's story about his painful experience from his early business life illustrates emotional distress as part of a wider emotional repertoire participants may evoke during fieldwork. The pain evoked is contextual and displayed in stories told and retold across contexts. The experience is narrated as a tellable story, recipient-oriented and tailored for a particular audience. The emotional stress is subjective and interpretive and the story works to connect and relate, calls for attention and relieves the stress. Some years later he narrated the same story as a straightforward experience about a troublesome bank, so stories come up in different versions, emotional and not, depending on the situation, audience and setting. This challenges the assumed 'authenticity' of experiences. We still have to relate to the storyteller's emotional state of mind in one way or another while being aware of the cultural and situated ways of interpreting emotions. Such stories may serve different ends and reflect complicated transactions in the field. Mahid finds it arrogant when I at times stop listening to his many stories so I have learnt to listen. At the same time Lee and Lee (2012: 45) remind us of bureaucratic bodies' commonsensical assumptions about 'sensitivity' and their concern with the researched. Experiences show that personal engagement in the research process also causes researchers stress based on feelings of guilt, powerlessness, frustration, physical and emotional exhaustion. So, there is also a time for boundaries, but no documents can ever tell us exactly when or where. There is no simple formula for the link between qualitative research and emotional stress.

Then, let us briefly look into a more profound criticism of the interventions by the research ethics regime in recent years. The power they exercise has made qualitative researchers rightly question their legitimacy.

CONTROVERSIES OVER THE CONTEMPORARY RESEARCH ETHICAL REGIME

Despite warnings and extensive reactions from qualitative researchers, many countries have institutionalized a new research ethical regime with local, rather bio-medical dominated research ethical committees (for illustrations see Gubrium et al., 2012, section VI; Hammersley, 2009, on the UK; and Mertens and Ginsberg, 2009, on the US). Qualitative researchers find it most peculiar that a positivist-informed external committee claims a special competence in these matters. The system has been described as an 'audit culture', a surveillance apparatus and an administrative and bureaucratic burden (Ryen, 2012). To copy the medical profession came with a cost. The opposition refers to the new committee system rather than to research ethics itself.[5]

Critics rightly argue that the new regime also obstructs the knowledge production by restricting legitimate topics and choice of methods (problematic when deviant from the bio-medical tradition such as covert observation and innovative methods). It also has made access to certain groups or subjects more problematic (for example when they fit the bio-medical image of 'vulnerable' such as the mentally ill and elderly) (Hammersley, 2009; Hammersley and Traianou, 2012).

---

[5]Violations of research ethics refers to a wide range of issues also other than between researcher and researched.

We may ask why is there this lack of understanding of qualitative research when the regimes' judgements themselves become ridden by everyday assumptions and scepticism? Henry A. Giroux describes a scenario linked up with a US right-wing anti-intellectualism and an instrumentalism in knowledge and higher education. In universities modelled after the business world and corporate interests, faculty increasingly are being stripped of their autonomy and critical aspects (2007: 8). In academic capitalism higher education and research have become part of a new global commercial growth industry (Kjeldstadli, 2010). The pressure for external funding comes with worries about litigation or lawsuits which fuel their interest in the new regulatory practice of research ethics (Ryen, 2012). This again makes our contracts with our research participants vulnerable and the regime potentially harmful. Critics also point to a mismatch between these demands and academic freedom.

This seems to go beyond qualitative research. Iranian and Chinese PhD students have been evicted from Norway based on assumptions that their home regimes may (mis)use their knowledge in the future, and director and writer Ulrik Imtiaz Rolfsen, known for a number of films, experienced a secret police service razzia in his home when they took his documentary material on a young Islamist, a hard to reach interviewee.[6]

CHAPTER SUMMARY AND FUTURE PROSPECTS

Knowledge production comes with a moral responsibility towards research participants. The rich literature on research ethics and qualitative research reflects the multitude of approaches informed by parallel, alternative epistemologies. This makes the question of how moral responsibility can best be attended to. This is a contested terrain. The contemporary governance of research ethics may itself actively participate in constituting qualitative research as a vulnerable field. My chapter is another effort to avoid naive assumptions about the nature of ethical dilemmas in qualitative research. It would be immoral to underestimate the complexity of research ethics. What we come to see as challenges and solutions to dilemmas in research ethics in practice is informed by epistemology (Ryen, 2008b and 2011), and ethics is itself a field socially constituted and situated (Ryen, 2004).

In our global times, we will need to be more aware of variations in ethics and research ethics. If our research is in another culture than our own, we may ask how we can then best work in ethically respectful ways. Our research ethical guidelines often come up short here. If they collide or if our own set of research ethical guidelines is inadequate,

---

[6]See Secret Police Service (Norway) and Rolfsen (2015) in references. This occurred after Norway got a new neo-liberal friendly government. The offended have taken their cases to court (the PhD students competed for their grants on ordinary terms with other applicants and were evicted towards the end of their period).

we need to sort out what to do. If local guidelines claim national ownership of data just as for other resources, we need to know under what condition we can bring the data to our home country for further analysis. This deals with the questions 'Whose field is it?' and 'Whose ethics?', and makes us reflect on how research ethics is intertwined with power (Ryen, 2008b). This calls for more knowledge of the philosophy and the culture of the context of our research, whether abroad or at home. These issues will add to the contemporary debate when we can no longer take 'the-taken-for-granted' for granted (Ryen, 2007). The contextual side of allegedly universal Western research ethics shows the limits of the either/or perspective.

As qualitative researchers we need to recognize the social processes through which things come to be seen as ethical or not. As claimed by Zygmunt Bauman: 'The foolproof – universal and unshakeably founded – ethical code will never be found' (1993: 2–27). These are the basic issues I have tried to raise. Qualitative research calls for moral responsibility in a field scattered with dilemmas, not for quick pre-fixed answers.

ACKNOWLEDGEMENTS

Thanks to Mike Emmison and David Silverman for their most relevant comments to an earlier draft of this chapter.

Study questions

1. Think of your research problem: try to identify possible ethical dilemmas. Which ones can be sorted out *before* you start your fieldwork, and which ones may come up *during* and *after* fieldwork?
2. How does epistemology inform research ethics?
3. Discuss research ethics when you do research in another culture than that of your own country.
4. If your field is located in another country, what are the research ethics guidelines here? If they do not overlap with those in your own country, what should you do?

Recommended reading

For an introduction to the standard ethical issues (consent, confidentiality and trust):
Gubrium, J. A., Holstein, J. A., Marvasti, A. B. and McKinney, K. D. (eds) (2012) *The Sage Handbook of Interview Research: The Complexity of the Craft.* Thousand Oaks, CA: Sage. 'Section VI: ethics of the interview', pp. 441-508.

Israel, M. (2014) *Research Ethics and Integrity for Social: Scientists Beyond Regulatory Compliance* (2nd edn). London: Sage.

Ryen, A. (2004) 'Ethical issues', in C. Seale, G. Gobo, J. F. Gubrium and D. Silverman (eds), *Qualitative Research Practice*. London: Sage, pp. 158–74.

Books that also discuss ethical dilemmas across the research *process*:

Liamputtong, P. (2010) *Performing Qualitative Cross-Cultural Research*. Cambridge: Cambridge University Press.

Miller, T., Birch, M., Mauthner, M. and Jessop, J. (eds) (2012) *Ethics in Qualitative Research*. London: Sage.

Publications where authors write about and discuss ethical dilemmas in their own research:

Jegatheesan, B. (ed.) (2008) *Access: A Zone of Comprehension, and Intrusion*. Bingley: Emerald. Offers good illustrations on topics like closeness, privacy, deception, IRBs, indigenous research, flirtation and self.

Qualitative Social Work: Research and Practice (2008) Special issue on research ethics, 7 (4). http://qsw.sagepub.com/content/vol7/issue4/. Offers an overview article and some good illustrations on IRBs, informed consent, trust etc.

Overview for the more advanced reader:

Hammersley, M. and Traianou, A. (2012) *Ethics in Qualitative Research: Controversies and Contexts*. London: Sage.

Mertens, D. M. and Ginsberg, P. E. (eds) (2009) *The Handbook of Social Research Ethics*. Los Angeles, CA: Sage.

You will also find the rich lists of references in these journals very helpful.

Qualitative Research (on the link between qualitative research and research ethics, Sage).

Research Ethics (Sage).

References

Baker, C. D. (2004) 'Membership categorization and interview accounts', in D. Silverman (ed.), *Qualitative Research: Theory, Method and Practice*. London: Sage, pp. 162–76.

Bauman, Z. (1993) *Postmodern Ethics*. Oxford: Blackwell.

Bourne-Day, J. and Lee-Treweek, G. (2008) 'Interconnected lives: examining privacy as a shared concern for the researched and the researchers', in B. Jegatheesan (ed.), *Access: A Zone of Comprehension, and Intrusion*. Bingley: Emerald, pp. 29–60.

Dingwall, R. (1980) 'Ethics and ethnography', *Sociological Review*, 28 (4): 871–92.

Duncombe, J. and Jessop, J. (2012) '"Doing rapport" and the ethics of "faking friendship"', in T. Miller, M. Birch, M. Mauthner and J. Jessop (eds), *Ethics in Qualitative Research*. London: Sage, pp. 108–21.

Fine, G. A. (1993) 'Ten lies of ethnography: moral dilemmas in field research', *Journal of Contemporary Ethnography*, (22) 3: 267–94.

Giroux, H. A. (2007) *The University in Chains: Confronting the Military-Industrial-Academic Complex*. Boulder, CO: Paradigm Publishers.

Gubrium. J. F. and J. A. Holstein (1997) *The New Language of Qualitative Research*. New York: Oxford University Press.

Gubrium, J. A., Holstein, J. A., Marvasti, A. B. and McKinney, K. D. (eds) (2012) *The Sage Handbook of Interview Research: The Complexity of the Craft*. Thousand Oaks, CA: Sage.

Hammersley, M. (2009) 'Against the ethicists: on the evils of ethical regulation', *International Journal of Social Research Methodology*, 12 (3): 211–25.

Hammersley, M. and Traianou, A. (2012) *Ethics in Qualitative Research: Controversies and Contexts*. London: Sage.

Kjeldstadli, K. (2010) *Akademisk kapitalisme*. Oslo, Norway: Res publica.

Lee, Y.-O. and Lee, R. M. (2012) 'Methodological research on "sensitive" topics: a decade review', *BMS/Bulletin of Sociological Methodology*, 114: 35–49.

Liamputtong, P. (2010) *Performing Qualitative Cross-Cultural Research*. Cambridge: Cambridge University Press.

McIntosh, M. J. and Morse, J. (2009) 'Institutional review boards and the ethics of emotion', in N. K. Denzin and M. D. Giardina (eds), *Qualitative Inquiry and Social Justice*. Walnut Creek, CA: Left Coast Press, pp. 81–107.

Mellick, M. and Fleming, S. (2010) 'Personal narrative and the ethics of disclosure: a case study from elite sport', *Qualitative Research*, 10 (3): 299–314.

Mertens, D. M., Cram, F. and Chilisa, B. (eds) (2013) *Indigenous Pathways into Social Research: Voices of a New Generation*. Walnut Creek, CA: Left Coast Press.

Mertens, D. M. and Ginsberg, P. E. (eds) (2009) *The Handbook of Social Research Ethics*. Los Angeles, CA: Sage.

Miller, T. and Bell, L. (2012) 'Consenting to what? Issues of access, gate-keeping and "informed" consent', in M. Mauthner, M. Birch, J. Jessop, and T. Miller (eds), *Ethics in Qualitative Research*. London: Sage, pp. 61–75.

Oakley, A. (1981) 'Interviewing women: a contradiction in terms', in H. Roberts (ed.), *Doing Feminist Research*. London: Routledge & Kegan Paul, pp. 30–61.

Punch, M. (1994) 'Politics and ethics in qualitative research', in N. K. Denzin and Y. S. Lincoln (eds), *Handbook of Qualitative Research*. Thousand Oaks, CA: Sage, pp. 83–97.

Riessman, C. K. (2005) 'Exporting ethics: a narrative about a narrative research in South India', *Health: An Interdisciplinary Journal for the Study of Health, Illness and Medicine*, 9 (4): 473–90.

Rolfsen, U. I. (2015) www.dagbladet.no/tag/ulrik_imtiaz_rolfsen (accessed 22 June 2015).

Ryen, A. (2004) 'Ethical issues', in C. Seale, G. Gobo, J. F. Gubrium and D. Silverman (eds), *Qualitative Research Practice*. London: Sage, pp. 158–74.

Ryen, A. (2007) 'Do Western research ethics work in Africa? A discussion about not taking "the taken-for-granted" for granted', *Mosenodi*, 15 (1/2): 31–45.

Ryen, A. (ed.) (2008a) A special issue on research ethics, *Qualitative Social Work, Research and Practice*, 7 (4). http://qsw.sagepub.com/content/7/4.toc (accessed 25 June 2015).

Ryen, A. (2008b) 'Trust in cross-cultural research: the puzzle of epistemology, research ethics and context', *Qualitative Social Work*, 7 (4): 448–65.

Ryen, A. (2008c) 'Wading the field with my key informant: exploring field relations', *Qualitative Sociology Review*, 4 (3). www.qualitativesociologyreview.org/ENG/archive_eng.php (accessed 10 January 2010).

Ryen, A. (2008d) 'Crossing borders? Doing gendered ethnographies of third-world organi-sations', in B. Jegatheesan (ed.), *Access: A Zone of Comprehension, and Intrusion*. Bingley: Emerald, pp. 141–64.

Ryen, A. (2011) 'Exploring or exporting? Qualitative methods in times of globalisation', *International Journal of Social Research Methodology*, 14 (6): 439–52.

Ryen, A. (2012) 'Assessing the risk of being interviewed', in J. F. Gubrium, J. A. Holstein, A. B. Marvasti and K. D. McKinney (eds), *The Sage Handbook of Interview Research: The Complexity of the Craft*. Thousand Oaks, CA: Sage, pp. 477–93.

Sacks, H. (1984) 'Notes on methodology', in J. M. Atkinson and J. Heritage (eds), *Structures of Social Action: Studies in Conversational Analysis*. Cambridge: Cambridge University Press, pp. 21–7.

Secret Police Service (Norway) www.bbc.com/news/world-middle-east-28488024; www.thelocal.no/20150312/expelled-chinese-phd-did-illegal-missile-research; www.dagbladet.no/tag/ulrik_imtiaz_rolfsen (all accessed 26 June 2015).

Silverman, D. (1998) *Harvey Sacks: Social Sciences and Conversational Analysis*. Cambridge: Polity Press.

Silverman, D. (2006) *Interpreting Qualitative Data*. London: Sage.

Stake, R. and Jegatheesan, B. (2008) 'Access: a zone of comprehension, and intrusion', in B. Jegatheesan (ed.), *Access: A Zone of Comprehension, and Intrusion*. Bingley: Emerald, pp. 1–13.

Stake, R. and Rizvi, F. (2009) 'Research ethics in transnational spaces', in D. M. Mertens and P. Ginsberg (eds), *Handbook of Social Science Research in Ethics*. Thousand Oaks, CA: Sage, pp. 521–36.

PART II
INTERVIEWS AND FOCUS GROUPS

Following Ryen's reminder of the importance of the researcher–researched relationship, the three chapters in Part II on interviews and focus groups show us that both respondents and social scientists actively construct meaning in each other's talk. Jody Miller and Barry Glassner address the issue of finding 'reality' in interview accounts. For Miller and Glassner, the focus of interview research should be fixed upon what stories are told and how and where they are produced. In their chapter, James Holstein and Jaber Gubrium show us how a focus on story and narrative structure demands that we recognize that both the gathering of interview data and interview analysis are active occasions in which meanings are produced. This means that we ought to view research 'subjects' not as stable entities but as actively constructed through their answers. Sue Wilkinson's chapter on focus groups carries forward Holstein and Gubrium's concern with how we construct the social world with our respondents. Wilkinson shows us that content analysis and a concentration on the mechanics of how to run a focus group are no substitute for theoretically informed and detailed data analysis of talk-in-action.

FOUR

The 'Inside' and the 'Outside': Finding Realities in Interviews

Jody Miller and Barry Glassner

About this chapter

In this chapter, we argue that in-depth interview accounts provide a meaningful opportunity to study and theorize about the social world. We reject the objectivist-constructivist divide, and show how the narrative accounts produced through in-depth interviews provide us with access to realities. Specifically, we suggest that interviews reveal evidence of the nature of the phenomena under investigation, including the contexts and situations in which they emerge, as well as insights into the cultural frames people use to make sense of these experiences and their social worlds. We illustrate by discussing two projects completed by one of the authors.

Keywords

in-depth interviewing, symbolic interactionism, narrative accounts, social worlds

In his *Interpreting Qualitative Data*, Silverman (2001) highlights the dilemmas facing interview researchers concerning what to make of their data. On the one hand, positivists seek to create the 'pure' interview – enacted in such a way that it comes as close as possible to providing a 'mirror reflection' of the reality that exists in the social world. This position has been thoroughly critiqued over the years in terms of both its feasibility and its desirability. On the other hand, emotionalists suggest that unstructured, open-ended interviewing elicits 'authentic accounts of subjective experience'. While this approach is 'seductive', a significant problem lies in the question of whether these 'authentic accounts' are actually, instead, the repetition of familiar cultural tales. Finally, radical social constructionists suggest that no knowledge about a reality that is 'out there' in the social world can be obtained from the interview, because the interview is exclusively an interaction between the interviewer and interviewee in which both construct narrative versions of the social world. The problem with looking at these narratives as representative of some 'truth', according to these scholars, is that they are context-specific, invented for the interactive context of the interview, and representative of nothing more or less.

For those of us who hope to learn about the social world and contribute knowledge that can expand understanding and help foster social change, the proposition that our interviews are meaningless beyond the context in which they occur is a daunting one. This is not to say that we accept the positivist view of the possibility of untouched data available through standardized interviewing, nor that we take a romanticized view of seamless authenticity emerging from narrative accounts. Instead, we simply are not willing to discount the possibility of learning about the social world beyond the interview in our analyses of interview data.

In this chapter, we try to identify a position that is outside of this objectivist–constructivist continuum yet takes seriously the goals and critiques of researchers at both of its poles. We will argue that information about social worlds is achievable through in-depth interviewing. The position we are attempting to put forward is inspired by authors such as Harding (e.g. 1987) and Latour (e.g. 1993), who posit explicitly anti-dualistic options for methodological and theorizing practices – options which recognize that both emulation and rejection of dominant discourses such as positivism miss something critically important. Dominant discourses are totalizing only for those who view them as such; they are replete with fissures and uncolonized spaces within which people engage in highly satisfying and even resistant practices of knowledge-making. We concur with Sanders that:

> There is a considerable difference between being skeptical about the bases of truth claims while carefully examining the grounds upon with these claims are founded (a conventional interactionist enterprise) and denying that truth - as a utilitarian and liberating orientation - exists at all. (1995: 93, 97)

In sum, we believe that qualitative interviews provide us access to social worlds, as evidence both of 'what happens' within them and of how individuals make sense of themselves, their experiences and their place within these social worlds. Next, we discuss further the bases on which we stake our position.

NARRATIVES AND WORLDS

'Narratives are central to human existence' (Presser and Sandberg, 2015: 1). In telling stories, interview subjects construct social worlds. For researchers in the interactionist tradition, then, 'the primary issue is to generate data which give an authentic insight into people's experiences' (Silverman, 2001: xx). Interactionists do not suggest there is:

> 'a singular objective or absolute world out-there' ... [but they] recognize 'objectified worlds'. Indeed, they contend that some objectification is essential if human conduct is to be accomplished. Objectivity exists, thus, not as an absolute or inherently meaningful condition to which humans react but as an accomplished aspect of human lived experience. (Dawson and Prus, 1995: 113)

Research cannot provide the mirror reflection of the social world that positivists strive for, but it can provide access to the meanings people attribute to their experiences and social worlds. While the interview is itself a symbolic interaction, knowledge of the social world beyond the interaction still can be obtained. In fact, it is only in the context of non-positivistic interviews, which recognize and build on their interactive components (rather than trying to control and reduce them), that 'intersubjective depth' can be achieved (and, with this, the achievement of knowledge of social worlds).

Those of us who aim to understand others' understandings choose qualitative interviewing because it provides us with a means for exploring the points of view of our research subjects, while granting these points of view the culturally honoured status of reality. As Charmaz explains:

> We start with the experiencing person and try to share his or her subjective view. Our task is objective in the sense that we try to describe it with depth and detail. In doing so, we try to represent the person's view fairly and to portray it as consistent with his or her meanings. (1995: 54)

Silverman and others accurately suggest that this portrayal of what we do is in some ways romanticized. We will address below some of the problems that make this the case. But the proposition that romanticizing negates the objectivity Charmaz defines, or the subjectivities with which we work, does not follow.

We acknowledge, for instance, that interviewees sometimes respond to interviewers through the use of familiar narrative constructs, rather than providing meaningful insights into their subjective view. Indeed, as Denzin notes:

> The subject is more than can be contained in a text, and a text is only a reproduction of what the subject has told us. What the subject tells us is itself something that has been shaped by prior cultural understandings. Most important, language, which is our window into the subject's world (and our world), plays tricks ... [W]hat is always given is a trace of other things, not the thing - lived experience - itself. (1991: 68)

The language of interviewing (like all other telling) fractures the stories being told. This occurs inevitably within a storyteller's narrative, because stories are always partial and particular tellings of 'what happened' and 'why'. With qualitative interviews, the research commits further fractures as well. The coding, categorization and typologizing of stories result in telling only parts of stories, rather than presenting them in their 'wholeness' (Charmaz, 1995: 60). Numerous levels of representation occur from the moment of 'primary experience' to the reading of researchers' textual presentation of findings, including attending to the experience, telling it to the researcher, transcribing and analysing what is told, and the reading.

Qualitative interviewers recognize these fissures, noting, for example, that stories are told to particular people and may take different forms with other listeners (see Miller, 2010). The issue of how interviewees respond to us based on who we are – in their lives, as well as the social categories to which we belong, such as age, gender, class and race – is a practical concern as well as an epistemological or theoretical one. For example, when we study groups with whom we do not share membership, interviewees may not trust us, they may not understand our questions, or they may purposely mislead us in their responses. Likewise, given a lack of membership in their primary groups, we may not know enough about the phenomenon under study to ask the right questions.

Studying adolescents, as we have done in our own research, provides a good example. On the one hand, the meaning systems of adolescents are different from those of adults, and adult researchers must exercise caution in assuming they understand adolescent cultures because they've 'been there'. On the other hand, adolescents are in a transitional life period, becoming increasingly oriented to adult worlds, though with 'rough edges' (Fine and Sandstrom, 1988: 60). As a consequence, 'age begins to decrease in importance as a means of differentiating oneself, and other dimensions of cultural differentiation, such as gender and class [and race], become more crucial' (Fine and Sandstrom, 1988: 66). These dimensions are thus critically important for establishing research relationships, rapport and trust, and for evaluating the information obtained and the interactions that occur within in-depth interviews.

To treat a young person's age as the determinant or predictor of his or her experiences neglects another key point about age-ordering as well:

> The idea of an ending of childhood is predicated upon a normative system wherein childhood itself is taken for granted. But childhood may also be 'ended' by narratives of personal or societal 'deviance' or by new stories reconstituting the modelling of childhood itself. (Rogers and Rogers, 1992: 153)

In our experience, much of what adolescents talk about in open-ended interviews is precisely how their acts seem wayward, delinquent, premature or otherwise not befitting proper youthful behaviour. Their discourse towards and with us (and for themselves) is much about where and who they are. It is about trying out social locations and identities:

Our approach is to treat the adolescents' reports as situated elements in social worlds … One cannot read the transcripts and fail to recognize that much of what goes on is two persons trying to understand topics that neither would consider in quite this manner or detail except in such special circumstances. The interviewees typically seem to enjoy the chance to 'think aloud' about such matters, and often they say this to the interviewer. Much of that thinking is directed at a major project of their present lives – figuring out what type of person they are and what type they want to be. The interview offers an opportunity to try out various possibilities on this older student who is asking questions, and with reference to how it fits with one's self-image or might work out if directed at other audiences. On the other hand, these ways of viewing self and world come from and build into the social world itself. Ways of thinking and talking derive from daily experiences. (Glassner and Loughlin, 1987: 34-5)

Key to these potential challenges is how we utilize 'who we are' in relation to our interviewees in order to further understanding (Miller, 2010), as our examples below will illustrate.

LIFE OUTSIDE THE INTERVIEW

Interactionist research starts from a belief that people create and maintain meaningful worlds. As interactionist research with adolescents illustrates, this belief can be accepted 'without assuming the existence of a single, encompassing obdurate reality' (Charmaz, 1995: 62). To assume that realities beyond the interview context cannot be tapped into and explored is to grant narrative omnipotence. The roots of these realities are 'more fundamental and pervasive' (Dawson and Prus, 1995: 121; see also Presser and Sandberg, 2015). Charmaz's work with the chronically ill provides a vivid illustration: they experience sickness, she notes, regardless of whether they participate in her interviews (1995: 50). Likewise, the adolescents in our studies experience their age-, gender- and racial/ethnic-based identities and fluidity of identity whether or not we interview them – and within our interviews.

Language shapes meanings but also permits intersubjectivity and individuals' ability to create meaningful worlds (Presser and Sandberg, 2015). Recognizing this, we cannot accept the proposition that interviews do not yield information about social worlds. Rather, 'we take it that two persons can communicate their perceptions to one another. Knowing full well that there are both structures and pollutants in any discussion, we choose to study what is said in that discussion' (Glassner and Loughlin, 1987: 33). While certainly 'there is no way to stuff a real-live person between the two covers of a text', as Denzin (in Schmitt, 1993: 130) puts it, we can describe truthfully, delimited segments of real-live persons' lives. Indeed, in so delimiting, we may get closer to people's lived experience. As Charmaz (1995) notes, many people do not want themselves revealed in their totality. Recognizing this and responding accordingly may result in deeper, fuller conceptualizations of those aspects of people's lives we are most interested in understanding.

Much the same deserves to be said about the interactionist researcher concerning the place and fullness of his or her life within the interview context. Scholarship should preserve 'in it the presence, concerns, and the experience of the [researcher] as knower and discoverer' (Smith, 1987: 92) so that the subjectivity that exists in all social research will be a visible part of the project, and thus available to the reader for examination. As Harding (1987: 9) notes, when 'the researcher appears to us not as an invisible, anonymous voice of authority, but as a real, historical individual with concrete, specific desires and interests' the research process can be scrutinized.

In addition, being a 'good listener' – while necessary to produce rich interview accounts – does not end the attention we should pay to how our positionality affects the production of qualitative interview data. Interviews are 'instances of social action – speech-acts or events with common properties, recurrent structures, cultural conventions, and recognizable genres' (Atkinson, 2005: 6; see also Presser and Sandberg, 2015). Moreover, what stories interviewees share with us, and how they tell their stories, may be shaped not just by the rapport established, but also by social similarities and distances between us and those we interview. Yet, rather than argue that this creates 'bias' or makes the data of limited utility, we suggest that paying attention to how our social positioning affects the interview exchange offers an important site for social inquiry (see Grenz, 2005; Miller, 2010; Panfil, 2015).

In our experience, interviewees will tell us, if given the chance, which of our interests and formulations make sense and non-sense to them. In our respective studies, we each have described instances in which the interviewer brought up a topic that was seen by the subject as irrelevant or misinterpretation, and they offered correction (Glassner and Loughlin, 1987: 36; Miller, 2001). Of paramount importance regarding how (and how much) we present ourselves is the influence this presentation has on interviewees' ability and willingness to tell various sorts of stories. Richardson notes, 'People organize their personal biographies and understand them through the stories they create to explain and justify their life experiences' (1990: 23; see also Presser and Sandberg, 2015). We believe a strength of qualitative interviewing is precisely its capacity to access self-reflexivity among interview subjects, leading to the telling of stories that allow us to understand and theorize the social world.

In-depth interviewing is a particularly useful method for examining the social world from the points of view of research participants. As Orbuch (1997: 455) explains, interview accounts offer a means of identifying 'culturally embedded normative explanations [of events and behaviours, because they] represent ways in which people organize views of themselves, of others, and of their social worlds'. Yet, we argue here that they do more than provide information on cultural and subjective meanings. Rigorous analysis of accounts provides two intertwined sets of findings: evidence of the nature of the phenomena under investigation, including the contexts and situations in which it emerges, as well as insights into the cultural frames people use to make sense of these experiences. Combined, they offer important insights for theoretical understanding.

TWO ILLUSTRATIONS

We have suggested that narratives emerging from interviews are situated in social worlds, they come out of worlds that exist outside of the interview itself. We argue not only for the existence of these worlds, but also for our ability as researchers to capture elements of these worlds in our scholarship. To illustrate some of the interactionist strategies for achieving that access we turn to two of the first author's research efforts (Miller, 2001; 2008).

One of the guys: studying gender inequality and gender ideologies in youth gangs

When analysing in-depth interviews in a study of young women's experiences in gangs, Miller was faced with an important discrepancy that required address. While most girls were adamant that they were 'equals' with the boys in their gangs, they simultaneously described systematic gender inequalities within these groups, which they themselves often upheld through their own attitudes about other girls. Thus, her analysis required her to make sense of the disconnect between girls' claims that they were 'one of the guys' (a cultural frame they used to situate themselves in the gang) and their descriptions of inequality (experiences situated in the gang context).

Successful interviewing involves the interviewee feeling comfortable and competent enough in the interaction to 'talk back' (Blumer, 1969: 22) – to label particular topics irrelevant, point out misinterpretations and offer corrections. When respondents talk back they provide insights into the meanings of their social worlds and into their experience within these worlds. One way Miller's interviewees talked back – to her and to imagined audiences like her – was their resistance to her efforts to discuss how gender inequality shaped their experiences in gangs. In doing so, they situated their personal narratives within larger cultural stories about girls in gangs, both by vigilantly challenging these stories, and by embracing them in their discussions of 'other' girls.

A dominant theme in Miller's interviews was girls' insistence that their gangs were a space of gender equality, where males and females were treated as equals. As one explained, 'they give every last one of us respect the way they give the males'. Another was visibly frustrated with her line of questions about gender, and repeatedly cut her off in response:

JM:	You said before that the gang was about half girls and half guys? Can you tell me more about that? Like you said you don't think there are any differences in terms of what -
Interviewee:	There isn't!
JM:	Ok, can you tell me more -
Interviewee:	Like what? There isn't, there isn't like, there's nothing - boy, girl, white, black, Mexican, Chinese.

Such exchanges were a direct challenge to one sort of cultural story about girls in gangs. A longstanding cultural stereotype of girls' roles in gangs is that they are peripheral or auxiliary members whose primary function is as sexual outlets for male gang members (Campbell, 1984). For the young women in Miller's study, claiming a normative space of equality was an important means of rejecting this interpretation of their experiences.

Despite this prevailing story of gender equality, the young women's descriptions of the activities and behaviours of gang members markedly contradicted these statements. Instead, without exception, girls described a distinct gender hierarchy within mixed-gender gangs that included male leadership, a sexual double standard, the sexual exploitation of some girls, perceptions of girls as 'weak' and boys as 'strong', and most girls' exclusion from serious gang crime – specifically, those acts that built status and reputation within their groups (Miller, 2001).

It would be easy to simply discount girls' claims of gender equality as wrong or misguided. Instead, making sense of such contradictions provides an important basis for building theoretical insight. Miller's task, then, was to explain the basis on which girls made claims to gender equality and the functions that such claims served. First, she looked carefully at *how* girls made the case that they were treated as equals. Examining their accounts closely, it became apparent that the means by which this was accomplished was not to make broad claims that all women should be treated as equals, but to differentiate themselves from *other* girls – and in the process, uphold the masculine status norms of their groups. As one explained:

> A lot of girls get scared. Don't wanna break their nails and stuff like that. So, ain't no need for them to try to be in no gang. And the ones that's in it, most of the girls that's in act like boys. That's why they in, 'cause they like to fight and stuff. They know how to fight and they use guns and stuff.

In addition, because the young women Miller interviewed also described a range of gender inequalities in their gangs, they had to account for these descriptions of girls' mistreatment, and do so in ways that were consistent with their central belief in the norm of gender equality. Again, this required looking at not only *what* they said about girls' mistreatment, but also *how* they made sense of it. Closely analysing their accounts, Miller discovered that young women drew on two types of frames: first, they individualized acts involving the mistreatment of females, describing them as unique or exceptional cases. When this was not possible – for instance, when the mistreatment was recurring or routine – they sought ways to hold girls accountable for their mistreatment. They did so by justifying particular acts as deserved because of the behaviours of the girls in question, and by characterizing *other* young women as possessing particular negative 'female' traits – having 'big mouths', being 'troublemakers', or being "ho's" or 'wrecks'.[1]

The other piece of the puzzle that required explanation was *why* young women both insisted on their equality and strongly differentiated themselves from other girls.

---

[1]Wreck was a slang term used to name girls who were seen as sexually promiscuous.

Answering this question was key to providing an analytic framework that could link the structures of gender inequality in gangs to the processes by which they were reproduced and maintained. Miller did so by situating their gang participation in the broader contexts of their environments and life experiences, concluding that the overarching gender hierarchy in girls' gangs was not unique, but was embedded within a broader social environment in which gender inequalities were entrenched.[2]

Thus, to the extent that there *was* normative space within gangs for 'gender equality' – however narrowly defined – gang participation provided young women with empowerment and self-definition that were not available in other contexts. But this required them to accept a 'patriarchal bargain' (Kandiyoti, 1988) by which *they* could lay claim to being 'one of the guys' only by supporting and justifying the mistreatment of *other* girls. Identifying with dominant beliefs about women, and rejecting such images for themselves, allowed them to construct a space of gender equality *for themselves*, and draw particular advantages from their gangs that were less available in other social spaces in their lives (see Miller, 2001, Chapter 8, for a more detailed account of the analysis).

Another challenge Miller faced was that her findings were counter to previous research on young women in gangs, which tended to uncover bonds of solidarity among young women. This also required explanation. She began by looking closely at what differences might exist between the gangs that previous researchers had studied and those in her sample. She noticed that the gender composition of most gangs in her sample was 'skewed', with a preponderance of male members. In contrast, other studies reported on gangs that were gender-balanced or all-female. This led her to hypothesize that group proportion shaped gender dynamics in gangs.

To do so, she employed a constant comparative method within her data, whereby she continuously 'attempt[ed] to find another case through which to test out [her] provisional hypothesis' (Silverman, 2006: 296). She carefully sought instances in her data in which girls strongly articulated their position as 'one of the guys', as well as instances in which girls were critical of gender inequalities and espoused supportive relationships with other girls. What she discovered supported her hypothesis – the few girls in her study in gender-balanced or all-female gangs did not match the pattern she had previously uncovered. Her distinct findings about 'one of the guys' were shaped by the gender composition of girls' gangs, with this pattern revealed through a constant comparative method in the analytic process.

'Running trains': the interview as joint accomplishment

Some scholars argue that researchers should be members of the groups we study, in order to have the subjective knowledge necessary to truly understand their life experiences (Collins,

---

[2]This insight emerged from stories girls told that were peripheral to their gangs, and from situating these stories within other research.

1990; Taylor et al., 1995). Such insights are important to remain attuned to; however, we suggest that *both* social differences and similarities can be put to use in analysing social worlds. We illustrate by drawing from Miller's (2008) project on violence against African American young women in urban neighbourhoods, in which interviews were conducted by several interviewers, with divergent positions of similarity and difference from the interviewees.

Miller's research uncovered the practice, as described by young men, of 'running trains' on girls: sexual encounters that involved two or more young men engaging in penetrative sexual acts with a single young woman. Nearly half of the young men interviewed described engaging in such behaviours. And while researchers classify such incidents as gang rape, and young women interviewed for the project did so as well, the young men defined girls' participation in 'trains' as consensual. Thus, it was important to examine how young men understood 'running trains', and especially, how they constructed these behaviours as consensual.

In this case, interviews conducted by two research assistants – one a white European man (Dennis), the other an African American woman who grew up in the same community as research participants (Toya) – revealed two distinct types of accounts of the behaviour, each of which revealed different dimensions of the meaning and enactment of 'running trains' for young men.

A striking feature of the accounts provided to Dennis was the adamancy with which boys claimed that girls were willing, even eager, participants. Moreover, their descriptions were particularly graphic, focusing specific attention on the details of their sexual performances. Consider the following example:

> I mean, one be in front, one be in back. You know sometimes, you know like, say, you getting in her ass and she might be sucking the other dude dick. Then you probably get her, you probably get her to suck your dick while he get her in the ass. Or he probably, either I'll watch, and so she sucking your dick, or while you fuck her in the ass. It, I mean, it's a lot of ways you can do it.

This account, which emerged in an interview conducted by a white male interviewer, emphasized young men's performance and was sexually graphic. Research on gang rape suggests that group processes play a central role: its enactment increases solidarity among groups of young men, and the victim is treated as an object (Franklin, 2004). Just as performance played a central role in young men's accounts of these incidents, their accounts were themselves a particular sort of masculine performance in the context of their interview exchange.

In contrast, when young men were interviewed about their participation in 'running trains' by Toya – the African American female interviewer – two different features emerged. First, their accounts were much less sexually graphic. Second, due in part to Toya's concern with issues of consent, she asked follow-up questions that challenged young men's construction of the events as consensual. This helped reveal how young men accomplished this construct. The following conversation with Terence is illustrative:

Terence:	It was some girl that my friend had knew for a minute, and he, I guess he just came to her and asked her, 'is you gon' do everybody?' or whatever and she said 'yeah'. So he went first and then, I think my other partner went, then I went, then it was like two other dudes behind me … It was at [my friend's] crib.
Toya:	Were you all like there for a get together or party or something?
Terence:	It was specifically for that for real, 'cause he had already let us know that she was gon' do that, so.
Toya:	So it was five boys and just her?
Terence:	Yeah.
Toya:	And so he asked her first, and then he told you all to come over that day?
Terence:	We had already came over. 'Cause I guess he knew she was already gon' say yeah or whatever. We was already there when she got there.
Toya:	Did you know the girl?
Terence:	Naw, I ain't know her, know her like for real know her. But I knew her name or whatever. I had seen her before. That was it though.
Toya:	So when you all got there, she was in the room already?
Terence:	Naw, when we got there, she hadn't even got there yet. And when she came, she went in the room with my friend, the one she had already knew. And then after they was in there for a minute, he came out and let us know that she was 'gon, you know, run a train or whatever. So after that, we just went one by one.

By Terence's account – revealed through Toya's questions – the young woman arrived at a boy's house that she knew and may have been interested in. Waiting for her on arrival were four additional young men whom she did not know or know well. And they had come in advance specifically for the purpose of 'running a train' on her. While Terence described the incident as consensual – because his friend said 'she was down', his description of what transpired provided evidence that the young woman had not freely consented. Terence constructed the act as consensual on the word of his friend, rather than identifying that unexpectedly being outnumbered was, for the girl, a coercive context.[3]

Likewise, Tyrell described 'running a train' on a girl, and also described it as consensual. Toya's question about the details of the event revealed contradictory evidence, so she asked him whether he thought the girl felt bad about what happened. Tyrell replied:

Tyrell:	I can't even say. I don't even know her like that. I really can't say. She do that kinda stuff all the time.
Toya:	She does?
Tyrell:	No. I'm just saying. I don't know. If she don't she probably did feel bad, but if she do she probably wouldn't feel bad … But if she didn't really wanna do it, she shouldn't have did it.

Tyrell slipped easily into noting that 'she do that kinda stuff all the time', which is in keeping with cultural scripts that blame women for their victimization. When pressed, though, he conceded that he had no basis on which to draw such a conclusion.

_____

[3]This interpretation is consistent with young women's accounts of having 'trains' run on them, which they described as non-consensual.

The role that social similarities and differences between the interviewers and interviewees played in producing these disparate accounts of the same phenomenon also cannot be discounted. Both revealed facets of the nature of 'running trains'. Dennis's interviews demonstrated its function as masculine performance. Indeed, young men's acts of *telling* Dennis about the events were masculine performances, constructed in response to *whom* they were doing the telling. In contrast, Toya's interviews revealed evidence of the processes by which young men construct their interpretations of girls' consent, and reveal how they do so by discounting the points of view of their female victims (see King, 2003). This example suggests that it is both necessary and useful to pay close attention to how the interview context shapes accounts. Doing so can reveal multifaceted features of behaviours and their meanings. Moreover, it reveals the benefits for data analysis that can emerge by utilizing diverse research teams, and using this diversity itself as a means of furthering the analysis (Miller, 2010).

Finding realities in interviews

We have suggested that a strength of qualitative interviewing is the opportunity it provides to collect and rigorously examine narrative accounts of social worlds. In Miller's illustrations, several facets of the interviews – the disjuncture between the cultural frames adopted and description of experiences, and the different types of accounts that emerge from interviews with different interviewers – provide important insights into how young people understand their place in gangs, their participation in troubling behaviours and the broader social worlds in which they live. We have suggested that it is possible to find realities within interviews – stories that reveal 'culturally embedded normative explanations' (Orbuch, 1997: 455) are a significant aspect of this reality, but so are accounts of events and activities that ultimately contradict these stories (see also Miller and Carbone-Lopez, 2015). By juxtaposing gang girls' stories of equality with incongruous descriptions of gender *inequality*, Miller (2001) built her theoretical discussion around the contradictory operation of gender within gangs. Likewise, comparing young men's descriptions of 'running trains' as they were told to different interviewers – one who shared their gender but not their race, and another who shared their race but not gender – provided insights into the role of masculinity in this behaviour, how such events played out and the ways that young men constructed them as consensual.

CHAPTER SUMMARY

Silverman argues that 'while "open-ended" interviews can be useful, we need to justify departing from the naturally occurring data that surrounds us and to be cautious about the "romantic" impulse which identifies "experience" with "authenticity"' (2001: xx). We agree, but with different words in scare quotes.

On the one hand, we have suggested that interviewers need not resort to romanticism, or to identifying experience as authenticity, in order to utilize interviewees' stories to produce authentic accounts of social worlds. On the other hand, we would put in scare quotes 'naturally occurring data', because we question the grounds for any neat distinction between the natural and cultural, in sociological data as elsewhere (cf. Douglas, 1986). In making such claims, it is not that we are 'not too sure whether interviews are purely local events or express underlying external realities', as Silverman (2001: xx) has suggested. Instead, we argue against the dualistic imperative to classify them as one or the other.

FUTURE PROSPECTS

Qualitative interviewing produces accounts that offer researchers a means of examining intertwined sets of findings: evidence of the nature of the phenomena under investigation, including the contexts and situations in which it emerges, as well as insights into the cultural frames people use to make sense of these experiences. Combined, they offer important insights for theoretical understanding. Two approaches to data collection and analysis point to future directions for research using this methodological approach. The use of comparative samples is one. This strategy allows for some specification of similarities and variations in social process and meaning systems across groups, settings, and/or over time. Second, interview-based research can be enhanced when it includes diverse research teams, and this diversity is taken into account in data analysis. Both strategies can strengthen internal validity by allowing for more refined analysis and greater contextual specification.

All we sociologists have are stories. Some come from other people, some from us, some from our interactions with others. What matters is to understand how and where the stories are produced, which sort of stories they are, and how we can put them to honest and intelligent use in theorizing about social life.

Study questions

1. How does the authors' constructionist position differ from positivism, emotionalism and radical social constructionism?
2. How do the authors make the case that interviews provide evidence of both the nature of social worlds and individuals' culturally embedded understanding of social worlds?
3. How do the authors argue that contradictory evidence in narrative accounts can lead to theoretical insights?
4. How do the authors argue that social distance and social similarity can be put to use in theorizing about social worlds?

Recommended reading

For a contemporary introduction to grounded theory, which is an analytic strategy frequently used by qualitative researchers who employ in-depth interviews, see:
Charmaz, K. (2006) *Constructing Grounded Theory: A Practical Guide Through Qualitative Analysis*. Thousand Oaks, CA: Sage Publications.

Part II of the following new volume includes essays by a diverse group of social scientists (in psychology, sociology and anthropology) who describe how they utilize narratives to understand biography, identity and culture. Part III includes essays by scholars who bring distinct insider/outsider positions to their research, and combined, they provide a meaningful dialogue about how positionality can be put to theoretical use:
Miller, J. and Wilson, P. (eds) (2015) *Qualitative Research in Criminology*. Volume 20, *Advances in Criminological Theory* (Parts II and III). Piscataway, NJ: Transaction Publishers.

Using crime as the common theme, the following edited collection provides a range of case studies from qualitative interview research to illustrate the analysis of stories for understanding social worlds:
Presser, L. and Sandberg, S. (eds) (2015) *Narrative Criminology: Understanding Stories of Crime*. New York: New York University Press.

For a thorough overview of interviewing, including concrete advice on data collection, see this classic text:
Spradley, J. P. (1979) *The Ethnographic Interview*. Fort Worth, TX: Harcourt Brace Jonanovich.

Recommended online resources

For articles about interviews, go to the online journal *Forum: Qualitative Social Research* and click 'search' then enter 'interview':
www.qualitative-research.net/fqs/fqs-eng.htm

References

Atkinson, P. (2005) 'Qualitative research – unity and diversity', *Forum: Qualitative Social Research*, 6 (3). www.qualitative-research.net/index.php/fqs/issue/view/4/10 (accessed 1 December 2015).

Blumer, H. (1969) *Symbolic Interactionism: Perspective and Method*. Englewood Cliffs, NJ: Prentice Hall.

Campbell, A. (1984) *The Girls in the Gang*. New York: Basil Blackwell.

Charmaz, K. (1995) 'Between positivism and postmodernism: implications for methods', *Studies in Symbolic Interaction*, 17: 43–72.

Collins, P. H. (1990) *Black Feminist Thought*. Boston, MA: Unwin Hyman.

Dawson, L. L. and Prus, R. C. (1995) 'Postmodernism and linguistic reality versus symbolic interactionism and obdurate reality', *Studies in Symbolic Interaction*, 17: 105–24.

Denzin, N. K. (1991) 'Representing lived experiences in ethnographic texts', *Studies in Symbolic Interaction*, 12: 59–70.

Douglas, M. (1986) *Risk Acceptability According to the Social Sciences*. New York: Russell Sage Foundation.

Fine, G. A. and Sandstrom, K. L. (1988) *Knowing Children: Participant Observation with Minors*. Newbury Park, CA: Sage.

Franklin, K. (2004) 'Enacting masculinity: antigay violence and group rape as participatory theater', *Sexuality Research & Social Policy*, 1: 25–40.

Glassner, B. and Loughlin, J. (1987) *Drugs in Adolescent Worlds: Burnouts to Straights*. New York: St Martin's Press.

Grenz, S. (2005) 'Intersections of sex and power in research on prostitution: a female researcher interviewing male heterosexual clients', *Signs*, 30: 2092–113.

Harding, S. (1987) *Feminism and Methodology*. Bloomington: Indiana University Press.

Kandiyoti, D. (1988) 'Bargaining with patriarchy', *Gender & Society*, 2: 274–90.

King, N. (2003) 'Knowing women: straight men and sexual certainty', *Gender & Society*, 17: 861–77.

Latour, B. (1993) *We Have Never Been Modern*. Cambridge, MA: Harvard University Press.

Miller, J. (2001) *One of the Guys: Girls, Gangs and Gender*. New York: Oxford University Press.

Miller, J. (2008) *Getting Played: African American Girls, Urban Inequality, and Gendered Violence*. New York: New York University Press.

Miller, J. (2010) 'The impact of gender when studying "offenders on offending"', in W. Bernasco and M. Tonry (eds), *Offenders on Offending: Learning about Crime from Criminals*. London: Willan Press, pp. 161–83.

Miller, J. and Carbone-Lopez, K. (2015) 'Beyond "doing gender": incorporating race, class, place and life transitions into feminist drug research', *Substance Use and Misuse*, Early Online: 1–15. DOI: 10.3109/10826084.2015.978646.

Orbuch, T. L. (1997) 'People's accounts count: the sociology of accounts', *Annual Review of Sociology*, 23: 455–78.

Panfil, V. R. (2015) 'Queer anomalies? Overcoming assumptions in criminological research with gay men', in J. Miller and W. Palacios (eds), *Qualitative Research in Criminology*. Piscataway, NJ: Transaction Publishers, pp. 169–89.

Presser, L. and Sandberg, S. (eds) (2015) *Narrative Criminology: Understanding Stories of Crime*. New York: New York University Press.

Richardson, L. (1990) *Writing Strategies: Reaching Diverse Audiences*. Newbury Park, CA: Sage.

Rogers, R. S. and Rogers, W. S. (1992) *Stories of Childhood*. Toronto: University of Toronto Press.

Sanders, C. R. (1995) 'Stranger than fiction: insights and pitfalls in post-modern ethnography', *Studies in Symbolic Interaction*, 17: 89–104.

Schmitt, R. L. (1993) 'Cornerville as obdurate reality: retooling the research act through postmodernism', *Studies in Symbolic Interaction*, 15: 121–45.

Silverman, D. (2001) *Interpreting Qualitative Data: Methods for Analysing Talk, Text and Interaction*. London: Sage.

Silverman, D. (2006) *Interpreting Qualitative Data: Methods for Analyzing Talk, Text, and Interaction* (3rd edn). Thousand Oaks, CA: Sage Publications.

Smith, D. E. (1987) 'Women's perspective as a radical critique of sociology', in S. Harding (ed.), *Feminism and Methodology*. Bloomington: Indiana University Press. pp. 84–96.

Taylor, J. M., Gilligan, C. and Sullivan, A. M. (1995) *Between Voice and Silence: Women and Girls, Race and Relationship*. Cambridge, MA: Harvard University Press.

FIVE

Narrative Practice and the Active Interview

James A. Holstein and Jaber F. Gubrium

About this chapter

This chapter frames the interview as an actively constructed conversation through which narrative data are produced. It views the resulting data as by-products of narrative practice, distinguishing the *whats* and *hows* of a communicative process involving the active subjectivity behind interview participants. This view of the active interview has profound implications for how interview data are analysed.

Keywords

active interview, narrative practice, narrative work, narrative environments, participant agency, interview narratives, interview interaction, bias and rigour, qualitative data analysis

Qualitative research's increasing sophistication includes a concerted appreciation for the ways empirical material is produced and analysed. On one front, this heightened sensitivity has reframed the interview as an occasion for narrative production, inviting new forms of narrative analysis. Charles Briggs (2007: 552), for example, has encouraged researchers to rethink how interviews 'produce subjects, texts, knowledge, and authority', pointing us to how interview material is assembled, communicated and circulates in particular settings, as well as to its varying functions and consequences. These concerns characterize what Susan Chase (forthcoming) calls the emerging 'maturity' of narrative analysis. As Paul Atkinson (1997: 341) insists, researchers are now obliged to examine narratives for their 'construction in use: how actors improvise their personal narratives'. He underscores the importance of attending to 'how socially shared resources of rhetoric and narrative are deployed to generate recognizable, plausible, and culturally well-informed accounts'.

This chapter frames the interview process in terms of narrative practice and discusses its analytic implications. We argue that *all* interviews are active, despite attempts to regiment, standardize and neutralize the process. Regardless of how interviewers try to restrain their presence in the interview exchange, and no matter how forthright respondents are in offering their views, the resulting narratives are interactional accomplishments, not communicatively neutral artefacts. Underscoring this view, we use the characterization of the *active interview* to distinguish it from the more commonly discussed, passive model of the interview process. The term, however, does not denote a distinctive type of interview, differentiating it from, say, the standardized survey interview or the minimally directive life story interview. Instead, it highlights the inherent interpretive activity of *all* interviewing (see Holstein and Gubrium, 1995), which needs to be taken into account analytically.

THE INTERACTIONAL BASIS OF INTERVIEWING

Interviews vary from highly structured, standardized, quantitatively oriented survey interviews, to semi-formal guided conversations, to free-flowing informational exchanges. They collaboratively produce narratives of people's lives and circumstances. These narratives may be as truncated as forced-choice survey answers or as elaborate as oral life histories, but they are all incited and shaped by the interview process. Traditionally, the research interview has been viewed as a relatively straightforward data excavation procedure. Respondents were contacted, interviews scheduled, a location determined, ground rules set and the interviews proceeded. Questions were designed to elicit respondents' answers in an anticipatable form. The respondent's job was to provide information pertinent to the research project. Knowing his or her role, the respondent waited until questions were posed before answering. Duties did not extend to managing the encounter or raising queries of his or her own. This was the interviewer's responsibility. If the respondent asked questions, they were treated as requests for clarification.

This model of the interview has informed social research for decades. Most people are now well acquainted with what it takes to play either role, recognize what it means to interview someone and broadly know the aims of the interview process. The requirements of interviewing are familiar, whether they take the form of demographic questionnaires, product use surveys, internet polls or health inventories. The roles and expectations cross the borders of scientific and professional interviewing.

While this model is archetypal, most researchers also acknowledge the interactional basis of interviewing (see Warren and Karner, 2005; Conrad and Schober, 2008). The technical literature, however, typically stresses the need to keep conversational bias in check. Guides to interviewing – especially those oriented to standardized surveys – are primarily concerned with maximizing the flow of valid, reliable information while minimizing distortions of what the respondent knows (Gorden, 1987; Fowler and Mangione, 1990). But a heightened sensitivity to the constitutive properties of communication has refocused attention on the *in situ* activeness of interviews (e.g. Kvale, 1996; Houtkoop-Steenstra, 2000). These perspectives view meaning as socially constituted; experience is the product of the actions undertaken to produce and understand it (see Cicourel, 1964; Garfinkel, 1967; Cicourel, 1974). Treating interviewing as a social encounter in which information is actively formed and shaped implies that the interview is not so much a neutral conduit or possible source of distortion as an occasion for constructing experiential knowledge (Gubrium and Holstein, 1995; Holstein and Gubrium, 1995; Gubrium and Holstein, 2012).

Interview situations inherently – not incidentally – shape the form and content of what is said. Interviews result in locally pertinent narratives – some longer than others – that represent versions of opinion, persons, events and the world at large. Indeed, Aaron Cicourel (1974) maintains that interviews impose particular ways of understanding reality upon subjects' responses. Thus, the circumstances of narrative production are deeply and unavoidably implicated in creating the meanings that ostensibly reside within individual experience. Meaning is not merely directly elicited by skilful questioning, nor is it simply transported through truthful replies; it is strategically assembled in the interview process (Holstein and Gubrium, 1995). Interview participants are as much practitioners of experiential information construction as they are repositories or excavators of experiential knowledge.

Consequently, technical attempts to strip interviews of their interactional constituents are futile (Houtkoop-Steenstra, 2000; Maynard et al., 2002). Instead of refining the long list of methodological constraints under which standardized interviews should be conducted, researchers should embrace the view that the interview is an active, interactional process activation and capitalize analytically upon interviewers' and respondents' constitutive contributions to the production of interview data. This entails conscientiously attending to the interview process as a form of narrative practice that not only produces results, but also points to the constructive work and auspices operating in varied interview encounters (Gubrium and Holstein, 2009).

In reconceptualizing interviews in these terms, researchers need to pay explicit attention to both the practical *hows* and the substantive *whats* of interviewing, taking care to give them equal status in both the research process and in reporting results (see Gubrium and Holstein, 1997, 2009). Understanding and describing *how* the narrative process unfolds in the interview is as critical as apprehending *what* is substantively said. As such, interaction, the immediate situation and institutional context are equally important. Both the *hows* and the *whats* always reflect the interview's circumstances and communicative practices.

This appreciation derives from ethnomethodologically informed, social constructionist and ethnographic sensibilities (see Holstein and Gubrium, 2008). Ethnomethodology, constructionism, poststructuralism, postmodernism and some versions of feminism are all variously attuned to activity, subjectivity, complexity, perspective and meaning-construction. In one way or another, all cast an analytic eye on narrative practice. If their concerns and debates often relate to the epistemological status of interview data, they do not lose sight of the everyday facets of experience. At the same time, while the perspective we describe has postmodern sensibilities, it does not abide the view that interviews are simply another unruly swirl of signifiers (see Gubrium and Holstein, 1997). Rather, animated as they might be, interview narratives reflect both socially grounded interpretive practices and the subject matter with which the practices are concerned.

Key points

- A traditional view of the ideal interview is that of a neutral conduit for excavating and conveying undistorted knowledge.
- Researchers now recognize the interview as a meaning-making conversation – a site of narrative practice.
- Interviewing is unavoidably interactional and constructive. In a word, the interview actively produces knowledge.

IMAGES OF SUBJECTIVITY

All models of the interview emanate from images of subjects behind interview participants (Holstein and Gubrium, 1995). These images provide the basis for theorizing the interview process, as well as for conferring varying degrees of epistemological agency upon interview participants. Conceiving of the interview as active radically transforms interview subjectivity from fundamentally passive to concertedly active and agentic. In traditional interviewing, respondents are envisioned as being vessels of answers to whom interviewers direct their questions. Respondents are seen as repositories of facts, reflections, opinions, sentiments and other traces of experience. For example, legendary journalistic interviewer Studs Terkel worked with the traditional image, claiming to simply turn on his tape recorder and ask people to talk. Writing of the interviews he did for his classic book, *Working*, Terkel (1972: xxv) explained:

> There were questions, of course. But they were casual in nature ... the kind you would ask while having a drink with someone; the kind he would ask you ... In short, it was a conversation. In time, the sluice gates of dammed up hurts and dreams were open.

Others have likened traditional interviewing to 'prospecting' for the true facts and feelings residing within the respondent (cf. Kvale, 1996). The image of prospecting turns the interview into a search-and-discovery mission, with the interviewer intent on detecting what is already there within more or less cooperative respondents. The challenge lies in excavating information as efficiently as possible, without contaminating it. Highly refined interview techniques ostensibly streamline, systematize and sanitize the process. Occasionally, researchers acknowledge that it may be difficult to obtain accurate or honest information, but the information is still imagined, in principle, as contained in pristine form within the respondent's vessel of answers. The challenge is to formulate reliable questions and provide an atmosphere conducive to open communication between interviewer and respondent. The challenge is all up-front, in recalcitrant respondents and feckless interviewers, not in the vessel of answers.

In the vessel-of-answers approach, the image of the subject behind the respondent is passive, even while the subject's respondent may be either cooperative, reluctant or otherwise difficult to deal with (see Adler and Adler, 2002). The subjects themselves are not engaged in the production of knowledge. If the interviewing process goes 'by the book' and is nondirective and unbiased, respondents will validly and reliably speak the unadulterated facts of their subjects' experience. Contamination creeps in from the interview setting, its participants and their interaction. The imagined subject, in contrast, is more-or-less communicative, and under ideal conditions, his or her respondent serves up accurate, authentic reports when beckoned.

Much of the traditional methodological literature on interviewing deals with the nuances of aligning respondents with a passive subjectivity. Understandably, the vessel-of-answers view leads interviewers to be careful in how they ask questions, lest their method of inquiry pollute or bias what lies within the subject. This has prompted the development of myriad procedures for obtaining unadulterated information, most of which rely on interviewer and question neutrality. Successfully implementing neutral practices elicits truths held uncontaminated in this vessel of answers. 'Good data' result from the successful application of these techniques.

This image evokes a complementary model of the subject behind the interviewer. Because the interviewer aims to extract information, he or she stands apart from the actual data; the interviewer merely unearths and collects what is already there. Interviewers are expected to avoid shaping the information they extract. This involves controlling one's opinions as an interviewer so as not to influence what the passive interview subject can communicate. Interviewers resist supplying particular frames of reference or personal information in the interview. Interviewers are expected to minimize reactivity – to keep themselves and their preferences out of the interview conversation. Neutrality is the byword. Ideally, the interviewer uses his or her interpersonal skills to merely encourage the expression of, but not help construct, the attitudes, sentiments and behaviours under consideration. The ideal interviewer is a facilitator, not a co-producer, of pertinent information. This stance relegates the interviewer's involvement in the interview to a necessarily restrained, pre-ordained role, one that is constant from one interview to another. Should the interviewer introduce anything other than minor variations on pre-specified questions, the viability of the interview is compromised.

As researchers increasingly appreciate the narrative agency of subjects behind interview participants, the interview is being recast as an occasion for actively constructing, rather than excavating, information. Participants are viewed as narrative practitioners in the enterprise, working together to discern and designate the recognizable and orderly features of the experience under consideration (see Clandinin, 2007; Riessman, 2008; Gubrium and Holstein, 2009; Bamberg, 2012; Chase, forthcoming; Riessman in this volume). This transforms the subject behind the respondent from a repository of information into an animated, productive source of narrative knowledge (see Polkinghorne, 1988). If the subject behind the respondent retains the details of his or her inner life and social world, in the very process of offering them up to the interviewer, he or she narratively assembles them into a coherent account. The respondent can hardly spoil what is otherwise subjectively constructed.

With active subjectivity also lurking behind the interviewer, his or her participation is not a matter of standardization or constraint; neutrality is not the issue. One cannot very well taint the solicitation of information if this knowledge does not exist in some pure form apart from the process of communication. Rather, the active subject behind the interviewer is a working narrative partner of the active subject behind the respondent. From the time one identifies a research topic, to respondent selection, questioning and answering, and, finally, to the interpretation of responses, the interviewing enterprise is a narrative project.

Key points

- All approaches to interviewing rest on images of subjects behind respondents and interviewers.
- Conventional approaches envision the subject behind the respondent as essentially passive.
- Images of subjects behind interview participants have important implications for how the interview process is conducted and how interview data are construed.

NARRATIVE PRACTICE

As brief or as extended as they may be, interview narratives are actively assembled using the interpretive resources at hand, in light of the working contingencies of the interview project. Yet, meaning is not constantly formulated anew, but reflects relatively enduring and recognizable forms of meaning (Foucault, 1979), such as the research topics presented by interviewers, locally accepted ways of orienting to those topics, institutionalized means of understanding and talking about things, participants' biographical particulars, and larger discourses deploying 'what everyone knows' (Gubrium and Holstein, 1997). Those resources are astutely and adroitly adapted to the demands of the occasion, so that meaning is neither predetermined nor absolutely unique. Neither established pattern nor novelty prevail.

The *whats* and the *hows*

One family of working contingencies involves the *whats* of interviewing, dealing with the substantive demands and circumstances of the research enterprise. They provide interpretive signposts and resources for developing interview narratives. The eventual narrative is, to some degree, always already present in the kind of response prompted by the research project through the interviewer. From there, it is constructively elaborated in terms that resonate with the salient circumstances involved in, and evoked by, the interview process. These circumstances constitute the interview's narrative environment, discussed below. As interviewing practices are deployed, participants are encouraged to narratively link the topics of interest to biographical particulars, taking account of the circumstantial contingencies of the interview process, producing a subject who both responds to and is affected by the narrative environment. Analysis must take these environments into consideration so that results are not merely apprehended without regard for context but are also examined for circumstantial and cultural resonances.

Another group of working contingencies entails the constructive *hows* of the interview process. Interview narratives develop within ongoing interaction. The interaction is not merely incidental; it is a constitutive part of the meanings and accounts that emerge. In this context, narratives don't simply flow forth, but instead, are formulated and shaped in collaboration between the respondent and the interviewer. Participants continually construct and reflexively modify their roles in the exchange of questions and answers as the interview unfolds. The *whats* of the interview have to be interactionally put into place, managed and sustained.

The distinction between the *hows* and *whats* of the interview process relates broadly to different methodologies, which can be applied together, reflexively, with the appropriate analytic attitudes to study narrative practice (see Gubrium and Holstein, 2009). The *hows* constitute the everyday work of practice, the process by which, in the case of interviews, the interview gets 'done', so to speak. The appropriate methodology on this front involves techniques for analysing the meaning-making work of talk and interaction. The *whats* constitute the everyday substances of talk and interaction. The appropriate methodology on this front entails the ethnographic examination of available accounts, their circulation, stakes, negotiation and likely consequences within pertinent narrative environments.

Narrative work

The active vision of the interview highlights the narrative work that constitutes interview conversations. The appropriate analytic attitude for studying narrative work is to bracket or temporarily set aside interest in the *whats* of the matter in order to pay attention to how particular *whats* are constructed. This temporarily focuses attention on the interactional activity through which narratives are assembled and sustained or reconfigured. Narrative work includes any communicative activity involved in producing interview accounts: how interview participants work up adequate responses and what they attempt to accomplish in the process. As the term 'work' suggests, interview participants purposefully and concertedly orient to a specified task. It is a collaboration that relies on the artful application of communicative skill. In general, narrative work is not done self-consciously; it is mostly seen but unnoticed. In the vision of the active interview, one goal for researchers is to open this work to view, display its mechanics and local contingencies, and describe how it operates.

Put differently, interview participants not only ask and answer questions, but also simultaneously engage in 'speech activities' – the integral and inexorable narrative work that even survey interview participants engage in as they ask and answer questions (see Mishler, 1986; Maynard et al., 2002; Schaeffer and Maynard, 2002). Some aspects of this work involve the conversational structures and discursive machinery necessary for the interviewer and the respondent to mutually construct and monitor speech exchanges. Focusing on these *hows*, researchers might explore the ways in which participants collaboratively produce their senses of the developing interview agenda. Even the slightest or most subtle, mundane speech act may be integral to an unfolding narrative. To eliminate them can, in effect, stop the conversation, hence the interview. Thus, researchers need to be analytically sensitive to interview participants' routine conversational practices.

For example, researchers might begin by examining narrative activation – the work and mechanisms that elicit and encourage interview narratives. Whereas the respondent actively constructs and assembles interview narratives, he or she does not simply 'break out' or continue talking. Neither elaborate stories nor one-word replies emerge without incitement and conversational facilitation. An animated sense of interviewing suggests that researchers delve into how this happens. Alternatively, researchers might consider the broader mechanics and activities of meaning-making, the process of linking together and composing meaningful interview accounts. Their focus might include the linkages that are drawn between things said and done, and the elaboration of these linkages into meaningful patterns. Or they might examine the performative contours of narrative presentation, the tactics and/or concerted collaboration of participants, or the interactional controls that participants use to constrain accounts. As they proceed, the interview researcher is guided by leading analytic questions: 'How can the process of composing interview accounts be conceptualized?' and 'How can the empirical process be described?'

Narrative environments

While actively constructed interview narratives convey a sense of personal agency and spontaneity, they are not without their substantive groundings. The applicable analytic attitude for studying the way narrative environments figure in accounts of experience is to bracket or temporarily set aside interest in the *hows* of narrative practice in order to pay attention to what is at stake in the construction process. According to Erving Goffman (1981 [1967]), individuals obtain narrative footing as they move through various moral environments. These environments provide the expectations, accountability structures and interpretive resources for understanding and conveying experience. Moral environments are also narrative environments. Everett Hughes (1984 [1942]) expands this observation to the institutional world at large, arguing that everyday 'going concerns' specify pertinent ways of making sense of everyday realities. Hughes is suggesting that social institutions broadly construed provide preferred and expectable narrative options – the landscape of more-or-less anticipatable narrative possibilities associated with particular social circumstances.

Every day, we present ourselves in a panoply of going concerns, from the myriad formal organizations in which we work, study, play and recover, to the countless informal associations and networks to which we belong, to our membership in racial, ethnic and gendered communities. Taken together, these concerns establish conditions of possibility (Foucault, 1979) for the construction of experience. Human service agencies, for example, narratively formulate the deepest enclaves of the self to ameliorate personal and social problems. Lives are storied in the process, along both formal and informal institutional lines. Self-help organizations proliferate, and their associated literatures clamour at us from the tabloid racks of most supermarkets and the shelves of every bookstore. 'Psychobabble' on radio and TV talk shows constantly prompts us to formulate (or reformulate) our stories, aiming to give voice to the selves we do or should live by. Political talk shows offer contrasting narrative templates, railing that individuals are bereft of personal or moral accountability or that social forces make it impossible for disadvantaged individuals to get a fair shake. Interviewing conversations are subject to all of these influences.

These contingencies coalesce into discernible narrative environments that suggest relevant questions for interviewers and pertinent answers for respondents. Personal responses are not dictated, but the conditions of possibility for situationally reasonable and accountable answers are firmly in place. These narrative environments may be as informal as the sequential context of the interview conversation or as formal as a census survey interview. Regardless of the setting, interviewing's narrative environments offer preferences that propose the *whats* of matters under consideration as well as shape the *hows* of narrative construction. While narrative work is an important operating component of interviewing, it tells only part of the story about the ways local relevancies mediate interview narratives. Researchers are obliged to examine what interview accounts mean in the substantive scheme of things as well as the way circumstances shape those accounts.

The landscape of consequential narrative environments that interview researchers might consider is virtually endless. They might consider how various orientations to intimate relationships or family life might shape what interview respondents tell us about the social and/or emotional contours of households or domestic arrangements. Alternatively, researchers might examine how local culture, social status, jobs and occupations, and formal organizational membership mediate the production of interview accounts. Just as importantly, the narrative environments of race, ethnicity, gender and sexuality may certainly provide analytic impetus for understanding a wide variety of interview accounts. In considering contextual matters that cross interview settings, researchers might analyse how participants in particular settings might shape and respond to accounts elicited and formulated in other settings.

To guard against overdetermining the role of either narrative environments or narrative work in the production of interview accounts, we must emphasize that interviewing refracts, but does not reproduce, the narratives deployed by going concerns. Interview participants, themselves, are biographically active in responding to the institutional mediations of the interview process. While institutional auspices provide resources for both asking questions and formulating answers, prescribe possible roles for interview participants, and privilege or marginalize certain accounts, these resources and roles are not automatically adopted and reproduced in practice. If participants are accountable to particular circumstances, such as conducting social-scientific research, completing job interviews or interrogating suspects in criminal procedures, they borrow from the variety of narrative resources available to them. They are more 'artful' (Garfinkel, 1967) than mechanistic in managing their roles and giving voice to experience.

As in producing jazz music, themes and improvisation are the hallmarks of narrative practice. Interview narratives are artfully assembled, discursively informed and circumstantially conditioned. They feature personal agency, novelty and innovation, while simultaneously evincing institutionalized patterns (Gubrium and Holstein, forthcoming). Because the stories we live by refract a world of competing going concerns, they do not uniformly reproduce a collection of accounts. The interplay of narrative work and narrative environments – the constructive *hows* and substantive *whats* of the matter which are alternately made visible by *analytic bracketing* (Gubrium and Holstein, 1997) – provides interviews with a discernible range of possibilities for asking and responding to questions about what we are and what our worlds are like. As Karl Marx (1956) might have put it, people actively narrate the contours of their lives, but not necessarily, or completely on, or in, their own terms.

Key points

- Interview participants concertedly engage in narrative work.
- This work takes place under the discernible auspices of narrative environments, which provide the conditions of possibility of intelligible and accountable interview narratives.
- The versions of meaningful experience that emerge from interviews are constituted in the reflexive interplay of the hows and the whats of the process.

FORMS OF RIGOUR

An emphasis on the active character of the interview might suggest to some that unacceptable bias is unavoidably introduced into the information-gathering process. 'Contamination' seems to lurk everywhere and understandably needs to be rigorously controlled. But this criticism only holds if one's point of departure is an image of passive participant subjectivity and a pristine vessel of answers. Bias is problematic if interview participants are viewed as purely information-producing commodities.

If the substance of interviewer responses is seen as a narrative product of the *hows* and *whats* of interviewing, interview data are neither preformed nor are they ever pristinely communicated. Thus, a different form of rigour is applicable. Any interview situation – no matter how formalized, restricted or standardized – relies upon interaction between participants who are constantly engaged in interpretive practice. Because interviewing is unavoidably collaborative, it is virtually impossible to free interaction from factors that could be construed as contaminants. All participants in an interview are inevitably implicated in meaning-making, even if that sometimes takes a highly constricted form.

While naturally occurring talk and interaction may appear to be more spontaneous than what transpires in an interview, this is true only in the sense that such interaction is staged by persons other than an interviewer. Seemingly spontaneous conversations are not necessarily more authentic, bias-free or unstructured. They simply take place in what have been conventionally recognized as non-interview settings. But these settings, too, play a definite role in the production of experiential knowledge – just like interview situations. Still, with the development of today's 'interview society', and the related increasing deprivatization of personal experience (see Gubrium and Holstein, 1995, 2002), the interview has become more and more commonplace, increasingly being a naturally occurring occasion in its own right.

Given an orientation to the active interview, how can one make sense of the validity of interview data? Once we acknowledge that all interactional and discursive data are products of interpretive practice, analysis begins to centre on the interplay of the *hows* and *whats* of interviewing. This stands in contrast to more traditional naturalistic research, which focuses mainly on the *whats* of the social worlds described in interviews (see Gubrium and Holstein, 1997). These interviews are typically analysed as more or less accurate descriptions of experience, as reports or re-presentations of reality, depending on how postmodern the author's sensibilities. Analysis takes the form of systematically grouping and summarizing the descriptions, and providing a coherent organizing framework that encapsulates and offers an understanding of experience or the social world respondents portray.

When researchers also consider the constructive activity operating in the interview process, the question of validity extends to the *hows* of the matter as they reflexively relate to the *whats*. Respondents' comments are not seen as reality reports delivered from a fixed repository. Instead, they are considered for the ways they narratively construct experiential reality in collaboration with the interviewer. The focus is as much on the assembly process as on what is assembled and conveyed. What is valid in this context draws not only from what is produced but also from the practice of its production.

Key points

- The concept of the active interview casts interview 'bias' in a new light. All participants in an interview are implicated in the construction of narrative reality. They are involved in narrative production, not contamination.
- The guiding question should not be whether interview procedures contaminate data, but how the interview constructively generates the information it does.
- Because interview data are products of narrative practice, data analysis demands a rigorous sensitivity to both the hows and whats of the interview process.

ORIENTING GUIDELINES

Following an active vision of the interview, we conclude with some general guidelines for orienting to interviews as narrative practice.

1. Treat the interview process and its informational by-products as the situated, collaborative, narrative accomplishment of interview participants, both respondents and interviewers.
2. Be alert to the communicative machinery through which interview narratives are produced. Consider how narratives are activated and cultivated in the context of the interview conversation.
3. Take care not to presume that the meaning of interview narratives is self-evident. Look for the linkages actively used to compose narratives in particular circumstances.
4. Focus on the work of meaning-making, documenting its contextual parameters. Don't assume that linkages will be drawn directly from inner formulations or automatically reproduce cultural or historical understandings.
5. Document how circumstances enter into the process of composing interview narratives. Look for distinctive patterns of linkage and composition, comparing and contrasting types of themes and informational content across and within circumstances.
6. Be alert to how the interviewer and respondent collaborate in the production of accounts. Consider the ways this is accomplished as well as how meaning within narratives is collaboratively shaped.
7. Be sensitive to, and ethnographically document, the ways in which interview narratives refract particular narrative environments.
8. Figure that even the slightest or most fleeting of relationships may be viewed as narrative environments. Orient to the ways these relationships are characterized in accounts of their organization, paying attention to the linkages drawn between their overall characterization and particular elements within and outside of them.
9. Observe formal institutional circumstances, such as organizational membership, for example, to identify the organizational resources and orientations that shape accounts. Listen to narratives with the aim of

showing how they are characteristic of organizational orientations and locations, taking note of how formalized categories are used to 'certify' or 'authorize' descriptions and accounts within and beyond the setting.

10. Attend carefully to ways in which interview accounts are informally embedded in organizational life, noting the institutional voices and preferences that are heard in individual narratives. If possible, compare the organizational narratives of various sites for differences and similarities in the construction of individual interview accounts.

CHAPTER SUMMARY AND FUTURE PROSPECTS

By way of summary, let's highlight the chapter's key points. First, the active interview is not a particular type of interview, to be distinguished from other forms of interviewing. Rather, we use the term 'active' to underscore the idea that all interviews are unavoidably active communicative enterprises. Even the standardized survey interview is active, because standardization actively structures the interviewer's input and restricts the respondent's range of responses.

Second, by specifying the vision of an active, animated interview, we are not offering an oblique criticism of traditional or standardized interviewing methods. Rather, by calling attention to the constitutive narrative activity inherent in all forms of interviewing, we are pointing to the wide array of interviewing practices that construct experience rather than privileging any particular version or foundational model of the interview. We are not suggesting that there is a gold standard for the design of interviews.

Third, at the same time, by focusing on the active character of interview narratives, we are not saying that 'anything goes'. Put into place, every image of subjectivity spawns its own operating rules. The concept of the active interview derives from an ontologically warranted basis for construing the production, collection and analysis of information in a particular way, and demands its own set of procedural and analytic guidelines.

The view of the narratively animated interview broadens the analytic purview of interview research to consider a wider array of questions than are typically considered in more traditional approaches. Researchers should no longer be content simply to catalogue what respondents say in an interview. The challenge of framing the interview as a thoroughly active process is to carefully consider what is said in relation to how, where, when and by whom narratives are conveyed, and to what end. Construing the interview as active provides a more richly variegated field of inquiry than ever before. This will require the continued development of contextually sensitive forms of narrative analysis (see Holstein and Gubrium, 2012; Chase, forthcoming) that capture the complexities of the realities under consideration.

Study questions

1. What does the term 'active interview' convey?
2. What is the view of participant subjectivity and agency in the active interview?
3. Distinguish between the hows and whats of narrative practice and how this can be applied to the interview.
4. How do narrative work and narrative environments shape interview narratives?

Recommended reading

Holstein, J. A. and Gubrium, J. F. (1995) *The Active Interview*. Newbury Park, CA: Sage.
This describes the active interview in greater depth. It provides extensive illustration of the interactional, interpretive activity that is part and parcel of all interviewing.

Kvale, S. (1996) *InterViews*. London: Sage.
An introduction to qualitative research interviewing. The book frames the issues in terms of the active view presented here.

Gubrium, J. A., Holstein, J. A., Marvasti, A. B. and McKinney, K. D. (eds) (2012) *The Sage Handbook of Interview Research: The Complexity of the Craft* (2nd edn). Thousand Oaks, CA: Sage.
This is a both a thematic and encyclopedic collection of state-of-the-art descriptions of different approaches to interviewing. The handbook covers theoretical, technical, analytic, and representation issues relating to interview research.

Gubrium, J. F. and Holstein, J. A. (2009) *Analyzing Narrative Reality*. Thousand Oaks, CA: Sage.
This offers an approach to analysing actively constructed narratives, including those produced by interviewing.

Holstein, J. A. and Gubrium, J. F. (eds) (2012) *Varieties of Narrative Analysis*. Thousand Oaks, CA: Sage.
This outlines an assortment of different approaches to narrative analysis from multiple disciples.

Riessman, C. K. (2008) *Narrative Methods for the Human Sciences*. Thousand Oaks, CA: Sage
This provides a comprehensive overview of qualitative research approaches to working with narrative materials.

Gubrium, J. F. and Holstein, J. A. (1997) *The New Language of Qualitative Method*. New York: Oxford University Press.
A variety of approaches to qualitative inquiry are presented. The authors then offer an analytics which reflexively attends to the *whats* and *hows* of interpretive practice.

Recommended online resources

Journal of Contemporary Ethnography:
http://jce.sagepub.com/

Qualitative Inquiry:
http://qix.sagepub.com/

References

Adler, P. A. and Adler, P. (2002) 'The reluctant respondent', in J. F. Gubrium and J. A. Holstein (eds), *Handbook of Interview Research*. Thousand Oaks, CA: Sage, pp. 515–36.

Atkinson, P. (1997) 'Narrative turn or blind alley?', *Qualitative Health Research*, 7: 325–44.

Bamberg, M. (2012) 'Narrative practice and identity negotiation', in J. A. Holstein and J. F. Gubrium (eds), *Varieties of Narrative Analysis*. Thousand Oaks, CA: Sage, p. 99–124.

Briggs, C. L. (2007) 'Anthropology, interviewing, and communicability in contemporary society', *Current Anthropology*, 48: 551–80.

Chase, S. E. (forthcoming) 'Narrative inquiry: toward theoretical and methodological maturity', in N. K. Denzin and Y. S. Lincoln (eds), *The Sage Handbook of Qualitative Research* (5th edn). Thousand Oaks, CA: Sage.

Cicourel, A. V. (1964) *Method and Measurement in Sociology*. New York: Free Press.

Cicourel, A. V. (1974) *Theory and Method in a Study of Argentine Fertility*. New York: Wiley.

Clandinin, D. J. (ed.) (2007) *Handbook of Narrative Inquiry*. Thousand Oaks, CA: Sage.

Conrad, F. G. and Schober, M. F. (2008) 'New frontiers in standardized survey interviewing', in S. N. Hesse-Biber and P. Leavy (eds), *Handbook of Emergent Methods*. New York: Guilford Press, pp. 173–88.

Foucault, M. (1979) *Discipline and Punish*. New York: Vintage.

Fowler, F. J. and Mangione, T. W. (1990) *Standardized Survey Interviewing*. Newbury Park, CA: Sage.

Garfinkel, H. (1967) *Studies in Ethnomethodology*. Englewood Cliffs, NJ: Prentice Hall.

Gorden, R. L. (1987) *Interviewing: Strategy, Techniques, and Tactics*. Homewood, IL: Dorsey.

Gubrium, J. F. and Holstein, J. A. (1995) 'Biographical work and new ethnography', in R. Josselson and A. Lieblich (eds), *The Narrative Study of Lives*, Vol. 3. Newbury Park, CA: Sage, pp. 45–58.

Gubrium, J. F. and Holstein, J. A. (1997) *The New Language of Qualitative Method*. New York: Oxford University Press.

Gubrium, J. F. and Holstein, J. A. (2002) 'From the individual interview to the interview society', in J. F. Gubrium and J. A. Holstein (eds), *Handbook of Interview Research*. Thousand Oaks, CA: Sage, pp. 3–32.

Gubrium, J. F. and Holstein, J. A. (2009) *Analyzing Narrative Reality*. Thousand Oaks, CA: Sage.

Gubrium, J. F. and Holstein, J. A. (2012) 'Narrative practice and the transformation of interview subjectivity', in J. F. Gubrium, J. A. Holstein, A. B. Marvasti and K. D. McKinney (eds), *The Sage Handbook of Interview Research: The Complexity of the Craft* (2nd edn). Thousand Oaks, CA: Sage, pp. 3–32.

Gubrium, J. F and Holstein, J. A (forthcoming) 'Analyzing novelty and pattern in institutional life narratives', in I. Goodson, A. Antikainen, M. Andrews and P. Skiles (eds), *International Handbook on Narrative and Life History*. London: Routledge.

Holstein, J. A. and Gubrium, J. F. (1995) *The Active Interview*. Newbury Park, CA: Sage.

Holstein, J. A. and Gubrium, J. F. (eds) (2008) *Handbook of Constructionist Research*. New York: Guilford.

Holstein, J. A. and Gubrium, J. F. (eds) (2012) *Varieties of Narrative Analysis*. Thousand Oaks, CA: Sage.

Houtkoop-Steenstra, H. (2000) *Interaction and the Standardized Survey Interview*. Cambridge: Cambridge University Press.

Hughes, E. C. (1984 [1942]) *The Sociological Eye: Selected Papers*. Chicago: Aldine.

Kvale, S. (1996) *InterViews*. London: Sage.

Marx, K. (1956) *Selected Writings in Sociology and Social Philosophy*, ed. T. Bottomore. New York: McGraw-Hill.

Maynard, D. W., Houtkoop-Steenstra, H., van der Zouwen, J. and Schaeffer, N. C. (eds) (2002) *Standardization and Tacit Knowledge: Interaction and Practice in the Survey Interview*. New York: John Wiley.

Mishler, E. G. (1986) *Research Interviewing: Context and Narrative*. Cambridge, MA: Harvard University Press.

Polkinghorne, D. E. (1988) *Narrative Knowing and the Human Sciences*. Albany: SUNY Press.

Riessman, C. K. (2008) *Narrative Methods for the Human Sciences*. Thousand Oaks, CA: Sage.

Schaeffer, N. C. and Maynard, D. W. (2002) 'Standardization and interaction in the survey interview', in J. F. Gubrium and J. A. Holstein (eds), *Handbook of Interview Research*. Thousand Oaks, CA: Sage, pp. 577–602.

Terkel, S. (1972) *Working*. New York: Avon.

Warren, C. A. B and Karner, T. (2005) *Discovering Qualitative Methods*. Los Angeles, CA: Roxbury.

SIX
Analysing Focus Group Data

Sue Wilkinson

About this chapter

This chapter examines two different approaches to analysing focus group data: content analysis and ethnographic analysis. It outlines key theoretical and epistemological issues associated with each. It provides an illustration of the use of each approach in analysing one segment of a particular focus group, in which women with breast cancer talk about the possible causes of their cancer. Finally, it briefly considers when it is most appropriate to use focus groups, and likely future developments in focus group research.

Keywords

breast cancer, content analysis, conversation analysis, ethnographic analysis, focus groups, interaction

---

Although the 'invention' of focus groups can be traced back to the 1920s, it was not until the 1990s that they became a common research method across a range of disciplines, including education, communication and media studies, health studies, feminist research, sociology and social psychology (for reviews see Morgan, 1996; Wilkinson, 1998a, 1998b, 1998c, 1999). The popularity of focus group research continues to rise, with 8,600 focus group studies published across the social sciences in the last three years, about a third of these in the area of health.

Focus group methodology is a way of collecting qualitative data, typically engaging a small number of people in an informal group discussion (or discussions), 'focused' around a particular topic or set of issues. This could be, for example, young women sharing experiences of body modification practices, new mothers comparing and contrasting their experiences of maternity services, or elite athletes evaluating different motivational techniques. The discussion is usually based on a series of questions (the focus group 'schedule'), and the researcher generally acts as a 'moderator' for the group: posing the questions, keeping the discussion flowing and enabling group members to participate fully.

Although focus groups are sometimes referred to as 'group interviews', the moderator does *not* ask questions of each focus group participant in turn, but rather facilitates group discussion, actively encouraging group members to interact with *each other*. This interaction between research participants – and the potential analytic use of such interaction – has been described as the 'hallmark' of focus group research (Morgan, 1988: 12).

Typically, the discussion is recorded, transcribed and then analysed using conventional techniques for qualitative data: most commonly, content or thematic analysis. Focus groups are distinctive, then, primarily for the method of data *collection* (i.e. informal group discussion), rather than for the method of data *analysis*. This prompts most accounts of the method to emphasize how to run an effective focus group, rather than how to analyse the resulting data. There is a plethora of advice on the methodological and procedural choices entailed in setting up and conducting a focus group – e.g. Wilkinson (2003), Kamberelis and Dimitriadis (2013), Hennink (2014), Krueger and Casey (2014), Stewart et al. (2014), Wilkinson (2015) – but remarkably little on the theoretical and epistemological choices entailed in analysing and interpreting focus group data. I begin to redress that imbalance here, drawing upon my own focus group research.

TWO APPROACHES TO DATA ANALYSIS

There are many ways of analysing focus group data: for example, content, thematic, ethnographic, phenomenological, narrative, experiential, biographical, discourse or conversation analysis (see other chapters in this volume). Here, I will compare just two of these approaches – content analysis and ethnographic analysis – highlighting what is distinctive about each, what theoretical and epistemological assumptions each includes, and what each has to offer the researcher.

Content analysis produces a relatively systematic and comprehensive summary or overview of the data set as a whole, sometimes incorporating a quantitative element. Ethnographic analysis is more selective, typically addressing the issue of 'what is going on' between the participants in some segment (or segments) of the data, in greater analytic depth and detail. The two different approaches relate, of course, to different types of research question and the 'results' produced by the two types of analysis look very different.

An initial sense of the distinction between them can be gained from a project on heart attack risk factors, which utilizes *both* types of analysis (Morgan and Spanish, 1984). Here, content analysis is used to address the question of how *often* different risk factors for heart attacks are mentioned, and what these factors *are*, while ethnographic analysis is used to address the question of exactly *how* (and could also perhaps address *why*) risk factor information is introduced and discussed, in this particular context.

Content analysis is based on examining data for recurrent instances of some kind; these instances are then systematically identified across the data set, and grouped together by means of a coding system. The researcher has first to decide on the unit of analysis: this could be the whole group, the group dynamics, the individual participants, or (as is most commonly the case) the participants' utterances (Carey and Smith, 1994; Morgan, 1995). The unit of analysis provides the basis for developing a coding system, and the codes are then applied systematically across a transcript (or transcripts). Once the data have been coded, a further issue is whether to quantify them via counting instances (many qualitative researchers would, of course, argue that this loses the most valuable features of qualitative data). However, such counts are an effective way of providing a summary or overview of the data set as a whole.

In contrast to content analysis, ethnographic analysis is rarely systematic or comprehensive: rather, it is much more selective and limited in scope. Its main advantage is to permit a detailed – more or less interpretive – account of mundane features of the social world. This account may be limited to processes within the focus group itself, or (more typically) it may take the focus group discussion as offering a 'window' on participants' lives. Ethnographic analysis aims to ground interpretation in the particularities of the situation under study, and in participants' (rather than analysts') perspectives. Data are generally presented as accounts of social phenomena or social practices, substantiated by illustrative quotations from the focus group discussion. Key issues in ethnographic analysis are:

- how to select the material to present
- how to give due weight to the specific context within which the material was generated, while retaining some sense of the group discussion as a whole
- how best to prioritize participants' orientations in presenting an interpretive account.

A particular challenge is to address the *interactive* nature of focus group data: a surprising limitation of focus group research is the rarity with which group interactions are analysed or reported (Kitzinger, 1994; Wilkinson, 1999). For exceptions see, for example, Duggleby (2005) and Warr (2005).

CONTENT ANALYSIS

Most focus group studies use some type of content analysis. At its most basic, content analysis simply entails inspection of the data for recurrent instances of some kind. This is irrespective of the type of instance (e.g. word, phrase, some larger unit of 'meaning');

the preferred label for such instances (e.g. 'items', 'themes', 'discourses'); whether the instances are subsequently grouped into larger units, also variously labelled (e.g. 'categories', 'organizing themes', 'interpretive repertoires'); and whether the instances – or larger units – are counted or not. Most analyses of focus group data report recurrent instances of some kind, and do so more or less systematically, so they are essentially content analyses.

To illustrate this, I show (in Box 6.1) two different content analyses – one quantitative, one qualitative – of the *same* piece of focus group data. The 'results' of the quantitative content analysis are presented as frequency counts, while the 'results' of the qualitative content analysis are presented as illustrative quotations. The data come from a segment of a focus group in which three women with breast cancer are talking about possible causes of the disease (see Wilkinson, 2000, for more context). Both analyses take the 'mention' of a cause as the unit of analysis, and organize these 'mentions' using a category scheme derived from Blaxter's (1983) classic study of talk about the causes of health and illness. However, the first analysis systematically records the *number* of 'mentions' within each category (including null categories), summarizing what these 'mentions' are, while the second records the *words* in which these 'mentions' are couched, presenting them as quotations under each category heading (excluding null categories).

BOX 6.1   Content analyses (causes of breast cancer)

(1)   Quantitative version

1. *Infection*: 0 instances
2. *Heredity or familial tendencies*: 2 instances – family history (×2)
3. *Agents in the environment*:

   a)   *'poisons', working condition, climate*: 3 instances – aluminium pans; exposure to sun; chemicals in food

   b)   *drugs or the contraceptive pill*: 1 instance – taking the contraceptive pill

4. *Secondary to other diseases*: 0 instances
5. *Stress, strain and worry*: 0 instances
6. *Caused by childbearing, menopause*: 22 instances – not breast feeding; late childbearing (×3); having only one child; being single/not having children; hormonal; trouble with breast feeding – unspecified (×4); flattened nipples (×2); inverted nipples (×7); nipple discharge (×2)
7. *Secondary to trauma or to surgery*: 9 instances – knocks (×4); unspecified injury; air getting inside body (×4)
8. *Neglect, the constraints of poverty*: 0 instances
9. *Inherent susceptibility, individual and not hereditary*: 0 instances
10. *Behaviour, own responsibility*: 1 instance – mixing specific foods
11. *Ageing, natural degeneration*: 0 instances
12. *Other*: 5 instances – 'several things'; 'a lot'; 'multi-factorial'; everybody has a 'dormant' cancer; 'anything' could wake a dormant cancer

(2) Qualitative version

Heredity or familial tendencies

• 'I mean there's no family <u>history</u>'

Agents in the environment:

a) *'poisons', working condition, climate*

   • 'I was once told that if you use them aluminium pans that cause cancer'
   • 'Looking years and years ago, I mean, everybody used to sit about sunning themselves on the beach and now all of a sudden you get cancer from sunshine'
   • 'I don't know [about] all the chemicals in what you're eating and things these days as well, and how cultivated and everything'

b) *drugs or the contraceptive pill*

   • 'You know, obviously I took the pill at a younger age'

Caused by childbearing, menopause

• 'Inverted nipples, they say that that is one thing that you could be wary of'
• 'Until I came to the point of actually trying to breast feed I didn't realize I had flattened nipples and one of them was nearly inverted or whatever, so I had a lot of trouble breast feeding, and it, and I was several weeks with a breast pump trying to get it right, so that he could suckle on my nipple, I did have that problem'
• 'Over the years, every, I couldn't say it happened monthly or anything like that, it would just start throbbing, this leakage, nothing to put a dressing on or anything like that, but there it was, it was coming from somewhere and it were just kind of gently crust over'
• 'I mean, I don't know whether the age at which you have children makes a difference as well because I had my eight year old relatively <u>late</u>, I was an old mum'
• 'They say that if you've only had <u>one</u> that you're more likely to get it than if you have a <u>big</u> family'

Secondary to trauma or to surgery

• 'Sometimes I've heard that <u>knocks</u> can bring one on'
• 'I then remembered that I'd <u>banged</u> my breast with this ... you know these shopping bags with a wooden rod thing, those big trolley bags?'
• 'I always think that people go into hospital, even for an exploratory, it may be all wrong, but I do think, well the <u>air</u> gets to it, it seems to me that it's not long afterwards before they simply find that there's more to it than they thought, you know, and I often wonder if the <u>air</u> getting to your inside ... brings on cancer in any form'

(Continued)

(Continued)

Behaviour, own responsibility

- 'I was also told that if you eat tomatoes and plums at the same meal'

Other

- 'He told them nurses in his lectures that <u>every</u>body has a cancer, <u>and</u> it's a case of whether it lays dormant'
- 'I don't think it could be one cause, can it? It must be multi-factorial'

These two content analyses, then, *look* very different, although they are derived from the same piece of data, and share an underlying theoretical framework. The second type is often described as a 'thematic' analysis (sometimes as a 'discourse' analysis) and may be presented with the quotations integrated into the text, rather than in tabular form (e.g. Braun and Wilkinson, 2003). Neither of these analyses has preserved the focus group interaction – although it is possible for a thematic analysis to do so (see, for example, Ellis, 2002; Braun and Wilkinson, 2005).

ETHNOGRAPHIC ANALYSIS

So far, we have seen that content analyses which look very *different* (i.e. providing quantitative or qualitative 'results') in fact treat the data in the *same* kind of way (i.e. inspecting the data systematically for recurrent instances). We can further note that these two types of content analysis share a *similar underlying epistemology*: one in which research participants' talk is taken as providing a 'means of access' to something that lies behind or beyond it ('essentialism'). In my content analyses of women's talk about the causes of breast cancer, the words of focus group participants are taken to provide a 'transparent window' onto what they understand, think or believe about – say – the role of reproductive factors in the aetiology of breast cancer. Self-report is used to infer the relatively stable 'cognitions' (beliefs, attitudes or opinions) assumed to underlie people's talk (and – at least sometimes – to inform their subsequent behaviour), to which the researcher has no independent access.

A similar (essentialist) epistemological status is commonly given to talk in focus group studies which are designedly *ethnographic* (rather than content analytic) in nature – that is, studies which aim to provide contextual, interpretive accounts of their participants' social worlds. For example, in Lyons et al.'s (1995) study of women with multiple sclerosis, the focus group talk is taken as 'revealing' the nature of daily life for people with a chronic physical illness; and in Agar and MacDonald's (1995) study of ex-users of LSD, their talk is seen as flagging up a 'significant issue' in the life 'territory' of the drug-experienced young. In both of these studies, the focus group discussion is used as a means of access to the – inner and outer – lives of the research participants, rather than treated as of interest in its own right (see Miller and Glassner and Holstein and Gubrium in this volume).

I will contrast this view of talk (i.e. talk as a means of accessing a pre-given social or psychological world) with an alternative: talk as *constituting* the social world on a moment-by-moment basis ('social constructionism'). This very *different* epistemological status radically affects both the kind of study undertaken and the kind of 'results' obtained. It allows the possibility of seeing the focus group discussion as a social context *in its own right*, and, further, the possibility of subjecting it to *direct* observation (rather than studying it in order to infer more distal social – or psychological – phenomena). The resulting study will *necessarily* be ethnographic, and will provide a detailed, contextual account of social processes. This is a radical proposal for most focus group researchers, including those working within an ethnographic tradition. Even though (most) ethnography is predicated upon direct observation, few focus group researchers conducting (broadly) ethnographic analysis have turned their attention to observation of 'what is going on' in the focus group itself; still fewer have paid detailed attention to focus group talk as constitutive of social – or psychological – life.

In taking such a (social constructionist) approach, I have drawn on the theoretical framework offered by ethnomethodology and conversation analysis (see Heritage in this volume; Sidnell and Stivers, 2013). Conversation analysis assumes that it is fundamentally *through interaction* that participants build social context. Central to its framework is the notion of talk as *action* – that is, as designed to *do* particular things within a particular interactional context. Within a focus group we can see how people (for example) tell stories, joke, agree, debate, argue, challenge or attempt to persuade. We can see the ways in which they present particular 'versions' of themselves (and others) for particular interactional purposes: (for example) to impress, flatter, tease, ridicule, complain, castigate or condone. Participants build the context of their talk *in* and *through* that talk itself, on a moment-by-moment basis. The talk itself, in its interactional context, provides the primary data for analysis. Further, it is possible to harness analytic resources intrinsic to the data: by focusing on participants' *own* understanding of the interaction – as displayed *directly* in their talk, through the conversational practices they use. In this way, a conversation analytic approach prioritizes the participants' (rather than the analysts') analysis of the interaction.

The traditions of ethnomethodology and conversation analysis rely primarily upon the use of naturally occurring data, i.e. data produced independent of the researcher. These data, however, encompass a range of institutional contexts (e.g. classrooms, courtrooms, doctors' surgeries), in which talk has been shown both to follow the conventions of 'everyday' conversation and systematically to depart from these (Heritage and Clayman, 2010). Likewise, data from focus groups range both across 'everyday' social actions (e.g. arguing, joking, teasing, complaining) and actions likely to be specific to the particular (research) context, e.g. asking elaborate questions (Puchta and Potter, 1999) or displaying opinions (Myers, 1998). However, while it may be useful to consider what goes on in focus group *qua* focus group, analysis need not be limited by the specificity of this particular context: it can also address more generic conversational phenomena (e.g. Schegloff, 1997).

To illustrate this approach, here is a sample ethnographic data analysis, based upon the principles of ethnomethodology and conversation analysis. It seeks to offer a detailed interpretive account of 'what is going on' within the talk which constitutes the focus group, and it theorizes this talk as action-oriented – in pursuit of particular, local interactional goals.

The data extracts for this analysis are presented below in Boxes 6.2 and 6.3. These two extracts are drawn from the *same* segment of the *same* focus group as used in the content analyses above, i.e. the part in which the three women are talking about possible causes of breast cancer. Here, I have identified myself ('SW') as moderator of the focus group, and I have called the participants 'Freda', 'Doreen' and 'Gertie'. The level of detail presented in the transcripts is appropriate to the level of analysis which follows: somewhere between a simple orthographic rendition and a full 'Jeffersonian' (conversation analytic) transcription (see Appendix for transcription conventions).

BOX 6.2   Data extract 1

	SW:	BCP12 (Causes extracts 1+2)
01	SW:	D'you have any idea what <u>caused</u> your breast cancer [pause] any of you?
02	Fre:	No- What <u>does</u> cause breast cancer do you think?
03	SW:	What do you think it <u>might</u> be?
04	Ger:	[cuts in] There's a lot of <u>stories</u> going about.=I was once told that
05		if you use them aluminium pans that cause cancer..hh I was also told
06		that if you- if you eat tomatoes and plums at the same meal that-
07	Dor:	[laughs]
08	Ger:	[to Doreen] Have you heard all these those things?
09	Dor:	[laughs] No
10	Ger:	Now that's what <u>I</u> heard and-
11	Dor:	[laughs] Mm
12	Ger:	Oh there's several things that if you <u>listen</u> to people [pause] we::ll-
13	Dor:	Mm
14	SW:	[to Gertie, laughingly] What else have they told you?
15	Ger:	Pardon?
16	SW:	[to Gertie, laughingly] What else have they told you?
17	D/SW:	[laughter]
18	Ger:	I can't think off hand I knew a- I knew a <u>lot</u> that I've heard over the
19		years from people who've passed on 'Oh yeah well that causes cancer'.

20	Dor:	Mm
21	Ger:	But I don't know but-
22	Dor:	[cuts in] I mean uhm-
23	Ger:	Now I've no views on this [To Doreen] have you?

Data extract 1 (Box 6.2) opens with my question (as moderator) about causes, and Freda's and Gertie's responses to this question. A content analysis (of the kind presented earlier) might code Freda's initial response (line 2) as 'I don't know', and Gertie's subsequent response (lines 4–6) as items in the categories 'agents in the environment' (aluminium pans) and 'behaviour, own responsibility' (choosing to eat tomatoes and plums at the same meal). An ethnographic analysis, by contrast, focuses on the immediate interactional context. Talk about causes can be interactionally tricky – particularly when a presumed 'expert' is asking questions, or when potentially equally knowledgeable others might have different or even conflicting opinions. Conversation analysts (e.g. Sacks, 1992: 340–7) have noted the asymmetry between being the first to express an opinion and being second: going first means you have to put your opinion on the line, whereas going second offers an opportunity either for agreement or for potential challenge. Consequently, speakers often try to avoid first position – and this is precisely what Freda does in response to the moderator's question. She declines to gives an opinion, and bounces the question right back to the moderator, as a 'counter' (Schegloff, 2007: 16–19). It is not simply then, as an (essentialist) content analysis might suggest, that Freda 'doesn't know' what causes breast cancer: from the perspective of a (social constructionist) ethnographic analysis, she is not here reporting a state of mind, but is engaged in a piece of local interactional business.

The moderator (SW) avoids answering Freda's direct question: instead she reformulates it (in the manner typically recommended for focus group moderators) to make clear she is interested in what the participants themselves 'think it might be' (line 3), rather than in any purported 'actual' (i.e. scientific) causes of breast cancer. With this reassurance, Gertie offers some 'stories' (i.e. folk wisdom, labelled as such), thereby putting herself in the vulnerable first speaking position, and attracting just the kind of second-speaker disagreement that Freda's counter enabled her to avoid: Doreen, the third member of the group, *laughs* at Gertie's response.

Within most other approaches, Gertie's references to 'stories', and to what she has 'heard over the years', would be taken as transparent reports of the *source* of her ideas about cause, i.e. as indicating a reliance on folk knowledge. Within this framework, however, the attribution of ideas about cause to folk knowledge is seen as an *interactional device* seeking to protect the speaker from challenge (although, here, it fails to avert ridicule).

Gertie's candidate causes, then, are presented as 'stories'. However, only moments later, even these 'stories' are retracted. By the end of Doreen and Gertie's subsequent exchange (at line 23), Gertie, like Freda before her, is claiming to have 'no views' on the causes of breast cancer.

Again – within this approach – this is not simply a straightforward report of a cognitive state. Rather, it arises out of the interactional sequence within which it is embedded, in the course of which both Doreen and the moderator have implied, through their laughter, that Gertie's candidate causes are rather implausible (indeed, the moderator's probe (line 14) can be heard as 'positioning' (Wilkinson and Kitzinger, 2003) Gertie as the sort of gullible person who believes anything she is told). Gertie responds first by reminding everyone that she is not reporting her own views, but those of others, and then she flatly refuses to offer further candidate answers, explicitly handing the floor to Doreen at (line 23).

BOX 6.3   Data extract 2

	SW:	BCP12 (Causes extracts 4+5)
65	Ger:	My sister was a <u>nurse</u> [pause] wa:y <u>back</u> in the 1920s she [indistinct].
66		And she-she was at what is Springfield General now.=She did her
67		training there and there was a doctor Patterson at the time.hh who
68		used to lecture to the nurses.hh and he told them <u>nurses</u> in his
69		lectures that <u>every</u>body has a cancer [pause] <u>and</u> [pause] it's a case
70		of whether it lays dormant
71	Fre:	Yes I've heard that
72	Dor:	Mm
73	Ger:	Have you heard that?
74	Fre:	Mm
75	Ger:	Well yes that she told us <u>that</u> and that came in her lectures.hh and
76		[pause] according to <u>him anything</u> could wake it up
77	Dor:	Mm
78	Ger:	a knock or whatever in the appropriate place.hh and <u>then</u> it would
79		develop but that's what-
80	Dor:	Mm
81	Ger:	that's what <u>she</u> was told
82	Dor:	Mm
83	Ger:	But when I-
84	Fre:	[cuts in] Sometimes I've heard that <u>knocks</u> can bring one on but I've
85		never (had any knocks) [indistinct]
86	Ger:	No
87	Fre:	[cuts in] (I don't think that) [indistinct]
88	Dor:	[cuts in] Well I'd heard <u>that</u> from somebody else and so when I-
89		when obviously this was sus- my lump was suspicious I then- I
90		then remembered I'd <u>banged</u> my breast with this.hh uhm [tch] you
91		know these shopping bags with a wooden rod thing.hh those big
92		trolley bags?
93	Fre:	Mm
94	Dor:	I-I-I >don't ask me how I do these stupid things< but I got it <u>wedged</u>

95		between the car door as I was getting out of the <u>car</u> I got it wedged
96		in the car door so it- so this [pause] appropriately sized *rod* that
97		was the size of this <u>lump</u> you know went into my breast and I- and I
98		queried that.hh and Mr Fell [consultant surgeon] said you know
99		'You're always looking for a <u>reason</u>' [laughs] d'you know
100		'You've always got to find something that might be the cause of it'
101		you know.hh but I thought 'Well I'd just better <u>mention</u> it' in case
102		it turned out to be.hh you know sort of they'll say-, they then come
103		round to me afterwards and say 'Are you sure you haven't d-
104		done some injury to yourself' >or that sort of thing< 'cos you know,
105		it just sprung to <u>mind</u>..hh 'Cos I-I'd mentioned it to the GP and
106		she'd sort of said 'No no.hh it's nearly always hormonal' so it'd
107		gone out of my <u>head</u> and an- but- but then she was saying 'No it'll be
108		be a *cyst*' >whatever< and when it wasn't a cyst then I started to
109		think of another cause you see but-.hh
110	Ger:	Mm
111	Dor:	uh:m I-I mean I sup- if-if they <u>knew</u> what the cause was they
112		would- they would be able to treat it wouldn't they.
113	Ger:	Well you know I-
114	Dor:	[cuts in]I don't think it could be <u>one</u> cause can it? It must be multi
115	Ger:	Mm
116	Dor:	.hh multi-factorial
117	Ger:	[cuts in] You've heard them say-
118	Dor:	whatever the word is

When Gertie re-enters the conversation (at line 65, in extract 2, Box 6.3), with a subsequent suggestion of a candidate cause (the theory that cancer is 'dormant' until woken), she is still attending to the danger of being laughed at. However, here she deals with the risk of ridicule by using a very different kind of footing (Goffman, 1981 [1967]): the 'dormant cancer' theory is painstakingly constructed as *someone else's* opinion – that of a specified medical expert, a Dr Patterson, at Springfield General Hospital (the hospital where most of these women have received treatment). She carefully monitors the reception of this theory, and even though Freda and Doreen affiliate with this view (at lines 71 and 72), she checks to be sure she has their support (line 73), and continues repeatedly to stress that this theory comes from her sister's nursing training: 'she told us that, and that came in her lectures' (line 75); 'according to him' (line 76); 'that's what <u>she</u> was told' (line 81). The effect of all this footing is to emphasize that these ideas are *not* her own, and that she is *not* to be held accountable for believing them.

Again, within a social constructionist framework, the attribution of views to others does not offer a 'transparent window' on what Gertie 'believes', nor does it indicate the 'source' of her information. Gertie is not simply repeating what her sister may or may not have told her Dr Patterson had said – rather, she is using footing as a conversational resource, in order to manage the delicate interactional business of presenting an opinion without sounding ignorant or stupid.

Doreen then rejoins the conversation (at line 88) to offer another candidate cause – a 'bang' on her breast. Her story, elaborated in lines 88–105, is apparently 'touched off' by Gertie's mention of 'a knock or whatever in the appropriate place' causing cancer to develop (line 78), followed by Freda's subsequent acknowledgement of the theory that *'knocks* can bring one on' (line 84). Just before Doreen begins her story, Gertie and Freda have both placed considerable distance between themselves and the 'knock' theory: Freda saying it is a theory she has 'sometimes heard', but that she has never had any knocks her-self (lines 84–85), and Gertie attributing the theory to her sister's nursing training, some 70 years earlier (lines 65–68 and 78–81). In telling a story about her own knock, then, Doreen can be seen to attend to the risk of aligning herself with a belief in knocks, and thereby possibly attracting scorn or censure (see Potter, 1996: 142–7, for a detailed discus-sion of distancing, neutrality and alignment; also Potter in this volume).

Doreen never actually says directly that she believes her breast cancer to have been caused by a knock to her breast. She simply 'remembered' (line 90) having banged her breast, and felt it necessary to 'mention it' (line 101) to her surgeon, thereby displaying to her co-conversationalists that she is a rational person who informed a medical profes-sional of the knock in order to check out all possibilities. The surgeon's reported response, 'You're always looking for a <u>reason</u>' (line 99), is a generalized formulation that does not dismiss the 'knock' theory *specifically*, but that even-handedly dismisses *any* theory (actu-ally or potentially) offered by Doreen – and, by implication, anyone else. Ventriloquizing the surgeon in this way enables Doreen to present the 'knock' theory as no more *or less* plausible than any other theory (to which the 'always looking for a reason' dismissal is equally applicable).

The surgeon's response, with its implicit suggestion that looking for 'reasons' and 'causes' is futile, also provides evidence for Doreen's later claim that 'they' (doctors) do not know the causes of breast cancer (line 111). If they do not, and if looking for causes is pointless, then the 'knock' theory is as plausible as any other. Likewise, the GP's dismissal of Doreen's theory is also reported in such a way that the 'knock' theory is left open as a possible cause: the competing cause offered by the GP ('it's nearly always hormonal', line 106) is explained as having been offered as a cause for a *cyst*, not cancer. The reported misdiagnosis has the added benefit of pointing to the fallibility of the medical profession (re-emphasized in lines 111–112).

Within a social constructionist framework, the concern is not with whether Doreen 'really' believes the 'knock' theory, or with whether medical professionals 'actually' dismissed her possible explanation. Rather, it is with how Doreen *designs* her talk to illustrate: (a) her own rationality (both in reporting the knock and in assessing its merits and demerits as a theory); (b) her own willingness to listen to the opinions of expert others; (c) the fallibility of the medical profession; and (d) the plausibility of a knock as a cause for breast cancer.

Doreen's final statement – that the causes of breast cancer must be 'multi-factorial' (line 116) – enables her to maintain the possibility that her injury was causally implicated, while not denying the potential relevance of other (more medically approved) causes. In this interaction, then, Doreen designs her talk to display to her co-conversationalists that she is a rational and open-minded person.

CHAPTER SUMMARY AND FUTURE PROSPECTS

In this chapter, I have outlined what is involved in analysing focus group data, with particular reference to the theoretical and epistemological issues entailed in two different types of analysis: content analysis and ethnographic analysis. Although I am a keen advocate of focus groups, I would not want to claim that they are always appropriate. Focus groups are a method of choice when the objective of the research is primarily to study *talk*, either conceptualized as a 'window' on participants' lives or their underlying beliefs and opinions, or – in a more limited way – as constituting a social context in its own right, amenable to direct observation. If, by contrast, the purpose of the research is to categorize or compare types of individuals or social groups, in terms of the lives they lead or the views they hold, then focus groups are less appropriate (although they are not uncommonly used in this way).

Focus group data readily lend themselves to analysis by content analytic or ethnographic methods, as well as by other qualitative techniques; and the resulting analyses can be presented in a variety of ways, ranging from numerical tables summarizing a whole data set, through prose accounts containing illustrative quotations, to detailed interpretive accounts of a relatively circumscribed single data extract. Focus groups offer particular opportunities for the study of interaction between research participants, and ethnomethodological and conversation analytic approaches may prove particularly useful for developing sustained analyses of interaction. This is one possible future direction for focus group research. Other ways in which focus group research seems likely to develop include increasing use of the method – appropriately adapted in culturally sensitive ways – in social and community contexts outside Western, developed countries (see Hennink, 2007); and increasing reliance on virtual (i.e. computer-mediated) focus groups (e.g. Stewart and Williams, 2005; Fox et al., 2007; Gaiser, 2008).

Study questions

1. What are the key differences between 'content analysis' and 'ethnographic analysis' of focus group data?

2.   What are the key differences between 'essentialist' and 'social constructionist' epistemologies?
3.   Why is the interaction between focus group participants important?
4.   How might you analyse such interaction?

Recommended reading

Wilkinson, S. (1998) 'Focus group methodology: a review', *International Journal of Social Research Methodology*, 1 (3): 181-203.
Good brief introduction to the method and the ways it has been used in various disciplinary contexts.

Barbour, R. (2007) *Doing Focus Groups*. London: Sage.
A very accessible introduction to using focus groups, with a variety of research examples.

Krueger, R. A. and Casey, M. A. (2014) *Focus Groups: A Practical Guide for Applied Research* (5th edn). Thousand Oaks, CA: Sage.
One of the best contemporary 'handbooks' on focus group research, comprehensive and practical.

Wilkinson, S. (2000) 'Women with breast cancer talking causes: comparing content, biographical and discursive analyses', *Feminism & Psychology*, 10 (4): 431-60.
Useful for more examples of different types of data analysis, and discussion of their implications.

Recommended online resources

Website for key focus group researcher Richard A. Krueger, with a section on 'Focus group inter-viewing' which includes practical tips, instructional guides, examples and reflections:
www.tc.umn.edu/~rkrueger/index.html

Article by Anita Gibbs in *Social Research Update*, with a brief overview of focus group methodology:
http://sru.soc.surrey.ac.uk/SRU19.html

Article by Jenny Kitzinger in the *British Medical Journal*, with a brief, accessible introduction to focus groups, especially for health researchers:
www.ncbi.nlm.nih.gov/pmc/articles/PMC2550365/pdf/bmj00603-0031.pdf

A selective annotated bibliography, particularly useful for health researchers:

Focus Groups, Volume II, A Selective Annotated Bibliography: Medical and Health Sciences by Graham Walden; available at Google Books.

References

Agar, M. and MacDonald, J. (1995) 'Focus groups and ethnography', *Human Organization*, 54 (1): 78–86.

Blaxter, M. (1983) 'The causes of disease: women talking', *Social Science & Medicine*, 17: 59–69.

Braun, V. and Wilkinson, S. (2003) 'The vagina: liability or asset?', *Psychology of Women Section Review*, 5: 28–42.

Braun, V. and Wilkinson, S. (2005) 'Vagina equals woman? On genitals and gendered identity', *Women's Studies International Forum*, 28 (6): 509–22.

Carey, M. A. and Smith, M. W. (1994) 'Capturing the group effect in focus groups: a special concern in analysis', *Qualitative Health Research*, 4 (1): 123–7.

Duggleby, W. (2005) 'What about focus group interaction data?', *Qualitative Health Research*, 15: 832–40.

Ellis, S. (2002) 'Doing being liberal: implicit prejudice in focus group talk about lesbian and gay human rights issues', *Lesbian and Gay Psychology Review*, 2 (2): 43–9.

Fox, F. E., Morris, M. and Rumsey, N. (2007) 'Doing synchronous online focus groups with young people: methodological reflections', *Qualitative Health Research*, 17: 539–47.

Gaiser, T. J. (2008) 'Online focus groups', in N. G. Fielding, R. M. Lee and G. Blank (eds), *Sage Handbook of Online Research Methods*. Thousand Oaks, CA: Sage, pp. 290–306.

Goffman, E. (1981 [1967]) *Forms of Talk*. Oxford: Basil Blackwell.

Hennink, M. M. (2007) *International Focus Group Research: A Handbook for the Health and Social Sciences*. Cambridge: Cambridge University Press.

Hennink, M. M. (2014) *Focus Group Discussions*. New York: Oxford University Press.

Heritage, J. and Clayman, S. (2010) *Talk in Action: Interactions, Identities and Institutions*. Chichester: Wiley-Blackwell.

Kamberelis, G. and Dimitriadis, G. (2013) *Focus Groups: From Structured Interviews to Collective Conversations*. Abingdon: Routledge.

Kitzinger, J. (1994) 'The methodology of focus groups: the importance of interaction between research participants', *Sociology of Health and Illness*, 16: 103–21.

Krueger, R. A. and Casey, M. A. (2014) *Focus Groups: A Practical Guide for Applied Research* (5th edn). Thousand Oaks, CA: Sage.

Lyons, R. F., Sullivan, M. J. L., Ritvo, P. G. with Coyne, J. C. (1995) *Relationships in Chronic Illness and Disability*. Thousand Oaks, CA: Sage.

Morgan, D. L. (1988) *Focus Groups as Qualitative Research*. Newbury Park, CA: Sage.

Morgan, D. L. (1995) 'Why things (sometimes) go wrong in focus groups', *Qualitative Health Research*, 5: 515–22.

Morgan, D. L. (1996) 'Focus groups', *Annual Review of Sociology*, 22: 129–52.

Morgan, D. L. and Spanish, M. T. (1984) 'Focus groups: a new tool for qualitative research', *Qualitative Sociology*, 7 (3): 253–70.

Myers, G. (1998) 'Displaying opinions: topics and disagreement in focus groups', *Language in Society*, 27: 85–111.

Potter, J. (1996) *Representing Reality: Discourse, Rhetoric and Social Construction*. London: Sage.

Puchta, C. and Potter, J. (1999) 'Asking elaborate questions: focus groups and the management of spontaneity', *Journal of Sociolinguistics*, 3: 314–35.

Sacks, H. (1992) *Lectures on Conversation*, ed. G. Jefferson. Oxford: Basil Blackwell.

Schegloff, E. A. (1997) 'Practices and actions: boundary cases of other-initiated repair', *Discourse Processes*, 23 (3): 499–545.

Schegloff, E. A. (2007) *Sequence Organization in Interaction: A Primer in Conversation Analysis*. Cambridge: Cambridge University Press.

Sidnell, J. and Stivers, T. (eds) (2013) *The Handbook of Conversation Analysis*. Oxford: Wiley-Blackwell.

Stewart, D. W., Shamdasani, P. N. and Rook, D. W. (2014) *Focus Groups: Theory and Practice* (3rd edn). Thousand Oaks, CA: Sage.

Stewart, K. and Williams, M. (2005) 'Researching online populations: the use of online focus groups for social research', *Qualitative Research*, 5 (4): 395–416.

Warr, D. J. (2005) '"It was fun ... but we don't usually talk about these things": analyzing sociable interaction in focus groups', *Qualitative Inquiry*, 11 (2): 200–25.

Wilkinson, S. (1998a) 'Focus groups in health research: exploring the meanings of health and illness', *Journal of Health Psychology*, 3 (3): 329–48.

Wilkinson, S. (1998b) 'Focus group methodology: a review', *International Journal of Social Research Methodology*, 1 (3): 181–203.

Wilkinson, S. (1998c) 'Focus groups in feminist research: power, interaction, and the co-construction of meaning', *Women's Studies International Forum*, 21 (1): 111–25.

Wilkinson, S. (1999) 'Focus groups: a feminist method', *Psychology of Women Quarterly*, 23: 221–44.

Wilkinson, S. (2000) 'Women with breast cancer talking causes: comparing content, biographical and discursive analyses', *Feminism & Psychology*, 10 (4): 431–60.

Wilkinson, S. (2003) 'Focus groups', in G. M. Breakwell (ed.), *Doing Social Psychology*. Oxford: Blackwell, pp. 344–76.

Wilkinson, S. (2015) 'Focus groups', in J. A. Smith (ed.), *Qualitative Psychology: A Practical Guide to Research Methods* (3rd edn). London: Sage, pp. 199–221.

Wilkinson, S. and Kitzinger, C. (2003) 'Constructing identities: a feminist conversation analytic approach to positioning in action', in R. Harré and F. Moghaddam (eds), *The Self and Others: Positioning Individuals and Groups in Personal, Political and Cultural Contexts*. New York: Praeger/Greenwood, pp. 157–80.

PART III
ETHNOGRAPHY

The three chapters on ethnography seek to rescue observational work from the pitfalls of mere 'description' and lazy coding and look towards exciting methodological and analytic directions for observational research. In Chapter 7, Giampietro Gobo and Lukas Marciniak show how observation is the basic tool of ethnographers. They demonstrate why, if we want to understand behaviour and interaction, it is not enough to ask questions. We must also observe the routines and practices of social actors, reliably and consistently. Moreover, as they note, ethnography, like any other methodology, is not simply an instrument of data collection. It is born at a particular moment in the history of society. Thomas Eberle and Christoph Maeder's chapter gives us more specific insights into how ethnographers go about studying organizations. Their chapter contains some illuminating case studies which demonstrate the methodological strengths of observing routine practices within organizations. They conclude with a helpful account of practical considerations in doing organizational ethnography, access and participation, ways to collect and analyse data, multi-sited ethnography, informant and field relations, reporting back, ethical questions and finally writing up. Marie Buscatto takes up the preceding chapters' concerns with the credibility of ethnographic research. She shows that a recognition of the observer's involvement in the field she studies is (or should be) a commonplace of all research. Her chapter on reflexivity calls for a balance between 'involvement' and 'detachment'. She helpfully sets out three principles of ethnographic detachment.

SEVEN

What Is Ethnography?

Giampietro Gobo and Lukas T. Marciniak

About this chapter

Ethnography is a methodology based on direct observation. Of course, when doing ethnography, it is also essential to listen to the conversations of the actors 'on stage', read the documents produced in the field under study, and ask people questions. Yet what most distinguishes ethnography from other methodologies is a more active role assigned to the cognitive modes of observing, watching, seeing, looking at and scrutinizing.

Ethnography, like any other methodology, is not simply an instrument of data collection. It was born at a particular moment in the history of society and embodies certain of its cultural features. The end of this chapter, embracing a theory of method, focuses upon why (right now, notwithstanding more than a century of history) ethnography has come into fashion.

Keywords

observation, ethnography, methodology, theory of method, applied methods

Ethnography is a methodology with more than one hundred years of history. It arose in the Western world as a particular form of knowledge about distant cultures (typically non-Western ones) which were impenetrable to analysis since we had only fleeting contact or brief conversations. Despite its good intentions (to gain deeper understanding), ethnography is still a colonial method that must be de-colonialized (for a detailed analysis of this see Gobo, 2011).

COMPETING DEFINITIONS OF ETHNOGRAPHY

Since the 1980s the meaning of ethnography has been expanded to such an extent that it encompasses forms of research that are extremely diverse from a methodological point of view. Everything is now ethnography: from life stories to analysis of letters and questionnaires, from autobiography to narrative analysis, from action research to performance, to field research lasting from a few days (see Knoblauch, 2005) to several years.

Leading scholars such as James Lull and David Morley have pointed out that what passes as ethnography in cultural studies fails to fulfil the fundamental requirements for data collection and reporting typical of most anthropological and sociological ethnographic research. *Ethnography* has become an abused buzz-word and has been diluted into a multitude of sometimes contrasting and contradictory meanings, sometimes becoming synonymous with qualitative studies.

Amid these multiple meanings, there are at least three terms that merge with 'ethnography': 'participant observation', 'fieldwork' and 'case study'. Though for many researchers these terms might all be used interchangeably (Delamont, 2004) they should not be mixed up. They all have many common features but still represent different concepts and practices.

- *Case study* denotes research on a system bounded in space and time and embedded in a particular physical and socio-cultural context. Research is conducted using diverse methodologies, methods and data sources, like participant observation, interviews, audio-visual materials, documents and so on.
- *Fieldwork* stresses the continuous presence of the researcher in the field, as opposed to 'grab-it-and-run' methodologies like the survey, in-depth interview or analysis of documents and recordings.
- *Participant observation* is a distinctive research strategy. Participant observation and fieldwork treat observation as a mere technique, while the term 'ethnography' stresses the theoretical basis of such work stemming from a particular history and tradition.

AN UPDATED DEFINITION

The stretching of the term 'ethnography' has emptied it of its original meaning. Ethnography was born as a technique based upon direct observation. By contrast, interviews and surveys are mainly based upon listening and asking questions. Of course, it is also essential in ethnography to listen to the conversations of the actors 'on stage', read the documents produced by them (diaries, letters, class essays, administrative documents, newspapers, photographs and audio-visual aids), ask people questions and so on. However they are ancillary sources of information because what most distinguishes ethnography from other methodologies is a more active role assigned to observation.

Ethnographic methodology comprises two research strategies: *non-participant* observation and *participant* observation. In the former case the researcher observes the subjects 'from a distance' without interacting with them. Those who use this strategy are uninterested in investigating the symbolic sphere, and they make sure not to interfere with the subjects' actions so as not to influence their behaviour. In participant observation the researcher joins a group and their activities, becomes a part of the group and the phenomena being studied, while at the same time taking care to observe and describe all events, behaviours and artefacts of the social setting. The scale of the established participant role of the researcher might be at least fourfold, from complete observer, through observer as participant, participant as observer, up to complete participant (Gold, 1958; Junker, 1960).

However, although most ethnographies include the necessity to access the field (for related ethical issues see Ryen, in this book), there are situations when access is not an issue. Whenever the ethnographer focuses on the accounts produced by people in the world and their activities of seeing, talking and recognizing, there is no particular participation. The researcher neither elects a side to 'do ethnography' nor a group or activity to 'become a part of'. The setting is already defined and publicly available. So the everyday world people live in becomes the topic as Edward Rose emphasized in his programme for ethnography (Rose, 1960, 1997).

Five distinctive characteristics of participant observation

- the researcher establishes a direct relationship with the social actors
- staying long in their natural environment
- with the purpose of observing and describing their social actions
- by interacting with them and participating in their everyday ceremonials and rituals, and
- learning their code (or at least parts of it) in order to understand the meaning of their actions.

THE ADVENT OF THE ETHNOGRAPHIC PERSPECTIVE IN ANTHROPOLOGY

The birth of ethnographic methodology is commonly dated to the period between the late nineteenth and early twentieth centuries.

Ethnography developed internally to ethnology, a discipline which in the first half of the 1800s split away from traditional anthropology, which was then dominated by physical and biological assumptions. Ethnology was more concerned to study peoples (through comparison of their material artefacts) and their cultures, and to classify their salient features. Before the advent of ethnographic methodology, ethnologists did not collect information by means of direct observation; instead, they examined statistics, the archives of government offices and missions, documentation centres, accounts of journeys, archaeological finds, native manufactures or objects furnished by collectors of exotic art, or they conversed with travellers, missionaries and explorers. These anthropologists considered the members of native peoples to be 'primitives': they were savages to be educated, and they could not be used as direct informants because they could not be trusted to furnish objective information.

Ethnographic methodology did not suddenly erupt in anthropology; rather it arose gradually through the work of various authors, among them the English anthropologist of Polish origin, Bronislaw K. Malinowski (1884–1942), and the English anthropologist Alfred R. Radcliffe-Brown (1881–1955). British social anthropology of an ethnographic stamp assimilated the positivist intellectual climate of its time and put itself forward, according to Radcliffe-Brown (1948), as a 'natural science of society' which was better able to furnish an objective description of a culture than the other methods used by anthropologists at the time. Radcliffe-Brown's polemic was directed against the then dominant speculative or 'desk' anthropology, which preferred to rely on secondary sources rather than undertake direct observation of social facts (customs, rituals, ceremonies) in order to uncover the 'laws' that govern a society.

Malinowski is commonly regarded as being the first to systematize ethnographic methodology. In his famous 'Introduction' to the *Argonauts of the Western Pacific* – the book which sets out his research conducted in the Trobriand Islands of the Melanesian archipelago off eastern New Guinea – Malinowski described the methodological principles underpinning the main goal of ethnography, which is to grasp the native's point of view, his relation to life, to realize his vision of his world. To this end, Malinowski lived for a total of two years (between 1914 and 1918) among the Kula of the Trobriand Islands. He learned their language (Kiriwinian), used natives as informants and directly observed the social life of a village, participating in its everyday activities. Malinowski inaugurated a view 'from within' that American anthropologists of the 1950s would call the 'emic' perspective – as opposed to the 'etic' or comparative perspective, which instead sought to establish categories, useful for the analyst but not necessarily important for the members of the culture studied.

SOCIOLOGICAL APPROACHES TO ETHNOGRAPHY

From the 1920s onwards, ethnographic methodology developed also in sociology – where it was adopted by researchers who mostly belonged to the University of Chicago's

Sociology Department (the Chicago School) – and then in psychology and (recently) political science. Before then, the French mining engineer and later sociologist Frédéric Le Play (1806–1882), in the late 1840s, and the English philanthropist Seebohm B. Rowntree (1871–1954), after 1886, used primordial forms of participant observation for their inquiries into poverty and the living conditions of the working class.

Although ethnography has a long tradition in sociology, there does not exist a unique shared mode but several sometimes contradictory approaches.

The period of 'nosing around' and the ex-post facto construction of a myth: the 'first' Chicago School

Ethnographic methodology was first introduced into sociology at the end of the 1910s by teachers and researchers at the Department of Sociology in the University of Chicago.

Its director, Robert Park (1864–1944), instructed his students in the following way:

> You have been told to go grubbing in the library, thereby accumulating a mass of notes and a liberal coating of grime. You have been told to choose problems wherever you can find musty stacks of routine records based on trivial schedules prepared by tired bureaucrats and filled out by reluctant applicants for aid or fussy do-gooders or indifferent clerks. This is called 'getting your hands dirty in real research'. Those who counsel you are wise and honorable; the reasons they offer are of great value. But one more thing is needful: first-hand observation. Go and sit in the lounges of the luxury hotels and on the doorsteps of the flophouses; sit on the Gold Coast settees and on the slum shakedowns; sit in the Orchestra Hall and in the Star and Garter Burlesque. In short, gentlemen, go get the seat of your pants dirty in real research. (Personal note by one of Park's students, reported in Bulmer, 1984: 97)

However, except for some particularly scrupulous and systematic researchers like Frederic M. Thrasher and Clifford Shaw, the research methods used by most of the Chicago School's members were rather primitive. As Madge (1962) recalls, 'a concern with method was left very much to the initiative of each investigator' (1962: 117) because 'the abiding fact [...] is that it is unified by its field of interest rather than by its methods' (1962: 125), which were always of secondary concern. Participant observation was given no particular importance, being just one of the many methods that the Chicago School used. Indeed, strictly speaking, the Chicago School's methods cannot be termed 'ethnography'; and its members themselves only expressly used the terms *ethnography* and *participant observation* after the 1940s.

What authors since the 1960s have retrospectively called 'ethnography' (thus creating a myth – see Platt, 1983; Hammersley, 1989) was nothing but a general form of qualitative research. If anything, the Chicago researchers produced case studies (Platt, 1983; Hammersley, 1989), monographs written using a mixture of methodologies and methods. But the marked methodological pluralism of the Chicago School was not the result of a deliberate choice. Observation was one of the methods that the criminologist Sheldon Messinger (1925–2002) called 'nosing around' (see Lofland, 1980: 4). Only much later did methodological problems – access to the field, the ethics of research, the relativity of informants' points of view – become important.

The institutionalization of ethnography: the 'second' Chicago School

During the 1930s, the Chicago Faculty of Sociology was joined by new members of staff, among them Louis Wirth (1897–1952), Herbert Blumer, Lloyd W. Warner (1898–1970) and Everett Cherrington Hughes. These scholars were distinguished, among other things, by a greater methodological awareness which had a strong impact on their pupils and followers (most notably William Foot Whyte, Howard Becker, Blanche Geer, Anselm Strauss, Melville Dalton, Erving Goffman, Fred Davis and Rosalie Wax), who after World War II produced a series of studies which revolutionized the current theories of deviance, education and work. And it was in this period, too, that ethnographic research became institutionalized by being taught, described in articles, subjected to methodological reflection, and eventually (after the 1960s) codified in textbooks.

Ethnographic methodology as we know it today came into being largely through the work of Everett Cherrington Hughes (1897–1983), who took up an appointment specifically to teach fieldwork at the university. He was convinced that participant observation was a method to collect data, which allowed us to understand the activities and experiences of certain actors. Participation was in this sense ancillary to observation, although it was its complement for the correct production of theoretical material.

Interactionism

The participant observation method was given a privileged role and specific theoretical importance by interactionism, an approach developed between the 1930s and 1950s by Herbert Blumer (1900–1987). He believed that social research must adopt a 'naturalistic' approach and rely on fieldwork in order to grasp the perspective of social actors and see reality from their point of view. Blumer thus furnished the theoretical-methodological bases for a research practice which the first Chicago School had commendably introduced but had confusedly used. The methodological principles of interactionism have been well summarized by Denzin (1970: 7–19) and Silverman (1993: 48, Table 3.2). Stated extremely briefly, they are:

1. relating symbols and interaction, showing how meanings arise in the context of behaviour
2. taking the actors' point of view
3. studying the 'situated' character of interaction
4. analysing processes instead of structures, avoiding the determinism of predicting behaviour from class, gender, race, and so on
5. generalizing from descriptions to theories.

'Grounded theory'

The task of introducing methodological rules and procedural rigour into interactionism fell to two sociologists of medicine: Barney G. Glaser and Anselm Strauss (1916–1996). Their book *The Discovery of Grounded Theory: Strategies for Qualitative Research* (1967) rapidly became the standard methodological reference work. It was the first study to organize ethnographic methodology into its various phases: the gathering of information, its classification and then its analysis. This was also by virtue of Strauss's wide experience as an ethnographer (see Charmaz and Bryant in this volume).

Structuralist ethnography

Another fruitful approach that has contributed to the prestige of ethnography is 'structural' analysis. The term denotes an approach less interested in the subjective aspects of action (contrary to interactionism) than in its social context. To use a celebrated phrase from Goffman (1967) (a representative of this approach), it is an approach concerned with: 'Not, then, men and their moments. Rather moments and their men' (1967: 3).

A protagonist of structuralist ethnography was William Foote Whyte (1914–2000). Between 1936 and 1940, he conducted ethnography in North End, a poor district of Boston (which he renamed Cornerville) inhabited by a large number of Italian immigrants. His aim was to study the relationship between everyday life in Boston's juvenile gangs, the formation of their leaderships and politics in the slums. His monograph, published with the striking title *Street Corner Society* (1943), was the first urban ethnography ever produced. Focusing on the bottom-up growth of political activities and their relations with the politics of the city in general, Whyte observed Cornerville in light of its dependent relation with the broader urban context. In this respect, his approach differed from that of the urban studies conducted by the Chicago School, which described the slums as autonomous and isolated spaces.

Whyte's ethnography is important both on the substantive and structural level and for its methodological implications. Whyte introduced what today is termed *reflexivity*: the self-aware analysis of the dynamics between researcher and participants, the critical capacity to make explicit the position assumed by the observer in the field, and the way in which the researcher's positioning impacts on the research process (see Buscatto in this volume).

Another leading representative of structural ethnography was the Canadian Erving Goffman (1922–1982). His method of empirical research was almost exclusively ethnographic observation. However, he was not a systematic researcher, and his works (with some exceptions) do not refer to specific settings. His research strategy reflected Hughes' approach, with its unusual comparisons among apparently antithetical categories, behaviours and professions: all mixed by an unsystematic procedure and an impressionistic style, which on Goffman's own admission, deliberately emulated the nineteenth-century German sociologist Georg Simmel. To conclude, therefore, methodology was not Goffman's principal concern.

Ethnomethodology

During the 1950s, alongside interactionism and the works of Goffman there arose a new approach developed by Harold Garfinkel (1917–2011), which he subsequently termed *ethnomethodology*. By this term, he meant the study of the means (*methods*) that people (*ethno*) use in their everyday lives to recognize, interpret and classify their own and others' actions. In the second half of the 1950s, Garfinkel conducted a series of ethnographic observations in institutional settings: he studied, for example, a courtroom jury (with Saul Mendlovitz) and the psychiatric staff of the UCLA School of Medicine (with Egon Bittner). These ethnographies were not conducted methodically and systematically probably because they were intended as *demonstrations* of the inescapable context-boundedness of everyday actions rather than as empirical *findings*. But they nevertheless opened the way for a new type of process-based ethnography which sought to grasp phenomena as they unfolded. This approach inspired a series of ethnographic studies conducted by Garfinkel's colleagues, assistants and pupils during the 1960s and 1970s in a variety of institutional settings: police departments, newspaper editorial offices, law courts, therapy sessions, hospitals, halfway houses and so on.

Cultural studies and reception ethnography

The approaches described in the previous section were current, with alternating fortunes, until the end of the 1970s. Thereafter new approaches arose (reception ethnography, postmodernist ethnography, feminist ethnography and so on) which critically distanced themselves from the previous ethnographic traditions, although the latter obviously did not disappear and continued to operate in parallel with the new approaches. The ethnographic panorama, consequently, grew highly diversified.

Prior to the 'ethnographic turn', media analysts had attributed enormous power to television in conditioning people's tastes and opinions (according to the Marxist theory of Althusser, and Adorno, Horkheimer and the Frankfurt School) which asserted that communication media were instruments used by the state to propagate the dominant ideology. The scholars working in the area of cultural studies were not entirely opposed to this view, in so far as they acknowledged that television was a powerful means of persuasion, but they criticized the doctrine's 'textual determinism' and its claim that a television programme was able *per se* (automatically and immediately, as if indeed by simple transfusion) to influence or predetermine its audience's opinions. Instead, according to Stuart Hall, another leading representative of cultural studies, consumers were not at all the passive recipients of meanings: they actively produced their own meanings, and they could even reject those proposed by the televisual text. Watching television was not the isolated activity performed in perfect silence, alone in a darkened room, that the academics imagined it to be (Hobson, 1982: 110). Rather, it took place in a broader domestic context which conditioned its reception: television programmes may, for example, be watched during dinner while those at the table discuss, intervene in and thus interrupt the media flow. There is consequently a space between the producer (of the programme) and the final consumer (the viewer) where domestic activities condition the programme's reception, with outcomes not easy to predict. Ethnography could describe consumption practices (Ang, 1991: 165) by delineating the meanings that media consumers attribute to the texts and technologies that they encounter in their everyday lives.

In the last decades many other approaches emerged: feminist ethnography, interpretative ethnography (Denzin, 1997), postmodern ethnography, constitutive ethnography (Mehan, 1979), institutional ethnography (Smith, 1986), performance ethnography (McCall, 2000), global ethnography (Burawoy et al., 2000). Each of them introduced new features, which empowered this methodology (see Gobo, 2008).

Participatory, collaborative and critical ethnographies

Two recent directions are more and more visible: the collaborative strategy and its committed nature. Collaboration and participation are both inevitable aspects of ethnographic research, since we cannot carry out the findings without engaging others and their actions in the everyday context of their lives. Collaborative ethnography makes collaboration the central feature, as Lassiter (2005) describes; it *deliberately* and *explicitly* emphasizes collaboration at every point in the ethnographic process. It is therefore not about doing ethnography *with* collaboration but *through* the consistent inclusion and participation of those being studied, local and native in the social setting.

This kind of ethnography is often recognized as a community-based research and has, besides its participatory character, visible engagement and an ideologically driven focus on addressing inequalities or injustice. Collaborative and critical ethnographers conduct their research with a sense of duty, taking responsibility not only for the methodological side of the research but also for the very practical results of their studies and the influence they wield on the others (Thomas, 1992; Madison, 2012). Collaborative and critical ethnography, then, are both methodological but also theoretical approaches for doing and writing ethnography.

THE 'OBSERVATION SOCIETY': TOWARDS A THEORY OF METHOD

As noted above, in the last 20 years there has been a trend (or a fashion) which has made ethnographic methodology both diffuse and well known. Why has this happened? Why

Table 7.1 Comparison between traditional versus participatory, critical and collaborative ethnography

Traditional	Participatory, Critical and Collaborative
✓ Reconstructs 'what is'	✓ Reveals 'what could be'
✓ Aims to describe artefacts, interactions, processes and cultures	✓ Aims to identify obscure influence of power, control and inequality
✓ Contributes mostly to issue-related knowledge and research domain	✓ Contributes mostly to emancipatory knowledge and social justice
✓ Ethnographer as a researcher (observer – participant)	✓ Ethnographer as an activist (adviser – propagator)
✓ Subjects as merely informants providing data	✓ Subjects as co-researchers jointly elaborating concepts
✓ Strives for deeper understanding of social mechanisms, processes and contextual aspects of studied phenomena	✓ Probes possibilities of challenging institutions and social practices that constrain individuals and communities
✓ Respects needs of people due to the ethical standards	✓ Unites needs of people with goals of research

does a methodology with more than one hundred years of history come to the fore only recently? Why now and not before?

Explaining the particular success and diffusion of some research methods in a certain historical period leads to an epistemological issue. As a matter of fact if we accept that there exists a circular and reflexive relationship between science and society (on how social beliefs have influenced knowledge and scientific theories, and *vice versa*) or between technology and society, then even the relationship between society and social research methods can be analysed with this perspective.

Previously Silverman (1997: 248) pointed out that interview and society were mutually constitutive: on the one hand, survey and in-depth interviewing required a particular type of society for them to come into being and develop; on the other, these research methods strengthen the society, which has produced them. Atkinson and Silverman (1997) have stated that we live in an 'interview society', a society in which interviewing has become a fundamental activity, and interviews seem to have become crucial for people to make sense of their lives.

Ethnography is becoming as fashionable as the interview became from the 1920s. If the 'interview society' is still the dominant societal model, the recent sudden increase of ethnography can be explained with the hypothesis that we are entering an 'observation society', a society in which observing (as interviewing) has become a fundamental activity, and watching and scrutinizing are becoming important cognitive modes alongside the others, like listening, feeling, hearing and eavesdropping, that are typical of the 'interview society'.

The clues that we are living in an 'observation society' are many: wherever we go there is always a television camera ready to film our actions (unbeknown to us): camera phones and the current fashion for making video recordings of even the most personal and intimate situations and posting them on the internet; or logging on to webcams pointed at city streets, monument, landscapes, plants, birds' nests, coffee pots, etc. to observe movements, developments and changes. Observing and being observed are two important features of contemporary Western societies. Consequently, there is increasing demand in various sectors of society – from marketing to security, television to the fashion industry[1] – for observation and ethnography. All of which suggests that ours is becoming an observation society.

THE ADDED VALUE OF ETHNOGRAPHY

As already noted, ethnographic methodology gives priority to observation as its primary source of information. The overriding concern is always to observe actions as they are performed in concrete settings. From this point of view, community studies are not usually ethnographies since, although the researchers may stay for a relatively long period of time in the environment of the group studied, their analyses are often based mainly on interviews, surveys and documents gathered on the spot. As Heritage stresses, if one is interested in action, the statements made by social actors during interviews cannot be treated 'as an appropriate substitute for the observation of actual behavior' (1984: 236). In fact, there is an oft-documented gap between attitudes and social actions (La Piere, 1934), between what people say and what they do (Gilbert and Mulkay, 1983).

The presence of researchers in the field enables them to gain a better understanding of the conceptual categories of social actors, their points of view (emic), the meanings of their actions and behaviour, and social and political processes. This is the main added value of this methodology compared to other methodologies: observing actions and behaviours instead of opinions and attitudes only. The consequences are not only theoretical (finding new or different results) but also practical, because a closer view of the routines and practices of social actors facilitates the crafting of remedies and solutions to social problems. In other words, it is easier to outline proposed social, political or organizational changes after having directly observed participants' actual social actions (see Bloor in this volume).

Ethnography is nowadays a recognizable approach to organizational change management, serving as a strategy for the in-depth exploration of the organizational culture and business performance. It is often a first choice method for initiating new developments in education, social policy or local self-government, political science or healthcare through

---

[1]The new demand for ethnography and the increase of professions based on observation are visible in marketing with commercial ethnography (the mystery shopper and related techniques), the fashion industry (the cool-hunter), management studies, ITC, ergonomics and action-research, industrial design (shadowing, flanking, focused ethnography), journalism (investigative and gossip journalism), the natural sciences (birdwatching), surveillance of leisure activities (lifeguards), police investigation and the politics of security, the politics of destabilization (crime and terrorism), art (photography, films and documentaries), tax investigations, paediatrics and so on.

the systematic study of the groups, communities and organizations and their needs, actions and resources. Ethnography successfully assists governments and institutions in outlining strategies and policies, for instance in the prison system (Jenness, 2010; Chomczynski, 2015) or healthcare (Savage, 2000).

ETHNOGRAPHY AND ITS ENEMIES

Notwithstanding the acknowledged usefulness of ethnography, however, it is still subject to the following well-known stereotypes and prejudices.

Some popular misunderstandings concerning ethnography

- Participants might present ideal/unreal behaviour during observation.
- Results are strictly limited to the context of the research.
- Results are mostly descriptive and not applicable.
- Research is not replicable thus methodologically doubtful.
- The research process is chaotic and unpredictable.
- Ethnography is a highly subjective method.

Is ethnography a highly subjective method?

It is often argued that ethnography is a *highly* subjective method, in the sense that it is very sensitive to the researcher's attitudes and perceptions. In other words, if different researchers visit the same setting, they will see different things, and their ethnographic notes will record different aspects. Instead, a questionnaire or an in-depth interview, if conducted correctly, are more likely to obtain similar replies (reliability) regardless of who the interviewer is. And yet experience shows that this idea has scant empirical grounding (Gobo, 2008).

A while ago, some students of Gobo conducted their ethnography in a bar. Two groups (formed of three students each) visited the same bar at a distance of a few days from each other. The fact that they had chosen the same bar was absolutely coincidental, in the sense that they had not agreed on this beforehand. Nevertheless, the two groups had a specific research design: to study the rituals, ceremonials and social actions of consumption in bars. They then produced a report. And, reading their reports, Gobo discovered that they had observed and discovered practically the same things.

Hence the research design makes a greater contribution to discovery (or construction of data) than do the researchers themselves. Ethnography, therefore, is anything but a *highly* subjective methodology (even if subjectivity is ever-present, as in all methodologies).

Behaviours are more consistent than attitudes and opinions

What does the experience just described tell us theoretically? In other words, why did six different observers in the same bar notice practically the same things? Because what an ethnography mainly observes are behaviours (rituals, routines, ceremonials), and these are much more stable over time than attitudes and opinions. Those who deal with organizations know very well that altering a behaviour requires more time than altering an attitude, not to mention opinions, which are sometimes so volatile that they change from one day to the next.

Can ethnographic research be replicated or reproduced?

From this it follows that, because behaviours are temporally rather stable, the results of ethnographic research can be repeated and reproduced. This depends upon two factors:

- the presence of a precise research design which has guided the research
- that no significant changes have taken place between one study and the next.

Ethnography and generalization

A recurrent criticism made of ethnographic methods is that their results are impossible to generalize because they are based on a few cases, and sometimes on only one. However, there are numerous disciplines which work on a limited number of cases: for instance palaeontology, archaeology, geology, ethology, biology, astrophysics, history, genetics, anthropology, linguistics, cognitive science, psychology (whose theories are largely based on experiments, and therefore on research conducted on non-probabilistic samples and on few cases). According to Becker (1998), these disciplines are unconcerned about their use of only a handful of cases to draw inferences and generalizations about thousands of people, animals, plants and other objects. Moreover, science studies the individual object/phenomenon not in itself but as a member of a broader class of objects/phenomena with particular characteristics/properties (Williams, 2000; Payne and Williams, 2005).

For these reasons it is anything but odd to think that the results of ethnographic research can be generalized. As Collins (1988) stated, much of the best work in sociology has been carried out using qualitative methods without statistical tests. This has been true of research areas ranging from organizational and community studies to micro studies of face-to-face interaction and macro studies of the world system. In addition, if the focus of ethnography is on behaviour, and given that this is stable in time, then it is likely that generalizations are possible. Obviously, precise criteria must be followed in the choice of samples (Gobo, 2008). Nevertheless ethnography is not precluded from making generalizations.

Two initiatives that aimed to reinforce ethnography as a method capable to generalize its results are worth noticing here:

- The concept of analytic ethnography as initially described by Lofland (1995) and then elaborated by Snow, Morill and Anderson (2003). Analytic ethnography seeks to produce generic understandings and conceptual propositions concerning social processes. Generalizations are possible through the theoretical extensions in which concepts developed from one particular field are transferred to another. To make it happen, researchers need to continually search for the aspects of the studied phenomenon that are more or less transcontextual, replacing 'thick descriptions' of the situation with analytic reconstructions of the processes and its details across diverse contexts.
- Ethnographers should develop concepts that transcend the contextual uniqueness of each setting and enable us to link ethnographic inquiries with one another. Following Prus's (1997) agenda for conducting ethnography, researchers need to simultaneously achieve familiarity with the setting at hand and use conceptual notions derived from other contexts as a source of comparisons, contrasts and complements.

Results and concepts have been transferred from the one setting to another as in Morrill's (1995) ethnography of conflict among managers or Prus and Grills' (2003) study of deviant behaviours. Results and concepts are also moved from the local context to the general level as in Ho's (2009) ethnography of Wall Street as a basis for reflection on the global financial market or Marciniak's (2015) ethnography of a bazaar that brought insight into the general social mechanism of market competition.

CONCLUSION

We have described some clues to the emerging demand for observation and ethnography in different social worlds. With the variety of approaches, from collaborative and critical ethnography to the multi-sited and analytic variants, and with a wide range of options from non-participant observation up to natural ethno-inquiry, ethnography nowadays has much to offer. The demand for ethnography as a method for both developing theory and social praxis is increasing every day.

We have tried to explain this phenomenon on the hypothesis that we are entering the observation society. Nevertheless, this is no more than a hypothesis: only the future will tell us how well founded it is.

CHAPTER SUMMARY

- Ethnography is a methodology based on direct observation. Other sources of information (such as interviews with participants or documents) are ancillary.
- We are entering into an 'observation society', a society in which observing has become a fundamental activity, and watching and scrutinizing are becoming important cognitive modes.

FUTURE PROSPECTS

Due to the added value of ethnography (the presence of researchers in the field, which enables them to gain a better understanding of the meanings of the social actions of social actors) this methodology has the potential to become a prominent approach in applied research.

Study questions

1. In term of research practices, what is the difference in doing research based on observation and research based on interviews?
2. What are the main features of participant observation?
3. Why is ethnography becoming so fashionable?

Recommended reading

Emerson, R. M., Fretz, R. I. and Shaw, L. L. (2011) *Writing Ethnographic Fieldnotes* (2nd edn). Chicago: University of Chicago Press.
A source of guidelines and practical advice showing how to transform direct observations into ethnographic descriptions; detailed, accurate and vivid enough to envision scenes and reflect their specificity.

Gobo, G. (2008) *Doing Ethnography.* London: Sage.
Comprehensive introduction to the theory and practice of ethnography, with a reflection on the methodological background and step-by-step guidance through the various phases of the inquiry.

Silverman, D. (2013) 'Instances or sequences?', in D. Silverman, *A Very Short, Fairly Interesting, Reasonably Cheap Book about Qualitative Research* (2nd edn). London: Sage, pp. 56–85.
A fundamental question for qualitative methodology, considered in the pivotal chapter of this very concise, fairly gripping and reader-friendly, nicely priced book for all qualitative researchers.

Recommended online resources

Ethnobase:
www.lse.ac.uk/collections/ethnobase/

Ethnographic Database Project:
www.ucl.ac.uk/~ucsalfo/EDP/Welcome.html

INCITE (Incubator for Critical Inquiry into Technology and Ethnography), Goldsmiths College, University of London (UK):
www.studioincite.com/

Interaction Design Centre, Middlesex University, London (UK):
www.mdx.ac.uk/our-research/centres/interaction-design-centre

Work, Interaction and Technology Research Group, King's College, London (UK):
www.kcl.ac.uk/sspp/departments/management/research/wit/index.aspx

References

Ang, I. (1991) *Desperately Seeking the Audience*. London: Routledge.

Atkinson, P. and Silverman, D. (1997) 'Kundera's *Immortality*: the interview society and the invention of self', *Qualitative Inquiry*, 3 (3): 324–45.

Becker, H. S. (1998) *Trick of the Trade*. Chicago and London: University of Chicago Press.

Bulmer, M. (1984) *The Chicago School of Sociology: Institutionalization, Diversity, and the Rise of Sociological Research*. Chicago: University of Chicago Press.

Burawoy, M., Blum, J. A., George S., Gille, Z., Gowan, T., Haney, L., Klawiter, M., Lopez, S. H., Riain, S. O. and Thayer, M. (2000) *Global Ethnography*. Berkeley: University of California Press.

Chomczynski, P. (2015) *Działania wychowanków schronisk dla nieletnich* [Juveniles and their activity in detention centers]. Lodz: Lodz University Press.

Collins, R. (1988) *Theoretical Sociology*. San Diego, CA: Harcourt, Brace, Jovanovich.

Delamont, S. (2004) 'Ethnography and participant observation', in C. Seale, G. Gobo, J. F. Gubrium and D. Silverman (eds), *Qualitative Research Practice*. London Sage, pp. 217–29.

Denzin, N. K. (1970) *The Research Act*. New York: McGraw Hill.

Denzin, N. K. (1997) *Interpretive Ethnography*. Thousand Oaks, CA: Sage

Gilbert, N. and Mulkay, M. (1983) 'In search of the action', in N. Gilbert and P. Abell (eds), *Accounts and Action*. Aldershot: Gower, pp. 8–34.

Glaser, B. G. and Strauss, A. L. (1967) *The Discovery of Grounded Theory: Strategies for Qualitative Research*. Chicago, IL: Aldine.

Gobo, G. (2008) *Doing Ethnography*. London: Sage.

Gobo, G. (2011) 'Glocalizing methodology? The encounter between local methodologies', *International Journal of Social Research Methodology*, 14 (6): 417–37.

Goffman, E. (1967) *Interaction Ritual*. New York: Doubleday Anchor.

Gold, R. (1958) 'Roles in the sociological field observations', *Social Forces*, 36: 217–23.

Hammersley, M. (1989) *The Dilemma of Qualitative Method*. London: Routledge.

Heritage, J. (1984) *Garfinkel and Ethnomethodology*. Cambridge: Polity.

Ho, K. (2009) *Liquidated: An Ethnography of Wall Street*. Durham, NC: Duke University Press.

Hobson, D. (1982) *'Crossroads': The Drama of Soap Opera*. London: Methuen.

Jenness, V. (2010) 'From policy to prisoners to people: a 'soft mixed methods' approach to studying transgender prisoners', *Journal of Contemporary Ethnography* 39 (5): 517–53.

Junker, B. (1960) *Field Work*. Chicago: Chicago University Press.

Knoblauch, H. (2005) 'Focused ethnography', *Forum: Qualitative Social Research*, 6 (3). www.qualitative-research.net/index.php/fqs/article/view/20/43 (accessed 2 December 2015).

La Piere, R. T. (1934) 'Attitudes vs. action', *Social Force*, 12: 230–7.

Lassiter, L. (2005) *The Chicago Guide to Collaborative Ethnography*. Chicago: Chicago University Press.

Lofland, J. (1995) 'Analytic ethnography', *Journal of Contemporary Ethnography*, 24: 30–67.

Lofland, L. H. (1980) 'Reminiscences of classic Chicago: "The Blumer-Hughes Talk"', *Urban Life*, 9 (3): 251–81.

Madge, J. (1962) *The Origins of Scientific Sociology*. New York: The Free Press of Glencoe.

Madison, S. (2012) *Critical Ethnography: Method, Ethics, and Performance*. London: Sage.

Marciniak, L. (2015) *Social Organization of the Vendors' Activities*. Lodz: Lodz University Press.

McCall, M. (2000) 'Performance ethnography', in N. Denzin and Y. Lincoln (eds), *Handbook of Qualitative Research* (2nd edn). London: Sage, pp. 421–35.

Mehan, H. (1979) *Learning Lessons*. Cambridge, MA: Harvard University Press.

Morrill, C. (1995) *The Executive Way: Conflict Management in Corporations*. Chicago: University of Chicago Press.

Payne, G. and Williams, M. (2005) 'Generalization in qualitative research', *Sociology*, 39 (2): 295–314.

Platt, J. (1983) 'The development of the "participant observation" method in sociology: origin, myth and history', *Journal of the History of the Behavioural Sciences*, 19 (4): 379–93.

Prus, R. (1997) *Subcultural Mosaics and Intersubjective Realities: An Ethnographic Research Agenda for Pragmatizing the Social Sciences*. Albany, NY: State University of New York Press.

Prus, R. and Grills, S. (2003) *The Deviant Mystique: Involvements, Realities, and Regulation*. Westport, CT: Praeger (Greenwood) Press.

Radcliffe-Brown, A. R. (1948) *A Natural Science of Society*. New York: Free Press.

Rose, E. (1960) 'The English record of a natural sociology', *American Sociological Review*, 25: 193–208.

Rose, E. (1997) 'The unattached society', *Ethnographic Studies*, 1: xv–43.

Savage, J. (2000) 'Ethnography and health care', *British Medical Journal*, 321: 1400–2.

Silverman, D. (1993) *Interpreting Qualitative Data*. London: Sage.

Silverman, D. (1997) *Qualitative Research: Theory, Method and Practice*. London: Sage.

Smith, D. E. (1986) 'Institutional ethnography: a feminist method', *Resource for Feminist Research*, 15: 6–13.

Snow, D., Morrill, C. and Anderson, L. (2003) 'Elaborating analytic ethnography', *Ethnography*, 4 (2): 181–200.

Thomas, J. (1992) *Doing Critical Ethnography*. London: Sage.

Whyte, W. F. (1943) *Street Corner Society*. Chicago: Chicago University Press.

Williams, M. (2000) 'Interpretativism and generalization', *Sociology*, 34 (2): 209–24.

EIGHT
Organizational Ethnography

Thomas S. Eberle and Christoph Maeder

About this chapter

Organizational ethnography means doing ethnography in and of organizations. We discuss the characteristics which distinguish organizational ethnography from general ethnography, and consider how it relates to (organizational) theory. We suggest sorting the great multiplicity of theoretical and methodological approaches in organizational studies along a continuum between theory- and data-guided poles, and present some important sociological approaches of organizational ethnography. We then discuss practical considerations in doing organizational ethnography such as field access and participation, data collection and data analysis, the distribution of organizational practice within space (multi-sited ethnography), informant and field relations, reporting back, ethical questions and finally writing up. We conclude by highlighting two major current developments and future prospects.

Keywords

organization, ethnography, organizational theory, research methods

The aim of this chapter is to introduce the field of organizational ethnography and to outline its central features and issues. In particular, we will focus on the following areas:

- What is organizational ethnography? What are the special characteristics of the field?
- What are the main theoretical and methodological approaches of organizational ethnography?
- Practical issues of doing organizational ethnography.

WHAT IS ORGANIZATIONAL ETHNOGRAPHY?

Organizational ethnography is a multi-method approach (observation, interviewing, document analysis, examination of the use of artefacts) whose pivotal feature is participant or non-participant observation of actions and practices in natural settings (see Gobo and Marciniak in this volume).[1] Most of what is written on the methodology of organizational ethnography is valid for any sort of ethnography. This can be well illustrated by the guidebook on how to become an organizational ethnographer by Daniel Neyland (2008). As it is impossible to formulate a fixed set of instructions, rules and procedures on how to do ethnography (Atkinson, 1990), Neyland discusses the crucial issues in the form of 'sensibilities'. Sensibilities do not have the same status as recipes or instructions but are not vague or incoherent either. They provide information and background, questions and a range of answers, and the tricks of the trade available for ethnographic consideration (Becker, 1998: 11). The author describes ten sensibilities:

1. Developing an ethnographic strategy in tandem with the situation, making initial choices about the type of group or activity, the place, material object or a very specific question, but keeping it fluid and flexible.
2. Choosing among the three principal approaches to knowledge: a realist ethnography that strives for objective representation; a narrative ethnography which accepts that different interpretations and accounts are possible; and a reflexive ethnography that reflects on how the processes of collecting, organizing and analysing the data produce the outcome.
3. Choosing locations and negotiating access.
4. Establishing field relations by close involvement with key informants and gatekeepers or even by becoming a group member. Establishing trust but not getting too close.
5. The time frame of an ethnographic study or field access may lead the research towards producing either thick or quick descriptions.
6. Observational skills and writing well-organized field notes are important, as well as keeping a kind of strangeness in order to see the ordinary.
7. Making choices about supplementing observations by interviews, audio-visual recordings and studying other technologies, like the virtual world of computers.
8. Choosing the form of writing, either for a broad (organizational) audience or for scholarly pursuit.
9. Ethical considerations should feature which areas are studied, who is incorporated into the research and how, what will be done with the observational data and if the researched have access to them (e.g. to the field notes or to recordings).
10. Exits should be considered at an early stage of ethnography and in relation to the time frame of the study, the phenomenon and field access.

Neyland (2008) illustrates each sensibility through a range of examples from ethnographic fieldwork in organizations that give insight into the practical tasks involved in doing organizational ethnography (and which are worthwhile reading).

---

[1]For the history of organizational ethnography see Schwartzman, 1993.

A fundamental difference between 'ethnographying' (Tota, 2004) modern organizations vs. tribal societies seems to be the geographical and cultural distance. To research an exotic tribe implied that an anthropological ethnographer would travel far from home, stay for two years, immerse him- or herself in an unfamiliar culture, learn a foreign language and live with a number of hardships. An organizational ethnographer does not need a toothbrush when leaving home (Bate, 1997: 1150), as he or she usually returns for the night. Ethnographers can work regular hours and enjoy multiple leisure time activities in between as the other members of the organization do. It is even possible – and common practice – to enter the field only sporadically, to move in for short periods and then move out again.

However, ethnographers have found cultural milieux in modern societies that differ greatly from 'regular' lifestyles and take ample time to investigate. In a similar vein, sophisticated work settings with high-tech equipment, such as for example scientific laboratories or surveillance and control rooms, require plenty of fieldwork in order to make adequate sense of what is going on (Latour and Woolgar, 1979; Knorr-Cetina, 1999; Knoblauch et al., 2000; Luff et al., 2000).

WHAT ARE THE MAIN THEORETICAL AND METHODOLOGICAL APPROACHES OF ORGANIZATIONAL ETHNOGRAPHY?

The paradigmatic diversity of organizational studies

As organizational ethnographers must interpret their data in relation to a theoretical framework, they face the practical problem of how to come to terms with this variety. Gareth Morgan (2006 [1986]) proposed a solution to this problem which is still relevant today. He suggested understanding the theoretical landscape as a collection of multiple images. Each theory represents an image that has its strengths and weaknesses. Each works like a metaphor, making some aspects of a phenomenon visible and having blind spots in regard to others. If you consider organizations as machines, you will see all their mechanistic aspects and overlook the non-mechanistic properties or treat them as disturbances or threats. The mechanistic image emphasizes technical precision, efficiency and rationality and is appropriate for constructing conveyer belts or analysing the rule-like, bureaucratic side of an organization, but it has difficulty taking account of the 'human factor'. Taylor's *Scientific Management* (1947) is an illustrative example of such a view. If, however, you choose a different image and regard organizations as holographic brains, for example, you will instead think in terms of information processes, cybernetic feedback loops, network designs, redundancies and variety, self-reference and self-organization. Each approach makes you ask different types of questions about how organizations learn, how they learn to learn, how processes of self-organization emerge and so on. Similarly, one can consider organizations as organisms, as political systems, as psychic prisons, as instruments of domination or as cultures. These metaphors create ways of seeing and shaping organizational life. Taking different perspectives when analysing an organizational problem, suggests Morgan, aids the identification of innovative solutions.

While much ethnography *of* organizations refers to such a kind of organizational theory (or image), there are many approaches to doing ethnography *in* organizations that focus on the *practices* of organizing and use different theoretical concepts. Overall, we can distinguish between more theory-guided and more data-guided approaches. Data-guided approaches such as ethnomethodology consider the term 'organization' not as a scientific but rather as a commonsense construct (cf. Silverman and Jones, 1976); they refrain from using theoretical concepts and restrict their focus on what the data reveal.

Selected sociological approaches of organizational ethnography

It would be futile attempting to account for all the diverse approaches of organizational ethnography. But this does not discharge us from at least mentioning some perceivable branches in organizational ethnographic research. We have a preference for approaches that are 'interpretive' and a theoretical affinity to 'social constructivism': the idea that social reality is inextricably produced in everyday life and its routines of action and interaction (Berger and Luckmann, 1966; Goffman, 1983). Although such a list is always somewhat arbitrary and necessarily cannot include everything that counts, it can help to orient the student reader about the possible range and some focal points of such research. Here are some examples:

- *social organization* where the organization is treated as a context in order to observe the social production of essential societal aspects of life within a particular type of organization. This concept is usually called 'the social organization of X'. Sudnow's *Passing On* (1967), Zerubavel's *Patterns of Time in Hospital Life* (1979), Gubrium's *Oldtimers and Alzheimer's* (1986), are but a few classic examples of this strategy in the realm of medical organizations. These studies – like most others in this tradition – raise and illuminate important issues and their features, which we almost exclusively can find embedded in particular organizations.
- *organizational culture* is another possibly defining topic for organizational ethnography (Jelinek et al., 1983). This seeks to understand organizations through the observation of language use. Linguistic concepts like metaphors, stories, narratives, forms of talk and others became employed by the researchers in order to represent and analyse reality construction in organizations and 'Organizations as *shared meaning*' (Smircich, 1983) became available for social research, be it in a bank (Weeks, 2004) or a cat shelter (Alger and Alger, 2003).
- *science and laboratory studies* introduced by Latour and Woolgar (1979), are concerned with the scrupulous reconstruction of how, under the organizational conditions of a lab, scientific facts become constructed. Taking ethnomethodological concepts like sense-making in interaction and organization as a joint production of accomplishments by scientists as a starting point, this approach led to the more general topic of epistemic cultures and the production of scientific knowledge in general (Knorr-Cetina, 1999).
- *workplace studies* conceptualize work and organization as related accomplishments of actors interacting in a given, often technologically sophisticated context (see Knoblauch et al., 2000; Luff et al., 2000).
- *grounded theory*, as developed chiefly by Barney Glaser and Anselm Strauss (1967), introduces many concepts often still used today, such as the ideas of trajectories of chains of linked interactions and processes, going concerns of the members of an organization or a profession, awareness contexts for doing things, etc. (see Charmaz and Bryant in this volume). Perhaps one of the most influential proposals from this

approach is the idea of looking at the negotiating that goes on nearly permanently in every social setting. While not everything is negotiable in a given situation, an astonishing number of judgements on properties at stake are. The idea of negotiating as a fundamental property of human communication led to what is known today as a 'negotiated order approach' (Strauss, 1978; Fine, 1984; Maines, 1985) and continues to inspire ethnographic organizational research.

- *overarching organizational schemes and discourses* as seen in the work of Beach and Carlson (2004) where the impact of a reorganization of the adult education system by the introduction of markets as a means of coordination is analysed by the use of ethnographic case studies. In their work they carefully look at the impact of an ideology upon local practices contained in organizations. A similar and even more general analysis of the connection between educational policies and the effects in school organizations, classrooms, etc. is provided by Hammersley (1999) and Troman et al. (2006).
- *emotion and organization* as a useful start into this realm of organization, work and ethnography can be found in Schweingruber and Berns' (2005) text on the emotion management of young salespeople and Garot's (2004) research on emotions and bureaucracy, while the locus classicus is Fineman (2003).
- *organizational memories* represent past knowledge of an organization, as individual memories of members as well as collectively shared memories, by means of organizational archives and practices of collective remembering as well as embodied routines (which include implicit or tacit knowledge). Organizational memories are socially distributed and linked to spaces (Middleton and Edwards, 1990; Walsh and Ungson, 1991; Eberle 2016). Special problems are involved in digital memories because of the obsolescence of hardware and software: Are old databases still readable? (Cliché question: Can NASA still fly to the moon? Linde, 2006.)

PRACTICAL ISSUES OF DOING ORGANIZATIONAL ETHNOGRAPHY

Research in 'live settings' or *in vivo* within an organization by the use of physical co-presence of the researcher and the researched involves typically, and at a minimum, the following tasks: (1) gaining access to the organization and finding an appropriate social role; (2) setting up a useful data collection process and defining an analytical framework for the data analysis; (3) establishing a working relation with at least some members of the organization; (4) finding a style of writing for the ethnographic text; (5) reporting findings and analyses back to the field while staying ethically alert and honest towards the people and their organization. These tasks should not be seen in linear order, but rather as constant elements of the exercise of 'muddling through' during the process of research in organizational ethnography. It is for this reason that ethnographers sometimes ironically refer to their work as doing 'dirty fieldwork'.

Field access and participation

Organizations usually regulate membership and access carefully. This can make them difficult sites for ethnographic research and sometimes even renders it impossible. Think, for example, of the ethnography of the secret service or a nuclear submarine. Even after the researcher has identified the organization he or she wants to study, a good reason is required for the local authorities to grant permission to enter, stay and to collect data.

This is why some ethnographers choose to do what is called participant observation by complete immersion in the field. This means the ethnographer tries to become a full member of the organization with a full job and duties against which he or she will be scrutinized. In such a case the ethnographer undertakes all entry routines into an organization as with the other members and he or she attains full membership status.

An example of this strategy of complete immersion into a field is Gary Alan Fine's (1996) text on the culture of work in restaurant kitchens. He worked in four different restaurants as a kitchen helper. While not hiding his research interest, he fully participated in the work and became a true member for a limited amount of time. Such an approach offers the unique chance of gathering first-hand knowledge on the hidden or backroom side of organizations. This can reveal informal aspects of social relations and gives the ethnographer the chance to experience personally some less apparent aspects of the organization such as, for instance, pride in the work or economic exploitation.

However, this ideal type of 'being there' does not work in every case. The same author used another more common approach in organizational research when he was doing ethnography on meteorologists: he participated as an observer without taking on any working responsibilities (Fine, 2007). The more specialized and professionally infused the work within organizations becomes, the more likely the researcher will have to use this second approach. The danger is that we end up with what is called 'quick and dirty' ethnography. In particular in the business field and the related realm of management studies, where time is money, this poses a sombre threat. It also poses a risk to the reputation of more serious ethnographic studies, because such 'quick and dirty' studies pretend to be ethnographic, but in fact they are only sketchy impressions without any theoretical ambitions. Like every serious business, organizational ethnography as a method and a scientific endeavour needs thorough training and lots of time. Only this allows us to advance to the 'thick description' (Geertz, 1973), the reconstruction of the polyphony of emic (participants') views and their relation to the practical social order in the field of research.

Of course, in many cases we can also find a public, accessible and open side to organizations. And these accesses can be used as research sites and topics too, as the French ethnographers Dubois (2010) and Weller (1999) demonstrated in their studies of the state bureaucracy 'at the counter window'. But such a coincidence of research question and accessibility to the setting is a rather rare exemption. If for instance Paul Atkinson (2006) in his seminal work on the opera or Buscatto (in this volume) in her research on female jazz singers had restricted themselves simply to presentation of the public part of the performance, we would have missed the most insightful points they made. And sometimes the ethnographer even has to accept real danger to life as the price of gaining field access. A very nice example of this can be found in Van Maanen's report (1988: 109–15) on his participation in police patrol work, where he ended up with his wish of 'don't shoot the fieldworker' (1988: 112).

Another important question besides the degree of involvement possible and/or needed refers to what is called 'researching up' or 'researching down'. Looking at an organization from the top down creates another set of data, shows other structures of relevance, and displays different practices from doing research 'at the bottom'. The last strategy is called 'researching up'. At first sight it might look more sympathetic than 'being with the chiefs'. But sympathy is not the point here, since ethnography as a form of description always distances the researcher from the researched to a certain degree. Even a study like Adler and Adler's (2004) book on hotel work, the ethnography of luxury resorts in which they 'research up' from the labourer's perspective, puts a remarkable distance between the researchers and the researched. And, as Melville Dalton's classic study *Men Who Manage* (1959) brilliantly documents, research within the upper echelons shows interesting and important features of organizations too. So, in the context of power structure, the organizational ethnographer must be aware that different hierarchical and functional positions within an organization evoke different systems of meaning, different practices, different perspectives and voices. But which strategy to choose depends on the research questions and the contacts available for field access.

Data collection and data analysis

One of the long-standing challenges of doing participant observation in organizational ethnography by the sole use of field notes is summed up in the question of why others should believe the ethnographer when he or she reports. Would another researcher not reach different conclusions if he or she were to visit the same place and make his or her field notes? While we do not think that the knowledge gained in the process of serious fieldwork is as arbitrary or sketchy as this question suggests, the advantages of having audio or video recordings in order to check and recheck an interpretation are convincing. On the other hand electronic devices pose tricky challenges insofar as the ethnographer needs the organization's permission to use this technology. This is not always obtainable because the people in an organization can also distinguish between bulletproof evidence of a technically recorded and infinitely reproducible strip of data and a researcher's memory. In particular, if you touch on sensitive issues like informal networks, unprofessional practices and so on, this tension will apply.

So it is advisable to have such a project and its potential empirical focus discussed with colleagues *before and as* you enter the field. This does not mean that the researcher cannot adapt to unanticipated but emerging and particularly interesting features of the field. Indeed this usually happens and is regarded here as one of the strengths of organizational ethnography. The authors' own research on human resources management serves as a useful example. We found a multinational company with a very belligerent wording when it came to the description of its staff: 'war for talents', 'high performance as a goal for everyone', etc., so we expected a hire and fire culture with a lot of people being dismissed. But to our surprise the observable practices were very different. The company offered a lot of training, help and care for those who were not complying with the performance management goals and it generally took a very long time (up to four years) before somebody was discharged. This was a surprising and interesting contradiction between the official language in use and the observable practice (Nadai and Maeder, 2008).

Data analysis is the next difficult job in such a project. Which concepts get employed and are useful is closely linked to the kind of ethnography one intends to do. For instance, while in grounded theory (see Charmaz and Bryant in this volume) the analysis will yield codes and categories in relation to trajectories, going concerns or conditional matrices, a more ethnomethodologically oriented project like a membership categorization analysis (membership categorization device analysis; Silverman, 2011: 256–70) will emphasize the properties and functioning of particular focused elements (e.g. the CEO) of organizations. There are many more ways to analyse field notes, documents and other data (semiotics, discourse analytic approaches, socio-linguistics, etc.) in organizational ethnography and we often find them combined. There is more than one way to properly design and conduct this kind of research, but the approach should be carefully and knowingly chosen.

An all-time challenge for analysis in organizational ethnography is the handling of the size of an organization. As an example, think of doing research in a huge multinational company, structured into functional divisions and with long chains of hierarchy dispersed over different national boundaries. Even if the ethnographer's freedom to move around is not hindered at all by the organization itself, the sheer size makes it impossible to gain something like 'the whole picture'. In order to do organizational ethnography on an analytical level one should avoid exaggerating the ideals of localized ethnographic fieldwork only, where the local phenomena are taken as the exclusive features of social reality and the rest of the world is left for good or just regarded as a narrative. There is always a multiplicity of specific places within an organization where relevant things are happening, launched, performed, enacted, coordinated, carried out, etc. This feature of the coordinated or at least orderly distribution of things within organizations leads to the idea of a 'multi-sited ethnography'. The term goes back to a discussion that was started in anthropology by George Marcus (1995), where the question arose of how to do ethnography in a globalized world system. The following debate has inspired not only promising developments in ethnography on larger social systems in general (see Falzon, 2009), but also on organizational ethnography in particular (Nadai and Maeder, 2009). The idea of following an actor or a group of actors or even of following an artefact (e.g. a document, a tool) on the path through the organization is but one strategy one can employ in this regard. What is rendered visible by doing so is the connectedness between, and the coordination of, practices, actions, artefacts and rules in organizations.

Informant and field relations; reporting back and ethical questions

As already mentioned, organizations do have boundaries and usually control access. The student of an organization therefore needs to find a way to cross these barriers. The usual way is to find a person who is a member of the organization and can provide access to it. Such persons are called 'informants' from the ethnographic point of view and 'members' from the organizational perspective. Whenever such a member becomes an informant for the ethnographer, he or she takes a certain degree of risk. This risk arises because informants are unlikely to be familiar with what the research person does and informants typically do not want to risk their position in the organization as a consequence of providing information to the ethnographer. This is particularly the case when ethnographers reconstruct informal habits, tacit knowledge, routine methods of working around official rules or any other aspect of an organization which belongs backstage and is regularly hidden from the public. Although such knowledge can be very important for understanding the everyday functioning of an organization, it is delicate to report. Furthermore, an ethnographer and the informant will sometimes develop close ties due to time spent together. So keeping good field relations becomes a subtle and often ambivalent task in organizational ethnography. As a consequence we strongly recommend that the student ethnographer of organizations considers informants not solely as data sources, but as special sorts of transient professional friends that deserve friendly treatment in many respects (see Ryen in this volume).

Another challenge in building and maintaining contact with informants is the fact that most of them are interested in the outcome of the ethnographic research. But ethnographic texts and analyses regularly put a distance between the researcher and the researched. Although the informants will recognize their organization in such a description, they might not agree, for example, with the importance ascribed by the ethnographer to certain features of the organization. Given the theoretical assumption that there can be many voices and viewpoints within an organization itself, the ethnographer's voice is surely allowed to differ. But sometimes the 'polyphony of the field' (the fact that there is seldom just one valid perspective) can make it necessary to write additional texts targeted at the members of the researched organization itself in addition to those for scientific publications.

Writing ethnography

In a broad sense, organizational ethnography is the description of the culture and everyday life that people in organizations share. So the term 'ethnography' indicates the challenge of writing and using a method in order to get a textual representation of that culture. Writing an organizational ethnography hence does not differ from writing any other sociological ethnography and the general categories to differentiate the writing styles in ethnography apply. According to Van Maanen's (1988: 4–23) well-received proposition, we distinguish the genres of 'ethnographic realism', 'confessional ethnography', 'dramatic ethnography', 'critical ethnographies' and 'self-' or 'auto-ethnography'. We do not elaborate these genres here (but see Marvasti in this volume), but want to bring our readers' attention to the fact that writing organizational ethnographies is not only a scientific, but to a certain degree also a literary challenge. While writing, we have to choose an audience, select a thesis and adapt a writing style. Of course, this rough description of the writing process does not tell it all. But it provides some structure and should make the student of organizations aware of the storytelling character of nearly every organizational ethnography. The only exception here is the study of 'institutional talk', informed by conversation analysis (Heritage in this volume), where the writing takes on a more 'scientific' format since it is based on the rigorous analysis of audio and video recordings.

CHAPTER SUMMARY

Organizational ethnography is a multi-method approach (observation, interviewing, document analysis, examination of the use of artefacts) whose pivotal feature is participant or non-participant observation of actions and practices in natural settings. The term 'organization' can refer to the everyday practices and routines of action going on within such a social structure ('ethnography in organization'), or the term and observations in the field can be linked to social theory of organization ('ethnography of organization').

When you do organizational ethnography, you must consider:

- the different strands of organizational ethnography, some more theory-guided and some more data-guided
- the vibrant change of modern organizations and their environments and the impact of new technologies
- the cluster of practical questions arising in such research when it comes to field access, informant relations, research ethics, data collection and writing ethnography
- the relative slowness of such research, because the researcher him- or herself has to be socialized in the field.

FUTURE PROSPECTS

What are the major current issues in organizational ethnography? First, organizations are changing rapidly through the use of information and communication technology such as computers, the internet, email, mobile phones, video-conferences, social media, ubiquitous web access and so on. This requires new research methods. Kozinets (2010) coined the term *netnography* to designate a new approach in qualitative research that draws together the terms 'internet' and 'ethnography'. A netnographer needs to be computer savvy and up-to-date with current developments on the web and state of the art hardware and software (cf. Hine, 2015; see Part VI in this volume). Others promote a multi-site approach (Marcus, 1998) as large corporations have become increasingly global, and meanwhile many organizational ethnographers work in research teams whose members are sometimes scattered around the world at different sites of a company. Knoblauch (2005) favours a 'focused ethnography', for instance combined with videography; indeed, if an organizational site changes fast, what is the advantage of a long-time stay in the same setting?

Second, new approaches have been developed. The most significant is probably the so-called 'representation crises' proclaimed by postmodern authors (Clifford and Marcus, 1986) which eventually led to 'non-representational methodologies' (Vannini, 2015). In such a perspective, organizational ethnographies do not strive for any sort of 'objective' representation, but rather for new vistas, new perspectives, new insights. Creativity, innovation and new ways of learning are their favoured goals. Beyes and Steyaert (2011, 2012, 2013), who avoid the sharp distinction and speak, following Lorimer (2005), of a 'more-than-representational' approach, developed an organizational ethnography of affects, of space and of aesthetics. Furthermore, there is an ascendency of practice-based studies (Gherardi, 2013) and discursive approaches (Rouleau et al., 2014: 4). Another approach that is widely used and that tries to replace social constructivism is actor-network theory (ANT). Nimmo (2011) discusses the relationship between ANT and ethnography as follows: they share the emphasis on practices, which requires a deliberately 'messy' methodology, an openness and sensitivity to heterogeneity and multiplicity. Disparate elements such as objects and environments, materials and techniques, taxonomies, categories and symbolic systems, are inextricably intertwined with practices so that any absolute distinction between subjective and objective or social and natural dimensions is rendered nonsensical (Mol, 1998: 31; Nimmo, 2011: 113). ANT's generalized symmetry gives more agency to non-human actors than most ethnographic approaches do. While postmodern theories spurred seminal debates and advanced reflexivity, our own position is far from 'anything goes' – we maintain, within the premises of the interpretive paradigm, the ideal of scientific rigour in empirical research, practising reflexivity in organizational ethnography (see Buscatto, 2008, and in this volume).

Given that modern societies show an unparalleled degree of organization and that most aspects of modern life are handled by, and regulated through, organizations, we are surely likely to see increased attention being given to organizational ethnography in the future. Ethnographic texts have enriched the description and expanded the understanding of this organizational world in which we live. In this sense organizational ethnography today is already much more than just 'tales from the trails'. From the interaction-oriented ethnomethodology, to organizations as shared meanings and cultures, right through to the idea of the negotiated order, there emerges a wide array of future possibilities for theoretical underpinnings and empirical observation.

Organizational ethnography will surely always remain empirically local, stay embedded in certain contexts in time and space, be limited in scope, and hardly ever be useful for quick fixes due to its methodological foundation (and slowness) in discovering the social aspects of organizations. The idea that any social order is produced and constructed by the actions and practices of people in a given context is the starting and the end point of such an endeavour.

Study questions

1. Explain how ethnography relates to theory, and list three major strands of organizational ethnography.
2. What are the key factors that will influence your field role in organizational ethnography?
3. Why do you have to be aware that the individual subjects of your ethnographic research may not share your view on the organization under investigation?
4. Which are the major current developments in organizational ethnography?

Recommended reading

Besides the organizational ethnographies cited in the text, we recommend the prospective researcher to have a look at the contents of the following books:

Kostera, M. (2007) *Organizational Ethnography: Methods and Inspirations*. Lund: Studentlitteratur AB. This book is an introduction to organizational ethnography for masters and doctoral students. It presents the ethnographic methodological tradition and different types of organizations as objects of ethnographic research. Observation, interview and text analysis are explained as main methods, but also how field notes and transcribed interviews are analysed, and how an ethnographic thesis is written.

Neyland, D. (2008) *Organizational Ethnography*. London: Sage.
This book covers the whole research project process, from research design all the way to negotiating an exit strategy. It is organized around the ten sensibilities that are quoted at the beginning of this chapter. It covers many practical issues during the different phases of the research process and illustrates them with many concrete examples of organizational ethnography.

Ybema, S., Yanov, D., Wels, H. and Kamsteeg, F. (2009) *Organizational Ethnography: Studying the Complexities of Everyday Life*. London: Sage.
As organizational studies have tended largely to ignore the everyday experiences of people working in organizations, this book presents an ethnographic perspective on organizations and organizational research. The chapters are written by leading scholars in organizational studies and cover many aspects, from gaining access to research sites to the problems of distance and closeness, the role of friendship relations in the field, ethical issues, writing styles and evaluation standards for ethnographic work. Contains a commented bibliography.

Recommended online resources

Journal of Contemporary Ethnography:
http://jce.sagepub.com/

Journal of Organizational Ethnography:
www.emeraldgrouppublishing.com/products/journals/journals.htm?id=JOE

Forum: Qualitative Social Research:
www.qualitative-research.net/

Qualitative Inquiry:
http://qix.sagepub.com/

Qualitative Research:
http://qrj.sagepub.com/

Ethnography and Education:
www.tandf.co.uk/journals/titles/17457823.asp

Qualitative Sociology Review:
www.qualitativesociologyreview.org

References

Adler, P. A. and Adler, P. (2004) *Paradise Laborers: Hotel Work in the Global Economy*. Ithaca, NY: ILR Press.

Alger, J. M. and Alger, S. (2003) *Cat Culture: The Social World of a Cat Shelter*. Philadelphia: Temple University Press.

Atkinson, P. (1990) *The Ethnographic Imagination: Textual Constructions of Reality*. London: Routledge.

Atkinson, P. (2006) *Everyday Arias: An Operatic Ethnography*. Lanham, MD: Altamira Press.

Bate, S. (1997) 'Whatever happened to organizational anthropology? A review of the field of organizational ethnography and anthropological studies', *Human Relations,* 50 (9): 1147–76.

Beach, D. and Carlson, M. (2004) 'Adult education goes to market: an ethnographic case study of the restructuring and reculturing of adult education', *European Educational Research Journal*, 3 (3): 673–91.

Becker, H. S. (1998) *Tricks of the Trade*. Chicago: Chicago University Press.

Berger, P. L. and Luckmann, T. (1966) *The Social Construction of Reality: A Treatise in the Sociology of Knowledge*. London and New York: Penguin Books.

Beyes, T. and Steyaert, C. (2011) 'The ontological politics of artistic interventions: implications for performing action research', *Action Research Journal*, 9 (1): 100–15.

Beyes, T. and Steyaert, C. (2012) 'Spacing organization: non-representational theorizing and the spatial turn in organizational research', *Organization*, 19 (1): 45–61.

Beyes, T. and Steyaert, C. (2013) 'Strangely familiar: the uncanny and unsiting organizational analysis', *Organization Studies*, 34 (10): 1445–65.

Buscatto, M. (2008) 'Who allowed you to observe? A reflexive overt organizational ethnography', *Qualitative Sociology Review*, 4 (3): 29–48.

Clifford, J. and Marcus, G. E. (eds) (1986) *Writing Culture: The Poetics and Politics of Ethnography*. Berkeley: University of California Press.

Dalton, M. (1959) *Men Who Manage: Fusions of Feeling and Theory in Administration*. New York: Wiley.

Dubois, V. (2010) *The Bureaucrat and the Poor: Encounters in French Welfare Offices*. Aldershot: Ashgate.

Eberle, T. S. (2016) 'Organizational memories – a phenomenological analysis', in A. L. Tota and T. Hagen (eds), *The Routledge International Handbook of Memory Studies*. London: Routledge, pp. 93–108.

Falzon, M.-A. (ed.) (2009) *Multi-sited Ethnography: Theory, Practice and Locality in Contemporary Social Research*. Aldershot: Ashgate.

Fine, G. A. (1984) 'Negotiated orders and organizational cultures', *Annual Review of Sociology*, 10: 239–62.

Fine, G. A. (1996) *Kitchens: The Culture of Restaurant Work*. Berkeley: University of California Press.

Fine, G. A. (2007) *Authors of the Storm: Meteorologists and the Culture of Prediction*. Chicago: University of Chicago Press.

Fineman, S. (2003) *Understanding Emotion at Work*. London: Sage.

Garot, R. (2004) '"You're not a stone": emotional sensitivity in a bureaucratic setting', *Journal of Contemporary Ethnography*, 33: 735–66.

Geertz, C. (1973) *The Interpretation of Culture*. New York: Basic Books.

Gherardi, S. (2013) *How to Conduct a Practice-based Study: Problems and Methods*. Cheltenham: Edward Elgar Publishing.

Glaser, B. G. and Strauss, A. L. (1967) *The Discovery of Grounded Theory: Strategies for Qualitative Research*. Chicago, IL: Aldine.

Goffman, E. (1983) 'The interaction order', *American Sociological Review*, 48: 1–17.

Gubrium, J. F. (1986) *Oldtimers and Alzheimer's: The Descriptive Organization of Senility*. Greenwich, CT: JAI Press.

Hammersley, M. (ed.) (1999) *Researching School Experience: Ethnographic Studies of Teaching and Learning*. London: Routledge.

Hine, C. (2015) *Ethnography for the Internet: Embedded, Embodied and Everyday*. London: Bloomsbury Academic.

Jelinek, M., Smircich, L. and Hirsch, P. (1983) 'Introduction: a code of many colors', *Administrative Science Quarterly*, 28 (3): 331–8.

Knoblauch, H. (2005) 'Focused ethnography', *Forum: Qualitative Social Research*, 6 (3). www.qualitative-research.net/index.php/fqs/article/view/20/43 (accessed 2 December 2015).

Knoblauch, H., Heath, C. and Luff, P. (2000) 'Technology and social interaction: the emergence of "workplace studies"', *British Journal of Sociology*, 51 (2): 299–320.

Knorr-Cetina, K. (1999) *Epistemic Cultures: How the Sciences Make Knowledge*. Cambridge, MA: Harvard University Press.

Kozinets, R. V. (2010) *Netnography: Doing Ethnographic Research Online*. Thousand Oaks, CA: Sage.

Latour, B. and Woolgar, S. (1979) *Laboratory Life: The Social Construction of Scientific Facts*. Thousand Oaks, CA: Sage.

Linde, C. (2006) 'Remembering the Moon: memory issues in NASA's lunar return', talk given at the annual meeting of the Society for the Sociological Study of Science, Vancouver.

Lorimer, H. (2005) 'Cultural geography: the busyness of being "more-than-representational"', *Progress in Human Geography*, 29: 83–94.

Luff, P., Hindmarsh, J. and Heath, C. (2000) *Workplace Studies: Recovering Work Practice and Informing System Design*. Cambridge: Cambridge University Press.

Maines, D. R. (1985) 'Social organization and social structure in symbolic interactionist thought', *Annual Review of Sociology*, 3: 235–59.

Marcus, G. E. (1995) 'Ethnography in/of the world system: the emergence of multi-sited ethnography', *Annual Review of Anthropology*, 24: 95–117.

Marcus, G. E. (1998) *Ethnography Through Thick and Thin*. Princeton, NJ: Princeton University Press.

Middleton, D. and Edwards, D. (eds) (1990) *Collective Remembering*. London: Sage.

Mol, A. (1998) 'Ontological politics: a word and some questions', *The Sociological Review*, 46: 74–89.

Morgan, G. (2006 [1986]) *Images of Organizations* (updated edn). Thousand Oaks, CA: Sage.

Nadai, E. and Maeder, C. (2008) 'Negotiations at all points? Interaction and organization', *Forum Qualitative Research*, 9 (1). www.qualitative-research.net/index.php/fqs/article/view/337/735 (accessed 2 December 2015).

Nadai, E. and Maeder, C. (2009) 'Contours of the field(s): multi-sited ethnography as a theory-driven research strategy for sociology', in M.-A. Falzon (ed.), *Multi-sited Ethnography: Theory, Practice and Locality in Contemporary Research*. Aldershot: Ashgate, pp. 233–50.

Neyland, D. (2008) *Organizational Ethnography*. London: Sage.

Nimmo, R. (2011) 'Actor-network theory and methodology: social research in a more-than-human world', *Methodological Innovations Online*, 6 (3): 108–19.

Rouleau, L., de Rond, M. and Musca, G. (2014) 'From the ethnographic turn to new forms of organizational ethnography', guest editorial, *Journal of Organizational Ethnography*, 3 (1): 2–9.

Schwartzman, H. B. (1993) *Ethnography in Organizations*. Thousand Oaks, CA: Sage.

Schweingruber, D. and Berns, N. (2005) 'Shaping the selves of young salespeople through emotion management', *Journal of Contemporary Ethnography*, 34: 679–706.

Silverman, D. (2011) *Interpreting Qualitative Data: Methods for Analysing Talk, Text and Interaction*. London: Sage.

Silverman, D. and Jones, J. (1976) *Organizational Work*. London: Collier Macmillan.

Smircich, L. (1983) 'Organizations as shared meanings', in L. R. Pondy, P. J. Frost, G. Morgan and T. C. Dandridge (eds), *Organizational Symbolism*. Greenwich, CT: JAI Press, pp. 55–65.

Strauss, A. L. (1978) *Negotiations: Varieties, Contexts, Processes, and Social Order*. San Francisco, CA: Jossey-Bass.

Sudnow, D. (1967) *Passing On: The Social Organization of Dying.* Englewood Cliffs, NJ: Prentice Hall.

Taylor, F. (1947) *Scientific Management.* New York: Harper.

Tota, A. L. (2004) 'Ethnographying public memory: the commemorative genre for the victims of terrorism in Italy', *Qualitative Research*, 4: 131–59.

Troman, G., Jeffrey, B. and Beach, D. (2006) *Researching Education Policy: Ethnographic Experiences.* London: Tufnell.

Van Maanen, J. (1988) *Tales of the Field: On Writing Ethnography.* Chicago: University of Chicago Press.

Vannini, P. (ed.) (2015) *Non-representational Methodologies: Re-envisioning Research.* New York: Routledge.

Walsh, J. P. and Ungson, G. R. (1991) 'Organizational Memory', *Academy of Management Review*, 16: 57–91.

Weeks, J. (2004) *Unpopular Culture: The Ritual of Complaint in a British Bank.* Chicago: University of Chicago Press.

Weller, J.-M. (1999) *L'État au guichet: sociologie cognitive du travail et modernisation administrative des services publics.* Paris: Desclée de Brouwer.

Zerubavel, E. (1979) *Patterns of Time in Hospital Life: A Sociological Perspective.* Chicago: University of Chicago Press.

NINE

Practising Reflexivity in Ethnography

Marie Buscatto

About this chapter

In this chapter I discuss the general defining principles of a reflexive epistemological framework that may be useful to sociologists practising the ethnographic method. This discussion leads to the presentation of specific techniques that may be used during the research process to ensure the scientific quality of sociological findings based on ethnographic 'data'. The reflexive framework, already operative in related disciplines – notably history and anthropology – will be illustrated with a few empirical examples designed to help students conduct their ethnographic sociological studies.

Keywords

ethnography, qualitative methods, reflexivity, artefacts, epistemology, involvement and detachment

I have never been impressed by the argument that, as complete objectivity is impossible in these matters (as, of course, it is), one might as well let one's sentiments run loose. As Robert Solow has remarked, that is like saying that as a perfectly aseptic environment is impossible, one might as well conduct surgery in a sewer (Geertz, 1973: 30).

The anthropologists who invented field studies in the late nineteenth century, most notably Bronislaw Malinowski and Edward E. Evans Pritchard, defined their way of proceeding to be scientific. The stated aim was to collect ethnographic data in an objective way. But anthropology was destabilizing the positivist scientific model – first in practice, then in discourse. Like archive work in history, ethnography – basically defined as direct observation conducted over time (for details, see Gobo and Marciniak in this volume) – soon appeared as incomplete, lacking and imperfect. It thus could not be practised with a blind respect for the positivist method based on the presumed superiority of the hypothetico-deductive model and the understanding that it will ensure objectivity for the 'data' collected. Realizing this, historians and anthropologists were quick to construct a reflexive scientific approach. This no longer adhered to the positivist model, while defending the possibility of producing scientific results, as is clear in the famous remark by Clifford Geertz quoted above.

REFLEXIVITY AS A SCIENTIFIC PRACTICE

Like historians and anthropologists, ethnographic sociologists very early on considered that ethnography, defined as long-term direct observations, was incompatible with the positivist framework. Because of the human relationship that gets established between researcher(s) and observed people, researchers in these disciplines realized that they could not follow a predetermined path 'as Lareau (1989: 189) observed, "Using qualitative methods means learning to live with uncertainty, ambiguity, and confusion, sometimes for weeks at a time. It also means carving a path by making many decisions, with only the vaguest guide posts"' (Grindstaff, 2002: 277).

Right from its beginning, the ethnographic method appeared as inevitably subjective; it could not proceed on the basis of positivist criteria which were then favoured in social studies based on questionnaires, statistics or systematic records (see Gobo and Marciniak in this volume). In the positivist method, researchers construct hypotheses, indicators and questions in order to ensure that they will not be caught up in or tripped up by preconceptions, which may conflict with the objectivity of the experimental method. But very soon, ethnographic researchers could not be considered as being protected from their theoretical or personal biases. They were potentially considered as systematically falling victims to them, becoming – potentially – like journalists, novelists or travellers. And being integrated into the community they were studying offered no external guarantee that they would be able to break free of their ideologies, assumptions or preconceptions. It was early on considered that researchers' past experience, personality and cultural orientations necessarily influence what they see and how they interpret it:

> Ethnography, therefore - like every non-standardized type of social research [...] must now and, above all, in the longer term be marked by a fundamental scepticism about the quality of the data provided by others. (Honer, 2004: 114)

Rejection of the 'postmodern' path

Faced with the impossibility of attaining the positivist ideal, some anthropologists and ethnographic sociologists, including Norman Denzin (1999), James Clifford and George E. Marcus (1986) or Patricia Clough (1992), chose the 'postmodern' path, in which their writings became not just scientific works but also literary ones where the first-person author is central to the researcher's account. Here the argument pertained to both the supposed nature of such study – too subjective to be objectified – and the understanding that it is impossible to grasp the complexity of the world as it operates in global, modern, many-faceted societies. Under these conditions, went this argument, ethnographers must aim to present the entire range of voices present in the societies they study, as this will eliminate the fundamentally inegalitarian character of anthropological research, research that 'naturally' gives precedence to dominant viewpoints:

> An existential ethnography offers a blueprint for cultural criticism, a criticism grounded in the specific worlds made visible in the ethnography. It understands that there can be no value-free, objective, dispassionate, value-neutral account of a culture and its ways. [...] Ethnography like art is always political. (Denzin, 1999: 512)

The choice of the postmodern path can even be used to denigrate one's colleague's work as 'non-scientific' as was done by Gary Alan Fine in his criticism of Loïc Wacquant's 'carnal sociology'. As shown below, most ethnographers do not relish such comments: the labelling of one's work as 'postmodern' is indeed associated with this work as being 'non-scientific':

> I must dissent with Gary Fine's (2004b: 505) proclamation of *Body and Soul* as 'the first sociological classic of reflexive autoethnography'. My book is reflexive in that it consciously features the ethnographer in the picture and ongoingly turns the sociological theory it develops back onto his field experiences, but it is decidedly not autoethnographic by any current acception of that ill-defined genre. [...] *Body and Soul* is moreover written against the grain of postmodernism and at crosscurrent with the narcissistic irrationalism that has informed autoethnographic efforts in the past decade. (Wacquant, 2005: 469-70)

A vast majority of ethnographers reject the postmodern path because it makes doing scientific research impossible. Since postmodern studies favour the restitution of actors' voices and points of view as unique and idiosyncratic views, they do reject the possibility of the production of systematic, rigorous and empirically founded analyses of observed social phenomena. Most academic ethnographers prefer another path – the reflexive approach presented here. So ethnographic sociologists like Whyte (1955 [1943]), Glaser and Strauss (1967), Hammersley (1999), Hertz (1997), Taylor (2002) or Burawoy (2003) all developed and formulated similar kinds of reflexive practice. Reflexive ethnography, 'that is, an approach to participant observation that recognizes that we are part of the world we study'

(Burawoy, 2003: 655), is understood to be the foundation of sociological practice, at least for advocates and practitioners of qualitative methods and sources such as observation, interviewing and archives.

A balance between involvement and detachment

How, then, can we guarantee that researchers do not become travellers, journalists or autobiographical novelists while at the same time ensuring that they are not constrained to practise ill-adapted procedures and investigation methods following an inept positive method? What is required above all is reconciling the opposites of involvement and detachment (Elias, 1956; Hughes, 1971). Constant and rigorous adherence to this principle will provide a solid basis for research without eroding its primary quality: the researcher's ability to adapt to the experience and realities of the people he or she is observing. Though involvement does imply constant flexibility and adaptability on the part of ethnographic researchers, they must still be vigilant about maintaining distance, remaining detached. Involvement is in fact one more construction that the researcher needs to analyse and negotiate with the actors in connection with the rules structuring the social system in which they operate.

In an ideal world, detachment is a continuous activity, as Glaser and Strauss recommend for the practice of the 'grounded theory'. It guides the researcher's choices in all phases of their involvement: determining how to behave, what strategies to implement, the limits to impose on their action and analysing collected observations in relation to the roles played. But in their involvement the researcher may go through phases of intense identification, as happened when Becker and Faulkner (2008) were studying the jazz world (see below). The processes underlying that kind of identification then have to be analysed, deciphered and contextualized so as to apprehend, if only after the fact, the workings of the action structuring the negotiated relationship between the researcher and the observed actors and to assess their implications for the study. These last activities are what is meant by detachment.

THREE PRINCIPLES OF DETACHMENT

Detachment thus requires the researcher to describe and critically question or probe their way of viewing the world and the social conditions in which 'data' are produced in the research act. But what exactly does that mean? There is no single set of formulas or practical guidelines that will suffice to attain the desired scientific quality or goal. While finely detailed techniques may be developed to help researchers achieve rigorous, controlled practice, in the reflexive approach those techniques cannot be seen as mere procedures to be followed, standards to evaluate or rules to follow and check off: 'A cookbook approach towards collecting data and writing up one's results is rejected here' (Rosen, 1991: 11).

Within the abundant literature on the subject, it is possible to distinguish at least three principles common to reflexive approaches to scientific activity:

1.   An assumption that truth is 'more or less true'.
2.   An attempt to analyse the social conditions under which a research study is produced.
3.   A reflection on the use of particular techniques for particular studies.

Those principles should guide not only the researcher's daily activity in the field but also how they account for and present findings. The scientific debate that is implied in the very act of doing research bears not only on evidence production and demonstration but also on the validity of the researcher's conceptualization. They are used by the researcher throughout all the stages of their study.

1. Truth that is 'more or less true'
Research that is contradictory and necessarily incomplete

Truth in the reflexive approach is not considered an attainable goal *per se*, at least not the absolute goal it represents in the positivist ideal. Once again, the facts described are never complete, massive or strictly objective:

> Like Harding, we argue that truth claims are organized along a gradient of 'better' and 'worse'. In locating ourselves as agents of knowledge and scrutinizing the influence of our positionality on the practice of ethnography, we have sought to achieve a stronger form of objectivity - an 'objectivity' that generates a 'better', more realistic claim than those offered by positivism or earlier versions of standpoint methodology. (McCorkell and Myers, 2003: 229)

All research involves dealing with contradictions, missing or forgotten material, the limitations of the particular field. Actors contradict themselves and each other; information gets lost; places change; new observation posts appear. There are necessarily several possible interpretations of what one has observed. Researchers therefore have to be careful and disciplined, like impassioned puzzle solvers working ceaselessly to reconstitute an image that is not readily accessible – but with additional difficulties in their case: several pieces are missing; there is more than one possible image, and the 'field' represents a constant source of distraction. The metaphor of the detective or puzzle solver is often used to illustrate this careful, constant vigilance and the cross-checking between theory and empirical data that the researcher must practise – the only means of ensuring research quality.

This principle is perfectly represented in the 'grounded theory' developed by Barney Glaser and Anselm Strauss as early as the 1960s (see Bryant and Charmaz in this volume). In direct opposition to the positivist principle of checking whether empirical material validates a 'pre-existing' – i.e. already constructed – theory, Glaser and Strauss explained that the researcher should be concerned first and foremost with constructing a theory 'grounded' in the 'data' they collect in the field. But this inductive proceeding was still suffused with the ideal of scientific rigour, and to formulate it in terms that would be acceptable at the time the authors used words very similar to those of the positivist scientific model. Theory construction was to be rigorous and carefully monitored; theories to be constructed on the basis of systematic, continuous data collection, coding and analysis. 'To further this view, we seek in this book to further the systematization of the collection, coding and analysis of qualitative data for the generation of theory' (Glaser and Strauss, 1967: 18). The rigorous, disciplined character of ethnographic analysis clearly follows on from this understanding that analysis of empirical research findings should be a continuous, cumulative process (Prus, 1987).

Varied techniques with many uses

There are already many articles and guidebooks like this one that describe specific techniques for ensuring rigorous ethnographic research and analysis (see Peräkylä in this volume). Those techniques include 'saturation', 'triangulation', counting and measuring, analysis of the social conditions in which 'data' are produced, collective research, combining comparable cases, note-taking technique, and sharing and 'discussing' research findings with observed actors. To convey how reflexive approaches are practised, I first briefly review a few ways in which researchers have used these techniques, then present a detailed example of the last one listed above: 'discussing' research findings with the observed.

In his study of the work of technicians in companies, Stephen R. Barley drew 'on a set of ethnographies to propose an empirically grounded model of technicians' work' (Barley, 1996: 404). Eight researchers studied the question over a five-year period. Barley's interpretation of what technicians' work had become in contemporary North America is therefore founded on systematic comparative analysis of those constructed cases. Following the same path, Randy Hodson based his empirical conclusions on workers' participation in organization on a comparison of 122 ethnographies led in North American organizations (Hodson, 2002).

Some researchers use the technique of quantification, not to ensure that observed practices are statistically representative, but rather to check observations and interpretations of them as rigorously as possible. Jean Peneff (1995) recommended that researchers measure and count different features of the work activity being studied so as to describe in the finest possible detail how labour is divided in a given organization: task timing, interaction frequency and duration, types of activities, guidelines used in action and customer relations. Jean-Pierre Hassoun (2000) collected, counted and compared all the nicknames of observed actors in the French financial world to obtain reliable findings on their social and symbolic meanings in this specific social context. And in my study of female jazz singers in France (Buscatto, 2003), I counted, measured and categorized the observed jazz musicians by certain social and musical characteristics – sex and age; musical style and reputation level – in order to better determine the social processes that account for the marginal position of women jazz singers in France. Counting and measuring musicians according to these criteria led me to the finding that musical style has little impact on female jazz singer marginalization and, conversely, that male musicians' reputation level was inversely proportional to the amount of time spent playing with female jazz singers: the more well-known an instrumentalist is, the less he plays with women singers, while little-known musicians often find themselves constrained to do so.

Sharing findings with observed actors: an ethnographic example

My last, more detailed example will illustrate how a specific technique can be used in the framework of reflexive practice either to ensure the relevance of post-observation analyses or to enhance them. Sharing constructed sociological findings with the people one has observed can produce, consolidate or qualitatively change findings and conclusions. What exactly does this mean?

The ethnographer's task is to identify what makes the people they are observing act the way they do by explicitly stating what, for the actors, is usually implicit; i.e. the different points of view, ways of proceeding and action choices that operate and interact within the field. By sharing their sociological findings with the actors and defending their analyses with arguments, the ethnographer can discover how many and which of those findings resonate with them, to what degree their arguments are receivable in light of scientific criteria, how fully they have grasped the complexity of a given situation. Through the researcher's exchanges with the actors, through their questions, points of resistance and even what they reject in their analysis, they can enrich it, refine it or even discard it altogether. They can renew and improve their analysis of how action works in the observed field. Sharing ethnographic findings with observed actors may of course constitute a component of action research, in which case the aim is to help the observed improve their practices by raising their awareness of their real effects. But it is also useful for the ethnographer as it enables them to ensure analysis quality through the detachment implied in the act of confronting the observed actors, regardless of whether or not they agree with the findings. By attaining an understanding of the actors' reactions to their analysis, ethnographers will be able to further fuel, refine, transform, enhance and indeed solidify that analysis.

Consider the example of a conflict that developed in June 1998 around what I shared at the end of a study conducted at the Hermès insurance company (Buscatto, 2008a). The encounter was particularly problematic since one of the written reports I had submitted to Hermès operations managers provoked their hostility and led to the radical demand that the report be either discarded or fundamentally altered. The first telephone exchanges were bitterly hostile; one director accused me of being irresponsible and writing analyses with no foundation. At the end of the exchange I received a telephone call from my key informant at Hermès, the head of the training department, who already knew what was happening. I explained how upset I was, and that I found such accusations incomprehensible. She reassured me and later contacted the operations managers, assuring them that the report was confidential but also requesting that they meet with me to discuss it. At this point the operations managers organized a meeting, at which it became apparent that they had rejected my report because of my analysis of the role of supervisors in the organization, which I had found to be virtually non-existent. In the course of our discussion I observed that the directors did not reject my conclusion about the supervisors' role ('Your observation is true', they repeatedly acknowl-edged), but they wanted to include historical and psychological explanations that would legitimate their managerial choices. Whereas for the operations managers the supervisors' career advancement had been slowed and in essence blocked due to their own psychological and cognitive difficulties – the managers saw the supervisors as old-fashioned, ill-adapted – my explanation concerned the complex collective action logic operative in this particular organization, which had reduced the supervisors' activity to a matter of purely formal execu-tion. Agreement between myself-as-observer and the managers-as-observed was impossible, but the latter did acknowledge a relative agreement between my report and the reality of the situation. Moreover, the arguments we exchanged further fuelled my analysis, namely regarding the phenomenon of 'social psychologization' at Hermès. The operations manage-ment office perceived the report as a radical critique of managerial qualities that were valued by the company's head office.

The operations managers 'won' on the points they were most concerned about: the report never circulated in the organization and I never discussed my findings at the com-pany. But the conflict, which contributed further material to the analyses I had already written up for my research report, became the matter of a scientific article, published in 2002 in the *Revue Française de Sociologie*, on the social phenomenon of 'social psychologi-zation' practised by various actors at Hermès and how it produced and legitimated stigma-tization of the company's mid-level employees (Buscatto, 2002).

However, as discussed by Emerson and Pollner (1988), based on their experience of such an exchange after their research in a psychiatric organization, the technique may not always be as efficient as stated in this example, when observed people's reactions are ambiguous and do not lead to clear interpretations by researchers. As always when adopt-ing a reflexive technique, the researcher should use multiple ways to elicit results and to confirm them over time, rather than relying on just one technique to ensure the quality of their final results.

2. Analysing the social conditions under which a research study is produced

The second principle that looms large in reflexive scientific approaches is taking into account the social conditions under which 'data' and data analysis are produced. Whereas historians situate archives in the social context that produced them at the time and in their own time, for reflexive sociologists the ethnographic study and interpretation of it are founded on the relation between the researcher(s) and the observed actors.

Observing the actors' relationships is the basis and bedrock of scientific interpretation

In reflexive sociological practice, the social conditions for producing empirical material are a fundamental component of the analysis when it comes to checking how you produce your 'data' and constructing a finding-based analysis. Anthropologists and ethnographic sociologists have identified several points in the process where it is helpful to practise detachment: formulating the research aim and constructing the observed population, determining how the researcher–observed actors relationship is produced and choosing tools to analyse the data collected. The process unfolds over time and, as explained, it cannot follow predefined rules.

The observers, therefore, detach themselves from the field in order to better control their entry into and action within it and to ensure that the meaning they attribute to the observations and discourses they collect in their analyses cleaves as closely as possible to the empirical material:

> It is ultimately by analyzing all the places that respondents assign her, either in parallel or consecutively, that the anthropologist will be able to understand both what they say to her and what she observes, because that way she will know who it is said to, who it is shown to. (Weber, 1989: 24)

The researcher tries out social positions in the field in order to open closed doors, elicit invitations, circumvent prefabricated discourse, gain access to the unsaid or taboo – and interpret rationally what they have observed. Those social positions are both defined by the field's possibilities and by the researcher's specific characteristics. For instance, if the researcher is to observe an organization, they may try to develop different social positions in the field – as an expert, as an academic, as a friend, as a worker – depending on who they are observing, when and how. But social positions are also defined by their social characteristics as perceived by the observed actors – age, professional status, physical appearance, sex or prior relationships with observed actors.

While the social relationship that develops with the actors is constantly being constructed and reconstructed in a chaotic, experimental way, the researcher is also analysing it in depth so as to discover the best way to interpret the experienced situations. Conducting a field study in a working-class milieu is not the same as doing a study with aristocrats or members of the *grande bourgeoisie* – or studying the jazz world discussed in the next section:

> These dimensions (age, class, gender) are thus of critical importance in establishing research relationships, rapport, and trust, and in evaluating both the information obtained and the interaction that occurs within in-depth interviews. (Miller and Glassner, 2004 [1997]: 128)

A field study of women jazz singers

During my study of women jazz singers in France (Buscatto, 2003, 2007), one of the observing positions I assumed was that of amateur jazz singer. The position of being a woman in a predominantly male world and a singer personally involved in the jazz world may at first sight appear to introduce strong and indeed insurmountable bias – and according to positive scientific logic, it does. In fact that position proved to be of great epistemological value, though it did require in-depth reflexive analysis. My position offered a range of different observation opportunities that then fuelled my analysis of the marginal situation of female singers in the French jazz world. Here I shall discuss two pre-cise examples of what reflexive practice contributed to my gender-specific analysis of the researcher–observed actors relationship: enhanced observation opportunities, and direct access to a 'sexual' imaginary.

My position as an amateur jazz singer often elicited a desire in male jazz musicians to invite me to meet and play with them – on a friendly basis and even in some cases in hopes of a love relationship. The paucity of women in this man's world makes their presence 'pleasant', say the musicians, and changes the 'nature' of the musical evenings, the subjects and tone of conversation, the 'jokes'. It also seems that the seductive power of women jazz singers plays an important role in their being invited by male jazz instru-mentalists. I had already had an opportunity to observe male musicians' attraction to my singer girlfriends, some of who invited me to join them in the encounters they had access to through training sessions, evenings with friends and vocal jam sessions, and I had of course noticed that several musicians openly flirted with me. My position as a woman in this world thus greatly increased my observation opportunities and enriched the study.

In parallel, I gradually became aware that due to the way I behaved on stage, my seductive power greatly increased with unknown spectators, who sometimes 'tried their luck' with me after a jam session or a concert, and with my male instrumentalist colleagues, often strongly attracted to 'the' singer. During the jams, musical evenings or classes, the way these men treated me varied radically depending on whether or not I had sung on stage. Several times it happened that an instrumentalist who had virtually ignored me before I went on stage came to talk to me, even flirt with me, afterwards. Clearly there was a prevailing myth in which the female singer is associated with considerable seductive powers.

This experience not only opened doors for me in the field I was observing, facilitating access to male jazz musicians, but more importantly, once I had analysed it and seen it reproduced in different musical contexts it also enabled me to grasp the negative effect of that experience on professional recognition of women singers. The remarkable seduc-tive power associated with female singers turns out to be correlated with deprecation of their professional abilities. Being perceived as 'desirable' works to inhibit the develop-ment of straightforward professional relations and to prevent women singers from being listened to 'neutrally' by their male musician colleagues. Women jazz singers have diffi-culty gaining recognition for their professional abilities, and it is their strong power of seduction that accounts to a considerable degree, though not entirely, for this situation (see Buscatto, 2003, 2007). While that seductive power could of course have been dis-covered by reading jazz magazines and analysing the photographs of 'seductive' women singers used in them, the impact it has – i.e. that it goes together with dismissal by male jazz professionals of women jazz singers' professional qualities – could only be grasped through my own experience and reiterated observation of that correlation in musical situations – that is, once I had analysed my experience and observations systematically, rigorously and with detachment.

3. Reflecting on the use of particular techniques for particular studies

The third principle of reflexive practice pertains directly to the research activity. It is important that the researcher not claim superiority for one or another technique 'in itself' but rather consider how effectively a given technique has been used and whether it is relevant for studying the given subject and developing an innovative, original set of research questions.

So, though some reflexive ethnographers here and there do claim absolute superiority for their method – observation – or their technique – participant observation as opposed to external observation for instance – over another, most researchers work instead to determine the heuristic advantages of a given method over another in studying a particular subject or identifying relevant research questions. This debate has even come up in discussion of different uses of the same method, as in the exchange between ethnographic sociologists Howard Becker and Robert Faulkner (2008) on their position as participant observers as opposed to external observers.

In a study of American jazz musicians' repertoires, Becker and Faulkner have elegantly deconstructed the debate on the possible superiority of participant observation – one is acting as a member of the observed group – over external or non-participant observation – one is observing the group without participating in its main activities. The *insider* position that these jazz musician sociologists were able to assume simply because they practise jazz (Faulkner plays trumpet, Becker piano) and their familiarity with the North American jazz world 'field' proved extremely helpful in identifying new knowledge, issues and questions. Their intimate familiarity with the musical language, existing styles and collective conventions specific to jazz helped them see what mattered during observations and interviews and to speak easily with musicians about immediate examples. But the insider participant observer position did limit the study strictly speaking and/or the analysis at times because it generated prejudices, convictions, preconceived notions. Faulkner and Becker have fixed ideas about the jazz repertoire, ideas that stem from their own musical tastes and habits, and this means they may not have seen what did not resonate with those habits. The question was not so much whether one is an insider or not or whether one is a *participant* observer or not. Rather it was knowing how to choose the right position for the field one intends to study, the position best adapted to the questions being raised, and to achieve the right balance between involvement and detachment during research. In their case, the subject under study – jazz repertoires – and the detachment practices they engaged in through exchange and comparison made for particularly effective participant observation.

Debates aimed at proving that one or another method is 'better' in absolute terms, without regard for the research topics chosen or the questions raised, therefore appear sterile and uselessly polemical. Along the same lines, the special issue of the journal *Ethnologie française* that I edited, 'L'art du travail' [Art at work] (Buscatto, 2008b), was pleased to accept an entire range of positions, strategies and researcher–observed actors relations in art worlds. The only selective criteria were that researchers examine varied empirical objects from different theoretical perspectives in accordance with their positions in the field and available observation opportunities. So while certain researchers took up the artistic practices they were studying in order to gain an insider's feeling for them, others adopted visual recording techniques – photography, video – to analyse art objects produced over time or to better grasp negotiations between actors. Whereas some used their external status to identify conflicting or 'excessively' natural social relations, others got themselves hired for several years in the field workplace to have direct access to complex social relations. These different examples illustrate the variety of uses that may be made of the ethnographic method and their respective value in connection with the particular sets of questions researchers develop (for complementary and useful examples in organizational ethnographies, see Eberle and Maeder in this volume).

CHAPTER SUMMARY AND FUTURE PROSPECTS

Ethnography requires reflexivity, but reflexivity is not exclusive to qualitative social sciences such as history and anthropology or use of the ethnographic method in sociology. It is also found in some so-called exact sciences – for example, particle physics (Knorr-Cetina, 1996).

If we look at the question more closely, we see that the hypothetico-deductive methods of the positivist model – modelling, laboratory experiments, written questionnaires – also run into social biases that disrupt the positivist ideal. Subjectivity as part of the researcher's experience is not specific to the ethnographic method (for further arguments, see Gobo and Marciniak in this volume). A number of different methodological studies have brought to light the social 'bias' that continuously mars the use of questionnaires, laboratory experiments, modelling and interviewing (see Peneff, 1988). 'Artefacts' (Silverman, 2007) are produced at different stages of both quantitative and qualitative research alike. Given that such biases undermine the supposed objectivity of the research, these studies might be improved if all researchers engaged in reflexive practice as defined in this chapter.

While up until now the sociologists in question, conscious of the difficulties, have explained how they control for or limit bias, or even 'put up with it' and render it scientifically relevant, reflexive practice could, to even better effect, pave the way for a rational encounter between quantitative and qualitative methods in sociology, as has happened in the related disciplines of history and anthropology. This would surely not impact much on rigorous quantitative researchers, as their practice is already highly reflexive, but it might open up fruitful, straightforward, intelligent debate between researchers whose scientific practices differ.

Study questions

1. What does the term 'reflexivity' convey?
2. Why is the 'postmodern path' rejected?
3. What are the three main principles underlying reflexivity?
4. Why might reflexivity also be used to do research with quantitative methods?

Recommended reading

Atkinson, P., Coffey, A., Delamont, S., Lofland, J. and Lofland, L. (eds) (2007) *Handbook of Ethnography*. London: Sage.
This book is both a thematic and an encyclopedic collection of state-of-the-art descriptions of theoretical traditions in ethnography and of relevant contemporary approaches to ethnography.

Burawoy, M. B. (2003) 'Revisits: an outline of a theory of reflexive ethnography', *American Sociological Review*, 68 (5): 645–78.
This article explores the ethnographic technique of the focused revisit when an ethnographer returns to the site of a previous study. In centring attention on ethnography-as-revisit, sociologists directly confront the dilemmas of participation in the world they study.

Glaser, B. G. and Strauss, A. L. (1968) *The Discovery of Grounded Theory: Strategies for Qualitative Research*. Chicago, IL: Aldine.
Most writing on sociological method has been concerned with how accurate facts can be obtained and how theory can thereby be more rigorously tested. In this historical book, the authors discuss how the discovery of theory from data – systematically obtained and analysed in social research – can be furthered.

Gobo, G. (2008) *Doing Ethnography*. London: Sage.
This book systematically describes the various phases of an ethnographic inquiry, provides numerous examples, and offers suggestions and advice for the novice ethnographer.

Hertz, R. (ed.) (1997) *Reflexivity and Voice*. Thousand Oaks, CA: Sage.
This volume presents an array of contemporary ethnographers grappling with the questions and new conventions of ethnographic writing. Authors deal with issues related to writing up their

studies and creating a new ethnography where the author's voice, as well as those of their participants, are fully realized for the reader.

Taylor, S. (ed.) (2002) *Ethnographic Research: A Reader*. London: Sage.
This book presents, in a single volume, a selection of ten recently published studies intended to
illustrate the variety of social research which is currently being conducted within the ethnographic
tradition.

Recommended online resources

Ethnography Journal:

www.uk.sagepub.com/journalsProdDesc.nav?prodId=Journal200906
Qualitative Sociology Review, special issue *Ethnographies of Artistic Work*:

www.qualitativesociologyreview.org/ENG/volume8.php
Journal of Contemporary Ethnography:

http://jce.sagepub.com

References

Barley, S. R. (1996) 'Technicians in the workplace: ethnographic evidence for bringing
    work into organization studies', *Administrative Science Quarterly*, 41: 404–41.
Becker, H. S. and Faulkner, R. R. (2008) 'Studying something you are part of: the view from
    the bandstand', *Ethnologie française*, 38 (1): 15–21.
Burawoy, M. B. (2003) 'Revisits: an outline of a theory of reflexive ethnography', *American
    Sociological Review*, 68 (5): 645–78.
Buscatto, M. (2002) 'Des managers à la marge: la stigmatisation d'une hiérarchie inter-
    médiaire', *Revue française de sociologie*, 43 (1): 73–98.
Buscatto, M. (2003) 'Chanteuse de jazz n'est point métier d'homme: l'accord imparfait
    entre voix et instrument en France', *Revue française de sociologie*, 44 (1): 33–60.
Buscatto, M. (2007) 'Women in artistic professions: an emblematic paradigm for gender
    studies', *Social Cohesion and Development Journal*, 2 (1): 69–77.
Buscatto, M. (2008a) 'Who allowed you to observe? A reflexive overt organizational eth-
    nography', *Qualitative Sociology Review*, 4 (3): 29–48.
Buscatto, M. (ed.) (2008b) *L'art au travail* [Art as Work], special issue of *Ethnologie française*,
    38 (1).
Clifford, J. and Marcus, G. E. (eds) (1986) *Writing Culture: The Poetics and Politics of
    Ethnography*. Berkeley: University of California Press.
Clough, P. T. (1992) *The End(s) of Ethnography: From Realism to Social Criticism*. New York: Sage.

Denzin, N. K. (1999) 'Interpretive ethnography for the next century', *Journal of Contemporary Ethnography*, 28 (5): 510–19.

Elias, N. (1956) 'Problems of involvement and detachment', *The British Journal of Sociology*, 7 (3): 226–52.

Emerson, R. M. and Pollner, M. (1988) 'On the use of members' responses to researchers' accounts', *Human Organization*, 47 (3) : 189–98.

Geertz, C. (1973) *The Interpretation of Cultures*. New York: Basic Books.

Glaser B. G. and Strauss A. L. (1967) *The Discovery of Grounded Theory: Strategies for Qualitative Research*. Chicago, IL: Aldine.

Grindstaff, L. (2002) *The Money Shot: Trash, Class, and the Making of TV Talk Shows*. Chicago: University of Chicago Press.

Hammersley, M. (1999) 'Not bricolage but boatbuilding: exploring two metaphors for thinking about ethnography', *Journal of Contemporary Ethnography*, 28 (5): 574–85.

Hassoun, J.-P. (2000) 'Le Surnom et ses usages sur les marchés à la criée du Matif: contrôle social, fluidité relationnelle et représentations collectives', *Genèses*, 41: 5–40.

Hertz, R. (ed.) (1997) *Reflexivity and Voice*. Thousand Oaks, CA: Sage.

Hodson, R. (2002) 'Worker participation and teams: new evidence from analysing organizational ethnographies', *Economic and Industrial Democracy*, 23 (4): 491–528.

Honer, A. (2004) 'Life-world analysis in ethnography', in U. Flick, E. Von Kardoff and I. Steinke (eds), *A Companion to Qualitative Research*. London: Sage: pp. 113–17.

Hughes, E. C. (1971) *The Sociological Eye: Selected Papers on Work, Self and the Study of Society*, Vol. 2. Chicago, IL: Aldine.

Knorr-Cetina, K. (1996) 'Le "Souci de soi" ou les "tâtonnements": ethnographie de l'empirie dans deux disciplines scientifiques', *Sociologie du travail*, 38 (3): 311–30.

McCorkell, J. A. and Myers, K. (2003) 'What difference does difference make? Position and privilege in the field', *Qualitative Sociology*, 26 (2): 199–231.

Miller, J. and Glassner, B. (2004 [1997]) 'The 'inside' and the 'outside': finding realities in interviews', in D. Silverman (ed.), *Qualitative Research: Theory, Method and Practice*. London: Sage, pp. 125–39.

Peneff, J. (1988) 'The observers observed: French survey researchers at work', *Social Problems*, 35: 520–35.

Peneff, J. (1995) 'Mesure et contrôle des observations dans le travail de terrain: l'exemple des professions de service', *Sociétés contemporaines*, 21: 119–38.

Prus, R. (1987) 'Generic social processes: maximizing conceptual development in ethnographic research', *Journal of Contemporary Ethnography*, 16 (3): 250–93.

Rosen, M. (1991) 'Coming to terms with the field: understanding and doing organizational ethnography', *Journal of Management Studies*, 28 (1): 1–24.

Silverman, D. (2007) 'Art and artefact in qualitative research' (unpublished paper), Improving the Quality of Qualitative Research Conference, The European Science Foundation, Kristiansand, Norway, June 25–27.

Taylor, S. (ed.) (2002) *Ethnographic Research: A Reader*. London: Sage.

Wacquant, L. (2005) 'Carnal connections: on embodiment, apprenticeship, and membership', *Qualitative Sociology*, 28 (4): 445–74.

Weber, F. (1989) *Le Travail à-côté: étude d'ethnographie ouvrière*. Paris: INRA, EHESS.

Whyte, W. F. (1955 [1943]) *Street Corner Society*. Chicago: Chicago University Press.

PART IV
TEXTS

Documents and texts have been a strangely neglected area for many social researchers. Even when they look at documents, researchers often prefer to treat them as a resource in their analysis of other data rather than as a topic in themselves. Both chapters in Part IV contest the majority view of documentary data in sociology and qualitative research that documents are detached from social action and are just 'background' material. Katarina Jacobsson shows how observing what people do with documents is just as important as analysing document content. She uses several fascinating case studies to demonstrate how we can study the ways in which documents are produced and used in particular social and economic contexts. Lindsay Prior develops Jacobsson's arguments about what happens when people 'do things with documents'. Prior shows us how we can instead focus on the ways in which a text instructs us to see the world. Using examples as diverse as a statistical summary of prevalence rates of mental illness and airline pilots' pre-take-off check lists, he reveals a thought-provoking toolbox that we can use when working with textual material.

TEN
Analysing Documents through Fieldwork

Katarina Jacobsson

About this chapter

Ethnographic methods can advance our knowledge of a setting through its documents as well as help the researcher to grasp a document in its setting. This chapter contests the idea that the study of documents only refers to close analyses of text. Taking pictures of documents, asking about documents and observing what people do with documents are approaches that can answer sociologically significant questions that cannot be addressed by merely analysing the content of a text. Moreover, audio and video recordings of interactions over documents enable analyses of how documents are produced *in situ* as well as how documents shape and pattern interaction. The recognition of such aspects of documentary data requires fieldwork rather than deskwork.

Keywords

fieldwork, documents-in-use, records, files, document practices, ethnography, constructionism

'I don't know how to do discourse analysis', says a student when we discuss the possibility of including documentary data in his Master's thesis. Another student turns down the same prospect because she thinks document analysis is boring compared to talking with people. They both imagine very narrow approaches to the study of documents. This chapter seeks to widen the scope of how we analyse documents.

The idea that analysing documentary data exclusively corresponds to close text analyses may give the impression that the researcher is primarily engaged in deskwork or in arm-chair research. Ample ethnographic research has demonstrated the contrary, and prominent scholars continually remind us of the research potential that documentary data hold (e.g. Prior, 2003; Hammersley and Atkinson, 2007; Silverman, 2011). Still, many contemporary ethnographers prefer to rely on observations and interviews, probably convinced that these methods offer more direct entry to the social realities that they study (Drew, 2006). When documents are included in the dataset, they tend to serve as 'background material', often for crosschecking oral accounts (Silverman, 2011).

Atkinson and Coffey (2011) traced the weak interest in documents to the history of ethnographic fieldwork originally carried out in fundamentally oral communities: 'Many qualitative researchers continue to produce ethnographic accounts of complex, literate social worlds as if they were entirely without documents or texts' (Atkinson and Coffey, 2011: 78). However, the empirical opportunities to analyse documents appear to be endless: newspaper articles, advertisements, policy documents, government reports, blogs, schedules, letters, posters, pamphlets, brochures, campaign materials, etc.

Everyday life offers a range of situations that involve forms and documents, particularly with regard to interpersonal encounters within various institutions. It takes paperwork to start school, get a job, declare one's income, get married, start up a bank account, have children, take out insurance, join a club and get divorced, not to mention the form-filling procedures that are set in motion when someone dies. When people seek medical help or judicial advice, register at the unemployment office or cross international borders, they are often asked to complete various forms. Everyday life is routinely categorized in and through pre-fabricated and culturally embedded stories and reports, boxes and forms, numbers and rules.

Despite numerous empirical opportunities, researchers interested in identifying situations 'where the action is' (Goffman, 1967: 149ff) may find it hard to recognize action in a pile of paper. The majority view of documentary data in sociology and qualitative research is that documents are detached from social action (Prior, 2003) – an approach that often stresses the unobtrusiveness of documents as a methodological asset (Webb et al., 2000). In contrast to an interview, the document appears more stable and fixed, whereas the content of an interview in general seems more fuzzy, dynamic and alive. The image of documents as cold, passive and disconnected from social action is contested by Lindsay Prior in *Using Documents in Social Research* (2003; see also his chapter in this volume). Documents can be quite lively agents in their own right rather than merely containers of text; they can tell people what to do, they can stir up conflicts and they can evoke emotions such as anger, relief, envy, pride and fatigue. Documents often trigger chains of interaction far beyond the original piece of paper. Additionally, people do things with documents: they use them for various purposes, both intended and unintended, they exchange documents, they hide documents and so forth. In order to recognize these aspects of documentary data, fieldwork rather than deskwork is required.

The study of documents is a growing field of inquiry pursued from various angles, but it is 'patchy' in character considering 'the sheer volume of "literate" record-keeping and documentation in contemporary society' (Hammersley and Atkinson, 2007: 129). This enormous ocean of documentary realities (Smith, 1974) – not only in organizations and social settings, but also linked to individuals, families and other social groups (Coffey, 2014: 369) – may explain the absence of coverage as well as a coherent notion of the study of documents. Prior identifies four distinct routes into the analysis of texts and records:

1.   the study of content
2.   the social construction of documents and records
3.   documents in 'the field'
4.   documents in action and documents in networks (Prior 2011; see also his chapter in this book).

This chapter focuses on research in the third and fourth routes of analyses, in which the use and function of documents are emphasized. Furthermore, this chapter draws on Prior's (2003) and Atkinson's and Coffey's (2011; Coffey, 2014) methodological contributions to the ethnographic analysis of documents, though my focus is more practical and more specific; practical in the sense that I emphasize the ethnographic methods through which researchers approach documents, as well as what kind of knowledge these methods capture or generate. My focus is specific in the sense that I have particular kinds of documents in mind. In general, I refer to *organizationally embedded* documents, specifically those found in human service organizations, with examples from my own fieldwork and the fieldwork of others. Nonetheless, I imagine that the reasoning described here is applicable to other empirical fields and may elicit additional ideas for how to do research on documentary data.

THE SITUATED STUDY OF DOCUMENTS

From a positivist or objectivist tradition, the vital methodological question is whether the data can be trusted. Are the documents authentic and credible? Do they represent reality 'as it really is'? A constructionist perspective on documents renders these questions superfluous simply because they are beside the point: 'Rather than ask whether a document offers a "true" account, or whether it can be used as "valid" evidence about a research setting, it is more fruitful to ask questions about the form and function of documents themselves' (Coffey, 2014: 377). According to this view, documents are not substitutes for other types of data, and should not be taken as factual evidence of what they represent. As people never engage with documents in a neutral way, stripped from context, documents need to be studied *in situ* while acknowledging the local context that shapes how people write and read documents.

The phrase 'documents-in-use' captures an approach in which the immediate setting, its people and the evolving situation are of interest (Rapley, 2007). 'Document practices' is another phrase that underlines interest in what people do with documents and what documents do with people. Rather than being part of a separate textual order, documents are viewed as an integral part of the social order. In the words of Berg (2004: 26), '"[t]he social", as a pure category, is a chimera: practices always also include artifacts, architectures, paper, machines'. In line with Prior, I prefer to think of this approach as an ethnography of documentation in which a document's use and function are as important as its content:

> Clearly, documents carry content - words, images, plans, ideas, patterns and so forth - but the manner in which such material is actually called upon and manipulated, and the way in which it functions, cannot be determined (though it may be constrained) by an analysis of content ... The text has meaning only in the context of its use and its nature is defined by its use. (Prior, 2011: 8)

Accordingly, ethnographers should not just be interested in a document's content, but also in how and why written accounts form an essential part of the social setting under study. Hammersley and Atkinson (2007: 132–3) suggested several ethnographic questions about texts. Here, I divide these questions into two categories depending on whether they are oriented towards the text *per se* or whether they are more oriented towards context:

Text	Context
What is recorded?	How are texts written?
What is omitted?	How are they read?
What is taken for granted?	Who writes them?
What does the writer seem to take for granted about the reader(s)?	Who reads them? For what purposes?
What do readers need to know in order to make sense of the text?	On what occasions? With what outcome?

Although answers to all of the above questions benefit from ethnographic knowledge of the setting in which the documentary data are gathered, the right-hand column in particular contains questions that call for complementary data beyond the text. How such data may be generated is the topic of this chapter, which is structured around five conceivable methods for the study of documents-in-use:

- capturing documents as objects
  - asking about documents
    - observing the production of documents
      - observing interaction over documents
        - shadowing the document

I picture these methods or techniques placed (from left to right) along a continuum with different analytical claims at its ends. At the left end, documents serve as clues that enable researchers to shed light over a setting (Coffey, 2014); at the right end, documents are studied for their constituent potency (Prior, 2011). To put it simply, it is a matter of studying settings through documents or documents through settings. This shift of emphasis is not always obvious and clear cut; rather, these approaches overlap and inform one another.

Capturing documents as objects

The importance of the physical document has become increasingly obvious as computerized routines are developed. Efforts to render paper redundant have not always had the desired effect. For example, Sellen and Harper (2003) noted that paper consumption in office environments has increased rather than decreased alongside computerized technology. This observation is consistent with a Swedish study of document practices in primary care centres (Thelander and Jacobsson, 2016). Despite the digitalization of medical records and the fact that nearly all rooms in these centres were equipped with a computer, papers were conspicuously present in everyday work, ranging from referrals and print-outs of (electronic) medical records to Post-it notes and lists of all kinds. One informant used hard copies to create 'a general overview'; she placed sheets of paper all over her desk, explaining that this procedure allows her to survey her workload better than her computer does.

The presence of documents in human service organizations is striking yet self-evident, which is why they can be hard to notice. Taking pictures of documents is a way to make the obvious visible, not only for the sake of presenting evidence or illustrations to the

Figure 10.1 'Creating an overview': a doctor's desk at a Swedish primary care centre

reader, but also to trigger analytical imagination in the researcher. A picture explicitly turns the document into an object and evokes questions about its physical shape and its spatial position. A picture of documents *in situ* can capture how they are arranged and yield insight into how to analyse the setting in which they occur.

Paper documents seem to be attractive for their 'at-a-glance-visibility' and their 'at-handedness', as Hartswood et al. (2011) put it. At the same time, their mere physical presence can be demanding and stir up stressful emotions. At another site, a social service unit, I was present when social workers discussed their superior's habit of placing documents on their chairs or keyboards to communicate the unmistakable message 'Take care of this ASAP!' This tactic of placing documents at strategic spots, or hanging up notices, may signal more than just the content of the document: do this or don't do that! The document itself appears to insist on (non)performance of a certain action. Stapling a sheet of paper to a bulletin board conveys that this message is important to someone, and it encourages passers-by to participate in the instructions, news or messages.

In Sweden, as in other countries, health care is increasingly imbued with economic management that emphasizes cost-efficient treatment and care (e.g. Pollitt and Bouckaert, 2011). During our fieldwork at several primary care centres (Thelander and Jacobsson, 2016), all staff commented on this expanding economic rationality, although managers' comments were less negative than were doctors' and nurses'. At one centre, the management nailed monthly results in the form of plots and bar graphs to a bulletin board, visualizing 'how well we did' in comparison to previous months. The bulletin board was placed directly outside the staff dining room, urging everyone to bring themselves up to date on the unit's results during their daily visits there.

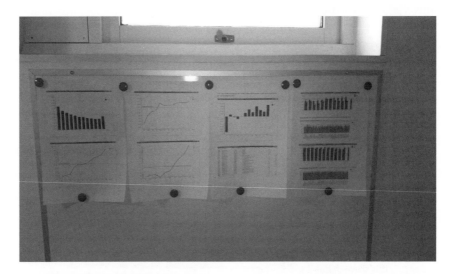

Figure 10.2 'How well we did': plots and bar graphs on a bulletin board outside the staff dining room at a Swedish primary care center

In sum, documents can be studied with regard to their visibility as physical objects in a particular setting. The placement of a document provides instructions on how we are supposed to read its content. Which documents are put on display or placed to signal importance in other ways, as well as how this notification is performed and received, can serve as clues to both the reading of the document and the interpretation of the setting in which the document occurs.

Asking about documents

Studying documents-in-use may be challenging due to the difficulties of being on site at the very moment that the documents are produced, read or used in other ways. Interviews are an option in these cases; questions about a particular document may generate talk about the practical reasoning that guides the respondent while using the document. In our Swedish study, we were interested in the growing emphasis on transparency within the social services (Carlstedt and Jacobsson, 2015), which for instance manifests annually in so-called 'open comparisons' among all municipalities in Sweden. Official authorities collect data for these comparisons via a survey that a manager or controller completes once per year; this survey is constructed for various social service areas such as child welfare, addiction treatment, homelessness and social security allowances. Examples of questions are whether the local district offers standardized assessment instruments, in what ways and when citizens can contact a social worker, and whether there is a career plan for employees. All of these questions aim to measure quality within the social services. The answers are mostly restricted to 'yes' and 'no', and the survey is constructed such that feedback is only solicited for plans, procedures and documentation systems that are required by the authorities. Accordingly, 'yes' means that the local district 'has' the requested item, which in turn is assumed to indicate quality.

For our interviews, we had the last year's questionnaire as a point of departure, and we asked the respondents to go through the document item by item. The respondents read aloud from the document, after which we discussed how they had answered (or would answer) each question. Most respondents provided elaborate accounts of their choices, yielding interesting material on their reasoning when ticking the 'yes' box as well as their doubts as to whether it was correct to do so in some cases. In the following extract, the respondent accounts for why she claimed that they had a career plan, although it was not yet in effect:

Respondent:	[reads the survey question aloud] 'On September 1, 2013, did you have a complete career plan for the employees' professional development?' Yes, we had, didn't we. But it wasn't running. /--/ [It was] very ambitious! It's still not put into practice, really. But it *is* there!
Interviewer:	It is there ... but it's not used?
Respondent:	Yes, it is there! Well, this is about, kind of, what would I respond? I would've said yes, you know. And my boss definitely would've said yes! So ... but ...

| **Interviewer**: | But what are they looking for in the questionnaire? Do they want to know that there is a plan, or do they want to know if it's used? |
| **Respondent**: | Exactly, and that's the question. I mean … /--/ We *have* a plan. And I mean, they [the authorities] must know this, of course, that I respond in a good way for *us*. |

The questionnaire was analysed for its content and used as a tool for generating talk about it – talk that was more specific than would have been elicited by questions of quality measurements in general (Carlstedt and Jacobsson, 2015). Is it ethical to claim that staff are skilled in method X when only 2 per cent have undergone training in it? Isn't it reasonable to assume that all districts likely sugarcoat their results a bit in order to perform well in comparison with other districts? The interviews laid bare various rationales for how the form-completer claimed to handle the survey questions.

Most texts are 'recipient-designed'; '[t]hey are produced with readers in mind and will therefore reflect implicit assumptions about who will be the reader' (Coffey, 2014: 375). Interviews can generate explicit assumptions; 'Who do you write for?' is a rewarding theme when interviewing professionals who keep files and records and who constantly are aware of the risk of having their actions assessed through records (Berg, 2004). The writer's ideas of who the reader is can bring energy to the analysis of texts. There are several potential readers, for example the patient/client/student, the auditing authorities, a colleague, a manager, other professionals or an investigative reporter. Social and cultural norms are conveyed in talk about one's motives for writing, as well as the motives of one's colleagues; these motives often appear to be linked to who the reader is. Furthermore, established norms are made visible in respondents' accounts for 'my way of writing' and in accounts for explicit rule violations (Scott and Lyman, 1968).

Observing the production of documents

Knowledge of the practices that precede the production of documents is instructive for how to interpret the content of the document, as well as the production *per se* (Garfinkel, 1967: 186ff). An example from the medical field demonstrates the misleading nature of the idea that doctors are sole authors of the medical record. Beck Nielsen's (2014) observations from staff meetings in geriatric wards show that records are authored through a process of co-production by staff members. Although the doctors dictate conclusions and treatment decisions for the record, they ensure the assistance of nurses and physiotherapists by encouraging them to share viewpoints and to answer questions. Nonetheless, this co-authorship is 'doctor-governed': the doctors' interactional and interpreting leadership is maintained and acknowledged by all participants (Beck Nielsen, 2014).

Observations in our ongoing Swedish study on how social workers produce text provide numerous examples of co-authorship in various forms. Text written by social workers was checked by the manager, who marked spelling and word choices on a paper copy and added or revised sentences for the social worker to revise in the electronic form of the document. Co-authorship was also evident in the habit of copying and pasting text between cases (or recycling text by the same author); a particularly well-formulated decision on temporary custody or a poignant description of a client's needs can be reused or borrowed by team members (see also Thomas and Holland, 2010). Some software programs used within human service organizations contribute suitable phrases and other ready-made comments, or a working team may cooperate on the task of constructing a 'phrase bank' that is tailored to organizationally relevant purposes.

Whereas analysis of client and patient records can elucidate person descriptions, decision rhetoric, constructions of social or medical problems and much more, the interactional accomplishments within an organization can only be captured via observation. How are decisions made? How and when are records written? How are people and problems written down *in situ*? Robert Emerson's (1994) analysis of constructions of violence, an instructive example, was based on audio-recorded legal interviews conducted by volunteers at a legal-aid office that helped women apply for restraining orders due to domestic violence. Emerson combined one recorded legal interview with all written material for one particular case to analyse how the interviewer moulded the applicant's story into a statement of serious violence with details relevant for the justice system. The materials allowed Emerson to show how the final version of the application, which was written in the first person, was the product of a struggle between the volunteer's efforts to make a strong case for a restraining order (stressing violence and victimhood) and the applicant's less clear-cut story in which she resisted picturing herself as a victim. This process would have escaped the analyst if only the final application were investigated.

It is also worth mentioning the possibility of comparing a written record with field notes, since these distinct data can inform one another. At a Swedish centre for juvenile delinquents, staff often discussed youngsters and incidents in ambivalent and hesitant terms; in contrast, the case records of the same youngsters or incidents were 'cleansed' of ambiguity, portraying the institution's remedies as faceless, uniform and collective (Wästerfors and Åkerström, 2015). This case history rhetoric identified by the authors stood out in strong relief against the field notes.

In any place where writing is a significant activity, more or less explicit rules and norms (official and local) about writing are developed. Examining how people honour such a writing culture, how they question, twist or confirm the rules while producing text, is one strategy for approaching document practices. During fieldwork at a cardiology clinic (Jacobsson, 2014), I noticed that the rounds served as an opportunity to teach younger doctors how to write a medical record as much as it was utilized to instruct them on medical conditions and treatment (c.f. Berg, 2004). Personal note-keeping by staff members also turned out to be bounded by subtle norms and implicit meanings. Note-taking practices varied depending on whether the note-taker was a doctor, nurse or assistant nurse. During the morning handover, nurses started a blank half sheet of paper for each new patient, putting the patient's name at the top left corner, the anamnesis on the right side of the paper and the current medical status on the left side. Although these notes were personal, they were all organized in this standardized way. Basically, the notes consisted of numerous abbreviations and medical terms for conditions and treatments; they did not contain orally reported issues about family ('his wife just died') or emotional state ('she was very upset the whole night'). Some nurses were more meticulous than others, using different ink colours or a highlighter to mark certain information. Throughout the day, the notes were kept in the nurse's uniform pocket and were actively used for remembering things about the patient or for adding new information.

From what I could tell, neither doctors nor assistant nurses kept personal notes, or perhaps were reluctant to do so while 'on the floor' around nurses and patients. A doctor that I followed excused himself for taking a look at his notes (which were hidden in his pocket) while we took the elevator; he called them a 'crib', as if he were cheating by looking at them. These observations suggest that the practice of writing and reading notes (or not) could be used by staff for matters beyond immediate practicalities, for example demonstrating one's position in the professional hierarchy, nurses by making quite a big thing of their notes (in contrast to assistant nurses), doctors by downplaying the need for notes (in contrast to nurses). Thus, observations of how, when, where and by whom documents are produced may indicate important things about a setting that cannot be captured by the document itself.

Observing interactions over documents

Audio and video recordings of interactions over documents have proven successful for establishing detailed interpretations of how documents are used. For instance, a written document can be used to sustain micro interactions, such as when professionals use the client record 'as a prop to deal with a sensitive issue' (Prior, 2003: 59). Likewise, Paul Drew (2006: 23) concluded that speakers often refer to documents when they are managing potentially problematic information (e.g. bad test scores, unwanted diagnoses), using the document as an objective record to stand proxy for the delivery of bad news.

Some documents demand full attention from the participants. A questionnaire is an example of a document that could be said to use its 'form-completer' rather than to be used *by* the respondent. A survey that is conducted by an interviewer and has fixed answers gives rise to 'text-governed' interaction; in a detailed and precise manner, the document directs or nearly dictates the conversation. Still, Maynard and Schaeffer (2006) showed that the interaction between interviewer and respondent affects the information that emerges from survey interviews. It goes without saying that the opposite is also true: the standardized survey interview affects how the interaction unfolds between interviewer and respondent. This side of the coin is particularly interesting in contexts other than those of research or polling, namely a professional context in which conversation-based 'meetings' or 'alliances' between clients and social workers traditionally have been highly valued by the professional ideology (e.g. Trevithick, 2005).

In social work today, several 'standardized assessment instruments' have gained promi-nence as part of evidence-based programmes (e.g. Broadhurst et al., 2010; Martinell Barfoed and Jacobsson, 2012). One such instrument is the Addiction Severity Index (ASI), which is prescribed by the Swedish state authorities and is currently in widespread use within the divisions of social services that address addiction treatment. Client treatment needs are surveyed and rated via personal interviews based on a questionnaire with fixed response alternatives. The interview has a profound impact on what is said during an ASI client meeting, given that it is composed of 180 questions that take approximately 90 minutes for the social worker and client to complete. The following extract is from an ASI inter-view with Carl, a good-humoured old man awaiting trial for drunk driving. He voluntarily enrolled in an addiction treatment programme. In the beginning of the interview, he was talkative and elaborated on his answers. Quite quickly, he grasped the logic of the survey and adjusted his speech accordingly. In this extract, near the end of the 180 questions, Carl is rather tired and his previous habit of telling a short story during the interview is gone:

Social worker:	Okay. Let's see … [reads from questionnaire:] Have you experienced severe depression over the past 30 days?
Carl:	No.
Social worker:	Earlier in life?
Carl:	No.
Social worker:	Have you experienced serious anxiety or severe stress conditions the past 30 days?
Carl:	No.
Social worker:	Earlier in life?
Carl:	No.
Social worker:	Have you experienced difficulties to understand, remember or be able to concentrate?
Carl:	No, no, no! [annoyed]
Social worker:	Not previously either? Have you experienced hallucinations?
Carl:	No.
Social worker:	Never?
Carl:	No.
Social worker:	Have you experienced difficulties in controlling violent behaviour?
Carl:	No.
Social worker:	No. Have you had serious thoughts of suicide over the past 30 days?
Carl:	No.
Social worker:	Earlier in life?
Carl:	No.
Social worker:	No. And no suicide attempts either?
Carl:	No.

By analysing the survey itself, we learn a great deal about how social problems are con-structed. The document also reveals an officially sanctioned approach that favours 'infor-mation' and 'facts' more than the client's 'subjective' narrative (Martinell Barfoed, 2014). Furthermore, the interview schedule takes the shape of an actor in so far as it drives the rhythm and sequencing of the interaction (Prior, personal communication). Data on how people interact over documents *in situ* disclose to what degree the document is used by, or uses, its reader. In the example above, the social worker strictly adhered to the survey. This is not to say that standardized interviewing by professionals is fully determined by the document at all times, although this is precisely what the authorities would want; social workers tend to adapt prescribed methods to the situation and to their previous working experiences (White et al., 2009). Text-governed or not, interaction over documents is shaped not only by the interlocutors, but also by the document itself.

In professions in which people's lives, problems and needs are written down in files, records or other templates, the interaction that precedes the process of writing affects the production of texts, as discussed previously. As illustrated above, the reverse statement is also true: the use of documents while talking to people significantly affects how the interaction unfolds. What kind of talk is produced when professionals rely on, for example, standardized assessment instruments or other technologies? In what ways do documents organize conversation? Observations, or better yet, recordings of human service encounters make it possible to answer such questions.

Shadowing the document

Mobile ethnographic methods are techniques in which the informant is shadowed by the researcher (Czarniawska, 2007), who both interviews and observes the informant (Kusenbach, 2003). Just as people in organizations may be shadowed, so can the researcher shadow documents through the organization in order to scrutinize the production of a document, its use and its circulation.

Ethnomethodologists have carried out sophisticated analyses of transformations from speech to text and text to speech by following documents in bureaucratic organizations (e.g. Komter, 2012). For example, Kameo and Whalen (2015) examined a document's constitutive role in organizing the work at a police and fire communications centre. The analysis sought to capture, in all their complexity, the speech and text that run through a computer-aided dispatch system in an often time-sensitive process:

1. someone calls for help
2. a call-taker writes an incident record on the computer screen while simultaneously asking the caller for clarification, and
3. a radio dispatcher receives the incident record electronically and turns the text into speech over a radio broadcast to police officers on the street.

Kameo and Whalen (2015) drew on recordings of all three steps, as well as a printout of the electronic document in one case of a 'possible burglary'. They showed how the caller's speech was condensed into codes and categories; during this process, qualifiers such as 'probably' or 'looks like' were removed. They also demonstrated how this scarce text must be elaborated and expanded upon when the dispatcher communicates it to patrolling police officers. The dispatcher brings 'the text into the conventions that govern talk' (Kameo and Whalen, 2015: 224). Following a document's production and use in detail enables a precise demonstration of how people and events are continuously constructed and reconstructed in the process of producing a factual version; in the words of Smith (1974: 260), such processes often aim to establish 'what actually happened'.

The above example illustrates rather tight shadowing of a document. Another strategy would be to shadow documents at a greater distance in order to map their dissemination and generative features. Which activities are generated by a document? What about its circulation and significance? What other documents and practices are linked to a specific document? What people, professions, clients, patients, etc. are involved? Such questions lead the researcher away from the original document and its immediate situation (cf. Rapley, 2007). Let us return to the ASI interview described above – the standardized assessment of drug addicts. The actual paper copy of the survey exists within a wide network of supporting infrastructure (cf. Timmermans and Epstein, 2010): ASI manuals, policies, in-service training, experts, an 'ASI net bank' in which individual interview results are registered, computer consultants, evaluations and research. Following the document in this sense means that the researcher can map networks that extend beyond organizational boundaries, paying attention to how a particular document is integrated into various contexts simultaneously.

CHAPTER SUMMARY AND FUTURE PROSPECTS

The various entries to the study of documents-in-use sketched above are associated with different analytical claims. Obviously, the choice of methods directs what claims can be made, and informs whether the aim is to investigate a setting through its documents or to investigate a document through its setting. At one end of this analytical continuum, documents are tools for interpreting social groups, organizations, times and lives. Taking pictures of documents, asking about documents and observing what people do with documents help the researcher to shed light over a setting (Coffey, 2014); the documents and the talk about them reveal prevailing norms, logics, discourses and rhetoric. At the other end of the continuum, where analytical claims are sharper, researchers seek to establish the constituent features of documents, how documents shape and pattern interaction (Prior, 2011). Such claims demand more precise data, preferably recorded interactions in which people are engaged in the use of documents.

A wide range of ethnographic methods can be used to advance our knowledge of a setting through its documents or to grasp a document through its setting. Returning to the student objections with which I introduced this chapter, this range illustrates that analyses of documents are certainly not restricted to close text analyses or boring deskwork.

As for future prospects, people's interaction with documents (digital or hard copies) is a promising field of research. As technological advancements seem to generate an increasing societal reliance on documentary realities, the possibilities for investigation and analysis multiply.

Study questions

1. Why are documents important (but often neglected) data in social science research?
2. What ethnographic questions about documents cannot be answered exclusively with content analysis?
3. Imagine a given site (for instance a school or a customs check), and exemplify in what ways it would be possible to study documents *in situ*.
4. What would close shadowing of a document through an organization entail? What features could be captured by a more distant shadowing?

Recommended reading

An inspiring and insightful text for various analytical strategies, particularly regarding the use and function of documents:
Prior, L. (2003) *Using Documents in Social Research*. London: Sage.

A collection of classical and contemporary texts on documents, which gives a thorough exposition of approaches to studying the content of documents as well as their use and function:
Prior, L. (2011) *Using Documents and Records in Social Research*, four volumes. London: Sage.

Important (constructionist) methodological contributions to the ethnographic analysis of documents:
Atkinson, P. and Coffey, A. (2011) 'Analysing documentary realities', in D. Silverman (ed.), *Qualitative Research* (3d edn). London: Sage, pp. 77–92.
Coffey, A. (2014) 'Analysing documents', in U. Flick (ed.), *The Sage Handbook of Qualitative Data Analysis*. London: Sage, pp. 367-79.

Examples of texts on documents that are now viewed as classics in the field:
Garfinkel, H. (1967) '"Good" organizational reasons for "bad" clinic records', in H. Garfinkel (ed.), *Studies in Ethnomethodology*. Englewood Cliffs, NJ: Prentice-Hall, pp. 186-207.
Smith, D. (1974) 'The social construction of documentary reality', *Sociological Inquiry*, 44 (4): 257-68.

References

Atkinson, P. and Coffey, A. (2011) 'Analysing documentary realities', in D. Silverman (ed.), *Qualitative Research* (3rd edn). London: Sage, pp. 77–92.

Beck Nielsen, S. (2014) 'Medical record keeping as interactional accomplishment', *Pragmatics and Society*, 5 (2): 221–42.

Berg, M. (2004) 'Practices of reading and writing: the constitutive role of the patient record in medical work', in E. Annandale, M. A. Elston and L. Prior (eds), *Medical Work, Medical Knowledge and Health Care*. Malden, MA: Blackwell Publishing, pp. 25–49.

Broadhurst, K., Hall, C., Wastell, D., White, S. and Pithouse, A. (2010) 'Risk, instrumentalism and the humane project in social work: identifying the informal logics of risk management in children's statutory services', *British Journal of Social Work*, 40: 1046–64.

Carlstedt, E. and Jacobsson, K. (2015) 'Indications of quality or quality as a matter of fact? "Open comparisons" in the social work sector' (unpublished paper). Workshop on the Modernisation of the State, Lund University, 24 September.

Coffey, A. (2014) 'Analysing documents', in U. Flick (ed.), *The Sage Handbook of Qualitative Data Analysis*. London: Sage, pp. 367–79.

Czarniawska, B. (2007) *Shadowing and Other Techniques for Doing Fieldwork in Modern Societies*. Malmö: Liber.

Drew, P. (2006) 'When documents "speak": documents, language and interaction', in P. Drew, G. Raymond and D. Weinberg (eds), *Talk and Interaction in Social Research Methods*. London: Sage, pp. 63–80.

Emerson, R. M. (1994) 'Constructing serious violence: processing a domestic violence restraining order', in J. A. Holstein and G. Miller (eds), *Perspectives on Social Problems*, 6. Stamford, CT: JAI Press, pp. 3–28.

Garfinkel, H. (1967) *Studies in Ethnomethodology*. Englewood Cliffs, NJ: Prentice-Hall.

Goffman, E. (1967) *Interaction Ritual: Essays on Face-to-face Behavior*. New York: Pantheon Books.

Hammersley, M. and Atkinson, P. (2007) *Ethnography: Principles in Practice* (3rd edn). London: Tavistock.

Hartswood, M., Rouncefield, M., Slack, R. and Carlin, A. (2011) 'Documents', in M. Rouncefield and P. Tolmie (eds), *Ethnomethodology at Work*. Farnham: Ashgate Publishing, pp. 151–72.

Jacobsson, K. (2014) 'Categories by heart: shortcut reasoning in a cardiology clinic', *Professions & Professionalism*, 4 (3): 1–15. https://journals.hioa.no/index.php/pp/article/view/763/868 (accessed 10 December 2015).

Kameo, N. and Whalen, J. (2015) 'Organizing documents: standard forms, person production and organizational action', *Qualitative Sociology*, 38: 205–29.

Komter, M. (2012) 'The career of a suspect's statement: talk, text, context', *Discourse Studies*, 14 (6): 731–52.

Kusenbach, M. (2003) 'Street phenomenology: the go-along as ethnographic research tool', *Ethnography*, 4 (3): 455–85.

Martinell Barfoed, E. (2014) 'Standardiserad interaktion – en utmaning i socialt arbete', *Socialvetenskaplig tidskrift*, 21 (1): 4–22.

Martinell Barfoed, E. and Jacobsson, K. (2012) 'Moving from "gut-feeling" to "pure facts": launching the ASI interview as part of in-service training for social workers', *Nordic Social Work Research*, 2 (1): 5–20.

Maynard, D. W. and Shaeffer, N. C. (2006) 'Standardization-in-interaction: the survey interview', in P. Drew, G. Raymond and D. Weinberg (eds), *Talk and Interaction in Social Research Methods*. London: Sage, pp. 9–27.

Pollitt, C. and Bouckaert, G. (2011) *Public Management Reform: A Comparative Analysis – New Public Management, Governance, and the Neo-Weberian State* (3rd edn). New York: Oxford University Press.

Prior, L. (2003) *Using Documents in Social Research*. London: Sage.

Prior, L. (2011) *Using Documents and Records in Social Research*, four volumes. London: Sage.

Rapley, T. (2007) *Doing Conversation, Discourse and Document Analysis*. London: Sage.

Scott, M. B. and Lyman, S. M. (1968) 'Accounts', *American Sociological Review*, 33: 46–62.

Sellen, A. J. and Harper, R. H. R. (2003) *The Myth of the Paperless Office*. London: The MIT Press.

Silverman, D. (2011) *Interpreting Qualitative Data* (4th edn). London: Sage.

Smith, D. (1974) 'The social construction of documentary reality', *Sociological Inquiry*, 44 (4): 257–68.

Thelander, J. and Jacobsson, K. (2016) *Den motvilliga administratören. Om datorjobb och pappersgöra på vårdcentralen*. Research reports in social work, School of Social Work, Lund University.

Thomas, J. and Holland, S. (2010) 'Representing children's identities in core assessments', *British Journal of Social Work*, 40 (8): 2617–33.

Timmermans, S. and Epstein, S. (2010) 'A world of standards but not a standard world: toward a sociology of standards and standardization', *Annual Review of Sociology*, 36: 69–89.

Trevithick, P. (2005) *Social Work Skills: A Practice Handbook* (2nd edn). Maidenhead: Open University Press.

Webb, E., Campbell, D., Schwartz, R. and Sechrest, L. (2000) *Unobtrusive Measures* (revised edn). Thousand Oaks, CA: Sage.

White, S., Hall, C. and Peckover, S. (2009) 'The descriptive tyranny of the Common Assessment Framework: technologies of categorization and professional practice in child welfare', *British Journal of Social Work*, 39 (7): 1197–217.

Wästerfors, D. and Åkerström, M. (2015) 'Case history discourse: a rhetoric of troublesome youngsters and faceless treatment', *European Journal of Social Work*, on-line first: http://dx.doi.org/10.1080/13691457.2015.1030366.

ELEVEN
Using Documents in Social Research

Lindsay Prior

About this chapter

This chapter focuses on the different ways in which documents enter 'the field'. Four distinct social scientific modes in which data about documents might be collected and analysed are identified. The respective modes involve studying documents as 'resource', as 'topic', in use and in action. It is argued that there has hitherto been an undue emphasis placed on the first of these modes and a relative neglect of the last of the modes. As a result, the study of document content has tended to dominate discussion in research methods texts. The author consequently seeks to broaden the range of data that might be collected under the rubric of documentary research, and points to a variety of approaches that can be usefully deployed for the study of documentation.

Keywords

agency, content analysis, documents, discourse, hermeneutics, networks, sociology of knowledge

FOUR APPROACHES TO THE STUDY OF DOCUMENTATION

In one of the most influential texts on social scientific research methods produced during the second half of the twentieth century, Glaser and Strauss (1967: 163) argued that, in matters of sociological investigation, documents ought to be regarded as akin 'to an anthropologist's informant or a sociologist's interviewee'. The authors subsequently devoted an entire chapter to how the principles of grounded theory could and should be deployed on inert text. A focus on documents merely as containers of data had, of course, been well established in social science from the earlier part of the twentieth century (Madge, 1953). And as a key source of data, it is nowadays recommended that document content be screened, counted and 'coded' for appropriate evidence in support or refutation of relevant hypotheses (Weber, 1990; Neuendorf, 2002; Krippendorf, 2004). Indeed, an understanding of documents as inert carriers of content is normally well reflected in most of the textbook discussions on research methods and often associated with the idea that the study of documents should be allied to the use of 'unobtrusive' methods (see, for example, Bryman, 2012; Babbie, 2013). So it will probably be as well for me to outline at this stage a range of alternative approaches that might be adopted for the study of documents. I shall begin by referring to Table 11.1.

Table 11.1 is aimed at offering an understanding of the various ways in which documents have been dealt with by social researchers. Thus, approaches that fit into Cell 1 have been dominant in the history of sociology and of social science generally. Therein documents (especially as text) have been scoured and coded for what they contain in the way of descriptions, reports, images, representations and accounts. In short, they have been mined for evidence. Data analysis strategies concentrate almost entirely on what is in the 'text'. This emphasis on content is carried over into Cell 2 type approaches with the key differences that analysis is concerned with how document content comes into being. The attention here is usually on the conceptual architecture and socio-technical procedures by means of which written reports, descriptions, statistical data and so forth are generated.

Table 11.1 Approaches to the study of documents

Focus of Research Approach	Document as Resource	Document as Topic
Content	(Cell 1) Approaches that focus almost entirely on what is 'in' the document	(Cell 2) 'Archaeological' approaches that focus on how document content comes into being
Use and Function	(Cell 3) Approaches that focus on how documents are used as a resource by human actors for purposeful ends	(Cell 4) Approaches that focus on how documents function in, and impact on, schemes of social interaction and social organization

Source: Prior (2008a)

Various kinds of discourse analysis have been used to unravel the conceptual issues, while a focus on socio-technical and rule-based procedures by means of which clinical, police, social work and other forms of record and reports are constructed has been well represented in the work of ethnomethodologists and social constructionists. In contrast, and in Cell 3, the research focus is on the ways in which documents are used as a resource by various and different kinds of 'reader'. Here, a concern with document content or how a document has come into being is marginal, and the analysis concentrates on the relationship between specific documents and their use or recruitment by identifiable human actors for purposeful ends. Thus, in the field of medical sociology for example, there are various studies that focus on how medical professionals call upon and use X-rays, charts, notes, files, images and the like in routine clinical settings (see Prior, 2011, Vol. 3). The approaches that fit into Cell 4 also position content as secondary. However, the emphasis here is on how documents as 'things' function in schemes of social activity, and with how such things can drive, rather than be driven by, human actors – i.e. the spotlight is on the *vita activa* of documentation (see Prior, 2011, Vol. 4).

In the following sections I shall outline some examples of work in each of the four frames and highlight some of the methodological issues that they raise. We should also note that throughout this chapter I refer to documentation as if it were equivalent to text – though that is clearly not so. Indeed, architectural and engineering drawings, paintings, theatrical performances, X-ray images, film, World Wide Web pages, Facebook pages, bus tickets, shopping lists, tapestries and sequences of DNA can all be considered as 'documents' – depending on the use that is made of such materials in specific circumstances (Prior, 2003). For heuristic purposes, however, I will ignore non-textual forms of data and proceed as if the terms 'text' and 'documentation' were synonymous.

Key points

- Documents are traditionally regarded as passive and inert sources of information and evidence.
- For that reason their role in the research process is often associated with the deployment of unobtrusive methods.
- In this chapter it is argued that such a view is unduly limited and that documents should also be recognized as active agents in the production of social life.
- Consequently, as well as looking at what is 'in' any given document, it is suggested that we should consider how the document content has been put together (constructed), how it is used in episodes of social interaction and how it functions as an 'actor' in its own right.

DOCUMENTS AS RESOURCE

In the history of social science the collection and study of written documents has, at various times, played a major role in the research process. Indeed, according to Platt (1996)

and Plummer (2001), documents such as diaries, written life histories and letters constituted the primary source of data for most fieldworkers during the first half of the twentieth
century. Indeed, they are media that function as significant sources of both qualitative and
quantitative data up to the present day; end-of-life diaries, activity diaries and expenditure
diaries are contemporary examples of the genre. All this aside from the fact that most social
scientific data are collected via the aid of documentation (field notes, interview schedules,
questionnaires, transcripts) and generated via the deployment of documentation

In everyday life documentation is, of course, ubiquitous, and in terms of what might
be called naturally occurring data (rather than researcher generated data) it requires
little effort to note that the social world is awash with text and documentation. We
need only walk down a city street with its interminable signs, adverts and instructions
(not to mention the ever-present acts of texting and on-line searching) to establish the
veracity of that claim. For the purposes of this chapter, however, it is probably more
profitable to think in terms of the rich textual data routinely produced by bureaucratic
organizations such as schools, corporations, health care agencies and government
offices, rather than the somewhat truncated and in-your-face documentation of the
street. For, in the former, such things as memos, monthly, quarterly and annual reports,
procedure manuals, spreadsheets, as well as policy and mission statements can be found
in abundance – and the analysis of what is contained within is invariably fundamental
to an understanding as to how organizations work.

In this section I shall focus on some of the basic methodological issues that are highlighted
by use of text in social research rather than on data analysis. Nevertheless, we do need to note
that the strategies that can be adopted for the analysis of documents are numerous. Thus, we
can choose forms of content analysis, or turn to thematic analysis or even to the aforemen-
tioned grounded theory when we consider our analytical approach. Beyond that, a focus on
narrative or rhetorical styles as well as on frames will undoubtedly assist us in getting a wider
overview of how the document functions in its social, cultural and organizational contexts.
Ultimately, however, all forms of qualitative analysis have to be based on an examination of
content in one form or another, and in the realm of documentation this means grounding
analysis in the words and concepts contained in the text at hand – rather than on 'codes' and
'themes' and concepts extraneous to the data. Let us consider an example.

The example that I offer is a recent report from the European Division of the World
Health Organization (WHO, 2013). The WHO develops global templates for almost all
aspects of health policy – ranging from the identification of health problems to detailing
and publishing strategies for tackling such problems. WHO templates are subsequently
adapted to the needs of the different regions of the world as well as to the individual countries within each region. In this example we are dealing with a regional report – entitled,
Health 2020: A European Policy Framework and Strategy for the 21st Century. The question is,
'How should we approach it in terms of its content?'

Inevitably and unsurprisingly we have to begin with a 'reading'. And a stock claim of most
undergraduate (and many postgraduate) qualitative research texts is that our fundamental

strategy should be to direct our reading to the subjective meanings, or subjective experience, views and understandings of our research subjects as expressed through the data (e.g. Smith et al., 2009). In fieldwork settings such assertions have a seeming plausibility because we are working and engaging, face-to-face, with live human actors. We can see and identify our thinking and acting subjects. With documentation, however, this is rarely, if ever, the case. Thus, in terms of our example we are not even clear as to who the 'authors' of the report are. There are of course names within the document (of WHO officials), together with photographs of individuals, but we should be wary of believing that a report such as the one being considered has a single author or producer. Much better for us to think in terms of an author function than of identifiable authors and assume that the report has been written and assembled by a discrete team (or teams) of actors and agents (see, for example, Harper, 1998). Given that assumption, searching for the subjective meanings of ghostly agents is not a practical possibility – even were we to believe that 'meaning' is, indeed, subjective. Instead we have little option but to focus in on the *language* of the documentation – for that is all that is immediately available to us. And there is another twist to the act of discerning 'meaning' in documentation – namely that the meaning we derive from our analysis will be a product not simply of the words already in the text (the words and sentences of the 'authors' if you like), but also of the 'reader' or readers. In short, meaning arises out of active engagement of the researcher with her or his materials. It was this fundamental observation that led Hans-Georg Gadamer to argue that in the study of text, a focus of subjectivity is nothing less than a 'distorting mirror' (1975: 245), and that the task of the analyst is not so much to 'understand' the text but to interpret it. Those who embrace the precepts of hermeneutics would argue that such a claim necessarily extends to the study of human interaction as well as to text (see, for example, Ricoeur, 1991).

In the context of social research, interpretation is, of course, an act that demands evaluation and assessment. Otherwise we are left in the position that 'anything goes' and that we should be free to read into the data whatever we wish (this is a perpetual danger for those who seek to detect 'latent' meanings of text). So a key problem concerns ways in which we might verify or validate an interpretation as feasible or otherwise. There are of course various strategies for validating the interpretation of qualitative data, but in the realm of documentation it is, above all, the text that has to stand as the bedrock of any interpretation – that is why forms of content analysis are particularly useful as exploratory methods in documentary research (Prior, 2014). Thus, claims to the effect that our selected document is, for example, much more strongly focused on, say, 'health' rather than 'disease', or on the 'social determinants' of health than on 'inequality', can be initially and very easily verified by a simple frequency count of the words as used. (Feel free to check this claim for yourself.)

In the context of qualitative research this kind of frequency counting and looking at the co-association of words and concepts in context (what might be called a study of intratextuality) offers just one of many possible entry points to a text. To understand how the words in the documents connect to the world beyond the text – to discourse, and to the actions of the policy-makers and professionals who produced the document as well as to the audience for whom the documents were intended – we would need to call upon many other sources of data (such as interview data, speeches and presentations). In carrying out that programme one would inexorably be led to examine how the content of any one text interlinked to that of other texts – that is, to explore aspects of what is known as intertextuality (Allen, 2011), or the dialogical properties of text. And as we move from words and sentences towards discourse we have, necessarily, to engage with much broader strategies of analysis. To focus on, say, how the text in documentation interweaves so as to produce a narrative or series of policy narratives (Roe, 1994) or how the text expresses a specific rhetorical style (Billig, 1996), or a specific 'account' of events and processes. By such means we may come to see how documents 'frame' economic, social, political and cultural problems and channel our attention to a given set of solutions to such problems, while simultaneously excluding or downgrading others. In short, even when we elect to focus simply on content, it is clear that documents have to be studied as components in much broader networks of action rather than as independent and inert 'things' that can be approached 'unobtrusively' (see Prior, 2011, Vol. 1).

Key points

- Approaching documents as a resource essentially means focusing on their content.
- A focus on content can be undertaken using content analysis, thematic analysis or grounded theory.
- Whatever style of analysis we choose, our interpretation of the document must be based first and foremost on the language within the text (rather than on preconceived codes, themes, concepts or ideas).
- We need also to be aware that the analysis of content is merely a precursor to an examination of how the document links to text and action in the world at large - that is, how the document exists as a component in a network of action.

DOCUMENTS AS TOPIC

A second way in which documents may be approached as research material involves the concept of topic. In this frame, instead of accepting the content of documentation as 'evidence', as data to be drawn down and used as fact, we ask questions about how the content came to assume the form that it did. Following the ideas of Michel Foucault (1972) we can characterize this orientation as one that engages us in an 'archaeology of documentation'. The virtues of the approach are best displayed by reference to the analysis of statistical reports – on crime, education, deprivation, illness, mortality and the like – though, in fact, any document can be analysed in the archaeological frame. Let us take an example.

Table 11.2 Prevalence of psychiatric disorders in private households in Great Britain in 2000 by gender (rates per thousand of population in past week)

Nature of Disorder	Females	Males
Mixed Anxiety and Depressive Disorder (MADD)	108	68
Generalised Anxiety Disorder (GAD)	46	43
Depressive Episode	28	23
All Phobias	22	13
Obsessive-Compulsive Disorder (OCD)	13	9
Panic Disorder	7	7
Any Neurotic Disorder	194	135
Psychotic Disorder*	5	6
Drug dependence*	21	54

* = Rates per thousand of population in past 12 months

Source: Based on data derived from Singleton et al. (2001)

I am looking at a table of research results (Table 11.2). It tells us about the community prevalence rates in Great Britain of certain types of what are sometimes called 'neurotic disorder', together with an estimate for 'psychotic disorder' and drug dependence. The table represents 'facts' about mental illness. It is intended to be used, together with others related to it, as a resource for researchers. Thus, we can, for example, refer to Table 11.2 as evidence for our statement that during the earliest years of the current century, in Great Britain, about 16 per cent of people in any one week showed symptoms of a neurotic disorder. But how were this and other facts arrived at? How was the report put together? And what would answers to such questions tell us about fundamental social processes?

The study of the manner in which data such as are found in Table 11.2 are produced has a long sociological pedigree. Some early markers in this particular history are available in the works of Kitsuse and Cicourel (1963), Douglas (1967) and Garfinkel (1967) who tended to focus on crime and suicide statistics. Dorothy Smith (1974) referred to the social production of documentary reality in this context – arguing that our knowledge of the world is filtered through the reports and analyses that statistical and other agencies produce. In all cases, however, the production of such realities depends on the existence of at least two mechanisms. The first of these concerns the availability of a conceptual or theoretical scheme, and the second concerns a set of rules and technical instructions by means of which events and occurrences can be allocated to categories. Now, the conceptual scheme in terms of which mental illness is routinely comprehended is that contained in the *Diagnostic and Statistical Manual of the American Psychiatric Association* (such as the *DSM-V*, American Psychiatric Association, 2013, for example). The latter contains a series of categories (diagnoses) relating to the various psychiatric maladies that people might be said to experience, and it also contains diagnostic criteria for recognizing the distinct disorders. Some of those disorders are listed in Table 11.2. The *DSM* is in itself a document of some interest and demonstrates one of the ways in which we 'sort things out' in Western culture (Bowker and Star, 1999). As such it is always worthwhile examining how psychiatric disorders appear in and disappear from the *DSM* nosology. Thus, Multiple Personality Disorder, for example, is a category that once was present in the *DSM* and which is no longer present, while Post Traumatic Stress Disorder was once absent and is now present. In the latest edition (*DSM-V*) normal grief (or bereavement) is classified, for the first time, as a psychiatric disorder – and so on. For now, however, let us focus on how the figures in Table 11.2 were obtained, rather than on the *DSM*.

The data in the table are derived from answers to a survey conducted in over 15,000 private households, some members of whom were asked to respond to a specific set of questionnaires (see Singleton et al., 2001); over 8,000 people did so. One of the questionnaires or instruments used was called the Clinical Interview Schedule (Revised) or CIS-R. The CIS-R is one of a variety of 'instruments' that produce clinical and other phenomena (for others see Singleton et al., 2001). In many respects documents such as the CIS-R are like machine tools – tools for producing 'facts'. Indeed, phenomena such as 'disability', types of psychiatric illness, 'quality of life' and wellbeing are conditions routinely manufactured by instruments of the kind referred to here. In the case of the CIS-R the tool operates through a system of questions and answers. For example, one such question asks, 'During the past month, have you felt that you've been lacking in energy?' Another question asks, 'Have you had any sort of ache or pain in the past month?' Respondents are required to answer 'Yes' or 'No'. Normally these responses are coded into a machine readable form. So a 'Yes' might be coded as, say, 1 and a 'No' as zero. The ones and zeros are then added so that for each respondent in the sample it is possible to determine at least two things; a total score for the individual concerned and a precise indication of which section of the questionnaire the scores came from. Should an individual score a total of 12 or more points on the CIS-R then they are usually regarded as a 'case' of psychiatric disorder. In that sense 12 is said to function as the cut-off point for 'caseness'. Whether a person is then to be allocated to the category of 'depression', 'compulsive disorder' or 'anxiety' is dependent on the distribution of scores ('yes's and 'no's) within the instrument. Note that at no point are subjects asked whether they suffer from Obsessive Compulsive Disorder or Depression or whatever, nor are they assessed (for this purpose) by a psychiatrist – the diagnosis is achieved via the deployment of machine driven algorithms. (Individuals who were identified as possible cases of personality disorder in the above survey were, however, allocated a clinical interview.)

So what does all of this suggest about our concept of psychiatric disorder? And what would happen if someone decided to set the cut-off point on the schedule to 10 or 18 rather than 12? Such questions are in many ways related. It is possible, for example, to select a different cut-off point. Moving the point to, say, 10 would increase the prevalence of mental illness in the community. Moving the point to 18 would decrease it. So there is a sense in which we can have as much or as little neurotic disorder in the community as we want. The acceptance of 12 as a cut-off point is merely a (useful) convention. In the same way, if we re-aligned the rules by means of which the different illnesses take precedence one over the other then our entire picture of the prevalence of the different disorders would change. So the 'facts' about psychiatric disorder in the community are in a sense malleable, and the same thing is true of the 'facts' about economic activity, crime, obesity, physical activity, mortality, well-being and other processes and behaviours (for some examples see Prior, 2011, Vol. 2).

Naturally, most social researchers prefer to use data of the kind just discussed as a 'resource' or evidence and often resent what they misinterpret as attempts to query the 'validity' of quantitative data such as we have referred to. However, what the discussion above suggests is that it is always worthwhile investigating such data as a 'topic' (on this distinction see Zimmerman and Pollner, 1971). That is to say, it is forever beneficial to ask how documents are produced; who, exactly, produced them; and how the production process was socially organized so as to generate a particular image of social reality.

Key points

- Approaching documents as topic essentially means focusing on how the documents were assembled and how the document generates a specific image of social reality.
- Such a task involves examining the conceptual structure on which the document is based together with a consideration of the technical rules and assumptions used in the production of facts and evidence within.
- Traditionally it has been reports on such things as crime and suicide rates, drugs, mental illness and economic activity that have been treated as topic, but it is possible to deconstruct documents of any kind - including news reports, court proceedings, police interviews and educational records; to name just a few possibilities.

STUDYING DOCUMENTS IN USE

It is quite clear that although documents contain things – text, image, instruction, reports and so forth – one of their primary qualities is that they can be and are used in everyday affairs. They are commonly used to *do* things as well as to say things, and one important line of approach to the study of documents is to consider the manner of their use in concrete and specific circumstances – to develop an ethnography of documentation as it were (see, Smith and Turner, 2014; and Jacobsson in this volume).

An early foray into such a field was that of Garfinkel (1967) in his masterful essay on why clinical records designed for one set of purposes were used for another. He entitled his essay '"Good" organizational reasons for "bad" clinical records'; subsequently research into clinical and medical records of all kinds emerged as a substantial area of inquiry. For example, in psychiatry there has been extensive discussion of the ways in which clinical notes have been used to do such things as construct patient identities and patient 'careers'

(Barrett, 1996). Other researchers (e.g. Berg, 1996) have noted how medical records are routinely used to represent and constitute both patient bodies and the organizations of which they are clients, while on a mundane level it has been noted how charts and end-of-bed records are used to monitor and organize the daily experiences of hospital patients. Indeed, Zerubavel (1979) long ago indicated how such charts and records are used to structure staff routines as well as those of patients.

Beyond the hospital, other researchers (e.g. Henderson, 1991) have indicated how such things as engineering drawings routinely function to constitute production teams as well as to demarcate employee roles on the factory floor. (Henderson speaks of documents as 'conscription devices' in such circumstances.) In like manner, Preda (2002) has indicated how economic reports and analyses that circulate in financial organizations routinely function as (social and economic) networking mechanisms. This capacity of documents, charts, drawings and records to create, sustain and mediate social relationships has also been observed in welfare, judicial, policing and educational organizations as well as medical and economic settings (for examples see, Prior 2011, Vol. 3). It is also increasingly clear that in many fields of everyday life, electronic documents – as contained on Facebook and the like – also function to create, sustain and redefine social relations. Above all, perhaps, they can be seen to function as identity-creating mechanisms and as such their existence underlines the ways in which documents can serve to objectify us (as humans) every bit as much as we objectify things.

Key points

- Focusing on documents in use involves an exploration of the ways in which human actors call upon and manipulate documents (records, forms, reports, images) in specific settings. Essentially it involves engagement with an ethnography of documentation.
- Of particular interest to researchers is the way in which documents function to facilitate networks and identities.
- In studying how humans use documents as 'things' we can also glimpse at how those things come to define humans.

STUDYING DOCUMENTS IN ACTION

The idea that documents can function as actors is probably difficult to accept for many. We are, after all, conditioned to regard human agency as the wellspring of action and in qualitative work there is an additional emphasis on the role and function of human consciousness in action. Indeed, 'social action' is more often than not defined in terms of consciousness (Giddens, 1984: 14). Yet there are good empirical and theoretical grounds for arguing that 'things', including documents, can be actors. To act is to make a difference, and documents often make a big difference to social arrangements (and so too does

the absence of documentation). In fact, it is possible to identify at least three different theoretical perspectives that might encourage us to view documents in action and as actors.

The first approach draws on ideas from 'speech-act' theory so as to examine how text
can 'perform' in both informal (everyday) and organizational settings. The origin of the
concept of a speech act can be traced to the work of J. L. Austin (1911–1960). Austin
was among the earliest philosophers of language to note that we often do things with
words (as well as merely speak them). For example, in saying 'I promise', I am doing
something (promising) as well as stating something. Later philosophers such as Searle
extended Austin's insights to cover a wide range of instances in which speech might be
said to 'do something' (see Green, 2014), and in a social scientific context Cooren (2004)
picked upon such categories of speech-act and suggested that there are multiple ways
in which 'texts make a difference' (2004: 374), and can therefore be said to act. Thus he
illustrates how text can inform, indicate, certify, proclaim and announce; as well as how
it can ban, authorize, notify and summon; not to mention declare, pardon, bequeath and
endorse. The anthropological task, then, is to identify not simply how text – as well as
physical objects – are created by humans but how such texts act back upon their creators
(see Prior, 2003).

A second line of approach is indicated in the work of writers such as Charles Bazerman
(1997), in so far as the latter draws on the ideas of Vygotsky and activity theory to highlight
ways in which documents interact with humans so as to shape and pattern what humans
actually do. Vygotsky (1978), in a Marxist frame, was interested in the ways in which tools
could influence their users (rather than how people used their tools), and with that theme
in mind Bazerman (1997) has written about 'discursively structured activities', one example of which concerns the airline pilot's checklist. Such a checklist, observes Bazerman,
structures the procedures of take-off, the perception and inspection of instruments and
the manipulation of aircraft controls. (Check levels of X, Y, Z, observe the readings for F
and G, examine P and Q, communicate with ground staff about C and D, etc.) There is
little room for manoeuvre or loose interpretation in the procedure – the checklist drives
the sequence and the activity. These same kinds of effect are visible when we complete
application forms, on-line questionnaires and the like, wherein the human respondent
is required to answer in a given sequence and simply not allowed to move to step 2 or 3
until the previous steps have been responded to in an exact manner. The form drives the
eye, the hands and the thought. Dorothy Winsor (1999) has also invoked activity theory
to demonstrate how documents (as tools in use) function so as to hold organizational systems together. Her examples are focused on the use of formal work orders in engineering
settings, but text and documentation do not have to be formal to have an effect – graffiti,
especially in politically sensitive contexts, can also function as notable actors in complex
systems of action (Peteet, 1996).

Thirdly and finally, it is possible to draw on actor-network theory or ANT to support
our claims that documents can function as actors. The idea of conceptualizing things and
objects as actors or 'actants' is a hallmark of actor-network theorists. And a key assertion

within ANT is that the traditional distinction – indeed, the asymmetry – between material objects and human beings should be not just problematized, but overturned. In the same way, it is argued that the traditional distinction between subject and object should be dispensed with. So, for example, non-human 'things' are not to be regarded as mere (passive) resources that merit consideration only when activated by human actors, but are to be viewed and understood as playing a vital role in economic, technological, scientific and all other forms of organizational life in their own right. That is to say, 'things' can be seen to instigate and direct as well as be directed. One of the best known studies of how human actors and non-human actants mesh into a network of action is that of Michel Callon (1986) in his analysis of scallop fishing in northern France – an analysis in which the scallops, as well as the fishermen, are seen to play a role. (Sadly documents get only one brief mention in the Callon study.)

CHAPTER SUMMARY

- Conceptualizing documents as actors involves focusing on how documents 'do' things with and to human agents.
- There are numerous theoretical grounds on which we might consider documents as actors, and three specific lines of thought have been referred to in this section - namely, speech-act theory, Vygotskyan activity theory, and actor-network theory (ANT).
- However, of the three, it is only ANT that emphasizes the role of documents in networks of action.

FUTURE PROSPECTS

There is little room to explore these issues at this point, but it is appropriate to indicate that the focus on networks of influence and the interconnections of 'actants' that is so characteristic of ANT is well worth adopting. Indeed, visualizing such networks has a useful role to play in social research (see Prior, 2008b), and it is in terms of such visualizations that important advances have still to be made. Given an increasing focus on 'big data' it also seems likely that researchers will be encouraged to move from forms of close or detailed reading of individual texts, to the 'distant reading' of substantial collections of (electronic) text.

Study questions

1. There are four distinctive ways in which we might focus on the role of documents in the field. What are they?
2. How might one distinguish between looking at documents as (a) a resource and (b) a topic?

3.   On what theoretical grounds can it be argued that documents function as 'actors' in social settings?
4.   In what ways can human identity ('who we are') be said to be shaped by documentation?

Recommended reading

Prior, L. (2003) *Using Documents in Social Research*. London: Sage.
Provides detailed examples on the production, consumption and exchange of documents in social life.

Prior, L. (2008) 'Documents and action', in P. Alasuutari, L. Bickman and J. Brannen (eds), *Sage Handbook of Social Research Methods*. London: Sage, pp. 479-92.
Indicates how visualizations of data as networks can add to our understanding of the role of documentation in social life.

Prior, L. (2011) 'Introduction', in L. Prior (ed.), *Using Documents and Records in Social Research*, Vol 1. London: Sage, pp. xxi-xxvii.
Provides an overview of the field and points to a range of studies that deploy the approaches referred to in this chapter.

Recommended online resources

For discussion of various topics in research methods including the study of documents search:
www.socresonline.org.uk/home.html
For a database of newspaper stories across the globe the lexisnexis database (available via most university libraries) is indispensable. See also:
http://academic.lexisnexis.com/
For more advanced examination of many of the theoretical terms used in this chapter – such as agency, hermeneutics, rhetoric and speech-act – as well as further information on thinkers such as Foucault, Gadamer, Ricouer and Searle, see *Stanford Encyclopedia of Philosophy* at:
plato.Stanford.edu/contents.htm

References

Allen, G. (2011) *Intertextuality* (2nd edn). Abingdon: Routledge.
American Psychiatric Association (2013) *Diagnostic and Statistical Manual of Mental Disorders (DSM-V)*. Washington, DC: American Psychiatric Association.
Babbie, E. (2013) *The Practice of Social Research* (13th edn). Belmont, CA: Wadsworth.
Barrett, R. (1996) *The Psychiatric Team and the Social Definition of Schizophrenia: An Anthropological Study of Person and Illness*. Cambridge: Cambridge University Press.

Bazerman, C. (1997) 'Discursively structured activities', *Mind, Culture, and Activity*, 4 (4): 296–308.

Berg, M. (1996) 'Practices of reading and writing: the constitutive role of the patient record in medical work', *Sociology of Health and Illness*, 18 (4): 499–524.

Billig, M. (1996) *Arguing and Thinking*. Cambridge: Cambridge University Press.

Bowker, G. C. and Star, S. L. (1999) *Sorting Things Out: Classification and Its Consequences*. Cambridge, MA: MIT Press.

Bryman, A. (2012) *Social Research Methods* (4th edn). Oxford: Oxford University Press.

Callon, C. (1986) 'Some elements of a sociology of translation: domestication of the scallops and the fishermen of St Brieuc Bay', in J. Law (ed.), *Power, Action and Belief: A New Sociology of Knowledge?* London, Routledge, pp. 196–223.

Cooren, F. (2004) 'Textual agency: how texts do things in organizational settings', *Organization*, 11 (3): 373–93.

Douglas, J. D. (1967) *The Social Meanings of Suicide*. Princeton: Princeton University Press.

Foucault, M. (1972) *The Archaeology of Knowledge*, tr. A. Sheridan. New York: Pantheon.

Gadamer, H.-G. (1975) *Truth and Method*. London: Sheed & Ward.

Garfinkel, H. (1967) *Studies in Ethnomethodology*. Englewood Cliffs, NJ: Prentice Hall.

Giddens, A. (1984) *The Constitution of Society*. Cambridge: Polity.

Glaser, B. G. and Strauss, A. L. (1967) *The Discovery of Grounded Theory*. Chicago, IL: Aldine.

Green, M. (2014) 'Speech acts', *The Stanford Encyclopedia of Philosophy* (Winter edn), ed. Edward N. Zalta. http://plato.stanford.edu/archives/win2014/entries/speech-acts/ (accessed 4 December 2015).

Harper, R. (1998) *Inside the IMF: An Ethnography of Documents, Technology, and Organizational Action*. London: Academic Press.

Henderson, K. (1991) 'Flexible sketches and inflexible data bases', *Science, Technology and Human Values*, 16 (4) :448–73.

Kitsuse, J. I. and Cicourel, A. (1963) 'A note on the use of official statistics', *Social Problems*, 11 (2): 131–9.

Krippendorf, K. (2004) *Content Analysis: An Introduction to its Methodology* (2nd edn). London: Sage.

Madge, J. (1953) *The Tools of Social Science*. London: Longmans.

Neuendorf, K. A. (2002) *The Content Analysis Guidebook*. Thousand Oaks, CA: Sage.

Peteet, J. (1996) 'The writing on the walls: the graffiti of the Intifada', *Cultural Anthropology*, 11 (2):139–59.

Platt, J. (1996) *A History of Sociological Research Methods in America, 1920–1960*. Cambridge: Cambridge University Press.

Plummer, K. (2001) *Documents of Life 2: An Invitation to Critical Humanism*. London: Sage.

Preda, A. (2002) 'Financial knowledge, documents, and the structures of financial activities', *Journal of Contemporary Ethnography*, 31 (2): 207–39.

Prior L. (2003) *Using Documents in Social Research*. London: Sage.

Prior, L. (2008a) 'Repositioning documents in social research', *Sociology*. Special Issue on Research Methods, 42: 821–36.

Prior, L. (2008b) 'Documents and action', in P. Alasuutari, L. Bickman and J. Brannen (eds), *Sage Handbook of Social Research Methods*. London: Sage, pp. 479–92.

Prior, L. (2011) *Using Documents and Records in Social Research*, four volumes. London: Sage.

Prior, L. (2014) 'Content analysis', in P. Leavy (ed.), *The Oxford Handbook of Qualitative Research*. New York: Oxford University Press, pp. 359–79.

Ricoeur, P. (1991) *From Text to Action: Essays in Hermeneutics II*, trans. K. Blamey and J. B. Thompson. London: Athlone Press.

Roe, E. (1994) *Narrative Policy Analysis, Theory and Practice*. Durham, NC: Duke University Press.

Singleton, N., Bumpstead, R., O'Brien, M., Lee, A., Meltzer, H. and Hinds, K. (2001) *Psychiatric Morbidity among Adults Living in Private Households*. London: TSO.

Smith, D. E. (1974) 'The social construction of documentary reality', *Sociological Inquiry*, 44 (4): 257–68.

Smith, D. and Turner, S. M. (eds) (2014) *Incorporating Texts into Institutional Ethnographies*. Toronto: University of Toronto Press.

Smith, J. A., Flowers, P. and Larkin, M. (2009) *Interpretative Phenomenological Analysis*. London: Sage.

Vygotsky, L. S. (1978) *Mind in Society: The Development of Higher Psychological Processes*. Cambridge, MA: Harvard University Press.

Weber, R. P. (1990) *Basic Content Analysis*. Newbury Park, CA: Sage.

WHO (World Health Organization) (2013) *Health 2020: A European Policy Framework and Strategy for the 21st Century*. Copenhagen: WHO.

Winsor, D. (1999) 'Genre and activity systems: the role of documentation in maintaining and changing engineering activity systems', *Written Communication*, 16 (2): 200–24.

Zerubavel, E. (1979) *Patterns of Time in Hospital Life: A Sociological Perspective*. Chicago and London: University of Chicago Press.

Zimmerman, D. H. and Pollner, M. (1971) 'The everyday world as a phenomenon', in J. D. Douglas (ed.), *Understanding Everyday Life*. London: Routledge & Kegan Paul, pp. 80–103.

PART V
TALK

These two chapters set out two related ways to analyse talk in interaction. Jonathan Potter discusses 'discursive psychology', also known as discourse analysis (DA), as a way of analysing naturally occurring talk in the constructionist tradition. DA allows us to address how versions of reality are produced which seem objective and separate from the speaker. Using examples drawn from television interviews with Princess Diana and Salman Rushdie, an excerpt from a *Friends* episode and talk from a relationship counselling session, he demonstrates how we can analyse the ways in which speakers disavow a 'stake' in their actions.

For Potter, DA focuses on rhetorical organization in the context of sequential organization. Conversation analysis (CA) is concerned squarely with sequential organization. John Heritage's chapter presents an accessible introduction to how conversation analytic methods can be used in the analysis of everyday interaction. Heritage helpfully sets out the nuts and bolts of doing CA. Using extracts of talk, he shows us how he goes about deciding whether a conversational practice is distinctive, how to locate it in a sequence and then how to determine its role or function. He concludes with a powerful reply to critics who maintain that CA cannot deal with the social context of talk.

TWELVE

Discursive Psychology and the Study of Naturally Occurring Talk

Jonathan Potter

About this chapter

This chapter introduces a style of discourse analysis known as discursive psychology. This is focused on the study of texts and talk as social practices. Basic theoretical and methodological features of discursive psychology are described as well as the kinds of questions that are developed in this style of work. Four characteristics that distinguish discursive psychology from conversation analysis are overviewed. This outline is followed by an illustration of the logic of analysis which is focused on the attempt to understand why the late Princess Diana used 'I dunno' twice during a high-profile interview on British television. This involves considering the way stake and interest become participants' concerns and the way that stake can be managed, or even 'inoculated' against, by using particular discursive constructions. This is further illustrated by analysing extracts from newspaper reports and relationship counselling sessions.

Keywords

discursive psychology, discourse analysis, interaction, stake, benefactives, fact construction, epistemics

This chapter will focus on the way discourse analysis can be used to study naturally occurring talk. Discourse analysis as a label can be a source of confusion as different forms of discourse analytic work have developed in the different disciplinary environments of linguistics, cognitive psychology, social psychology, sociolinguistics and poststructuralism (for overviews see Phillips and Jørgensen, 2002; Wooffitt, 2005). This chapter will focus on a strand of discourse research often called discursive psychology (sometimes DP below). This is not just a method; it is a broad approach to social life that combines meta-theoretical assumptions, theoretical ideas, analytic orientations and bodies of work. It is a perspective that draws heavily on conversation analytic work (see Heritage in this volume).

DISCURSIVE PSYCHOLOGY

Discursive psychology is a constructionist perspective. That is, DP emphasises the way versions of the world, of society, events and inner psychological worlds are produced in discourse. This leads discursive psychologists to be concerned with participants' constructions and how they are accomplished and undermined (Potter and Hepburn, 2008). This focus on practical epistemics presages and overlaps with the more recent conversation analytic focus on knowledge and sequence (see Potter, 1996, for an overview of the connections). Indeed, this perspective treats realism, whether developed by participants or researchers, as a rhetorical production that can itself be decomposed and studied (Edwards et al., 1995).

DP has an analytic commitment to studying discourse as *texts and talk in social practices*. That is, the focus is not on language as an abstract entity such as a lexicon and set of grammatical rules (in linguistics), a system of differences (in structuralism), a set of rules for transforming statements (in Foucauldian genealogies). Instead, it is the medium for interaction; analysis of discourse becomes, then, analysis of what people do. One theme that is particularly emphasized here is the rhetorical or argumentative organization of talk and texts; claims and versions are constructed to undermine alternatives (Billig, 1996).

DP is neither squarely psychological nor sociological. On the one hand, DP has eaten away at traditional psychological notions by reformulating them in discursive terms. For example, a classic psychological notion such as a cognitive script can be reworked by considering what people do by 'script formulating' descriptions of their own or others' behaviour (Edwards, 1994). DP exposes a territory of study that has remained untouched by mainstream psychology (Edwards, 1997; Edwards and Potter, 1992, Potter and Edwards, 2013).

On the other hand, the micro–macro distinction has also been made problematic. It has been blurred by three kinds of work. First, there is now a range of conversation analytic studies which are concerned with the way in which the institutionally specific properties of a setting such as a news interview, a doctor–patient consultation or an award ceremony are constituted in talk rather than being structurally determined in any simple way (Heritage and Clayman, 2011; see Heritage in this volume). For example, pedagogic interaction certainly happens in school classrooms, and yet much of what happens in classrooms is not pedagogic (playing around, chatting) while much recognisably pedagogic interaction ('test' questions, encouraging discovery) happens over family breakfast tables or with a partner in front of the television. Second, there is work on the way people produce descriptions or stories of social organization in their talk. For example, Wetherell and Potter (1992) studied the way particular constructions of social groups, processes of conflict and influence, histories and so on were drawn on as practical resources for blaming minority groups for their own disadvantaged social position. That is, social structure becomes part of interaction as it is worked up, invoked and reworked (Wiggins and Hepburn, 2007). Third, there is recent work in DP that attempts to highlight the way psychological notions are constructed in and for institutions, and how they can constitute some of the characteristic features of organizations (Edwards, 2008; Butler et al., 2010).

In contemporary DP the overwhelming analytic focus is on the analysis of naturalistic materials: audio or video recordings of people interacting in everyday or institutional settings. Although much earlier discursive work used open-ended interviews, the virtues of working with naturalistic materials and the shortcomings of interviews have become more and more apparent (see Potter and Hepburn, 2005; Silverman, 2007). DP is overwhelmingly qualitative, although the principled argument is not against quantification *per se*, but against the way counting and coding often obscure the activities being done with talk and texts (see Heritage in this volume; Peräkylä in this volume; Schegloff, 1993).

DISCURSIVE PSYCHOLOGY AND METHOD

In traditional stories of method in social research you have a question and then you search for a method to answer that question. For example, you may be interested in the 'factors' that lead to condom use in sexual encounters, and ponder whether to use an experiment with vignettes, some open-ended interviews or discourse analysis to check them out. Adopting DP in this way is a recipe for confusion. Some questions are simply not suited to DP. For example, the kinds of assumptions about factors and outcomes that underpin a lot of thinking in traditional social psychology and sociology do not mesh with its rhetorical and normative logic. Rather than conceiving of a world of discrete variables with discrete effects, in DP there are constructions and versions that may be adopted, responded to or undermined. Thus a categorization, say, may be undermined by a particularization; no upshot is guaranteed (Billig, 1991). Norms are *oriented to*: that is, they are not templates for action but provide a way of interpreting deviations. The absence of a return greeting does not disconfirm a regularity, rather it is the basis for inference: the recipient is rude, sad, deaf perhaps (Heritage, 1988). The general point is that the phenomena that DP studies are highly ordered but not determined – the patterning is a product of ordered choices as interaction unfolds in settings.

So what kinds of questions are coherent within DP? Given the general focus is on texts and talk as social practices, there has been a dual focus on the practices themselves and on the resources that are drawn on in those practices. Take gender inequalities for example. Studies have considered both the way in which such inequalities are constructed, made factual and justified in talk, and they have also considered the resources ('interpretative repertoires', identities, category systems, metaphors) that are used to manufacture coherent and persuasive justifications that work to sustain those inequalities (Wetherell et al., 1987; Clarke et al., 2004; Stokoe, 2011).

NATURALLY OCCURRING TALK AS TOPIC

I am going to focus here on DP specifically as applied to naturally occurring talk. Naturally occurring talk is spoken language produced entirely independent of the actions of the researcher, whether it is everyday conversation over the telephone, the records of a company board meeting, or the interaction between doctor and patient in a surgery. It is natural in the specific sense that it is not 'got up' by the researcher using an interview schedule, a questionnaire, an experimental protocol or some such social research technology. The appropriate test for whether the talk is naturally occurring is whether the talk would have taken place in much the same way if the researcher had been taken ill that morning. Experiments, focus groups and interviews would have had to be cancelled; recordings of therapy sessions or family mealtimes would have carried on regardless.

It is important to note what is distinctive about the considerable body of earlier discursive psychological work that has used open-ended interviews. When interviews are treated as a machinery for harvesting psychologically and linguistically interesting responses, the research is inevitably focused on those elements of interviews contributed by the participant rather than those from the researcher. However, it is possible to conceptualize interviews as arenas for interaction between two or more parties. That is, we can treat them as a form of natural conversational interaction, by analysing them in the same way that we might a telephone conversation between friends or the cross-examination in a courtroom.

How is discursive psychology related to ethnomethodology and conversation analysis?

Contemporary discursive psychology draws heavily on the analytic methods of conversation analysis (see Heritage in this volume). There are a number of areas of divergence:

1. *Construction*: DP is constructionist in the sense that it takes a specific focus on the way versions and descriptions are assembled to perform actions. The construction and use of descriptions is a topic of study

(Potter, 1996). Many of the themes in the discursive psychology work on fact construction are developed further in conversation analysis (particularly in the emerging fields of epistemics and benefactives).

2. *Rhetoric*: whereas conversation analytic work is focused on sequential organization, discursive psychology is focused on that but also focused on rhetorical organization – the way versions are put together to counter alternatives. An understanding of sequential organization is often a prerequisite for understanding rhetorical organization.

3. *Cognition*: discursive psychology is an alternative to dominant cognitivist perspectives in psychology. It rejects the aim of explaining action by reference to underlying cognitive states. The difficult issue of the status of cognition in ethnomethodology and CA is a source of some disagreement (see papers in te Molder and Potter, 2005). Edwards (1995a) has offered an anti-cognitivist reading of Sacks; Potter (2006) has provided an analysis of cognitivist assumptions in some of Drew's conversation analytic work (e.g. Drew, 2005). Te Molder (2016) gives a recent summary of issues in this area.

Up to now I have addressed a number of background issues for discourse analytic research. There is a range of other concerns to do with transcription, interview conduct, coding, forms of validation, writing up discourse research that there is no space to discuss here (see Potter, 2012). For a more detailed coverage of these see Antaki et al. (2003), Hepburn and Potter (2003), Potter and Wetherell (1987), McKinlay and McVittie (2008), Wetherell et al. (2001a, 2001b), and Wiggins and Potter (2008). For the rest of this chapter I will focus on a particular example, with the aim of illustrating the analytic mentality involved in discourse analytic research on talk.

DISCURSIVE PSYCHOLOGY AND NATURALLY OCCURRING TALK

There is a wide range of different ways of analysing discourse. It is useful to make a distinction between studies that focus on the kinds of resources drawn on in discourse and the practices in which those resources are used. The emphasis here will be on the latter kind of study. What I will do is highlight some of the concerns that analysis works with, and one of the best ways of doing this is to work with some specific materials. It will try to avoid the common goal in writing about method that is to provide justifications to other academics rather than assist in the conduct of analysis itself.

Princess Diana and 'I dunno'

I have chosen to start with a piece of talk that is interesting and is easily available on YouTube in its entirety. It comes from an extended BBC television interview; the interviewer is Martin Bashir and the interviewee is the late Princess Diana (see the Appendix for transcription conventions).

Extract 1

Bashir:	The -Quee:n described nineteen ninety tw↓o: (0.2)
	as her (0.2) ‹annus (0.4) horribilis›. (0.5)
Princess:	[((adjusts posture))　　]
Bashir:	[.Dhh and it was in that] year: that (0.2) Andrew
	Morton's book about you was published.
Princess:	Mhm. ((nods and blinks))
Bashir:	Dhhh did ↑you ever: (0.6) meet ↓Andrew Morton,
	[or personally (.) help him with the] book?
Princess:	[((raises eyebrows, shakes head))]
Princess:	I never- (0.3) I [never met him.]
Princess:	[((shakes head))]
	(0.4)
Princess:	No.
	[(1.5)]
Princess:	[((shakes head and purses lips))] (0.8)
Bashir:	Did you ever (0.2) personally (0.2) assist
	him with the writing of his book.
	(0.8)
Princess:	A lot of people.hhh ((clears throat))
	saw the distress (0.4) that my life (.) was (.) in. (0.8)
Princess:	And they felt- (0.8) felt it was a supportive thing to h:elp. (1.0)
Princess:	In the way that they did. [(2.4)]
Princess:	[((purses lips))]
Bashir:	Did you: (0.6) allow your frien:ds, ›your
	close friends‹ to speak to Andrew °Morton°?
Princess:	Yes I did. (1.0)
Princess:	((nodding)) Ye[s I d]id.
Bashir:	[°Why°.] (0.7)
Princess:	Hh I was: [(0.5) at the end of my tether.]
Princess:	[(((shaking head))]
	(0.4)
Princess:	I was: [(0.9) desperate.]
Princess:	[((shaking head))]
	(1.5)
Princess:	›I ↑think I was so fed up with being‹ (0.2).h
	see:n (0.3) as someone who was a ba:sket case. (0.8)
Princess:	Cos I am a very strong person,.h (0.2)
	and I know (0.3).h that causes complications. (0.8)
Princess:	In the system (.) that I (0.4) live in.
	[(4.0)]
Princess:	[(((smiles then purses lips))]
Bashir:	How would a book (0.7) change that?
Princess:	[↑I dunno..hh]
Princess:	[(((raises eyebrows, looks away))]
	Maybe people have a better understanding, (0.6)
	maybe there's a lot of women out there,.h
	who suffer. (0.9)

Princess: On the same level but in a different environment? (0.2)
Princess: Who are unable to:.h (0.2) stand up for themselves? (0.2)
Princess: Becau:se (0.3).h their self-esteem is (0.2)
                           c-cut [into two, (0.2) I dun↑no]
Princess: [((shakes head))   ]

(from *Panorama*, BBC1, 20 November 1995)

The first thing to note here is that even a short sequence of interaction of this kind is enormously rich, and could be the startpoint for a wide range of different studies. For example, conversation analysts have considered the way the different interactional roles of interviewer and interviewee are produced, and the way issues such as neutrality and evasiveness are managed (Clayman and Heritage, 2002). I am going to pick up a theme more characteristic of discursive psychology in particular. I am going to focus principally on just the two lines that have been arrowed – the two 'I dunno's. Why these? There are three reasons, all of which illustrate different facets of doing discursive psychological research.

First, these fragments of talk relate to broader and established analytic concerns with fact construction and the role of descriptions in interaction. The point, then, is that although I have not come to this material with a pre-set hypothesis of the kind that a social psychologist might have when designing an experiment, my way into it is related to a wide range of prior interests, knowledge and concerns. However, there is nothing particularly special about the topic of fact construction; a range of different established interests could be brought to bear on this same material.

Second, these fragments are easily treated as the trivial details of interaction. If we were to make a precis of the interaction we would probably not draw attention to them. On the video they sound almost throwaway. However, one of the features of talk that has been strongly emphasized by Harvey Sacks (1992) and other conversation analysts is that what may seem to be minor details can be highly significant for interactants. Social scientists often treat talk as a conduit for information between speakers: there is a message and it is passed from one person to another. When we use this picture it is easy to imagine that what is important is some basic package of information, and then there is a lot of rather unimportant noise added to the signal: hesitations, pauses, overlaps, choice of specific words and so on. For discursive psychologists this view is fundamentally misguided. Rather than treating these features of talk as simply a blurred edge on the pure message, these features are treated as determining precisely what action is being performed as well as providing a rich resource that both participants and analysts use for understanding what that activity is.

It is for this reason that talk is carefully transcribed as it is delivered rather than being rendered into the conventional 'playscript' that is common in many kinds of qualitative work. Note that it is sometimes complained that such transcription is unnecessary, unhelpful or even – sin of sins – positivistic! However, it is important to remember that the playscript that often passes for transcript is itself highly conventionalized and makes a set of mainly inexplicit assumptions about interaction.

The third reason for focusing on 'I dunno' is that it provides a neat way of contrasting discursive psychology with a cognitive psychological approach to talk. What might a cognitive psychologist make of 'I dunno's? There are all sorts of possibilities, but one approach that might be taken is to treat such utterances as 'uncertainty tokens'; that is, words or expressions that people use to report states of uncertainty. This would be in line with the general cognitive psychological approach of relating language use to an individual's cognitive processes and representations (Edwards, 1997). Considering 'I dunno's therefore has the virtue of allowing us to compare and contrast a cognitive and discursive approach to talk.

One of the notable features of discourse research is that the best way to start making sense of a set of materials like this may be to consider *other* materials or *other* sorts of findings. At its most basic, a good feel for some of the standard features of everyday and institutional talk is essential for producing high-quality analyses. In this case, I suggest that one of the ways into Princess Diana's 'I dunno's is to consider the way issues of stake and interest have been conceptualized in discursive psychology.

Stake as a participant's concern

Work in the ethnomethodological and conversation analytic tradition has highlighted the centrality of accountability in interaction. Discursive psychologists dealing with psychological issues have emphasized the significance that participants place on issues of stake and interest (Edwards and Potter, 1992). People treat each other as entities with desires, motives, institutional allegiances and so on, as having a stake in their actions and those actions is seen to benefit some parties rather than others. Referencing stake is one principal way of discounting the significance of an action or reworking its nature. For example, a blaming can be discounted as merely a product of spite; an offer may be discounted as an attempt to influence. This work covers ground that has been more recently addressed by conversation analysts using the notion of benefactives (Clayman and Heritage, 2014).

Here is an explicit example where the speaker invokes an interest to undercut a (reported) claim. The extract is from a current affairs programme in which the author Salman Rushdie is being interviewed by David Frost. Frost is asking about the *fatwa* – the religious death sentence on Rushdie.

Extract 2

      Frost: And how could they cancel it now? Can they cancel it - they say they can't.

→   **Rushdie**:   Yeah, but you know, they would, wouldn't they, as somebody once said. The thing is, without going into the kind of arcana of theology, there is no technical problem. The problem is not technical. The problem is that they don't want to.

                                         (Public Broadcasting Service, 26 November 1993 - their transcript)

Rushdie's response to the claim that the *fatwa* cannot be cancelled is to discount the claim as obviously motivated. The familiar phrase 'they would, wouldn't they' treats the Iranians' claim as something to be expected: it is the sort of thing that people with that background, those interests, that set of attitudes *would* say; and it formulates that predictability as shared knowledge. This extract illustrates the potential for invoking stake and interest to discount claims.

Both discourse and conversation analysts have stressed that where some difficulty or issue is widespread, there are likely to be some well-developed procedures for dealing with it. For example, given the established procedures that exist for managing turn taking we would expect there to be some procedures to exist for terminating conversations, and this is what is found (Schegloff and Sacks, 1973). Or, to take a more discourse analytic example, given that scientists tend to keep separate the inconsistent repertoires of terms they use for justifying their own claims and undermining those of opponents, we would expect that some devices would be developed for dealing with situations where those repertoires come together; and this is what is found (Gilbert and Mulkay, 1984).

Such features of discourse can be understood by a medical analogy. People can avoid catching a disease such as tuberculosis by being inoculated against it. Perhaps in the same way conversationalists and writers can limit the ease with which their talk and texts can be undermined by doing a *stake inoculation* (Potter, 1996). Just as you have a jab to prevent the disease, perhaps you can inject a piece of discourse to prevent your talk being undermined.

'I dunno' as a stake inoculation

So far, then, I have emphasized some background considerations that might help us understand what Princess Diana's 'I dunno's in Extract 1 are doing. One helpful way to continue the analysis is to collect some more examples of a similar kind. More formally, we might think of this as building a corpus for study or even coding a set of data. Whatever we call it, the goal is to help the analyst see patterns and to highlight different properties of particular constructions. Although some of the initial procedures are superficially similar, the goal is not the content analytic one of providing counts of occurrences of particular kinds of talk within categories.

A search for 'I don't know's through a set of materials taken from relationship counselling sessions provided Extract 3 below. The extract comes from the start of a long story in which the speaker, Jimmy, is describing a difficult evening in a pub with his wife, Connie. As well as Connie and Jimmy there is a counsellor present. One of the themes in the session is a series of complaints by Jimmy about Connie flirting with other men. At the same time Connie has made a number of suggestions that he is pathologically jealous and prone to seeing harmless sociability as sexual suggestion (Edwards, 1995b).

Extract 3

Jimmy:	This ↑one particular <u>night</u>, (0.2)	
	anyway (0.2) there was uh: (1.2) I didn't-	
	Connie had made ar<u>range</u>ments to ↑<u>meet</u> people.	
	(1.8)	
	And I didn't <u>want</u> to. (0.6)	
	It <u>was</u>n't any <u>o</u>ther thing.	
	(1.6)	
	A:nd (0.8) we <u>sat</u> in the pub and	
	we (.) <u>start</u>ed to discuss=	
	=>we had a <u>little</u> bit of a <u>row</u>.< (2.0)	
	In the pub. (0.6)	
	And <u>argu</u>ing about the time. (0.8)	
	U:m (.) whe:n these people came in. (.)	
	>It was:< (.) John and Caroline. (1.0)	
	And then they <u>had</u>- (.)	
	this <u>other</u> fella <u>Dave</u>.	
	oWith them as well.o	
	[6 lines omitted]	
	they <u>all</u> came in the pub anyway. (1.0)	
	Well (.) Connie sat beside (0.6) Caroline.	
	And I sat (further back).	
	So you was (.) you was split between us.	
	They <u>sat</u> in- on the <u>o</u>ther side.	
	(1.0)	
	[16 lines omitted]	
	And uh:: (1.0)	
1→	Connie had a short skirt on	
2→	I don't know. (1.0)	
	And I kn<u>ew</u> this- (0.6)	
	uh ah- maybe I <u>had</u> met him. (1.0) Ye:h. (.)	
	I musta met Da:ve before. (0.8)	
	But I'd <u>heard</u> he was a bit of a la:d ( ).	
	He <u>didn't</u> care: (1.0) <u>who</u> he (0.2) chatted up or (.)	
	<u>who</u> was in Ireland (.) y'know	
	those were (unavailable) to chat up with.	
	(1.0)	
	So <u>C</u>onnie stood up (0.8)	
	pulled her skirt right up her side (0.6)	
	and she was looking <u>straight</u> at Da:ve (.)	
	>olike thato< (0.6)	

(DE:C2:S1:10-11)

Let us start by considering Jimmy's description of Connie's skirt length (arrow 1). For Jimmy this description does some important business related to why they are here for counselling, and who has the problems that need fixing. The short skirt exemplifies something about Connie's character. It is a building block in the construction of Connie as 'flirty', making this an objective particular rather than just Jimmy's opinion. He is merely reporting something that she chose to wear rather than engaging in psychological judgement. However, the description is an especially delicate one, which means that Jimmy's stake in it is likely to be something to be scrutinized. The problem for Jimmy is that the description could be turned round and used as evidence that he is *precisely* the sort of pathologically jealous guy who obsessively remembers every detail of his partner's skirt length. That is, his description might generate problems for him as much as for Connie. How can he manage this delicacy?

It is immediately after the description of the skirt length that Jimmy says 'I don't know' (arrow 2). Why might he be saying just this just here? Let us consider the possibility that it attempts to head off the potential counter that Jimmy was jealously inspecting Connie's clothing, that he was *already* concerned about it even before the evening was under way? This interpretation is consistent with the detail of the sequence. Jimmy provides a description of Connie's skirt length that is part of his picture of *her* flirtatious behaviour, which, in turn, makes *his* own strong reaction more accountable. At the same time the expression of uncertainty works against the idea that *he* is saying this, noticing this, because *he* is pathologically jealous.

Why not treat the 'I don't know' as Jimmy straightforwardly reporting his uncertainty about this feature of the narrative? This would be in line with the cognitive psychological account of such utterances as 'uncertainty markers'. Can we adjudicate between these different interpretations of 'I don't know'? There are various ways we might go about this. One approach that discourse analysts have found particularly fruitful has been to look for variability between different versions. Variability is to be expected where people are constructing their talk in different ways to perform different actions – variability in and between versions can be an important clue to understanding what action is being done. In this case, for example, we can search the materials for other references to Connie's skirt length. We do not have to look very hard! The very first thing Connie says after Jimmy's long narrative is the following.

Extract 4

Connie: My skirt <u>prob</u>ably went up to about there. ((gestures))
Jimmy: ((gives a sharp intake of breath))
Connie: <u>May</u>be a bit <u>short</u>er. It was <u>done</u> for <u>no</u>- I never <u>look</u>ed at that particular bloke when I did it it was my friend commented
Oh you're <u>show</u>ing o:ff a lot o' leg tonight.

(DE:C2:S1:11)

Two things are particularly worth highlighting here. First, note that despite various dramatic events in Jimmy's long narrative of which this is just a fragment (including a suicide attempt) the very first thing that Connie picks out to contest is the description of her skirt length. In doing this she is displaying a skilled awareness of the relationship of descriptions to moral categories. This is a display that we can use to help support our own understanding of the working of this description.

Second, note that *here* Jimmy does not seem to be in any doubt about the precise length of Connie's skirt. His sharp, highly audible, in-breath is a display of disagreement with Connie's gestural measure of her skirt length that occasions a grudging modification by Connie. The point, then, is that there is no evidence of Jimmy's cloudy memory – there is no 'I dunnoness' here; precision in skirt length now seems to be the order of the day. This variability supports the tentative discursive psychological interpretation of this 'I dunno' as a stake inoculation and it does not fit with the plain vanilla cognitive account in which the speaker merely reports their lack of certainty.

Let us return now to Martin Bashir's interview with Princess Diana. We are now in a better position to make some systematic suggestions about the 'I dunno's in this passage of talk. We can start to make sense of their role in the management of stake and interest, and in particular their operation as stake inoculations.

The first thing we need to be confident of is that there is an orientation to issues of stake in this material. It is not hard to find. Bashir opens the sequence by formulating the relation between Andrew Morton's book and a hard year for the Queen (her well-known *annus horribilis*). Bashir then pursues a line of questioning with the Princess about her involvement with this book. He attempts to tease out for the viewing audience how responsible she is for this (negatively constructed) book.

Princess Diana responds to these questions with a series of denials, evasions, accounts and implicit versions of the role of the book (in that order in response to the first three questions). However, having accepted that she had some involvement with the book, if only via her friends, she is now faced with a tricky question about how the book make a positive contribution (how would a book change that?). This question is so tricky because of its potential for suggesting that Princess Diana has acted as a spurned and vindictive ex-wife, getting her revenge for a book that Prince Charles was involved with (mentioned soon after this extract). Given this issue of stake, we can make sense of the placement of the two 'I dunno's. The uncertainty displayed in the answer to 'how would a book change all of that?' precisely manages the danger that she will be seen as calculating and malevolent, a woman who has carefully planned her revenge. The 'I dunno's help break the connection between her action of helping with the book and the potentially noxious identity implied in this action. Note the coordination of verbal and non-verbal here. Her first 'I dunno' is accompanied by what might be called a display of wondering – she looks into the distance as if never having been asked this before or had to think about it before. It is a lovely exhibition of psychological matters being attended to by both vocal and non-vocal actions.

This is by no means a definitive account of the role of 'I dunno' in Extract 1. And, of course, it does not address the very many other live and relevant features of the extract. However, what I have tried to do is show some of the procedures that can help build an interpretation of a piece of discourse, and the mentality that goes with such analysis. Let me list some of these features

THEMES IN THE ANALYSIS OF DISCOURSE

This chapter has attempted to overview some of the issues that arise when analysing discourse. Developing analytic skills is best characterized as developing a particular mentality. Discursive psychology is more inductive than hypothetico-deductive; generally work starts with a setting or particular discursive phenomenon rather than a preformulated hypothesis. The focus is on texts and talk as social practices in their own right. Part of the procedure of discursive psychology may involve the coding of a set of materials, but this is an analytic preliminary used to build a corpus of manageable size rather than a procedure that performs the analysis itself. There is nothing sacred about such codings and extracts are often freely excluded and included in the course of a programme of research.

Discursive psychology follows the conversation analytic assumption that any order of detail in talk and text is potentially consequential for interaction, and for that reason high-quality transcripts are used in conjunction with audio or video recordings. In addition, discursive psychology research generally avoids trading on analysts' prior assumptions about what might be called ethnographic particulars (e.g. participants' status, the nature of the context, the goals of the participants), preferring to see these as things that are worked up, attended to and made relevant in interaction rather than being external determinants.

Discursive psychology does not use talk and texts as a pathway to underlying cognitions; indeed, discursive psychology resolutely steers clear of cognitive reduction, instead treating purportedly cognitive phenomena as parts of social practices. It has focused, for example, on the way participants invoke stake and interest to understand and undercut accounts, and how such undercutting may be resisted by performing actions via accounts that are constructed as factual. It has focused on the way who will benefit is subtly embedded in the construction of descriptions without being necessarily marked through explicit grammar (cf. Clayman and Heritage, 2014).

In this chapter I illustrated these themes by way of a discussion of 'I dunno' and 'I don't know'. I have considered only a small number of examples. However, I hope that the insights are more general. Let me end with an extract from the US sitcom *Friends*. Even with my minimal, cleaned up transcription I think we can start to see the way the humour in the sequence depends on the sorts of features of 'I don't know' discussed above, and in particular the way each 'I don't know' manages the delivery of a piece of subtle psychological insight that generates trouble for the recipients. The sequence starts with Ross talking to a psychologist, Rodge, about his ex-wife.

Extract 5

Ross: You see that's where you're wrong! Why would
            I marry her if I thought on any level that
            she was a lesbian?

Rodge:	I don't know. ((shrugs)) Maybe you wanted your ← marriage to fail. ((laughs))
Ross:	Why, why, why would I, why, why, why?
Rodge:	I don't know. Maybe ... Maybe low self esteem, ← maybe to compensate for overshadowing a sibling. Maybe you w-
Monica:	W- w- wait. Go back to that sibling thing.
Rodge:	I don't know. ((shrugs)) It's conceivable that ← you wanted to sabotage your marriage so the sibling would feel less like a failure in the eyes of the parents.
Ross:	Tchow! That's, that's ridiculous. I don't feel guilty for her failures.

(*The One with the Boobies*, 27 June 1996 - Ross is Monica's brother, Rodge is a psychologist boyfriend of Ross and Monica's friend. Note, each 'I don't know' is heavily emphasized)

CHAPTER SUMMARY

This chapter overviewed discursive psychology. It described basic theoretical and methodological themes and distinguished discursive psychology from conversation analysis. The analytic approach of discursive psychology was introduced by way of an exploration of the role of 'I dunno' in different kinds of materials. This was interpreted in terms of participants managing their stake in particular delicate actions that they are performing.

FUTURE PROSPECTS

In the past decade discursive psychological work has increasingly focused on building programmes of work on large collections of talk taken from different institutional settings (helplines, neighbour mediation). It has moved beyond making theoretically targeted demonstrations of points to building full-scale studies that accumulate into programmes of work.

At the same time there has been an increasingly close engagement with conversation analysis such that at times the two perspectives overlap or merge. The enormous analytic rigour and system of conversation analysis has been an important influence on the development of discursive psychological work. It is likely that this close engagement will continue bearing analytic fruit as well as interesting debates.

In the past few years discursive psychologists have started to focus on video recordings of face-to-face interaction in family settings, with a particular focus on the coordination of action and how traditionally developmental issues (what can young children do?) become live for the participants. Work of this kind will continue with a focus on applied questions, for example relating to issues of health and the delivery of social services.

Study questions

1. Summarize the differences between discursive psychology and conversation analysis. Try to decide which differences are most consequential for their different analytic practices (if any).
2. Compare the analysis of 'I dunno' here with that developed by Weatherall (2011). How do they complement one another? Are there points of tension?
3. Go through the *Friends* extract from the end of the chapter and carefully examine each 'I dunno' and consider the way it draws attention to the kinds of stake inoculation that such constructions can perform.

Recommended reading

Edwards, D. (1997) *Discourse and Cognition*. London and Beverly Hills, CA: Sage.
Highlights the interplay of discursive psychology, ethnomethodology and conversation analysis with a range of analyses of psychological matters. A major work that rewards close study.

Potter, J. and Hepburn, A. (2008) 'Discursive constructionism', in J. A. Holstein and J. F. Gubrium (eds), *Handbook of Constructionist Research*. New York: Guildford, pp. 275–93.
This shows how recent analytic work has combined discursive psychology and conversation analysis with a focus on the epistemic and practical business done by descriptions.

Wiggins, S. and Potter, J. (2008) 'Discursive psychology', in C. Willig and W. Hollway (eds), *The Sage Handbook of Qualitative Research in Psychology*. London: Sage, pp. 72–89.
An overview of the different stages in discursive psychological research.

Potter, J. and Edwards, D. (2013) 'Conversation analysis and psychology', in J. Sidnell and T. Stivers (eds), *The Handbook of Conversation Analysis*. Oxford: Wiley-Blackwell, pp. 701-25.
This explores the way psychological matters can be consistently understood from a conversational perspective.

Recommended online resources

The ethnomethodology and conversation analysis wiki is a source of new publications, conferences, and includes a comprehensive bibliography of discursive psychology:
www.emcawiki.net/
The Loughborough Discourse and Rhetoric Group website includes an up-to-date bibliography, information about methods, and examples of transcription alongside sound and video files. Many articles can be downloaded directly:
www.lboro.ac.uk/departments/socialsciences/research/groups/darg/

References

Antaki, C., Billig, M., Edwards, D. and Potter, J. (2003) 'Discourse analysis means doing analysis: a critique of six analytic shortcomings', *Discourse Analysis Online*, 1.

Billig, M. (1991) *Ideologies and Beliefs*. London: Sage.

Billig, M. (1996) *Arguing and Thinking: A Rhetorical Approach to Social Psychology* (2nd edn). Cambridge: Cambridge University Press.

Butler, C. W, Potter, J., Danby, S., Emmison, M. and Hepburn, A. (2010) 'Advice-implicative interrogatives: building "client centred" support in a children's helpline', *Social Psychology Quarterly*, 73: 216–41.

Clarke, V., Kitzinger, C. and Potter, J. (2004) '"Kids are just cruel anyway": lesbian and gay parents' talk about homophobic bullying', *British Journal of Social Psychology*, 43: 531–50.

Clayman, S. E. and Heritage, J. C (2002) *The News Interview: Journalists and Public Figures on the Air*. Cambridge: Cambridge University Press.

Clayman, S. E. and Heritage, J. C. (2014) 'Benefactors and beneficiaries: benefactive status and stance in the management of offers and requests', in P. Drew and E. Couper-Kuhlen (eds), *Requesting in Social Interaction*. Amsterdam: John Benjamins, pp. 55–86.

Drew, P. (2005) 'Is confusion a state of mind?', in H. te Molder and J. Potter (eds), *Conversation and Cognition*. Cambridge: Cambridge University Press, pp. 161–83.

Edwards, D. (1994) 'Script formulations: a study of event descriptions in conversation', *Journal of Language and Social Psychology*, 13 (3): 211–47.

Edwards, D. (1995a) 'Sacks and psychology', *Theory and Psychology*, 5: 579–96.

Edwards, D. (1995b) 'Two to tango: script formulations, dispositions, and rhetorical symmetry in relationship troubles talk', *Research on Language and Social Interaction*, 28: 319–50.

Edwards, D. (1997) *Discourse and Cognition*. London and Beverly Hills, CA: Sage.

Edwards, D. (2008) 'Intentionality and *mens rea* in police interrogations: the production of actions as crimes', *Intercultural Pragmatics*, 5: 177–99.

Edwards, D., Ashmore, M. and Potter, J. (1995) 'Death and furniture: the rhetoric, politics and theology of bottom line arguments against relativism', *History of the Human Sciences*, 8: 25–49.

Edwards, D. and Potter, J. (1992) *Discursive Psychology*. London: Sage.

Gilbert, G. N. and Mulkay, M. (1984) *Opening Pandora's Box: A Sociological Analysis of Scientists' Discourse*. Cambridge: Cambridge University Press.

Hepburn, A. and Potter, J. (2003) 'Discourse analytic practice', in C. Seale, D. Silverman, J. Gubrium and G. Gobo (eds), *Qualitative Research Practice*. London: Sage, pp. 180–96.

Heritage, J. C. (1988) 'Explanations as accounts: a conversation analytic perspective', in C. Antaki (ed.), *Analysing Everyday Explanation: A Casebook of Methods*. London: Sage, pp. 127–44.

Heritage, J. C. and Clayman, S. (2011) *Talk in Action: Interactions, Identities and Institutions*. London: John Wiley.

McKinlay, A. and McVittie, C. (2008) *Social Psychology and Discourse*. London: Wiley Blackwell.

Phillips, L. J. and Jørgensen, M. W. (2002) *Discourse Analysis as Theory and Method*. London: Sage.

Potter, J. (1996) *Representing Reality: Discourse, Rhetoric and Social Construction*. London: Sage.

Potter, J. (2006) 'Cognition and conversation', *Discourse Studies*, 8: 131–40.

Potter, J. (2012) 'Discourse analysis and discursive psychology', in H. Cooper (editor-in-chief), *APA Handbook of Research Methods in Psychology: Vol. 2. Quantitative, Qualitative, Neuropsychological, and Biological*. Washington, DC: American Psychological Association Press, pp. 119–38.

Potter, J. and Edwards, D. (2013) 'Conversation analysis and psychology', in J. Sidnell and T. Stivers (eds), *The Handbook of Conversation Analysis*. Oxford: Wiley-Blackwell, pp. 701–25.

Potter, J. and Hepburn, A. (2003) 'I'm a bit concerned: early actions and psychological constructions in a child protection helpline', *Research on Language and Social Interaction*, 36: 197–240.

Potter, J. and Hepburn, A. (2005) 'Qualitative interviews in psychology: problems and possibilities', *Qualitative Research in Psychology*, 2: 281–307.

Potter, J. and Hepburn, A. (2008) 'Discursive constructionism', in J. A. Holstein and J. F. Gubrium (eds), *Handbook of Constructionist Research*. New York: Guildford, pp. 275–93.

Potter, J. and Wetherell, M. (1987) *Discourse and Social Psychology: Beyond Attitudes and Behaviour*. London: Sage.

Sacks, H. (1992) *Lectures on Conversation*, Vols I and II, ed. G. Jefferson. Oxford: Basil Blackwell.

Schegloff, E. A. (1993) 'Reflections on quantification in the study of conversation', *Research on Language and Social Interaction*, 26: 99–128.

Schegloff, E. A. and Sacks, H. (1973) 'Opening up closings', *Semiotica*, 7: 289–327.

Silverman, D. (2007) *A Very Short, Fairly Interesting and Reasonably Cheap Book about Qualitative Research*. London: Sage.

Stokoe, E. (2011) '"Girl – woman – sorry!": on the repair and non-repair of consecutive gender categories', in S. A. Speer and E. Stokoe (eds), *Conversation and Gender*. Cambridge: Cambridge University Press, pp. 85–111.

Te Molder, H. (2016) 'What happened to post-cognitive psychology?', in C. Tileagă and E. Stokoe (eds), *Discursive Psychology: Classic and Contemporary Issues*. London: Routledge, pp. 87–100.

Te Molder, H. and Potter, J. (eds) (2005) *Conversation and Cognition*. Cambridge: Cambridge University Press.

Weatherall, A. (2011) 'I don't know as a pre-positioned hedge', *Research on Language and Social Interaction*, 44 (4): 317–37.

Wetherell, M. and Potter, J. (1992) *Mapping the Language of Racism: Discourse and the Legitimation of Exploitation*. London: Harvester, New York: Columbia University Press.

Wetherell, M., Stiven, H. and Potter, J. (1987) 'Unequal egalitarianism: a preliminary study of discourses concerning gender and employment opportunities', *British Journal of Social Psychology*, 26: 59–71.

Wetherell, M., Taylor, S. and Yates, S. (eds) (2001a) *Discourse Theory and Practice: A Reader*. London: Sage.

Wetherell, M., Taylor, S. and Yates, S. (eds) (2001b) *Discourse as Data: A Guide for Analysis*. London: Sage.

Wiggins, S. and Hepburn, A. (2007) 'Discursive research: applications and implications', in A. Hepburn and S. Wiggins (eds), *Discursive Research in Practice: New Approaches to Psychology and Interaction*. London: Sage, pp. 281–91.

Wiggins, S. and Potter, J. (2008) 'Discursive psychology', in C. Willig and W. Hollway (eds), *The Sage Handbook of Qualitative Research in Psychology*. London; Sage, pp. 72–89.

Wooffitt, R. (2005) *Conversation Analysis and Discourse Analysis: A Comparative and Critical Introduction*. London: Sage.

THIRTEEN

Conversation Analysis: Practices and Methods

John Heritage

About this chapter

This chapter focuses on the process of identifying, defining and understanding the meaning of specific interactional practices deployed in ordinary interaction. This process involves extracting the practice from a large variety of contexts in order to establish the extent to which it is context-free. Once this is determined, the practice (together with many others) can become the basis for narrowing the range of plausible interpretations of context, intention and meaning indefinitely in many other scenes of inter-action. A worked example - oh-prefacing an answer to a question - is presented as a typical example of conversation analytic practice.

Keywords

context, sequence, practice, reflexivity, comparison, ethnography

In this chapter, my aim is to give an overview of conversation analytic (CA) methods with a particular focus on ordinary conversation. To understand these methods, it is helpful to remember that they are designed to deal with fundamental features of human action and interaction. By the 1960s, there was a broad consensus on a number of these features:

1. *Human actions are meaningful and involve meaning-making*: Human actions (whether spoken or otherwise) are meaningful. Unlike the processes of the physical universe, they are goal directed and based on reasoning about the physical and social circumstances that persons find themselves in (Schütz, 1962; Blumer, 1969). This reasoning involves knowledge, socio-cultural norms and beliefs, and a grasp of the goals and intentions of others. Because goals, intentions and the 'state of play' in interaction can change rapidly, this knowledge and reasoning is continuously updated during the process of interaction itself (Garfinkel, 1967). Social interaction also involves *meaning-making*. Actions, no matter how similar or repetitive, are never identical in meaning (Garfinkel, 1967; Blumer, 1969). Each of them is singular, if only because it takes place in a new and singular situation. Each action therefore is, in some degree, creative in the meaning it creates and conveys.

2. *Actions achieve meaning through a combination of their content and context*: meaning-making is frequently creative just by virtue of the creative power of language. However, to this creativity of content must be added the creative power of context. The meaning of even the most formulaic of actions (such as 'okay', 'mm hm' and so on) is in fact differentiated by context. The contextual variation (and specification) of action is a profound feature of human socio-cultural life, and a second major source of creativity and meaning-making in interaction that works in tandem with the creative power of language. Analysis of action cannot avoid this contextual variation without appearing superficial and irrelevant, not least because human beings exploit context in the construction of action. 'Context' is complex and layered. It embraces the immediately preceding action (someone just said or did something you have to respond to), through medial (that someone is an old friend), to distal (she is rather closer to your significant other than to you).

3. *To be socially meaningful, the meaning of actions must be shared*: human actions are socially meaningful only to the extent that their meaning is shared by the actor, the recipient(s) of the act and (sometimes) other observers. Absent this and actions will be unintelligible to others and will fail to achieve their desired objectives. The shared meaning of actions is constructed by the common use of methods for analysing actions-in-context (Garfinkel, 1967). This means that there must be procedures for persons to check whether their understandings about the meanings of earlier actions are correct, and of whether their responses are 'on target'. As persons construct interaction in an unfolding sequence of moves, they will also have to keep score of 'where they are' in the interaction and of the interaction's 'state of play'. Like 'context', shared (or 'intersubjective') meaning is also layered on a gradient from the most public (I asked you a question and you replied 'No'), to less public but available to some observers (your response betrays the fact that you are not an expert), to more private (your 'No' is rationalizing an unstated anxiety, or reflects a private promise you made to someone else).

4. *Meanings are unique and singular – actions function in particular ways to create meanings that are particular*: implicit in the first three principles is the idea that actions and their meanings are highly particularized. At first sight the extraordinary singularity of human action would seem inimical to any sustained achievement of coherent meaning. Yet it works – somehow! Context elaborates the meanings of utterances. A similar principle applies in interaction: 'Is it serious?' is understood differently in the context of a sprained ankle and a cancer diagnosis. Context specifies meaning.

These four features of action have been extensively discussed within the fields of anthropology and sociology, where they have often been viewed as potential obstacles to a natural science of society. Nonetheless these are the characteristics that a conception of interaction must come to terms with. Social participants somehow manage their interactions in daily life while coping with, and in fact actually exploiting, these characteristics of human conduct. Conversation analysis is a discipline that was developed to come to terms with, and model, these capacities.

BASIC PRINCIPLES OF CA

Sequence

The foundational principles of CA tackle these four fundamental facts of human action by exploiting the concept of *sequence* (Schegloff, 2007). The basic idea is that the most elementary context in which a turn at talk occurs is the immediately preceding turn at talk. It is a default assumption in human conduct that a current action should be, and normally will be, responsive to the immediately prior one. Indeed persons have to engage in special procedures (e.g. 'Oh by the way …') to show that a next action is *not* responsive to the prior.

The inherent turn-by-turn contextuality of conversation is a vital resource for the construction of understanding in interaction. Since each action will be understood as responsive to the previous one, the understanding that it displays is open for inspection. For example, in the following case, Ann's turn in line 1 is treated as an invitation by a response that 'accepts' it:

```
(1)
    Ann: Why don't you come and see me some[times.
    Bar:                      [I would like to
```

By contrast, Barbara could have responded with an apology and an excuse:

```
(2)
    Ann: Why don't you come and see me sometimes.
    Bar: I'm sorry. I've been terribly tied up lately.
```

However, then it would be apparent that Barbara had understood Ann's initial utterance as a complaint rather than an invitation (Heritage, 1984a).

These two understandings are built into the design of the two different responses. They are apparent to observers but, and this is the important point, they are apparent to the participants too. As a result, however the sequence plays out, Ann will find from Barbara's response how Barbara understood her and that Barbara has, or has not, understood her correctly.

We can take this analysis a step further by recognizing that at this point Ann knows how Barbara understood her turn, but Barbara does not know whether she understood it correctly. Continuation of the sequence allows Barbara to make this judgement (Schegloff, 1992):

```
(3)
    Ann: Why don't you come and see me some[times.
    Bar:                 [I would like to
    Ann: I would like you to.
```

Ann's 'accepting' response to Barbara's acceptance confirms Barbara in her belief that she understood Ann correctly. But it could have gone otherwise:

```
(4)
     Ann: Why don't you come and see me some[times.
     Bar:                   [I would like to
     Ann: Yes but why don't you
```

In this second scenario, Barbara would see that her understanding of Ann's first turn at talk as an invitation was mistaken. Ann's response, which renews and indeed escalates her complaint, conveys that her original utterance was in fact intended to have been just that.

The sequential logic inherent in these examples is central to the construction of human interaction as a shared sense-making enterprise, regardless of its social context. Because it is the foundation of courses of conduct that are mutually intelligible, this logic underwrites both the conduct of social interaction and its analysis (see the Appendix for transcription conventions).

Practices

CA investigates interaction by examining the practices which participants use to construct it. A 'practice' is any feature of the design of a turn in a sequence that (a) has a distinctive character, (b) has specific locations within a turn or sequence, and (c) is distinctive in its consequences for the nature or the meaning of the action that the turn implements. Here are three examples of conversational practices:

- Turn-initial address terms designed to select a specific next speaker to respond (Lerner, 2003):

```
(5)
     A:   Gene, do you want another piece of cake?
```

- Elements of question design that convey an expectation favouring a 'yes' or a 'no' answer: in this case the word 'any' conveys an expectation tilted towards a 'no' (Heritage et al., 2007):

```
(6)
     Prof: Do you have any questions?
```

- Oh-prefaced responses to questions primarily conveying that the question was inapposite or out of place (Heritage, 1998):

```
(7)
     Ann: How are you feeling Joyce.=
     Joy: Oh fi:ne.
```

Organizations

The practices that CA finds in interaction cluster into organized collections that centre on fundamental orders of conversational and social organization. Clusters of practices are associated with taking a turn at talk:

- practices of repair that address systematic problems in speaking, hearing and understanding talk
- practices associated with the management of reference to persons and objects in the world (Schegloff, 2006).

Other organizations of practices address more broadly social dimensions of interaction:

- the management of ties of social solidarity and affiliation between persons, favouring their maintenance and militating against their destruction
- the management of epistemic rights to knowledge between persons which is an important dimension of personal identity (Heritage, 2008).

Key points

CA research works at three main levels:

1. sequences of actions
2. the interactional practices that are involved in the construction of actions
3. larger organizations of practices focused on the management of interaction, and of social relationships more generally.

METHODS FOR STUDYING PRACTICES

CA methods for isolating and studying interactional practices have a good deal in common with the method of analytic induction, and in particular the constant comparative method and the search for deviant cases (Glaser and Strauss, 1967). The method, of course, is specified to the interactional subject matter of conversation analysis as follows.

Stage 1: Deciding that a practice is 'distinctive'

First some practice, or candidate practice, will emerge as 'interesting' or worthy of pursuit. For simplicity, we will exemplify this with a fairly well-researched practice: the oh-prefacing of responses to questions and other 'first actions' (Heritage, 1984b, 1998, 2002). Initially the practice will very likely emerge as 'vague' or 'imprecise' (Schegloff, 1997). For example, at first sight, (8) and (9) below look rather similar. In (8) Steve and Lesley are talking about the late publishing magnate Robert Maxwell. Steve mentions that Maxwell's parents had suffered at the hands of the Nazis, whereupon Lesley infers that Maxwell is Jewish. Steve confirms this at line 8, beginning his turn with an 'oh' that is intonationally 'run into' the next component of his response as a single unit of talk (a single turn constructional unit, Sacks et al., 1974).

```
(8) [Field:2:3:9]
1    Ste: Well he didn't either 'ee had a bad start I mean 'ee had 'iz
2    1-> (0.3) .t.k.hh father shot by the Nazis 'nd is uh .hh mother
3       died in: Auschvitz yih kno:w [so
4    Les:           [Oh really:?=
5    Ste: =So eez [had the: ( ] )-
6    Les: 2-> [Oh 'z a Je:w] is he Je:w?
7       (.)
8    Ste: 3-> Oh yeah.
9       (.)
10   Ste:  He's had k- 'eez a Czechoslovakian Jew so ...
```

In (9) as part of an arrangements-making sequence, Ivy's question at line 5 is countered by one from Jane (lines 6–7). Ivy responds with 'oh' and subsequently a response to the question. Her 'oh' is intonationally distinct and seems to be its own unit of response, temporally separated from the subsequent answer (lines 8–10). At this point in the investigation, while it is clear that the two responses are distinctive in that the first 'oh' is 'run into' the next component of the response while the second is not, it is not clear that the distinction makes a difference in terms of the meaning of the actions they are performing.

```
(9) [Rah:C:1:(16):3]
1    Ivy:  An' then (.) she'll pick you up on the way: down then as
2       ah said.
3       (0.3)
4    Jan:  Well it's a [bit eh in a[h it
5    Ivy: 1->      [Is  [Is that too early.
6    Jan: 2-> eh- No: no it's not too early it's jist uh how long is she
7       gon'to be in Middles[ber. Thi[s's the th[ing.
8    Ivy: 3->        [.hhh [Oh:. [She's got tuh be
9       ho:me by .hh i-jis turned half past eleven quartuh tih
10      twelve.
```

So now we have a candidate practice: beginning a turn with the word 'oh'. We don't really know much about its meaning yet, and we don't really know whether 'beginning' means being part of the same unit of the talk that follows, or whether 'free-standing' cases followed by more talk from the same speaker are part of the same practice.

Stage 2: Locating the practice sequentially

At the end of stage 1, we have identified our phenomenon – the production of 'oh' at the beginning of a turn. We have located the practice within the turn, but not within particular sequences. As we now search for other instances, these will start to get clearer. Cases like the following start to pile up.

(10) [Heritage:01:18:2]

```
1   Jan:    .t Okay now that's roas:' chick'n isn'it. Th[at ]=
2   Ivy:                          [It-]=
3   Jan:    =[roasting chick'n‹]
4   Ivy: 1-› =[i t h a s bee:n ] cooked.
5        (.)
6   Ivy:   1-› It's been co[oked.
7   Jan: 2-›   [Iz ↑BEEN cooked.=
8   Ivy: 3-› =Oh yes.
9   Jan:   Oh well thaz good......
```

(11) [NB:II:2:R:7]

```
1   Nan:    .....hhh one a'the other girls hadda leave
2        1-› fer something en there I sit with all these (h)you(h)ng
3        1-› fellas I fel'like a den [mother.
4   Emm:                      [°Uh huh°
5   Nan:    .hhh[hh
6   Emm: 2-›     [Are you th:e ol:dest one the cla:ss?
7   Nan: 3-›  °Oh: w- by fa:r.°
8   Emm:   ↑Are yih rill[y?↑
9   Nan: 3-›         [°Oh: ya:h.°
10  Emm:   Didju learn a lo:t'n cla:ss?
```

These cases are strongly consistent with (8). In each case, the first speaker (1->) makes an observation which is the object of a pretty obvious inference by the second (2->), and then the first speaker re-affirms it (3->), perhaps conveying that the second speaker was questioning something 'obvious' that didn't need to be asked.

A further product of looking at these cases is that (9) starts to look different from the others. In this case a questioner turns out to have made incorrect assumptions about the situation being inquired into (arrow 1). Following the correction (arrow 2), the speaker uses a stand-alone 'oh' (arrow 3) to acknowledge the new understanding (Heritage, 1984b) – and by implication her earlier misapprehension – before going on to address the newly revealed circumstances. This difference is reinforced by cases like (12) which concerns a mutual acquaintance who has been looking for a job:

(12) [Rah:II:1]

```
1   Ver:   And she's got the application forms.=
2   Jen: 1-› =Ooh:: so when is her interview did she sa[:y?
```

```
3  Ver:         [She
4  2-> didn't (.) Well she's gotta send their fo:rm
5     back. Sh[e doesn't know when the [interview is yet.
6  Jen: 3->  [O h : : .    [Oh it's just the
7     form,
```

Once again an initial question (1->) turns out to be based on faulty assumptions (2->), and a free-standing 'oh' registers that fact before its speaker goes on display a revised understanding of the situation (3->). We are ready, then, to say that (9) and (12) are distinctive from (8), (10) and (11).

Stage 3: Determining the distinctive role or meaning of the practice

It is clear enough from the materials to hand that oh-prefaced responses to questions often emerge in contexts where a speaker questions something that has already been stated or strongly implied, and the answer to the question is therefore obvious or self-evident. But is there evidence that the participants orient to this role or meaning for the practice?

The clearest evidence emerges when the questioner who got an oh-prefaced response then defends the relevance of the question. This is what happens in (13) and (14):

```
(13) [TG:10]
1  Bee:  Dihyuh have any-cl- You have a class with Billy this te:rm?
2  Ava:  Yeh he's in my abnormal class.
3  Bee:  mnYeh [ how-]
4  Ava:      [Abnor]mal psy[ch.
5  Bee: 1->         [Still not gettin married,
6  Ava: 2=> .hhh Oh no. Definitely not.[married.]
7  Bee: 3->         [No he's] dicided [defin[itely?]
8  Ava: 4=>               [.hhh [O h ] no.
9  Bee: 5-> `hh Bec'z [las'] time you told me he said no: but he wasn't su:re,
10 Ava:      [ No.]
11 Ava:  n:No definitely not. He, he'n Gail were like on the outs,
12     yihknow,
```

Here Bee defends her question at line 5, by reference to earlier statements she attributes to Ava about Billy's marital intentions being 'not sure' (3-> and 5->). And in (14) Ann defends her initial question by reference to what somebody else had told her about Joyce's health. As it turns out, Joyce had been unwell, but not very recently (line 5).

```
(14) [Frankel QC:I:2SO:1]
1  Ann:  How are you feeling Joyce.=
2  Joy:  Oh fi:ne.
3  Ann:  'Cause- I think Doreen mentioned that you weren't so well?
```

```
4       A few [weeks ago:?]
5   Joy:    [Yeah,   ] Couple of weeks ago.
6   Ann:  Yeah. And you're alright no:[w?
7   Joy:            [Yeah.
```

In other cases, questioners may register that they already knew the answer, as in (15):

```
(15) [Frankel:TC:l:1:17]
1   Sus:   =Yeh you guys er g'nna drive up aren'tchu,
2   Mar:   Oh yea:h.
3   Sus: -> That's what I figu[red.
4   Mar:            [Yeh,=
```

Or that they have temporarily forgotten the circumstances that make the question inappropriate, as in (16), lines 4 and 6:

```
(16) [Frankel TC:1:1:15-16]
1   Sus:   .hhh So if you guys want a place tuh sta:y.
2       (0.3)
3   Mar:   .t.hhh Oh (w-) thank you but you we ha- yihknow Victor.
4   Sus: -> ↑OH that's ↑RIGHT.=
5   Mar:   =That's why we were going [(we)
6   Sus: ->            [I FER↑GO:T. Completely.
```

Key points

Our practice - oh-prefacing a response to a question - is now very robust:

1. It has a definite 'shape:': the 'oh' must be turn-initial and part of a larger unit of talk, not a separate free-standing element of it.
2. It is located in a specific sequential position: in response to a question.
3. It has a determinate 'meaning' that is reflected in a variety of responses to its production.

The position our analysis has arrived at is presented in Table 13.1 below:

Table 13.1   Two types of turn-initial 'oh'

Type of Turn-initial 'Oh'	Position	Role or Meaning of the Practice
Prefacing 'Oh'	As a response to a question	Showing that the answer to a question was self-evident and that the question need hardly have been asked
Free-standing 'Oh' + more talk	As a response to an answer to a question	Registering the answer to the question as informative

A CONTEXT-FREE PRACTICE

One of the chief objectives of basic CA is to identify bedrock practices of interaction, whose meaning and significance are fundamental and obdurate. To this end, an important test is to make sure that practices operate in a stable way across a wide range of social contexts.

With this in mind, consider the following example from a broadcast interview with Sir Harold Acton, conducted by the British broadcaster Russell Harty. The topic is Acton's life in China and his work as a teacher of T. S. Eliot's poetry at Beijing University. At this point, Harty ventures to ask him if he speaks Chinese:

```
(18) [Chat Show: Russell Harty–Sir Harold Acton]
1   Act:   ....hhhh and some of thuh- (0.3) some of my students
2          translated Eliot into Chine::se. I think thuh very
3          first.
4          (0.2)
5   Har:   Did you learn to speak (.) Chine[:se.
6   Act: ->              [.hh Oh yes.
7          (0.7)
8   Act:   .hhhh You cah::n't live in thuh country without speaking
9          thuh lang[uage it's impossible .hhhhh=
10  Har: ->          [Not no: cour:se
```

Acton's response (line 6) is oh-prefaced, and plainly treats it as self-evident that he 'speaks Chinese'. And he elaborates it with an observation about how necessary it is to speak the language of a host country (lines 8–9). For his part, Harty acknowledges the self-evident truth of this observation with his *sotto voce* 'Not no: cour:se' (line 10). Here then the practice is deployed to very similar effect in a very different social setting – a celebrity interview – than in the cases we have seen so far. News interviews contain very many instances of this type.

Similarly in the following case, a doctor finds himself on the receiving end of this practice – in this case, the patient is quite elderly:

```
(19) [Routine physical]
1   DOC:   Hi Missis Mar[:ti:n,
2   PAT:        [Hi (there)
3   DOC:   How are you toda:[:y,
4   PAT: 1->       [Oh pretty goo:d,
5        (.)
6   DOC:   How are you fee:ling.
7   DOC: 2-> The l[ast time I saw you you had broken that ↑ri:b.↑=
8   PAT:   [Oh oka:y,
9   PAT:   =Mm hm:,
10  DOC:    Are you doing a little bit better:,
```

Similar to (14), the doctor's 'how are you' question (line 3), together with his 'follow-up' 'how are you feeling' (line 6) solicit health 'updates' from the patient (Robinson, 2006).

Both, however, inherit oh-prefaced responses. By line 7, the doctor defends the relevance of his question by invoking the patient's earlier broken rib as grounds for his inquiry. Here too, in the context of the medical consultation, our practice is robust.

A CONTEXT-SENSITIVE PRACTICE AND EXPLOITATIONS

Robust interactional practices like oh-prefacing have the property of 'reflexivity:' they can convey the meaning that is anchored in routine exchanges in non-routine situations. Here is an example from the celebrated trial of O. J. Simpson in Los Angeles, as narrated by a journalist:

> (20) [Margolick, 1995]
>
> 'She [Marcia Clark] also asked Mr. Kaelin whether the place Mr. Simpson took him to eat earlier that evening was not a McDonald's but a Burger King. It was a clear reference to published reports, heretofore entirely unsubstantiated, that Mr. Simpson and Mr. Kaelin went out in the evening of June 12 not to purchase hamburgers and french fries but drugs. 'Oh no', Mr. Kaelin replied, almost in wonder that such a question would be asked'.

And, transparently exploitative is this reply from one of the police officers on trial for the infamous beating of Rodney King who is asked about the videotaped evidence that was used in the prosecution case:

> (21) [Goodwin, 1994: 618]
> 1 Pro: You can't look at that video and say that every
> 2   one of those blows is reasonable can you.
> 3   (1.0)
> 4 Powell: -> Oh I <u>can</u> if I put my perceptions in.

As Goodwin (1994) shows, the defence case rested entirely on reinterpreting the apparently incriminating video record, and it is the determination to insist on this reinterpretation which is expressed in Powell's oh-prefaced response to a prosecutor's question which implies that the record is a self-evident basis for a conviction.

Key points

- We began with a practice - oh-prefacing - that we started to distinguish from starting a turn with a free-standing 'oh'.
- We distinguished environments in which this practice was used: these clustered around 'redundant' questions that re-invoked or re-questioned something that had already been said or strongly implied.

(Continued)

(Continued)

- We looked at other aspects of the sequence that showed the parties' orientation to the self-evident nature of what was questioned.
- We showed that this meaning of oh-prefacing could be exploited in contexts where what is being questioned is not at all self-evident or redundant. In these latter contexts, this 'why are you asking' meaning of an oh-prefaced response is used manipulatively.

It is often suggested that CA lacks a sensitivity to 'context' and yet, if my comments about the motivation of CA at the beginning of this chapter have any meaning, this suggestion is quite paradoxical. In fact, basic CA is highly focused on the contexts of talk, *but this focus is deployed in the interest of exploring the limits of the context-free meaning of a practice, as well as its context-sensitive uses.* It is these limits and these uses that we have been looking at in this chapter.

ETHNOGRAPHIC CONTEXT AND THE USES OF CA

Every defined sequential context has its context in the larger conversation, in the sequence of such conversations that have occurred between these participants, in the enduring social relations between the participants together with their biographical and emotional tenor, and in the webs of social relations in which the participants are enmeshed both separately and together. Can CA help in exhibiting the 'traces' of these relationships and structural connections in the concrete details of interactions? In this section, I will illustrate what I take to be the 'ethnographic' value of CA in this kind of a context, using the practice – oh-prefacing – that we have been working with.

Consider the following datum in which a patient is asked a series of 'lifestyle' questions. Here the patient, a middle-aged woman, the owner-manager of a restaurant with a daughter aged 28, who is hypertensive and on medication, is asked about her alcohol use (line 11). The question is devoid of a verb and is ambiguous between the polar question 'Do you use alcohol?' and the more presupposing 'How much alcohol do you use?' This design allows the clinician to circumvent the 'yes/no' question, while permitting the patient to decide how to frame a response. After a one second silence (a substantial period of time in an engaged state of interaction) during which the patient assumed a 'thinking' facial expression, the patient articulates a sound which conveys pensiveness ('hm::'), and then offers an estimate ('moderate'), concluding her turn with 'I'd say' which retroactively presents her response as a personal judgement, albeit a 'considered' one. Though presented as a 'considered opinion', the patient's estimate is unanchored to any objective referent and, starting at line 15, the physician now attempts to get a more precise understanding:

(22) [MidWest 3.4:6]
1   DOC: Are you married?
2   (.)
3   PAT: No.
4   (.)
5   DOC: You're divorced (°cur[rently,°??)
6   PAT: [Mm hm,
7   (2.2)
8   DOC: tch D'you smoke?, h
9   PAT: Hm mm.
10   (5.0)
11 DOC: -> Alcohol use?
12   (1.0)
13 PAT: Hm:: moderate I'd say.
14   (0.2)
15 DOC: Can you define that, hhhehh ((laughing outbreath))

16 PAT: Uh huh hah .hh I don't get off my- (0.2) outa
17   thuh restaurant very much but [(awh:)
18 DOC: ->   [Daily do you use
19 alcohol or:=h
20 PAT: Pardon?
21 DOC: -> Daily? or[:
22 PAT: => [Oh: huh uh. .hh No: uhm (3.0) probably::
23   I usually go out like once uh week.
24   (1.0)
25 DOC: °Kay.°

The physician begins this effort by inviting the patient to 'define' moderate (line 15). As he concludes his turn, he looks up from the chart and gazes, smiling, directly at the patient, and briefly laughs. Laughter in interaction is quite commonly associated with 'misdeeds' of various sorts (Jefferson, 1985; Haakana, 2001). Because the laughter in this case is not targeted at a single word or phrase (Jefferson, 1985) but follows the physician's entire turn, it will, by default, be understood as addressing the entire turn. In this case, it appears designed to mitigate any implied criticism of the patient's previous estimate.

In her reply, the patient begins to laugh in response (Jefferson, 1979) but does not offer a 'definition'. Instead she takes a step back and remarks: 'I don't get … outta thuh restaurant very much but', but her subsequent development of this line is interdicted by the clinician (line 18). While this remark may be on its way to a revised estimate, its immediate significance is to convey the context of her alcohol use, or 'how' she drinks. In particular, it purports to indicate that her drinking is 'social': she does not drink alone in her apartment, nor does she drink on the job. In this way, the patient introduces a little of her 'lifeworld' circumstances into the encounter, conveying that her drinking is 'healthy' or at least not suspect or problematic.

At line 18 the clinician pursues a measurable metric for the patient's alcohol use by asking, 'D<u>ai</u>ly do you use alcohol or:=h'. The question invites the patient to agree that she uses alcohol on a daily basis, thereby permitting her to take a step in the direction of acknowledging a 'worst case scenario' (Heritage, 2010) for alcohol use. The movement of the word 'daily' from its natural grammatical position at the end of the sentence to the beginning, has the effect of raising its salience, presenting a frequency estimate as the type of answer he is looking for. Finally, the 'or' at the end of the sentence invites some other measure of frequency, and thereby reduces the physician's emphasis on 'daily' as the only possible (or most likely) response for the patient to deal with.

At this point, although the physician and patient are no more than two feet apart, the patient's response to the question (line 20) is to ask for its repetition. Drew (1997) observes that these kinds of repeat requests are produced in two contexts: (a) when there is a hearing problem or, alternatively, (b) when there is a problem in grasping the relevance of the talk to be responded to.

A hearing problem is out of the question because of the objective circumstances of the participants, and it is subsequently ruled out by the conduct of both of them. Not so the 'relevance' problem. After all the patient's remark at lines 9 and 10 (that she didn't get out of the restaurant 'very much') was most likely on its way to suggesting that she didn't have many opportunities to drink. The transition from this implication to an inquiry about whether she drinks on a 'daily' basis may indeed have been somewhat jarring, and difficult to process.

Earlier it was suggested that the parties ruled out a 'hearing problem' as the basis for the patient's request for repetition. The physician rules this out when, rather than fully repeating his previous question, he repeats a reduced form (line 21) in which only the two most salient words are left: 'daily' and 'or'. Only a full repeat would have been compatible with a belief that his patient had not heard him. A drastically reduced repeat like this one conveys, to the contrary, that he believes she heard him. For her part, the patient confirms this analysis when she proves fully able to respond to this abbreviated repeat, beginning before it is even concluded. Here then the objective circumstances of the interaction and the actual conduct of the parties are compatible with only one interpretation of the patient's 'Pardon?': that it expressed a difficulty with the relevance of the question.

This same difficulty is expressed in a different way when the patient begins to respond. The response includes 'huh uh', a casual and minimizing version of 'no' designed to indicate that 'daily?' is far off the mark. It is also oh-prefaced which conveys that the question was irrelevant or inapposite. *Here we see the patient exploits our target practice to assert the fundamental inappropriateness of the physician's question and to exert 'push back' against its terms.*

After she rejects the physician's frequency proposal of 'daily' as an estimate of her alcohol consumption, the patient finally comes up with an estimate of her own: 'once a week'. However she packages this as an estimate of how frequently she 'goes out'. This framing has two consequences: (a) it estimates her actual drinking in an implicit way, leaving it to the clinician to draw the relevant inferences, and (b) it renews her insistence on the social, and morally acceptable, nature of her drinking, implicitly ruling out, for example, solo drinking at work, or at night after work.

With lines 22–3, physician and patient have arrived at a compromise: the physician has a frequency estimate of the patient's drinking, while the patient has been able to retain her focus on 'how' she drinks. At line 24, the physician turns to the patient's chart and starts to write, subsequently acknowledging the patient's response with a sotto voce 'okay' and terminating the sequence.

The transactions of this sequence will be relatively familiar to most qualitative sociologists who study medicine. Physicians need anchored, and preferably quantitative, information as a basis for clinical judgements; patients are often inclined to give more contextualized descriptions. These different orientations were conceptualized by Elliot Mishler (1984) in terms of the 'voice of medicine' with its technical priorities, and the 'voice of the lifeworld' with its experiential grounding. Mishler portrayed these two orientations as in conflict with one another, and this conflict is apparent in this datum. Yet it is a conflict which is effectively mandated by the positions of clinician and patient. In particular, there may be a special vulnerability for patients who offer quantitative estimates of their drinking too readily or too 'technically' (e.g. 'twenty units a week'). Patients who are tempted to respond in this manner may reflect that it could be treated as portraying too great a preoccupation with alcohol consumption, a preoccupation which is itself suspect and may attract further inquiry. Persons do not 'talk this way' about alcohol in everyday life and, even in the doctor's office, too radical a departure from ordinary ways of talking about ordinary concerns may be undesirable (Sacks, 1984).

Here then, though it is but one practice of many deployed in this sequence, our findings about the nature of oh-prefaced responses give us an element of solid interpretive anchorage in this sequence. They do so because, as we already know, these findings are highly robust.

CHAPTER SUMMARY

In this chapter, we have worked with a practice which is robust, and which has been directly validated, not by surveys or psychological testing, but by direct observation of the conduct of persons in a wide variety of settings. This gives our observations about this practice exceptional validity, and allows it to be reliably used as an interpretive resource in ethnographic interpretations of data, and as a quantitative measure or index, if required (cf. Clayman et al., 2007; Heritage et al., 2007).

This practice is but a small cog in a large organization of practices concerned with the management of epistemic relations between persons. These relations concern who knows what, who has rights to know it, and describe it, who knows better than whom, with what certainty, recency and authority. Large numbers of practices are devoted to this business and it is not surprising that they are, because personhood and identity are deeply implicated in the ways in which we patrol the boundaries of our knowledge preserves, and defend our sovereign epistemic territories against overzealous incursion by others, or trampling by invaders who care little for who we are. In the end, it is the cumulative weight of all these practices that allows interactants to live in a densely organized and meaningful social world, and which gives the world of social interaction, and the institutions instantiated in social interaction, their robustness and nuance. For all these reasons and more these practices matter for CA. CA's wholesale effort to map the entire 'genome' of interactional practices is mandated by their extraordinary significance.

FUTURE PROSPECTS

The last ten years have witnessed a wholesale expansion of CA as a research method in a wide variety of fields, including education, medicine, legal process, human-machine interaction and software engineering. CA is currently practised in around half the world's countries. Applied and cross-linguistic work is proceeding apace. The time has arrived for more attention focusing on the fundamentals of CA – in particular, the analysis of basic conversational practices – on which applied research ultimately depends.

Study questions

1. Which elements of methodology are shared by CA and ethnography?
2. How are these elements specified in CA research?
3. How do the methods differ?
4. How are practices 'located' in interaction?
5. What is meant by the 'reflexive' feature of practices?
6. How does CA embody two different ways of approaching the role and significance of 'context' in interaction?

Recommended reading

Schegloff, E. A. (2007) *Sequence Organization in Interaction: A Primer in Conversation Analysis*, Vol. 1. Cambridge: Cambridge University Press.
An authoritative guide to CA by one of the founders of the field.

Sidnell, J. and Stivers, T. (2013) *The Handbook of Conversation Analysis*. Oxford: Wiley-Blackwell.
A wide-ranging 'state of the art' introduction to CA.

Heritage, J. and Clayman, S. (2010) *Talk in Action: Interactions, Identities and Institutions*. Oxford: Blackwell-Wiley.
An introduction to the application of CA in institutional interactions.

ten Have, P. (2007) *Doing Conversation Analysis: A Practical Guide* (2nd edn). Thousand Oaks, CA: Sage.
Gives a 'nuts and bolts' introduction to doing CA.

Recommended online resources

EM/CA Wiki is a general information site for the field:
emcawiki.net/Main_Page
Emanuel A. Schegloff's transcription training module:
www.sscnet.ucla.edu/soc/faculty/schegloff/TranscriptionProject/
Loughborough University CA website:
www-staff.lboro.ac.uk/~ssca1/sitemenu.htm
International Society for Conversation Analysis:
isca.clubexpress.com

References

Blumer, H. (1969) 'The methodological position of symbolic interactionism', in H. Blumer (ed.), *Symbolic Interactionism: Perspective and Method*. Englewood Cliffs, NJ: Prentice Hall, pp. 1–60.

Clayman, S. E., Heritage, J., Elliott M. N. and McDonald, L. (2007) 'When does the watchdog bark? Conditions of aggressive questioning in presidential news conferences', *American Sociological Review*, 72: 23–41.

Drew, P. (1997) '"Open" class repair initiators in response to sequential sources of trouble in conversation', *Journal of Pragmatics*, 28: 69–101.

Garfinkel, H. (1967) *Studies in Ethnomethodology*. Englewood Cliffs, NJ: Prentice-Hall.

Glaser, B. G. and A. L. Strauss (1967) *The Discovery of Grounded Theory: Strategies for Qualitative Research*. Chicago, IL: Aldine.

Goodwin, C. (1994) 'Professional vision', *American Anthropologist*, 96 (3): 606–33.

Haakana, M. (2001) 'Laughter as a patient's resource: dealing with delicate aspects of medical interaction', *Text*, 21 (1): 187–219.

Heritage, J. (1984a) *Garfinkel and Ethnomethodology*. Cambridge: Polity Press.

Heritage, J. (1984b) 'A change-of-state token and aspects of its sequential placement', in J. Maxwell Atkinson and J. Heritage (eds), *Structures of Social Action*. Cambridge: Cambridge University Press, pp. 299–345.

Heritage, J. (1998) 'Oh-prefaced responses to inquiry', *Language in Society*, 27 (3): 291–334.

Heritage, J. (2002) '*Oh*-prefaced responses to assessments: a method of modifying agreement/ disagreement', in C. Ford, B. Fox and S. Thompson (eds), *The Language of Turn and Sequence*. Oxford: Oxford University Press, pp. 196–224.

Heritage, J. (2008) 'Conversation analysis as social theory', in Bryan Turner (ed.), *The New Blackwell Companion to Social Theory*. Oxford: Blackwell.

Heritage, J. (2010) 'Questioning in medicine', in A. F. Freed and S. Ehrlich (eds), '*Why Do You Ask?' The Function of Questions in Institutional Discourse*. New York: Oxford University Press, pp. 42–68.

Heritage, J., Robinson, J. D., Elliott, M., Beckett, M. and Wilkes, M. (2007) 'Reducing patients' unmet concerns: the difference one word can make', *Journal of General Internal Medicine*, 22: 1429–33.

Jefferson, G. (1979) 'A technique for inviting laughter and its subsequent acceptance/ declination', in G. Psathas (ed.), *Everyday Language: Studies in Ethnomethodology*. New York: Irvington Publishers, pp. 79–96.

Jefferson, G. (1985) 'An exercise in the transcription and analysis of laughter', in T. A. Dijk (ed.), *Handbook of Discourse Analysis*, Volume 3. New York: Academic Press, pp. 25–34.

Lerner, G. (2003) 'Selecting next speaker: the context sensitive operation of a context-free organization', *Language in Society*, 32: 177–201.

Margolick, D. (1995) 'Simpson friend testifies of events before killings', *The New York Times*, 23 March 23, p. A8.

Mishler, E. (1984) *The Discourse of Medicine: Dialectics of Medical Interviews*. Norwood, NJ: Ablex.

Robinson, J. D. (2006) 'Soliciting patients' presenting concerns', in J. Heritage and D. Maynard (eds), *Communication in Medical Care: Interactions between Primary Care Physicians and Patients*. Cambridge: Cambridge University Press, pp. 22–47.

Sacks, H. (1984) 'On doing "being ordinary"', in J. Maxwell Atkinson and J. Heritage (eds), *Structures of Social Action*. Cambridge: Cambridge University Press, pp. 413–429.

Sacks, H., Schegloff, E. A. and Jefferson, G. (1974) 'A simplest systematics for the organization of turn-taking for conversation', *Language*, 50: 696–735.

Schegloff, E. A. (1992) 'Repair after next turn: the last structurally provided defence of intersubjectivity in conversation', *American Journal of Sociology*, 95 (5): 1295–345.

Schegloff, E. A. (1997) 'Practices and actions: boundary cases of other-initiated repair', *Discourse Processes*, 23 (3): 499–545.

Schegloff, E. A. (2006) 'Interaction: the infrastructure for social institutions, the natural ecological niche for language and the arena in which culture is enacted', in N. J. Enfield and S. C. Levinson (eds), *The Roots of Human Sociality: Culture, Cognition and Interaction*. New York: Berg, pp. 70–96.

Schegloff, E. A. (2007) *Sequence Organization in Interaction: A Primer in Conversation Analysis*, Volume 1. Cambridge: Cambridge University Press.

Schütz, A. (1962) 'Commonsense and scientific interpretations of human action', in M. Natanson (ed.), *Alfred Schütz Collected Papers, Volume 1: The Problem of Social Reality*. The Hague: Martinus Nijhoff, pp. 3–47.

PART VI
EXPANDING TECHNOLOGIES

The internet is now perhaps the prime site where words and pictures circulate. Markham and Stavrova point out that the internet not only collapses distance, it also can disrupt the way in which time is relevant to interaction. Markham and Stavrova show the importance of distinguishing research studies which simply use the internet as a tool to gather data (e.g. online interviews) from studies of internet practices and social media networks as phenomena in their own right (e.g. the mechanics of online dating or chatrooms). Following this latter option, we learn, as in the other chapters in this book, how participants actively construct meaning.

Nalita James and Hugh Busher next provide a helpful account of the mechanics of online interviews. They unpick the differences between such interviews which can be textual or visual, asynchronous or synchronous, one-to-one or group. Particularly useful to beginners is their discussion of how to build research relationships to facilitate online interviewing and how researchers can address the ethical considerations that can arise when we interview online.

Of course, understanding the mechanics and ethics of gathering data is only half the battle. In some senses, it is much more important to know how to *analyse* your data. Joanne Meredith's chapter addresses this very issue exploring how to use the specific analytic frames of conversation analysis (CA) and discursive psychology (DP) for the analysis of online data. Her chapter begins with a lively address of one data extract and later uses many examples from online forums and instant messaging data to demonstrate the power of these frames to illuminate how participants' construct meaning in the context of the opportunities and limits of particular online technologies.

CA and DP are not the only analytic frames available for analysing online data. The final chapter here by Johann W. Unger, Ruth Wodak and Majid KhosraviNik outlines the approach of critical discourse studies (CDS) and suggests how it may be applied to social media data. They helpfully explain what makes data in digitally mediated contexts different and interesting for researchers who adopt a critical perspective to social phenomena. Students will also find useful their description of how eight methodological steps from one approach to CDS (the discourse-historical approach) can be applied to social media data.

FOURTEEN

Internet/Digital Research

Annette Markham and Simona Stavrova

About this chapter

This chapter reviews key characteristics of digital media, internet culture and networked sociality. Whether conceptualized as a tool for research, a place for social and cultural formations, or a way of being in the twenty-first century, the internet provides many opportunities and challenges for qualitative researchers. Ethical considerations of internet research are also discussed.

Keywords

digital culture, networked sociality, sense of presence, multi-modality, informed consent, context sensitivity, perceived privacy

---

The term 'internet' originally described a network of computers that made possible the decentralized transmission of information. Now, 'the internet' is an umbrella term for innumerable technologies, capacities, uses, and social spaces. Because the types of social interaction made possible by the internet vary so widely, qualitative researchers find it necessary to define the concept more narrowly within individual studies. This is complicated by the fact that the study of the internet cuts across all academic disciplines. There are no central methodological or theoretical guidelines and research findings are widely distributed and decentralized.

Twenty years ago, most internet use occurred while sitting at a desktop computer. From here, we could send messages back and forth using email or an instant messaging program, shop or view news on the web, and interact with others in groups in various immersive text-based environments. At this time, most of us who did qualitative research of digital contexts conceptualized the internet as a social phenomenon, a tool or a fieldsite for qualitative research. Today, internet technologies are ubiquitous and mobile. We carry the internet with us in our pockets or on our wrists. We use multiple devices at once. We stitch the capacity of the internet into our clothing. On a larger scale, sensors embedded in our appliances, vehicles and buildings weave the digital and analog elements of our world together in what has been called the Internet of Things (IOT). This results in a number of significant shifts in how social life occurs whether or not one is online, or directly connected to the internet.

One shift in the past decade is the rise of personalization of what we see online and proceduralization of how we move through various online platforms. As we surf the web, chat with our friends and walk with GPS connected devices, we produce digital signals. Collected and combined with other data, our data are processed by automated or self-learning software programs.

A second shift is that people who might have once only consumed digital information can now quite easily produce and distribute their own content, mostly through the capacity of what we call Web 2.0 technologies. Rather than being just a user or a producer of media, people will be both, simultaneously, engaging in what Bruns (2008) calls 'produsage'. Social media platforms facilitate the sharing of user-generated content. Through YouTube, Facebook, Instagram, Twitter and various blogging platforms, people present the self across multiple platforms and for multiple audiences, both visible and invisible.

A third shift is that internet technologies are becoming less visible and at the same time more prominent as a mediator of social life. As the internet grows increasingly 'embedded, embodied, and everyday' (Hine, 2015), it challenges taken-for-granted frameworks for how identities, relationships, cultures and social structures are constructed. As the internet becomes more and more ubiquitous, it saturates literally every part of our civic, social and professional lives. Whether we use the technologies themselves or not, the internet has become a deeply embedded foundation for personal identity, politics, social life and commerce in the twenty-first century. Thus, the internet challenges how we understand and conduct qualitative inquiry (Markham and Baym, 2009).

THE RESEARCHER'S PERSPECTIVE

Depending on the role the internet plays in the qualitative research project or how it is conceptualized by the researcher, different theoretical, logistical and ethical considerations will come into play. This will become apparent in other chapters in this book.

The internet is often *conceptualized as a tool* for collecting information because of how easily researchers can gain access to groups, download texts, capture conversations, observe individual and group behaviours, or interact with participants conveniently or at a distance. A researcher might also utilize various capacities and interfaces available via the internet to augment or replace traditional qualitative methods of collecting, storing, sorting and analysing information. The internet is also associated with the use of data analysis software, even if the internet is not strictly necessary to enable the functioning of such analytical tools.

The internet can also be experienced *as a place*, thus the researcher might conceptualize it as *a fieldsite of culture*. The internet facilitates the formation of relationships and communities. If these cultural formations rely on the internet for their composition or function, they are considered 'internet-mediated' or 'digitally saturated'. Researchers of such cultural formations or networked sociality might take their methods from a wide range of disciplines. Ethnography remains a strong framework, since it can be adapted to the 'place' features of many online communities and groups. Another suitable approach in this category is to mix a range of methods, sometimes experimentally, since the contexts can be quite complex – crossing multiple platforms, blending both online and offline modalities, and including obvious as well as embedded technologies.

Because the internet is interwoven into many aspects of social life, whether or not one is online, scholars have recognized the importance of studying the internet as a *way of being*. This perspective takes seriously the idea that our social lives are essentially and thoroughly mediated (Horst and Miller, 2012), and thus, the study of contemporary culture naturally involves the internet. Along similar lines, scholars might focus on the network, technologies or capacities of the internet. This research scenario is distinguished from the previous one because of a greater focus on various features and implications of this globe-spanning network of connectivity, rather than those social phenomena resulting from internet use.

The researcher's own perceptions about what the internet *is* will influence the way he or she delimits the object of analysis or the ethnographic field, defines bodies, persons, agency and thus what counts as 'communication' or 'interaction' or 'presence' in a particular situation, and makes decisions about what to include or exclude as relevant data for study. Taking three hypothetical cases as an example, the researcher in case 1, studying how breast cancer survivors frame their experiences, might conceptualize the internet as a tool, using various internet media to contact participants, schedule interviews, distribute open-ended question lists, collect research diaries, organize and sort data and so forth. The researcher in case 2, studying how women feel about being members of a Facebook breast cancer group, may conceptualize the internet as a fieldsite, observing interaction practices and group norms among participants. The researcher in case 3, studying how frames of meaning surrounding breast cancer are negotiated and reproduced, might focus on the networked features of blogging, studying the hyperlinks between websites, mapping the network of connections created by repeated elements across multiple sites. In case 1, the information processing and transmitting features of the internet are salient, but only inasmuch as these tools function effectively. It is essential to consider how these tools are operating, but the internet itself or the internet-mediated aspects of sense-making are not the subjects of study. In case 2, the internet-mediated characteristics of the group become salient if one is attempting to study the uniqueness of an online community. In case 3, the networks of connections constitute the phenomenon; links between users might constitute the primary focus for analysis.

The perspectives we mention above are not all inclusive. They're also not necessarily mutually exclusive. Researchers studying an online community may conceptualize the internet simultaneously as a tool for collecting information, the fieldsite and also an object of analysis. A researcher mapping the way text messages flow through networks during local or global crises may use the internet as a tool for collecting data or measuring speed of transmission. At the same time, they might explore the social impact of this mapping or examine the social life of the messages themselves as they travel beyond the individual (for a good example of how researchers blend qualitative and quantitative methods, discuss social practices at different levels, and think about the networks of sociality at both large and small scale, see Bruns and Burgess, 2012).

These examples are oversimplified to demonstrate that one's definitional and conceptual framework for the internet will shift depending on one's ontological and epistemological premises, research goals and the specific form of the research question. Rigorously analysing the connections between one's questions, the subjects of inquiry and the possible methods of collection, analysis and interpretation is an essential part of all good qualitative inquiry. Qualitative research is inductive, meaning it naturally shifts over the course of a project. Therefore, as the purpose of research is identified and the study unfolds, certain characteristics of the internet will become more meaningful than others. In internet studies specifically, reflecting on various characteristics of the internet is a crucial part of this iterative process.

Key points

- If you're using the internet as a tool for communicating with participants, certain media will be second nature to some users while completely foreign for others.
- If you're studying cultural formations in online places, placeness and presence are likely to be important features of the research design.
- If you're studying sociality or life in the digital era where the internet is a way of being, you may need to use a mix of methods to access and understand the more interwoven, less visible aspects of the internet.

Below, we review some basic characteristics of the internet or networked sociality that might be salient to one's project. This list is not exhaustive but provides a starting point for thinking about the challenges of internet research. These are characteristics that tend to cause problems for qualitative researchers, raise challenging questions about research methods, or create new opportunities for researchers. Reflecting on these characteristics with a specific case study in mind can help researchers make wise choices as they investigate potentially unfamiliar forms of mediation, new technologies or unique research environments. These characteristics can apply to almost any internet-mediated research context, regardless of the specific technologies involved. These characteristics are also felt to differing degrees by users (and researchers), depending on the specific situation and/or relation.

SALIENT CHARACTERISTICS OF NETWORKED SOCIALITY

Communicating and connecting

As a medium for communication, the internet provides multiple means and modes of interaction, offering many choices and platforms for performing self-identity, building relationships and developing communities. We use the internet to help with many communicative activities. Most of us probably appreciate the way the internet enables us to transmit and receive information; offers – through various apps – a range of visual, textual and audio forms for interacting with others; allows us to bookmark, combine or remix units of information for particular audiences, in different formats such as internet memes, Pinterest boards, video mashups, reaction gifs, Tumblr blogs and so forth.

For the most part, users focus less on the actual platforms for performance or networks of connections than the communities made possible by these networks or the texts, still and moving images, and sounds facilitated by these networks. People use the internet in ways that parallel but depart from or extend earlier media for communication, such as letter writing, telephone, Post-it notes, bulletin boards and so forth. People also use many different platforms simultaneously, connecting to multiple global networks. One's use of the media can be asynchronous or synchronous; one-to-one, one-to-many, or many–many; anonymous or not. The presentation of self may be represented in writing, sound, moving and still images, live or pre-recorded video, avatars, various displayed artefacts and so forth.

Whether the researcher is using chat as a tool for conducting interviews, exploring the cultural norms of chat in an immersive game, or analysing the sociality of people chatting about a political event, it is important to be aware that communication functions at both the level of content (what is being said) and relationship (what is meant by what is said). Use of a particular form of internet medium may appear homogeneous at the surface level of behaviour when, in fact, there are as many motives and purposes as there are conversations. For example, the seemingly simple practice of posting on Instagram or Facebook could be conceptualized variously as: a conversation continuer, a marker of presence, a sign of status, a possibility to represent oneself authentically, a move of resistance, an opportunity to wear a mask, a location device or a signal for unified action. Thus, while paying attention to content and form is important, so too is paying attention to the context and relation (Watzlawick et al., 1967).

If used as a tool for research, the internet and its capabilities should be matched to the goals, topics or participants of the project. There are many creative possibilities. For example, collecting life histories via Skype interview may be satisfactory, but allowing participants to create ongoing life history accounts on multimedia platforms they can design themselves may yield richly textured results. Using photo or video blogging would yield yet another outcome for analysis. For an interview study, real-time text-based interfaces may provide anonymous participation and spontaneous conversation, but that may be inadequate for certain participants or research questions. Interviewing via video-conferencing may be preferred by some participants, but others might provide more information or be more comfortable using a chat interface. Email interviews may be better suited to participants who have busy schedules or desire time to consider their responses, but may be unsuitable for users more familiar with shorter snippet forms of interaction.

Presence and placeness

The internet is geographically dispersed, meaning people can congregate or have a sense of togetherness despite great distances. The internet extends our senses, allowing us to see, listen and reach well beyond our local sensory limits. The telegraph, radio, television and phone did the same, as McLuhan articulated in the 1960s, but the digital and networked qualities of information, as well as the multiple modalities for interacting with it, yield significant differences in experience. One can experientially connect to situations far removed from one's physical location, or be engaged in multiple, distinctive situations simultaneously.

Having a sense of presence without actually being there is a hallmark of the internet. Presence becomes a more complicated concept because it is determined by participation more than proximity. Meyrowitz (1985) discussed this as a separation of social from physical presence. Waskul complicates this by arguing that 'places are transmitted from one locality to any and all users' varied geographic "space"' (2005: 55). In this way, our sense of presence and the sociality of presence does not require our physical presence. For me, this is most evident in game environments. For example, a player might deliberately assign a random 'twitch' to their avatar, so that when their in-game character might seem lifeless because it is listening or resting instead of moving, their character will still appear to be breathing – that is to say, existing. This feature can also function to maintain a social presence even when the player's not paying attention, as when they activate the twitch while they are away from the game, making dinner. Gergen (2002) would call this 'absent presence'.

The internet facilitates the development of varied cultural forms. Researchers might study communities that exist solely online in immersive environments. These 'virtual worlds' can have defined boundaries and stable cultural patterns (Boellstorff et al., 2012). Alternatively, researchers might study how placeness or presence is more a temporary assemblage. We have witnessed many moments when citizens coalesce around crises such as the Japan earthquake (2011) or the Occupy movements (2011). These were experienced as strong cultural formations. They were decentralized, combined online and offline modes of interaction, and challenged standard notions of place. Even if one is only using the internet as a tool to carry out interviews or collect discourse, it is important to note that as people use the internet in their everyday lives, they will have different responses to the environment. While certainly not everyone will feel a sense of presence, there are still many ways interface design, technical affordances and geographic dispersion can influence experience. Good research design will take this into consideration, even if these aspects may not be variables the researcher can control.

Malleable time

As well as collapsing distance or making it irrelevant, internet technologies can disrupt time, shifting it from an unchanging or universal flow to a malleable variable in everyday interactions. Once a novelty, we now take for granted the ability to stop and start time in the midst of a conversation to consider and adjust our interactive choices. Most of us don't notice that we are, in effect, manipulating time to suit our purposes. This is a relevant feature in contemporary social relations, so time/temporality may become relevant as an object of analysis.

Time is also shifted in ways we cannot control and may not notice, by the interface we're using, the quality of our network connection and other factors. This may be a significant feature of a social situation, if the researcher is studying an internet-based social context, such as a Facebook group, game or social virtual world, or the development and enactment of internet-mediated social relationships.

Interaction via the internet occurs in multiple modes, alternately or simultaneously. Whether sponsored by software and hardware, a person's individual use, or the emergence of dyadic or group norms over time, these multiple modes operate on the sense-making practices of users. This particular time-related function, *multi-modality*, is meaningful when designing or capturing interactions in the research context.

In their everyday interactions with technology, users generally employ more than one internet-based modality at once. A user might be sending status updates to their social network, playing interactive games with friends, downloading music, updating their blog and watching streaming video. When instant messages pop up on the screen, they are prompted to type a reply within a new or continued conversation. Much more than mere technical accomplishments, these activities can be seen as adaptive, evolving means of constituting and maintaining networked identities in a media-saturated environment. These can be studied as phenomena or used as tools to augment the ways that researchers engage and communicate with participants.

These and many other malleable features of time in internet-mediated contexts can assist researchers in conducting interviews. In addition to the ways discussed by James and Busher (in this volume), researchers can use multiple modalities at once. For example, a researcher could interview via one medium or forum with a group and simultaneously use different 'back channels' with individuals to interact privately while the larger group activity is occurring. These non-disruptive 'whispers' can add valuable data that might not otherwise be captured.

Technologies and platforms afford certain time/space possibilities for users. At the same time, users also actively adapt or hack technologies to use them in ways unintended by the designers. This may be important to consider as one designs the research, but is also likely to emerge in unexpected ways as one interacts with people in their own specific contexts. Also, one should be aware that many of these modes may be functioning invisibly to an outsider looking at the situation or the participant.

Contexts of social construction

As we write this chapter, various programs on our computers and smart phones collaborate to present filtered versions of not only our own worlds, but also our understandings of the whole world. We filter news, we follow links sent by friends, and we follow random or not-so-random paths of information to build knowledge of the world. As we use various apps, we might find ourselves moving through different information flows. We might just watch and listen, or we might contribute to various social networks.

In this milieu, one of us might perform multiple versions of the self. Every post or update is authored or shared by a slightly different version of 'me' and targeted to slightly different audiences. I might be a cook posting new recipes. I might have an account where I post satirical photos to make fun of selfie culture. I might use Snapchat with only three of my closest friends to give them unedited versions of what I perceive to be my authentic self.

For many, this is everyday life in the twenty-first century. Of course, the saturated, multiphrenic self (Gergen, 1991) emerged well before the internet. But the extent to which our identities are saturated with media, networked with others, and intermingled with information and communication technologies is a recent phenomenon, one worthy of study and reflection. This is not just a sociological issue, but a methodological issue, as 'the sociological subject is powerful, shifting, and in terms of qualitative research design, confusing. Our research models do not fit the multiphrenic subject very well' (Baym and Markham, 2009: x).

The internet comprises discursive forms of presentation and interaction that can be observed immediately and archived. This capacity facilitates the researcher's ability to witness and analyse the structure of talk, the negotiation of meaning and identity, the development of relationships and communities, and the construction of social structures as these occur discursively. Linguistic and social structures emerging through social interaction via the internet provide the opportunity for researchers to track and analyse how language builds and sustains social reality.

The internet is unique in that it leaves visible traces of actions, movements and interactions. Internet technologies allow the researcher to see the visible artefacts of this negotiation process in forms divorced from both the source and the intended or actual audience. This can give researchers a means of studying the way social realities are displayed or how these might be negotiated over time.

Key points

- Assess how the research participants themselves define the internet and frame their communication behaviours.
- Adapt to the needs of the specific situation by building a strong awareness of the range of possible meanings.
- Rather than adopting universal procedures and tools, try adapting the medium and method to the participant's preferences and comfort zones, or the emerging needs of specific situations.

ETHICAL CONSIDERATIONS

In line with the basic principles outlined in international ethics documents, the Association of Internet Researchers (AoIR) finds the following principles to be fundamental to an ethical approach to internet research:

- The greater the vulnerability of the community/author/participant, the greater the obligation of the researcher to protect the community/author/participant.
- Because 'harm' is defined contextually, ethical principles are more likely to be understood inductively rather than applied universally. That is, rather than one-size-fits-all pronouncements, ethical decision-making is best approached through the application of practical judgement attentive to the specific context.
- When making ethical decisions, researchers must balance the rights of subjects (as authors, as research participants, as people) with the social benefits of research and researchers' rights to conduct research. In different contexts the rights of subjects may outweigh the benefits of research.
- Ethical issues may arise and need to be addressed during all steps of the research process, from planning to publication and dissemination.
- Ethical decision-making is a deliberative process, and researchers should consult as many people and resources as possible in this process, including fellow researchers, people participating in or familiar with the contexts/sites being studied, research review boards, ethics guidelines, published scholarship (within one's discipline but also in other disciplines), and where applicable, legal precedent.

Internet contexts present persistent ethical dilemmas for social researchers. Here, we briefly mention three: perceptions of privacy, personally identifiable information and informed consent.

Perceptions of privacy

Researchers struggling with the practical and methodological challenges surrounding the issue of privacy find themselves on constantly shifting conceptual terrain. The term 'privacy' is almost always discussed as a binary that contrasts private with public. This binary may seem useful in determining whether the material is a public (published) text or a private person, or to determine whether and how privacy needs to be protected. But this model breaks down in the digital/internet era.

Commonly, people use publicly accessible information spaces but maintain strong expectations of privacy. This experience of perceived, rather than actual, privacy, has guided much of our current thinking about privacy and ethical social internet research. Sveningsson (2004) argues that not only is privacy a continuum, it is also a concept understood in relation to the sensitivity of content or context.

More recent scholarship finds that even continua like these inadequately describe how people feel about information and privacy. For example, youth interviewed by Boyd and Marwick (2011) felt angry that their Facebook information was used by teachers and administrators in a school-wide public presentation to illustrate the dangers of posting private information in public spaces. They knew the information was relatively public. It was the manner in which it was used that made them feel violated (2011: 6). Context, more than type of information, was the critical consideration.

Privacy is also defined generationally or culturally. For some users, privacy is a disintegrating condition or state, seemingly impossible to protect. For others, privacy – in any traditional sense – has never been a perceived right or concern. In internet or digital contexts, as Nissenbaum points out, 'what people care most about is not simply restricting the flow of information but ensuring that it flows appropriately' (2010: 2). So to consider how we might protect participants, researchers may need to consider a different set of questions, such as: 'What is a person's relationship to their information in this context?' or more specifically, even: 'How does a person feel about his or her relationship to his or her information?' (Markham, 2012). This question can be extended, of course, to larger groups or to discussions of data flow more broadly.

Informed consent

The process of obtaining 'informed consent' is a regulatory term used by many local and national institutions to ensure that persons understand and accept the potential risks of research and willingly participate (see Ryen in this volume). This formulation is based on certain premises: first, it assumes that the researcher can literally see the potential participant to verify demographic information, which then helps determine whether or not the participant falls into a known category of vulnerability. Second, it assumes that procedures, purpose and potential risks and benefits can be delimited and explained adequately.

In internet or digitally-related research contexts, the objective of informed consent may be well-intended but problematic. At the most basic level, we can ask: how can a researcher ensure they have gained actual consent from participants who are not physically co-located? This challenge grows more complicated when we add anonymity: how can we gain consent from anonymous chatroom or online forum participants? How can we ensure our participants don't fall into a vulnerable category? How can we obtain informed consent when we're using a person's information rather than interacting with the person? What sort of protection should we afford information in large-scale digital databases? These questions have compelled reconsideration of the goals and even the concept of informed consent. Case studies illustrate how sometimes obtaining informed consent can actually cause harm, how informed consent is sometimes impossible, and how informed consent can be counterproductive. In light of these cases, the AoIR ethics committee suggests that researchers should make decisions about whether and how to obtain informed consent by returning to the rationale or premises for informed consent rather than taking for granted the regulatory norms for obtaining informed consent in *a priori* fashion. This stance would enable a more proactive role in determining how best to enact beneficence, justice and respect for persons.

(Protection of) Personally identifiable information

Much of the discussion of privacy and ethics in the first decade of internet research focused on protecting the privacy and anonymity of individuals and groups in online contexts. Now, in an era of big data, we face daunting challenges associated with data protection. As noted by the US National Research Council, 'There is so much information that is freely and openly available about individuals that informational risk is ubiquitous in society' (2014: 83). As it gets easier to collect data in large-scale and automated ways, data and personally identifiable information becomes an increasingly complicated category. Archiving everyday deliberate activities, such as surfing patterns or demographic information, is commonplace. But it is also possible to collect non-deliberate activities, such as backspacing and deleting. Programs can archive information passively or incidentally, as when a restaurant recommendation site not only tags but also stores one's geolocation, or when a self-tracking exercise device logs, statistically manages and then archives one's physical data over time (sleep cycles, weight gain or loss, heart rate, running times, blood pressure, medication schedules and so forth).

Snowden's 2013 revelation that the NSA was secretly collecting personally identifiable information increased public awareness of the crumbling myth of data privacy. For research communities, too, this issue is a growing ethical concern. While there is no consensus on how to handle and effectively protect personally identifiable information, the problem is recognized as a universal priority.

It is important to note that ethical issues continue to grow more complicated as new technologies and capacities develop. Although the above terms point to persistent concerns, others may emerge. Thus, it is important that ethical decision-making remains active and case-based, rather than passive acceptance of or adherence to existing norms and parameters of regulatory bodies. This is an important shift in how regulators, policy-makers and research communities are talking about how ethical guidelines are best applied in actual research situations.

REFLEXIVITY AND CONTEXT-SENSITIVITY

Given the complexity of internet-related contexts for research, we conclude by emphasizing how good internet research is a matter of evaluating what the 'internet' means to both the researcher and in the context of the study. This context-sensitivity is accomplished by being attentive, reflexive and adaptive (see also Buscatto in this volume). Since methods might differ radically, we do not specify what tools or techniques one should use. Instead, we offer these general conceptual guidelines:

- Research environments utilizing various internet media must undergo careful evaluation, as each decision one makes throughout the course of a research project makes a difference. Testing various mediated environments and reflecting on the associated characteristics can help one discern which might be most suitable for the particular participants or research questions. Evaluating the research environment is not just a matter of looking at the tools and technologies but also reflexively interrogating the self as a researcher, to understand one's own assumptions and habitual practices.
- Reflection and adaptation are necessary as one integrates internet communication technologies into qualitative research design. Adapting to the internet is one level of reflexivity; as we use new media for communication, the interactional challenges and opportunities can teach us about how to use these methods. Adjusting to the individual is another level; as in face-to-face contexts, a skilled researcher will pay close attention to how the participant conceptualizes and uses digital technologies.
- Adapting to the context requires the willingness and ability to be methodologically agile, particularly as our networked selves and social forms do not appear to be getting any less complex. If researchers cannot adjust to the particular features and capacities of internet technologies, they may miss the opportunity to understand these phenomena as they operate in context.
- In studying novel contexts or emerging technologies, researchers will likely need to embrace the need for innovation, adaptation and a willingness to creatively adapt one's methods to meet the needs of the context. Still, good qualitative research principles remain the same, and one should keep at least one foot solidly grounded in the core practices and principles of qualitative inquiry.

CHAPTER SUMMARY AND FUTURE PROSPECTS

This chapter focuses on salient characteristics of the internet that influence social life, the research context and research design. It also addresses ethical challenges in conducting internet research. Throughout, it emphasizes that depending on one's perspective and definition of the internet, the research design may vary. Some researchers might use the internet as a tool for collecting, storing and analysing data. Other researchers might study the internet as a place or context where meaningful social action and cultural formation happens. Still other researchers might study how the internet is becoming a way of being in the twenty-first century. Certainly, platforms, devices and other internet-mediated technologies continue to infuse into everyday life. This is not likely to go away. While qualitative researchers will always have close, local, personal, face-to-face-settings to study, these are more and more interwoven with the digital. As this interweaving becomes invisible, whatever we once referred to as 'the internet' or 'the digital' will look more and more like simply 'social life'. This will continue to challenge and energize qualitative researchers.

Study questions

1. Given the salient characteristics of the internet described above, what might be key concerns for different approaches, such as ethnography, discourse analysis or case study research?
2. In what ways are internet contexts becoming more invisible or absorbed into everyday life?
3. What strategies can researchers develop to grapple with the embedded characteristics of the future internet?

Recommended reading

For an overview of central trajectories and concerns within the fields of internet studies and digital media studies, see:

Consalvo, M. and Ess, C. (2011) *The Handbook of Internet Studies*. Oxford: Wiley-Blackwell.

Hartley, J., Burgess, J. and Bruns, A. (2013) *A Companion to New Media Dynamics*. Chichester and Malden, MA: Wiley-Blackwell.

For interesting examinations of the social, technical, relational and economic elements of networked society, see:

Baym, N. (2015) *Personal Connections in the Digital Age*. Malden, MA: Polity Press.

José van Dijck (2013) *The Culture of Connectivity: A Critical History of Social Media*. New York: Oxford University Press.

Papacharissi, Z. (ed.) (2011) *A Networked Self: Identity, Community and Culture on Social Network Sites*. New York: Routledge.

For a solid set of practical concepts, see:

McKee, H. and Porter, J. (2009) *The Ethics of Internet Research: A Rhetorical, Case-based Process*. New York: Peter Lang.

For in depth information on various methodological issues and strategies relating to qualitative internet research, the following readings are recommended:

Boellstorff, T., Nardi, B., Pearce, C. and Taylor, T. L. (2012) *Ethnography and Virtual Worlds: A Handbook of Method*. Princeton: Princeton University Press.

Hine, C. (2015) *Ethnography for the Internet: Embedded, Embodied and Everyday*. London and New York: Bloomsbury.

Horst, H. and Miller, D. (2012) *Digital Anthropology*. London and New York: Berg.

Markham, A. and Baym, N. (2009) *Internet Inquiry: Dialogue among Scholars*. Thousand Oaks, CA: Sage.

Here are some book-length qualitative analyses that demonstrate a vast range of perspectives and techniques, which explore the experience of online community using a mixture of qualitative methods to collect and analyse communication practices and relationships:

Baym, N. (2000) *Tune In, Log On: Soaps, Fandom, and Online Community*. Thousand Oaks, CA: Sage.

Kendall, L. (2002) *Hanging Out in the Virtual Pub*: *Masculinities and Relationships Online*. Berkeley, CA: University of California Press.

For an introduction to a now longstanding practice of exploring how people experience the internet by starting offline rather than online, see this classic work on the ground in Trinidad, which has been followed by many interesting ethnographic studies around the world:

Miller, D. and Slater, D. (2000) *The Internet: An Ethnographic Approach*. Oxford: Berg.

Other scholars explore the internet by diving into immersive worlds like Second Life or multiplayer online games, such as:

Boellstorff, T. (2008) *Coming of Age in Second Life: An Anthropologist Explores the Virtually Human*. Princeton, NJ: Princeton University Press.

Nardi, B. (2010) *My Life as a Night Elf Priest: An Anthropological Account of World of Warcraft*. Ann Arbor, MI: University of Michigan Press.

Taylor, T. L. (2006) *Play Between Worlds: Exploring Online Game Culture*. Cambridge, MA and London: MIT Press.

For recent explorations of identity in networked sociality, one might enjoy:

Boyd, D. (2014) *It's Complicated: The Social Lives of Networked Teens*. New Haven: Yale University Press.

Marwick, A. (2013) *Status Update: Celebrity, Publicity, and Branding in the Social Media Age*. New Haven: Yale University Press.

Recommended online resources

For overviews of ethical issues in internet studies, the Association of Internet Researchers (AoIR) has produced two guides for *Ethical Decision Making and Internet Research*. For this and other resources, see the wiki at:

http://aoir.org/ethics/

References

Baym, N. and Markham, A. (2009) 'Introduction: making smart choices on shifting ground', in A. Markham and N. Baym (eds), *Internet Inquiry: Dialogue among Scholars*. Thousand Oaks, CA: Sage, pp. vii–xix.

Boellstorff, T., Nardi, B., Pearce, C. and Taylor, T. L. (2012) *Ethnography and Virtual Worlds: A Handbook of Method*. Princeton: Princeton University Press.

Boyd, D. and Marwick, A. (2011) 'Social privacy in networked publics: teens' attitudes, practices, and strategies', paper presented at the Oxford Internet Institute Decade in Internet Time Symposium, Oxford, UK, September 22.

Bruns, A. (2008) *Blogs, Wikipedia, Second Life, and Beyond: From Production to Produsage*. New York: Peter Lang.

Bruns, A. and Burgess, J. (2012) 'Analysing Twitter activity in crisis contexts', paper presented at the European Communication Conference (ECREA), Istanbul, 26 October.

Gergen, K. (1991) *The Saturated Self*. New York: Basic Books.

Gergen, K. (2002) 'The challenge of absent presence', in J. E. Katz and M. Aakhus (eds), *Perpetual Contact*. Cambridge: Cambridge University Press, pp. 227–41.

Hine, C. (2015) *Ethnography for the Internet: Embedded, Embodied and Everyday*. London and New York: Bloomsbury.

Horst, H. and Miller, D. (2012) *Digital Anthropology*. London and New York: Berg.

Markham, A. N. (2012) 'Fabrication as ethical practice', *Information, Communication and Society*, 15 (3): 334–53.

Markham, A. and Baym, N. (eds) (2009) *Internet Inquiry: Dialogue among Scholars*. Thousand Oaks, CA: Sage.

Meyrowitz, J. (1985) *No Sense of Place: The Impact of Electronic Media on Social Behavior*. New York and Oxford: Oxford University Press.

Nissenbaum, H. (2010) *Privacy in Context: Technology, Policy, and the Integrity of Social Life*. Stanford, CA: Stanford Law Books.

Sveningsson, M. (2004) 'Ethics in internet ethnography', in E. A. Buchanan (ed.), *Virtual Research Ethics: Issues and Controversies*. Hershey, PA: Idea Group, pp. 45–61.

US National Research Council (2014) *Proposed Revisions to the Common Rule for the Protection of Human Subjects in the Behavioral and Social Sciences: Report by the Committee*. Washington, DC: The National Academies Press.

Waskul, D. (2005) 'Ekstasis and the internet: liminality and computer-mediated communication', *New Media and Society*, 7 (1): 47–63.

Watzlawick, P., Beavin, J. and Jackson, D. (1967) *Pragmatics of Human Communication: A Study of Interactional Patterns, Pathologies, and Paradoxes*. New York: W. W. Norton and Company.

FIFTEEN
Online interviewing
Nalita James and Hugh Busher

About this chapter

This chapter discusses the possibilities and challenges that online interviews offer to researchers. It examines the different types of online interviews, including textual and visual, asynchronous and synchronous, one-to-one and group. The chapter also examines the importance of building research relationships to facilitate online interviewing and how researchers can address the particular ethical considerations that can arise.

Keywords

(a)synchronous, ethics, interviews, online, text, visual

This chapter discusses the potential, versatility and challenges of conducting online interviews in social science research. It will reflect on how these types of interviews are designed and used as methods of data collection, and where they are located epistemologically, methodologically and ethically.

Over the last few decades, the technological changes and growth of the internet have developed opportunities for online interviewing in qualitative inquiry and have reduced the problems related to face-to-face interviews (Hooley et al., 2012). The internet has altered the nature of the context in which research can take place and how knowledge is constructed by offering a different space and dimension in which conventional research designs and methods can be used and adapted. The use of online research methods in social science research has enabled researchers to communicate with geographically dispersed individuals and groups, not only with real-time and non-real time conversation but also with the ability to actually see the person on the other end of the technological device.

Online interviews can be used to gather original data via the internet with the intention of analysing these to provide new evidence in relation to a specific research question. This is in contrast to secondary internet research, that uses existing documents or information sources found online (Hewson, 2010). Online interviews can be conducted asynchronously (in non-real-time) and synchronously (in real-time) and involve audio, textual as well as video/visual exchanges. Emails, bulletin boards and discussion/focus group/forums are the most commonly used methods for asynchronous online interviewing (Orgad, 2005; James and Busher, 2009; Hooley et al., 2012). (Web)Blogs and wikis also offer qualitative researchers innovative ways to interview participants (Chenail, 2011). Synchronous approaches have focused on text-based chat rooms, instant messenger protocols, and video-conferencing and Voice-Over Internet Protocol (VOIP) to ask and answer questions and to see interview participants while conversing (Stewart and Williams, 2005; Stieger and Göritz, 2006). Researchers can also use online communication services such as Skype to conduct online 'face-to-face' interviews in real-time (Sullivan, 2012).

USING ONLINE INTERVIEWS FOR DATA COLLECTION

In synchronous interviews the interaction and sharing of experiences are framed by the researcher and participant(s) online presence. The real-time nature of online interviews, whether one-on-one or focus group interviews, as in face-to-face interviews, can encourage spontaneous interactions between participants and the researcher, whether they are involved in text-based one-on-one or group interviews or multi-channel visual interviews.

Online synchronous interviewing facilitated by online communication platforms such as Instant Messenger (IM), an electronic online communication system that combines the facilities of telephone-synchronous conversations and email, can lead to rapid, real-time chat (Hincliffe and Gavin, 2009). IM is a faster, more conversational way of communicating than email, and is inexpensive (free to download in most cases), convenient and attractive for those who dislike or find opinion expression difficult during face-to-face interviews. As such, they can dispel participant apprehension, allowing participants who are reticent or shy in face-to-face contexts to have more confidence to 'speak' freely and contribute to a research study (Orgad, 2005). Creative use of interactive visual stimulus also means they can be valuable platforms for facilitating immediate and dynamic group interactions and creating new forms of knowledge (Moore et al., 2015). These interactions can elevate participants' awareness of each other and narrow the psychological distance between participants as well as enhance the feeling of joint involvement (Bowker and Tuffin, 2004). Alternatively researchers can set up their online forum or use external providers such as Networked Virtual Reality, or Graphical MUDs, to offer both synchronous text communication and a graphical representation of the environment (Stewart and Williams, 2005).

One issue that can be challenging for both researchers and participants of online interviews is the fast-paced nature of online discussions can lead to both researchers and participants lagging behind. The distinction between responding and sending can become blurred or responses brief and made up of very few words. Bowker and Tuffin (2004) overcame this problem by meeting with participants offline prior to the commencement of the interviews. In their research, the synchronous online interviews created less opportunity to relate with participants by reciprocating disclosure of experiences:

Natilene: if u don't mind me asking – (I feel very nosey asking u all these questions, but I never know what interesting tales u have to tell and what would be useful for my research) – how did they help?
Daniel: ok, they helped me with info
Daniel: I'm still on their email list
Daniel: they provide good info
Daniel: it helped me to know I wasn't alone.

(Bowker and Tuffin, 2004: 235)

Increased bandwidth and the availability of inexpensive, easy-to-use technologies have made it more viable to conduct synchronous online audio and video interviews. For example, using Skype, either for telephone or video-conferencing research, allows geographical flexibility and it is possible for researchers to record computer-to-computer and computer-to-telephone conversations. Skype calls allowed Cater (2011) to interview her participants at a time that fitted their schedules. Some interviews were broken into segments, while others lasted for up to two hours. The research protocol called for 90 minutes per participant. Some calls were Skype-to-Skype and others were Skype-to-phone with the participants determining the type of calls.

Synchronous online focus groups can be set up with tools such as instant messaging and chat rooms (Fox et al., 2007) and can offer a less threatening interview environment as they offer no visual clues about other participants, although participants have to be made aware by the researchers that they are taking part in a research project. Researchers too need to be proactive in establishing a permissive and friendly atmosphere (Mann and Stewart, 2000). In part, researchers take on a moderating role in order to manage the dynamics of the group (Busher and James, 2012). Moderating and taking part in an online text-based focus group can also require fast typing skills and some experience with the style of real-time discussion. Synchronous online chat can be fast and furious, leading to a high level of immediacy, interaction and engagement with the topic being discussed (O'Connor and Madge, 2003). The complexity of participant interactions can also result in a chaotic transcript, characterized by real-time 'threading', which can be frustrating for the novice researcher to interpret (Fox et al., 2007). Containing the group size and increasing moderating experience can attenuate this difficulty. This also depends on the individual personalities of those taking part, their proficiency with technology, and the appropriateness of interventions made by moderators seeking to direct focus group discussions (Moore et al., 2015).

Asynchronous interviews that are conducted in non-real time are far easier to set up than synchronous interviews in terms of technological requirements. For example, using email can offer an asynchronous online method of interviewing to generate detailed qualitative data or reflexive accounts of individuals' experiences and life histories but require clear protocols for how the interviews are to be conducted (James and Busher, 2006). Similarly, blogs can be used to collect naturalistic data in a textual diary format and the creation of immediate text without the resource intensiveness of tape recorders and transcription (Hookway, 2008). However, researchers need to have permission from the authors to gain access to these blogs for research, or need to help participants to set them up for a particular research project. These approaches can be used for longitudinal research which has important implications for understanding participants' everyday experiences and how they make sense of these over time (James, 2007). They can also be used for asynchronous focus groups to construct virtual ethnographic studies of naturally occurring online forums (Busher and James, 2012).

Textual data collected asynchronously are in written form so there is no need to transcribe. This increases the accuracy of the transcripts and removes the potential for error. It may also enhance interpretation for researchers. Participants may compensate for the lack of non-verbal cues by ensuring that their descriptions portray the level of meaning and emotion that they wish to communicate, allowing a greater level of transparency and sensitivity to the original context of the data. The explicit expression of emotion in written language can be more easily interpreted and incorporated into analyses than the implicit emotional nuances offered in spoken communication (Williams et al., 2012).

While these types of interview can be simple to administer by researchers sending interview questions to participants and then just waiting for a reply, they can take several days or even weeks as participants do not necessarily reply to questions in the time frame set by the researcher (James and Busher, 2009). Further, there is a greater risk of non-response from participants than with synchronous interviews as participants can be distracted by other demands on their time and not feel pressed to respond. Participants' everyday lives, let alone exceptional circumstances, of which a researcher may be unaware, can inhibit participation in a research project, interrupting the flow of the online interview. In the worst circumstances this can lead to a participant's prolonged if temporary disengagement from the project or withdrawal from it altogether. Researchers may have to work hard to maintain a rapport with participants who engage spasmodically with a research project. Probes or prompts to main questions can get lost in participants' email traffic. It is relatively easy for participants to delete or ignore emails with requests for further information if they are too busy or lose interest in the research project, especially if they do not wish to 'open up' (James, 2007). However, because asynchronous interviews can last for weeks, they aid the collection of in-depth data and closer reflection on interview issues through the repeated interactions between participants and researchers. On the other hand, spontaneity of interaction can be lost if participants digress to subjects outside the research project, making it difficult to maintain the flow of the dialogue (Sanders, 2005).

Key points

Advantages of online interviews:

- savings of costs
- location, geography and travel
- flexibility
- venue
- engagement in the online interview
- speed.

Disadvantages of online interview:

- time lags in the online conversation
- distracted participants
- participants' interest and motivations
- language use
- technical competence and failing technology
- access
- identity verification
- absence of verbal cues.

ACCESSING PARTICIPANTS AND ESTABLISHING RESEARCH RELATIONSHIPS

When conducting online interviews, researchers must decide how they are going to access the population and obtain informed consent from all participants. When using video-conferencing with certain populations, access and availability can be greatly improved because individuals are not only connected through their home computers but also on their phones, iPods, laptops, reading devices or at internet cafes. For most people, this is not a problem, but older people or those with disabilities, for example, may not have access to or be able to take part in an online interview (Sullivan, 2012). Younger people tend to be familiar with synchronous online chat. Fox et al. (2007) chose to recruit young participants online as they were more likely to have both access to and some experience of using the internet.

Purposive or convenience sampling is something that is often applied to online interviewing. James and Busher (2006) chose research methods that acknowledged their participants had ready access to email and were familiar with using it in their professional lives. Online focus groups have the potential to use larger sample sizes than face-to-face studies (Stewart and Williams, 2005), allowing researchers to gain access to a wider range of perspectives in a study. Despite this, many researchers using online methods have chosen to replicate sample sizes recommended for face-to-face focus groups, perhaps to stay true to the aims of qualitative research and gain a deeper understanding of experience from a smaller sample of people (Moore et al., 2015). For video-conferencing interviews, the pool of possible participants can increase if, for example, the researcher finds individuals who liked a page on Facebook or belonged to a certain website, in addition to the normal modes of sampling.

Whichever mode (synchronous or asynchronous interview) or type (one-to-one or group interview, video/visual or audio) researchers choose for their online research, they need to consider how they are going to establish a research relationship with their participants and the impact of the online interaction on those being researched. In face-to-face interviews, the presentation of self is based not only on what participants choose to show, for example through gesture or tone of voice, but also on how that is perceived by others in the space of social interaction (Matthews, 2006). In online text-based interviews, the written word becomes the sole means of building rapport and trust. When face-to-face contact is absent, researchers 'cannot ignore the potential obstacles that anonymity and disembodiment pose in attempting to arrive at a relationship of trust with other people online' (Orgad, 2005: 55). Where visual and social gestures and cues in online interviews are not visible, such as simple gestures (nodding, agreeing, eye contact), these have to be translated into text and researchers must, perhaps, more quickly and with greater explicit clarity, 'establish their bona fide status and the boundaries of the online interview … than they might in a face-to-face situation' (Sanders, 2005: 78). Some online researchers have provided personal information about themselves such as family life and work to construct a certain level of rapport with participants (Kivits, 2005), especially where research interviews have involved sensitive topics. Others have tried to facilitate this by providing prompt replies to their participants' messages to demonstrate their commitment to their written texts and their textual exchanges with their participants (Orgad, 2005).

Unless researchers are using web-cameras or video-conferencing, participants and researchers are hidden from each other by the 'smoked mirror' of the internet, affording them visual anonymity and the opportunity for pseudonymity if they wish. This can reduce researcher-participant effects as the physical characteristics of the other are absent, if not their orthographical ones, and make it easier to discuss more sensitive topics or state unpopular views. On the other hand, written texts generated during online exchanges make it easier for people to play with their views and perspectives and identities (James, 2007), allowing the possibility of the creation of personae that bear little relationship to a participant's 'interactional self in everyday "non-screen life"' (Denzin, 1999: 114).

Any interview situation – no matter how formalized, restricted or standardized – relies upon interactions between participants who are constantly engaged in interpretive practice (Holstein and Gubrium in this volume). When using the internet as a communicative social space (Orgad, 2009) to host interactions between participants, researchers need to consider critically the data that they obtain and interpret and their authenticity. Interviews that occur online or use a mixture of face-to-face and online media are not less authentic or truthful than offline data. However, some researchers think that meeting participants offline helps to authenticate online texts, because they believe that people's online interactions are deeply embedded in their offline relationships (Bowker and Tuffin, 2004). Other researchers argue that online discourses and inter-textual constructions of self are valid in themselves and do not need to be verified offline (Lee, 2006). Standards of authenticity should be seen as situationally negotiated and sustained (Hine, 2000) by researchers facilitating open and honest dialogues with their participants (Busher and James, 2012). Gatson and Zweerink (2004) found that the identities portrayed by their participants emphasized the importance of discourse and experience in shaping both the real and virtual worlds. People's actions happen not only in physical places but also in spaces containing multiple locations in hybrid online/face-to-face worlds (Busher and James, 2015).

Researchers' decisions not to look for offline data on their participants will be context sensitive and driven by an understanding of their participants' perceptions of online communications, face-to-face engagement and the interactions of both. However, using online and offline discussions together in a research project can add depth to a researcher's interpretations of participants' online texts as their relationships transcend both online and offline boundaries (Busher and James, 2015). Collecting offline data may add context, enhance information and yield insights that are consequential to the research but would have otherwise remained invisible if only online data had been collected (Hine, 2000). What must guide researchers' choices of research methods are the particular research contexts, the demands of their research goals and an analytical position about the status of the data with which they work (Orgad, 2009).

Key points

- Combining offline/online interviews depends on the purposes of the research project and the characteristics and circumstances of participants' lives.
- Building relationships with participants online can generate authentic dialogue.
- Participants can shape the process and direction of the online interview thus aiding authenticity and credibility.
- Online and offline interviews can present different types of discourses and need to be carefully analysed.

Ethical concerns

Irrespective of the type of online interview chosen by researchers, every research project has to negotiate its own agreed norms between researchers and participants to establish an ethical framework of process. This negotiation is central to persuading participants that they are adequately protected from intentional or unintentional harm and so free to (re) present themselves truthfully if they join a research project. When research is carried out online, researchers encounter conflicts between the requirements of research and its possible benefits on the one hand, and human subjects' rights to and *expectations* of autonomy, privacy, informed consent, etc. on the other (Ess and the Association of Internet Researchers (AoIR), 2012). While such issues are not uncommon in research conducted face-to-face, researchers wanting to conduct online interviews must also recognize that the internet has opened up a wide range of ways to examine human (inter-)actions in different contexts, which inevitably present additional ethical challenges to individual privacy and confidentiality, greater challenges to a researcher in gaining informed consent, and more difficulty in assuring and ascertaining trustworthiness and data authenticity, as also noted above (Ess and the AoIR, 2012).

Informed consent and safety

The grounds for informed consent in face-to-face interviews also apply when interviews are conducted in online environments. Researchers need to gain participants' informed consent to take part in a research project from the time they join it and before online interviews are begun (James and Busher, 2007). To gain that, researchers will need to identify themselves and the purposes of the project to potential participants. They will also need to explain the medium that they are going to use for interviews, whether conducted on a private website, public bulletin board or by email, and how they intend to protect the privacy and anonymity of participants' communications with them in the project as well as maintain data confidentiality. This is necessary because identifying information, coupled with names, email addresses, accompanying photographic or video material or partially disguised pseudonyms, may be inadvertently disclosed either when the data are being collected or, more commonly, when they are stored on a networked computer connected to the public internet. Emphasizing to participants that certain measures will be adopted to maximize confidentiality is necessary. Examples of these measures include the use of pseudonyms and hiding the user names, domain names and any other personal identifiers when publishing or storing interview data (Meho, 2006).

An important element of the informed consent that participants give to researchers when joining a project is the voluntary nature of their participation that allows them to withdraw at any time. While the technology of the internet facilitates this it can also lead to uncertainty. 'Silence' or the lack of any obvious signal by participants during the course of an online interview or focus group can be an indication that they are, even if only temporarily, withdrawing from a project (Kivits, 2005). In online interviewing the reasons for participants dropping-out of the research may not be transparent or amenable to investigation (Hodgson, 2004). This re-emphasizes the provisional nature of the informed consent that participants give to a researcher. It is not merely garnered at the start of a project but must be sustained throughout the online interview. This includes empowering participants to feel comfortable to also withdraw consent when they wish (Hewson, 2010). Moore et al. (2015) found the process of obtaining consent for online focus groups similar to that for face-to-face contexts. However, the blurred distinction between public and private dialogues in the online setting placed a greater responsibility on them to protect the privacy and confidentiality of participants, as well as to ensure that the storage and use of information provided online were both secure for, and made clear to, participants.

Ensuring privacy, confidentiality and anonymity

Ess and the AoIR (2012) argue that researchers are more likely to persuade participants to disclose personal information if they establish a secure online environment that minimises the risk to participants' privacy, confidentiality and anonymity of data at all stages of the research process, during all interactions with participants, when data are transmitted between participants and researchers, when these are stored and when they are published. These might include a project-dedicated website or chat-room to collect, curate and disseminate interview data, instead of an open environment such as email. When conducting online focus group interviews, careful consideration of where this will be hosted is essential to ensuring the safety and confidentiality of participants. For example, maintaining privacy or obtaining informed consent might be more difficult if the study site is merely a separate area on an existing online resource (Williams et al., 2012).

Protecting participants' privacy is a particular issue in online interviews that seek to gather personal or sensitive data. For individuals whose social confidence can be compromised by appearance-related concerns, the online environment can offer a veil of privacy, and this anonymity can contribute to an enjoyable participation experience in an online interview (Fox et al., 2007). However, the extent to which participants may be willing to be open and honest with researchers is likely to depend heavily on the extent to which the researchers can construct a secure environment for communication and one which protects participants' anonymity. For example, researchers can use existing Virtual Learning Environments (VLEs) to host their focus group on their own custom-made site, creating a secure, confidential and safe environment for research participants (Peacock et al., 2009). This allows participants to feel confident that their privacy is protected and the risk of harm to them is minimised to a level acceptable to them.

Much then depends on the personal relationships researchers are able to develop with participants that allow them to build trust. James and Busher (2006) wanted their participants to feel confident that their privacy was adequately protected 'in their eyes' if they self-disclosed, and the risk of harm to them or their communities was minimised to a level acceptable to them. However, as the projects were conducted via email rather than a dedicated project website, they had to make the participants aware that the research conversations were not taking place in a private setting, allowing them to make an informed choice about whether or not to participate. The openness of online technology also threatens the confidentiality of participants' records.

Information collected from the internet or by email and stored on institutional computers and servers, even if carefully processed, can make participants' conversations instantly visible. The further addition of online photographic data as an adjunct to online interviews compounds this problem (Busher and James, 2012). If participants' email addresses, especially their domain names, contain part or all of their real names this makes it possible in public sites to retrieve messages (Eysenbach and Till, 2001). Further, email addresses often contain identifiers such as name, organization and geographical location. Such data will be retained on whichever servers participants and researchers use, and are potentially accessible to whoever services those servers. However, although certain elements of emails and other online postings appear to indicate the origin of a message, the real origin and thus authorship of messages can be relatively easily hidden (Lee, 2006). The risk of a breach of confidentiality is particularly important when online researchers are dealing with sensitive topics unless information is stored in a coded form or anonymously or in separate silos. If researchers know the private email addresses of their participants and these participants have given their written consent to take part in a project, which has to include their real names regardless of whatever aliases they use online, it is relatively easy for anybody to find out who the participants are physically, where they live and to link their data to them (Fox et al., 2007).

Key points

- To reduce the risk of confidentiality do not store research data on institutional servers, but on project-dedicated laptops and computer drives.
- Keep online consent data on a separate computer drive and limit accessibility to those directly working on the research project.
- Give participants a dedicated and different email address from that of the research project/ project website for them to contact researchers.
- Construct a dedicated project website that has restricted access segments on it on which participants and researchers can converse or exchange views without these being visible or public.

In online interviews, unlike face-to-face interviews, participants do not have to divulge any personal information and can remain invisible and anonymous. The anonymity of the online context also means that participants may be relatively unselfconscious about what they write since they remain hidden from view. This can reduce participants' appre-hension about speaking and being recorded since the records of interviews are more likely to be accurate and can easily be checked by participants during the course of an interview for accuracy. This is useful for research into sensitive topics or other scenarios where par-ticipants do not want to be identifiable. Online interviews, especially those conducted in chat rooms, can be conducted on an anonymous basis, so long as participants are made aware that researchers are engaging in research. It allows online researchers to read mes-sages and observe without disturbing the natural conversations and linguistic behaviour of their participants engaged in real-time chat. Participants engaged in the 'chat' can also observe the ongoing actions of others, especially if they do not have the confidence to fully participate and share their values (James and Busher, 2009).

While the internet offers a sense of freedom and anonymity to research participants, this may not always be the case as qualitative researchers can often know who their research participants are. Nevertheless, it is important for researchers to change participants' names and locations, if necessary, to allow for privacy, not least because conducting interviews on the internet allows conversations, locations and identities to be tracked (Busher and James, 2012). Skype even has the right to record conversations although this is not always clear when participants have been signed up. To address these types of issues, a researcher could state the possibility of this occurring, and could also create dummy Skype accounts with dummy email addresses for the participants to use, which would then make it much more time consuming and difficult for others to track (Sullivan, 2012).

Constituting public and private spaces

Another ethical concern faced in online research is knowing what constitutes private and public conversations. Although an online focus group interview might be accessible to the public the conversations taking place might represent confidential and personal informa-tion that individuals may not want to have shared in the public domain (Elgesem, 2002). Some researchers see online texts as both publicly private and privately public (Waskul and Douglass, 1996). This is because on the internet, 'privacy need not be expressly linked to concealment' (Joinson, 2005: 26). Further, inviting participants of a discussion forum to become part of a research project might be perceived by them as an invasion of private space because the research is perceived as irrelevant to the focus of their discussions. To gain access ethically to such discussion forums would involve a researcher approaching the mod-erator of the forum and waiting for her/him to respond after discussing the request with members of the forum to gain approval before beginning the research (Fox et al., 2007).

Having a researcher legitimately present in an online focus group makes it problematic for participants to know to what extent they should divulge personal information because of concerns about such data being broadcast in a public domain. Researchers are more likely to persuade participants to disclose personal information if they establish a safe online environment, such as a dedicated project website (Ess and the AoIR, 2012). In asynchronous focus group interviews using regular listserv or bulletin boards, the interaction will be less private and this may lead participants to be less candid than in email interviews. Even email records of conversations might make participants visible, as discussed earlier. Participants have to take seriously that during their conversations with other members of an online community, whether or not constructed for research, strangers may be 'lurking' on this and possibly harvesting information without their consent (James and Busher, 2009). 'Lurking' on discussion forums is unethical and akin to eavesdropping on conversations without first gaining permission from the other participants to do so (Coleman, 2006). Researchers should declare their presence and purpose when entering an online group.

Researchers also have to define carefully what they mean by private spaces in a research project as it can compromise their research integrity if they use open internet or email communication with participants. For example, blogs are firmly located in the public domain, not only in the sense of being publicly accessible but also in how they are defined by users (Waskul and Douglass, 1996). Blogging is a public act of writing for an implicit audience despite blogs being interpreted by bloggers as 'private' (Hookway, 2008). As discussed earlier they can be used for online asynchronous interviews. When researchers use their institutional email addresses for online interviews, it can be relatively easy for participants to identify them and their geographical locations. Researchers also need to consider the extent to which they share personal information with participants and ask them to do the same in an attempt to develop respectful, trusting and collaborative online relationships with participants (James and Busher, 2009). Such issues potentially undermine the ethical basis of research projects (Orgad, 2005).

CHAPTER SUMMARY

The development of the internet has created exciting ways to examine human interactions in new contexts/sites and offers researchers alternative ways of interviewing individuals and groups which might not be possible onsite and face to face. The written, anonymous and asynchronous nature of some online interviews can facilitate greater self-disclosure, increased reflexivity, and an opportunity to collect details of participants' experiences over time. Visual/video communication in online interviewing has broadened the scope for researchers and participants to simulate face-to-face exchanges and enhance synchronous online conversations. These possibilities add to the media richness of the interview, while raising a new set of questions. Thus, researchers are still faced with the dilemmas of ensuring that their research projects are carried out with professional integrity and an ethical respect for their participants.

In choosing to use online interviewing, researchers need to establish their online research practice, rather than just adapting face-to-face research methods for the virtual world linked to the cautious epistemology of qualitative research. This includes developing a coherent ethical framework for online research to deal with the potential ethical risks.

Key points

- In developing the online interview consider the nature of the social interaction and communication that exists in the online setting and how individuals participate.
- Choose a mode of communication (asynchronous/synchronous) which suits the aims and purposes of the research study.
- Consider how you will organize and participate in the online interview and the ethical implications of how researchers announce their online identity and presence.
- Review the online interview as it progresses to ensure that the research relationship is maintained and that participants feel safe and protected in the online environment.

The use of online interviews in social research should not be seen as an easy option, although such instruments do provide a range of methods that complement face-to-face interactions. Researchers need to justify use of the internet to conduct their research by making explicit what benefits it can bring to their research projects. The effectiveness of online research interviews of all sorts is dependent on who is being researched, what is being researched, and why.

FUTURE PROSPECTS

Although traditional face-to-face interviews remain prominent, innovative technologies have facilitated new modes of communication. Further, the continued advances in these technologies are likely to offer more possibilities than ever to conduct qualitative interviews online, and are also likely to influence the development of online interview methods and approaches to data collection. As Markham (2008: 255) suggests with the use of the internet for research, 'a researcher's reach is potentially global, data collection is economical, and transcribing is no more difficult than cutting and pasting'. Researchers can collect interview data faster and cheaper, and research participants can now be offered an alternative interview if they cannot be physically present in research (on site), without decreasing the quality of the research. As such, the use of multiple and simultaneous methods for different participants addressing the same research topic offers exciting possibilities. However, consideration also needs to be given to the relationship between these technologies when used to conduct online interviews and face-to-face interviews, the various theoretical perspectives of qualitative research, and whether relationships differ between the data collection and data analysis stages of the research. As emerging technologies offer new spaces and places to conduct online interviews in qualitative research, more research is needed to better understand how such technologies can challenge the basic assumptions of the traditional face-to-face interview, and alter human social interrelations. In turn this will help researchers improve their methodological understanding and the use of online interviews in qualitative research.

Study questions

1.   What is the researcher's motivation for conducting interviews online?
2.   What kind of phenomena will online interviews investigate (real-world, online, both)?
3.   How do participants respond to the process of being interviewed online?
4.   What types of online data will be collected and are these adequate for the purposes of the study?
5.   How can the data allow the researcher to construct, analyse and generate conclusions?

Recommended reading

Salmons, J. (2014) *Qualitative Online Interviews: Strategies, Design, and Skills*. Thousand Oaks, CA: Sage.
Encourages researchers to extend the reach of their studies by using methods that defy geographic boundaries by focusing on designing, conducting and assessing research that relies on data from interviews and related observations, materials or artefacts collected online.

Hooley, T., Marriott, J. and Wellens, J. (2012) *What is Online Research? Using the Internet for Social Science Research*. New York: Bloomsbury Academic.
Covers the key issues and concerns for social scientists using clear case studies, online surveys, focus groups, interviews, ethnographies and experiments, as well as discussing the implications of social media and online research ethics.

James, N. and Busher, H, (2009) *Online Interviewing*. London: Sage.
Helps the reader to understand the theoretical, methodological and epistemological challenges of carrying out online interviews in the virtual environment. They highlight the many new ethical issues that face researchers in this medium.

Fielding, N., Lee, R. and Blank, G. (eds) (2008) *The Sage Handbook of Online Research Methods*. Thousand Oaks, CA: Sage.
The chapters cover both methodological and procedural themes, offering readers a sophisticated treatment of the practice and uses of internet and online research that is grounded in the principles of research methodology.

References

Bowker, N. and Tuffin, K. (2004) 'Using the online medium for discursive research about people with disabilities', *Social Science Computer Review*, 22: 228–41.
Busher, H. and James, N. (2012) 'Ethics of research in education', in A. Briggs, M. Coleman and M. Morrison (eds), *Research Methods in Educational Leadership and Management*. London: Sage, pp. 90–105.

Busher, H. and James, N. (2015) 'In pursuit of ethical research: studying hybrid communities using online and face-to-face communications', *Special Issue, Educational Research and Evaluation: An International Journal on Theory and Practice*, 21: 168–81.

Cater, J. K. (2011) 'SKYPE: a cost-effective method for qualitative research', *Rehabilitation Counsellors and Educators Journal*, 4: 3–4.

Chenail, R. J. (2011) 'Qualitative researchers in the blogosphere: using blogs as diaries and data', *The Qualitative Report*, 16: 249–54. www.nova.edu.sss/QR/QR16-1/blog.pdf (accessed 3 May 2015).

Coleman, S. (2006) 'Email, terrorism, and the right to privacy', *Ethics and Information Technology*, 8: 17–27.

Denzin, N. K. (1999) 'Cybertalk and the method of instances', in S. Jones (ed.), *Doing Internet Research: Critical Issues and Methods for Examining the Net*. London: Sage, pp. 107–25.

Elgesem, D. (2002) 'What is special about the ethical issues in online research?', *Ethics and Information Technology*, 4: 195–203.

Ess, C. and the Association of Internet Researchers (AoIR) (2012) 'Ethical decision-making and internet research: recommendations from the AoIR Ethics Working Committee (Version 2.0)'. http://aoir.org/reports/ethics2.pdf (accessed 20 May 2015).

Eysenbach, G. and Till, J. E. (2001) 'Ethical issues in qualitative research on internet communities', *British Medical Journal*, 323: 1103–5.

Fox, F. E., Morris, M. and Rumsey, N. (2007) 'Doing synchronous online focus groups with young people: methodological reflections', *Qualitative Health Research*, 17: 539–47.

Gatson, S. N. and Zweerink, A. (2004) 'ethnography online: "natives" practising and inscribing community', *Qualitative Research*, 4: 179–200.

Hewson, C. (2010) 'Internet-mediated research and its potential role in facilitating mixed methods research', in S. N. Hesse-Biber and P. Leavy (eds), *Handbook of Emergent Methods*. New York: Guilford, pp. 543–70.

Hinchcliffe, V. and Gavin, H. (2009) 'Social and virtual networks: evaluating synchronous online interviewing using instant messenger', *The Qualitative Report*, 14: 318–40.

Hine, C. (2000) *Virtual Ethnography*. London: Sage.

Hodgson, S. (2004) 'Cutting through the silence, a sociological construction of self-injury', *Sociological Inquiry*, 74: 162–79.

Hookway, N. (2008) '"Entering the blogosphere": some strategies for using blogs in social research', *Qualitative Research*, 8: 91–13.

Hooley, T., Wellens, J. and Marriott, J. (2012) *What Is Online Research? Using the Internet for Social Science Research*. New York: Bloomsbury Academic.

James, N. (2007) 'The use of email interviewing as a qualitative method of inquiry in educational research', *British Educational Research Journal*, 33: 963–76.

James, N. and Busher, H. (2006) 'Credibility, authenticity and voice: dilemmas in web-based interviewing', *Qualitative Research Journal*, 6: 403–20.

James, N. and Busher, H. (2007) 'Ethical issues in online educational research: protecting privacy, establishing authenticity in email interviewing', *International Journal of Research & Method in Education*, 30: 101–13.

James, N. and Busher, H. (2009) *Online Interviewing*. London: Sage.

Joinson, A. N. (2005) 'Internet behaviour and the design of virtual methods', in C. Hine (ed.), *Virtual Methods: Issues in Social Research on the Internet*. Oxford: Berg, pp. 21–34.

Kivits, J. (2005) 'Online interviewing and the research relationship', in C. Hine (ed.), *Virtual Methods: Issues in Social Research on the Internet*. Oxford: Berg, pp. 35–50.

Lee, H. (2006) 'Privacy, publicity and accountability of self-presentation in an online discussion group', *Sociological Inquiry*, 76: 1–22.

Mann, C. and Stewart, F. (2000) *Internet Communication and Qualitative Research: A Handbook for Research Online*. London: Sage.

Markham, A. (2008) 'The internet in qualitative research', in L. Given (ed.), *The Sage Encyclopedia of Qualitative Research Methods*. New York: Sage, pp. 454–8.

Matthews, S. (2006) 'On-line professionals', *Ethics and Information Technology*, 8: 61–71.

Meho, L. (2006) 'E-mail interviewing in qualitative research: a methodological discussion', *Journal of the American Society for Information Science and Technology*, 57: 1284–95.

Moore, T., McKee, K. and Mclouglin, P. (2015) 'Online focus groups and qualitative research in the social sciences: their merits and limitations in a study of housing and youth', *People, Place and Policy*, 9 (1): 17–28.

O'Connor, H. and Madge, C. (2003) 'Focus groups in cyberspace: using the internet for qualitative research', *Qualitative Market Research: An International Journal*, 6: 133–43.

Orgad, S. (2005) 'From online to offline and back: moving from online to offline relationships with research participants: online interviewing and the research relationship', in C. Hine (ed.), *Virtual Methods: Issues in Social Research on the Internet*. Oxford: Berg, pp. 51–66.

Orgad, S. (2009) 'How can researchers make sense of the issues involved in collecting and interpreting online and offline data?', in A. Markham and N. Baym (eds), *Internet Inquiry: Conversations about Method*. Thousand Oaks, CA: Sage, pp. 33–53.

Peacock, S., Robertson, A., Williams, S. and Clausen, M. (2009) 'The role of learning technologists in supporting E-research', *ALT-J*, 17: 115–29.

Sanders, T. (2005) 'Researching the online sex work community', in C. Hine (ed.), *Virtual Methods: Issues in Social Research on the Internet*. Oxford: Berg, pp. 67–80.

Stieger, S. and Göritz, A. S. (2006) 'Using instant messaging for internet-based interviews', *Cyberpsychology & Behavior*, 9: 552–9.

Stewart, K. and Williams, M. (2005) 'Researching online populations: the use of online focus groups for social research', *Qualitative Research*, 5: 395–416.

Sullivan, J. R. (2012) 'Skype: an appropriate method of data collection for qualitative interviews?', *The Hilltop Review*, 6 (1): Article 10. http://scholarworks.wmich.edu/hilltopress/vol6/iss1/10 (accessed 3 May 2015).

Waskul, D. and Douglass, M. (1997) 'Cyberself: the emergence of self in on-line chat', *Information Society*, 13: 375–98.

Williams, S., Giatsi, M., Robertson, A. and Peacock, S. (2012) 'Methodological reflections on the use of asynchronous online focus groups in health research', *International Journal of Qualitative Methods*, 11: 368–83.

SIXTEEN

Using Conversation Analysis and Discursive Psychology to Analyse Online Data

Joanne Meredith

About this chapter

This chapter explores how to use conversation analysis and discursive psychology for the analysis of online data. It investigates the challenges of analysing online data and, using examples from online forum and instant messaging data, demonstrates how these methods can illuminate participants' interactional practices in the context of particular technological affordances.

Keywords

conversation analysis, discursive psychology, instant messaging, online forums, technological affordances

```
FranchiseThis 24 Mar 2010, 4:11PM
P:  I always get a little suspicious when posters
    who I have never seen before get in really
    quick to say how wonderful our government is
    and get a hat full of recommendations
```

```
      in no time flat.
      A cynic might think it was an organised effort
      rather than the
      opinions of one individual.

 FT:  Quite.
      Ironically they also accuse other posters
      of being from Tory HQ.
      Takes a paid apparatchik to know one, eh, Hughesy?
```

This post is a fairly simple example of one type of qualitative online data from an online forum discussion about UK politics. We see one poster (FT) responding to another (P), expressing some suspicion about other posters' impartiality. The question for qualitative researchers is how to analyse these sorts of data. One option is contacting the people who posted these messages and interviewing them to discuss their use of online communication, and their aims or motivations behind the posts (Androutsopoulos, 2008). Such research would be extremely interesting and valuable, but does not allow for the analysis of the interaction itself. Analysing the interaction is important as other posters in the forum only have access to the words on the screen and do not have the ability to interview other users face-to-face. So, if we are interested in interaction, we need to find a way of analysing the words that appear on screen. Clearly, common qualitative methods, such as thematic analysis (TA) and grounded theory (GT), could be used to analyse the data with the aim of finding patterns and themes (see, for example, Malik and Coulson, 2008; Lawlor and Kirakowski, 2014). Such a study of online forum posts would give us some sense of the patterns that occur across different posts and the general types of discussions that occur online. However, methods like TA and GT tend to condense data into themes or categories, and in doing so, lose the sense of how the data are produced in a specific context (Potter and Hepburn, 2005). In other words, we may miss how any post produced in a forum is part of an interaction. Consider the post above: FT's response is seemingly to P's post, but is also directed at a different poster (Hughesey) and therefore is part of an interaction. However, if a post does not receive a response, could we still consider it an interaction? There are other questions which could also be posed about this online forum post:

- Why does FT not simply ask the poster directly if they are being paid by Tory HQ, rather than hedging it as they do?
- Did the online medium and its various technological features impact upon the conduct of the interaction?

These are all questions which can be addressed using conversation analysis (CA; see Heritage in this volume) and discursive psychology (DP; see Potter in this volume), and will be discussed in more detail throughout the chapter. Rather than focusing on patterns in talk or text, CA and DP focus instead on how talk and text are rhetorically and sequentially situated in a particular context. These interactional methods have been developed for, and are most commonly used with, spoken interaction. However, there is growing use of these methods to study online communication (Meredith and Potter, 2013; Giles et al., 2015).

This chapter will demonstrate how online forums and instant messaging can be analysed using CA or DP, while also showing how these methods can illuminate the impact of the technological affordances on the interaction. While only two types of data are used in this chapter, it is hoped that the analysis presented will prove instructive for the analysis of other forms of online data. Before moving on to the analysis, it is necessary to discuss some of the more theoretical and conceptual issues about treating online data as an interaction.

ONLINE DATA AS AN INTERACTION

The first issue to be addressed is how we can understand all online communication as interactional. After all, not every post in an online forum will get a response, not every tweet receives a reply, and not all Facebook statuses receive comments. However, we can suggest that online data are 'designedly' interactional, meaning that even if there is no apparent interaction, online data can still be analysed for how they are designed for particular recipients (see Stokoe, 2011, for example). This idea draws on the concept of 'recipient design', which is fundamental to both CA and DP. It is described as:

> The multitude of respects in which talk by a party in a conversation is constructed or designed in ways which display an orientation and sensitivity to the particular other(s) who are the co-participants. (Sacks et al., 1974: 727)

Discussing co-participants in online data is more complicated than in spoken talk, because there can be a number of participants interacting online. Consider this example: a tweet is sent from Hillary Clinton to Barack Obama, but Obama never responds to the tweet. The initial tweet is designed for Obama, who is the *direct* recipient. However, if a person follows both Clinton and Obama, the tweet will appear in their timeline and so they will be *indirect* recipients. In addition, there may be people who come across the tweet via a news report or on another website. These readers are not necessarily 'ratified' participants in this interaction, but instead are 'overhearing' recipients (Goffman, 1981). There are, then, a number of potential recipients for that one tweet – the direct, indirect and overhearing recipient. Similarly, the post at the start of this chapter could be seen as being designed for P who is the direct recipient. However, it is also designed for Hughesey who could be seen as a direct recipient, as they are named in the post. The post is also, though, designed for all the other people who may be reading it, who are the overhearing recipients.

The definition of recipient design can, therefore, be rephrased for the current focus:

> recipient design is the multitude of respects in which online communication is constructed or designed in ways which display an orientation and sensitivity to the particular or more general other(s) who are receiving or co-participating in this electronic communication. (Meredith and Potter, 2013: 372)

The approach that CA and DP take to online data, then, is to focus on the data as rhetorically and sequentially organized to 'do' some action. Unlike methods such as computer-mediated discourse analysis (Herring, 2004), the aim is not to try and understand people's decision-making processes, gender-bias in posting or any other underlying issues, but is instead to analyse online data as a social practice in its own right (Lamerichs and te Molder, 2003). In other words, CA and DP move away from treating *internet-data-as-resource* to understand people's lives and instead move towards treating *internet-data-as-topic* (Zimmerman and Pollner, 1970; Rapley, 2001); that is, seeing this as a topic of study in its own right.

Key points

- CA and DP treat all online communication as designedly interactional or 'recipient-designed'
- There are a number of potential recipients for online communication: direct, indirect and overhearing.
- CA/DP move away from treating internet data as a way to get at the people 'behind the screen', but instead examine online interaction as a topic in its own right.

CONVERSATION ANALYSIS, DISCURSIVE PSYCHOLOGY AND ANALYSING ONLINE INTERACTION

CA and DP have been applied to online interaction, although DP is more prominently used as it 'extends more readily to studies of written text' (Potter and Edwards, 2013: 702). DP is more broadly interested in the rhetorical organization of talk and text although it also engages with CA, merging an interest in how facts are constructed and how actions are made accountable, with an interest in interaction (Potter, 2012). DP has most often been applied to asynchronous forum data (e.g. Horne and Wiggins, 2009; Lester and Paulus, 2011) and often emphasises the topic of discussion, rather than devoting attention to the local interactional context. Indeed it has tended to model online interaction on everyday interaction in terms of its rhetorical organization (Lamerichs and te Molder, 2003; Flinkfeldt, 2011).

CA has more commonly been used for analysing the sequential organization of online interaction. This research has focused on a variety of practices, including how participants maintain coherence (Berglund, 2009), manage turn-taking (Garcia and Jacobs, 1999) and deal with potential trouble in interaction (Meredith and Stokoe, 2014). We might, though, ask questions about the suitability of a method which, by its very name, appears to focus on spoken conversation. Reed and Ashmore (2000) note that when CA studies of textual interaction were first published, they were criticized – by some – for being an inappropriate type of interaction to study. Questions have also been raised about the appropriateness of applying a method of analysis developed for spoken interaction to written interaction (Androutsopoulos and Beisswenger, 2008). Similar arguments have been made about extending CA to visual conduct and visual objects (Greiffenhagen and Watson, 2009). However, from the very outset conversation analysts have been interested in, and have analysed, embodied conduct, such as hand gestures, posture, gaze and so on (e.g. Heath and Luff, 2013). For example, Robinson (1998) examined how gaze and body position are used in medical consultations by doctors and found that such embodied conduct indicates doctors' engagement or disengagement with particular social actions. Heath (2013) has studied auctions in detail, and has demonstrated the importance of even minor non-verbal actions in buying and selling items. These studies, and numerous others like them, show that embodied and multi-modal conduct can be subject to the same analysis as spoken interaction. The focus of CA is not, then, on 'conversation' in and of itself, but rather on 'the practical accomplishment of social action and activity' (Heath and Luff, 2013: 286).

Another issue to consider is how to take account of the context when analysing the data. CA argues that the meaning of any particular action is differentiated by the context, but interactional practices are also context-free as well as context-specific (Heritage in this volume). While this can be seen to be equally true of online interaction, it is also important to discuss the technological context. However, it should not be presumed that any technological features or affordances (Hutchby, 2001) necessarily impact upon the interaction. Instead, participants' conduct should be examined to see if, and how, their practices *orient* to any particular context or affordance. In other words, we should start with the interaction as the object of interest, and then see how participants' conduct may orient to the particular mediated context in which their interaction takes place.

A brief note on data collection

CA and DP both aim to collect interactions as they occur in people's lives, and as they are understood by participants (Mondada, 2013). Therefore, rather than asking people about how they live their lives using an interview or an experiment, researchers record the actual events (Potter and Edwards, 2001). The same principles apply to collecting data from online sources. The use of laboratory or experimental settings for collecting qualitative data is less preferable to using naturally occurring data taken directly from the internet. Those working within the perspective of CA/DP will want, as far as possible, to collect materials from participants' ordinary use of PCs or other devices rather than setting up such materials in laboratory or other formal settings. At the same time the focus should be on people's use of their familiar programmes. If features of new programmes have to be learnt for the purposes of data collection, this is likely to have an important and not easily explicated impact on the material generated. It is, of course, adequate to work with data collected directly from the site of interest. However, to be able to conduct a good interactional analysis, it is important that as much information is collected as possible. This requirement means at a minimum collecting the timings and context of any online posting, such as, for example, screen shots of online forums or timings of each tweet sent in a Twitter conversation.

The data discussed in this chapter were collected from two online sources: Facebook 'chat' and a newspaper comment site. Facebook 'chat' is an instant messaging facility which, at the time of data collection, allowed for quasi-synchronous interaction; that is, posters had to be logged on at the same time in order to interact, but the interaction was not synchronous due to the separation of message construction and sending. Timed transcripts of Facebook chats were collected by research participants, having first gained consent from their co-participant.

The comment threads, from which the first example in this chapter also comes, were collected on the day of the annual budget in the UK from *The Guardian*'s 'Comment is Free' site. This site functions as a discussion board where users are encouraged to comment on articles published in the newspaper's opinion section. It allows for asynchronous interaction, that is, posters do not have to be logged on at the same time in order to interact. The first 50 posts of one thread and the second 50 posts of another related thread were collected as posted (including spelling errors), along with the name of the poster and the time of each post.

In the following sections I will use examples from both sets of data to demonstrate the insights that CA and DP can provide into such data. Although I use DP for the analysis of forum data and CA for instant messaging, this should in no way suggest that each method should only be used for that type of data.

Key points

- Both CA and DP can be used to analyse online interaction. However, DP may be more suitable for studies of written text as it focuses in more depth on the rhetorical organization of talk, whereas CA tends to focus on the sequential organization.
- We can examine the interaction itself to understand how participants' interactional practices orient to the mediated context.
- Data should be collected which are, as far as possible, naturally occurring. As much context as possible should be collected, particularly the timings of the data.

ANALYSING FORUM DATA

This section focuses on the analysis of asynchronous forum data from *The Guardian*'s 'Comment is Free' website. The analysis will demonstrate the insights that a DP analysis can provide, and also how such analysis can illuminate certain technological affordances.

In the first example in this section, we see the original post which was quoted at the start of this chapter. In this post, Peason1 is indirectly responding to another poster's positive comments about the government.

Extract 1

Peason1, 24 Mar 2010, 4:06PM
```
1    P:    I always get a little suspicious when posters
2          who I have never seen before get in
3          really quick to say how wonderful
4          our government is and get a hat full
5          of recommendations in no time flat.
6          A cynic might think it was an
7          organised effort rather than
8          the opinions of one individual.
```

Peason1 builds an argument that implies that another poster may be posting as part of an 'organised effort' (line 7) rather than as an individual and as such they can be seen as having a stake or interest in posting a particular viewpoint. Peason1 builds their accusation in a way which also manages what Edwards (2005) describes as the 'subject-side' of the post, which refers to how speakers manage the potential inferences that can be made about them (Edwards, 2005). We might question whether individuals posting anonymously on an online forum would necessarily be concerned about the opinions of other, equally anonymous, individuals, but as Sacks notes, people will control for 'an impression of themselves for somebody who couldn't matter less' (1992, cited in Silverman, 1998: 16). So, Peason1 manages the subject-side of their post to ensure that any potential for counter-claims or accusations can be mitigated.

Firstly, Peason1 does not make an explicit accusation towards a particular person, but rather talks about 'posters I have never seen before', as a general category of posters. The formulation of this complaint means that objective measures (such as when the poster signed up to the site) cannot be used to discern who the post is directed at. Instead, in order to offer any counter-argument, the poster would have to implicitly place themselves within the subjective category of posters Peason1 had never seen before.

Secondly, the post contains extreme case formulations (ECFs) (Edwards, 2000), such as 'never' (line 2), 'a hat full' (line 4) and 'no time flat' (line 5). ECFs function to emphasize or highlight the point while also signalling 'a speaker's investment in that point'

(Edwards, 2000: 364). They can also be used as a way of performing irony, teasing or joking. So, Peason1 uses ECFs to show their investment in their point, but the teasing or ironic formulation of the accusation allows them to soften it, and deny that it should be taken seriously.

In the latter half of the post (from line 6) Peason1 moves from talking about what *they* think, to talking about what a particular *category* of person might think. This move shifts from a subjective evaluation to a categorial description and can be heard as more objective. Peason1 does not directly state that the other poster is posting on behalf of the government, but rather states that someone who classed themselves as a 'cynic' might think this. However, Peason1 also describes themselves as 'suspicious', which could be heard as being a characteristic, or predicate, of someone who placed themselves within the category of 'cynic'. They therefore implicitly place themselves within that category. Thus, Peason1 works to make the accusation hearably objective, but by using a category of which they are implicitly incumbent, enables recipients to infer that Peason1 is the one making the accusation.

Through using a DP analysis, then, we can start to build up a picture of how such posts are built rhetorically to do particular actions. Peason1 builds up an accusation, while at the same time managing any potential inferences or counter-claims by building it in such a way that it is merely an *implicit* accusation. It is also notable that these types of accusations are reliant on posters being able to use a pseudonym and therefore being anonymous. The analysis shows that this technological feature is an affordance which participants can draw upon when constructing their posts.

The following example demonstrates further how posts are recipient-designed and how anonymity is a resource drawn on by participants to do particular interactional work.

Extract 2

```
Hughesey, 24 Mar 2010, 4:03PM
1   H:    Shinsie
2         So you are saying Ashcroft has
3         pulled the wool over the Tories
4         eyes again it will probably take another
5         10 years for them to figures this out.
6         Or maybe you have been sent from
7         Tory Central Office to put us all of the scent. <
8         I wonder which it is.
```

In this example, Hughesey is responding to a post by Shinsie. Hughesey questions whether Shinsie may in fact be posting on behalf of 'Tory Central Office' (line 7). There are a number of similarities with the previous example. For example, Hughesey also works to manage the subject-side of their post, through avoiding making an outright accusation (such as 'you are from Tory Central Office'), but rather softening it by posing it as a question and using the word 'maybe' in line 6. This construction manages the possibility that were Hughesey to be held accountable for the accusation, they could deny that it was meant (too) seriously.

There are also notable differences with the previous example, not least that this post is directed *at* a specific recipient. The post is, therefore, explicitly designed for Shinsie, as evidenced by the use of Shinsie's name in line 1. However, other posters – the indirect and overhearing participants – are also able to read this post, and so the content will also be designed for them. This analysis is not merely my interpretation, but is in fact warranted by Hughesey implicitly orienting to other recipients by mentioning 'us all' in line 7. Using DP to analyse these data allows us to demonstrate empirically how participants construct their posts for multiple audiences.

This post again demonstrates how anonymity can be used as a rhetorical device, through Hughesey implying that Shinsie may not be an impartial commentator. However, it also demonstrates how participants manage the multi-party nature of the interaction. In particular, the use of an address term at the outset ensures that it is clear who Hughesey is responding to, which manages the difficulties of interacting in a multi-party forum.

One final point of note about Extract 2 is the organization of the post. The first part of the post consists of Hughesey responding to Shinsie, with the second part working to undermine Shinsie as a poster and the final part comprising a – potentially rhetorical – question. Sacks et al. (1974) note that in spoken interaction turns often have a similar three-part structure, where the first part of the turn addresses the prior turn, the second part is 'involved with what is occupying the turn' (1974: 722), and the final part addresses the next turn in the series. There are, then, some potential similarities which can be identified between turn design in online and offline interaction.

Key points

- Posts are recipient-designed for direct and indirect recipients.
- Posters attempt to manage the subject-side of their post through using ECFs, mitigating their accusations and using categories.
- Anonymity is a resource which is drawn on by participants, and is relevant to the interaction.
- Posts are organized sequentially and practices used which maintain the coherence of the interaction in a multi-party environment.

ANALYSING INSTANT MESSAGING CHATS

This section uses data drawn from the corpus of Facebook chats and will demonstrate how these chats can be analysed using CA and how such analysis can illuminate participants' orientations to the medium. To start, consider this extract, where the participants (Joe and Isla) are discussing what they have done and are planning to do that day.

Extract 3 (JM/IS20/B: 96-125)

```
1    Joe:   I have showered and cooked
2                   (4.0)
3    Joe:   that is all
4                   (21.0)
5    Joe:   some one tried to add
6           photos of me from friday ☺
7                   (1.0)
8    Isla:  yeah I need to cook
9                   (11.0)
10   Isla:  and I think we might watch a film
11          too
12                  (1.0)
13   Joe:   yea you need cock? ….......what?
14                  (1.0)
15   Isla:  who>>
16                  (11.0)
17   Joe:   lol
18                  (2.0)
19   Isla:  its says cook joe
20                  (1.0)
21   Isla:  lol
22                  (0.0)
23   Joe:   a girl
```

In this extract, it is noticeable that the sequence does not develop as we might expect in spoken interaction, with first pair parts and second pair parts adjacent to one another. Instead, turn adjacency, which is so critical in spoken talk (Schegloff, 2007), is disrupted. For example, in lines 1–3 Joe is talking about what he has done that day, before starting a new topic in lines 5–6, which is the first pair part of an adjacency pair. A second later Isla posts a message which responds to Joe's messages in lines 1–3. The second pair part of the adjacency pair is therefore dislocated from the first pair part. Disrupted turn adjacency has been found in many types of online interaction (Herring, 2007) and it has been suggested that this disruption occurs because the construction of a message occurs 'privately' and separate from the sending of the message to the public space. In other words, disrupted turn adjacency occurs because the participants cannot mutually coordinate their turns as in spoken interaction. For example, in Extract 3 we could surmise that Isla and Joe were writing at the same time between lines 4 and 8 due to Isla posting her message only one-second after Joe's (line 8). The turn disruption occurs because both parties may have been constructing their messages at the same time, but neither party will have known when the other would send their message. However, we must be careful about presuming that the separation of message construction and sending necessarily determines that turn adjacency will be disrupted. Participants may be aware that their co-participant is writing due to a small 'writing' icon in the corner of the screen. Therefore, participants could try to avoid overlaps in writing and so avoid disrupted turn adjacency. Yet participants do not do this and indeed sometimes appear to cause more disruption. For example, consider Isla's turn in lines 10–11 in Extract 3. Joe's turn in lines 5–6 has been sent to the chat window, but Isla does not respond to that in her next turn, but instead posts a continuation of her previous turn about planning to watch a film. Consequently, her response to Joe's turn in lines 5–6 does not occur until line 15, and is thus dislocated from its first pair part.

It is notable that, as with online forums, participants seem to maintain coherence with little difficulty. For example, we can understand that Isla's turn in line 8 is responsive to Joe's in line 1, firstly because the use of the word 'yeah' at the start of the turn suggests that it is an answer to a previous turn. Secondly, her repetition of the word 'cook' provides a link to Joe's use of the word 'cooking'. So we could potentially suggest that 'disrupted' turn adjacency is not actually 'disruptive' for participants at all (Greiffenhagen and Watson, 2005), but rather sequentiality functions differently online.

The following extract demonstrates that there are some, perhaps surprising, similarities in the sequential placement of certain features in online and spoken interaction. Here, Joe and Isla are discussing whether to meet up for training the following morning.

Extract 4 (JM/IS18/B: 89-93)

```
1    Isla: erm like 9am?
2         (7.0)
3    Isla: too early for you joe😛
4         (9.0)
5    Joe:  ☹10 is a maybe
```

In this extract, both Isla and Joe make use of smilies; Isla uses a smiley – a face with its tongue sticking out – at the end of line 3 and Joe uses a 'sad face' smiley at the start of his turn in line 5. In spoken interaction, such features are 'organized in [...] fine detail to coordinate with and sometimes sustain on-going actions' (Potter and Hepburn, 2010: 1543). We find something similar here. Isla places the smiley in her turn at the end to indicate that the action of her turn in line 3 is 'teasing', rather than, say, asserting or assessing. In contrast, Joe *starts* his turn with a 'sad face' smiley, which displays his stance towards Isla's turn as well as potentially his own. Therefore, we can see that as with stance markers and facial expressions in spoken interaction, smilies do different actions depending on their sequential placement (Herring, 2007; Markman and Oshima, 2007). We can also see how the use of smilies orients to, and indeed manages, the lack of face-to-face contact in online interaction.

Key points

- Paired actions in online interaction are not necessarily adjacent, but this does not appear to cause problems in understanding or maintaining coherence.
- The 'disruption' of turn adjacency shows an implicit orientation to the inability to mutually coordinate turns.
- Participants use smilies to indicate stance, and these are – as with spoken interaction – sequentially placed to do certain actions.

CHAPTER SUMMARY

The objective of this chapter was to explore how qualitative online data can be analysed using interactional methods such as CA and DP. I have demonstrated how online data can be analysed as a form of interaction that is designed for a recipient, sequentially organized and builds actions. Whether the data are asynchronous (such as from a forum, or from Twitter) or quasi-synchronous (from chat rooms or instant messaging services) they should be treated as a social practice, rather than as a resource for understanding the individuals behind the screen. I have demonstrated, through using sample analysis, how an approach informed by both CA and DP can be fruitful in explicating participants' orientations and revealing the way in which the varied affordances of specific technology and software are relevant to interaction. CA and DP approaches to online interaction can also be integrated into wider projects, where the focus might be on much broader issues. Research questions which focus on, for example, online education, health support online and online relationships, as well as questions around online interactions, norms and practices, could feasibly include some analysis using either CA or DP.

FUTURE PROSPECTS

There are great opportunities for individuals interested in online interaction to develop the use of CA and DP in the analysis of online data. There is an ever-growing range of sites where people can interact online, and this offers the potential to technically ground comparative work on different forms of chat, forums, blogs and so on. This comparative work will be somewhat analogous to work comparing different institutional settings in spoken interaction (i.e. news interviews, police interviews, research interviews and so on). There are also some potential challenges, not least for researchers attempting to keep up with the development of the internet. There may also be more conceptual challenges around using the same terminology for both spoken and online interaction, when the same terms may describe different practices. In addition, as the technology develops for interacting online, it will be important to develop new and innovative methods of data collection for collecting data not only from laptops but also from other internet-enabled devices. In particular, screen-recordings can be used for collecting data, which would provide analysts with access to what is 'live' for the participant at that time and would therefore provide more insight into how online interaction unfolds.

Study questions

1. Consider a number of different types of online communication (e.g. Instagram, YouTube, etc.). In what ways could the content of these sites be thought of as recipient designed?
2. Why is discursive psychology potentially more suitable for written text than conversation analysis?
3. Look again at Extract 3. What practices do Isla and Joe use to maintain coherence in this section of interaction?

Recommended reading

Benwell, B. and Stokoe, E. (2006) *Discourse and Identity*. Edinburgh: Edinburgh University Press. Includes a chapter on virtual identity, with a good overview of broader issues around online discourse.

Hutchby, I. (2001) *Conversation and Technology*. Cambridge: Polity Press.
One of the key texts about CA and technology, it discusses issues around affordances in more detail.

Schegloff, E. A. (2002) 'Beginnings in the telephone', in J. E. Katz and M. A. Aakhus (eds), *Perpetual Contact: Mobile Communication, Private Talk, Public Performance*. Cambridge: Cambridge University Press, pp. 284–300.
Based on a talk given by Schegloff, this chapter does not focus on online interaction but does provide insight into how conversation analysts can approach the analysis of new technology.

References

Androutsopoulos, J. (2008) 'Potentials and limitations of discourse-centred online ethnography', *Language@Internet*, 5 (8). www.languageatinternet.org/articles/2008/1610 (accessed 10 December 2015).
Androutsopoulos, J. and Beisswenger, M. (2008) 'Introduction: data and methods in computer-mediated discourse analysis', *Language@Internet*, 5 (9). www.languageatinternet.org/articles/2008/1609 (accessed 10 December 2015).

Berglund, T. Ö. (2009) 'Disrupted turn adjacency and coherence maintenance in instant messaging conversations', *Language@Internet*, 6 (2). www.languageatinternet.org/articles/2009/2106 (accessed 10 December 2015).

Edwards, D. (2000) 'Extreme case formulations: softeners, investment, and doing nonliteral', *Research on Language and Social Interaction*, 33 (4): 347–73.

Edwards, D. (2005) 'Moaning, whinging and laughing: the subjective side of complaints', *Discourse Studies*, 7 (1): 5–29.

Flinkfeldt, M. (2011) '"Filling one's days": managing sick leave legitimacy in an online forum', *Sociology of Health & Illness*, 33 (5): 761–76.

Garcia, A. C. and Jacobs, J. B. (1999) 'The eyes of the beholder: understanding the turn-taking system in quasi-synchronous computer-mediated communication', *Research on Language and Social Interaction*, 32 (4): 337–67.

Giles, D., Stommel, W., Paulus, T., Lester, J. and Reed, D. (2015) 'Microanalysis of online data: the methodological development of 'digital CA', *Discourse, Context & Media*, 7: 45–51.

Goffman, E. (1981) *Forms of Talk*. Oxford: Basil Blackwell.

Greiffenhagen, C. and Watson, R. (2005) '"Teoria" e "método" na CMC: identidade, género e tomada-deturno: uma abordagem etnometodológica e analítico conversacional' ['Theory' and 'method' in CMC: identity, gender, and turn-taking: an ethnomethodological and conversation analytic approach], in A. Braga (ed.), *CMC, Identidades e Género: Teoria e Método*. Covilhã: Universidade da Beira Interior, pp. 89–114.

Greiffenhagen, C. and Watson, R. (2009) 'Visual repairables: analysing the work of repair in human-computer interaction', *Visual Communication*, 8 (1): 65–90.

Heath, C. (2013) *The Dynamics of Auction: Social Interaction and the Sale of Fine Art and Antiques*. Cambridge: Cambridge University Press.

Heath, C. and Luff, P. (2013) 'Embodied action and organizational activity', in J. Sidnell and T. Stivers (eds), *The Handbook of Conversation Analysis*. Oxford: Wiley Blackwell, pp. 281–307.

Herring, S. C. (2004) 'Computer-mediated discourse analysis: an approach to researching online behavior', in S. A. Barab, R. Kling and J. H. Gray (eds), *Designing for Virtual Communities in the Service of Learning*. New York: Cambridge University Press, pp. 338–76.

Herring, S. C. (2007) 'A faceted classification scheme for computer-mediated discourse', *Language@Internet*, 4 (1). www.languageatinternet.org/articles/2007/761 (accessed 10 December 2015).

Horne, J. and Wiggins, S. (2009) 'Doing being "on the edge": managing the dilemma of being authentically suicidal in an online forum', *Sociology of Health and Illness*, 31 (2): 170–84.

Hutchby, I. (2001) 'Technologies, texts and affordances', *Sociology*, 35: 441–56.

Lamerichs, J. and te Molder, H. F. M. (2003) 'Computer-mediated communication: from a cognitive to a discursive model', *New Media & Society*, 5 (4): 451–73.

Lawlor, A. and Kirakowski, J. (2014) 'When the lie is the truth: grounded theory analysis of an online support group for factitious disorder', *Psychiatry Research*, 218 (1): 209–18.

Lester, J. N. and Paulus, T. M. (2011) 'Accountability and public displays of knowing in an undergraduate computer-mediated communication context', *Discourse Studies*, 13 (6): 671–86.

Malik, S. H. and Coulson, N. (2008) 'The male experience of infertility: a thematic analysis of an online infertility support group bulletin board', *Journal of Reproductive and Infant Psychology*, 26 (1): 18–30.

Markman, K. M. and Oshima, S. (2007) 'Pragmatic play? Some possible functions of English emoticons and Japanese Kaomoji in computer-mediated discourse', paper presented at the *Association of Internet Researchers Annual Conference 8.0: Let's Play!* Vancouver, BC, Canada, 18 October. www.academia.edu/2666102/Pragmatic_play_Some_possible_functions_ of_English_emoticons_and_Japanese_kaomoji_in_computer-mediated_discourse (accessed 10 December 2015).

Meredith, J. and Potter, J. (2013) 'Conversation analysis and electronic interactions: meth- odological, analytic and technical considerations', in H. Lim and F. Sudweeks (eds), *Innovative Methods and Technologies for Electronic Discourse Analysis*. Hershey, USA: IGI Global, pp. 370–93.

Meredith, J. and Stokoe, E. (2014) 'Repair: comparing Facebook "chat" with spoken inter- action', *Discourse & Communication*, 8 (2): 181–207.

Mondada, L. (2013) 'The conversation analytic approach to data collection', in T. Stivers and J. Sidnell (eds), *The Handbook of Conversation Analysis*. Oxford: Wiley-Blackwell, pp. 32–56.

Potter, J. (2012) 'Discourse analysis and discursive psychology', in H. Cooper (ed.), *APA Handbook of Research Methods in Psychology: Vol. 2. Quantitative, Qualitative, Neuropsychological and Biological*. Washington: American Psychological Association, pp. 111–30.

Potter, J. and Edwards, D. (2001) 'Discursive social psychology', in P. W. Robinson and H. Giles (eds), *The New Handbook of Language and Social Psychology* (2nd edn). Oxford: Wiley, pp. 103–18.

Potter, J. and Edwards, D. (2013) 'Conversation analysis and psychology', in T. Stivers and J. Sidnell (eds), *The Handbook of Conversation Analysis*. Oxford: Wiley, pp. 701–25.

Potter, J. and Hepburn, A. (2005) 'Qualitative interviews in psychology: problems and pos- sibilities', *Qualitative Research in Psychology*, 2 (4): 281–307.

Potter, J. and Hepburn, A. (2010) 'Putting aspiration into words: "laugh particles", manag- ing descriptive trouble and modulating action', *Journal of Pragmatics*, 42: 1543–55.

Rapley, T. J. (2001) 'The art(fulness) of open-ended interviewing: some considerations on analysing interviews', *Qualitative Research*, 1 (3): 303–23.

Reed, D. and Ashmore, M. (2000) 'The naturally-occurring chat machine', *M/C: A Journal of Media and Culture*, 3 (4). http://journal.media-culture.org.au/0008/machine.php (accessed 10 December 2015)

Robinson, J. D. (1998) 'Getting down to business: talk, gaze, and body orientation dur- ing openings of doctor-patient consultations', *Human Communication Research*, 25 (1): 97–123.

Sacks, H., Schegloff, E. A. and Jefferson, G. (1974) 'A simplest systematics for the organiza- tion of turn-taking in conversation', *Language*, 50 (4): 696–735.

Schegloff, E. A. (2007) *Sequence Organization in Interaction: A Primer in Conversation Analysis*. Cambridge: Cambridge University Press.

Silverman, D. (1998) *Harvey Sacks: Social Science and Conversation Analysis*. Oxford: Oxford University Press.

Stokoe, E. (2011) '"Girl – woman – sorry!": on the repair and non-repair of consecutive gender categories', in S. A. Speer and E. Stokoe (eds), *Conversation and Gender*. Cambridge: Cambridge University Press, pp. 84–111.

Zimmerman, D. H. and Pollner, M. (1970) 'The everyday world as a phenomenon', in H. B. Pepinsky (ed.), *People and Information*. Oxford: Pergamon Press, pp. 33–66.

SEVENTEEN

Critical Discourse Studies and Social Media Data

Johann W. Unger, Ruth Wodak and Majid KhosraviNik

About this chapter

This chapter outlines key theoretical and methodological aspects of critical discourse studies (CDS) and suggests how they may be applied to social media data. After a brief overview of the main features of CDS, there is a discussion of what makes data in digitally mediated contexts different and interesting for researchers who adopt a critical perspective to social phenomena. Eight methodological steps from one approach to CDS, the discourse-historical approach, are presented with specific reference to how they can be applied to social media data. In the final part of the chapter, a case study analysing some aspects of the 'life of protest movements' (Arab Spring, Occupy) on Web 2.0 is used by way of illustration.

Keywords

social media, critical discourse studies, digital discourse, context, Facebook, genre, discourse-historical approach, Twitter, Flickr, Tumblr, Arab Spring, Occupy, multilingualism, hegemony, intertextuality, recontextualization, interdiscursivity

INTRODUCING CRITICAL DISCOURSE STUDIES (CDS)

Since the late 1980s, critical discourse analysis (CDA), or as it has more recently come to be called critical discourse studies (CDS), has become a well-established field in the social sciences. CDS can be defined as a problem-oriented interdisciplinary research programme, subsuming a variety of approaches, each with different theoretical models, research methods and agenda. What unites all approaches is a shared interest in the semiotic dimensions of power, injustice and political-economic, social or cultural change in society. 'Semiotic' here refers to systems of signs, such as words, sounds and images that are used in meaningful ways by motivated individuals and groups in society. For example, protesters carrying banners are engaging in multiple semiotic acts: their banners may have writing or pictures on them, they may be chanting slogans using their voice, and their very presence, en masse, in a public space, may be seen as carrying meaning (see Kress and van Leeuwen, 2006: 7ff for a further discussion of different approaches to semiotics).

CDS scholars do not study a specific linguistic unit *per se* but rather social phenomena which are necessarily complex and thus require an approach that draws on different disciplines and makes use of different methods. The objects under investigation do not have to be related to only negative or exceptionally 'serious' social or political experiences or events. This is a frequent misunderstanding of the aims and goals of CDS where the term 'critical' does not mean 'negative' as it does in common usage (see Chilton et al., 2010). Any social phenomenon lends itself to critical investigation, to be challenged and not taken for granted.

All CDS approaches are problem-oriented, and thus necessarily interdisciplinary and eclectic. CDS is characterized by a common interest in de-mystifying ideologies and power through the systematic and transparent investigation of semiotic data (written, spoken, visual or other meaningful forms and practices). CDS researchers attempt to make their own positions and interests explicit while retaining their respective scholarly methodologies and while remaining self-reflective about their own research process.

CDS scholars see discourse – language use in speech and writing – as a form of 'social practice'. Describing discourse as social practice implies a two-way relationship between a particular discursive event and the situation(s), institution(s) and social structure(s), which frame it: the discursive event is shaped by them, but it also shapes them. Since discourse is so socially consequential, it gives rise to important issues of power. Discursive practices may have major ideological effects – that is, they can help produce and reproduce unequal power relations between (for instance) social classes, genders and ethnic/cultural majorities and minorities through the ways in which they represent things and position people (Fairclough and Wodak, 1997). As a broad research programme, most critical studies of discourse are based on the analysis of a topic-related body of linguistic data positioned and explained in relation to a socio-political context with a critical angle. Within this broad framework, texts are analysed against genre-specific (institutional, media) backgrounds to address the processes of distribution. This includes providing some background to:

- the nature of the data
- how is the text received (e.g. number of likes or shares, what is the nature of the comments)
- the possibilities provided by the genre of communication
- the semiotic features of the language used (see for example Wodak, 2011, 2014, on the four-level context model of the discourse-historical approach; and KhosraviNik, 2010, on the interaction of context levels).

Three important concepts: critique, ideology and power

Work within CDS encompasses varied understandings of the terms 'critical', 'criticism' and 'critique':

- Critical analysis of discourse can imply that researchers 'make the implicit explicit' – making explicit the implicit relationship between discourse, power and ideology, challenging surface meanings, and not taking anything for granted.
- 'Being critical' in CDA includes being self-reflective and self-critical. In this sense, CDA does not only mean criticizing others. It also means critiquing the 'critical' itself.
- Critical analysis itself is a practice that may contribute to social change – bringing the socio-political and structural context into the analysis and interpretation of textual meanings.
- Naming oneself 'critical' implies explicit ethical standards: an intention to make the researcher's position, interests and values explicit and their criteria as transparent as possible, without feeling the need to apologize for the critical stance of their work (Reisigl and Wodak, 2001: 32ff; van Leeuwen, 2006: 293; Wodak, 2013; Angermuller et al., 2014; Wodak and Meyer, 2015).

Although the core definition of ideology as a *coherent and relatively stable set of beliefs or values* has remained the same in political science over time, the connotations associated with this concept have undergone many transformations. Clearly it is not easy to capture ideology as a belief system and simultaneously to free the concept from negative connotations (Knight, 2006: 625). It is the functioning of ideologies in everyday life that intrigues CDS researchers. Moreover, we have to distinguish between ideology (or other frequently used terms such as stance/beliefs/opinions/*Weltanschauung*/positioning) and discourse (Purvis and Hunt, 1993: 474ff).

'Ideology' is usually (more or less) closely associated with the Marxist tradition, whereas 'discourse' has gained much significance in the linguistic turn in modern social theory 'by providing a term with which to grasp the way in which language and other forms of social semiotics not merely convey social experience but play some major part in constituting social objects (the subjectivities and their associated identities), their relations, and the field in which they exist' (Purvis and Hunt, 1993: 474).

Power is the third concept which is central for CDS: CDS researchers are interested in the way discourse produces and reproduces social domination, that is, power abuse of one group over others, and how dominated groups may discursively resist such abuse. This raises the question of how CDS researchers define power and what moral standards allow them to differentiate between power use and abuse – a question which has so far had to remain unanswered (Billig, 2008). Holzscheiter (2005) points out that much CDS research is concerned with differentiating the modes of exercising power *in discourse* and *over discourse* in the field of politics:

- *Power in discourse* here means actors' struggles over different interpretations of meaning.
- *Power over discourse* is defined as processes of inclusion and exclusion (Wodak, 2007).
- *Power of discourse* relates to 'the influence of historically grown macro-structures of meaning, of the conventions of the language game in which actors find themselves' (Holzscheiter, 2005: 61).

In texts, discursive differences are negotiated; they are governed by differences in power that is in part encoded in, and determined by, discourse and by genre. Therefore texts are often sites of struggle in that they show traces of differing discourses and ideologies contending for dominance.

CDS AND SOCIAL MEDIA

When considering how the framework can be applied to social media, we are careful to acknowledge differences in data types and new affordances that account for the overall qualities of texts before engaging in more detailed analysis. However, the separation of the 'online world' as a strikingly different discursive arena, as advocated by early studies in computer-mediated communication (CMC), does not sit well theoretically with the socially critical aspirations of CDS research. Thus, just as CDS scholars would not endorse an analytical approach that strictly separates the data from their immediate or broader contexts, they should also not treat 'offline' and 'online' as separate and independent of one another, a world view that Jurgenson (2012) terms 'digital dualism'.

Any text may be seen as existing within multiple contexts (see for example, van Dijk, 2005, or Reisigl and Wodak, 2009, for two different approaches to context in CDS). For social media data specifically, it is worthwhile paying some attention to the media practices and the affordances of the technologies that allow social media data to be produced and shared, just as for newspaper texts, journalistic and editorial practices may be a legitimate focus of attention.

Although interactivity and the possibility of users changing roles, from text consumers to text producers, is an overall characteristic of the participatory web, this dynamic is not always present in various sub-genres of the web. Communicative practices in the participatory web often involve a bundle of relatively static organizationally controlled texts, e.g. adverts and 'about' pages, as well as what is more usually seen as social media data, namely interactive and dynamically evolving user-generated texts, such as comment threads on newspaper sites or under Facebook posts. For a CDS study involving social

Table 17.1 Medium and situation factors (from Herring, 2007, quoted in Page et al., 2014)

Medium factors	Synchronicity	Asychronous–synchronous
	Message transmission	One-to-one; one-to-many; many-to-many
	Persistence of the transcript	Ephemeral – archived
	Size of the message	Amount of text conveyed
	Channels of communication	Words, images, sounds, videos
	Privacy settings	Public, semi-public, semi-private, private contexts
	Anonymous	Extent to which the participants' identities are represented within a site
	Message format	Architecture for displaying interactions
Situation factors	Participation structure	Number of participants involved
	Participant characteristics	Stated or assumed demographic and ideological characteristics
	Purpose	Goals of interaction (at either individual or group level)
	Topic	Subject matter
	Tone	Formal or informal
	Norms	Accepted practices established by the group
	Code	Language variety and choice of script

media data, these institutional texts should be viewed and analysed within their new interactive context, while bearing in mind that the social nature of communication is the core quality of textual practice in the participatory web.

The table above (Table 17.1) shows some of the factors that can be considered in linguistic and semiotic analyses of social media data in general, and some of these are then taken up in our case study to illustrate how they can be integrated into a CDS approach.

HOW TO CONDUCT A CRITICAL DISCURSIVE ANALYSIS OF SOCIAL MEDIA DATA

There are some confounding logistical issues regarding harnessing and defining analytical materials in social media, for instance:

- How to collect and select data from the vast amounts available on some social media platforms.
- How to deal with the inherent non-linearity of text production and consumption processes.
- How to define context vis-à-vis social media.
- How to deal with the fleeting nature of data and constant changes in the format and functions of platforms.

- How to incorporate systematic observations to account for media and genre-specific contexts of communication.
- How to decide on an ethical framework that respects individuals' rights and their understanding of how public their data should be.

The non-linear forms of communication on the participatory web (see Markham and Stavrova in this volume) indicate the usefulness of more observational research approaches, in other words attending to communicative events and practices rather than treating communicative data just as texts to be studied in isolation. Participant-observer methods (at least in the initial stages of a study) seem a good way to study how users communicate, what affordances platforms permit, their interconnectivity, the features of different genres and the broader media context. Hence, a case-study approach to data and analysis seems to suit a CDS approach. We suggest three broad orientations:

1. As discourse analysts we consider the social context of the users and their communication.
2. As critical discourse analysts we are not satisfied with the mere description of genre, content and communication.
3. As social-media scholars we view the participatory Web as part of a media apparatus which is used by individuals in society, hence we do not treat digitally mediated texts as part of a 'virtual' world that is separate from the physical world and 'reality', despite acknowledging that digitally mediated contexts have specific features that may affect our analyses.

For the purposes of this chapter we will outline the eight methodological steps identified within the discourse-historical approach to CDS (Reisigl and Wodak, 2015), and give some indications for how these can be applied in the context of social media research:

1. *Activation and consultation of preceding theoretical knowledge* (i.e. recollection, reading and discussion of previous research): many of the explanatory theories from traditional applications of CDS (e.g. concerned with politics, the traditional media, institutions) may continue to be relevant, because social media data are still a part of society and its uses often relate to political, media or other institutions. However, there is a growing critical body of work on social media (Fuchs, 2014), and in related areas such as participatory media (Bruns, 2008), citizen journalism (Bruns, 2005), and digitally mediated activism (Potts et al., 2014) that should be consulted depending on the nature of the research.
2. *Systematic collection of data and context information* (depending on what the research question, various discourses and discursive event and social fields, as well as actors, semiotic media, genres and texts are focused on): this can form part of the initial ethnographic/participant observations, or can involve reading more broadly about the history and traditions of a particular social media platform or digitally mediated community. Where information is scarce, interviews or focus groups with users of a platform or members of a community can provide context but could also be part of the data.
3. *Selection and preparation of data for specific analyses* (selection and downsizing of data according to relevant criteria, transcription of tape recordings, etc.): many social media platforms make it relatively easy to acquire huge volumes of related information, because they are often searchable, and they have built-in systems to link different groups or texts thematically (e.g. through (hash)tags, personalized suggestions or algorithmic ordering of search results that are 'most relevant for you'). Of course, ethnographic/observational or participant-oriented work can help in making such difficult decisions.
4. *Specification of the research question and formulation of assumptions* (on the basis of a literature review and a first skimming of the data): as suggested above, consulting previous work on digitally mediated discourse can help researchers identify the most salient categories of analysis, hopefully avoiding the

rather unfruitful exercise of just pointing out the differences between social media data and non-social media data.

5. *Qualitative pilot analysis* (allows testing categories and first assumptions as well as the further specification of assumptions): building in an additional participant stage to confront the creators/typical audiences of the social media data being used with the initial analysis, and making adjustments where appropriate, can be very valuable here. However, qualitative analysis may also comprise the communicative events or contexts directly, the results of which can then be juxtaposed with previous theoretical insights (step 1) or contextual information (step 2)

6. *Detailed case studies* (of a whole range of data, primarily qualitative, but in part also quantitative): as in step 3 above, the availability of data is not usually the issue. However, gathering these data ethically (see Markham and Stavrova, and Ryen, both in this volume) and also narrowing down the volume of data to a manageable amount can be a challenge.

7. *Formulation of critique* (interpretation of results, taking into account the relevant context knowledge and referring to the three dimensions of critique): while not every CDS project has necessarily to be critical of the technologies and commercial priorities underlying many social media platforms, this should nevertheless be something that researchers are aware of when formulating their critique.

8. *Application of the detailed analytical results* (if possible, the results might be applied or proposed for application): it is almost trivially easy to make the results of research available publicly to anyone who is interested, and this is becoming more commonplace in academia in general. When the object of investigation is also social media, it seems appropriate to share research results via social media when possible, for example using accessible blog posts or easily digestible infographics.

It is beyond the scope of this chapter to give a detailed list of linguistic and semiotic phenomena that a CDS researcher who is interested in social media might analyse, but many of the classic analytical categories used in various approaches to CDS (see Wodak and Meyer, 2015), such as modality, presupposition, syntax, nominalization or metaphors, can often still be relevant, and can be combined with the factors listed by Herring (2007). It is important to note that the choice of which categories to analyse is highly context and genre-dependent. Herring (2013) distinguishes between different kinds of genres in the participatory web: familiar (e.g. email or text-based chat), reconfigured (e.g. review websites, which now tend to include primarily user-generated rather than expert-generated content) and emergent (e.g. microblogs like Twitter). It is important to keep these genre differences in mind when establishing analytical categories, as phenomena that are highly salient in one genre (for instance, jokes and irony used in a formal speech by a politician) may be less so in social-media contexts, or vice versa.

CASE STUDY: THE ROLE OF TECHNOLOGIES AND MULTILINGUALISM IN DIGITALLY MEDIATED PROTEST

In this case study we ask in what ways digitally mediated technologies cause or facilitate, complicate or frustrate communication by, to and between protestors. The data are a collection of images taken by protestors and journalists of signs and placards at physical locations associated with particular protest movements. These 'texts' are retrieved from a Google image search using specific search terms. We follow an *abductive approach* in moving between textual features and theories related to protests, social movements and globalization.

Since the protests and uprisings in the Middle East and North Africa region, the so-called 'Arab Spring', the various manifestations of the 'Occupy' movement and the protests against austerity measures in London and various other affluent cities, scholars in politics, media studies and various other socially engaged disciplines have been trying to unpack the role that social media have played in these contexts.

Much of the media coverage of the Arab Spring and other protest movements such as Occupy has involved photographs and videos of events happening in public spaces in large cities, many of them provided by protestors using their own cameras or smart-phones. But even for people not holding a device in their hands while on Tahrir Square or on the steps of the London Stock Exchange, their physical realities will have been mediated in some way by social media. Thus, Tufekci and Wilson (2012: 3) maintain that 'Social media alter the key tenets of collective action [...] and, in doing so, create new vulnerabilities for even the most durable of authoritarian regimes'. Their overall finding implies that social media accelerated, but were not wholly responsible for, those vulnera-bilities (as some mainstream Western media would have had us believe at the time). The changes in 'key tenets of collective action' could be seen in the content, form, distribution and consumption of images. For example, the image below (Figure 17.1) is of signs laid out in Tahrir Square protesting against the Egyptian President, Hosni Mubarak, who was ousted in 2011 after massive protests across Egypt, and particularly in Tahrir Square in one of the key events of the Arab Spring.

These signs will have been seen by thousands of people in their physical location but they may also have been seen by thousands if not hundreds of thousands more people as images circulated on the web, via social media and on websites associated with more traditional news media. While the analysis of the image itself (the various texts, languages and linguistic varieties used, the arrangement of semiotic elements, for instance drawing on Kress and van Leeuwen (2006) and their grammar of visual semiosis) is an important theme for CDS, in this case study we are focusing on the bigger picture: the relation of images such as these to broader media ecologies and global socio-political changes. The image appears on the first results page of a Google image search for 'Tahrir Square signs' (see below), suggesting Google's algorithms rate it highly. This may be because it is widely linked to, because it is frequently clicked on, or for various other reasons that Google algorithms have decided to indicate an image worthy of attention. The metadata available with the image also give some clues. At the time of writing, it has been viewed approxi-mately 2,500 times on its source page, Al Jazeera's English Flickr page, which is not a huge number, but in addition to being on Flickr, it is also visible on the Wikimedia Foundation page from which it was retrieved for this chapter.

While there are currently no Wikipedia pages linking to it, a Google image-match search shows that this version of the photo has been used on a number of online news sites. The Flickr page also gives a considerable amount of information about the image, for instance that it was taken on a particular type of camera (an entry-level single-lens reflex camera) that might be used by a keen hobby photographer or perhaps a freelance journalist, rather than a mobile device or a professional-level camera. However, the fact that the image is found on Al Jazeera's official Flickr page suggests that it was taken either by a journalist associated with the media corporation, or that they bought the image from someone who was not previously affiliated. All this is valuable information for an analysis of the media/institutional context, and it gives us some clues as to the production and consumption of this digitally mediated image, though it does not of course give all the information that might be revealed through further ethnographic work or contact with the image producer(s).

There is of course value in doing ethnographic work in the physical spaces where events related to a protest are taking place. Through 'on-the-ground' ethnographic work we can gain access to local (or glocal?) representations (or misrepresentations?) of global movements, but to grasp fully how global media (mis)represent local voices, we of course need to include texts drawn from these media in our analysis.

Figure 17.1   Anti-Mubarak signs in Tahrir Square

Source: *Al Jazeera English* under a CC:BY:SA licence

Moreover, many of these movements are not about global problems but about local (or at least national) ones, or local manifestations of global problems. Many of the most powerful actions and images from various protests since 2011 have been oriented towards achieving local objectives – though they have then been photographed, videoed, described in blogs, put on Twitter and then reproduced and *recontextualized* globally. What many activists have been successful in doing is using *intertextual references* to highlight the links and similarities between different movements – where these exist – and in using previous successes (e.g. Tunisia) to present visual and verbal arguments pertaining to their present plight. Thus, we argue that many of these movements are at best quasi-global.

We might ask why these local protests with their quasi-global orientations happen in particular places and at particular times. We draw on the notion of *political opportunity structures* that Kitschelt (1986: 58) finds are 'comprised of specific configurations of resources, institutional arrangements and historical precedents for social mobilization, which facilitate the development of protest movements in some instances and constrain them in others'. This notion seems highly compatible with the critical, context-sensitive analysis of institutions as well as accounting for socio-political contexts of communication (see above). In the present case, the conditions that led to the Arab Spring long preceded the advent of social media: repressive political or military regimes, restrictions on free communication, poverty and violence, heavy-handed policing and many other factors contributed. However, as Tufekci and Wilson (2012) argue, the advent of social media helped to facilitate and accelerate different kinds of communication and we argue that social networking sites should thus be regarded as one element of the political opportunity structures.

In this example we are particularly interested in specific 'technologies of protest'. The argument is that protestors in any context will make use of the technologies that are available to them, and they will utilize these to the maximum extent possible within their affordances. One technology we were particularly struck by was the use of banners, posters or placards – often handwritten or hand-painted – and the subsequent appearance of these signs in images shared via social media. The use of signs of this kind is of course not new, and their appearance in mainstream press photographs has a similarly long pedigree. What is relatively new, however, is the speed at which images of these signs can be spread to viewers not physically co-present and shared and recontextualized on various social media platforms. This thus provides us with a compelling reason for studying digitally mediated texts in this context: the strategic (and perhaps sometimes accidental) distribution of specific images from a physical protest location via social and traditional media has become a vital link within and between social movements. However, at the same time that protesters are trying to get their message out, garner more support, seek help from abroad, etc., they are working unpaid for social media corporations and generating advertising revenue.

The strong *intertextual and interdiscursive* links between signs in various contexts also warranted further examination. For instance, one image of a handheld sign in Tahrir Square, photographed in February 2011, bears the slogan 'Egypt Supports Wisconsin Workers:

One World, One Pain', thus expressing support for workers in the US State of Wisconsin, who were at the time protesting against proposed laws attacking their employment rights and pensions (see http://crooksandliars.com/scarce/sign-tahrir-square). The full extent of this intertextuality becomes apparent when digitally mediated texts are brought into the physical environment of a protest, e.g. a poster showing a Facebook 'Like' icon or Twitter hashtag, which is then remediated by being photographed and posted and shared via social media. Furthermore, various ways of challenging dominant ideologies, e.g. drawing on anti-capitalism or calls for political freedom, as well as connections between events, e.g. references to the Tunisian revolution in the Egyptian uprising, are intertextual bridges between different, but related, more-or-less mediated contexts.

We might ask whether it is the emergence of digital and social media that has made these sorts of strong intertextual links between different protest movements possible in the first place. This is not to suggest that the technologies literally cause the protests, but it is evident that they form part of the political opportunity structures. However, new structures around protests, such as flat hierarchies, shared decision-making and the absence of leaders that have characterized movements like Occupy, may have been made possible by changes in communication structures; in other words, they may have fundamentally changed the relationships between affected individuals and groups, as predicted by Graham (2006). This is supported by González-Bailón et al.'s (2011: 5–6) analysis of the use of Twitter in the Spanish May protests. They found that communication via Twitter involves a:

> trade-off between global bridges (controlled by well connected users) and local networks: the former are efficient at transmitting information, the latter at transmitting behavior. This is one reason why Twitter has played a prominent role in so many recent protests and mobilizations: it combines the global reach of broadcasters with local, personalized relations.

Our key finding, however, is that the relationships between protest movements across the globe are not unlike those between linguistic communities, whereby global languages (particularly English) often dominate. Furthermore, the hegemonic power structures found in the global economic system are partially reproduced in the way technologies and texts flow between protests, much as in the case of academic publishing, where 'Western' publications in the English language are seen as more prestigious and desirable in many disciplines (see for instance Meriläinen et al., 2008). We make these claims for two reasons: first, while some research points to the many multilingual and intertextual signs found in Tahrir Square (e.g. Aboelezz, 2014), we have found very little evidence that the protests around Occupy Wall Street or in London were similarly multilingual. They were strongly intertextual – but what was notably absent from these contexts was much engagement with other global resistance movements. This is easily supported by systematic content and structural analysis of the most popular image search results for 'Tahrir Square signs' vs 'Occupy Wall Street signs', just a few of which are depicted in Figures 17.2 below, and image blogs such as 'wearethe99percent' on Tumblr. Again, the details of the analysis go beyond the scope of this case study, but these involved categorizing each image according to which language(s) and language variety(ies) were used in the signs, and specific categories that arose from the data themselves related to the messages on the signs (e.g. regime-critical, ironic, intertextual references, etc.).

The disparity in languages used and between references to and from each protest location may of course refer to the pictures and descriptions of the protests that we detected during our period of data collection and were already mediated by news organizations, bloggers and tweeters, which/who focus on data that are globally accessible, i.e. in English. But it is mainly these globally accessible images and reports that have the potential to forge links between protest movements. Iconic images emerge, and by being shared and linked to repeatedly, they become more prominent in search results, which then makes them more likely to be reused.

It is the most popular images – the ones linked to, reproduced, recontextualized – that constitute the global discourse on the protest movements. Thus, we argue that these are an appropriate site for research in themselves and carry the same, if not higher, levels of 'authenticity' as data sources when considering global flows of media production, consumption and 'prosumption' (see Ritzer and Jurgenson, 2010). There are of course references to the Arab Spring by the protestors in Occupy protests and even in interviews conducted with UK rioters. In fact, Tahrir was central to the formation of Occupy, if we take the *Adbusters*' call to occupy Wall Street as the starting point: 'Are you ready for a

Figure 17.2 Google Image search results for 'Tahrir Square signs' on 8 October 2014, limited in this chapter to images labelled for reuse with modification

Tahrir moment? On 17 September, flood into lower Manhattan, set up tents, kitchens, peaceful barricades and occupy Wall Street' (*Adbusters*, 2011).

We found that in the signs and texts produced by the occupiers, these references were mainly instrumentalized in three ways:

- in arguments about the right to protest
- in attempts to highlight the hypocrisy of governments that support protests abroad while suppressing them at home
- as a symbolic claim about of the global nature of the movement, even when no direct engagement with or links between these protestors and those in other global resistance movements was indicated.

An additional reason for our claims about global hegemonic flows is that much of the infrastructure for the social media platforms and digital devices used to augment the physical protests is based in the United States or other 'Western' countries, and most of this infrastructure is run by companies that are owned by shareholders who are expecting a return on their investment. This feeds to the narratives of the protests presented in the 'Western' media, particularly with the labels 'Twitter revolution' or 'Facebook revolution'. While the mainstream English-language media have often presented a compelling narrative of 'liberation, democratization and social change caused by "Western" technology', the reality is considerably more complex.

With regard to linguistic practices, particularly notable changes in the channels and modes of communication can be detected, rather than in the linguistic forms being used. These are not, however, restricted to social struggles but are common to many forms of digital communication in the public sphere. Social and digital media have undoubtedly played a role in organizing these protests, in making the views of protestors public and in holding public figures to account (as suggested by Tufekci and Wilson, 2012). Their particular value to protesters has been in drawing global attention to local issues and in circumventing traditional media outlets that are restricted by state control or commercial interests. Nevertheless, they are themselves also susceptible to state or commercial control, and thus we should not be too optimistic about their role. With regard to multilingualism, the picture is highly complex: much as in international business and politics, English occupies a hegemonic position in the global communication of issues being protested about. Multilingualism appears at times to be symbolic – and to be heavily instrumentalized, or even commodified, as part of local protest goals.

CHAPTER SUMMARY

In this chapter we have presented some relevant considerations when applying critical discourse studies to social media data. We have outlined some of the key theoretical and analytical categories from traditional applications of CDS and discussed some additional ones that are useful in digitally mediated contexts. Eight methodological steps from the methodology of the discourse-historical approach are described in terms of how they can be applied to social media, and finally we demonstrate the application of some of these concepts and methods in a specific case study.

FUTURE PROSPECTS

CDS is constantly developing to take account of new theoretical and methodological developments, and being adapted to new sites and contexts of research. In one sense, social media are just another such set of sites/contexts. However, given the sweeping changes to communication practices across the world, particularly in more affluent countries, that have accompanied the growth of digital communication technologies, we feel that it is necessary for CDS to go beyond the affordances of these technologies. We also need to consider how discourse is organized, shaped and disseminated, e.g. not only through automated algorithms, manipulation of 'news feeds' and the interconnectedness of various platforms, but also the specific methods that can be used to study data, such as in accounting for new forms of communication such as in-text annotation, tagging, 'likes' and 'sharing'. This also applies to the growing body of theoretical work on social media, for example explaining new forms of media power that provide new concepts and frameworks to be integrated into CDS.

Study questions

1. What are the main methodological steps for a discourse-historical analysis, and what particular factors do you need to consider when analysing digital media?
2. Thinking about some social media data that interest you, how might different levels of context affect how you analyse texts (e.g. the broader socio-political context, the technical restrictions and affordances of the social media platform, or the texts or images which accompany a text)?
3. What texts or images other than the ones mentioned in the case study above could you analyse in relation to protest movements? How might this change your findings?

Recommended reading

Page, R., Barton, D., Unger, J. W. and Zappavigna, M. (2014) *Researching Language and Social Media*. London: Routledge.
An accessible introduction to linguistic research into social media, including a chapter on ethics, one on qualitative research, and two on ethnographic research.

Fuchs, C. (2014) *Social Media: A Critical Introduction*. London: Sage.
A useful and thought-provoking introduction to social media from a critical (Marxist) perspective.

KhosraviNik, M. and Unger, J. W. (2015) 'Critical discourse studies and social media: Power, resistance and critique in changing media ecologies', in R. Wodak and M. Meyer (eds), *Methods for Critical Discourse Analysis* (3rd edn). London: Sage, pp. 205-33.
Presents an extended discussion of the theoretical aspects underlying critical discourse studies of social media.

Wodak, R. and Wright, S. (2006) 'The European Union in cyberspace: multilingual democratic participation in a virtual public sphere?', *Journal of Language and Politics*, 5 (2): 251-75.
One of the earliest applications of critical discourse studies to social media data (in this case a multilingual discussion forum).

KhosraviNik, M. and Zia, M. (2014) 'Persian nationalism, identity and anti-Arab sentiments in Iranian Facebook discourses: critical discourse analysis and social media communication', *Journal of Language and Politics*, 13 (4): 755-80.
Analyses Facebook discussions on Iranian national identity.

Angouri, J. and Wodak, R. (2014) 'They became big in the shadow of the crisis: the Greek success story and the rise of the far right', *Discourse & Society*, 25: 540-65.
Presents an analysis of discourse on the Greek exit from the Eurozone in newspaper website comments.

Recommended online resources

Research portal for discourse studies:
www.discourseanalysis.net/
Critical Approaches to Discourse Analysis across Disciplines website, open access journal, conference announcements and other useful content:
http://cadaad.net/
Website of Axel Bruns on participatory media, citizen journalism and useful research methods and tools for large volumes of digital data:
http://snurb.info/
New Media, New Social Science blog:
http://nsmnss.blogspot.co.uk/

References

Aboelezz, M. (2014) 'The geosemiotics of Tahrir Square: a study of the relationship between discourse and space', *Journal of Language and Politics*, 13 (4): 599–622.
Adbusters (2011) '#OCCUPYWALLSTREET'. www.adbusters.org/blogs/adbusters-blog/occupy-wallstreet.html (accessed 14 December 2015).

Angermuller, J., Maingueneau, D. and Wodak, R. (eds) (2014) *The Discourse Studies Reader: Main Currents in Theory and Analysis*. Amsterdam: John Benjamins Publishing Company.

Billig, M. (2008) 'The language of critical discourse analysis: the case of nominalization', *Discourse & Society*, 19 (6): 783–800.

Bruns, A. (2005) *Gatewatching: Collaborative Online News Production*. New York: Peter Lang.

Bruns, A. (2008) *Blogs, Wikipedia, Second Life, and Beyond: From Production to Produsage*. New York: Peter Lang.

Chilton, P., Tian, H. and Wodak, R. (2010) 'Reflections on discourse and critique in China and the West', *Journal of Language and Politics*, 9 (4): 489–507.

Fairclough, N. and Wodak, R. (1997) 'Critical discourse analysis', in T. A. van Dijk (ed.), *Discourse as Social Interaction*. London: Sage, pp. 258–84.

Fuchs, C. (2014) *Social Media: A Critical Introduction*. London: Sage.

González-Bailón, S., Borge-Holthoefer, J., Rivero, A. and Moreno, Y. (2011) 'The dynamics of protest recruitment through an online network', *Scientific Reports*, 1: 1–7.

Graham, P. (2006) *Hypercapitalism: New Media, Language, and Social Perceptions of Value*. New York: Peter Lang.

Herring, S. C. (2007) 'A faceted classification scheme for computer-mediated discourse', *Language@Internet*, 4.

Herring, S. C. (2013) 'Discourse in web 2.0: familiar, reconfigured, and emergent', in D. Tannen and A. M. Trester (eds), *Discourse 2.0: Language and New Media*. Georgetown: Georgetown University Press, pp. 1–25.

Holzscheiter, A. (2005) 'Discourse as capability: non-state actors' capital in global governance', *Millennium: Journal of International Studies*, 33 (3): 723–46.

Jurgenson, N. (2012) 'When atoms meet bits: social media, the mobile web and augmented revolution', *Future Internet*, 4 (1): 83–91. doi:10.3390/fi4010083.

KhosraviNik, M. (2010) 'Actor descriptions, action attributions, and argumentation: towards a systematization of CDA analytical categories in the representation of social groups', *Critical Discourse Studies*, 7 (1): 55–72.

Kitschelt, H. P. (1986) 'Political opportunity structures and political protest: antinuclear movements in four democracies', *British Journal of Political Science*, 16 (1): 57–85. doi:10.1017/S000712340000380X.

Knight, K. (2006) 'Transformations of the concept of ideology in the twentieth century', *American Political Science Review*, 100 (4): 619.

Kress, G. and van Leeuwen, T. (2006) *Reading Images: The Grammar of Visual Design*. London: Routledge.

Meriläinen, S., Tienari, J., Thomas, R. and Davis, A. (2008) 'Hegemonic academic practices: experiences of publishing from the periphery', *Organization*, 15: 584–97.

Page, R., Barton, D., Unger, J. W. and Zappavigna, M. (2014) *Researching Language and Social Media*. London: Routledge.

Potts, A., Simm, W., Whittle, J. and Unger, J.W. (2014) 'Exploring "success" in digitally augmented activism: a triangulated approach to analyzing UK activist twitter use', *Discourse, Context and Media*, 6: 65–76. doi:10.1016/j.dcm.2014.08.008

Purvis, T. and Hunt, A. (1993) 'Discourse, ideology, discourse, ideology, discourse, ideology…', *British Journal of Sociology*, 4 (33): 473–99.

Reisigl, M. and Wodak, R. (2001) *Discourse and Discrimination: Rhetorics of Racism and Antisemitism*. London: Routledge.

Reisigl, M. and Wodak, R. (2009) 'The discourse-historical approach (DHA)', in R. Wodak and M. Meyer (eds), *Methods of Critical Discourse Analysis* (2nd edn). London: Sage, pp. 87–121.

Reisigl, M. and Wodak, R. (2015) 'The discourse-historical approach (DHA)', in R. Wodak and M. Meyer (eds), *Methods of Critical Discourse Analysis* (3rd edn). London: Sage, pp. 23–61.

Ritzer, G. and Jurgenson, N. (2010) 'Production, consumption, prosumption: the nature of capitalism in the age of the digital prosumer', *Journal of Consumer Culture*, 10: 13–36.

Tufekci, Z. and Wilson, C. (2012) 'Social media and the decision to participate in political protest: observations from Tahrir Square', *Journal of Communication*, 62 (2): 363–79. doi:10.1111/j.1460-2466.2012.01629.x.

van Dijk, T. A. (2005) 'Contextual knowledge management in discourse production', in R. Wodak and P. Chilton (eds), *A New Agenda in (Critical) Discourse Analysis*. Amsterdam: John Benjamins, pp. 71–100.

van Leeuwen, T. (2006) 'Critical discourse analysis', in K. Brown (ed.), *Encyclopedia of Language and Linguistics*, Vol. 3 (2nd edn). Oxford: Elsevier, pp. 290–4.

Wodak, R. (2007) 'Discourses in European Union organizations: aspects of access, participation, and exclusion', *Text & Talk: An Interdisciplinary Journal of Language, Discourse Communication Studies*, 27 (5–6): 655–80.

Wodak, R. (2011) 'Complex texts: analysing, understanding, explaining and interpreting meanings', *Discourse Studies*, 13 (5): 623–33.

Wodak, R. (2013) 'Editor's introduction: critical discourse analysis', in R. Wodak (ed.), *Critical Discourse Analysis*, Vol. 1. London: Sage, pp. xx–xliii.

Wodak, R. (2014) 'Discourse and politics', in J. Flowerdew (ed.), *Discourse in Context*. London: Bloomsbury, pp. 321–46.

Wodak, R. and Meyer, M. (eds) (2015) *Methods for Critical Discourse Analysis* (3rd edn). London: Sage.

PART VII
VISUAL DATA

Like documents and electronic data, it can be argued that visual data are under-used in qualitative research. Michael Emmison reviews the development of visual data analysis, reflecting upon the shift towards involving participants in the generation and analysis of visual data. This leads on to his argument that visual researchers have worked with inadequate theories. For instance, most tend to identify visual data with such artefacts as photographs and, to a lesser extent, cartoons and advertisements. Although such work can be interesting, it is, in a sense, two-dimensional. If we recognize that the visual is also spatial, a whole new set of three-dimensional objects emerge. By looking at how people use objects in the world around them, we can study the material embodiment of culture.

Like Emmison, Christian Heath differentiates the wide-ranging interest in the 'visual' in sociology and cognate disciplines, from research that uses video recordings to analyse conduct and interaction in everyday, naturalistic settings. Heath shows how CA can be used to study visual conduct and how the physical properties of human environments are made relevant within the course of social interaction. He argues that the most significant contribution of video-based research has been to our understanding of work and organization through what has become known as 'workplace studies'. Heath uses fascinating audio-visual data from an auction to analyse its unfolding interactional order. Heath also provides highly practical information for students about field relations when using video and how best to record and transcribe such data. He concludes by showing the relevance of these insights to studies of the workplace, including human–computer interaction.

EIGHTEEN

Visual Inquiry: Issues and Developments

Michael Emmison

About this chapter

This chapter has two principal tasks. In the first place it aims to conduct a stock-taking exercise of the various modalities through which visual research is currently being conducted. I focus in particular on recent developments which have seen a shift from the older social documentary tradition, in which the research subjects were passive objects for the researcher's camera, to approaches which involve the active participation of those under investigation. I look in detail at how participant-centred studies are conducted and offer some reasons why they have become so dominant. A common feature of virtually all existing modes of visual inquiry is that they focus in some way upon the generation, use and analysis of photographic and other forms of images. The chapter's second goal is to suggest that this is unduly restrictive and that visual inquiry needs to consider a range of other sources of data besides the two dimensional photographic image. An alternative approach which focuses instead on the visible aspects of social life, and the contexts in which these are observed or encountered, is sketched. The chapter proposes a number of theoretically informed types of visual information or data and offers examples of how visual research could be conducted in each of these conceptually distinct arenas.

Keywords

image, photography, photo-elicitation, observation, space, place

Interest in 'researching the visual' – understood either as a distinctive methodological approach, as a substantive domain of inquiry or indeed some combination of both of these – in the social sciences and humanities shows no signs of abating. The visual has become not only a focus of concern in its traditional homelands of anthropology and sociology, but something which has engaged the interests of scholars in many disciplines which had previously shown little or no interest in this topic. The complaint, once regularly voiced by visual sociologists, that their field was marginalized and ignored by mainstream social scientists can clearly no longer be justified. The plethora of theoretical and methodological discussions, handbooks and edited collections, not to mention original research articles, which have appeared over the last decade or so testifies to the legitimacy of this field within the broader domain of qualitative research practice.

Agreement as to what visual inquiry entails or how it should be conducted is, however, less forthcoming. Simply put, there appears to be no single way of doing visual research and newcomers must of necessity make strategic choices as to how to frame their research questions and designs. Perhaps the most basic is the decision as to whether they should generate the data they seek to analyse or alternatively confine their attention to the numerous images which are already available. But the field has now extended well beyond these foundational approaches so at the outset, therefore, it is helpful to begin with an overview of the various modalities through which visual inquiry has been, and in part continues to be, conducted. Although this is not an exhaustive typology I argue that the vast bulk of visual social research falls into one of four principal modes or approaches. Some of these have existed almost from the inception of visual inquiry as a recognizable field; others are of more recent provenance. In summary form these approaches are as follows:

1. *The use of researcher produced visual materials - the researcher as photographer*. The generation of photographic images, and to some extent film, has been the traditional mode of conducting visual research. Photography has been principally associated with ethnographers in the fields of social anthropology and sociology, and has been variously understood as an additional means of documenting social and cultural settings and processes. Historically, still photography played a prominent part in the development of visual inquiry (Becker, 1974; Wagner, 1979) and there are some studies (e.g. Bateson and Mead, 1942) which are widely respected as exemplars of the craft. However, it has frequently faced charges that it fails to meet the rigour required by the standards of social science research, and cannot be readily distinguished from the illustrative use of images associated with journalistic or social documentary traditions. Today this form of ethnographic still photographic work is much less popular, and its prospects seem relatively stagnant. It appears to have been largely replaced by work conducted in other modes, particularly participant-centred approaches.

2. *The analysis of existing materials - decoding or coding and counting*. Alternatively visual research can be undertaken on the numerous existing images that are readily available. The ubiquity of visual imagery has been seen as one of the defining features of our postmodern societies, and the rise of internet-based visual digital culture has witnessed a dramatic increase in the sheer volume of images that are available, as well as facilitating their ease of access to these materials. A variety of methods are on offer for the investigation of existing or 'found' visual data as it is sometimes referred to. A great deal of research has traditionally been conducted on print media content, such as advertising images, primarily by cultural studies scholars who are interested in decoding their hidden ideological and cultural messages. Much of

this work has been carried out on single case studies or small samples from which wider generalizations may often be difficult to make. However, the extensive records which are generally available, for example in the form of newspaper and magazines archives, means that such material can be subject to more rigorous investigation via traditional methods of content analysis. Although attention has more recently shifted to the investigation of internet-based visual imagery and the voluminous images posted on social media websites, it has not fundamentally altered the ways in which researchers seek to analyse this content.

3.   *The use of video technology – seeing social interaction in detail.* Approaches to visual inquiry which rely on the use of video recording provide a third distinctive mode in which visual research is currently being undertaken. Despite the increasing use of video as a private or domestic media technology, the systematic use of video for research purposes poses particular challenges. As noted above, ethnographic film making did play a part in the early development of disciplines such as social anthropology but for a variety of reasons it fell out of favour. Isolated instances of film being used in other social science disciplines to study aspects of human movement and work activities can be found throughout the twentieth century but it is only comparatively recently, with the availability of affordable digital recording equipment, that the potential video offers for social researchers has been recognized. However, the use of video technology appears to be marked by a fundamental analytical division. One branch (e.g. Pink, 2007) has sought to disassociate itself from the earlier scientific-realist appropriation of the moving image and instead advocates its use largely as a tool for conducting reflexive or experimental ethnographic research with the video recording typically viewed as a collaborative undertaking between researcher and researched. In contrast a second group of researchers, those working with the ethnomethodological tradition, see video's potential as lying precisely in its ability to capture the embodied details of social life – the 'elusive phenomena' (Heath et al., 2010: 5; see also Heath in this volume) comprising everyday interactional conduct. In this tradition the use of video has been equated with the role that the microscope has played in the biological sciences.

4.   *Participant-centred approaches – recruiting the respondent in the analysis of visual materials.* The defining feature of work in this modality is that it involves the research subjects actively participating at some point in the research process rather than remaining as passive objects for the researcher's camera as in the earlier documentary tradition. The extent of this involvement is variable, ranging from being invited to comment on visual material in an interview, through to more extensive engagement as image producers, photographing sub-cultural worlds which are largely inaccessible to the researcher. These different approaches have been given a variety of labels such as 'photo-elicitation', 'auto-photography', 'photovoice' or 'visual storytelling'. Involving research participants in producing and commenting on their own visual material was first undertaken in pioneering anthropological research but in recent years participatory visual approaches have become popular in sociology in fields such as adolescence and youth studies, health and illness, race and ethnicity, and gender relations. More generally they have been identified as a possible means for achieving an emancipatory style of qualitative research among scholars investigating marginalized or subordinate groups (Packard, 2008).

Space does not permit a detailed discussion of each of these modalities. The pioneering social documentary tradition in visual sociology appears to be of limited relevance today as it has been largely eclipsed by the participant-centred approaches. Becker's classical discussions of the relationship between photography and sociology (e.g. Becker, 1974, 2002) can still be profitably read today but they retain most relevance for the historian of the discipline. The analysis of existing images has received extensive coverage in the literature and there are useful discussions and illustrations of the two principal methodological approaches (semiotics and content analysis) which have been adopted for the investigation of this material readily available elsewhere (e.g. Ali, 2004; Lutz and Collins, 1993).

The voluminous visual material which is now available on photo sharing and other social media websites has not unsurprisingly attracted interest from scholars from several disciplines. For example those who adopt what Rose has termed 'the anthropological approach' (Rose, 2007: Chapter 10) in studying family photograph albums now have available public web-based material with which to compare the older private analogue collections (e.g. Pauwels, 2008). The use of video technology to capture interactional conduct is a highly specialized field and as it is the subject of a separate chapter in this volume (Heath) I shall not provide further comment on this.

Instead I propose to consider the developments which have assumed an unexpected prominence on the visual research agenda over the last decade or so. At the heart of this new agenda is the active participation of the research subjects. Although images might still be taken (by researcher or by participant) less is made of the visual material *per se* and rather more on what the research subjects are motivated to say about these images. This is a change of profound importance and one which I suspect would sit uneasily with the social documentary pioneers. Rather than their photographic work enjoying central place in the research process – and carrying the analytic burden – the new agenda places the research subjects and their interpretations of the images at the heart of the investigation. Indeed Rose (2014: 28) has gone as far as claiming that now 'Almost all VRM [visual research methods] involve talk between the researcher and the researched'. This is not hyperbole. The focus on talk has become so prevalent now that it can be often difficult to assess whether a particular publication can be construed as a contribution to visual inquiry. Whereas once a visual sociological article could virtually always be identified by the inclusion of photographic images these are now often seen as optional extras clearly subordinate to whatever comments they have generated. It is talk about the images or talk about issues touched off by the images which is now seen as essential. This epistemological shift in the form of knowledge which can be generated through visual inquiry has come about at a staggering pace. As recently as 2002 Harper offered a useful overview of participatory approaches, largely covering photo-elicitation methods. A measure of the growth of this style of visual research practice can be seen in the fact that he was able to individually comment on all of the then published studies. Such a feat would be inconceivable today.

So what lies behind the exponential growth of these participatory visual studies? At least part of the answer no doubt lies in the fashionable currents – reflexivity, postcolonialism, empowerment – informing the wider social science agenda, the challenges these pose for established research protocols and the undermining of the authority of the researcher as the sole repository of knowledge. But I would suggest that there are more mundane matters at play in the shift towards the participatory visual agenda. Put simply, eliciting talk from your research subjects can be a reassuring and generally productive analytical gambit for a visual researcher who may be uncertain as to how to proceed with a purely visual study. By scaffolding their inquiries on the tried and tested techniques of the interview method, participatory visual researchers are provided with a means by which they can generate material (talk) which is recognisable as data and perhaps more to the point, readily analysable. But does this come at a cost for the integrity of such studies as 'visual'? Before we consider this matter let us look first at the practical details of doing participatory visual inquiry for this also gives us some clues as to their popularity.

PARTICIPATORY APPROACHES: CORE THEMES AND TECHNIQUES

Over the last decade qualitative visual researchers have embraced participatory methodologies in ever increasing numbers. Studies drawing on photo-elicitation, photovoice, auto-photography and so on have been conducted on homeless people (Johnsen et al., 2008), socially excluded black youth (Wright et al., 2010), chronic disease self-management in adolescents (Drew et al., 2010), women's experience of their postnatal body shape (Nash, 2014), pain management in older adults (Baker and Wang, 2006), prostate cancer survivors (Oliffe and Bottorff, 2007), personal space in organizations (Vince and Warren, 2012) and identity construction in mature age body builders (Phoenix, 2010). These studies, and many others like them, follow a very similar format. Rose (2007: 241–2) suggests that there is a basic template to much of this research which involves six steps or ingredients and, although not all of these are included in every participatory visual study, for ease of exposition I follow her outline of the steps with illustrations from some of the studies referred to above.

Step 1 is an initial interview conducted with the research participants. The purpose of the interview is to explain the aims of the research and why the respondents have been recruited or chosen. Typically at this stage there is no, or only minimal, discussion of the role photography will play in the research; instead the focus is on the broader questions to which the eventual photographs will play a part in answering.

Step 2 involves providing the research participants with a camera as well as some instruction in its use if this is required. Although digital cameras are now relatively cheap, most researchers prefer to use some form of single-use or disposable camera. The assumption here seems to be to minimize the degree of researcher control of the images which digital technology would permit and to maximize the 'spontaneity' or unedited character of the visual material which is generated. For example, in their auto-photographic study of socially excluded black youth in the UK, Wright et al. (2010) gave disposable cameras to their research participants and simply asked them to take pictures of 'family, friends and anyone else who has been a source of support and people they enjoyed being with'. In other cases where the research question is more specific the researcher may exercise more control over this stage. In their study of how young people coped with chronic health conditions Drew et al. (2010) asked their participants to create a series of photographs to show a) what it was like to live with an ongoing health condition and b) the sorts of things they might do to take care of their health.

Step 3 is for the photographs to be developed and, in some cases, for the research subjects to write brief comments about them prior to meeting with the researcher for a second time. Several researchers note that this can be a very time consuming process, particularly if the research involves marginalized groups. In their study of homeless people in two sites in the UK Johnsen et al. (2008) comment that the need of some of their participants to find somewhere safe to eat and/or feed a 'habit' inevitably outweighed their desire to complete the research exercises. A number of their participants failed to return their cameras, some reported that they were lost or stolen (and they add that it is not unrealistic to assume that some may have been sold). However, assuming that the cameras are successfully returned and the film developed, a crucial phase in participatory visual design then needs to be confronted concerning the issue of respondent anonymity and/or ownership of the images. Drew et al. (2010) took particular care to ensure that their research participants were able to make decisions about whether the photographs they had taken could be incorporated into the project data. A written information sheet stressed that the adolescent would be the first to view the developed images and that they would have an opportunity at the start of the interview to remove any images they did not want the researcher to see. In contrast Johnsen et al. (2008) approach the issue of image inclusion in a different way. Their research participants were provided with a disposable camera and asked to carry this with them for a week and to take pictures of the places that they utilized in everyday life and/or that were in some way important to them. However, upon return of the cameras two sets of photographs were developed – one for the research participants to keep and one for the research team's records.

Step 4 involves the researcher carrying out a second interview with the participants during which the photographs they have taken are discussed in detail. All researchers comment on the importance of this step and how the presence of the visual material serves to facilitate the interview process and elicit verbal material which may not otherwise have surfaced. In their study of prostate cancer survivors Oliffe and Bottorff (2007) note the general reluctance of men to admit to, let alone talk about, illness and discuss a number of ways in which the photographs helped to overcome this. A number of their respondents dwelt on the objects or possessions depicted in the photos and this helped generate a sense of shared 'men's talk' within the overall formality of the interview. At other times when the topic of the interview turned to more sensitive matters, such as the specific details of their recovery or their feelings of mortality, the men 'found respite and refuge in the photographs' and, by speaking in the third person about others they had encountered during hospitalization, were able to distance themselves from the overall cancer experience.

Step 5 is the actual analysis of both the photographs and the interview materials in accordance with some established social scientific technique or procedure, or with the aim of exploring a particular theoretical concept or issue. There is considerable variability to be found here and the decision as to how to proceed is largely determined by the initial research question(s). The techniques chosen can be either quantitative or qualitative or perhaps some combination. A recent auto photographic study, which employed a systematic quantitative research design, was a large-scale comparative investigation of children's photographic practices (Sharples et al., 2003). In this study a total of 180 children from three different age levels (7, 11 and 15) recruited from five European countries were provided with single use cameras. The resulting photographs could be understood in terms of two axes – one which differentiated between photographs taken indoors as opposed to outdoors, and a second dimension which distinguished between photographs of people and those of objects or scenes – and where the photographs were located on these axes was significantly shaped by the age and gender of the children. For example, the photographs of the older girls were most likely to feature their friends. Sharples et al. argued that their research had challenged the view that children were immature or untutored users of cameras. Children's photographs should not be seen simply as their 'view of the world' but as an important means for them to articulate their sense of identity in relation to both parents and friends.

Quantitative participatory visual studies are, however, the exception and it is more common to find qualitative or interpretive approaches used in the analysis. In her auto photographic study of mature age body builders, Phoenix (2010) arrives at the concept of the 'body-self' after reviewing the photographs her respondents had taken and their commentaries on these. Three different 'body-self' identities were revealed: a 'healthy body-self', a 'performing body-self' and a 'relational body-self'. The diverse identities which her mature age body builders exhibited appeared to challenge 'stereotypical assumptions' that such people were obsessed with their weight training and generally lead anti-social lives. In their study of marginalized black youth Wright et al. turned to Goffman's well-known distinction between 'front stage' and 'back stage' regions (Goffman, 1959) in their analysis of the images and the comments made by their respondents during the interviews. Front stage regions comprised 'public spaces, schools, parks, streets, city centre' and so on. Back stage regions, in contrast, are those spaces such as family homes, bedrooms, living rooms and relationships with friends. Wright et al. suggest that the limited number of photographs taken of front regions might be one way in which the young people tried to account for their exclusion. In contrast the more numerous photos of their back regions typically depicted relationships with friends which were a source of support in managing their perceived exclusion.

Step 6, the final step, concerns the way that the completed research is presented to a wider audience and this involves decisions about the balance between a focus on 'the talk', the interview discussions about the photographs, and a focus of the images. As I have observed it is the former which is given priority with the visual material used as illustrations of key conceptual points. In some cases the visual material may not even be included. The absence of images may be the result of cost constraints; publishers of social science journals (and books) are often reluctant to include high quality illustrations and colour images are generally out of the question. A further factor is that because the images have not been professionally taken they may not be of a suitable standard for publication. Finally, of course, given that empowerment is seen as a major dimension to this research, if the research subjects are reluctant to have their images viewed by a wider community then authors are unlikely to challenge this.

There seems little doubt that this participatory style of visual inquiry is likely to attract more adherents over the coming decades. For the reasons I have outlined – its appeal to qualitative researchers from many disciplines, its natural affinities with established qualitative methods such as the in-depth interview or focus group – it is not an exaggeration to suggest that eventually it may come to be seen as the sole way in which researchers who wish to employ photography as a research method must proceed. To the extent that the proliferation of participatory visual research has succeeded in having visual methodological concerns bought to the attention of the wider social scientific community then it can be welcomed. But has it also come at a cost? Glancing through the participant-centred studies reviewed earlier it seems clear that they are preoccupied with finding answers for a vast array of disciplinary-specific research questions but the answers are primarily found in respondent talk. However, the extent to which they are also seeking to contribute to a cumulative advance in our theoretical and methodological understanding of 'the visual' as a particular modality is not at all apparent. It seems ironic to say the least that only a few decades since the pioneers of visual sociology urged us to consider new methods of generating data by canvasing the explanatory potential of photography and image making, that visual methods appear to have attenuated to the point that they are in danger of becoming almost indistinguishable from the established research techniques.

VISUAL RESEARCH BEYOND THE PHOTOGRAPHIC IMAGE

Whether they are generating their own images, analysing existing visual material or eliciting respondent talk about their self-generated photographs, visual researchers are united in the belief that the image is central to their field. In the remainder of the chapter I want to consider what an agenda for visual research which goes beyond the photograph might entail. The principal message I want to convey is the need to think of visual inquiry as embracing *more* than the study of images. Elsewhere with colleagues (Emmison and Smith, 2000; Emmison et al., 2012) I offer book length explorations of this issue and so the following observations must of necessity be schematic. Since we first presented these ideas over a decade ago signs have emerged that our message has begun to be taken note of by the wider visual research community. For example, in his proposal for an 'integrated framework' for visual social research, Luc Pauwels argues that the field is founded on 'the idea that valid scientific insight in society can be acquired by observing, analysing and theorizing its visual manifestations: behaviour of people and material products of culture' (Pauwels, 2010: 546). What is intriguing about this statement is that it contains no reference to visual inquiry being predicated on the camera or the photograph. Formulations such as this would have been inconceivable 30 years or so ago when visual sociology re-emerged as a speciality after a lengthy period of quiescence. Moreover throughout her overview of visual methodologies Gillian Rose (2007) uses the phrase 'visual object' interchangeably with the term 'image'. Although Rose doesn't offer a precise explanation of what a 'visual object' is, the point that she wishes to make seems clear enough: visual researchers need to embrace data which go beyond the typical photograph or two dimensional image with which they have been traditionally preoccupied. Rose confesses that her book will deal with a 'narrow selection of things visual' and suggests that the methods she outlines could equally well apply to 'buildings, built landscape and sculpture' (2007: xv). Pauwels, in the article to which I have already referred, ventures into similar territory though even more explicitly. He points out that the phenomenon of material culture, which constitutes one of the core empirical referents of visual inquiry, 'includes artefacts and objects (boardrooms, home settings, art objects) and larger visible structures (e.g. urban areas, cemeteries) that may provide useful information about both the material and the immaterial traits (in as much as they embody values and norms) of a given society' (Pauwels, 2010: 553).

Both Pauwels and Rose allude in these statements to a visual research practice which extends far beyond the photographic image. However, neither of them look systematically at what this requires. In our earlier, more detailed, consideration of these issues we advance this agenda through a number of key propositions. The first, and less contentious, is to think of images not simply as a realm of representation but also as containing information which can be brought to bear on the investigation of social and cultural processes. It is this theme – that the visual is a realm of data, not simply a domain amenable to cultural or interpretive modes of inquiry – which is at the heart of this alternative programme. In part, thinking of the visual as data may require going beyond the reliance on the photograph and to consider the possibilities inherent in other forms of visual material of the kind we refer to as 'two-dimensional'. For example, newspaper cartoons offer unexpected insights into the wider political and economic systems in which they are located (Emmison et al., 2012: 81–91). Other forms of two-dimensional visual data such as directional signs, maps and instructional diagrams can be used to explicate the claims of ethnomethodologists about the significance of commonsense reasoning. Here the focus is not so much on the discovery of cultural meanings by the academic analyst but rather the ways in which ordinary actors use or make sense of such visual information and incorporate it into their everyday practical routines (see also Prior in this volume).

However, the equating of 'the visual' only with such two-dimensional images is also curiously short-sighted and unduly restrictive. Social life is visual in diverse and counter-intuitive ways. Consequently there are many more forms of visual data than the photograph, the advertisement or the cartoon. Accordingly we propose that visual research should also recognize the existence of three-dimensional data. We have in mind here the elements of material culture which operate as purposive or accidental signifiers in social life. These range from the items of everyday life in the home which carry personal meanings to those in public spaces, such as statues, which represent official public discourses. Our argument is that such objects provide a rich vein of visual information which can be read for clues about selves and societies. While they can be analysed in traditional semiotic terms, they are also implicated in human actions. Object-centred visual inquiry has obvious methodological affinities with an older – and these days somewhat neglected and unfashionable – branch of social research, the use of unobtrusive or non-reactive measures (e.g. Webb et al., 1999). The sheer visibility of many kinds of objects means that it is possible to explore social life covertly. Because respondents are not required for many kinds of object-based research we can circumvent the usual problem of normative responding – providing the researcher a socially acceptable answer. This may be particularly useful in researching fields such as crime and deviance or urban disorder.

Pushing further down this analytical path we also argue that the physical spaces and places in which humans conduct their social lives – suburban homes and gardens, educational institutions, shopping malls, boardrooms, as well as larger geographical spaces – parks, city centres and the like – are also amenable to visual inquiry. Such settings constitute 'lived visual data' where both actions and sign systems can be read to unpack their cultural significance. A dual focus is possible looking at both the place or setting itself and on the ways in which action is patterned in response to the physical locale – for example 'successful' public spaces are generally those which encourage or enable interaction (Whyte, 1980). Finally, of course, these spaces and places are generally populated by humans in interaction and this in turn provides us with a further analytic category of data. People are 'living visual data' and interaction in contemporary urban environments is significantly regulated by norms about display, dress, eye contact. Clothing, gesture and body language are signs which we use to establish identity and negotiate public situations. To research these one does not necessarily require the fine-grained power of the video recording. Simple observation, provided it is theoretically informed can offer a way to answer diverse questions about the ordering of human conduct.

In all of these areas there are rich supplies of material for the visual researcher. In giving up the idea that visual research is only the study of photographs or advertisements, then a far broader range of data becomes available for investigation. From this vantage point visual inquiry is no longer just the study of the image, but rather the study of the seen and observable. Photographs may be helpful sometimes in recording the seen dimensions of social life. Usually they are not necessary. Our insistence on the need to think beyond 'the photograph' in broadening the agenda for visual inquiry was one which caused considerable consternation within the established visual research community (e.g. Wagner, 2002; Prosser, 2008), but it is one that is essential if visual research is to genuinely connect with the broader themes in social and cultural inquiry.

CHAPTER SUMMARY AND FUTURE PROSPECTS

The use of visual data and visual methods are here to stay but future developments are not easy to predict and are likely to be uneven. A major growth area is almost certainly to be in the use of video technology given the affordability of new digital technologies and their widespread adoption outside the academy. But the gulf between the experimental ethnographic use of video and the multi-modal analysis of interaction by ethnomethodologists and conversation analysts is one that seems likely to remain. The possibilities for conducting research on the ever increasing world of digital imagery are immense but paradoxically some of the most animated discussions are to be found among quantitative researchers where it has been subsumed under the concept of 'big data' and the challenges that this profusion of online social and transactional data poses for the viability of established empirical sociology (Burrows and Savage, 2014). As indicated earlier the growth in qualitative visual inquiry is likely to be in the use of participatory methods but with the danger that such approaches will increasingly come to resemble mainstream interview techniques and that the distinctive character of the visual mode for conducting research will accordingly be lost.

In moving towards an agenda for a revitalized visual inquiry which is respectful of the spirit (if not the letter) of the pioneers of the field I have argued that too much of what is offered up as visual research relies upon a largely unreflexive use of the photographic image. A failure to distinguish between the disparate kinds of information which photographs inevitably contain and the use of photographs as the means by which this information can be disseminated has led to a confusion about the status of visual inquiry and a failure to appreciate its divergent theoretical possibilities. If we move away from the commonsense equation of visual research as a purely image-based activity and embrace the claims I have advanced here, then it is possible to regard many aspects of twentieth-century social science, and many of the major figures (for example Simmel, the Chicago School, Foucault) in these disciplines, as contributing to the development of visual research. Thinking of visual research more as the study of the seen and the observable, rather than as something which can only be conducted through recording technology, can facilitate important conceptual connections to be made between 'the visual' as a domain of inquiry and the work of many classical and contemporary theorists alike who might not otherwise be regarded as contributing to this field. In addition this may well open up visual inquiry to students whose substantive research interests might otherwise lead them to overlook the possibility of visual methodologies.

Study questions

1. What are some of the problems with basing visual research solely on the use of photographs?
2. Do you think participant-centred visual studies are advancing the methodology of visual research?
3. Identify an example of two-dimensional visual data other than a photograph and suggest how it could be analysed.

Recommended reading

Banks, M. (2008) *Using Visual Data in Qualitative Research*. London: Sage.
Provides an overview of the ways in which visual data, primarily in the form of images, can be utilized in qualitative research. Suitable for both advanced undergraduate and postgraduate students.

Emmison, M., Smith, P. and M. Mayall (2012) *Researching the Visual* (2nd edn). London: Sage.
Offers an innovative way of conducting visual research which extends the field beyond the use of photographic images and shows how visual inquiry can connect with many of the core theoretical traditions in the social sciences.

Margolis, E. and Pauwels, L. (eds) (2011) *The Sage Handbook of Visual Research Methods*. London: Sage.
A comprehensive edited handbook which addresses a range of visual research methods and debates with contributions from many of the leading figures in the field.

Rose, G. (2007) *Visual Methodologies: An Introduction to the Interpretation of Visual Materials* (2nd edn). London: Sage.
Provides a systematic overview of the various methodological approaches which can be utilized for conducting research into visual culture. Covers both qualitative and some quantitative techniques.

Recommended online resources

The Visual Sociology Group of the British Sociological Association:
www.visualsociology.org.uk

International Visual Sociology Organization (IVSA):
www.visualsociology.org/

Mass Observation Project:
www.massobs.org.uk/

References

Ali, S. (2004) 'Using visual materials', in C. Seale (ed.) *Researching Culture and Society* (2nd edn). London: Sage, pp. 265–78.

Baker, T. and Wang, C (2006) 'Photovoice: use of a participatory action research method to explore the chronic pain experience in older adults', *Qualitative Health Research*, 16 (10): 1405–13.

Bateson, G. and Mead. M (1942) *Balinese Character: A Photographic Analysis*. New York: New York Academy of Sciences.

Becker, H. S. (1974) 'Photography and sociology', *Studies in the Anthropology of Visual Communication*, 1: 3–26.

Becker, H. S. (2002) 'Visual evidence: *A Seventh Man*, the specified generalization and the work of the reader', *Visual Studies*, 17 (1): 3–11.

Burrows, R and Savage, M. (2014) 'After the crisis? Big data and the methodological challenges of empirical sociology', *Big Data & Society*, April–June: 1–6.

Drew, S., Duncan, R. and Sawyer S. (2010) 'Visual storytelling: a beneficial but challenging method for health research with young people', *Qualitative Health Research*, 20 (12): 1677–88.

Emmison, M. and Smith, P. (2000) *Researching the Visual: Images, Objects, Contexts and Interactions in Social and Cultural Inquiry*. London: Sage.

Emmison, M., Smith, P. and Mayall, M (2012) *Researching the Visual* (2nd edn). London: Sage.

Goffman, E. (1959) *The Presentation of Self in Everyday Life*. New York: Doubleday Anchor.

Harper, D. (2002) 'Talking about pictures: a case for photo elicitation', *Visual Studies*, 17 (1): 13–26.

Heath, C., Hindmarsh, J. and Luff, P. (2010) *Video in Qualitative Research*. London: Sage.

Johnsen, S., May, J. and Cloke, P. (2008) 'Imag(in)ing "homeless places": using auto-photography to (re)examine the geographies of homelessness', *Area*, 40 (2): 194–207.

Lutz, C. and Collins, J (1993) *Reading National Geographic*. Chicago, IL: University of Chicago Press.

Nash, M. (2014) 'Shapes of motherhood: exploring postnatal body image through photography', *Journal of Gender Studies*, 24 (1): 18–37.

Oliffe, J. and Bottorff, J. (2007) 'Further than the eye can see? Photo elicitation and research with men', *Qualitative Health Research*, 17 (6): 850–8.

Packard, J. (2008) '"I'm gonna show you what it's really like out here": the power and limitation of participatory visual methods', *Visual Studies*, 23 (1): 63–77.

Pauwels, L. (2008) 'A private visual practice going public? Social functions and sociological research opportunities of web-based family photography', *Visual Studies*, 23 (1): 34–49.

Pauwels, L. (2010) 'Visual sociology reframed: an analytical synthesis and discussion of visual methods in social and cultural research', *Sociological Methods & Research*, 38 (4): 545–81.

Phoenix, C. (2010) 'Auto-photography in aging studies: exploring issues of identity construction in mature body-builders', *Journal of Aging Studies*, 24: 167–80.

Pink, S. (2007) *Doing Visual Ethnography: Images, Media and Representation in Research* (2nd edn). London: Sage.

Prosser, J. (2008) 'The darker side of visual research', ESRC National Centre for Research Methods, Working Paper 9.

Rose, G. (2007) *Visual Methodologies: An Introduction to the Interpretation of Visual Materials* (2nd edn). London: Sage.

Rose, G. (2014) 'On the relation between "visual research methods" and contemporary visual culture', *The Sociological Review*, 62: 24–46.

Sharples, M., Davison, L., Thomas, G. and Rudman, P. (2003) 'Children as photographers: an analysis of children's photographic behaviour and intentions at three age levels', *Visual Communication*, 2 (3): 303–30.

Vince, R. and Warren, S. (2012) 'Participatory visual methods', in G. Symon and C. Cassell (eds), *Qualitative Organizational Research: Core Methods and Current Challenges*. London Sage, pp. 275–95.

Wagner, J. (ed.) (1979) *Images of Information: Still Photography in the Social Sciences*, Beverley Hills, CA: Sage.

Wagner, J. (2002) 'Contrasting images, complementary trajectories: sociology, visual sociology and visual research', *Visual Studies*, 17 (2): 160–71.

Webb, E. J., Campbell, D. T., Schwartz, R. D. and Sechrest, L. (1999) *Unobtrusive Measures: Non-reactive Research in the Social Sciences* (rev. edn). London: Sage.

Whyte, W. (1980) *The Social Life of Small Urban Spaces*. New York: Project for Public Spaces.

Wright, C. Y., Darko, N., Standen, P. J. and Patel, T. G. (2010) 'Visual research methods: using cameras to empower socially excluded black youth', *Sociology*, 44 (3): 541–58.

NINETEEN

Embodied Action: Video and the Analysis of Social Interaction

Christian Heath

.

About this chapter

Video provides unprecedented opportunities for social science research. It offers new and distinctive ways of collecting data, of analysing social actions and activities, and in presenting observations and findings to academics, practitioners and the public. In this chapter we draw on ethnomethodology and conversation analysis to discuss how we can use video recordings to examine social interaction in organizational settings and the ways in which we can begin to consider how visible conduct as well as talk – embodied action – features in the accomplishment of workplace activities.

Keywords

video, social interaction, work and organization

INTRODUCTION

In recent years we have witnessed the emergence of a growing corpus of studies that use video to analyse social action and interaction. These studies have generated a substantial range of insights and findings concerning the social organization of activities within a broad range of everyday environments including the workplace, the home and more public settings such as museums and galleries. In different ways, these studies have built on and developed the rich and diverse range of research concerned with language use and talk that arose over the last three decades or so and have powerfully demonstrated the ways in which social actions and activities are accomplished in and though the visible, the material, as well as the spoken. This growing interest in embodied action and multi-modal communication is reflected in the growing commitment to using video in naturalistic research throughout a range of disciplines, including sociology, organization studies, applied linguistics, education, psychology and management, and to readdress areas and issues that have long been of concern to the social science, including learning, health care, professional practice, technology, markets and the emotions (see for example Luff et al., 2000; Knoblauch et al., 2006; Goldman et al., 2007; Jewitt, 2009; Streeck et al., 2011).

This chapter discusses the ways in which we can use video to explore everyday activities as they arise in ordinary, naturally occurring settings. We focus in particular on the analysis of social interaction and the ways in which social interaction not only underpins the accomplishment of everyday activities, but also provides a methodological resource with which to prioritize the participants' perspective. Drawing on ethnomethodology and conversation analysis, the chapter addresses how we can explore the situated production of social action and activity and examine the resources and competencies on which participants rely in accomplishing their own actions and making sense of the actions of others. The chapter suggests that we can develop a distinctive approach to the analysis of embodied action and contribute to our understanding of a range of analytic and substantive issues in the social sciences. Video, audio-visual recordings of naturally occurring activities provide a critical resource in this regard.

It is important, as Knoblauch et al. (2006) suggest, to differentiate the wide-ranging interest in the 'visual' both in sociology and cognate disciplines (see for example Pink, 2007; Rose, 2007; Banks, 2008; Kissmann, 2009; Margolis and Pauwels, 2011; Emmison et al., 2012), from research that uses video recordings to analyse conduct and interaction in 'naturally occurring' day-to-day settings. It is the latter with which we are concerned and it is ethnomethodology and conversation analysis that have primarily provided the analytic and conceptual resources that have enabled researchers from a range of disciplines to use video to address the social and interactional organization of everyday practical activities.

EMERGING FIELDS OF VIDEO-BASED RESEARCH

The flowering of video-based studies of social interaction has given rise to an impressive corpus of research of a broad variety of everyday settings and situations including both formal and informal environments. So, for example, we find studies of driving, children's play, dinner parties, cooking, watching television, visits to museums, computer games, the use of mobile phones, shopping, virtual environments and interaction in various institutional settings (Hindmarsh et al., 2000; vom Lehn et al., 2001; Dant, 2004; Büscher, 2005; Goodwin, 2006; Laurier and Philo, 2006; Peräkylä and Ruusuvuori, 2006; Asch, 2007; Goldman et al., 2007; Heath and vom Lehn, 2008; Mondada, 2011; 2012; Haddington et al., 2013; Licoppe, 2015). Perhaps the most significant contribution of video-based research has been to our understanding of work and organization and the ways in which work is accomplished in and though social interaction. Indeed, over the past couple of decades or so we have witnessed the emergence of what have come to be known as 'workplace studies'. This substantial corpus of research has addressed the ways in which specialized tasks and activities are accomplished through embodied activity, activities that involve the interplay of talk, visible conduct and the use of various objects and artefacts, tools and technologies. This corpus of research includes for example studies of control rooms, operating theatres, street markets, medical consultations, call centres, news rooms, financial trading rooms, architectural practices, construction sites and offices (see for example, Clark and Pinch, 1995; Engeström and Middleton, 1996; Heath and Luff, 2000; Luff et al., 2000; Suchman, 2007; Llewellyn and Hindmarsh, 2010; Streeck et al., 2011; Szymanski and Whalen, 2011).

One of the more important contributions of video-based studies of organizations has been to our understanding of the ways in which tools and technologies, ranging from highly complex digital systems to seemingly simple artefacts, such as pen and paper, feature in the collaborative accomplishment of workplace activities. These studies stand in marked contrast to more traditional research on technology and system use found within the social sciences in both sociology and fields such as human–computer interaction (HCI). For example, research has examined the ways in which advanced systems for traffic management and surveillance, for instance in rapid urban transport, rely upon operators' ability to participate in, and coordinate, concurrent activities and to remain 'peripherally aware' of the selective contributions of others, both within the immediate environment and beyond (see for example Goodwin and Goodwin, 1996; Suchman, 1996; Heath and Luff, 2000; Luff and Heath, 2002; and for a discussion of related issues see Hindmarsh and Pilnick, 2002; Mondada, 2003; Koschmann et al., 2007). It has also examined, for instance, how the use of systems to document and retrieve information in service encounters, emergency dispatch centres and medical consultations is systematically interleaved with the interaction between the client and the professional and the ways in which the system shapes and is shaped by the emergent and contingent contributions of the participants (Luff and Heath, 1993; Whalen, 1995; Whalen and Vinkhuyzen, 2000). These video-based studies of technology in action have also addressed how the accomplishment of workplace activities, even in highly complex organizational environments, relies upon the use of mundane artefacts and material resources such as sketches, plans, records, flight strips, paper timetables, Post-it notes, markers, pens and pencils, and how these objects and artefacts gain their sense and significance in and through interaction (Heath, 1986; Luff and Heath, 2000; Büscher, 2005; Luff et al., 2009). In other words, these video-based studies have powerfully shown how tools and technologies rely upon a body of socially organized practice and reasoning, practice that emerges within and is sustained through the forms of social interaction that arise within particular organizational settings. As Barley and Kunda (2001) suggest, this growing corpus of research has begun to refocus studies of organization on work and work's practical accomplishment and demonstrated how the analysis of the fine details of social interaction provides a distinctive understanding of contemporary work that builds on and extends the ethnographic tradition of studies of occupations and organization.

There is a growing and diverse range of research that uses video to analyse naturally occurring activities, research that draws distinct analytic traditions and has differing theoretical commitments. In this regard, ethnomethodology and conversation analysis have proved particularly fruitful, not only by virtue of a methodological framework that drives analytic attention towards the interactional and sequential character of mundane activities, but also in the light of the substantial corpus of findings and insights that emerged over some years concerning the organization of talk and in particular talk in interaction (see for example Sacks et al., 1974; Drew and Heritage, 1992; Sacks, 1992; Heritage and Maynard, 2006; Peräkylä and Sorjonen, 2012; Stivers and Sidnell, 2013). Studies of naturally occurring conversation and, over the last couple decades or so, talk at work or institutional interaction have provided both the analytic resources and substantive findings with which to address embodied action and activity. In this regard, there are three principal analytic commitments that have underpinned a substantial corpus of video-based research, commitments that resonate with a range of qualitative research, but have particular significance for ethnomethodology and conversation analysis (see Garfinkel, 1967; Heritage, 1984; Sacks, 1992). They are:

1.   *Social action is situated*: action is produced with regard to the emerging context and the meaning or intelligibility of an action or activity is bound to, and inseparable from, the circumstances and framework of action in which it is produced.
2.   *Social action is an emerging practical accomplishment*: participants, in concert and collaboration with others, are ongoingly engaged in the production of action and in making sense of the actions of others.
3.   *Social action relies upon a methodology*: practice(s), reasoning and commonsense knowledge in and through which people produce their own actions and make sense of the actions of others.

Analysis therefore proceeds on a case by case basis in which we scrutinize extracts or fragments of data, the original video recording accompanied transcripts, to examine the ways in which participants produce and orient particular actions with regard to the contributions of others – co-participants. Social interaction becomes both a topic of inquiry and a resource for analysis, providing the resources through which we can examine how participants' themselves orient to each other's conduct in the production of particular actions and activities. It is worthwhile considering a brief extract drawn from a substantial corpus of video recordings of auctions of fine art and antiques, recordings gathered both in the UK and abroad (see Heath, 2013).

SEQUENCE AND PARTICIPATION IN WORKPLACE ACTIVITIES

Auctions of fine art and antiques consist of repeated episodes of intense forms of interaction with up to 500 lots sold in one day. Each episode rarely lasts more than 30 seconds but within those brief moments the price of goods can rise more than five times the starting figure. At any one time there may be up to a hundred people at an auction, many of whom are potential bidders for any of the objects that come up for sale. There may also be a number of people who have booked telephone lines with the auction house to enable them to bid on particular lots through sales assistants and others who have registered to bid over the internet. The auctioneer has to deploy an organization that encourages and coordinates the contributions of bidders, bidders who not only are in competition with each other, but may have a very different idea of the value of the goods in question. At its most basic the auctioneer, in cooperation with bidders, has to implement an organizational arrangement whereby the potential contributions of multiple participants, many of whom might wish to bid if the price is right, are organized through an orderly sequence of turns, where those turns, to corrupt Sacks et al. (1974), are 'valued', literally in this case.

Consider the following fragment, a brief extract from a recent auction of antiquities at a sales room in London. For convenience, we have simplified and abbreviated the transcript and represented bidding by [B bids], numbering particular bidders [B.1 bids] in the order that they first enter the bidding.

Fragment 1

A: Lot One Hundred and Six. There it is. Lot One Hundred and Six

        .

A: Eight hundred
       [B.1 bids]

A: Eight fifty
       [B.2 bids]

A: Nine hundred
       [B.1 bids]

A: Nine fifty
       [B.2 bids]

A: A thousand <u>the</u>re:
       (0.4) [B.1 bids]

A: Eleven here
       (.) [B.2 bids]

A: Twelve hundred
       [B.1 bids]

A: Thirteen hundred
       [B.2 bids]

A: Fourteen hundred
        [B.1 bids]
A: Fifteen hundred

        .

A: Two two:: the standing bidder (0.2) last chance [glances at B.3] (0.2) two thousand two hundred
        pounds:::
        (0.6)
        {knock}

From the transcript alone we can see that the interaction differs markedly from the organization of other activities and events with which we might be familiar. There is only one
speaker, the auctioneer (A), and talk consists largely of numbers, namely price increments.
Those increments remain stable at £50 up until £1,000 and then change to £100. Once
begun, the incremental structure projects the series of prices at which people bid irrespective of the values they may have in mind. Moreover, it can be seen that bidding alternates
between two principal protagonists, B.1 and B.2. A little later at £1,800, not included in
the transcript, B.1 withdraws and the auctioneer then finds a new bidder, and alternates
the bidding between B.2 and B.3. This ordering principle is known as the 'run' and is used
within many forms of auctions; irrespective of the number of people who try to bid, the
auctioneer establishes two bidders and no more than two bidders at any one time.

  It is clear from the transcript that visible or bodily conduct plays an important part in the
organization of the event. First and foremost, 'turns' at bidding are accomplished through
gestures (e.g. a nod or a wave) rather than through talk. The participation of potential buyers is largely limited to agreeing or declining to bid at a price. Secondly, given that there
may be up to a hundred or so people in the sales room, and a number of people eager to
bid, it is clear that the visible conduct of the auctioneer may play an important part in enabling individuals to know when it is their turn to bid. Thirdly, bidders and all those present
need to know when a bid has been successful and who, at any moment, has bid the highest
price. In other words, the organization of participation during the event, the distribution
of opportunities to bid and the rapid escalation of price, rests upon the visible conduct of
the auctioneer and potential buyers. To explore this further it is worthwhile considering a
section of the run. Take for example the announcement of the increment 'Twelve hundred'.

  From the images in Figure 19.1, one can see that the auctioneer alternates between gestures with his right hand and gestures with his left. The gestures are accompanied by shifts
in his visual alignment in which he turns from the bidder on his right (B.1) to the bidder
on his left (B.2). As he begins to announce 'Eleven here' (bid by B.1), he turns towards B.2.
His gaze arrives with the word 'here'. He withdraws his right hand and starts to raise his
left to gesture towards B.2. The moment he looks at and gestures towards B.2, she nods,
agreeing to the projected next increment. The visible realignment and the gesture, coupled with the announcement, enable the buyer to know when it is her turn and the price
that she is expected to bid. It also enables the bid to be accomplished through the most
minimal of actions – a head nod.

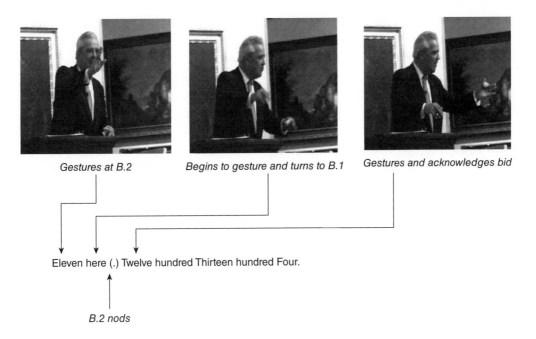

Gestures at B.2   Begins to gesture and turns to B.1   Gestures and acknowledges bid

Eleven here (.) Twelve hundred Thirteen hundred Four.

B.2 nods

Figure 19.1   Inviting a bid

The fragment points to a number of analytic consideration that enable us to unpack the methodological commitments that were mentioned earlier.

Firstly, we begin to see how visible conduct, like talk, performs social actions and activities. In the case at hand, potential buyers produce turns, bids, within the developing course of the interaction, not through talk but rather through visible or bodily conduct. The bidder on the right of the auctioneer raises his catalogue, the bidder on the left nods her head. Moreover, the invitation to bid is accomplished not only through the announcement of the current increment, for example 'a thousand <u>the</u>re:', but also by virtue of the auctioneer's accompanying bodily conduct, his visual realignment towards the under-bidder and a gesture that offers the opportunity to bid. Visible conduct therefore, both with and without talk, is used to produce specific actions and engender a response from a particular participant.

Secondly, the location or position of the participants' conduct within the developing course of the interaction is critical to its sense and its ability to perform a particular action. For example, a head nod serves to produce a bid of £1,200 by virtue of its immediate juxtaposition with the announcement of the increment coupled with the auctioneer's turning and gesturing towards the participant. The head nod is produced and is seen as responsive to the auctioneer's invitation to bid and bid at the projected next increment. Similarly, the announcement of the increment and the gesture with which it is accompanied are intelligible by virtue of the ways in which they stand in contrast to the preceding action of the auctioneer and the conduct of the protagonist. The actions of the participants, whether visible, spoken or a combination of both, are accomplished by virtue of the ways in which they are oriented to the (immediately) preceding action(s) and create opportunities for subsequent action, not infrequently in the next turn.

Thirdly, the actions of the participants are accomplished in and through sequences of actions and these sequences inform how people produce their conduct and make sense of the actions of others. For example, the run is dependent upon a social and interactional arrangement that alternatively places particular participants under the obligation to respond to an invitation to bid. The invitation is produced through the announcement of a figure, an increment, accompanied by the auctioneer's reorienting and gesturing towards a particular individual. The invitation renders relevant, implicates, an action from a potential buyer, to accept or decline to bid, in this case the acceptance, enabling the auctioneer immediately to invite the protagonist to bid the next increment. The participants' actions therefore, and indeed the systematic escalation of price at auction, are accomplished through alternating sequences of action, through which particular participants are provided with the opportunity to bid or withdraw. The remarkable economy of action established through this sequential organization enables auctioneers to rapidly establish the value of goods and secure their exchange – goods that may be worth a few pounds or many millions (see Heath, 2013).

Within these rapidly emerging sequences of activity we find evidence of a social organization that informs the emerging production of each and every action, however minimal or seemingly irrelevant. Consider, for example, the gesture that accompanies the announcement of the increment, a gesture that on close inspection appears systematically in the course of its production to accomplish at least two actions (Figure 19.2). As B.2 bids in response to the increment and accompanying pointing gesture and bodily realignment, the auctioneer immediately turns away from her and towards B.1, simultaneously announcing the price that she has bid. As she begins to nod in response to the invitation, he transforms his gesture, flipping the hand up and down. The flip of the hand displays acknowledgement of the bid and, as it is raised up and down, the participant turns to one side and ceases her head nod. As the hand flips up and down, the auctioneer begins to turn to the protagonist and announces the current increment, namely 'Twelve hundred'. In turn, we can consider the ways in which visible behaviour, like talk, is systematically shaped, designed, in the course of its production, to accomplish particular actions with regard to the context at hand, a 'context' that is emerging in the light of the concurrent conduct of the co-participant(s).

In this way, we can begin to see how people ongoingly fashion the forms of participation that arise during interaction and thereby give that interaction its particular institutional character or quality. In this regard, it is worthwhile recalling Goffman's (1981) discussion of participation framework:

'Participation framework': when a word is spoken all those who happen to be in perceptual range of the event will have some sort of participation status relative to it. The codification of these various positions and the normative specifications of appropriate conduct with each provide an essential background for interaction analysis - whether (I presume) in our own society or any other. (Goffman, 1981: 3)

Figure 19.2   Bidding and the transformation of gesture

In the case at hand, we can begin to see how auctions rely upon an interactional order that selectively organises both the opportunities to participate and the forms of participation in which people engage within the developing course of the activity. These forms of participation are emergent, accomplished, even within the emerging production of an action, sensitive to the emerging conduct of the co-participant(s). In this way, a particular institutional arrangement, which enables the transaction of goods worth many billions of dollars each year, is established and maintained in and through a fine-grained interactional organization that rests upon the situated deployment of socially organized practice and procedure.

Analysis of a single fragment of a video recording can provide the resources with which we can begin to examine the social and interactional organization on which these highly complex events rely. We might then proceed to assemble collections of particular actions or action sequences and compare and contrast their character and organization.

The analysis of the interactional organization of social actions and activities provides the resources with which to address the ways in which participants themselves orient to, and display an understanding of, each other's actions. For instance, in considering the auctioneer's announcement of the increment and the accompanying visual alignment and gesture, we can examine how the recipient responds to the action, in this case 'in next turn' in order to consider how the participant herself is treating the auctioneer's conduct. Moreover, by considering how the auctioneer himself, in turn, responds to the bidder's actions, by flipping the hand, announcing the next increment and inviting the protagonist to bid, we can discern how he is treating the head nods of the woman. In other words, the interactional organization of the participants' actions, their emergent and sequential character, provides a vehicle to analyse the very ways in which participants themselves display an understanding of each other's conduct in subsequent action and activity. While analysis may well go on to consider numerous instances of this sequential organization, the detailed examination of a single case provides the resources through which we can begin to explicate the characteristics of particular activities and prioritize the participants' orientation to each other's conduct (see Sacks et al., 1974; Goodwin, 1981; Sacks, 1992; Schegloff, 2007; Heath et al., 2010).

DATA COLLECTION AND TRANSCRIPTION

The analytic standpoint the researcher adopts has important implications for data collection. There are long-standing debates concerning how best to record the visual and audible aspects of human conduct and interaction exemplified in the intense discussion between Margaret Mead and Gregory Bateson where they debate the advantages and disadvantages of fixed and roving cameras (see Brand, 1976). With the emphasis on interaction, and exploring the ways in which people respond to and participate in each other's conduct, there are some clear implications for data collection and identifying materials that will serve analytic purposes. First and foremost, it is critical to record the conduct and contribution of all active participants in an activity's accomplishment to enable analysis to address the ways in which particular actions and activities emerge in and through social interaction. Secondly, where possible fixed, rather than roaming, cameras are adopted for two principal reasons: in attempting to follow action there is often a small delay before the camera begins to capture the action in question, thereby missing its onset; and in following the action, people remain highly sensitive, and in some cases orient, to the recording – the researcher becomes an active participant within the scene of action. Thirdly, using a fixed camera position, even if it requires using multiple cameras, enables the researcher to maximize the quality of sound and vision and focus the scene that is best for analysis. In this way, data can be gathered that enable a range of analytic interests to be brought to bear upon the analysis of the material. In the case of auctions we found that in many cases it was necessary to use three cameras simultaneously to record the event. In this way, we were able to access recordings of potential buyers, other participants such as sale assistants and clerks, as well as the auctioneer (see Heath, 2013).

These methodological commitments also point to the importance of transcription and transcription as part of the analytic process rather than simply as a means to represent the data in a particular form. Of particular importance is clarifying the position or location of action in order to examine the ways in which an action is sensitive to the preceding and concurrent contributions of others. In analysing a fragment, an episode or event, we begin by transcribing the talk using the orthography developed by Gail Jefferson, a system that is now widely used within conversation analysis and cognate approaches to the analysis of language use and discourse. We then use either a software program or transpose the transcript of the talk to graph paper or the equivalent and, laying the talk horizontally, systematically map at least the onset and completion of the participants' visible conduct (see Heath et al., 2010). Mapping fragments in this way enables one to identify with some precision the position of particular actions and the components of those actions and to examine the potential relations between the actions of the different participants within the interaction. It also provides a vehicle for scrutinizing the original recording and noting the complex details of the participants' actions and interaction. These maps of the interaction are for analytic purposes and rarely used within presentations or publications, though it is not unusual to provide simplified versions of the original transcripts.

FIELDWORK AND VIDEO ANALYSIS

The video recording is the principal vehicle for analysis and, with a commitment to demonstrating how participants themselves orient to each other's actions, provides the resources through which we develop evidence for particular observations and warrant our findings and explanations. Fieldwork, however, can prove invaluable both in collecting data, including recorded data, and in subjecting these materials to analysis. The importance of fieldwork in undertaking video-based analysis is perhaps of particular importance to studies of the workplace and more complex organizational environments. It can provide invaluable information concerning the setting and in gaining the trust of the participants.

So, for example, in our study of auctions, we undertook extensive fieldwork that enabled us not only to resolve certain problems that arose in gathering recorded data, but also to become familiar with some of the techniques and resources on which auctioneers rely in conducting sales. Matters such as why auctioneers begin the bidding at particular prices, how they structure increments, the information documented on the sales sheets, the ways in which they plan a sale and discriminate certain lots proved invaluable in analysing the recordings. Or, for example, consider the picture in Figure 19.3 of a station supervisor in an operations room on London Underground, a setting in which we have undertaken research for some years (see, for example, Heath et al., 2002; Luff et al. 2008).

To begin to understand the activities of participants in a domain as complex as the operations rooms it is necessary to become familiar with the resources on which personnel rely.

Figure 19.3   The station operations room at Victoria Station on London Underground

For example, a seemingly simple public announcement to inform passengers and staff that the station is overcrowded and is being temporarily closed will involve the supervisor in scrutinizing successive CCTV monitors, reviewing the timing of trains, keying area codes into the public address system, radioing selective station staff and, following the event, entering information into 'the failure and delay' sheets. The supervisor's action and the interaction through which it emerges is dependent upon the 'occasioned' use of these resources and analysis can only proceed by understanding those resources and how they are used within the emerging accomplishment of particular activities.

Notwithstanding the necessity to undertake fieldwork, the recording, the video record, remains the principal analytic resource and the vehicle through which we can warrant our observations and findings with regard to the actions of the participants themselves. In this way, video recordings do not simply stand as an additional way in which we can gather qualitative data or illustrate events that may be of ethnographic interest, but rather provide the critical methodological resource that enables us to begin to come to terms with one of the central commitments of qualitative research, that is developing analyses that are sensitive to and demonstrate how participants themselves rely upon particular practices and procedures in the concerted accomplishment of social actions and activities.

CHAPTER SUMMARY

Video provides an unprecedented resource for social science research and enables the application of various methodological interests and commitments (see, for example, Knoblauch et al., 2006). In this chapter, we have discussed a particular use of video, an application that exploits video as an 'investigative technology', a technology that enables us to record activities as they arise in ordinary everyday settings and subject them to detailed scrutiny. Drawing on analytic developments within sociology, namely ethnomethodology and conversation analysis, these recordings can provide us with the resources with which to address the key principles of qualitative research with its commitment to the situated character of practical action, the orientations of the participants themselves and the practices through which they accomplish social actions and activities. Social interaction is critical in this regard, forming both the topic and resource of analysis and enabling us to examine the concerted production of social action and the ways in which people make sense of each other's conduct. It is not surprising therefore that in recent years we have witnessed the emergence of a burgeoning corpus of qualitative research that uses video to examine embodied action, research that provides highly distinctive insights into the social and interactional organization of everyday activities:

- Video provides unprecedented resources for the analysis of social action and interaction in everyday settings and in building a corpus of data can be subject to a range of analytic and substantive interests.
- Drawing on ethnomethodology and conversation analysis, video can enable the investigation of embodied action and interaction and the ways in which activities are accomplished through the interplay of talk, visible conduct and use of various tools and technologies, objects and artefacts.

- Video coupled with methodological resources that drive analytic attention to the social and interactional accomplishment of everyday activities, can provide highly distinctive insights into topics of contemporary interest in the social sciences such as the delivery of health care, economic action and the operation of markets, and engagement in the cultural and creative industries.

FUTURE PROSPECTS

Developments in quality of digital recording, coupled with widespread use of pictures and video in interpersonal communication provide unprecedented resources for social science research and opportunities for the detailed analysis of social interaction. They also pose significant methodological challenges, not simply in the ways in which we gather data and transcribe multi-modal activities, but rather with regard to how we define and identify action and sequences of action and build evidence for how participants themselves orient to particular practices and structure.

Study questions

1. What opportunities and resources can video provide for qualitative research?
2. How can we use video to examine the social and interactional accomplishment of everyday activities?
3. In what ways does transcription provide resources for analysis?
4. Why is it helpful to undertake fieldwork as well as record people's actions and activities?

Recommended reading

Knoblauch, H., Schnettler, B., Raab, J. and Söffner, H.-G. (eds) (2006) *Video-Analysis: Methodology and Methods Qualitative Audiovisual Data Analysis in Sociology*. Frankfurt am Main: Lang-Verlag. Provides a wide-ranging exposition of qualitative video analysis built around a series of empirical studies adopting different approaches and techniques.

Kissmann, U. T. (ed.) (2009) *Video Interaction Analysis: Methods and Methodology.* Frankfurt-am-Main: Peter Lang. Presents a collection of various approaches to the analysis of video, drawing on leading scholars from linguistic anthropology, conversation analysis, ethnography and phenomenology.

Heath, C. C., Hindmarsh, J. and Luff, P. (2010) *Video in Qualitative Research: Analysing Social Interaction in Everyday Life*. London: Sage. Provides an introduction to using video for qualitative research and discusses gaining access and ethics, data collection, the analysis of video recordings of everyday activities, the presentation of data and findings, and future developments.

Recommended online resources

See the following for ethical guidelines and procedures:

British Psychological Society (2006):
www.bps.org.uk/the-society/code-of-conduct/code-of-conduct_home.cfm

British Sociological Association: Visual Sociology Statement of Ethical Practice (2006):
www.visualsociology.org.uk/about/ethical_statement.php

Economic and Social Research Council, 'Research Ethics Framework' (2015):
www.esrc.ac.uk/files/funding/guidance-for-applicants/esrc-framework-for-research-ethics-2015/

References

Asch, D. (2007) 'Using video data to capture discontinuous science meaning making in nonschool settings', in R. Goldman, R. Pea, B. Barron and S. J. Derry (eds), *Video Research in the Learning Sciences*. London: Routledge, pp. 207–26.

Banks, M. (2008) *Using Visual Data in Qualitative Research*. London: Sage.

Barley, S. R. and G. Kunda (2001) 'Bringing work back in', *Organization Science*, 12(1): 76–95.

Brand, S. B. (1976) '"For God's sake, Margaret": conversation with Gregory Bateson and Margaret Mead', *CoEvolutionary Quarterly*, 10: 32–44.

Büscher, M. (2005) 'Social life under the microscope', *Sociological Research Online*, 10 (1). http://socresonline.org.uk/10/1/buscher.html (accessed 10 December 2015).

Clark, C. and Pinch, T. (1995). *The Hard Sell: The Language and Lessons of Street Wise Marketing*. New York: HarperCollins.

Dant, T. (2004) 'Recording the 'Habitus', in C. Pole (ed.), *Seeing Is Believing? Approaches to Visual Methodology*, Studies in Qualitative Methodology, Vol. 7. Amsterdam: Elsevier, pp. 43–63.

Drew, P. and Heritage, J. C. (eds) (1992) *Talk at Work: Interaction in Institutional Settings*. Cambridge: Cambridge University Press.

Emmison, M., Smith, P. and Mayall, M (2012) *Researching the Visual* (2nd edn). London: Sage.

Engeström, Y. and Middleton, D. (eds) (1996) *Cognition and Communication at Work*. Cambridge: Cambridge University Press.

Garfinkel, H. (1967) *Studies in Ethnomethodology*. Englewood Cliffs, NJ: Prentice Hall.

Goffman, E. (1981) *Forms of Talk*. Oxford: Blackwell.

Goldman, R., Pea, R., Barron, B. and Derry, S. J. (eds) (2007) *Video Research in the Learning Sciences*. London: Routledge.

Goodwin, C. (1981) *Conversational Organization: Interaction between Speakers and Hearers*. London: Academic.

Goodwin, C. and Goodwin, M. H. (1996) 'Seeing as a situated activity: formulating planes', in Y. Engeström and D. Middleton (eds), *Cognition and Communication at Work*. Cambridge: Cambridge University Press, pp. 61–95.

Goodwin, M. H. (2006) *The Hidden Life of Girls: Games of Stance, Status and Exclusion*. Oxford: Blackwell.

Haddington, P., Mondada, L. and Nevile, M. (eds) (2013) *Interaction and Mobility: Language and the Body in Motion*. Berlin: De Gruyter.

Heath, C. C. (1986) *Body Movement and Speech in Medical Interaction*. Cambridge: Cambridge University Press.

Heath, C. C. (2013) *The Dynamics of Auction: Social Interaction and the Sale of Fine Art and Antiques*. Cambridge: Cambridge University Press

Heath, C. C., Hindmarsh, J. and Luff, P. (2010) *Video in Qualitative Research: Analysing Social Interaction in Everyday Life*. London: Sage.

Heath, C. C. and Luff, P. (2000) *Technology in Action*. Cambridge: Cambridge University Press.

Heath, C., Luff, P. and Sanchez Svensson, M. (2002) 'Overseeing organisations: configuring the environment of action', *British Journal of Sociology*, 53 (2): 181–203.

Heath, C. C. and vom Lehn, D. (2008) 'Construing interactivity: enhancing engagement with new technologies in science centres and museums', *Social Studies of Science*, 38: 63–96.

Heritage, J. C. (1984). *Garfinkel and Ethnomethodology*. Cambridge: Polity.

Heritage, J. C. and Maynard, D. (eds) (2006). *Practising Medicine: Talk and Action in Primary Care Encounters*. Cambridge: Cambridge University Press.

Hindmarsh, J., Fraser, M., Heath, C. and Benford, S. (2000) 'Object-focused interaction in collaborative virtual environments', *ACM Transactions on Computer-Human Interaction (ToCHI)*, 7 (4): 477–509.

Hindmarsh, J. and Pilnick, A. (2002) 'The tacit order of teamwork: collaboration and embodied conduct in anaesthesia', *Sociological Quarterly*, 43 (2): 139–64.

Jewitt, C. (ed.) (2009) *Routledge Handbook of Multimodal Analysis*. London: Routledge.

Kissmann, U. T. (ed.) (2009) *Video Interaction Analysis: Methods and Methodology*. Frankfurt-am-Main: Peter Lang.

Knoblauch, H., Schnettler, B., Raab, J. and Söffner, H.-G. (eds) (2006) *Video-Analysis: Methodology and Methods Qualitative Audiovisual Data Analysis in Sociology*. Frankfurt-am-Main: Lang-Verlag.

Koschmann, T., LeBaron, C., Goodwin, C., Zemel, A. and Dunnington, G. (2007) 'Formulating the triangle of doom', *Gesture*, 7 (1): 97–118.

Laurier, E. and Philo, C. (2006) 'Natural problems of naturalistic video data', in H. Knoblauch, J. Raab, H.-G. Soefnner and B. Schnettler (eds), *Video Analysis: Methodology and Methods*. Frankfurt-am-Main: Peter Lang, pp. 181–90.

Licoppe, C. (2015) 'Video communication and "camera actions": the production of wide video shots in courtrooms with remote defendants', *Journal of Pragmatics*, 76: 117–34.

Llewellyn, N. and Hindmarsh, J. (eds) (2010) *Organization, Interaction and Practice: Studies in Ethnomethodology and Conversation Analysis*. Cambridge: Cambridge University Press.

Luff, P. K. and C. C. Heath (1993) 'Some practicalities of menu use: improvisation in screen based activity', *Journal of Intelligent Systems*, Special Issue on the Social Context of Intelligent Systems, 3 (2–4): 251–96.

Luff, P. K. and Heath, C. C. (2000) 'The collaborative production of computer commands in command and control', *Journal of Human Computer Studies*, 52: 669–99

Luff, P. and Heath, C. C. (2002) 'Broadcast talk: technologically mediated action in a complex setting', *Research on Language and Social Interaction*, 35 (3): 232–64

Luff, P., Heath, C. and Pitsch, K. (2009) 'Indefinite precision: the use of artefacts-in-interaction in design work', in C. Jewitt (ed.), *Routledge Handbook of Multimodal Analysis*. London: Routledge, pp. 213–24.

Luff, P., Heath, C. and Sanchez Svensson, M. (2008) 'Discriminating conduct: deploying systems to support awareness in organisations', *International Journal of Human Computer Studies*, 24 (4): 410–36.

Luff, P., Hindmarsh, J. and Heath, C. (eds) (2000) *Workplace Studies: Recovering Work Practice and Informing System Design*. Cambridge: Cambridge University Press.

Margolis, E. and Pauwels, L. (eds) (2011) *The Sage Handbook of Visual Research Methods*. London: Sage.

Mondada, L. (2003) 'Working with video: how surgeons produce video records of their actions', *Visual Studies*, 18: 58–73.

Mondada, L. (2011) 'The interactional production of multiple spatialities within a participatory democracy meeting', *Social Semiotics*, 21 (2): 283–308.

Mondada, L. (2012) 'Talking and driving: multiactivity in the car', *Semiotica*, 191: 223–56.

Peräkylä, A. and Ruusuvuori, J. (2006) 'Facial expression in an assessment', in H. Knoblauch, J. Raab, H.-G. Soefnner and B. Schnettler (eds), *Video Analysis: Methodology and Methods*. Frankfurt: Peter Lang, pp. 127–42.

Peräkylä, A. and Sorjonen, M.-L. (eds) (2012) *Emotion and Social Interaction*. Oxford: Oxford University Press.

Pink, S. (2007) *Doing Visual Ethnography: Images, Media and Representation in Research* (2nd edn). London: Sage.

Rose, G. (2007) *Visual Methodologies: An Introduction to the Interpretation of Visual Materials* (2nd edn). London: Sage.

Sacks, H. (1992) *Lectures in Conversation* (Vols I and II). Oxford: Blackwell.

Sacks, H., Schegloff, E. A. and Jefferson, G. (1974) 'A simplest systematics for the organisation of turn-taking for conversation', *Language*, 50 (4): 696–735.

Schegloff, E. A. (2007) *Sequence Organisation in Interaction: A Primer in Conversation Analysis, Volume 1*. Cambridge: Cambridge University Press

Stivers, T. and J. Sidnell (eds) (2013) *Handbook of Conversation Analysis*. Oxford: Wiley-Blackwell.

Streeck, J., Goodwin, C. and LeBaron, C. (eds) (2011) *Embodied Interaction in the Material World*. Cambridge: Cambridge University Press

Suchman, L. (1996) 'Constituting shared workspaces', in Y. Engeström and D. Middleton (eds), *Cognition and Communication at Work*. Cambridge: Cambridge University Press, pp. 35–60.

Suchman, L. A. (2007) *Human-Machine Reconfigurations: Plans and Situated Actions* (2nd edn). Cambridge: Cambridge University Press.

Szymanski, M. H. and J. Whalen (2011) *Making Work Visible: Ethnographically Grounded Case Studies of Work Practice*. Cambridge: Cambridge University Press.

vom Lehn, D., Heath, C. C. and Hindmarsh, J. (2001) 'Exhibiting interaction: conduct and collaboration in museums and galleries interaction', *Symbolic Interaction*, 24 (2): 189–217.

Whalen, J. (1995) 'Expert systems vs. systems for experts: computer-aided dispatch as a support system in real-world environments', in P. Thomas (ed.), *The Social and Interactional Dimensions of Human-Computer Interfaces*. Cambridge: Cambridge University Press, pp. 161–83.

Whalen, J. and Vinkhuyzen, E. (2000) 'Expert systems in (inter)action: diagnosing document machine problems over the telephone', in P. Luff, J. Hindmarsh and C. Heath (eds), *Workplace Studies: Recovering Work Practice and Informing System Design*. Cambridge: Cambridge University Press, pp. 92–140.

PART VIII
QUALITATIVE DATA ANALYSIS

This section deals with the more 'nuts and bolts' issues of doing qualitative research. Tim Rapley clearly and informally reveals what he calls the 'pragmatics' of qualitative data analysis. Rapley offers invaluable advice about how to do good qualitative data analysis, emphasizing the importance of detailed readings, reviewing and refining your categories and using your provisional analysis to inform how you collect, transcribe and analyse data when you return to the field. As Rapley argues, good qualitative research is about 'living in the detail'.

Kathy Charmaz and Antony Bryant elucidate the elements of grounded theory (GT) and show what, in their view, has been right and wrong about criticisms of the GT approach. They then go on to demonstrate how grounded theory already contains under-used strategies that increase both its methodological power and the credibility of its data analysis. Like Rapley, they explain the nitty-gritty of data analysis from doing line-by-line initial coding and writing memos, to conducting theoretical sampling. Using helpful illustrations from their own data analysis, they demonstrate what a 'constructivist' GT methodology can look like in practice, showing how we can achieve analytic and theoretical credibility.

In her chapter on narrative inquiry (NI), Catherine Riessman continues this hands-on, student-friendly approach to the pragmatics of data analysis. Her aim is to distinguish such work from GT and from other methods of analysing interview data. For Riessman, NI involves resisting what she calls the 'seductive power' of stories. Instead, it asks: why was the story told *that* way? How do narrators position themselves in their stories? What other readings are possible, beyond what the narrator may have intended? Her argument that the research interview is a collaborative conversation ties in nicely with Holstein and Gubrium's earlier chapter on interview data.

As every student is taught, elegant data analysis presupposes a well-defined research topic, based on a review of earlier studies. Mary Dixon-Woods asks how we can make our literature reviews more robust. As she argues, a key question concerns the extent to which conventional systematic review methodology, with its focus on estimating the effectiveness of a particular intervention on average, can be consistent with aspirations of those aiming to produce more interpretive forms of overview of bodies of research evidence.

From the point of view of the research student, there remains the problem that we can spend so much time on literature reviews that we have too little time to gather and analyse our data. As I suggest in *Doing Qualitative Research*, one quick solution to this problem is to work with secondary data. Libby Bishop helpfully discusses the ethics of using such data and distinguishes the different ways it can be used in research design and methodological development. She supports her argument with case studies of school leavers' essays, migration and parenting and oral history interviews which show the degree to which general methodological debates are relevant to this form of research practice.

Like Bishop and Dixon-Woods, Anssi Peräkylä is concerned with the credibility of qualitative research. He is particularly interested in how qualitative research can offer reliable and valid descriptions of its data. Following Heritage's chapter, Peräkylä illustrates his argument with CA research. Recognizing that CA is a specialist field, in this newly revised chapter Peräkylä now extends his argument to qualitative research as a whole. Validity questions are discussed in terms of the comparative method and 'deviant case analysis' as well as specifically CA methods, such as validation through 'next turn'. He also demonstrates one way of generalizing from case studies and discusses the uses and limits of quantitative techniques in qualitative research.

Ultimately, good qualitative data analysis is expressed in how well we write. Amir Marvasti argues that novice researchers need to learn the basic skills or craft of writing. In qualitative research, there is no such thing as a format for 'the standard scientific paper'. Marvasti shows that different genres are available to us and describes the stylistic choices available and their advantages and limitations. He also comments upon the strategic choices authors have to consider as they try to publish their work and make it accessible to various audiences. He suggests that a 'perfect paper' is one that strikes a balance between craft skills, genre and intended audience. In this new version of his chapter, Marvasti helpfully outlines the possibilities of online publishing.

TWENTY

Some Pragmatics of Qualitative Data Analysis

Tim Rapley

About this chapter

This chapter gives you access to some of the routines, procedures, phases and tactics that are common in qualitative analytic reasoning and practice. Initially I focus on four routinely cited approaches to qualitative data analysis in order to explore their similarities and differences. I then describe some of the pragmatic issues you might need to consider alongside some of the qualities or states of mind you might seek to cultivate.

Keywords

coding, memos, data reduction, sampling, deviant case analysis

SOME INITIAL THOUGHTS ON 'ANALYSIS'

Anyone new to qualitative analysis will be faced with a quandary: what should I do with all these data? You look at various journal articles, and often see the same key phrases again and again. People keep telling you they did 'grounded theory', or conducted a 'phenomenological analysis', and then give you various levels of details about what that did. Some are quite rich descriptions; others just use a couple of phrases and a single reference. Above all, whatever you read, you realize that you need the right kind of label in your methods section.

The practices of good (or even adequate) qualitative data analysis can never be adequately summed up by using a neat label. They can also never be summed up by a list of specific steps or procedures that have been undertaken. Above all, you need to develop a hands-on knowledge of analysis. This should enable you to develop a 'qualitative analytic attitude'.

SOME EXAMPLES OF ANALYTIC APPROACHES

The novice is often faced with a second quandary: which of the many approaches I've read about should I use? Rather than offer you an exhaustive account of all the potential approaches available to you, I'm going briefly to focus on and compare four routinely cited approaches to qualitative data analysis. In Table 20.1, you'll see that each column outlines, in very basic terms, some of the key actions related to each analytic method.

I've chosen two quite popular and relatively discipline-free approaches, 'thematic analysis' and 'grounded theory', alongside 'framework analysis', which is often tied to applied and/or policy research, and a relative newcomer, 'interpretative phenomenological analysis' (IPA), which is increasingly cited in some qualitative psychology. These four were chosen, in part, as they already have quite clear 'guidelines' about the key tactics researchers might employ.

I need to add a warning here. The table is an heuristic device. Do not simply follow the phases outlined in the table. If you like the look of any of them, go and read about them.

As you'll see, in their most basic terms they all share some family resemblances, in that they seek to move from the particular to the abstract. By that I mean they all start with a close inspection of a sample of data about a specific issue. This close inspection is used to discover, explore and generate an increasingly refined conceptual description of the phenomena. The resulting conceptual description therefore emerges from, is based on, or is grounded in the data about the phenomena. The focus shifts from:

- what is said by participants, what you've observed them doing or what you read in a text (the level of description and summary); to
- exploring and explaining what is 'underlying' or 'broader' or to 'distil' essence, meaning, norms, orders, patterns, rules, structures, etc. (the level of concepts and themes).

What, if anything, can we learn from all these different approaches to qualitative data analysis? The central methods that appear to cut across these (and other forms of data analysis methods like analytic induction, alongside data analysis phases in things like ethnography, discourse analysis) appear to be as follows:

Table 20.1 Comparison of key processes from different analytic approaches

Framework analysis (see Ritchie et al., 2003)	Thematic analysis (see Grbich, 1999; Braun and Clarke, 2006)	Interpretative phenomenological analysis (see Smith and Osborn, 2008)	Constructivist grounded theory (see Charmaz, 2014)
1 Familiarize yourself with the dataset (note initial themes or concepts)	1 Familiarize yourself with the dataset (note initial comments and ideas)	1 Read single transcript (note initial comments and ideas)	1 Initial coding and memo writing (line-by-line coding, compare new codes with old, evaluate, alter, adjust, write notes)
2 Generate thematic framework (themes, sub-themes from data and interview topic guide)	2 Generate initial codes (systematically code whole dataset)	2 Generate initial themes (transform comments into themes)	2 Focused coding and memo-writing (select and then code key issues, keep comparing, write notes to refine ideas)
3 Indexing (apply thematic framework, label data with number or term)	3 Search for themes (collate similar codes into potential themes, gather all data for potential theme)	3 Create initial list of themes	3 Collect new data via theoretical sampling (strategically sample to further develop categories and their properties)
4 Sort data by theme or concept and summarize (create thematic charts)	4 Review themes (check if themes work in relation to the dataset, check for examples that do not fit, generate a thematic map/diagram)	4 Cluster themes (order the list of themes into connected areas)	4 Continue to code, memo and use theoretical sampling (develop and refine categories until no new issues emerge)
5 Develop descriptive accounts (develop and then refine categories)	5 Refine themes (refine specifics of each theme and linkages between them, generate propositions, look for complexity, associations)	5 Create a list/ table with superordinate themes and sub-themes	5 Sort and integrate memos (refine links between categories, develop concepts, write an initial draft of a theory)
6 Develop explanatory accounts (look for patterns, associations, clustering and explanations)		6 Go to new transcript (repeat above process and refine list/ table of themes)	
		7 Create a final list/table with superordinate themes and sub-themes	

Some fundamentals

- *Always start by engaging in some kind of close, detailed reading of a sample of your data.*

  o   And close, detailed, reading means looking for key, essential, striking, odd, interesting things people or texts say or do, as well as repetition.
  o   You should make notes, jottings, markings, etc., either on the pages or somewhere else.

- *Always read and systematically code your archive of data.*

  o   Code key, essential, striking, odd, interesting things.
  o   Code similar items with the same code.
  o   These codes can be drawn from ideas emerging from your close, detailed reading of your data archive, as well as from your prior reading of empirical and theoretical works.
  o   With each new application of a code, review your prior coding practices and see if what you want to code fits what has gone before. If yes, use that code. If no, create a new one. If it fits somewhat, you may want to modify your understanding of that code to include this.

- *Always reflect on why you've done what you've done.*

  o   Come up with a document that lists your codes. It might be useful to give some key examples, to write a sentence or two that explains what you are trying to get at, what sort of things should go together under specific codes.

- *Always review and refine your codes and coding practices.*

  o   For each code, collect together all the data you've given that code to. Ask yourself whether the data and ideas collected under this code are coherent, and ask yourself what are the key properties and dimensions of all the data collected under that code?
  o   Try to combine your initial codes, look for links between them, look for repetitions, exceptions and try to reduce them to key ones. This will often mean shifting from more verbatim, descriptive codes to more conceptual, abstract and analytic codes.
  o   Keep evaluating, adjusting, altering and modifying your codes and coding practices.
  o   Go back over what you've already done and recode it with your new schema or ideas.

- *Always focus on what you feel are the key codes and the relationship between them.*

  o   Make some judgements about what you feel are the central codes and focus on them.
  o   Try to look for links, patterns, associations, arrangements, relationships, sequences, etc.

The above fundamentals should be read as general statements about the analytic process. They seem to be embedded, to various degrees, in a whole range of traditions. Interestingly, they are all quite accessible. Some other methods, although I personally feel they are central, only appear in some how-to discussions.

Some options

- *Always make notes of your thinking behind why you've done what you've done.*

  o   Make notes on ideas that emerge before, during or while you're engaged in coding or reading related to your research project.

    o   Make some diagrams, tables, maps, models that enable you to conceptualize, witness, generate and show connections and relationships between codes.

- *Always return to the field with the knowledge you have already gained in mind and let this knowledge modify, guide or shape the data you want to collect next.*

Despite some apparent family resemblances in Table 20.1, even a brief reading shows that there are some telling differences. You should note that each approach has its own analytic language. So, for example, grounded theory talks in terms of moving from 'codes' to 'categories and their properties', whereas IPA talks of moving from 'themes' to 'superordinate themes'.

Each approach also has its own specific norms and rules of application. For example, both IPA and framework assume that the dataset is made up of some kind of recorded interviews. Given IPA's commitment to the specifics of each case, it is suggested that the analyst should focus on a very small number of qualitative interviews. With framework, they suggest that you work with a range of 'thematic charts'. So, for example, you'd initially establish a table where you list all the themes and sub-themes and quotes from each interview. You then begin to finely code that data, and then you refine those codes to more abstract codes. In the case of constructivist grounded theory the focus is on developing substantive theory of a particular process, situation or (inter)actions. You constantly note and develop your ideas in memos, encouraging you to shift your thinking from just this moment of data to more abstract reasoning. The iterative process of rounds of data collection, coding and memo-writing encourages conceptual development. Unlike the other approaches, thematic analysis has no coherent groups of academics claiming, defining and shaping its trajectory. So, the specific analytic etiquette of doing thematic analysis seems to vary broadly between authors.

Key points

- There is a range of approaches to qualitative analysis, but they share a common focus.
- They initially focus on a close reading and description of the collected data.
- Over time, they seek to discover, explore and generate connections and patterns underlying the data.

SOME OBSERVATIONS ON ASPECTS OF A QUALITATIVE ANALYTIC ATTITUDE

I now want to focus on some descriptions of some aspects of qualitative analytic practice and reasoning. I'm interested in trying to give you access to some of the very practical things you might need to consider or do alongside some of the qualities or states of mind you might seek to cultivate.

On uncertainty, intuition and hunches

When undertaking analysis you need to be prepared to be led down novel and unexpected paths, to be open and to be fascinated. Potential ideas can emerge from any quarter – from your reading, your knowledge of the field, engagements with your data, from conversations with colleagues – and from any phase in the life-cycle of the project. Whatever you do, remember to write it down! You also need to listen to and value your intuition and hunches. At some points you follow up a hunch, you go back over the data, and look again at your data (your transcripts, texts, field notes, coding, memos, journal articles, etc.) with a sense of joy as you feel you might be on to something.

Sometimes this ends in frustration, as your idea does not hold water; either the interviewee did not say something that radically different, or your idea echoes something already well developed in the literature. Sometimes the idea only comes to fruition much later in the project, or acts as a spark that instigates a new trajectory of thought. Centrally, try and cultivate a sense of creative, even playful, engagement with your data. If you spot a potential pattern, then search your data to see if this is coherent. Ideas emerge in all sorts of ways, but you *must* be immersed in the detail of your data to be really able to generate and fully explore them.

On coding

There is something very interesting about adding some sort of code to your data archive. In learning to code, you begin to develop, to borrow a phrase from Goodwin (1994), a 'professional vision' directed at your data. By that I mean you make some analytic choices about which lines, chunks or sections of data to highlight. In highlighting some things as belonging to a particular code, you begin inductively to create a local coding schema, a specific way to see and understand the phenomena. It does involve quite a lot of skill and requires some degree of confidence.

At the start of the data-coding process, being faced with a large stretch of text to be highlighted and coded can be quite scary, and adding your first 'official' code can be quite odd. If you are at all unsure, the trick is, rather than mark a specific day as 'the day I start coding' and maybe delay the process until you've collected some more data or done some more reading, just read the text and make some notes on it. Just underline or mark it in some way or add a note about whatever interests you. These initial engagements, what Layder (1998) calls pre-coding, are vital. Give yourself time to reflect and ponder.

On your initial systematic engagements

At some point, you need to start engaging in a more systematic, albeit preliminary, style of coding. You are really doing this for three reasons:

1. It forces you to engage, word by word, line by line, section by section, with the detail, to ask specific questions about and of your data. Reading in and for detail is essential practice.
2. You simply will not be able to remember all the things you've seen that you feel are important, so coding helps you to recall issues.
3. You can then easily gather all the data you've collected under a specific code and use this, alongside your related notes, to review the issue you are exploring, to help you to establish connections, commonalties and any overarching orders.

When starting to systematically code, I would suggest working with a paper and pen rather than a computer. Computers can overly constrain the options you have for marking up a text, whereas with paper and pen you can scrawl all over the text. You will often find that initial marked-up text will be very messy, both in a practical sense – in that things will be underlined, crossed out, commented on – and in a conceptual sense – in that you may have a very large number of, sometimes competing, codes. Remember that, especially at the start, what you choose to highlight and the code you choose to apply to it are the product of your *understanding so far*. Don't worry if the next day you feel you have to come back and do it again or if you think it's not quite right. At the start all you are trying to do is to establish the *possible dimensions* of the phenomena, so just try and make sense about what each word, line and section are about. Coding practices are always provisional and over the life of the project you will continually modify, refine and sometimes recode whole chunks of texts as your understanding shifts.

On living in the detail

Whether you prefer to think broadly and conceptually or prefer to live in the detail, with the first few rounds of coding texts, I would always recommend forcing yourself to start out doing line-by-line coding, and if you really can't face that, at least paragraph-by-paragraph coding. This initial tight focus can really help you concentrate on working *with* the data, and help avoid importing too many *a priori* presuppositions. That is not to say that you cannot draw on your prior reading, knowledge or experiences from the field. In thinking about and designing your interview schedule, setting up interviews or observations, or collecting documents or recordings you will already be making and forming certain analytic ideas. However, these ideas should never wholly overshadow your sense-making. They are tools which you can draw on to enable and enhance engagement with your data. Above all, follow the data.

The practicalities of coding are as simple as: highlight a word, line, sentence or paragraph and then give it a label. These codes can range from the quite descriptive to the abstract and conceptual. But what do you even use as a code? You have a whole array of possibilities, ranging from single 'key words' that do some nice summing up, to a few words, to phrases or even sentences. And these can emerge from using the specific words that people use, as well as modifying, somewhat, those phrases. This is often referred to as '*in vivo* coding' (see Charmaz, 2014). You can also draw on your repertoire of ideas, using words or phrases that draw out the key issue or idea.

Some words of caution

Despite repeated warnings in the literature to retain 'the participant's voice', don't feel that you need to stick to exactly the phrase used, that to modify it, you are somehow being disrespectful to that person's 'lived experience'. This can lose the point of good analysis and cause confusion. First, you need to remember that creating a list of key verbatim descriptions is not the end stage of analysis, it is the start. Second, in notes to yourself and in publications, you will probably end up using verbatim quotes, and so give others access to these 'voices'.

Relatedly, grouping relatively large chunks of text together, using large theoretical codes like 'power' or 'identity work', is rarely a good way to start. Such grand ideas may be present or shaping your data. However, this can easily close down the analysis far too quickly, in the sense that you've already decided that the specific focus is on issues such as this. Such broad concepts may be the end-point of a careful process of analytic work. By starting and only working with such theory-driven macro-codes, you often fail to grasp the specifics of the phenomena. The point is to try to explore how, when and why specific processes, practices and structures happen.

Finally, be aware of the context of people's talk and actions. For example, an interviewee's talk about a particular topic emerges from and responds to an interviewer's prior question, and so it is shaped by it. So rather than just code a specific phrase or action, and then later in your analysis only focus on that, try to retain the context of the issue you are interested in. Above all, be sensitive to the way things are often organized in sequences. It can really help to pay attention to people's ordering of what they do (Silverman, 2011: Chapter 3)

On knowing how to see things to highlight and code

How do you learn to read for the detail? Put simply, like most crafts, this takes practice and time. Alongside working with someone who has got some experience, and both working on the same data and then discussing your analytic reasoning and practices, it is worth looking at some of the texts available that offer you an overview of specific ways of coding. For example, Bernard and Ryan (2010) offer 12 simple techniques to begin to identify what they call, following Opler (1945), themes. These include focusing on such aspects as 'repetitions', 'similarities and differences' and 'indigenous typologies and categories'. Saladaña (2013) describes over 20 approaches to early-phase coding, with these grouped into different genres. For example, the genre 'elemental methods' includes *in vivo* coding, whereas the genre 'literary and language methods' includes narrative coding (so focus on narrative structure). Finally, Gibbs (2007) describes 12 aspects that you could focus on, from 'specific acts and behaviour', to 'relationship and interaction' and 'meanings'. What all these overviews share is a quite practical focus, offering a wide range of techniques for you to work with. Above all, read these and other texts, things that offer you quite practical and worked-through examples.

Finally, be aware that the initial stages of coding often take up a lot of time. It is routine to be hesitant, to find yourself pondering about what specific code to apply. Keep asking yourself: does this make sense, is that really about X, Y or Z or something else? Remember, you are attempting to create your own coding scheme rather than apply someone else's. With that comes some responsibility; most importantly, that your schema actually has some connection to the data! However idiosyncratic your coding practice, others should be able to come to your data and, with your support, be able to follow your reasoning.

Key points

- Be open, listen to your hunches and write your initial ideas down.
- Early coding is provisional; over the life of your project you will modify and refine your codes.
- Focus on the detail; look for similarities and differences.

On splitting, combining, simplifying and reducing

Alongside living in the detail, you also need to have your eye on the broader picture. You always need to be able to step back and think bigger, to start to get a sense of connections between different parts of your data. As Miles and Huberman (1994) argue, you always need to engage in a process of 'data reduction'. They describe this as:

> [t]he process of selecting, focusing, simplifying, abstracting and transforming the data that appear in written field notes or transcriptions [or texts]. ... As data collection proceeds, further episodes of data reduction occur (writing summaries, coding, teasing out themes, making clusters, making partitions, writing memos). ... Data reduction is a form of analysis that sharpens, sorts, focuses, discards, and organises data in such a way that 'final' conclusions can be drawn and verified. (1994: 10)

Centrally, data reduction is an ongoing activity. The simple act of highlighting and coding something, or of giving the same code to two distinct sections of the same or different texts, is in essence a way to reduce data.

Over the project you are often moving through rounds of splitting the data into separate codes, reviewing those fragments (and notes about them) collected under specific codes, trying to see how the ideas underlying each code combine, relate or diverge. You work to group certain codes together, to redefine and rename them, to drill down to explore the detail and dimensions of these new emerging issues. As you move through this process, you start to focus on specific issues and to discard some ideas as no longer central to your argument.

Over the project the process of highlighting and coding becomes quicker and you become less hesitant. With each new engagement with your data, your coding schema needs less tailoring and refining. You will generally reach a point when you've got a sense of what the key issues are so far. At the very least you now need to turn to a new piece of data or, even better, return to the field, to further refine your ideas. In an ideal world, as this process is going on you will be regularly meeting with others (be they colleagues or supervisors) to discuss your emerging findings. People may not always agree with everything, but such discussions will definitely sharpen and direct your thinking.

You're aiming for something that is representative of your dataset, yet relatively abstract. To be utterly representative you'd need to give everyone all your data; instead you offer them 'categories' or 'themes' that demonstrate the key issues. Dey (2007), albeit speaking about grounded theory, outlines some aspects of the analytic attitude central to much qualitative work:

> [seek] the underlying logic of apparently disparate events, recognizing causal inferences at work through our categorizations, checking, revising, amplifying interpretations through comparisons across settings, and using representational techniques to evaluate and explore connections between categories. (2007: 188)

Carefully and creatively, you need to conceptualize, abstract and render the central aspects of a phenomenon to make it available to others.

On repetition and boredom

Alongside moments of elation and frustration, at points, doing analysis can be quite boring. Boredom can be your friend. There are two potential ways that you can find yourself 'bored'.

First, it emerges when you're seeing the same issues again and again and certain codes seem to be emerging as dominant. Discovering repetition can be a good thing. Qualitative research is in part about finding and describing patterns and structures. When you've seen the same thing again and again, you may be onto something. In the early stages of analysis, seeing repetition can be useful. However, in these early stages, it can also mean that your codes are just too large, that you are not thinking with your data at an adequate level of detail. In the later stages, when you're trying to verify your ideas, being bored can be quite useful as it may signify that you've potentially hit gold.

Second, it can emerge as you are faced with an ever growing amount of data to analyse. This can lead you to cast too casual a glance at your data. You can get into a habit of glossing over some sections of your data or just giving it a rather grand code. The trick is to be aware of potential surprises. This often emerges when you've collected a lot of data and have not had time to engage with it. You're faced with having to manage large amounts of coding and related writing. This is, to be frank, a bad practice. Qualitative research is an iterative practice; its strength can lie in the process of collecting something, drawing out key issues, then going on to discover, in your next round of data collection (or reading), how relevant that issue is in a different context, with a different person.

On returning

For me, engaging in rounds or cycles of fieldwork and officework is essential practice. The reason we engage in qualitative research is to discover a phenomenon, in all its textures and nuances, to focus on and explore. The easiest way really to achieve this is to flip between phases of officework and fieldwork, so that they mutually inform each other. This means you need to think a lot about sampling. Our claims stand and fall on drawing out ideas from quite small (albeit deeply rich) collections of cases. We should work hard to choose those cases with some care. Only relying on a convenience sampling – all those you have access to and that said 'yes' – is not good practice. Also, only relying on a retrospective conceptualization of your sample, discovering the diversity *post hoc* and then describing it as a 'maximum variation sample', is not that useful.

After your initial rounds of sampling, you really need to follow that up with further rounds of sampling that are driven by your emerging analytic findings. Patton (2002) has a useful list of the 14 different styles of sampling to guide your choices. Your emerging data and ideas about it suggest further criteria for selecting additional cases, texts or settings, and you specifically seek more data to develop those ideas. You may want to go in search of similar cases, in order to further explore your ideas or more variable cases which may challenge your ideas.

At some point, you need to make the decision to stop collecting data. There are really no hard and fast rules about when this should happen. Ideally this would happen when you've had time to explore all the questions that office and fieldwork raise, that you've generated a rich and coherent account, and further rounds will not generate any substantial new directions. Given the nature of academic timelines and your willingness to devote your time to a single phenomenon, you'll never be able to answer all your questions, to follow up all the potential leads. What is central is that the key ideas and claims have been thoroughly thought through and investigated.

Key points

- Start your coding early!
- Look at how specific codes combine, relate or diverge.
- Talk to others; show them your data and codes; discuss your emerging ideas.
- Use your data and ideas to suggest further criteria for selecting additional cases, texts or settings.

On writing

I cannot stress enough how key this is. The focus that writing enables is incredibly helpful in establishing what you know (and don't know) and assisting you in making conceptual leaps. Transforming your thoughts onto paper or onto the screen, throughout the project, inscribes them with form and solidity. The act of writing is a rich and analytic process as you find yourself not only attempting to explain and justify your ideas, but also developing them. Thinking with data via some brief or extended period of writing will transform your ideas.

Making your ideas 'concrete' enables you to reflect, to see gaps, to explore, to draw other texts in. By writing, I mean from those moments when you have an idea and spend five minutes noting it down, to those moments when you might be spending hours writing. You should get into the habit of writing about anything that might be helpful. An idea may emerge from something you've read, seen, discussed or overheard. It is not only writing, but also working with diagrams, lists, tables, basically anything that offers you a way to conceptualize your ideas.

Two traditions of qualitative research already understand the value of writing. Writing in the form of memos is one of the essential foundations of all styles of grounded theory. For ethnographers, the practice of writing and working from field notes is vital. Irrespective of whether you're doing grounded theory, or ethnography, go and read some of the practitioners' discussion (see Emerson et al., 1995; Montgomery and Bailey, 2007). Rather than read these accounts as definitive guides about how to construct, manage and use writing, draw on them creatively. Whatever happens, you should never feel that writing is for the final stage of analysis, it is actually an essential practice at all stages of the analytic trajectory (see Marvasti in this volume).

On exceptions

At the start of your analysis, it is not an understatement to say that exceptions will be *everywhere*. Analysis is about focusing on 'similarity and difference'. As soon as you begin to look at a transcript, field note or text, you will be focusing not only on what it tells you about the phenomenon, but also on how it compares with what you already know. Exceptions can generally be found when you find yourself asking: where does that go?

In the early stages of analysis, finding 'exceptions' that make you change your ideas or coding practices is a routine and everyday affair. Each new line or page of text can make you question your ideas, as something new emerges which means you have to generate a new code or revise your thinking about an old one. You often find something that could potentially fit into multiple codes and so you may need to refine it, or accept that it works for multiple codes.

Over time, over rounds of data collection, coding and writing, these exceptions become less visible. At this point, when you do notice something that does not fit with what has gone before, it can really start to stand out, and in rarer case it can become vital for your argument. At these later stages, exceptions take three forms. These are what are known as the negative or deviant case (see Peräkylä in this volume) where the issue or case does not fit your current understanding of the phenomenon:

1. Those that, despite being different, *actually support your finding*, as people themselves understand them and orientate to them as 'exceptions to the rule' and in so doing show you the 'rule'.
2. Those that, through their difference, *mean you need to re-evaluate or change* your ideas.
3. Those that are different for *very specific, idiosyncratic and contingent reasons* that either do not support your findings or mean you need to re-evaluate your ideas.

You may want to go in search of them – some people do, in that they deliberately sample potentially atypical cases, in order to check and refine their ideas.

SOME CLOSING COMMENTS

An important thing to remember is that when you initially read about and start to apply a form of qualitative data analysis that is novel to you, you will find yourself engaging in it in a very procedural way. First, you might read some how-to descriptions, and maybe write down a step-by-step way of going about analysis. This initial 'recipe' is quite abstract and should contain the key stages and practices you need to go through. As you begin to apply this 'recipe' you'll generally find you have to go back to the how-to descriptions, to check if what you're doing makes sense in relation to the guidebooks. It is only through a process of 'getting your hands dirty' with data that some of the ideas you've read about begin to make sense. That is fine. No level of description can adequately prepare you for analysing your specific data-set. Over time, you can begin to improvise, to follow the spirit of analytic principles of your chosen approach.

CHAPTER SUMMARY

- There is a range of approaches to qualitative analysis, but they share a common focus on shifting from the level of description and summary to exploring and explaining the underlying essences, patterns, processes and structures.
- You should systematically code your data, constantly reviewing and refining your coding practices. Initially, focus on a sample of your data and look at this in detail. As you analyse more data, try to see how the ideas underlying each code combine, relate or diverge. Focus on specific issues and discard those ideas that are no longer central. Drill down to explore the detail and dimensions of key issues.
- Writing short and extended notes - about your hunches, ideas, coding practices, personal reflections, project-related reading - over the life of the project can help develop your analytic thinking.
- Engaging in rounds of data collection and then analysis can enable you to explore, refine and check your emerging ideas.

FUTURE PROSPECTS

Different analytic approaches will emerge and those currently in use will evolve somewhat. However, the core analytic routines, procedures, phases and tactics outlined in this chapter will remain central.

Study questions

1. What are the core aspects of qualitative data analysis?
2. Why does good analysis mean more than simply summarizing your data?
3. Why should you bother to code your data?
4. Why is writing part of the process of analysis?
5. Why is looking for exceptions in your data important?

Recommended reading

Bernard, H. R. and Ryan, G. W. (2010) *Analyzing Qualitative Data: Systematic Approaches*. Thousand Oaks, CA: Sage.
A good general overview of a range of practical approaches to coding your data.

Miles, M. B., Huberman, A. M. and Saladaña, J. (2014) *Qualitative Data Analysis* (3rd edn). Thousand Oaks, CA: Sage.
A very comprehensive, albeit at times idiosyncratic, guide to working with qualitative data.

Saladaña, J. (2013) *The Coding Manual for Qualitative Researchers* (2nd edn). Thousand Oaks, CA: Sage.
A good, general overview of a range of practical approaches to coding your data.

Recommended online resources

For a good overview of learning materials to support (computer assisted) qualitative data analysis, see:
http://onlineqda.hud.ac.uk/

A good report you can download that reviews key issues in qualitative research is:
www.hta.ac.uk/fullmono/mon216.pdf

References

Bernard, H. R. and Ryan, G. W. (2010) *Analyzing Qualitative Data: Systematic Approaches.* Thousand Oaks, CA: Sage.

Braun, V. and Clarke, V. (2006) 'Using thematic analysis in psychology', *Qualitative Research in Psychology*, 3 (2):, 77–101.

Charmaz, K. (2014) *Constructing Grounded Theory* (2nd edn). Thousand Oaks, CA: Sage.

Dey, I. (2007) 'Grounding categories', in A. Bryant and K. Charmaz (eds), *The Sage Handbook of Grounded Theory*. London: Sage, pp. 167–90.

Emerson, R., Fretz, R. and Shaw, L. (1995) *Writing Ethnographic Fieldnotes.* Chicago, IL: University of Chicago Press.

Gibbs, G. R. (2007) *Analysing Qualitative Data.* London: Sage.

Glaser, B. (1978) *Theoretical Sensitivity: Advances in Grounded Theory.* Mill Valley, CA: Sociology Press.

Goodwin, C. (1994) 'Professional vision', *American Anthropologist*, 96: 606–33.

Grbich, C. (1999) *Qualitative Research in Health: An Introduction.* London: Sage.

Layder, D. (1998) *Sociological Practice: Linking Theory and Social Research.* London: Sage.

Miles, M. B. and Huberman, A. M. (1994) *Qualitative Data Analysis* (2nd edn). Thousand Oaks, CA: Sage.

Montgomery, P. and Bailey, P. (2007) 'Field notes and theoretical memos in grounded theory', *Western Journal of Nursing Research*, 29 (1): 65–79.

Opler, M. E. (1945) 'Themes as dynamic forces in culture', *American Journal of Sociology*, 51 (3): 198–206.

Patton, M. Q. (2002) *Qualitative Research & Evaluation Methods* (3rd edn). Thousand Oaks, CA: Sage.

Ritchie, J., Spencer, L. and O'Connor, W. (2003) 'Carrying out qualitative analysis', in J. Ritchie and J. Lewis (eds), *Qualitative Research Practice: A Guide for Social Science Students and Researchers*. London: Sage. pp. 219–62.

Saladaña, J. (2013) *The Coding Manual for Qualitative Researchers* (2nd edn). Thousand Oaks, CA: Sage.

Silverman, D. (2011) *A Very Short, Fairly Interesting and Reasonably Cheap Book about Qualitative Research* (2nd edn). London: Sage.

Smith, J. A. and Osborn, M. (2008) 'Interpretative phenomenological analysis', in J. A. Smith (ed.), *Qualitative Psychology: A Practical Guide to Methods* (2nd edn). London: Sage, pp. 53–81.

References

[illegible faded text]

TWENTY ONE

Constructing Grounded Theory Analyses

Kathy Charmaz and Antony Bryant

About this chapter

This chapter focuses on grounded theory as an interactive, iterative and comparative qualitative method. Grounded theory offers flexible yet systematic methodological strategies that demystify the research process. Researchers who take up these strategies discussed here can increase the methodological rigour, theoretical reach and credibility of their studies – and expedite their work.

Keywords

grounded theory, constructivist grounded theory, coding, memo-writing, theoretical sampling

Grounded theory is a systematic method consisting of flexible strategies for conducting qualitative research. Its originators, Barney G. Glaser and Anselm L. Strauss (1967), aimed to construct fresh sociological theories through using comparative methods in an iterative process using inductive qualitative data. They contended that researchers could increase the abstract level and explanatory power of their emerging theories by going back and forth between gathering specific data and analysing them. Adopting key grounded theory strategies enables you to accomplish the following objectives:

- to move your analysis beyond description
- to define patterns in the data
- to develop new concepts, rather than rely on earlier theories
- to theorize processes in the data
- to complete your research projects.

Glaser and Strauss first argued that qualitative researchers could construct theories at a time when qualitative inquiry was imperilled in the United States. They also articulated a compelling rationale for legitimizing inductive qualitative studies that inspired numerous scholars who neither understood the logic of grounded theory nor how to use it. Over the decades, grounded theory has become a general method that has swept across disciplines and professions but whose strategies have become generalized and diffuse. Many researchers who claim to use grounded theory create descriptive and thematic analyses rather than abstract theories. Nonetheless, some grounded theorists fulfil the promise of using data in service of constructing and linking theoretical categories (e.g. Lois, 2010; Snow and Moss, 2014).

Glaser and Strauss's (1967; Glaser, 1978) contributions reach beyond grounded theory. They not only developed this method but also contributed to methodological practices throughout qualitative inquiry. Many qualitative researchers now adopt Glaser and Strauss's innovation of conducting simultaneous data collection and analysis. Coding, or labelling excerpts of data, has become standard practice in qualitative analysis, as has memo-writing, an intermediate form of writing between coding and drafting a report, in which researchers explore their codes.

Our objectives in this chapter are twofold: (1) to clarify what the grounded theory method is and (2) to focus on how its key basic strategies engage researchers with their data and emerging analyses. This method contains underused strategies that increase its methodological rigour, theoretical promise and the power of the subsequent analysis. We offer ideas for shaping data collection to enhance theory construction but emphasize grounded theory analytic strategies. In particular, we stress coding for actions, doing line-by-line initial coding, writing memos and conducting theoretical sampling, a distinctive grounded theory strategy. Theoretical sampling means sampling to fill out the properties (i.e. characteristics) of a tentative theoretical category. When these properties are saturated with data and no new properties emerge, the researcher ends collecting data and integrates the analysis.

THE GROUNDED THEORY APPROACH AND THE CONSTRUCTIVIST REVISION

Several variants of grounded theory exist but all share a set of methodological strategies. We grounded theorists begin with inductive data, engage in simultaneous data collection

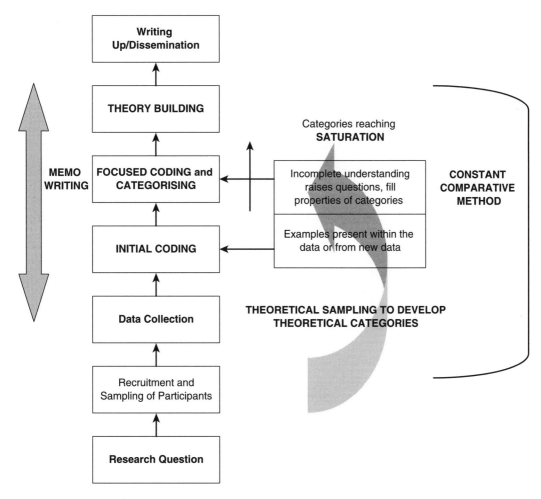

Figure 21.1   A visual representation of a grounded theory

Source: an earlier version of this figure originally appeared in Alison Tweed and Kathy Charmaz (2011) 'Grounded theory for mental health practitioners', in D. Harper and A. Thompson (eds), *Qualitative Research Methods in Mental Health and Psychotherapy: A Guide for Students and Practitioners*. London: Wiley-Blackwell, p. 133. Alison Tweed constructed the original figure.

and analysis, adopt comparative methods, favour analysing actions over general themes and topics, engage in coding data, examine our codes and ideas in memos, and check these ideas. We compare data with data, data with codes, codes with codes, codes with tentative theoretical categories, and categories with categories. We code data for actions and study how these actions might contribute to fundamental processes occurring in the research setting or in their research participants' lives. Through comparing data with codes and codes with codes, grounded theorists decide which codes to treat and test as tentative theoretical categories.

A contemporary version of grounded theory, *constructivist grounded theory*, revises the principles of the method. The constructivist approach adopts the grounded theory strategies above but also attends to methodological developments in qualitative inquiry over the past 50 years. As a result, a constructivist stance towards the research process and product differs from earlier versions of grounded theory. Unlike earlier versions, the constructivist stance assumes research occurs within specific historical moments, social structures, and situational and interactional conditions, and thus directs its proponents to learn how these conditions influence their studies. This approach leads researchers to locate themselves within inquiry whereas earlier grounded theorists' stance assumed they remained neutral observers outside of inquiry. Hence, constructivists take into account both researchers' and research participants' starting points and standpoints, and remain alert to how and when these shift during inquiry. Constructivists also aim to get as close to the studied phenomenon as possible. Gaining a close view fosters learning how participants' meanings and actions are connected to larger discourses and social structures of which they may be unaware. Earlier grounded theorists seldom made such links.

Constructivist grounded theorists view data as constructed, not simply out there in the world waiting to be discovered and gathered (Bryant and Charmaz, 2007). Similarly, constructivists assume that conducting and writing research flows from views and values and thus demand continual reflexive examination. In contrast to earlier versions of grounded theory, constructivist grounded theorists also accept the notion of multiple realities, reject assumptions that prior knowledge impedes constructing new theories, and aim to understand difference and variation in the research site(s) and/or among the research participants.

Key points

- Grounded theory is a method of theory construction that enables researchers to study processes.
- Grounded theorists start with inductive data, engage in simultaneous data collection and analysis, use comparative methods, code data, write memos, define theoretical categories and check these categories with more data.
- Constructivist grounded theory acknowledges the positions of the researcher and the research situation, attends to the researcher's actions and views data and analyses as constructed.

Grounded theory strategies prompt researchers to keep interacting with their participants, data and analyses throughout the research process. In the past, researchers viewed grounded theory primarily as a method of data analysis. Recent developments (Charmaz and Belgrave, 2012; Charmaz, 2014), however, also address its implications for data collection. We explore how data collecting, coding, memo-writing and theoretical sampling shape grounded theory practice about using these strategies.

COLLECTING DATA

What stands as solid and sufficient data is currently contested throughout qualitative inquiry. Like other forms of qualitative research, questions have arisen about the amount, depth and quality (i.e. accuracy) of data in grounded theory studies as well as about the methods invoked for obtaining them. These questions eclipsed the considerable strengths of grounded theory for informing data collection.

Grounded theory may be used with ethnographic materials, documents and interviews, although interviewing is the most common data collection method. Thus several comments about interviews are in order. Interviews are, of course, retrospective accounts that often explain and justify behaviour. Yet they may also be special social spaces in which research participants can reflect on the past and link it to the present and future in new ways (e.g. Conlon et al., 2015). An interview may be a performance, whether stories tumble out or are strategically calculated and enacted, but that does not disqualify interviews from providing rich data and sparking analytic insights (see Miller and Glassner, Gubrium and Holstein, and Riessman, in this volume). An interviewer's questions may frame the research participant's performance and seem to make the co-construction of data explicit. However, research participants may monitor what they say and how they say it. Much interaction and interpretation may proceed without words.

The interview excerpt below from Karen, a 46-year-old woman, illustrates what may occur during an interview (see Table 21.1). Karen viewed her devastating neck injury as leading to multiple health problems that included chronic fatigue syndrome and possible fibromyalgia. Note how a simple question, 'Were you married at the time then when your first accident occurred in '93?', produced an elaborate response in Table 21.1. The amount of non-stop detail belies the substantial non-verbal interaction that occurred and thus the co-construction of the interview. The content of this non-verbal interaction also challenges common assumptions about the researcher and participant's relative power to control the interview. Participants may have stories to tell and tales to tread on softly or to sidestep entirely. Thus, they may exert control over the content of the interview – and the situation by avoiding areas that might elicit probing questions.

From a grounded theory standpoint, asking few rather than many interview questions encourages research participants to tell their stories and discourages their interviewers from preconceiving the content of the interview, or, for that matter, its direction. Such a strategy is particularly useful during early interviews but may change as the researcher moves back and forth between data collection and analysis.

Theory construction can occur during telling moments during an interview, in the midst of an observation, or while reading a text. Being attuned to analytic issues sharpens data collection. Constructivist grounded theory emphasises going into emergent phenomena and defining their properties. By taking a phenomenon apart, grounded theorists build explicit 'what' and 'how' questions into the data collection, as other qualitative researchers do (Gubrium and Holstein, 2008). Grounded theorists, however, can use these questions to begin shaping a theoretical analysis. These questions elicit content that becomes the grist of the analysis and lead towards explicating processes. The question below gets at the properties of surrendering as well as this interviewee's meanings of it. When we think analytically while interviewing, the lines blur between data collection and analysis. Both rely on the researcher's actions and interpretations.

In addition to preparing an interviewee for asking detailing meanings, the pacing and tone of a direct 'what' or 'how' question does much to defuse the interviewee's possible interpretation of the following question as confrontational.

Sara:	... But, fortunately, I had the experience of at some point surrendering, you know.
Interviewer:	What does that mean to you, surrendering?
Sara:	It means that I don't have, I can't control it and to look at what it has to teach me. Just, you know, let it tell me what it needs to tell me. You know, that willingness and that acceptance.

In this excerpt, Sara brought up the term, 'surrendering'. Note that Kathy (Interviewer) immediately asked what it meant to her. Sara's response sparked ideas about the properties of 'surrendering to illness', a code Kathy subsequently raised to a category of her analysis of adapting to impairment.

By starting with 'what' and 'how' questions about the studied experience, you bring an analytic edge to the tales told during interviews, even at the beginning of research. These questions also serve a grounded theory emphasis on process. Subsequently, researchers can link events that otherwise might seem disparate. Inquiring about the person's circumstances, views and priorities illuminates data about social locations, standpoints and situations. Adding 'when' and 'to what extent' questions moves data collection towards specifying conditions under which the studied phenomenon or process occurs or changes. Similarly, asking questions about sequence of actions gets at process and implications as well as uncovering specific meanings and actions. Whatever questions are asked, researchers gain further insights through studying the sequences given in talk as participants tell their stories (Silverman, 2007).

GROUNDED THEORY CODING

Grounded theory coding consists of at least two sequential types: initial coding, in which we attempt to be open to defining whatever we see happening in fragments of data, and focused coding that uses the most frequent and/or significant initial codes to check against new data. The kind of data matters here. Researchers may prefer coding incidents or paragraphs with ethnographic data but use line-by-line coding with early intensive interviews and narratives. Line-by-line coding is an heuristic device to prompt the researcher to study each line of data and begin to gain a conceptual handle on them. Completing initial coding as quickly as possible fosters spontaneity and fresh ideas.

Coding in grounded theory differs from descriptive and thematic coding, which sorts and synthesizes data but seldom takes them apart, as grounded theorists do. We ask what constitutes the code. In the example above, of what does surrendering to illness consist? What are its properties? Then, too, we take coding a step further by coding for actions, invoking comparative methods, and discerning meanings of actions and events. We compare bits of data within the same data such as an interview, between pieces of data in different interviews, and compare codes to tease out their respective properties. How does 'surrendering to illness' differ from 'giving up'?

Using gerunds, a pivotal part of grounded theory coding, helps us to make distinctions. A gerund is the noun form of the verb such as 'defining', 'experiencing' or 'questioning'. Conducting line-by-line coding with gerunds helps to capture, crystallize and connect fragments of data – and thus helps us see processes that might otherwise remain invisible. Gerunds aid the researcher in defining what is happening in the data, identifying the theoretical direction implicit or explicit in the code, and discerning lines of an emerging analytic story in the data. Using gerunds can be difficult at first for English-speakers who think in structural terms of topics and themes, not in processual terms, but practice builds speed.

Observe that the codes in Table 21.1 reflect different levels of abstraction. The idea of a 'disintegrating self' is more abstract than the concrete interview statement. Is this legitimate? Yes, because the researcher tests the code against other data and writes memos explicating the comparisons involved in these tests. If the code does not hold up as a tentative conceptual category then the researcher drops it and pursues codes that do. Early coding allows time to ask analytic questions about the code and data that emerge from the material at hand, not from a preconceived coding framework. In this case, we can compare the data and code against other interview statements and ask questions such as:

- What are the properties of this self?
- How, when and to what extent are these properties discernible?
- To whom?
- With which consequences?
- What happens when they are taken as real and discernible to certain key actors but not to others?
- How, if at all, is this code related to other codes?
- What kind of additional data do I need to explore this code?

Are the codes in Table 21.1 the most fruitful for developing a grounded theory? Not necessarily. Another researcher from different standpoints, social locations and situations might come up with more compelling codes. If we took experiencing a disintegrating self as a tentative category, we could ask how it is related to other codes such as 'questioning survival of self' and 'feeling forced to be family emotional anchor'. The latter might contribute to the former and both may contribute to experiencing a disintegrating self. Are these the only way to use these codes? Not at all. Other analytic directions could include reconstructing the past, questioning identity, accounting for and to self, or the properties and process of constructing disclosure and myriad additional possibilities depending on

Table 21.1   Initial grounded theory coding

Examples of Codes	Initial Narrative Data to be Coded
	K: Were you married at the time then when your first accident occurred in '93?
Describing life	Yes, I was living in Springview and I was married to my third husband and we lived on a ranchette with a pasture, with farm animals, and a garden, and country life, pool, gym, it was very nice, and I was out there for six and a half years. My ex-husband had kind of a double life going on as it turns out; he would disappear for two or three days at a time which became increasingly worse. He had colitis ... part of it was his colitis but part of it, [as] it turned out was a hidden cocaine addiction so I couldn't continue to – in my chronic pain condition and his behavior, just kept me so stressed out where I couldn't function emotionally and physically to a point. That's why I say my survival was at stake ... it hurt me. And there was no support there for my pain issue. ... I always had to be the one who had to be strong because he'd be gone on these disappearing things and then somebody had to hold down the fort and keep everything going when this would happen. And then sometimes it would take him a week to recover because whatever he was doing would cause his colitis to flare up, so I was always forced to be in the position of the emotional anchor in the family and it was so exhausting to me and again I had to keep escalating that pain medication then to continue on and normally, then, at the time the disk was fully herniated so I was being treated for chronic pain but there was still some questions to the validity of my pain factor whether it was emotionally induced or physically and some question as to whether it was a lot psychological, that I was perhaps, you know, had a painful addiction and was just self-medicating.
Evaluating living situation	
Telling the time length	
Living with ex-husband's double life	
Disappearing husband	
Escalating disappearances	
Accounting for husband's disappearances	
Defining hidden addiction	
Alluding to limits for self	
Explaining distress	
Being unable to function	
Disintegrating self	
Questioning survival of self/of way of life	
Feeling hurt/betrayed	
Wanting husband's support for *her* pain	
Carrying doubled responsibilities	
Expressing resentments (in tone of voice)	
Keeping life (family and business) together	
Detailing ex-husband's lapses	
Timing then husband's recovery/explaining his complicating illness	
Feeling forced to be family emotional anchor	
Being exhausted	
Feeling forced to escalate pain meds	
Seeing pain meds as allowing a normal life	
Explaining extent of injury	
Externalizing questions about pain	
Revealing ambiguous cause of pain – physical and/or psychological	
Questioning the possibility of addiction	
Raising the spectre of self over-medicating	
Disclosing a plausible identity	
Over-lapping emotional and psychological pain	
	Most of this data excerpt appeared in Charmaz (2008: 165)

the relationship of the viewer to the viewed. Similarly, different researchers may develop dissimilar lines of coding of the same data, given their theoretical sensitivities and substantive interests.

Constructivist grounded theorists view coding as emergent and interactive. Therefore, coding has novel properties that draw on but are not determined by the researcher's interests, standpoints and relative and changing positions during data collection and analysis. A quest for inter-coder reliability does not make sense but a test of the robustness and usefulness of codes through comparative analysis does.

Initial coding generates the bones of an emergent theory. Focused coding identifies the bones with potential for carrying the weight of the analysis. Grounded theorists conduct focused coding when they construct codes that portend of becoming tentative categories. When researchers conduct focused coding, they take the most frequent and/or significant codes and see how well they account for large batches of data. Thus, focused coding winnows the array of initial codes, shapes the direction of analysis and forecasts its content.

MEMO-WRITING

Memo-writing consists of recording analytic conversations with yourself. Memos are analytic narratives for exploring your ideas about the codes and categories. Grounded theorists write memos from the beginning of research. Much of your analytic work takes place as you write progressively more abstract and precise memos. Thus, memo-writing becomes a crucial grounded theory strategy for bridging coding and report writing.

Your codes give you a way of looking at your data. Memos record what you see – and help you raise questions about what you don't see. Systematically recording your ideas and questions in memos helps you avoid losing flashes of insight and collecting thin, unfocused data. Writing memos increases your awareness of what is happening in your data and decreases your chances of failing to follow up on important questions and areas.

In early memos, you discuss hunches and take your data and codes apart to explore meanings and actions. Writing memos is an emergent process that builds on your interactions with data, codes and categories as well as your participants – and your earlier memos. You bring an analytic lens to your research and remain alert to potential analytic leads in your memos. Memos provide the site where you explore promising focused codes as tentative categories and preserve the data that speak to your categories and comparisons. Recording your comparisons enables you to construct incisive specific categories that you can subsequently compare with each other through making more penetrating comparisons with each other and the literature in later memos.

In Table 21.2, Kathy begins to define what 'experiencing a deteriorating self' means, what it assumes, when people define it and how it affects them. She wove Karen's statement into the memo and began to compare her situation with others.

Table 21.2 Excerpt from an early memo: experiencing a deteriorating self

Experiencing a deteriorating self indicates that the person identifies losing aspects of self - and sees the loss in his or her current existence. This type of loss is comparative because the person implicitly or explicitly recognizes and measures his or her present self against a past self. But what does the past self mean? Given that people define their past selves from the vantage point of present experience and the images of self in this present, they may elevate, romanticize, or select past selves. Karen witnessed her past self crumbling away as her responsibilities and pain simultaneously soared.

Karen said, 'I couldn't continue to - in my chronic pain condition and his behavior, just kept me so stressed out where I couldn't function emotionally and physically to a point. That's why I say my survival was at stake ... it hurt me. And there was no support there for my pain issue.' Her comment not only anchors her image of self in her ability to function, but also shows her awareness of how embedded she was in the situation in which she found herself. Self and situation are intricately bound and that situation relies on interwoven relationships and actions.

In other cases such as Tom's, family and friends viewed him as having a deteriorating self and marked his physical and mental changes although he evinced no awareness of them. He might have been ignoring or discounting these changes. People may not connect gradual changes that others observe with their experience until a major setback occurs.

THEORETICAL SAMPLING

The strategy of theoretical sampling is a major strength of grounded theory but its potential remains largely untapped. In addition to filling out the properties of their tentative categories, researchers also use theoretical sampling to define variation in a studied process or phenomenon or to establish the boundaries of a theoretical category. Theoretical sampling relies on using abductive reasoning to explain an intriguing or puzzling finding. The researcher considers all plausible theoretical explanations and tests them against new data (Reichertz, 2007). In the excerpt below, Kathy had already developed the category, 'situating the self in time' and had divided it into the past, present and future. Here, the elusiveness of the category and her lengthy acquaintance with the participant influenced how she posed questions pertaining to her category. How and when a grounded theorist probes for meaning may change as the relationship with a respondent and the iterative research process proceeds.

I followed up on an earlier conversation about locating oneself in time. I asked her where she now located herself in time. Note how I follow her statements and return to key points that she raised.

Patricia:	I'm in the present.
Kathy:	You're in the present.
Patricia:	Oh yeah.
Kathy:	And that's a change, isn't it?
Patricia:	Where was I before?
Kathy:	In the future.
Patricia:	Future. Yeah. Yeah. [said thoughtfully] I'm right here - today.
Kathy:	And has all this [what we had talked about in the preceding hour and a half] brought you to today?

Patricia: The whole process? Yeah.

Kathy: And what does tomorrow look like?

Patricia: Tomorrow's hopeful.

Kathy: How much of tomorrow do you see today with you [being] right here today?

Patricia: I see some. I can see quite a bit of tomorrow, I think. But what I see is that part ... I feel like because I – I have much more control over my – my life today that tomorrow will be better as a direct result of how I live today. But I also know that there's a great deal of unknown in there. But I think there are a lot of unknowns for a lot of people, for everybody. And that I have the advantage over everybody else because I'll be able to deal with it.

Kathy: Hmm, that's interesting. And your today is, when your self is in today, what does that mean to you?

Patricia: When myself is in today, what I'm probably saying about today is, *today* – actually today. (Charmaz, 2009: 54)

Theoretical sampling increases the depth and precision of your categories and knowledge of your participants' situations. Because conducting theoretical sampling often requires finesse, tacit negotiations may ensue about what researchers may ask and when they can ask it. It helps to listen to stories participants want to tell before redirecting the conversation to ask questions pertaining to your tentative theoretical categories.

The analytic strength of grounded theory resides in using its iterative process effectively. We can check hunches, follow leads in earlier data, select telling codes as tentative categories, test these categories against data, and demonstrate relationships between them. Our actions make these categories more abstract and useful by increasing their scope and interpretive power. Relatively few grounded theorists use theoretical sampling in a systematic way or at all. Yet this strategy can make a study distinctive and theoretically sophisticated, and thus increase the value of its contribution.

In their study of protest movements, David Snow and Dana Moss (2014) used theoretical sampling as they developed a theory of spontaneity in collective actions, and specified its links between time and action. They drew upon their prior research in social movements and conducted a textual analysis of ethnographic, historical and investigative studies of major protest events that contained detailed first-hand accounts. They explicated the conditions that spurred spontaneous actions and then coded and compared these conditions with subsequent cases. Snow and Moss argue that spontaneous action involves cognition – thinking – but it is compressed in time when compared with prior deliberation and arises during pivotal ambiguous moments. Spontaneous individual actions then spur collective actions. Snow and Moss not only show how spontaneity often is an important element in collective action but also specify associated triggering conditions under which spontaneity arises.

WRITING THE GROUNDED THEORY REPORT

Before assembling a first draft of their studies, grounded theorists sort and integrate memos. By this time, they have written progressively more abstract memos. They have made their analyses increasingly precise by gathering specific data to answer emergent analytic questions and then further develop their categories by checking against further data. So how do you next proceed? You integrate the memos according to the analysis you have instructed. Your analysis may be essentially complete but requires work before you have a finished paper.

When a researcher has theorized a process, the memos readily fit together as Kathy Charmaz's (2011: 179) Figure 21.2 illustrates.

In Figure 21.2, note that two major processes are depicted, losing and regaining a valued self. This figure outlines how the categories in the analysis fit together. Experiencing a disrupted self shares some properties with losing a valued self, but in contrast does not occur under continued uncertainty. The sub-processes of both losing and regaining a valued self emanate directly from the codes. The curved line represents the journey from loss of self to regaining a valued self and the possibility that loss may occur again.

The first draft of your report represents your initial attempt to provide a coherent statement of your analysis (see also Marvasti in this volume). You need to present and define your theoretical categories, show what constitutes them, provide evidence for your claims about these categories, explain how they are connected, and tell where they lead. We advise writing the first draft for yourself before thinking of your audiences – including your thesis committee. Say what you need to say. You can revise this draft later. An early draft is a time of discovery, for learning more about your categories and their implications. Analysis proceeds into the writing process.

After you have drafted your rendering of the analysis, draw out its implications in the conclusion. Last, write the introduction and state your purpose for *this* paper and the

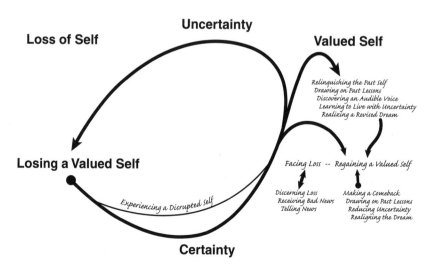

Figure 21.2   Effecting intentional reconstruction of self: losing and regaining a valued self

Source: Wertz et al., 2011, © Kathy Charmaz. Reprinted with permission of Guilford Press.

argument that flows from your purpose. New scholars often make the common mistake of using the same argument for their completed analyses that they made in their research proposals. Conducting a grounded theory study shifts and changes as a researcher becomes involved in his or her study. Each analysis serves a specific purpose and corresponding argument.

Similarly, each analysis requires a new literature review that fits the new ideas you have generated. Grounded theory spawns fresh ideas and original categories, which subsequently become the source of forming your literature review. Early grounded theorists insisted conducting a literature review before beginning the research would generate preconceived findings and import extant theories to account for them. We disagree. Like Cian Dunne (2011) and Robert Thornberg (2012), we contend researchers can take a critical view of the literature and earlier theories without being seduced by either.

Key points

- Grounded theory prepares researchers to follow up on emergent analytic leads immediately while collecting data.
- Coding with gerunds is an heuristic device to fracture and examine data and to define actions and processes.
- Memo-writing prompts grounded theorists to explore their codes and categories, make comparisons between them, and learn where they have gaps in their data.
- Theoretical sampling is a distinctive grounded theory strategy to fill out the properties of an abstract category.
- Writing the report entails writing for discovery, which fosters creating further analytic insights, and writing for reporting the study to audiences and thus involves genre, purpose, argument, style and organization.

CHAPTER SUMMARY AND FUTURE PROSPECTS

Grounded theory offers flexible methodological strategies that can generate strong analytic concepts and the evidence to support them. Three underused strategies of grounded theory are (1) initial coding with gerunds, (2) conducting comparisons throughout inquiry, and (3) theoretical sampling. We have explicated these strategies to make the method more accessible and applicable. Grounded theorists code with gerunds to the extent indicated by the data. Doing so allows us to make connections and to grasp actions and process, even when recounted in interviews.

Generally, grounded theorists stick closely to patterns that we define in our data and treat as categories. Yet in the past, relatively few grounded theorists understood how coding with gerunds could help them see invisible patterns and move their analyses from static topics to dynamic processes. Coding with gerunds also aids in using comparative methods because of the specificity of the codes. Making systematic comparisons leads us to raising our codes to tentative categories. Subsequently, we can discern their properties and make distinctions between categories. Theoretical sampling solidifies these categories and increases their analytic weight and by extension the significance of a grounded theorist's contribution. Adopting all these strategies will not only increase the credibility of grounded theory studies but also decrease their likelihood of being judged by imported criteria from another form of inquiry.

The constructivist revision of grounded theory resolves earlier problematic epistemological assumptions and knowledge claims. Past grounded theory proponents had treated data collection as unproblematic and reflexivity as unnecessary. However, the new constructivist dual emphasis on attending to data collection and engaging in reflexivity advances grounded theory practice and products.

Grounded theory continues to spread across fields ranging from traditional areas in the social sciences, health, education and management to new areas such as architecture, maths and science education, engineering, environmental science and applied linguistics. This method also spreads across multiple research purposes: academic knowledge, policy-formation, professional practice and a quest for social justice.

Thus, the prospects for grounded theory shaping diverse forms of knowledge are high. Given the increasing explication of the method, researchers have sharper tools to complete compelling grounded theory studies. Hence, the prospects for increasing numbers of theoretically sophisticated studies are also high. Growing numbers of grounded theory studies link individual meanings and actions with larger social structures. Yet in the past, most studies that claimed to do grounded theory instead consisted of thematic analyses or analytic description, despite lofty talk of theorizing. Similarly, like most qualitative researchers in general, grounded theorists of the past seldom located their research in the conditions of its production and their analyses in larger social structures. But now we have methods and exemplars that foster making these connections.

On the surface, grounded theory strategies may appear to generate concrete, mechanical analyses in which researchers simply follow leads given in their data and emerging analyses. True, some researchers use grounded theory in this way. However, the method fosters creating new ideas and possibilities for making imaginative interpretations of social life. And that is the beauty of grounded theory.

Study questions

1. What is constructivist grounded theory?
2. What are the main features of grounded theory coding?
3. How does theoretical sampling differ from other forms of sampling?

Recommended reading

Bryant, A. (2016) *Grounded Theory and Grounded Theorizing: Pragmatism in Research Practice.* New York: Oxford University Press.

The book situates GTM against an extended discussion of research practice and research methods. It draws on accounts from the work of some of Professor Bryant's doctoral students, and also includes consideration of Pragmatism as a key feature in understanding and implementing GTM. Other chapters offer specific examples of the method in action, including one that uses a large number of GTM research papers as its source of data. A final chapter discusses GTM as a 'Guide to good research practice'.

Charmaz, K. (2014) *Constructing Grounded Theory* (2nd edn). London: Sage.

This extensively expanded edition of *Constructing Grounded Theory* provides an up-to-date, accessible explication of the grounded theory approach with detailed worked examples, reflections by grounded theorists and discussions of exemplary grounded theory studies. The book emphasises researchers' interactions with their participants, data and emerging analyses while showing how to construct a grounded theory.

Corbin, J. and Strauss, A. (2015) *Basics of Qualitative Research* (4th edn). Los Angeles, CA: Sage.

Juliet Corbin continues to demonstrate how grounded theory evolves in the fourth edition of this classic text she first co-authored with Anselm Strauss. The book discusses pertinent topics and responds to novices' questions with explanations and advice.

Glaser, B. G. and Strauss, A. L. (1967) *The Discovery of Grounded Theory: Strategies for Qualitative Research.* Chicago, IL: Aldine.

In this original statement of the grounded theory method, Glaser and Strauss argue that researchers can use qualitative data to construct new theories. They opposed methodological traditions of the day that favoured quantitative over qualitative research, relied on deductive logic, separated data collection and analysis and viewed theorizing as the realm of a privileged elite.

Recommended online resources

Antony Bryant, research training 2-day workshop on grounded theory method:
www.youtube.com/watch?v=fmWKf5LOmfA

'The grounded theory method', a lecture by Antony Bryant:
www.youtube.com/watch?v=AK7WFo4inR4

Kathy Charmaz, British Sociological Association, MedSoc 2012, 'The power and potential of grounded theory':
www.youtube.com/watch?v=zY1h3387txo

A discussion with Professor Kathy Charmaz on grounded theory, interview by Graham R. Gibbs:
http://youtube/D5AHmHQS6WQ

Barney Glaser, 'Grounded theory is the study of a concept!':
www.youtube.com/watch?v=OcpxaLQDnLk

Anselm Strauss webpage:
http://dne2.ucsf.edu/public/anselmstrauss/index.html

References

Bryant, A. and Charmaz, K. (2007) 'Grounded theory in historical perspective: an episte-mological account', in A. Bryant and K. Charmaz (eds), *The Sage Handbook of Grounded Theory*. London: Sage, pp. 31–57.

Charmaz, K. (2009) 'Recollecting good and bad days', in A. Puddephatt, W. Shaffir, and S. Kleinknecht (eds), *Ethnographies Revisited: Constructing Theory in the Field*. London and New York: Routledge, pp. 48–62.

Charmaz, K. (2011) 'A constructivist grounded theory analysis of losing and regaining a valued self', in F. J. Wertz, K. Charmaz, L. J. McMullen, R. Josselson, R. Anderson and E. McSpadden, *Five Ways of Doing Qualitative Analysis: Phenomenological Psychology, Grounded Theory, Discourse Analysis, Narrative Research, and Intuitive Inquiry*. New York: Guilford, pp. 165–204.

Charmaz, K. (2014) *Constructing Grounded Theory*. London: Sage.

Charmaz, K. and Belgrave, L. L. (2012) 'Qualitative interviewing and grounded theory analysis', in J. F. Gubrium, J. A. Holstein, A. Marvasti and K. M. Marvasti (eds), *Handbook of Interview Research* (2nd edn). Thousand Oaks, CA: Sage, pp. 347–65.

Conlon, C., Carney, G., Timonen, V. and Scharf, T. (2015). 'Emergent reconstruction' in grounded theory: learning from team based interview research', *Qualitative Research*, 15 (1): 39–56.

Dunne, C. (2011) 'The place of the literature review in grounded theory research', *International Journal of Social Research Methodology*, 14 (2): 111–124.

Glaser, B. (1978). *Theoretical Sensitivity*. Mill Valley, CA: Sociology Press.

Glaser, B. G. and Strauss, A. L. (1967) *The Discovery of Grounded Theory: Strategies for Qualitative Research*. Chicago, IL: Aldine.

Gubrium, J. and Holstein, J. (2008) 'From the individual interview to the interview society', in J. Holstein and J. Gubrium (eds), *Handbook of Constructionist Research*. New York: Guilford, pp. 3–32.

Lois, J. (2010) 'The temporal emotion work of motherhood: homeschoolers' strategies for managing time shortage', *Gender & Society*, 24 (4): 421–46.

Reichertz, J. (2007) 'Abduction: the logic of discovery in grounded theory', in A. Bryant and K. Charmaz (eds), *The Sage Handbook of Grounded Theory*. London: Sage, pp. 214–28.

Silverman, D. (2007) *A Very Short, Fairly Interesting and Reasonably Cheap Book about Qualitative Research*. London: Sage.

Snow, D. and Moss, D. (2014) 'Protest on the fly: toward a theory of spontaneity in the dynamics of protest and social movements', *American Sociological Review*, 79 (6): 1122–43.

Thornberg, R. (2012) 'Informed grounded theory', *Scandinavian Journal of Educational Research*, 55 (1): 1–17.

Wertz, F. J., Charmaz, K., McMullen, L. M., Josselson, R., Anderson, R. and McSpadden, E. (2011) *Five Ways of Doing Qualitative Analysis: Phenomenological Psychology, Grounded Theory, Discourse Analysis, Narrative Research, and Intuitive Inquiry*. New York, Guilford Press.

TWENTY TWO

What's Different about Narrative Inquiry? Cases, Categories and Contexts

Catherine Kohler Riessman

About this chapter

Narrative inquiry is different in several ways from other qualitative approaches. It focuses closely on particular cases and their contexts of production. After introducing some key narrative concepts, I show them in action with a research example. Narrative inquiry is well suited to analysing the performance of identity in interviews.

Keywords

narrative analysis, narrative inquiry, storytelling, category-centred research, narrative form

One of the questions students frequently pose in my research seminars is the difference between narrative inquiry and other qualitative approaches. Having used several analytic methods and combined them successfully with narrative in several studies (Riessman, 1990, 2002a, 2002b, 2005), I always relish the question. This chapter allows me to take up the question again, articulating several dimensions of narrative analysis that distinguish it from the data analytic phase of grounded theory and other thematically oriented qualitative methods that work from interviews.

There is great diversity in modes of narrative inquiry that I cannot survey here (but see Riessman, 2007; De Fina and Georgakopoulou, 2015; Livholts and Tamboukou, 2015). My approach to the methodology was initially shaped by the sociolinguistic tradition that influenced scholars in the social sciences in the 1980s and by a network of colleagues since. But the field of narrative inquiry has mushroomed into something that is now very broad. As in other qualitative approaches, epistemological positions differ; both constructivists and logical positivists take up the idea of data as a 'story', the widely used popular term.

The softening of boundaries between the humanities and the social sciences has drawn many to a narrative vocabulary in interpreting diverse materials (not always critically, as discussed below). However, there is an increasing unfortunate trend to celebrate biographical accounts instead of systematically analysing them (Atkinson and Delamont, 2005).

My focus in this chapter will be limited to narratives generated in interviews. Research interviews are not the only context in which narratives appear; there are studies influenced by Harvey Sacks's groundbreaking work on children's stories (Sacks, 1972) that looks at storytelling in everyday settings (Polanyi, 1989), medical consultations (Clark and Mishler, 1992) and other contexts. Following a brief introduction to several key concepts that should guide a narrative inquiry, I present a research example below that illustrates concepts in practice.

CATEGORY VS. CASE-CENTRED RESEARCH

The vast majority of contemporary qualitative research is category-centred rather than case-centred. In the former – grounded theory is a familiar example – detail and specificity slip away in favour of general statements about the phenomenon of interest. Interview data are fractured into segments that are coded thematically – into conceptual categories – that are then grouped and compared to similar segments from other interviews. The goal is to generate theoretical concepts inductively, that is, generalizations about human processes that hold across individual participants (see Charmaz and Bryant in this volume).

By contrast, in case-centred research – practised in oral history, auto/biographical studies and narrative inquiry – the investigator preserves and interrogates particular instances and sequences of action, the way participants negotiate language and narrative genres in conversations, and other unique aspects of a 'case', which could be an individual, family, community, group, organization or other unit of social life. As Mishler (1996: 80) writes, case-based methods grant research participants 'unity and coherence through time, respecting them as subjects with both histories and intentions'. Human agency, consciousness – socially constructed, to be sure – and particularity are preserved. This becomes difficult when cases are pooled to generate general statements about the group as a whole.

Case-centred methods can nevertheless generate 'categories', that is, theoretical concepts and observations about general processes. The history of medicine is filled with studies of particular instances – cases where pathologies were noted and studied closely, leading to new disease categories. Similarly, in social research, knowledge about general aspects of social organization has sprung from the close study of particular action in a specific instance. Garfinkel's (1967) case study of Agnes, a transgender person who successfully passed as female, generated theory that challenged, and eventually transformed, the binary concept of gender. Narrative analysts have also compared cases to construct arguments about a process of social change (for examples from the women's health movement, see Bell, 1988, 1999).

Narrative analysis (NA) opens up a 'methodological repertoire' (Quinn, 2005: 6) that investigators can draw upon and expand to suit the demands of a particular project. In this spirit of methodological diversity, I have developed elsewhere a typology and illustrative exemplars of four general approaches to interpreting narrative: thematic, structural, dialogic/performative and visual analysis methods (www.qualitative-research.net/index.php/fqs/article/view/1418). In different ways, these analytic approaches resist preoccupation with content, i.e. primary attention to *what* is communicated substantively by a research participant.

There is a philosophy of language, of course, underlying the focus on content that many qualitative researchers share: viewing language as a transparent container of meaning. Such research assumes a direct connection between a speaker's words and the objects to which language refers. In everyday life, we operate with such a view, but, in analysing data, many in NA argue that it is useful to problematize meaning and the seemingly easy relationship between sign and signifier. We can ask, for example:

- In what context was this account generated?
- Why was the story told *that* way?
- What did the story accomplish for the speaker?
- What do the specific words a participant uses carry on their backs from prior uses?
- What other readings are possible, beyond what the narrator may have intended?

Narrative seduction (Chambers, 1984) is the illusion created by a skilful narrator that 'a story "is as it is" and needs no interpretation' (Bruner, 1991: 9). The artifice predisposes the listener to one and only one way of understanding meaning. By resisting seduction, the narrative researcher can challenge the 'automatic interpretive routine' of everyday life and begin 'unrehearsed interpretive activity' (Bruner, 1991: 9). Readers can be invited to question the omniscient narrator and focus instead on how an account was generated, its structure and effects, the positioning of characters and other aspects of narrative construction (see Holstein and Gubrium in this volume). Language use can come into view – an angle of vision typically missing from grounded theory studies.

A NARRATIVE VOCABULARY

Narrative terminology is important for anyone contemplating a narrative project, especially given the current 'promiscuity of the idea of narrative' in public discourse (Brooks, 2001). Journalists and politicians have adopted the literary term to refer to what in the past would have been called an ideological position or argument. Many qualitative researchers are appropriating a narrative vocabulary to refer to interview segments of any kind, even to all research reports. In many cases we have 'promiscuity' without rigorous, incisive analysis. If social science investigators plan to use narrative concepts analytically, terminology needs to be taken seriously.

Sociolinguists generally make a sharp distinction between narrative and story:

- Narrative refers to the broad class of discourse types that have certain properties in common (identified below).
- A story is one prototypic form of narrative that recounts a discrete set of events with 'sequential and temporal ordering' (De Fina, 2003: 13).

Following Aristotle, De Fina reserves the term 'story' for oral discourses 'that include some kind of rupture or disturbance in the normal course of events ... an action that provokes a reaction and/or adjustment' (2003: 13).

In a recent paper I drew on ideas of temporality and rupture to compose a written account of traumatic illness (Riessman, 2015a). All scholars, particularly those working with the subtype 'story', owe a debt to the canonical work of Labov (1972, 1982) and prior work of Labov and Waletzky (1967), even if they did not always make a distinction between 'narrative' and 'story', and the field has moved beyond their theory of narrative. As narrative studies have developed over the decades, our language and conceptual apparatus have grown more precise.

Accepting that narrative refers to a broad class of discourse types (of which the 'story' is only one), what are the defining features that distinguish narrative from other kinds of interview discourse, such as brief question and answer exchanges, expository statements of beliefs, chronicles, listings and other speech acts? Bell builds on Hinchman and Hinchman (1997) to define narrative as:

a sequence of ordered events that are connected in a meaningful way for a particular audience in order to make sense of the world or people's experience in it ... This definition assumes one action is consequential for the next, that a narrative sequence is held together with a 'plot', and that the 'plot' is organized temporally and spatially ... More than a list or chronicle, a narrative adds up to 'something ...'. (Bell, 2009: 8)

Determining that 'something', of course, is a central task for the listener and subsequently the analyst as they interpret meaning, or the 'point' the speaker wishes to make. A long story about a particular moment must be worth telling to take up so much space in a conversation.

Rather than thinking in binary terms – a segment is either narrative or not – and yet preserving some distinctions, Paley and Eva argue for degrees of narrativity, with the 'story' meeting the highest threshold: 'an arrangement of events [plot] and people [characters] designed to elicit a response [a reaction from an audience]' (2005: 89). Storytelling in conversational settings typically recapitulates discrete moments, whereas other forms of narrative telling are better suited for eliciting a response from the listener/question about the general course of things. These discourse forms – not always event-centred – include habitual, hypothetical, associative/episodic narrative and other forms (Riessman, 1993). A participant's causal claim – 'this is what x was like for me' – can be made more persuasively perhaps with a form other than a story about a particular incident.

FORM FOLLOWS FUNCTION

To resist the pull towards narrative seduction, the investigator can interrogate what the narrative accomplishes and precisely how the form of telling achieves that end. Drawing on the familiar modernist architectural adage, form follows function.

There are many ways we can narrate an experience. It is the analyst's role to interrogate what is being accomplished with the particular choices a speaker makes. There are recognizable genres of narrative – farce, tragedy, the travel saga, the conversion tale, among others – which serve as cultural resources for any speaker. They provide familiar models for constructing 'human plights [and] they achieve their effects by using language in a particular way' (Bruner, 1991: 14). The analyst can ask:

- Why was a narrative segment developed *that* way at *that* point in an unfolding conversation?
- What does the speaker accomplish by adopting a particular narrative form?
- Does a story of a particular moment serve to persuade the listener of a preferred position perhaps, or put the speaker in an advantaged moral light ('I am a good person despite what I did')?

Personal narratives contain many performative features that enable the 'local achievement of identity' (Cussins, 1998). Tellers intensify words and phrases; they enhance segments with narrative detail, reported speech, appeals to the audience, gestures and even sound effects (Wolfson, 1982; Bauman, 1986). Analysts can ask additional questions of a performance:

- In what kind of a story does a narrator place herself?
- How does she position herself to the audience, and vice versa?
- How does she position characters in relation to one another, and in relation to herself?
- How does she position herself to herself, that is, make identity claims? (Bamberg, 2005)

Social positioning in stories – how narrators position audience, characters and themselves – is a useful point of entry because 'fluid positioning, not fixed roles, are used by people to cope with the situations they find themselves in' (Harré and van Langenhove, 1999: 17).

Narrators can position themselves, for example, as victims of one circumstance or another in their tales, giving over to other characters the power to initiate action. Alternatively, narrators can position themselves as active beings that assume control over events and actions: they purposefully initiate and cause action. They can shift among positions, giving themselves agentic roles in certain scenes, and passive roles in others. To create these fluid semantic spaces for themselves, narrators rely on particular grammatical resources to construct how they want to be known – verbs, for example, that frame actions as voluntary rather than compulsory, or grammatical forms that intensify their vulnerability (Capps and Ochs, 1995).

These positionings in a narrative performance are enacted in an immediate discursive context – for an audience. Put differently, narratives are not simply a record of a past experience; they are purposeful: composed for the listener/questioner and perhaps other invisible audiences to accomplish something – to have an effect. In a word, narratives *do things*; they are motivated, if not always consciously (Freeman, 2002: 9). Echoing the warning about narrative seduction, Atkinson and Delamont (2006) caution us to avoid the assumption we have 'captured' someone's private experiences through our interviews. As social constructionists argue, there is no unmediated access to a participant's 'lived-experience' – a claim often made in the qualitative research literature to describe what in-depth interviewing yields (see Holstein and Gubrium in this volume). Most narrative analysts would eschew the simplistic claim.

INTERACTIONAL CONTEXT

Oral narratives develop in dynamic conversations with listeners/questioners. Yet many qualitative researchers ignore the audience and constraints of the setting in their analysis. In interview research the unfortunate practice follows from the view that a participant's 'story' is the focus of interest, which is independent of the conditions of its production. If investigators believe they can gain unmediated access to a life story, they will not attend to the interactional contexts that shaped the particular version of it.

In contrast to the naive position, many of us in narrative studies attend to the research relationship, the unfolding interview conversation and the positioning of a story in it. Valuing reflexivity (Riessman, 2015b), we interrogate the influence of the setting, historical context, our preferred theoretical positions and other dimensions that shape the data we generate. The extent to which an investigator represents these dimensions will vary of course with the purpose of a project, but to neglect them entirely strips context from a piece of research.

Interviewers are active participants in interviews, subtly prodding participants to 'say more' about a topic or by pausing at key points in the expectation that 'more' could be said. By our receptive stance narrative interviewing encourages disclosure; we invite stories rather than discourage 'digressions' from a predetermined focus of interest (Mishler, 1986). Attention to the actions of all participants brings the dynamics of conversation into view – an essential element of the local context. Excluding the action of the questioner/listener and other aspects of the production of narrative reflects a rationalist and monologic philosophy of language, and it can encourage essentialist thinking: the properties of an 'experience' as conveyed in a narrator's speech exist independent of context, that is, when, how and to whom it is described.

If we accept that the research interview is a collaborative conversation, a discursive event involving give and take between speakers who operate within the constraints of the setting and broader social discourses (a topic illustrated in the example below), it is hard to justify excluding the listener/questioner from an inquiry. Perhaps the omission reflects unacknowledged power relations in the research relationship (see DeVault, 1999; Gubrium and Holstein, 2002) – all too common in qualitative research.

Many narrative researchers are incorporating visual technologies into their recording practice, thus expanding understandings of the context of an utterance. Particularly in ethnographic studies taking place in institutional settings (schools, health care settings, etc.), the use of video recording is increasing. What is commonly called 'body language' – relational positioning of the speakers in space, gaze and gesture – can come into the analysis, aiding greatly the interpretation of spoken discourse. (For recent examples, see Örluv and Hydén, 2006; Riessman, 2007: 141–82; Luttrell, 2010; Heath in this volume).

Key points

In sum, my argument points to several key concepts for the beginning investigator who wants to incorporate narrative methods in a case study:

- Be precise in your use of a narrative vocabulary.
- In analysing particular narrative segments, interrogate the relation between form and meaning - the way a segment of data is organized and why.
- Do not neglect the local context in your analysis, including the questioner/listener, setting and position of an utterance in the broader stream of the conversation.
- Identify underlying social discourses that may be taken for granted and infiltrate the speech of participants in the conversation.

Taken together, these dimensions (among others) distinguish narrative analysis from other forms of qualitative inquiry. The research example to follow illustrates the concepts in action.

THE SOCIAL WORLD IN A PERSONAL NARRATIVE

The example comes from my research on childless women conducted in Kerala, South India. Elsewhere (Riessman, 2000, 2005) I describe the fieldwork in detail, which included an ethnographic component. My analysis of the interview data was initially category-centred, looking thematically across more than 30 conversations. Several detailed case studies were added when I noticed a deviation among the older women from the pattern of stigma and discrimination in reports of the younger women. Although few in number in my sample, the older women had constructed lives that defied the master narrative of compulsory motherhood for married women in India (for a case study comparison, see Riessman, 2002a). Defying stigma, they appeared to be leading successful lives.

One of the participants was a woman I call 'Gita': 55 years old, married and childless, Hindu, and from a lower caste. Because of progressive social policies and related opportunities in her South Indian state, Gita is educated, has risen in status and works as a lawyer in a small municipality. The particular interview segment represented in the transcript (see Transcript 1 below) took place after she and I had talked in English for nearly an hour in her home about a variety of topics, most of which she introduced – her schooling career, how her marriage was arranged, and her political work in the 'liberation struggle of Kerala'. We enter the interview as I reintroduce the topic of fertility – the stated purpose of our meeting. My transcription conventions are adapted from Gee (1991): lines about a single topic are grouped into stanzas, which I then group into scenes. Except for my opening question, I have not represented my brief utterances (they are marked '=' in the transcript) but bring my participation into the analysis in other ways.

Transcript 1

Cathy: Now I am going to go back and ask some specific questions.
Were you ever pregnant?

Gita: Pregnant means - You see it was 3 years [after the marriage]   Scene 1
then I approached [name of doctor]
then she said it is not a viable - [pregnancy].
=
So she asked me to undergo this operation, this D&C
and she wanted to examine him [husband] also.
Then the second time in 1974 - in 75,   Scene 2
next time - four months.
Then she wanted [me] to take bed rest
advised me to take bed rest
Because I already told you   Scene 3
it was during that period that [name] the socialist leader
led the gigantic procession against Mrs. Indira Gandhi,
the Prime Minister of India, in Delhi.
And I was a political leader [names place and party]
I had to participate in that
So I went by train to Delhi
but returned by plane.
After the return I was in [name] Nursing Home

for 16 days bleeding
And so he [husband] was very angry   Scene 4
he said 'do not go for any social work
do not be active' this and that
But afterwards I never became – [pregnant]
=
Then my in-laws, they are in [city]   Scene 5
they thought I had some defect really speaking
So they brought me to a gynecologist,
one [name], one specialist.
She took three hours to examine me
and she said 'you are perfectly – [normal], no defect at all'
even though I was 40 or 41 then.
'So I have to examine your husband'.
Then I told her [doctor] 'You just ask his sister'.
She was – his sister was with me in [city].
So I asked her to ask her to bring him in.
He will not come.
Then we went to the house
So then I said 'Dr. [name] wants to see you'.
Then he [husband] said 'No, no, I will not go to a lady doctor'.
Then she [sister-in-law] said she would not examine him
they had to examine the – what is it? – the sperm in the laboratory.
But he did not allow that.

Source: Riessman (2002a: 700)

Although Gita could have answered my question ('were you ever pregnant?') directly ('yes'), she chose instead to develop a complex narrative. She describes terminated pregnancies, going to a political demonstration, coming home to her husband's anger, whereupon the scene shifts to the actions of in-laws and her husband's refusal to be examined for infertility. The account was unlike any other: although temporally organized, Gita's plot spans many years and social settings – she does not tell a story about a discrete sequence of events. Unlike other women's accounts, there is no reference to sadness, disappointment or other emotions common to narratives of miscarriage and infertility.

In an effort to interpret the segment, I struggled to define some boundaries, initially deciding to end my representation of the narrative with what seems like a coda at the end of Scene 4: 'But afterwards I never became – [pregnant]'. The utterance ends the sequence about pregnancy – the topic of my initial question. Eventually, as I began to focus on identity construction, I decided to include the next scene. As a general rule, the choice of a segment for closer analysis – the textual representation of a spoken narrative and the boundaries chosen – is strongly influenced by the researcher's evolving research questions. In these ways, the investigator variously 'infiltrates' a transcript (see Riessman, 2007: Chapter 2).

Infertility in the Indian context is laden with stigma for women; it was a major theme in my interviews, especially with younger women. I turned to sociological theory to think critically about stigma and its management. As Goffman (1963, 1969) suggests, social actors can stage performances of a desirable self to preserve 'face' in difficult situations, thus managing potentially 'spoiled' identities. These identity performances are situated and accomplished: participants negotiate in conversation how they want to be known. Rather than 'revealing' an essential self, they perform the preferred self, selected from the multiplicity of selves or persona that we all switch between as we go about our lives. Approaching identity as a 'performative struggle over the meanings of experience' (Langellier, 2001: 3) opens up analytic possibilities that are missed with static theories of identity that assume a singular unified 'self'.

Returning to my conversation with Gita, she had agreed to be interviewed about infertility, but the absence of motherhood did not seem to be a salient topic for her (I was always the one to introduce it); nor did she express negative self-evaluation, as younger women did. Gita had built a life around principles other than motherhood – as a lawyer and political activist. Close examination of the conversation reveals precisely how she constructs this preferred identity, solving the problem of stigma and subordination as a childless woman in South India.

Gita carefully positions the audience (me) and various characters in the discursive construction of the story – a complex performance that I have represented in five 'scenes'. Each offers a snapshot of action, located in a different time and setting. Unlike the discrete stories told by other women, there is a complex structure to this narrative. Let us look at how the scenes are organized within the performance.

The first two scenes are prompted by a request ('were you ever pregnant?') – my attempt after an hour's conversation to reposition Gita in a world of fertility. It was supposed to be the topic of our meeting and I wanted to get back it. She reluctantly moves into the role of pregnant woman in these brief scenes, quickly chronicling two pregnancies several years apart – the outcomes of which I have to clarify (in lines marked '=' on the transcript). She does not provide narrative detail or elaborate meanings – the audience must infer a great deal. The first two scenes contain only one character – a doctor – aside from Gita herself. She 'approached' the doctor, who 'asked' her to have a D and C. A quick aside states the doctor wanted to examine the husband, but we infer this did not happen. (With this utterance, Gita prefigures her husband's responsibility, anticipating the final scene and the point of the narrative.) She casts the doctor as the active agent again in Scene 2: she 'wanted' and 'advised' bed rest. By choice of verbs and positioning of characters, Gita constructs scenes in which she plays a relatively minor role. The audience infers from the lack of narrative detail that the events in the plot up to this point are not particularly meaningful to her.

The narrator's position and the salience of events radically change in the third scene. Gita shifts topics, from pregnancy to 'to what I already told you' – the primacy of her political life. She constructs a scene where she is the central character and agent of action: a 'political leader' in her Kerala community who 'had to' participate in a demonstration in Delhi against Mrs. Indira Gandhi, who was seeking re-election. A well-known component of her policy was forced sterilization. Ironically, this public discourse intersects Gita's personal experience of fertility.

Notice how in Scene 3 verbs frame the narrator's intentional actions, situated in the political exigencies of the time. There is considerable narrative elaboration in sharp contrast to the spare, 'passive' grammar of the previous scenes, where she was the object of the doctor's actions. Gita locates her private fertility story in the public story of 'Mother India' and its socialist movement – the audience is not left wondering which is more important. Ignoring her doctor's advice 'to take bed rest' during her second pregnancy, she travels to Delhi to participate in a mass demonstration, which probably involved a three-day train trip in 1975. Despite her return by plane and a 16-day nursing home stay for 'bleeding', we infer Gita lost the pregnancy (a fact I confirm a few lines later). She constructs a narrative around oppositional worlds – family life, on the one hand, and the socialist movement of India on the other. The personal and the political occupy separate spheres of action.

Gita shifts the action in the next two scenes to the family world. In Scene 4, she again introduces her husband as a character, and reports that he was 'very angry' at her 'social work', meaning her political activism. She communicates a one-way conversation: not giving herself a speaking role, she positions herself as the object of her husband's angry speech. We do not know what she said to him, if anything. Her passive position in this scene is in sharp contrast to her activity in the previous one. Is she displaying here the typical practice in South Indian families – wives are expected to defer to husbands' authority (Riessman, 2000)? If so, her choice of language is intriguing – he said 'this and that'. Could she be belittling his anger and directives here? She concludes Scene 4 with a factual utterance ('But afterwards I never became – [pregnant]').

In the fifth and final lengthy scene, Gita introduces new characters (her parents-in-law, an infertility specialist, a sister-in-law) and an intricate plot, before the narrative moves towards its point: infertility is not Gita's responsibility. The final scene has the most elaboration, suggesting importance, and the performance of identity is most vivid here. Gita begins by constructing a passive, stigmatized position for herself: in-laws 'brought' her for treatment to a gynecologist in the major South Indian city where the parents live, because 'they thought I had some defect'. As in earlier scenes involving pregnancy, others suggest or initiate action. She intensifies meaning and thematic importance with repetition ('defect') in the next stanza – the gynecologist determined after a lengthy examination that Gita has 'no defect at all'. She is 'perfectly' normal. Blame for infertility, Gita intimates, resides elsewhere. Using the linguistic device of reported speech, she performs several conversations on the topic of getting her husband tested. Everyone is enlisted in the effort – gynecologist, sister-in-law – but he refuses: 'No, no, I will not go to a lady doctor'. Nor is he willing to have his sperm tested in a laboratory. (Gita returned several other times in our interview to his refusal to be tested.) The narrator has crafted a performance – akin to a legal brief reviewing the evidence – where she has no responsibility whatsoever for infertility.

Looking critically at the conversation, we can wonder. By resisting seduction the analyst can interrogate the narrator's attributions. Gita ignored her physician's advice to 'take bed rest' during her second pregnancy, choosing to travel instead to Delhi. She gave priority to political commitments, valuing work in the socialist movement over her gendered position in the home. She was also '40 or 41' years old when she was finally examined by a specialist. Age may have been a factor. Gita had conceived twice, but could not sustain pregnancies – suggesting a possible 'defect'.

The performance, however, signals how Gita wants to be known: as a 'perfectly' normal woman 'with no defect at all'. This is the message of the narrative, realized through its form. How she organizes scenes within the performance, choices about positioning and the grammatical resources employed have effects and put forth a preferred identity – committed political activist, not disappointed would-be mother. Later in the interview, Gita supported my interpretation here. In a clear statement she resisted once again my attempt to position her in the world of biological fertility: 'Because I do not have [children], I have no disappointments, because mine is a big family'. She continued with a listing of many brothers, their children and particular nieces who 'come here every evening … to take their meals'. With these words, I become the defective subject with naive binary notions of parental status – either you have children or you do not. Although I did not 'get it' at the time of our conversation, I sense that she did get it and worked hard to counter my positioning of her. She performed a gender identity that defied my assumptions as well as the master cultural narrative – biological motherhood is the central axis of identity for married women in India. With time and analytic reflection, I was able to historicize Gita's account, and locate her in an evolving cultural discourse about women's 'proper' place in modern India, a 'developing' nation that is developing new spaces (besides home and field) for women to labour (Riessman, 2000, 2002a, 2002b).

CONCLUSION

The analytic strategy in the case study is generalizable to other narrative projects, particularly those concerned with identity work. The data segment was a complex extended narrative from a research interview that moved across vast expanses of time and space. The analysis paid close attention to how the narrative was composed, to whom it was directed and with what effect. Form was linked to function – what the narrative was *doing* in the particular interactional and cultural context.

Research participants can employ their lives in a variety of ways; they 'select and assemble experiences and events so they contribute collectively to the intended point of the story … why it is being told, in just this way, in just this setting' (Mishler 1999: 8). If we resist seduction into the manifest content of narratives, form and function can come into view.

CHAPTER SUMMARY

Because narrative is a primary mode of human understanding (Ricoeur, 1981; Freeman, 2015), scholars in the human sciences have been drawn to narrative. Research has often been directed to the process of identity construction – how narrators craft their situated identities through the telling of stories. In a word, identity is constructed in situ. To make identity work visible, we can analyse scenes, the positioning of characters, self and audience, and we can 'unpack' the grammatical resources narrators chose to make their points. We can analyse how narrators position their audience (and, reciprocally, how the audience positions the narrator). Preferred identities are constituted through such performative actions.

FUTURE PROSPECTS

Narrative inquiry offers opportunities for the disciplined study of interviews, naturally occurring conversations, political discourse, as well as epistolary and visual materials. There is a need for culturally sensitive applications of the methods in non-Western contexts with focused attention to language translation issues.

Study questions

1.   What are some key differences between grounded theory and narrative analysis of data?
2.   What are some of the key points to keep in mind in analysing transcribed texts as narrative?

Recommended reading

Andrews, M., Squire, C. and M. Tamboukou (eds) (2013) *Doing Narrative Research* (2nd edn). London: Sage.
A guide to inquiry including forms of narrative analysis, reflexivity, interpretation and research contexts.

Emerson, P. and S. Frosh (2009) *Critical Narrative Analysis in Psychology: A Guide to Practice* (rev. edn). London: Palgrave Macmillan.
Working with a single 'case', the reader learns levels of analysis from micro to macro.

Riessman, C. K. (2008) *Narrative Methods for the Human Sciences*. Thousand Oaks, CA: Sage.
An accessible introduction to some analytic approaches with exemplars from several social sciences.

Recommended online resources

Website for narrative researchers looking for courses, papers and colleagues:
www.uel.ac.uk/cnr

Website for narrative events and colleagues in Australia/New Zealand:
http://narranetau.academia.edu

Website for model programme in working with epistolary narrative:
www.oliveschreinerletters.ed.ac.uk

Duque, R. L. (2010) 'Review: Catherine Kohler Riessman (2008) *Narrative Methods for the Human Sciences*', *Forum: Qualitative Social Research*, 11 (1):
www.qualitative-research.net/index.php/fqs/article/view/1418

References

Atkinson, P. and P. Delamont (2006) 'Rescuing narrative from qualitative research', *Narrative Inquiry*, 16: 164–72.

Bamberg, M. (2005) '"I know it may sound strange to say this, but we couldn't really care less about her anyway": form and function of 'slut-bashing' in male identity constructions of 15-year-olds', *Human Development*, 47: 331–53.

Bauman, R. (1986) *Story, Performance, and Event: Contextual Studies of Oral Narrative*. Cambridge: Cambridge University Press.

Bell, S. E. (1988) 'Becoming a political woman: the reconstruction and interpretation of experience through stories', in A. D. Todd and S. Fisher (eds), *Gender and Discourse: The Power of Talk*. Norwood, NJ: Ablex, pp. 97–123.

Bell, S. E. (1999) 'Narratives and lives: women's health politics and the diagnosis of cancer for DES daughters', *Narrative Inquiry*, 9: 1–43.

Bell, S. E. (2009) *DES Daughters: Embodied Knowledge and the Transformation of Women's Health Politics*. Philadelphia: Temple University Press.

Brooks, P. (2001) 'Stories abounding', *The Chronicle of Higher Education*, 47 (24): B11.

Bruner, J. (1991) 'The narrative construction of reality', *Critical Inquiry*, 18: 1–21.

Capps, L. and Ochs, E. (1995) *Constructing Panic: The Discourse of Agoraphobia*. Cambridge, MA: Harvard University Press.

Chambers, R. (1984) *Story and Situation: Narrative Seduction and the Power of Fiction*. Minneapolis: University of Minnesota Press.

Clark, J. A. and Mishler, E. G. (1992) 'Attending to patients' stories: reframing the clinical task', *Sociology of Health and Illness*, 14: 344–70.

Cussins, C. M. (1998) 'Ontological choreography: agency for women patients in an infertility clinic', in M. Berg and S. Mol (eds), *Differences in Medicine: Unraveling Practices, Techniques and Bodies*. Durham, NC: Duke University Press, pp. 166–201.

De Fina, A. (2003) *Identity in Narrative: A Study of Immigrant Discourse*. Amsterdam and Philadelphia: John Benjamins.

De Fina, A. and A. Georgakopoulou (eds) (2015) *The Handbook of Narrative Analysis*. Malden, MA: Wiley.

DeVault, M. L. (1999) *Liberating Method: Feminism and Social Research*. Philadelphia, PA: Temple University Press.

Freeman, M. (2002) 'The presence of what is missing: memory: poetry and the ride home', in R. J. Pellegrini and T. R. Sarbin (eds), *Critical Incident Narratives in the Development of Men's Lives*. New York: Haworth Clinical Practice Press, pp. 165–176.

Freeman, M. (2015) 'Narrative as a mode of understanding: method, theory, praxis', in A. De Fina and A. Georgakopoulou (eds), *Handbook of Narrative Analysis*. Malden, MA: Wiley.

Garfinkel, H. (1967) *Studies in Ethnomethodology*. Englewood Cliffs, NJ: Prentice Hall.

Gee, J. P. (1991) 'A linguistic approach to narrative', *Journal of Narrative and Life History/ Narrative Inquiry*, 1: 15–39.

Goffman, E. (1963) *Stigma: Notes on the Management of Spoiled Identity*. Englewood Cliffs, NJ: Prentice Hall.

Goffman, E. (1969) *The Presentation of Self in Everyday Life*. New York: Penguin.

Gubrium, J. F. and Holstein, J. A. (2002) 'From the interview to the interview society', in J. F. Gubrium and J. A. Holstein (eds), *Handbook of Interview Research: Context and Method*. Thousand Oaks, CA: Sage, pp. 3–32.

Harré, R. and L. van Langenhove (eds) (1999) *Positioning Theory*. Malden, MA: Blackwell.

Hinchman, L. P. and S. K. Hinchman (eds) (1997) *Memory, Identity, Community: The Idea of Narrative in the Human Sciences*. Albany: State University of New York Press.

Labov, W. (1972) *Language in the Inner City: Studies in the Black English Vernacular*. Philadelphia, PA: University of Pennsylvania Press.

Labov, W. (1982) 'Speech actions and reactions in personal narrative', in D. Tannen (ed.), *Analyzing Discourse: Text and Talk*. Washington, DC: Georgetown University Press, pp. 219–47.

Labov, W. and J. Waletzky (1967) 'Narrative analysis: oral versions of personal experience'. in J. Helm (ed.), *Essays on the Verbal and Visual Arts*. Seattle: American Ethnological Society/University of Washington Press, pp. 12–44.

Langellier, K. (2001) '"You're marked": breast cancer, tattoo and the narrative performance of identity', in J. Brockmeier and D. Carbaugh (eds), *Narrative Identity: Studies in Autobiography, Self, and Culture*. Amsterdam and Philadelphia: John Benjamins, pp. 145–84.

Livholts, M. and Tamboukou, M. (2015) *Discourse and Narrative Methods*. London: Sage.

Luttrell, W. (2010) '"A camera is a big responsibility": a lens for analyzing children's visual voices', *Visual Studies*, 25 (3): 224–37.

Mishler, E. G. (1986) *Research Interviewing: Context and Narrative*. Cambridge, MA: Harvard University Press.

Mishler, E. G. (1996) 'Missing persons: recovering developmental stories/histories', in R. Jessor, A. Colby and R. A. Shweder (eds), *Ethnography and Human Development: Context and Meaning in Social Inquiry*. Chicago, IL: University of Chicago Press, pp. 74–99.

Mishler, E. G. (1999) *Storylines: Craftartists' Narratives of Identity*. Cambridge, MA: Harvard University Press.

Örluv, L. and Hydén, L. C. (2006) 'Confabulation: sense-making, self-marking and world-making in dementia', *Discourse Studies*, 8: 647–73.

Paley, J. and Eva, G. (2005) 'Narrative vigilance: the analysis of stories in health care', *Nursing Philosophy*, 6: 83–97.

Polanyi, L. (1989) *Telling the American Story: A Structural and Cultural Analysis of Conversational Storytelling*. Cambridge, MA: MIT Press.

Quinn, N. (2005) *Finding Culture in Talk: A Collection of Methods*. New York: Palgrave Macmillan.

Ricoeur, P. (1981) 'Narrative time' in W. J. T. Mitchell (ed.), *On Narrative*. Chicago, IL: University of Chicago Press, pp. 165–86.

Riessman, C. K. (1990) *Divorce Talk: Women and Men Make Sense of Personal Relationships*. New Brunswick, NJ: Rutgers University Press.

Riessman, C. K. (1993) *Narrative Analysis*. Newbury Park, CA: Sage.

Riessman, C. K. (2000) 'Stigma and everyday resistance practices: childless women in South India', *Gender & Society*, 14: 111–35.

Riessman, C. K. (2002a) 'Analysis of personal narratives', in J. A. Gubrium and J. F. Holstein (eds), *Handbook of Interview Research*. Newbury Park, CA: Sage, pp. 695–710.

Riessman, C. K. (2002b) 'Positioning gender identity in narratives of infertility: South Indian women's lives in context', in M. C. Inhorn and F. van Balen (eds), *Infertility Around the Globe: New Thinking on Childlessness, Gender, and Reproductive Technologies*. Berkeley, CA: University of California Press, pp. 152–70.

Riessman, C. K. (2005) 'Exporting ethics: a narrative about narrative research in South India', *Health: An Interdisciplinary Journal for the Social Study of Health, Illness and Medicine*, 9: 473–90.

Riessman, C. K. (2007) *Narrative Methods for the Human Sciences*. Thousand Oaks, CA: Sage.

Riessman, C. K. (2015a) 'Ruptures and sutures: time, audience and identity in an illness narrative', *Sociology of Health & Illness*, 37 (7): 1055–71.

Riessman, C. K. (2015b) 'Entering the hall of mirrors: reflexivity and narrative research', in A. De Fina and A. Georgakopoulou (eds), *Handbook of Narrative Analysis*. Malden, MA: Wiley, pp. 219–38.

Sacks, H. (1972) 'On the analyzability of stories by children', in J. Gumperz and D. Hymes (eds), *Directions in Sociolinguistics*. New York: Holt, Rinehart and Winston, pp. 325–45.

Wolfson, N. (1982) *The Conversational Historical Present in American English Narrative*. Dordrecht: Foris.

TWENTY THREE

Systematic Reviews and Qualitative Studies

Mary Dixon-Woods

About this chapter

This chapter focuses on methods for conducting overviews of bodies of evidence that include qualitative research studies. Systematic review methodology – which treats the production of a review as a scientific process – has emerged partly to counter the apparent fallibilities of traditional literature reviews. It typically uses pre-specified protocols for the conduct of a review, which formalize and codify the review question; eligibility criteria for studies to be included; searching strategies to be used; quality appraisals to be undertaken; and methods to be used in synthesizing the included studies. This approach poses a number of challenges when the aim is to include qualitative research studies. Methodological approaches for incorporating qualitative research in systematic reviews vary along a spectrum from those that remain fairly close to the conventional systematic review template to those that seek a redefinition of systematic review as an approach.

Keywords

systematic review, research synthesis, literature review, qualitative research

INTRODUCTION

Undertaking reviews of the literature is perhaps one of the most fundamental and routine tasks of any academic. Such reviews are used, for example, to identify gaps in knowledge, theory or evidence, or to provide an overview of a field or sub-field. The question of how literature reviews should best be conducted has become a focus of increasing interest and debate. In tracing the outlines of these debates, it is useful, to begin with, to characterize the various approaches to conducting reviews in terms of caricatures. Two are especially helpful in introducing the area, and I will term these:

- the 'authorship' approach
- the 'contractual' approach.

The authorship approach is one that has long dominated much of the social sciences. Here, a literature review is seen as the product of a special kind of expertise and scholarly sensibility, gained by gradually internalizing the modes of conduct proper to competent members of the scholarly community. The skill of literature reviewing is learned as part of long and difficult effort aimed at gaining mastery not only over a body of knowledge, but also over the rhetorical tactics needed to persuade readers of the correctness of the author's interpretation. These tactics may include:

- showing that the author is aware of what are generally held to be the 'key papers' in a field and can mount a satisfying critique of them
- demonstrating that the argument being fashioned is coherent and plausible
- mobilizing persuasive modes of vocabulary and organizing the material in a manner likely to convince the reader.

Memorably described by Howard Becker (2007), the process of skill acquisition in this form of literature review is one of acculturation and socialization, part of the larger project of developing the ability to write social science. The annotation 'stink! stink! stink!' by way of comment on one of his manuscripts was just one of the purgatories Becker endured on his way to acquiring this ability.

In contrast to this is the contractual approach to literature reviewing. The defining characteristic of this approach is the proceduralization of the process of review. Here, literature review is viewed as a scientific process governed by a set of explicit and demanding rules oriented towards demonstrating comprehensiveness, immunity from bias, and transparency and accountability of technique and execution. This is the idea that finds its concrete expression in the methodology of the systematic review, which is conventionally understood to have specific characteristics (Table 23.1).

In systematic review, method is a way of expunging the author through a regime of accountability; the various techniques are intended to operate as a means of distancing the author from the material on which they work by disciplining and calling to account what

Table 23.1   Characteristics of a systematic review

A systematic review:

- uses explicit study protocol
- addresses a formal, pre-specified, highly focused question
- defines the eligibility criteria for studies to be included in the review in advance
- is explicit about the methods used for searching for studies, including any efforts to track down unpublished work or studies published in foreign languages
- screens publications for inclusion in the review against *a priori* criteria
- conducts formalized appraisals to assess scientific quality and otherwise limit the risk of bias
- uses explicit methods to combine the findings of studies

they do and how they report it. Learning how to do a literature review, in the contractual approach, involves learning the formal rules and displaying their conscientious application; systematic review is therefore just as much engaged in using rhetorical devices as a means of persuasion as the author-based review, but the nature of the rhetoric is different. A judgement about whether a systematic review has been done well will depend on an assessment of the extent to which it conforms to the procedural requirements governing its conduct. It can thus be understood as a contract-based form of activity, in which performance is assessed against specific standards. It is markedly distinct from a view of the literature review as a product of the author's innate, tacit skill, a form of cultural competence to be judged by attending to the quality of the argument and the aesthetics of the presentation. In this chapter, we examine what the turn towards systematic review means for reviews of qualitative studies.

THE RISE OF SYSTEMATIC REVIEW METHODOLOGY

The rise of 'systematic review' as a distinct methodology for conducting reviews of evidence has an interesting and instructive history. The need to produce unbiased overviews of the results of empirical studies was recognized as far back as 1753, when James Lind's treatise on scurvy noted the need to have a full and impartial view of the evidence. Methods for summarizing and synthesizing bodies of research have since taken several forms.

One important strand has been the development of statistical methods for aggregating and comparing the results of different quantitative studies. The statistician Karl Pearson (1904) is thought to have been the first to combine the findings of independent studies to produce an overall estimate, when he sought to compare infection and mortality among soldiers who had and had not volunteered for inoculation against typhoid fever. Techniques for statistical pooling of quantitative data continued to develop throughout the twentieth century, particularly within the fields of psychology and education studies. They were christened with the term 'meta-analysis' by the educationalist Gene Glass, who sought an alternative to what he saw as 'casual, narrative discussions of research studies' (1976: 3). Though sometimes (mis)appropriated, the term 'meta-analysis' is now properly used in a circumscribed way to describe the quantitative pooling of study findings. Meta-analysis is just one of the techniques that can be used in a systematic review: meta-analysis and systematic review are far from synonymous, and it is possible (indeed, very common) to have a systematic review without a meta-analysis.

The more general significance of the development of meta-analysis was in adding to a growing view throughout the 1980s and 1990s that unstructured and poorly disciplined reviews of quantitative studies were likely to be flawed because, confronted with a large body of evidence, reviewers are susceptible to a range of heuristics, biases, prejudices and sloppy practices. Reviewers may, for example:

- focus on a small sub-set of studies but not describe how they selected them
- be influenced by their own perspective and expert opinions
- fail to address the quality of studies they review
- combine the findings of studies in inappropriate ways
- not adequately account for publication bias (the problem that studies with positive findings are more likely to be published than those with negative findings)
- marshal the evidence in support of their preferred theories.

The correct remedy to the fallibilities of the author-based approach was seen to lie in the routinization of processes of review. This argument gained particular force in medicine, where both the failure to conduct systematic reviews and the lack of scientific rigour in published reviews came to be seen as an unacceptable threat to patient safety. For example, tens of thousands of babies are thought to have suffered or died unnecessarily because of a failure to conduct a systematic review and meta-analysis of clinical trials of steroids for premature labour (Evans et al., 2006). The discovery of many similar examples, together with the increasingly rapid development of methods for systematic review, helped fuel the rise of what came to be known as the evidence-based practice and policy movement, which has now spread from its initial origins in medicine to many diverse fields.

This highly influential movement has taken a number of institutionalized forms, including the founding of organizations engaged in publishing guidance on how to undertake systematic reviews and coordinating the production of reviews. In healthcare, the Cochrane Collaboration and the UK NHS Centre for Reviews and Dissemination (NHS CRD) are among the best known of these. The newer Campbell Collaboration has used the Cochrane model as the basis of an international network to produce systematic reviews on the effects of social interventions, particularly in the areas of education, crime and social welfare. The evidence-based approach has become popularized through blogs and columns, including the work of Ben Goldacre (see www.badscience.net), and others. The James Lind library (www.jameslindlibrary.org), and the freely available book 'Testing Treatments' (www.testingtreatments.org) have also sought to bring principles of systematic review and evidence-based policy and practice to a wider audience.

CONTROVERSY ABOUT SYSTEMATIC REVIEWS

Much of the work within the broad church of the evidence-based movement focuses on addressing questions of effectiveness or 'what works?', and, perhaps unsurprisingly, it has had considerable appeal to policy-makers and decision-makers. The production of systematic reviews is now a large-scale activity, undertaken in support of a wide range of important areas of policy and practice, and increasingly relied upon to support decision-making in areas as diverse as anti-bullying interventions, the effects of interview and interrogation methods on confession rates in criminal suspects, and the health and social effects of housing improvements.

As systematic review has become established as a scientific research methodology in its own right, it has become a political and social force to be reckoned with, to the extent that systematic reviews are now seen, in many influential quarters, as having a special kind of scientific authority. This has led to sometimes conflict-ridden debates, which to some extent represent the perpetuation of long-standing tensions about what should count as scientific method in the social sciences.

One side of the debate sees immense benefit in using systematic review methodology to synthesize bodies of available evidence, revealing to external scrutiny the basis of decisions about which studies have and have not been included in a review, making explicit and systematic the processes of summarizing data across multiple studies, and, where appropriate, increasing the statistical power of estimates of effect. The other side is critical of the argument that systematic review is the only evidence that counts as evidence, especially when systematic reviews are extended beyond the evaluation of therapeutic interventions in healthcare. Systematic review methodology has been attacked for allegedly positivist, reductionist leanings, its rigidities and the apparently limited, or even absurd, nature of the conclusions of some reviews (Hammersley, 2005; MacLure, 2005).

A particular (though not exclusive) focus of criticism of early forms of systematic review methodology was that they offered little or no place for qualitative research findings. The original 'hierarchy of evidence' ranked different study designs in terms of the quality of evidence they yielded, excluding qualitative research altogether or putting it at (or close to) the bottom of the pyramid. Such an approach can lead to a number of important problems, including:

- the risks that the question of the review might be inappropriately defined
- the outcomes of interest might be inappropriately specified
- the variables to be studied might be inappropriately selected
- potentially relevant data might be excluded
- inappropriate conclusions might be reached (Dixon-Woods et al., 2001).

The arguments in favour of including qualitative research in reviews might be stated briefly as follows: not everything we need to know about the world can be measured or counted, and other forms of data are often needed to form a comprehensive view or understanding of an area.

Recent years have seen explicit acknowledgement of the relevance and utility of qualitative research in systematic reviews, and a number of developments aimed at enabling qualitative research studies to be synthesized or summarized either on their own or with quantitative research findings. Recent guides (NHS Centre for Reviews and Dissemination, 2009; Higgins and Green, 2011) devote considerable attention to discussing the inclusion of qualitative research studies in or alongside systematic reviews of effectiveness.

METHODS FOR CONDUCTING REVIEWS OF RESEARCH EVIDENCE

Multiple methods for conducting reviews of qualitative (or qualitative and quantitative) studies are now available (Table 23.2), though they are at varying stages of development and evaluation (Dixon-Woods et al., 2005; Thomas and Harden, 2008). Some of the available approaches represent 'new' methods specifically designed to tackle the issue of synthesis, or modifications of these methods; others are primary research methods that have been adapted for the purpose of review and synthesis. Some are directed towards synthesis of qualitative research studies only; others offer methods for synthesizing both qualitative and quantitative findings. New methods continue to emerge – including Best Fit Framework Synthesis (Carroll et al., 2013) – and other methods continue to evolve. The scale and pace of methodological development has meant, however, that several approaches have different names but are actually very similar; the same terms are sometimes used to describe quite different things ('meta-synthesis' being one of these); some publications claim to use particular methods, but on more detailed inspection turn out not to have done so, or to have do so very poorly (France et al., 2014); and, overall, confusion about terminology and defining features abound.

The methods themselves are diverse. At one end of the spectrum, some approaches remain broadly within the frame offered by what might be termed 'conventional' systematic review (the contractual approach described above), and thus are characterized by pre-specified protocols, *a priori* question definition, formalized searching strategies, standardized quality appraisal and formal methods of synthesis. At the other end of the spectrum are more interpretive methods that make a more fundamental challenge to the idea, premises and methods of conventional systematic review (though some continue to lay claim to the label of 'systematic review' as a means of legitimation). Expressing unease at the lack of fit between the frame offered by conventional systematic review methodology and the kinds of epistemological assumptions and research practices more usually associated with qualitative research, these latter approaches attempt to redefine in some sense what is meant by a systematic review, and may therefore modify or otherwise reject some or all of the requirements of the methodology. And some approaches involve hybrids of conventional systematic review methodology and more interpretive strategies.

Table 23.2 Examples of methods that may be used in conducting a synthesis of qualitative studies

Bayesian meta-analysis

Content analysis

Case survey methods

Case-case analysis

Qualitative comparative analysis

Narrative summary

Thematic analysis

Grounded theory

Meta-ethnography

Realist synthesis

Critical interpretive synthesis

Meta-narrative mapping

'Best-fit' framework synthesis

In selecting a method, clarifying the specific purpose of the review is critically important, because it determines almost all of the decisions that follow. Just as primary research requires different methods and different theoretical perspectives depending on the purpose of the research, so too will reviews. This may seem rather an obvious point, but it tends to be one that gets rather lost in many of the controversies.

One useful way of thinking about the purpose of a review is to consider whether your aim is primarily aggregative or interpretive. *Aggregative syntheses* focus on *summarizing data*, and they may often – though far from always – be organized around assessing the effectiveness of various interventions or programmes. In answering 'does it work?' questions – for example, does a mentorship programme help reduce offending rates in young offenders? – an aggregative synthesis may be a highly appropriate choice. A conventional systematic review approach might be best suited to ensuring that all the relevant evidence has been identified and included, and moreover that attention has been given to the quality of the available data. Both qualitative and quantitative forms of evidence can contribute to this kind of review, and some techniques – such as Bayesian meta-analysis – can be used to allow qualitative evidence to influence quantitative estimates of effects.

Interpretive syntheses are concerned with the development of concepts and the specification of theories that integrate those concepts (for example, how can we best explain why mentorship might affect offending behaviours?). Interpretive synthesis involves processes similar to primary qualitative research, in which the concern is with *generating* concepts that have maximum explanatory value. For example, they may seek to characterize the mechanisms through which an intervention works, or may produce insights that deepen understanding of a particular field. This approach – which again may include quantitative and qualitative evidence – achieves synthesis through incorporating the concepts identified in the primary studies into a more subsuming theoretical structure. This structure may include concepts not found in the original studies but that help to characterize the data as a whole. This kind of work may be best undertaken using something closer to an authorial, interpretive approach, but perhaps disciplined by some explicit rules.

The distinction between an aggregative and an interpretive synthesis is very much an heuristic one; the difference is one of emphasis. For instance, aggregative syntheses can fulfil theoretical or interpretive functions, perhaps, for example, in the form of theories of causality, and they may also include claims about generalisability. Similarly, an interpretive synthesis should not be seen as floating free of any empirical anchor: an interpretive synthesis of primary studies must be grounded in the data reported in those studies. Further, many reviews may attempt hybrids of aggregative and interpretive activities. The discussion that follows will briefly consider some of the issues that arise when working with different approaches within the methodological template offered by systematic review methodology.

Defining the review question

Defining the review question is one of the principal tasks of conventional systematic review. The normal procedure is to specify a clear set of criteria focused around a specific question. These will usually define the study designs to be included (e.g. randomized controlled trials, case control studies, etc.) as well as characteristics related to the question, including populations of interest and outcomes of interest. They may be very precisely specified – for example, 'young' offenders may be defined as those under the age of 18. If the aim is an aggregative review, then it may be important to define the question in a way that conforms to expectations of a conventional systematic review. This, however, is far from straightforward, and will often require some kind of scoping exercise before the parameters of the review are determined. Even then, challenges may continue to arise about definitional decisions and choices about categorization.

If the question is one requiring an interpretive account of the literature, a more iterative approach to question specification might be used. This would treat the question and its parameters as fundamentally unsettled and open to critique. For example, it might question the idea of 'an offender' and look at how definitions are applied to categorize some individuals as offenders, but not others (such as so-called 'white collar' criminals). Such a review might seek to modify the question in response to search results and findings from retrieved items, and might search across disciplinary boundaries or fields of study. Thus, rather than something defined very precisely in advance, the precise terms of an interpretive review question might not be determined until closer to the end of a review.

Finding qualitative research

Conventional systematic review methodology, in keeping with its highly protocolized model, strongly emphasises the importance of rigorous and systematic searching to identify the population of relevant material for the parameters of the review. An effort is then made to identify all studies relevant to the criteria specified in the review question. Making sure that the entire set of relevant studies has been identified is usually seen as important to avoiding bias, especially if a meta-analysis is to be conducted, since leaving out relevant studies could bias any estimates of effect. This approach places particular stress on having a clear account of how searching was conducted, with the aim of ensuring that the search methods can be inspected and potentially reproduced. Searching may involve a range of strategies, but typically relies heavily on electronic bibliographic databases. The development and evaluation of search strategies is itself a sub-field of systematic review methodology. Typically, searching utilises the indexing systems of controlled keywords (known as thesaurus terms or subject headings) that are used to catalogue the records on major bibliographic databases. Other strategies include referencing chaining (where the list of references for papers already identified are checked) and contact with experts in the field. It is usual, in reporting systematic reviews, to give full details of the search strategies used, including lists of keywords.

When the aim is to apply such approaches to qualitative research, a number of challenges arise. Some of these are essentially technical in nature. Despite substantial improvements in recent years, attempts to identify qualitative studies using formalized search strategies remain often frustrating; the thesaurus terms that describe qualitative methodologies are still limited and vary across databases, and qualitative researchers do not always provide the kinds of abstracts and keywords that facilitate ready identification of the study designs they have used.

When the interest is in producing a more interpretive review with the review question and its parameters only provisionally defined at the outset, practical problems may arise in trying to use a formalized and easily audited search strategy. Subjecting a question to continual review and refinement may make it much more difficult to demonstrate, as required by conventional systematic review methodology, the transparency, comprehensiveness and reproducibility of search strategies. These problems go beyond being merely technical. Those used to more authorial forms of scholarship may find it constraining and frustrating to have to work within tightly defined parameters, especially if their embodied expertise means that they are aware of relevant literature but cannot find a way to show the inclusion of that literature to be legitimate within the frame of conventional systematic review. For example, a reviewer looking at ways of reducing 'inappropriate' admissions to hospitals through hospital emergency departments might recognize the relevance of literature in the completely different area of police processing of suspects because of the conceptual similarity of the nature of the tasks of classification and categorization that both settings undertake. At the same time, such a reviewer might struggle to find a way of showing that such work could meet formalized criteria for inclusion under conventional systematic review methodology.

Selection of material for inclusion

One of the important principles of conventional systematic review is that all possible data that might contribute to the synthesis should be identified, as exclusion of relevant data might affect estimates. A meta-analysis, for instance, is concerned with quantifying the effectiveness, *on average*, of a particular intervention, and will therefore want to include all relevant data that might assist in estimating that average. Inappropriate exclusion of relevant data might lead to the wrong estimate being made. As a check on the impact of including and excluding certain studies, quantitative syntheses use methods such as sensitivity analysis.

For interpretive syntheses, it could be argued that the same logic that governs sampling for primary qualitative research might apply. Here, the notion of theoretical saturation might have value. In primary research, theoretical sampling is conducted with a view towards the evolving theoretical development of the concepts. A researcher continues sampling until theoretical saturation is reached – where, after each new interview or observation, no new relevant data seem to emerge regarding a category, either to extend or contradict it (Strauss and Corbin, 1990). Under such a process, a reviewer might identify the papers that, on the basis of intuitive 'feel' are the most significant in a particular field, and might even deliberately sample outside of that field in order to test or refine the emerging synthesis.

Several problems arise in using theoretical sampling as a means of limiting the number of papers to be included in a review, however. First, within the frame of conventional systematic review methodology, it could be argued that once systematic reviews fail to be *explicit* and *reproducible*, and are allowed to include (apparently) idiosyncratically chosen literatures and to use non-transparent forms of interpretation to determine the synthesis of the included studies, they are no longer systematic. In fact, it could be asserted, reviews of this type are nothing new: they are simply literature reviews of the type that have always been done. Second, in employing sampling as an alternative to *comprehensiveness*, it has to be acknowledged that sampling research papers is fundamentally not like sampling people. Unlike people, research papers have a vested interest in being different from one another. Missing out some papers may therefore risk missing out potentially important insights.

Appraising qualitative research

Systematic appraisal of quality of evidence is undertaken by those conducting systematic reviews to reduce the possibility of bias. For quantitative systematic reviews, it is usual to devise broad inclusion criteria – for example adequate randomization for randomized controlled trials – and to exclude studies that fail to meet these. More detailed assessments of papers that are included in the review may also be undertaken to identify specific defects. If a meta-analysis is to be undertaken as part of the systematic review, techniques such as sensitivity analysis may be used to explore the effects of such defects on the conclusions of the synthesis, or the synthesis may be adjusted in other ways. For example, a randomized controlled trial (RCT) with only a very small number of participants might be given a lower 'weighting' than a bigger trial.

Whether or how to make judgements of the quality of qualitative research reports has been much contested in the context both of conventional systematic review and more interpretive reviews. No consensus has yet emerged. Some propose that there is an obligation to exclude 'weak' studies, but others disagree.

What is clear is that a decision to exclude qualitative studies from a review on the grounds of quality is not straightforward to execute. Because of the diversity of qualitative study designs and approaches, it is at present impossible to specify universally agreed *a priori* defects, equivalent to inadequate randomization for RCTs, that would indicate that a qualitative study is fatally flawed. Assessment of the quality of qualitative papers has therefore traditionally relied on much more detailed appraisals, often using checklist-type approaches. The use of such checklists has been the subject of heated debate. Nonetheless, a striking proliferation continues of checklists, quality criteria and standards for qualitative research, often adopting non-reconcilable positions on a number of issues. Few have distinguished between different study designs or theoretical approaches, thereby tending to treat qualitative research as a unified field; many represent attempts by their developers to impose a dominant view of what 'good' qualitative research should be like.

Appraisal checklists have themselves rarely been systematically appraised, but one study that compared two checklist-type approaches to unprompted judgement found that agreement between reviewers and between methods of appraisal was slight (Dixon-Woods et al., 2007). Reviewers disagreed not only on the quality of papers, but also on whether papers were reporting qualitative research and whether papers were relevant to the topic of the review. Greatest agreement between reviewers appears to occur when they used expertise-based judgements.

Excluding qualitative studies judged to be too weak might be one strategy for dealing with poor quality research, but less clear is what to do about assigning weights to studies of variable quality. Precisely how 'weak' qualitative findings should be attenuated or excluded in any synthesis is not yet clear. The feasibility and value of attempting some form of sensitivity analysis – where the effects of including or excluding particular qualitative findings are evaluated – remains to be assessed.

CONDUCTING A SYNTHESIS

Choices about methods for summarizing and/or synthesizing bodies of evidence will be strongly influenced by the purpose of the review. The methods listed in Table 23.2 vary in their degree of procedural specification and in the kinds of interpretive and aggregative work they require. Some require the conversion of one form of data into another. For example, Bayesian meta-analysis uses qualitative research to improve quantitative estimates. Other methods, such as meta-ethnography, proceduralize some aspects of the review process, but still rely on some level of interpretation by the reviewer. Some, such as realist synthesis, require a high level of creativity and critical interpretation on the part of reviewers. Critical interpretive synthesis is in many (though not all) ways a codification and formalization of the traditional authorial approach to reviewing.

Data extraction is one problem worth mentioning. In conventional systematic review, quantitative data are extracted onto pre-specified forms that have categories under which data are entered (e.g. male, female, tumour type, treatment A, treatment B). Standardized data extraction of this type is considerably more difficult to use with qualitative research reports. It is often not really clear what *are* the data – are they just quotations or extracts from field notes, or are they interpretations? Should material in the discussion sections of papers be included, or just findings? How should standardized headings be devised under which such data can be assigned, and in what format should it be extracted? No consensus has yet appeared on these issues.

Recent analysis (Lee et al., 2015) has suggested that conducting a synthesis of qualitative research may in fact involve many types of hidden labour that remain obscured in reports of such syntheses. Lee et al. identify in particular that intensive, repetitive and highly active reading is a key activity. They also argue that the hoped-for conceptual innovation that might result from synthesis work may be constrained by the 'thin', poorly conceptualized nature of the categories used in the primary research, and when the analytic constructs in a particular field are dominated by policy 'style-of-thought' concepts. A way of tackling the latter problem might be to charge those conducting syntheses with responsibility for conducting *critique* (Dixon-Woods et al., 2006) that treats the literature as warranting scrutiny in its own right. Such critiques may be especially attentive to, for example, the commonsense (and unexamined) assumptions about phenomena and categories that underlie studies, to the appropriateness of the match between the research problem and the method used in studies (for instance, was a qualitative approach used when an experiment would have been better-suited? Were interviews used when naturalistic data, such as ethnography, would have been more apt?), and what was the nature and warrantedness of the inferences that researchers in these studies have made (Silverman, 2007).

CONCLUSIONS

Systematic review is important both scientifically and politically; overviews of evidence conducted using conventional systematic review methodology enjoy special kinds of authority, but have not escaped criticism and challenge. Many debates can be understood as a playing out both of the inherent tensions between the 'authorial' and 'contractual' models of review, but more generally reflect the long history of epistemological contest between different paradigms. Different sides of the debate often have legitimate criticisms to make of the other. While the contractarians point to the tendency of authors to be chaotic, negligent or simply biased in their selection and assembly of literature, the 'authors' may condemn the apparently mechanical and stifling effects of systematic review methodology.

It is now accepted that qualitative research does have a valuable role to play in reviews of research evidence, and a plurality of methodological approaches to review is now beginning to emerge. Questions can be asked about whether apparent differences between the strategies reflect superficial differences in terminology and the degree to which methods have been specified. At least some differences may reflect how approaches have developed in isolation, rather than more fundamental points of divergence. Work comparing the results of applying different methods of synthesis is now beginning to appear, and will be increasingly useful in distinguishing trivial from non-trivial differences between methods. Also appearing are standards and guides, including statements on enhancing the reporting of qualitative research syntheses (Tong et al., 2012).

One key question concerns the extent to which conventional systematic review methodology, with its origins in the 'what works' template, and its focus on estimating the effectiveness of a particular intervention on average, can be consistent with aspirations of those aiming to produce more interpretive forms of overview of bodies of research evidence. Many innovations, in attempting to incorporate qualitative research, strain the epistemological and methodological assumptions that underlie systematic review, and raise questions about the precise remit and defining characteristics of this form of scientific activity. There is therefore need for sustained reflection on whether 'systematic review' describes a very specific methodology with very well-defined characteristics, or whether it is becoming a broad framework that allows multiple forms of evidence synthesis to be undertaken. With the diversity of techniques now beginning to appear, those using 'new' or evolving techniques will need to be highly reflexive and critical, and to produce critical accounts of their experiences of using the methods. By doing so, they will allow others to benefit from their learning and for the methods to be improved and become more sophisticated.

FUTURE PROSPECTS

The field of systematic review has evolved rapidly over the last two decades, and both its methodological and philosophical underpinnings look set to change as the limitations of rigid and stifling approaches become more apparent. Particularly noticeable is a movement towards characterising the theoretical basis of interventions and towards recognising the importance of contextual influences. As the field develops, the need for systematic reviews to retain discipline and structure will remain, but the specific forms they take may diversify. We are likely to see growing emphasis on the need for interventions and contexts to be more fully described in primary reports and accounted for in reviews, at the same time as the distinction between intervention and context may increasingly be questioned. As systematic review begins to be understood as more than a set of technical tasks, the need for social scientists and philosophers to engage in its methods and practices will become vividly clear.

CHAPTER SUMMARY

- Conventional systematic review methodology has emerged in response to criticisms that informal reviews may be incomplete or misleading
- Systematic review conventionally requires *a priori* specification of the review question, the methods of searching, methods of quality appraisal and methods of synthesis
- Methodological innovations aimed at including qualitative research in systematic reviews vary from those that remain fairly close to the conventional systematic review template to those that offer a more fundamental challenge to the approach

ACKNOWLEDGEMENTS

This chapter is based on work funded by ESRC Research Methods Programme grant H333250043. I thank my co-investigators Bridget Young, Andrew Booth, David Jones, Alex Sutton, Tina Miller, and Jonathan Smith.

Study questions

1. Identify a question that would be well suited to conventional systematic review. What makes it a good candidate for this approach?
2. What are the advantages and disadvantages of the 'authorial' approach to reviewing literature?
3. Why can it sometimes be difficult to work with highly specified protocols when including qualitative research in a review?

Recommended reading

For practical, structured, policy-oriented guides to systematic review methods with useful critique and commentary, the following are recommended:

Gough, D., Oliver, S. and Thomas J. (2012) *An Introduction to Systematic Reviews*. London: Sage.
Petticrew, M. and Roberts, H. (2006) *Systematic Reviews in the Social Sciences: A Practical Guide*. Oxford: Blackwell.

For a recent critique of the evidence-based movement in healthcare and how it might be re-imagined: Greenhalg, T., Howick, J. and Maskrey, N. (2014) 'Evidence based medicine: a movement in crisis?', *BMJ*, 348: g3725.

For a research agenda on the development of methods for systematic review of complex interventions: Noyes, J., Gough, D., Lewin, S., Mayhew, A., Michie, S., Pantoja, T., Petticrew, M., Pottie, K., Rehfuess, E., Shemilt, I. and Shepperd S. (2013) 'A research and development agenda for systematic reviews that ask complex questions about complex interventions', *Journal of Clinical Epidemiology*, 66 (11), pp.1262-70.

References

Becker, H. S. (2007) *Writing for Social Scientists: How to Start and Finish your Thesis, Book, or Article* (2nd edn). Chicago, IL: University of Chicago Press.

Carroll, C., Booth, A., Leaviss, J. and Rick, J. (2013) '"Best fit" framework synthesis: refining the method', *BMC Medical Research Methodology*, 13: 37.

Dixon-Woods, M., Agarwal, S., Jones, D., Young, B. and Sutton, A. (2005) 'Synthesising qualitative and quantitative evidence: a review of possible methods', *Journal of Health Services Research and Policy*, 10 (1): 45–53.

Dixon-Woods, M., Cavers, D., Agarwal, S., Annandale, E., Arthur, A., Harvey, J., Hsu, R., Katbamna, S., Olsen, R., Smith, L., Riley, R. and Sutton, A. J. (2006) 'Conducting a critical interpretive synthesis of the literature on access to healthcare by vulnerable groups', *BMC Medical Research Methodology*, 6: 35.

Dixon-Woods, M., Fitzpatrick, R. and Roberts, K. (2001) 'Including qualitative research in systematic reviews: opportunities and problems', *Journal of Evaluation in Clinical Practice*, 7 (2): 125–33.

Dixon-Woods, M., Sutton, A. J., Shaw, R. L., Miller, T., Smith, J., Young, B., Bonas, S., Booth, A. and Jones, D. (2007) 'Appraising qualitative research for inclusion in systematic reviews: a quantitative and qualitative comparison of three methods', *Journal of Health Services Research and Policy*, 12 (1): 42–7.

Evans, I., Thornton, H. and Chalmers, I. (2006) *Testing Treatments: Better Research for Better Healthcare*. London: British Library.

France, E. F., Ring, N., Thomas, R., Noyes, J., Maxwell, M. and Jepson, R. (2014) 'A methodological systematic review of what's wrong with meta-ethnography reporting', *BMC Medical Research Methodology*, 14: 119.

Glass, G. V. (1976) 'Primary, secondary, and meta-analysis of research', *Educational Researcher*, 5 (10): 3–8.

Hammersley, M. (2005) 'Is the evidence-based practice movement doing more good than harm? Reflections on Iain Chalmers' case for research-based policy making and practice', *Evidence & Policy*, 1: 85–100.

Higgins, J. and Green, S. (2011) 'Cochrane handbook for systematic reviews of interventions version 5.1. 0 [updated March 2011]', The Cochrane Collaboration, http://hand book.cochrane.org/ (accessed 10 December 2015).

Lee, R. P., Hart, R. I., Watson, R. M. and Rapley, T. (2015) 'Qualitative synthesis in practice: some pragmatics of meta-ethnography', *Qualitative Research*, 15 (3): 334–50.

MacLure, M. (2005) '"Clarity bordering on stupidity": where's the quality in systematic review?', *Journal of Education Policy*, 20 (4): 393–416.

NHS Centre for Reviews and Dissemination (2009) *Systematic Reviews: CRD's Guidance for Undertaking Reviews in Health Care*. York: Centre for Reviews and Dissemination.

Pearson, K. (1904) 'Report on certain enteric fever inoculation statistics', *British Medical Journal*, 2: 1243–6.

Silverman, D. (2007) *A Very Short, Fairly Interesting and Reasonably Cheap Book about Qualitative Research*. London: Sage.

Strauss, A. L. and Corbin, J. M. (1990) *Basics of Qualitative Research: Grounded Theory Procedures and Techniques*. Newbury Park, CA: Sage.

Thomas, J. and Harden, A. (2008) 'Methods for the thematic synthesis of qualitative research in systematic reviews', *BMC Medical Research Methodology*, 8: 45.

Tong, A., Flemming, K., McInnes, E., Oliver, S. and Craig, J. (2012) 'Enhancing transparency in reporting the synthesis of qualitative research: ENTREQ', *BMC Medical Research Methodology*, 12: 181.

TWENTY FOUR

Secondary Analysis of Qualitative Data

Libby Bishop

About this chapter

Secondary analysis means reusing data created from previous research projects for new purposes. Usually this implies that at least some of the people re-analysing the data were not involved in collecting it. While secondary analysis of quantitative data such as surveys is well established, it has been less common for qualitative data until recently. In this chapter, I will explain various forms of qualitative secondary analysis (QSA), provide tips for getting started, discuss examples of how others have done it, and close with key debates about QSA and its future prospects.

Keywords

secondary analysis, QSA, reuse, data archives, data analysis, qualitative data

INTRODUCTION

Secondary analysis of qualitative data (also called qualitative secondary analysis or QSA) as a method has grown rapidly to become widely practised and accepted (Bishop and Kuula-Lummi, forthcoming). This growth is explained by more general trends promoting openness and sharing such as the open data movement, research funder and journal policies promoting research transparency, and researchers seeing benefits of sharing all manner of resources through social networks. Reusing data can also be a good way to investigate hard to reach populations, such as prisoners (Fielding and Fielding, 2000). It also avoids burdening vulnerable populations, such as those with rare medical conditions (HERG, 2015).

Partly because this is a new area, the terminology is still changing. The most common phrase for this activity is 'secondary analysis'. It is correct, but inelegant. There is also some concern that the word 'secondary' may be interpreted as 'second-class' or less good. So the terms 're-use', 'reuse' and 'reworking' are also fairly common. There have been several attempts to define these terms more precisely (Hammersley, 2010; Irwin and Winterton, 2011). The best way to figure out exactly what QSA is and whether it works is to look at how researchers have reused data, and assess their methods and results. Let's look at one example to get started.

Example 1: School leavers' essays

In 2009, Dawn Lyon and Graham Crow began working with data collected by Ray Pahl and his colleagues in the 1970s about the Isle of Sheppey and held at the UK Data Service. Sheppey is an island in southeast England. Pahl and his team had collected all kinds of data about Sheppey communities – work, education, housing and more. They looked at just a subset of that data: a collection of essays written by school leavers in 1978, and the archived notes from Pahl's preliminary analysis of these data (Lyon and Crow, 2012).

The Pahl collection includes 141 essays written by school leavers at about age 16 in 1978 (52 girls and 89 boys). As an exercise, they had been asked to imagine themselves towards the end of their lives and looking back. They then had to write an essay about how their lives had turned out. These students were not facing an easy future. Unemployment rates were high that time, and even worse for young people, and worse yet on Sheppey. Lyon and Crow conducted a similar exercise with 110 young people in 2010 and were able to compare the two groups of essays.

Some findings were, perhaps, not too surprising. There are many fewer references to apprenticeships in 2010, and fewer young people mention marriage. Nonetheless, the scale of some of the changes is startling: in 1978, no girls wrote about going to university; by 2010, 39 per cent did so. Less hopefully, the numbers who expected to own their own homes declined markedly by 2010. The essays are detailed and imaginative – compelling data indeed.

Pahl wrote only one short magazine article on these essays; they remained an unmined source of data. Even when a famous researcher has written widely, there still may be lots of rich data left to be explored.

VARIED WAYS OF REUSING DATA

Here are just a few of the ways qualitative data are typically reused. There are many more examples in a bibliography at the UK Data Service (UKDS, 2015).

- *Description*: data from previous research can be used to better understand the attributes and behaviour of individuals, groups or societies at the time of the original project. This way of using data is broadly similar to doing a literature review with the benefit of looking at all the data, not just the published extracts. The objective is to build background knowledge, and access to data allows deeper understanding than reading the research results (Bornat, 2005; Gillies and Edwards, 2005).

- *Research design and methodological advancement*: this involves designing a new study or developing a methodology or research tool by studying sampling methods, data collection and fieldwork strategies, and topic guides. Although researchers often publish a section on methods used, researchers' own field-work diaries or analytic notes can offer much insight into the history of the research. Comparing an original interview schedule with how questions were actually asked during an interview can shed light on how interviewers flexibly adjust their questions during a semi-structured interview (Mauthner et al., 1998; Savage, 2010).

- *Re-analysis*: re-analysis asks new questions of the data and makes different interpretations from the original researcher. It approaches the data in ways that were not originally addressed, such as using data for investigating different topics of study. The more in-depth the material, and the more contextualized the raw data, the more possible this becomes. This does not involve attempts to undermine researcher's previous analysis (Thomson et al., 2012; Knight et al., 2015).

- *Re-purposing*: in this approach, the data are re-used, but for a purpose or research question very different from the goals of the original research. For example, Seale and Charteris-Black (2008) used comparative keyword analysis of illness narratives that had been collected for an educational website to study gender effects. Walker (2013) used video of parent–child interactions to investigate children's transgressions and laughter.

- *Learning and teaching*: older 'classic' studies and more contemporary research can provide rich case material for learning and teaching in both research methods and substantive areas across a range of social science disciplines (Bishop, 2012; Haynes and Jones, 2012; Haaker, forthcoming).

HOW TO GET STARTED WITH QSA

As with learning any new skill, it is useful to read about QSA and how others have done it, but eventually, you just have to try it for yourself. Below I have distilled some very practical basic steps for getting started. I am drawing heavily on the work of other researchers and teams with whom I have worked over the years; two of them are described below. That said, research of any kind is not like following a recipe so it would be misleading to set out precise steps. This is one suggested path; you will need to find (or make!) your own.

Timescapes

The Timescapes study used qualitative longitudinal methods to explore how personal and family relationships develop and change over time. The Timescapes project included both collection of primary data and QSA. Some of the points below are from a guide that was developed by Sarah Irwin and Mandy Winterton (2012a).

(Continued)

(Continued)

The Parenting Identities and Practices

The Parenting Identities and Practices (PIP) project is part of the National Centre for Research Methods Narratives of Everyday Lives and Linked Approaches (NOVELLA) programme. The project draws on two studies that use narrative methods to explore migration, parenting and other topics. Transforming Experiences, led by Ann Phoenix, is a psychosocial study of adults looking back on their 'non-normative' childhoods, in that their parents were mostly migrants. Fathering over the Generations, led by Julia Brannen, is a sociological study of fatherhood across three family generations (adapted from Elliott et al., 2013).

Finding data

A major factor enabling qualitative data reuse has been improved services and infrastructure, such as the UK Data Service, which provides access to hundreds of data collections. Recently, over 1,000 qualitative and mixed methods datasets per year were being downloaded from the Service. There has also been growth in qualitative data held in archives and institutional repositories in many parts of the world (Corti, 2011; Neale and Bishop, 2011; Bishop and Kuula-Lummi, forthcoming). As the later examples will show, it is still challenging to locate data, but improvements are rapid, including the pilot phase of a UK research data discovery service (Jisc, 2015).

The big picture – the project and the contexts of data production

The obvious starting point is to ask questions about the original project:

- Why was the project done?
- What were its aims?
- What were the research questions?
- Why were the particular methods chosen?

Addressing these questions helps to uncover why particular methods were used or why topics that seem obvious to you were not studied.

Knowing more about the contexts of data production can also be useful. Even when asked about 'the same' topic, such as fatherhood, the accounts fathers give can be shaped differently if one project emphasized managing family life, whereas another focused on fatherhood as part of male identity.

> we worked across data from two of the Timescapes projects: Work and Family Lives, and Men as Fathers. Within both projects, men were interviewed about aspects of their experiences and identities as fathers. However, in the different project contexts we saw examples of rather different kinds of accounts of fatherhood, even where particular lines of questioning were quite similar. (Irwin and Winterton, 2012a: 3)

Some accounts focused on the practicalities of managing family life. Others were more concerned with issues relating to the social psychological dynamics and social identities.

The best sources of information are often funding applications and published articles. If data are from a repository, all the related project materials may have been assembled into project documentation; this is the case for most of the data collections held at the UK Data Service.

Building an understanding of the sample

As more data become available, the problem becomes not too little but how to choose. It is difficult to know if text, audio or images might be useful without reading, listening or examining them. If you have to read the whole thing to decide, it means being strategic about what to look at.

Irwin and Winterton describe going about this phase using a filtered search. Because some basic socio-demographic data were recorded on every Timescapes participant across all projects, they could select men (and exclude women), in a certain age category, with additional demographic characteristics. They were able to sample selectively for factors such as men accepting a conventional division of labour and those who were much more engaged with daily, hands-on care for their children. Regardless of approach, they conclude:

> it is important to offer clarity and transparency as to why particular cases are chosen to evidence an argument, and to show how they are situated relative to other cases, and how typical they are. (Irwin and Winterton 2012a: 4)

Really getting to know the data

The PIP researchers had a wide range of backgrounds; some had been involved with collecting the original data, but others had not. Only the primary team was permitted access to the audio, but the entire team could read transcripts. They employed a strategy of reading the interviews aloud in the group. This kind of reading risks improperly portraying the original interactions, e.g. by not conveying pauses or inflection, but there were compensations. Reading aloud slowed down the process of analysis. The researchers paused to share what they expected to happen next in the text, then read, then reflected on what actually did (and did not) happen and why their expectations were met or not. This process revealed assumptions – usually unconscious – about what the researchers thought was going on (Thomson et al., 2012; Elliott et al., 2013, Phoenix et al., forthcoming). Moreover, the PIP team shared their analyses with the original interviewer to help prevent misinterpreting the interview.

THREE CASES OF REUSING DATA

In this section, I explore three cases of reusing data. Each case deals with the major issues of QSA: context, sampling and ethics. (I will say more about them later.) It is easier to understand these issues through examples where the abstract concepts are grounded in actual research. These cases demonstrate the richly diverse topics people investigate, from a history of gerontology, to single motherhood, to young people's sense of domestic space. The sampling methods are also varied and well described, which is especially helpful for those learning QSA.

Oral history interviews to study the history of geriatrics

This first case is a history of the medical speciality of geriatrics. Often perceived as a 'poor cousin' in the medical family, the history of geriatrics sheds light on how a new specialization emerged and established a niche in the dominant field. This example also illustrates several issues for reusing data:

- how a new research question can arise from existing data
- how to design research to enable a 'dialogue between these datasets' (Bornat et al., 2012: 10.1)
- identifying the ethical responsibilities secondary analysts have towards the primary researchers whose data they are using.

Getting a new idea from old data

In 1991, Margot Jefferys investigated the origins of geriatrics by conducting oral history interviews with 72 people in various roles, 54 of them geriatricians. Joanna Bornat was editing a book to which Jefferys was contributing a chapter and, checking the interview summaries, was struck by multiple references to Indian or South Asian doctors. Notably, only one of Jefferys' informants had been South Asian, and Bornat wanted to learn more about their experiences.

With her colleagues, Parvati Raghuram and Leroi Henry, Bornat wanted to extend and complement the original work by interviewing South Asian geriatricians. A central aim of this reuse project was to bring forward the experience of South Asian doctors; that had not been part of Jefferys' purpose:

> Her interest had not been postcolonial relationships, nor was she explicitly interested in the South Asian doctors' careers. By going back to her data we were reconceptualizing her findings, introducing an interpretation which took the South Asian doctors from the margins of narratives of the speciality to centre them in the story in a new way. (Bornat et al., 2012)

This example shows how over time, changes in debates about colonialism and race revealed previously unseen features in data, just as river water flowing through a canyon exposes new layers of sedimentation. It would make no sense to criticize earlier geologists for not seeing the previously unexposed layers; the passage of time and water are necessary to be able to tell the more complex, layered story.

How to create a new sample to match an existing one

In order to get the views of South Asian doctors, Bornat et al. needed to define a new sample. One possibility could have been to interview young doctors just entering the profession. This would have been appropriate if the primary focus was on change in the profession over time. Instead, the team wanted to make the two samples easy to compare, so both groups of doctors had to be able to reflect on their lives and geriatrics during the same time period. They needed South Asian doctors who had been practising during the same period as the British white doctors interviewed by Jefferys. They obtained a sample of 40 retired and 20 active doctors qualified in South Asia who had worked or were working in England or Wales. To ensure that at least some of the South Asian doctors were contemporaries of the original sample, participants needed to have started working in the UK before 1976. Gender was also a concern, as all but five of the new sample were men, but this broadly corresponded with the gender mix in the occupation at that time.

An ethical issue

An ethical question arose over the possible harm to the reputation of the primary researcher, Jefferys. Bornat et al. found that some of the interviews had material that, by contemporary standards, might be seen as colonialist or containing racist beliefs held by the interviewees. Moreover, there were subtle indications of Jefferys herself using language that could be seen as 'colluding' in discriminatory language when raising the issue of recruitment of South Asian doctors. The ethical question was how to respect the reputation of the original researcher in the face of discomfiting evidence (Bishop, 2013).

I have described elsewhere the steps the team took to not judge Jefferys by the standards of a more recent era.

> Bornat and her colleagues … set Jefferys' words within the context of what they knew of her other recorded materials, her writings and formal statements, made at the time of the interviews as well as her recent work. They also sought information from other sources about Jefferys as an individual and about the project she had undertaken, for example, by interviewing her son. (Bishop, 2013: 42).

Why did they choose to speak out? I believe it was because the risk of harm was small, many steps were taken to mitigate it, and the value of openness is extremely high. It is a central tenet of academic scholarship and a core value for the research community.

With great sensitivity, Bornat et al. (2012: 10) reflect on parallels between how they approached Jefferys with the prospect of how future researchers might view them:

that she [Jefferys] might also have been aware of the role of posterity in her research is something we can't know and we are conscious that we too, in time, may also be exposed to similar investigation. We hope that in raising ethical issues we are pointing the way towards good practice in re-use while not seeking to limit debate or critical questioning.

Bornat has opened her research to future scrutiny by making these data available for others to use (Bornat, 2013).

Life stories to study single motherhood

April Gallwey relates her use of life stories from the Millennium Memory Bank (MMB) to investigate the experience of single motherhood. The case demonstrates two significant features regarding the reuse of data:

- she documents the painstaking process of assembling the relevant sample of interviews to meet the needs of her research questions
- she sought information about the context of the creation of the MMB and incorporated that understanding into her analysis.

Gallwey's research was conducted for her PhD thesis, demonstrating unequivocally that pre-existing data can be the source of new knowledge. The summary below paraphrases sections of her article (Gallwey, 2013).

Getting research ideas from attending workshops

Gallwey was interested in single motherhood in England in the second half of the twentieth century. It was during an oral history workshop at the British Library where she heard one particularly vivid story – that of Ann Hoad – that convinced her of the potential of this material. The interview was part of the Memorial Memory Bank, and Gallwey began to search for similar data.

Building a sample – one step at a time

Her search was made easier by the British Library's electronic catalogue and the fact that most MMB interviews have content summaries. From her previous research, she knew relevant keywords to use such as 'war widow', 'divorced', 'unmarried mother', 'teenage pregnancy', 'single mother' and 'one-parent family'. Even so, with 6,069 recordings, this took a lot of searching, making further filtering necessary, such as removing divorced but childless women. Each record included characteristics of the women: date of birth, school leaving age, occupation, marital status, geographical location and number of children. She was then able to exclude childless women from the divorced sub-sample.

She constructed a sample of 50 interviews to form five generational cohorts of women born between 1910 and 1971 who became single mothers. These interviews covered all routes into single motherhood, from wartime widowhood to separation, divorce and pregnancy outside marriage. The MMB represents all of the UK and her sub-sample maintained that diversity.

She had relatively strict criteria and, not surprisingly, it was a challenge to find data. By drawing on interviews from several archives, she was able to create a sufficient sample, despite some initial failures. It is important to note that qualitative data holdings, while growing (more below) are still not extensive. Researchers should be realistic and not presume data will exist. On the other hand, as this case shows, persistence can pay off.

Gallwey demonstrates how to search in a rigorous and reflexive manner. She generated a wide range of search terms and used them successfully. However, she was also sensitive to the fact that some terms were more abstract, and thus less likely to show up in interview transcriptions. She was also attentive to the time-boundedness of certain terms, and how changes in classifications, 'single' vs. 'unmarried' woman, had to be understood in the broader context of how women's relationships to the welfare state were being reframed.

Working with, and without, contextual information

Gallwey was surprised, and puzzled, to find very little contextual information about the project in the MMB, especially given its scale of over 6,000 interviews. There were no profiles of the speakers providing key characteristics, such as age, gender and employment. Moreover, apart from one or two articles, there was very little information about how the MMB came to be. The interviews were classified into 16 themes that had been produced by an academic panel primarily as a tool for the interviewers. Gallwey noted the absence of class, gender and ethnicity as themes, which she regarded as core concepts for social analysis. In interviews with scholars associated with the project, several reasons emerged for the omission. The project was not intended only as a research resource, it also had been produced by the BBC for radio documentaries and thus was shaped by the prioritization of entertainment over education in late twentieth-century media. Indeed, part of the reason for focusing on other themes was the sense on the part of the MMB that some themes, such as 'war and work', were of less interest to viewers.

The example highlights very well the role of context and its importance for reuse. Gallwey perceived what she saw as a discrepancy between what she expected, certain kinds of classifications, and what she found. She was persistent, and was fortunate it was possible to persist because people associated with the project design were alive and willing to be interviewed.

Reusing qualitative longitudinal data for methodological reflection

As the cases above demonstrate, new insights are possible from existing data. That said, using existing data to address methodological challenges is equally valid. One example is Sarah Wilson's reuse of a sample from the Siblings and Friends data from the Timescapes project (Wilson, 2014) to reflect on her own methodologies.

Using QSA to think about how you do your own work

The aim of her work was to explore the concepts and methods of the original researchers more fully than would have been possible with only the published sources. The topic was quite specific: the conceptualizations of domestic spaces and how young people understand them. Moreover, Wilson's work to date had focused on young people whose parents misused substances; she wanted to investigate research by others on similar topics who had drawn on a more 'ordinary' sample.

Finding data is hard – new data, old data, any data

Given the quite specific nature of her question, finding suitable data was 'difficult'. She described some of the same problems as Gallwey: no centralized data portal and incomplete documentation. She became acquainted with the Timescapes programme, and one of its projects – Siblings and Friends – had gathered data from young people about their home lives (Siblings and Friends, 2015).

Using this source, Wilson then had to read substantial quantities of data to establish whether or not each case (person) met her requirements. Her experience confirms that of others whom I have helped to locate data: the time needed to find and assess data can be considerable. It is for this reason that I think it is misguided to suggest that QSA will always be faster than collecting original data. It will depend on the complexity of the data and the quality of documentation. The time may be spent searching and assessing, rather than recruiting and negotiating gatekeepers, but whether primary or secondary, qualitative data research takes time. There are no shortcuts.

Another problem Wilson identified was acquiring a comprehensive picture of all the project data available. The Siblings project following young people who had participated in an earlier project. Then two further waves of data collection took place, involving multiple kinds of data. Some forms were typical, such as interviews, questionnaires and essays, but there were also more complex and visual formats (e.g. relational maps, timelines, photos and video). It was a lot of data to absorb, and filtering on personal characteristics was also a challenge, even with excellent cooperation from the Siblings researchers.

In some cases, such information is comprehensively tabulated (the UK Data Service includes data lists with most studies), however, this data may be partial, or not collected at all. There can be legitimate reasons for not making some personal or sensitive information available, namely, protecting participant confidentiality. However, in most cases at least minimal information can be shared, and even made public. Where it cannot, two versions, one limited but public, and one detailed and restricted, can be produced.

Seeing others' work puts your own in a new light

The reading of the Siblings interviews revealed what Wilson saw as omissions in her earlier work (Wilson, 2014: 4.11). For example, homework and extra-curricular activities featured prominently in the Siblings interviews. Wilson realized she did not focus on these topics, and speculates that one possibility might have been funders' 'unexamined assumptions' that such activities were less important or less valued in the 'difficult' lives of the young people in her sample.

Similarly, Wilson learned from the Siblings data that a 'sense of belonging' was not limited to primary homes, but included other family members' and friends' homes. Wilson had reached similar findings with her sample, but the comparative data showed that this inclusive sense of belonging was not limited to children in less advantaged home situations, but in fact was common in 'ordinary' families too.

Thus, reading original research on closely related subjects, but different samples, allowed Wilson to become aware of unconscious assumptions in her own work. She became more deeply reflexive in her sociological research.

REPRISE: CONTEXT AND ETHICS

As the examples above show, the issues of context and ethics recur when doing QSA. These debates are documented in detail elsewhere, so only brief highlights will be provided with references to other sources.

Context – the importance of 'being there'

Some critics of QSA claim that when data are reused without complete context – immersion in the original data collection – that essential features of the data are lost, making it impossible for another researcher to reinterpret the original data. He or she was not at the scene when the data were collected, and lacks what are sometimes called 'head notes' – the tacit experience of being present when data were generated. In this view, the primary researcher has a privileged position to the data by virtue of having 'been there', that is, by having unique knowledge of the original context (Mauthner et al., 1998).

A number of scholars challenge this argument. First, just like everyone else, the primary researchers may make mistakes, even about their own data! 'We should not, of course, assume that what a primary researcher "knows" and "understands", in terms of context, is always right' (Hammersley, 2010: 3.6). Another argument agrees that tacit knowledge is rich, and that no matter how good the notes and records, secondary researchers will never reproduce it. But deriving insights from data does not rely solely on closeness to the data. Researchers' analytical capabilities, what they make of the data, is equally important.

> With Hammersley (2010) we argue that sociological data will support different theoretical understandings, and researchers' presence at data generation is not the final arbiter of the adequacy of such understandings. (Irwin and Winterton, 2012b: 2.5)

There are more practical replies also. First, if primary researchers describe and document their work thoroughly, this can go a long way towards providing adequate context for later researchers. Moreover, context is always dependent on the actual research question being asked and the type of data. In many cases the complete context of the original work is less relevant to the new enquiry if there is an entirely different question or methods posited in the later research (Bishop, 2006; Bishop and Kuula-Lummi, forthcoming).

Ethical issues – balancing multiple responsibilities

Critics of QSA pose ethical challenges, primarily around the risks of harm to participants from misuse of data. Much qualitative data is collected through personal interactions, often involving relationships of mutual trust. Even if the primary researchers ask participants to give their consent for other researchers to use the data, is that enough? Can consent for future, unknown research projects be regarded as 'informed consent', as required by many ethical guidelines (Parry and Mauthner, 2005; Bishop, 2009; Broom, 2009)?

One response reconsiders the requirements of what it means to be 'informed' (see Ryen in this volume). In such an approach, researchers give participants information about the ways data may be used, who typical re-users may be, and the security measures in place protecting their confidentiality (Neale and Bishop, 2012). Similar strategies, called generic or enduring consent, are common for genetic data and biobanks (Millet and O'Leary, 2015). Data archives and repositories provide resources and advice to researchers about how to talk to participants about reuse. But limitations have to be acknowledged: it is not possible to specify future research questions or outcomes in detail, and future researchers may interpret data differently, as we saw in the geriatrics case

QSA advocates also point out that in fact, re-using data can be part of fulfilling broader ethical responsibilities. These responsibilities include ensuring participants' data is used as widely as possible, and duties to be transparent about research (Neale and Bishop 2012).

CHAPTER SUMMARY

No method is suitable for every question, and QSA is no exception. For example, to use ethnographic data such as field notes from observational study for a question closely related to the original project might be problematic. Or if pursued, it would be best to do so in collaboration with at least some of the primary researchers (Morrow et al., 2014).

That said, I believe one of the strengths of QSA is that it often enables richer and more creative comparative work than is otherwise possible. Samples for qualitative research need not be large, but it can be a challenge to identify, locate and recruit a theoretically relevant sample. With QSA, it can be possible to add a comparative dimension – across time or geography – and as Irwin and Winterton (2012a) say, bring them 'into conversation' with one another.

FUTURE PROSPECTS

Consent for data reuse is a challenging area, affecting many types of data. For example, most tweets are public, yet there is an ongoing debate about both consent and anonymization for tweets and other social media (COSMOS, 2015). The usual forms of consent are infeasible for administrative, social media and other data – much research would be prohibitively expensive or impossible should consent be required for all cases. However, participants' rights to privacy must be respected. The extent of consent required for data reuse is being reviewed as part of revisions to data protection regulation in Europe (European Council, 2015). There are no easy answers.

In the face of challenges, there are many positive signs for QSA. Publications involving qualitative data and secondary analysis have increased nearly every year from 1995 (Bishop and Kuula-Lummi, forthcoming) and the Economic and Social Research Council continues to fund proposals that reuse data, including qualitative data. I used to have to search hard to find high quality examples of reuse; now there are so many I cannot keep up with all the new publications. That is a good problem to have.

ACKNOWLEDGEMENTS

Writing this chapter allowed me to read the work of many friends and colleagues who do QSA. My work would not be possible without that community. I would like to thank Maureen Haaker (University Campus Suffolk and UK Data Service) and the many others whose research I have cited here for their comments on earlier drafts.

Study questions

1. Get a taste of looking at someone else's data. Log in to QualiBank here: http://discover.ukdata service.ac.uk/QualiBank. The School Leavers and The Edwardians are two open collections. Look at one example of each.

   o   What are your reactions to the essay?
   o   What can you tell about the interviewer's approach after reading a few pages from The Edwardians?

2. What do you think about the value of 'being there' when reusing data? Do you think it is necessary, or not? Why?

3. Identify an ethical issue that might arise when using someone else's data? How might you resolve the issue?

Recommended online resources

Much QSA is done in teams, often with a mix of primary researchers and those new to the data. In some – but not all – cases, the teams produce, share and investigate data held in a dedicated repository. The summaries below have been adapted from their websites.

The Health Experiences Researcher Group (HERG) at Oxford has conducted qualitative interviews with people with varied health conditions; summaries have been published at: www.healthtalkonline.org

Inventing Adulthoods is a qualitative longitudinal study of over 100 young people, following them from their teens to their early thirties. Up to seven interviews with each participant provide a rich body of data about growing up in the twenty-first century. The anonymized digital interview transcripts for 50 participants are available at the UK Data Service or the Timescapes Repository at Leeds University, along with non-digital questionnaires and other written assignments: www.restore.ac.uk/inventingadulthoods/

NOVELLA (Narratives of Varied Everyday Lives and Linked Approaches) looked at habits and routines of families, because families often shape these practices. Some of the project's aims were to develop innovative methods in combining QSA and narrative approaches, linking quantitative longitudinal data with narratives, and matching narratives across studies: www.novella.ac.uk/about.html

The Timescapes projects explored how personal and family relationships develop and change over time. The broad aim was to scale up and promote qualitative longitudinal research, and it achieved this aim through a network of empirical projects, the creation of a new repository at the University of Leeds, and a secondary analysis programme: www.timescapes.leeds.ac.uk/

References

Bishop, L. (2006) 'A proposal for archiving context for secondary analysis', *Methodological Innovations Online*, 1 (2): 10–20. www.methodologicalinnovations.org.uk/wp-content/uploads/2013/07/2.-Bishop-pp10-20.pdf (accessed 23 September 2015).

Bishop, L. (2009) 'Ethical sharing and reuse of qualitative data', *Australian Journal of Social Issues*, 44 (3): 255–72.

Bishop, L. (2012) 'Using archived qualitative data for teaching: practical and ethical considerations', *International Journal of Social Research Methodology* (Special Issue: Perspectives on Working with Archived Textual and Visual Material in Social Research), 15 (4): 341–50. doi: 10.1080/13645579.2012.688335.

Bishop, L. (2013) 'The value of moral theory for addressing ethical questions when reusing qualitative data', *Methodological Innovations Online* (Special Issue: Ethical Issues in Using Archived Data), 8 (2): 36–51. www.methodologicalinnovations.org.uk/wp-content/uploads/2013/12/3.-Bishop.pdf (accessed 23 September 2015).

Bishop, L. and Kuula-Lummi, A. (forthcoming) 'Developments in reusing digital qualitative data in the UK and beyond', *Digital Representations: Opportunities for Re-using and Mining Digital Qualitative Data and Enhanced Publishing*, special issue of *Sage Online*.

Bornat, J. (2005) 'Recycling the evidence: different approaches to the reanalysis of gerontological data', *Forum: Qualitative Social Research*, 6 (1): Art 42.

Bornat, J. (2013) *Overseas-Trained South Asian Doctors and the Development of Geriatric Medicine, 1955–2000*. [data collection] UK Data Service. SN: 7264, http://dx.doi.org/10.5255/UKDA-SN-7264-1.

Bornat, J., Raghuram, P. and Henry, L. (2012) 'Revisiting the archives: a case study from the history of geriatric medicine', *Sociological Research Online*, 17 (2). www.socresonline.org.uk/17/2/11.html (accessed 23 September 2015).

Broom, A., Cheshire, L. and Emmison, M. (2009) 'Qualitative researchers understandings of their practice and the implications for data archiving and sharing', *Sociology*, 43 (6): 1163–80, doi:10.1177/0038038509345704.

Corti, L. (2011) 'The European landscape of qualitative social research archives: methodological and practical issues', *Forum Qualitative Sozialforschung/Forum: Qualitative Social Research* [S.l.], 12 (3). www.qualitative-research.net/index.php/fqs/article/view/1746 (accessed 23 September 2015).

COSMOS (Collaborative Online Social Media Observatory) (2015) *Ethics Resource Guide*. www.cs.cf.ac.uk/cosmos/ethics-resource-guide/ (accessed 23 September 2015).

Elliott, H., Brannen, J., Phoenix, A., Barlow, A., Morris, P., Smart, C., Smithson, J. and Bauer, E. (2013) 'Analysing qualitative data in groups', NCRM NOVELLA Working Paper, Institute of Education, August. http://eprints.ncrm.ac.uk/3172/1/jointanalysis paper200813.pdf (accessed 23 September 2015).

European Council (2015) 'Data protection: council agrees on a general approach'. www.consilium.europa.eu/en/press/press-releases/2015/06/15-jha-data-protection/ (accessed 23 September 2015).

Fielding, N. G. and Fielding, J. L. (2000) 'Resistance and adaptation to criminal identity: using secondary analysis to evaluate classic studies of crime and deviance', *Sociology*, 34 (4): 671–89.

Gallwey, A. (2013) 'The rewards of using archived oral histories in research: the case of the Millennium Memory Bank', *Oral History*, 41 (1): 37–50.

Gillies, V. and Edwards, R. (2005) 'Secondary analysis in exploring family and social change: addressing the issue of context', *Forum: Qualitative Social Research* 6 (1): Art. 44.

Haaker, M. (forthcoming) 'Developing research-led teaching: two case studies of practical data reuse in the classroom', *Sage Open*.

Hammersley, M. (2010) 'Can we re-use qualitative data via secondary analysis?', *Sociological Research Online*, 15 (1). www.socresonline.org.uk/15/1/5.html (accessed 23 September 2015).

Haynes, J. and Jones, D. (2012) 'A tale of two analyses: the use of archived qualitative data', *Sociological Research Online*, 17 (2). www.socresonline.org.uk/17/2/1.html (accessed 23 September 2015).

HERG (2015) Health Experiences Research Group. The HERG Data Archive. www.phc.ox.ac.uk/research/health-experiences/news-and-courses/news (accessed 23 September 2015).

Irwin, S. and Winterton, M. (2011) 'Debates in qualitative secondary analysis: critical reflections', Timescapes Working Paper No. 4, ISSN: 1758 3349.

Irwin, S. and Winterton, M. (2012a) *Qualitative Secondary Analysis: A Guide to Practice*. Timescapes Methods Guides Series, Guide No. 19. www.timescapes.leeds.ac.uk/assets/files/methods-guides/timescapes-irwin-secondary-analysis.pdf (accessed 23 September 2015).

Irwin, S. and Winterton, M. (2012b) 'Qualitative secondary analysis and social explanation', *Sociological Research Online*, 17 (2). www.socresonline.org.uk/17/2/4.html (accessed 23 September 2015).

Jisc (2015) 'UK research data discovery: making research data discoverable'. www.jisc.ac.uk/rd/projects/uk-research-data-discovery (accessed 23 September 2015).

Knight, A. Brannen, J. and O'Connell, R. (2015) 'Re-using family history sources on food and family life in World War One', *Oral History*, 43 (1): 63–72.

Lyon, D. and Crow, G. (2012) 'The challenges and opportunities of re-studying community on Sheppey: young people's imagined futures', *Sociological Review*, 60 (3): 498–517.

Mauthner, N., Parry, O. and Backett-Milburn, K. (1998) 'The data are out there, or are they? Implications for archiving and revisiting qualitative data', *Sociology*, 32 (4): 733–45.

Millett, S. and O'Leary, P. (2015) 'Revisiting consent for health information databanks', *Research Ethics*. doi:10.1177/1747016115587964.

Morrow, V., Boddy, J. and Lamb, R. (2014) 'The ethics of secondary data analysis: learning from the experience of sharing qualitative data from young people and their families in an international study of childhood poverty', NCRM NOVELLA Working Paper. London: Institute of Education. www.younglives.org.uk/publications/WP/ethics-secondary-data-analysis-novella/novella_morrow-et-al_wp (accessed 23 September 2015).

Neale, B. and Bishop, L. (2011) 'Qualitative and qualitative longitudinal resources in Europe', *IASSIST Quarterly (IQ)*, 34 (3–4) and 35 (1–2): 6–11.

Neale, B. and Bishop, L. (2012) 'The Timescapes archive: a stakeholder approach to archiving qualitative longitudinal data', *Qualitative Research*, 12 (1): 53–65

Parry, O. and Mauthner, N. (2005) 'Back to basics: who re-uses qualitative data and why?', *Sociology*, 39 (2): 337–42.

Phoenix, A., Brannen, J., Elliott, H., Smithson, J., Barlow, A., Morris, P., Smart, C. and Bauer, E. (forthcoming) 'Group analysis in practice: narrative approaches to qualitative data', *Forum for Qualitative Research*.

Savage, M. (2010) *Identities and Change in Britain since 1940: The Politics of Method*. Oxford: Oxford University Press.

Seale, C. and Charteris-Black, J. (2008) 'The interaction of age and gender in illness narratives', *Ageing and Society*, 28 (7): 1025–45. http://dx.doi.org/10.1017/S0144686X0800737X.

Siblings and Friends (2015) 'Siblings and Friends: the changing nature of children's lateral relationships'. www.timescapes.leeds.ac.uk/research/siblings-friends/ (accessed 23 September 2015).

Thomson, R., Moe, A., Thorne, B. and Nielsen, H. (2012) 'Situated affect in travelling data: tracing meaning-making in qualitative research', *Qualitative Inquiry* 18 (4): 310–22.

Walker, G. (2013) 'Young children's use of laughter after transgressions', *Research on Language and Social Interaction*, 46 (4): 363–82. doi:10.1080/08351813.2013.810415.

Wilson, S. (2014) 'Using secondary analysis to maintain a critically reflexive approach to qualitative research', *Sociological Research Online*, 19 (3). www.socresonline.org.uk/19/3/21.html (accessed 23 September 2015).

UKDS (UK Data Service) (2015) *Reusing Qualitative Data – Reuse Articles*. http://ukdata service.ac.uk/use-data/secondary-analysis/reusing-qualitative-data/reuse-articles (accessed 23 September 2015).

TWENTY FIVE
Validity in Qualitative Research
Anssi Peräkylä

About this chapter

The validity of research concerns the interpretation of observations: whether or not the inferences that the researcher makes are supported by the data, and sensible in relation to earlier research. This chapter describes processes of validation in conversation analysis, ethnography and interviews. In discussing validity, examples drawn from conversation analysis serve as a point of departure; the perspective arising from them is then applied to other modes of qualitative research. Validation issues include the analysis of the next speaker's interpretation of the preceding action as an instance of validation of the researcher's interpretations, deviant case analysis, specifying with reference to data the claims concerning the relevance of an institutional context of interaction, comparisons within and between institutional settings, generalizing results of case studies as possibilities of social interaction, as well as use of quantitative techniques. At a more general level, the considerations of validity in all qualitative research are the same, involving meticulous testing and consideration of the credibility of analytic claims.

Keywords

validity, deviant cases, comparisons, generalization, quantification

The aim of social science is to produce descriptions of a social world – not just any descriptions, but descriptions that in some controllable way correspond to the social world that is being described. Even though all descriptions are bound to a particular perspective and therefore represent the reality rather than reproduce it (Hammersley, 1992), it is possible to describe social interaction in ways that can be subjected to empirical testing. *Reliability* and *validity* are the technical terms that refer to the objectivity and credibility of research.

In research practice, enhancing objectivity is a very concrete activity. It involves:

- assuring the accuracy and inclusiveness of research data (reliability)
- testing the credibility of the analytic claims that are being made about those recordings (validity).

The researcher's efforts to ensure validity take different shapes according to the type of data on which the research is based. In interview research, one key question of validity is whether the views expressed by the interviewees reflect their experiences and opinions outside the interview situation, or whether they are an outcome of the interview situation itself (see Silverman, 2010: 225–9). In observational research, on the other hand, one key issue is the reconstructive nature of the researcher's field notes and descriptions based upon them, i.e. that the descriptions to a degree are bound to represent the researcher's (and not the participants') cultural and cognitive perspectives (Hammersley and Atkinson, 2007: 203–5; Gobo, 2008).

This chapter will deal with issues of validity in research based on audio or video recordings and transcripts, in interview-based research and in ethnography. I began my own research career as an ethnographer (Peräkylä, 1989). However, for the last two decades, I have employed conversation analysis – an approach which uses recordings to analyse talk in interaction (Peräkylä, 1995; and Heritage in this volume). In discussing different dimensions of validity, I will therefore use CA as a point of departure, and then expand the discussion to comprise interview research and ethnography. I will show that even though specific questions concerning validity are to a degree different in other qualitative methods, the basic concerns, as well as many techniques for ensuring validity, are the same.

WHAT IS VALIDITY?

The validity of research concerns the interpretation of observations: whether or not 'the researcher is calling what is measured by the right name' (Kirk and Miller, 1986: 69; see also Guba and Lincoln, 2005: 205–9; Silverman, 2010: 275–86). In discussions about validity, especially in the context of quantitative research, there is an underlying background assumption about a separation between the 'raw' observations and the issues that these observations stand for or represent. Responses to questionnaires, for example, can be more or less valid representations of underlying social phenomena, such as the respondents' attitudes or values (see Bryman, 2004: 72–4). In conversation analysis, questions of validity are articulated in a rather different way. The core aim of conversation analytical research is to investigate talk-in-interaction, not as a representation of other social phenomena, but as a phenomenon in its own right. This commitment to naturalistic description of interaction gives a distinctive shape to the issues of validation in CA. These include:

- the transparency of analytic claims
- validation through 'next turn'
- deviant case analysis
- questions about the institutional character of interaction
- the generalizability of conversation analytic findings
- the use of statistical techniques.

Key points

- The researcher's interpretations of observations are valid when they are in a credible and demonstrable way based on the data.
- Even though the term 'validity' is not used by all qualitative researchers, the concern for credibility of interpretations is the same in all strands of qualitative research.
- Many of the concrete techniques to assure validity are shared by different strands of qualitative research.

THE TRANSPARENCE OF ANALYTIC CLAIMS

The results of (good) conversation analytic research exhibit, in a positive manner, what Kirk and Miller (1986: 22) called *apparent validity*: once you have read them, you are convinced that they are transparently true. A conversational activity called 'fishing' may serve as an example. Anita Pomerantz showed in a classical paper published in 1980 how participants in a conversation can indirectly 'fish' for information from one another by telling what they themselves know. Descriptions of events displaying their producer's 'limited access' to the relevant facts may work as a device for inviting the other party to disclose his or her authorized version of the same issues (assuming, of course, that the other party is in a position of having privileged access to the relevant facts). Such dynamics are at work in cases like the following (see Appendix for transcription conventions):

Extract 1

1 B: Hello::.
2 A: HI:::.
3 B: Oh:hi:: 'ow are you Agne::s,
4 A: Fi:ne. Yer line's been busy.
5 B: Yeuh my fu (hh)- .hh my father's wife called me
6 ..hh So when she calls me::, .hh I can always talk
7 fer a long time. Cuz she c'n afford it'n I can't.
8 hhhh heh .ehhhhhh

(Pomerantz, 1980: 195)

In Extract 1 above, the description based on limited access to relevant facts given by A (bolded) works as what Pomerantz called 'a fishing device', successfully eliciting B's insider's report in the next turn. By telling her observations about the line having been busy, A makes it relevant for B to disclose to whom she was talking.

The description of an activity like 'fishing' tends to 'ring a bell' as soon as anyone stops to think about it. 'Fishing' is something in which everybody has participated in different roles. But until Pomerantz's article, this activity had not been described formally. The results of Pomerantz's analysis are very simple. Her argument is transparently true, or, in Kirk and Miller's (1986) terms, it has a genuine 'apparent validity'.

Arguably, something like apparent validity is associated to the results of all credible qualitative research. Silverman (2015) quotes Riessman's personal communication: 'Every reader has had the experience of encountering a piece of research and thinking "but of course ..." even when the argument an author was making was counterintuitive'. Together with Riessman and Silverman, we need to ask where this 'of course' comes from.

VALIDATION THROUGH 'NEXT TURN'

Even though the meaning of any expression, if considered in isolation, is extremely open-ended, any utterance that is produced in talk-in-interaction will be locally interpreted by the participants of that interaction. In the first place, their interpretation is displayed in the next actions after the utterance. Hence, any interpretations that conversation analysts may suggest can be subjected to the 'proof procedure' outlined by Sacks et al. (1974: 728–9): the next turn will show whether the interactants themselves treat the utterance in ways that are in accordance with the analyst's interpretation.

Therefore in Extract 1 shown above, the utterance produced by B in lines 5–8 provides a proof procedure for the interpretation suggested by Pomerantz concerning A's turn in line 4. (What Pomerantz suggested was that 'telling my side' (what A did in line 4) can operate as a 'fishing device', which indirectly elicits an authoritative version of the events from the interlocutor.) And as we see, Pomerantz's interpretation passes the test: in lines 5–8, B gives her first-hand account of what had happened.

In much everyday conversation analytic work, things are not as nice and simple as in Extract 1: the next turn may be ambiguous in relation to the action performed in the preceding turn. However, the 'proof procedure' provided by the next turn remains the primordial criterion of validity that must be used as much as possible in all conversation analytic work.

In a narrow and technical sense, validation through next turn is a procedure that is used in CA only, because only in CA, the data is organized strictly in terms of turns at talk. However, in a broader sense, the same insight applies to other modes of qualitative research, and especially interviews. Paying close attention to the ways in which interactants treat each other's utterances should be an essential aspect of the analysis of interview data. As Rapley (2004) and Silverman (2015) point out, interviewers and interviewees are inevitably engaged in collaborative meaning-making. Questions, even the very open-ended invitations to tell about 'such and such' inevitably guide the interviewees, as do the interviewer's reactions to answers (for example by treating an answer as sufficient, or inviting more talk through minimal feedbacks or requests for specification). Recognizing this sequential context of descriptions, accounts and categories, is of utmost importance in securing the validity of interpretations in interview research.

DEVIANT CASE ANALYSIS

By examining the relations between successive turns of talk, conversation analysts aim at establishing *regular patterns* of interaction (Heritage, 1995). The patterns concern relations between actions (such as the relations between 'telling my side' and 'giving an authoritative report' in the case of 'fishing' described above). After having established a pattern, the analyst's next task is to search for and examine *deviant cases*: cases where 'things go differently' – most typically, cases where an element of the suggested pattern is not associated with the other expected elements.

The deviant case analysis in CA closely resembles the technique of 'analytic induction' often used in ethnographic studies (see Silverman, 2015). For the analyst, those cases that do not fit the inductively constructed pattern are deviant. Rather than putting aside these discrepant cases, the analyst is encouraged to focus particular attention on them.

In her paper on 'fishing', Pomerantz (1980: 186–7) presents a deviant case in which a description of events displaying its producer's 'limited access' does *not* lead the other party to disclose her authorized version of the event:

Extract 2

```
1   A: ...dju j'see me pull us?=
2   B: =.hhh No:. I wz trying you all day. en the line
3   wz busy fer like hours
4   A: ohh:::::, oh:::::, .hhhhhh We::ll, hh I'm g'nna
5   c'm over in a little while help yer brother ou:t
6   B: Goo:d
7   A: Goo.hhh Cuz I know he needs some he::lp,
8   ((mournfully))
9   B: .hh Ye:ah. Yeh he'd mention' that tihday.=
10  A: =M-hm,=
11  B: .hhh Uh:m, .tlk.hhh Who wih yih ta:lking to.
```

(Pomerantz, 1980: 186-7)

In Extract 2 above, B reports her experience about A's line having been busy (lines 2–3). In terms of the interactional pattern identified by Pomerantz, this kind of telling should make relevant a subsequent disclosure of the details of the event by the other, more knowledgeable party. In the extract above, however, this does not happen. Instead, A shifts the topic in her subsequent turn (lines 4–5). Therefore, within the framework of the analysis of 'fishing', we can consider Extract 2 as a deviant case.

Clayman and Maynard (1994) have outlined three different ways that deviant cases, like Extract 2, can be dealt with:

1. Sometimes deviant cases can be shown to exhibit the interactants' orientation to the *same* considerations and normative orientations that produce the 'regular' cases. In those cases, something in the conduct of the participants discloses that they, too, treat the case as one involving a departure from the expected course of events. If the deviant cases show this kind of property, they provide *additional support* for the analyst's initial claim that the regularities found in the first phase of the data analysis 'are methodically produced and ori- ented to by the participants as normative organizations of action' (Heritage, 1988: 131). Extract 2 above is an example of this type of deviant case. After A has failed to respond to B's initial 'fishing' turn by an authorized report of the events, B asks directly to whom A had been talking (line 10). Through her question, she openly requests the information which the fishing device (lines 2-3), according to Pomerantz's analysis, solicited indirectly. This shift to open information seeking after an unsuccessful 'fishing' attempt indirectly confirms B's initial orientation to the 'fishing' as a device which can be used in indirect solicitation of information.

2. However, there are deviant cases that cannot be integrated within the analysts' construction of the partic- ipants' orientations that normally produce the regular cases. In dealing with these cases, the analyst may need to change his or her construction of the participants' orientations. A classic example is Schegloff's (1968) analysis of a single deviant case in his corpus of 500 telephone call openings. In this single case, unlike the other 499, the caller spoke first. The analysis of that single case led Schegloff to abandon his initial hypothesis (according to which there is a norm obligating the answerer to speak first) and to recon- ceptualize the very first moves of telephone calls in terms of the adjacency pair 'summons (telephone ringing)-answer'. In the deviant case, the answerer did not produce the relevant second pair part, and, accordingly, the caller reissued the summons by speaking first.

3. Some deviant cases cannot be integrated either into the existing or into a reconceptualized hypothesis concerning the participants' orientations (Clayman and Maynard, 1994). In these cases, an explanation can be sought from the individual contingencies of the single case. Normative orientations or strategic considerations other than those that usually inform the production of the pattern may be invoked by the participants in single cases, and these other orientations or considerations may explain the deviance.

Just as in CA, deviant case analysis is a central part of validation in other types of qualita- tive research. ethnography and interview-based research. The idea of deviant case analysis originates in grounded theory (Glaser and Strauss, 1967) and it is a central part of the ana- lytic induction – a procedure used in ethnography (Gobo, 2009). Therefore, in any strand of qualitative study, the researcher should consider deviant cases not as a nuisance, but as a treasure. The meticulous analysis of those cases gives impetus, strength and rigour to the development of the analytic arguments.

VALIDITY OF CLAIMS CONCERNING THE INSTITUTIONAL CONTEXT

In both qualitative and quantitative research, a central dimension of validity involves the relations between theoretical concepts and the observations that are supposed to represent those concepts. 'Construct validity' is a term that is often used in this context (Kirk and Miller, 1986: 22; Bryman, 2004: 73). The primary emphasis that CA places on naturalistic description de-intensifies the relevance of many ordinary concerns of construct validity. However, the expansion of conversation analytic research on institutional interaction (see Arminen, 2005; Heritage and Clayman, 2010; Heritage in this volume) has reinforced the need to consider the relation between observations and concepts also in conversation analytic studies.

In conversation analytic research on institutional interaction, a central question of validity is this: what grounds does the researcher have for claiming that the talk he or she is focusing on is in any way 'connected to' some institutional framework? The fact that a piece of interaction takes place in a hospital or in an office, for example, does not *per se* determine the institutional character of that particular interaction (Drew and Heritage, 1992: 18–21). Institutional roles, tasks and arrangements may or may not be present in any particular interactions; they may or may not be present at particular *moments* in particular interactions. If they are, the conversation analytic programme presupposes their presence is observable to the participants and the analyst alike.

Schegloff (1987, 1991) points out that there are indefinitely many aspects of context potentially available for any interaction: we may categorize one another on the basis of gender, age, social class, education, occupation, income, race and so on, and we may understand the setting of our interaction accordingly. In the momentary unfolding of interaction, Schegloff argues, 'the parties, singly and together, select and display in their conduct which of the indefinitely many aspects of context they are making relevant, or are invoking, for the immediate moment' (1987: 219).

There is a danger of 'importing' institutional context to data. The professional analyst may be tempted to assume, without going into the details of data, that this or that feature of talk is an indication of a particular context (such as 'medical authority' or 'professional dominance') having affected the interaction. Such stipulation for context may, Schegloff (1991: 24–5) argues, result in the analysis being terminated prematurely, so that the inherent organization within the talk is not thoroughly understood.

The question about the institutional context of interaction is equally important in inter-view studies, but it takes somewhat different forms than in CA. First, it is important for the researchers to acknowledge that *interview itself* is an institutional context. Institutional identities of interviewer and interviewee are made relevant by parties of the interview. Anything that the participants say about *other* institutions (those that they are talking about, such as medicine, education, business or family), they say, as it were, under the auspices of the institution of interview. Adopting the perspective arising from Schegloff (1991) and Silverman (2013), we might say that the interview as an institution is *procedurally consequential* for the data produced. Therefore, the interpretation of the data needs to be sensitive to the institution of interview.

Another important issue pertaining to institutional context in interview studies involves the multiple identities that can be invoked in interview talk (Holstein and Gubrium, 1995;

Silverman, 2013). Talking as a nurse, say, or as a patient is not the same all the time: the identities of nurses and patients alike (and any institutional roles and identities) can have different facets. For example, in my own study on caring for the dying, the talk of both hospital staff and patients vacillated between identities oriented to the medical realities, everyday realities and the psychological realities of emotion and cognition (Peräkylä, 1989). It is the challenge of the analysis of interview data to recognize such different institutional identities, and to show how they are made use of in the management of the interview situation, as well as in the management of the social situations that are referred to in the interview talk.

GENERALIZABILITY OF RESEARCH FINDINGS

A crucial dimension of validity in any research concerns the generalizability of findings (Bryman, 2004: 76–7, 284–5). Owing to their work-intensive character, many conversation analytic studies are based on relatively small databases. How widely can the results, derived from relatively small samples, be generalized?

In studies of ordinary conversation (everyday interactions outside specific institutional settings), the baseline assumption is that the results are or should be generalizable to the whole domain of ordinary conversations, and to a certain extent even across linguistic and cultural boundaries. Cross-linguistic and cross-cultural comparisons are being done to elaborate this (Stivers et al., 2009; Enfield et al., 2012).

In conversation analytical study of institutional interaction, the problem is posed in different terms. Do the findings of a particular study hold true in settings other than the one that was studied in this particular case? The answer to this question can be articulated in different ways, depending on the institution that has been studied.

Some types of institutional setting are, by now, covered by a set of cumulative CA studies. Primary care medical consultation is a case in point. There are strings of CA studies on different phases of the consultation: opening, verbal and physical examination, diagnosis, treatment recommendation and the like (see Heritage and Maynard, 2006). Any new study on medical consultation can, and has to, reflect its findings in the light of the earlier studies, specifying the results of the earlier ones.

Comparison across institutions is another avenue for generalization. What is being compared can be an action or a practice that can be found in different institutional settings, and which takes somewhat different shapes in these different settings. Ruusuvuori and Voutilainen (2010; see also Voutilainen et al., 2010) compare professionals' responses to patients' emotional expressions in general practice, homeopathy and psychotherapy, showing how the different responses are geared to facilitate the different professional tasks in each setting. Thus, for example, in general practice, the professionals' empathizing utterances are geared to close down the discussion on emotional experiences (and to move on to medical business) whereas in psychotherapy, they project topicalization and further talk of that experience.

Weiste and Peräkylä (2013) investigated formulations – utterances that suggest a gist or upshot of the preceding talk (Heritage and Watson, 1979) – in a study that compared two schools of psychotherapy, cognitive and psychoanalytic. They showed that some types of formulations were used in both strands of psychotherapy (embodying what is called common factors in psychotherapy), while others were used exclusively in one or another type of therapy. In psychoanalysis, the therapists used *relocating formulations* where the client's experiences were transferred to other times and places (by means of, for example, stating that the grief the adult client is now feeling is in fact the same grief that they felt as a child) while the cognitive therapists used *exaggerating formulations* where the therapist rephrased the client's description of problematic experience description in such a way that the experience became absurd and something to be questioned.

It is likely that as the databases and analyses of institutional interaction gradually accumulate, studies like Ruusvuori and Voutilainen's and Weiste and Peräkylä's will become more common. The comparative approach directly tackles the question of generalizability by demonstrating the similarities and differences across a number of settings. For the time being, however, many studies on institutional interaction are more like case studies.

Many case studies on institutional interaction are based on data collected from one or only a few sites. The number of subjects involved in such studies usually is relatively small. There are perhaps two overlapping ways in which issues of generalization can be tackled in case studies. One involves *finding the generic from the particular*: through the study of a single case, the researcher can come up with results that constitute claims or hypotheses regarding the organization of human interaction in a most generic level. Some studies by Charles Goodwin are a case in point. In studies that focus on particular occasions in interaction, such as a schoolchild doing homework with her father (2007), students and scholars undertaking archeological excavation in a field school (2003a, 2014) or an aphasic man communicating without almost any words (1995, 2014), Goodwin shows 'the constellation of language, environment, body and action' in bringing about joint attention, action packages and, ultimately, human social and cognitive worlds (see especially Goodwin, 2007: 61). In other words, Goodwin is not primarily trying to tell us what is peculiar in doing homework, archeological excavation or even the aphasic man's communication. Instead, he uses activities in these settings as specimens of the ways in which humans (in general) employ the resources of language, body and physical environment in bringing about their shared worlds that they attend to and know about. In this way, we might say, Goodwin finds the generic from the particular.

The other way to tackle the problem of generalization in case studies involves the notion of *possibility*. In terms of the traditional 'distributional' understanding of generalizability, case studies on institutional interaction cannot offer much. Studying one or only a few sites does not warrant conclusions concerning similarities in the professionals' and their clients' conduct in other settings that may be different in ways that cannot be specified without studying them. The concept of possibility, however, gives a new perspective to this. *Social practices that are possible*, i.e. *possibilities of language use*, are the central objects of all conversation analytic case studies on interaction in particular institutional settings. The possibility of various practices can be considered generalizable even if the practices are not necessarily actualized in similar ways across different settings. The study can show *how* the specific practices are made possible, by the participants skilful use of the linguistic and interactional resources (see Peräkylä, 1995).

As for ethnography and interview research, the questions of generalizability are as pressing as conversation analytical case studies. The ethnographer and the interview researcher can also resort to 'theoretical sampling' (Glaser and Strauss, 1967): as the coding of the data proceeds and hypotheses emerge, the researcher can return to the field to make new observations or interviews in settings that can allow for testing the emerging hypotheses.

Key points

- Accumulation of research results concerning a particular institutional setting can lead to generalizable results.
- Systematic comparison of interactional practices across different settings can enhance generalizability.
- It is also possible to find generic properties of interaction through detailed case studies, and to show, in a generalizable way, how highly context-bound practices are made possible.

QUANTIFICATION

Use of large databases and quantification involves another kind of strategy for ensuring the generalizability (and also other aspects of the validity) of the conversation analytical research findings. As Stivers (2015) argued in her recent review, conversation analysis involves inherently analytic procedures – such as classification of interactional events on the basis of position and composition of utterances – that make it amenable for quantitative applications perhaps more than many other qualitative approaches (see also Heritage in this book).

Quantification means, basically, coding and counting of interactional behaviours. In CA based quantitative research, the codes are based on qualitative analysis of composition and sequential location of utterances, initially pursued by means of more 'traditional' CA (Stivers, 2015). Thus, for example, in Stivers and Majid's (2007) study on racial bias in routine paediatric medical consultations, the coding was based on CA analysis of the verbal and non-verbal ways of addressee selection. The statistical analysis of the coded behaviours showed that black children and Latino children of low-education parents were less likely to be selected to answer questions than their white peers of the same age irrespective of education. Thus, there was an implicit race bias in the doctor's way of conducting interaction.

Some interactional practices are more amenable to coding than other. There are practices that involve such complexity that subsuming them under simple (and mutually exclusive) categories is difficult. Too much relevant insight may be lost, and achieving satisfactory inter-rater reliability may become virtually impossible. The other problem concerns sampling (Silverman, 2015). In order for quantitative analysis to provide a basis for generalization, the selection of cases to be studied should follow adequate statistical procedures so as to ensure their representativeness. In studies of CA, anything like random sampling is rarely possible. If the relation between the sample and the population remains unclear, statistical tests, if they are used, may yield results that should be understood heuristically only.

Quantitative applications make possible for CA to address new kinds of research questions. These can have to do with historical change in interactional practices (e.g. Heritage and Clayman, 2013), or the associations between interactional practices and variables exogenous to interaction, such as demographic variables pertaining to participants (Stivers and Majid, 2007), or the clinical or other outcomes of interactions (Heritage et al., 2007).

Quantification is a possible avenue also in ethnography and in interview research. In ethnography, coding and counting can be used to show the extent of the phenomenon observed, or to test hypotheses (Gobo, 2008). Simple calculations can also be used in qualitative interview studies. For example, Dutton et al. (2001; discussed in Silverman, 2015) compared manager's accounts on successful and unsuccessful 'issue selling episodes', i.e. interactions where they tried to influence the organizational decisions. By comparing the frequencies of the kinds of moves or efforts that were mentioned in the interviewee accounts on successful vs. unsuccessful episodes, the authors could validate their interpretations regarding the managers' contextual knowledge about issue selling.

CHAPTER SUMMARY

The main procedures of validation of the researcher's analytic claims in all conversation analytic research include the analysis of the next speaker's interpretation of the preceding action (next turn proof procedure), and deviant case analysis. Validation also involves the anchoring in data of the claims concerning the relevance of an institutional or psychological context of interaction, comparisons within and between institutional settings, issues of generalizability of the results of case studies, as well as use of quantitative techniques. None of these procedures is unique to conversation analysis: they, or variants of them, are used also in ethnographic studies and interview-based studies. Deviant case analysis has its origins in ethnographic research, and the procedures employed in CA are quite similar to those employed there. Issues related to generalization of research results certainly arise in all kinds of qualitative research. The use of quantitative techniques alongside the qualitative work is an option available in various strands of qualitative research. At a more general level, the considerations of validity in CA are indeed similar to those in any other kind of qualitative research: all serious qualitative research involves meticulous testing and consideration of the credibility of analytic claims.

FUTURE PROSPECTS

Regarding techniques of validation, the use of quantitative techniques will become more frequent, as well as the comparisons within and between institutions. Case study design will prevail especially in video-based analysis of complex working environments (see Heath in this volume).

Study questions

1.   What does 'validity' mean?
2.   Why might there be different techniques of validation in different qualitative approaches?
3.   What procedures of validation do conversation analysis and ethnography share?

Recommended reading

Seale, C. (1999) *The Quality of Qualitative Research*. London: Sage.
A thorough account of issues of validity and reliability in qualitative studies.

Sidnell, J. (2013) 'Basic conversation analytic methods', in J. Sidnell and T. Stivers (eds), *The Handbook of Conversation Analysis*. Oxford: Wiley-Blackwell, pp. 77–100.
Describes the process and principles of interpretation and argumentation in conversation analysis.

Silverman, D. (2015) *Interpreting Qualitative Data: Methods for Analysing Talk, Text and Interaction* (5th edn). London: Sage. Chapter 4.
Gives a compact account of validity and reliability in different schools of qualitative research.

Recommended online resources

Ethnomethodology and conversation analysis newsletter 'EM/CA wiki':
http://emcawiki.net/Main_Page

The International Institute for Ethnomethodology and Conversation Analysis:
www.iiemca.org/

International Society for Conversation Analysis:
http://isca.clubexpress.com

References

Arminen, I. (2005) *Institutional Interaction: Studies of Talk at Work*. Aldershot: Ashgate.

Bryman, A. (2004) *Social Research Methods* (2nd edn). Oxford: Oxford University Press.

Clayman, S. E. and Maynard, D. W. (1994) 'Ethnomethodology and conversation analysis', in P. ten Have and G. Psathas (eds), *Situated Order: Studies in the Social Organization of Talk and Embodied Activities*. Washington, DC: University Press of America, pp. 1–30.

Drew, P. and Heritage, J. (1992) 'Introduction: analyzing talk at work', in P. Drew and J. Heritage (eds), *Talk at Work: Interaction in Institutional Settings*. Cambridge: Cambridge University Press. pp. 3–65.

Dutton, J. E., Ashford, S. J., O'Neill, R. M. and Lawrence, K. A. (2001) 'Moves that matter: issue selling and organizational change', *Academy of Management Journal*, 2001 (4): 716–36.

Enfield, N., Dingemanse, M., Baranova, J., Blythe, J., Brown, P., Dirksmeyer, T., Drew, P., Floyd, S., Gipper, S., Gísladóttir, R., Hoymann, G., Kendrick, K. H., Levinson, S. C., Magyari, L., Manrique, E., Rossi, G., San Roque, L. and Torreira, F. (2012) 'Huh? What? – a first survey in 21 languages', in M. Hayasthi, G. Raymond and J. Sidnell (eds), *Conversational Repair and Human Understanding*. Cambridge: Cambridge University Press, pp. 343–80.

Glaser, B. G. and Strauss, A. L. (1967) *The Discovery of Grounded Theory: Strategies for Qualitative Research*. Chicago, IL: Aldine.

Gobo, G. (2008). *Doing Ethnography*. London: Sage.

Goodwin, C. (1995) 'Co-constructing meaning in conversations with an aphasic man', *Research on Language and Social Interaction*, 28 (3): 233–60.

Goodwin, C. (2003a) 'The body in action', in J. Coupland and R. Gwyn (eds), *Discourse, the Body, and Identity*. Houndsmill and New York: Palgrave/Macmillan, pp. 19–42.

Goodwin, C. (2003b) 'Pointing as situated practice', in S. Kita (ed.), *Pointing: Where Language, Culture and Cognition Meet*. Mahwah, NJ: Lawrence Erlbaum, pp. 217–42.

Goodwin, C. (2007) 'Participation, stance and affect in the organization of activities', *Discourse & Society*, 18 (1): 53–73.

Goodwin, C. (2014) 'The intelligibility of gesture within a framework of co-operative action', in M. Seyfeddinipur and M. Gullberg (eds), *From Gesture in Conversation to Visible Action as Utterance: Essays in Honor of Adam Kendon*. Amsterdam: Benjamins, pp. 199–216.

Guba, E. G. and Lincoln, Y. S. (2005) 'Paradigmatic controversies, contradictions, and emerging confluences', in N. K. Denzin and Y. S. Lincoln (eds), *The Sage Handbook of Qualitative Research* (3rd edn). Thousand Oaks, CA: Sage, pp. 191–216.

Hammersley, M. (1992) *What's Wrong with Ethnography: Methodological Explorations*. London: Routledge.

Hammersley, M. and Atkinson, P. (2007) *Ethnography: Principles in Practice* (3rd edn). London: Routledge.

Heritage, J. (1988) 'Explanations as accounts: a conversation analytic perspective', in C. Antaki (ed.), *Analysing Everyday Explanation: A Case Book of Methods*. London: Sage, pp. 127–44.

Heritage, J. (1995) 'Conversation analysis: methodological aspects', in U. M. Quatshoff (ed.), *Aspects of Oral Communication*. Berlin: Walter de Gruyter. pp. 391–418.

Heritage, J. and Clayman, S. (2010) *Talk in Action Interactions, Identities, and Institutions*. Chichester: Wiley-Blackwell.

Heritage, J. and Clayman, S. (2013) 'The changing tenor of questioning over time: tracking a question form across US presidential news conferences, 1953–2000', *Journalism Practice*, 7 (4): 481–501.

Heritage, J. and Maynard, D. (eds) (2006) *Communication in Medical Care: Interaction Between Primarycare Physicians and Patients*. Cambridge: Cambridge University Press.

Heritage, J., Robinson, J., Elliott, M., Beckett, M. and Wilkes, M. (2007) 'Reducing patients' unmet concerns in primary care: the difference one word can make', *Journal of General Internal Medicine*, 22 (10): 1429–33.

Heritage, J. and Watson, R. (1979) 'Formulation as conversational objects', in G. Psathas (ed.), *Everyday Language: Studies in Ethnomethodology*. New York: Irvington, pp. 123–62.

Holstein, J. A. and Gubrium, J. F. (1995) *The Active Interview*. Newbury Park, CA: Sage.

Kirk, J. and Miller, M. L. (1986) *Reliability and Validity in Qualitative Research*. London: Sage.

Peräkylä, A. (1989) 'Appealing to the experience of the patient in the care of the dying', *Sociology of Health and Illness*, 11 (2): 117–34.

Peräkylä, A. (1995) *AIDS Counselling: Institutional Interaction and Clinical Practice*. Cambridge: Cambridge University Press.

Pomerantz, A. (1980) 'Telling my side: "limited access" as a "fishing device"', *Sociological Inquiry*, 50: 186–98.

Rapley, T. (2004) 'Interviews', in C. Seale, D. Silverman, J. Gubrium and G. Gobo (eds), *Qualitative Research Practice*. London: Sage, pp. 15–33.

Ruusuvuori J. and Voutilainen L. (2010) 'Comparing interaction in different types of health care encounter', in M. Haakana, M. Laakso and J. Lindström (eds), *Talk in Interaction: Comparative Dimensions*. Helsinki: Finnish Literature Society, pp. 206–30.

Sacks, H., Schegloff, E. A. and Jefferson, G. (1974) 'A simplest systematics for the organization of turn-taking for conversation', *Language*, 50: 696–735.

Schegloff, E. A. (1968) 'Sequencing in conversational openings', *American Anthropologist*, 70: 1075–95.

Schegloff, E. A. (1987) 'Between macro and micro: contexts and other connections', in J. Alexander, B. Giesen, R. Munch and N. Smelser (eds), *The Micro–Macro Link*. Berkeley and Los Angeles: University of California Press, pp. 207–34.

Schegloff, E. A. (1991) 'Reflections on talk and social structure', in D. Boden and D. H. Zimmerman (eds), *Talk and Social Structure: Studies in Ethnomethodology and Conversation Analysi*s. Cambridge: Polity, pp. 44–70.

Silverman, D. (2010) *Doing Qualitative Research* (3rd edn). London: Sage.

Silverman, D. (2013) *A Very Short, Fairly Interesting, Reasonably Cheap Book about Qualitative Research* (2nd edn). London: Sage.

Silverman, D. (2015) *Interpreting Qualitative Data: Methods for Analysing Talk, Text and Interaction* (5th edn). London: Sage.

Stivers, T. (2015) 'Coding social interaction: a heretical approach in conversation analysis?', *Research on Language and Social Interaction*, 48 (1): 1–19.

Stivers, T., Enfield, N. J., Brown, P., Englert, C., Hayashi, M., Heinemann, T., Hoymann, G., Rossano, F., de Ruiter, J. P., Yoon, K.-E. and Levinson, S. C. (2009) 'Universals and cultural variation in turn-taking in conversation', *Proceedings of the National Academy of Sciences of the United States of America*, 106 (26): 10587–92.

Stivers, T. and Majid, A. (2007) 'Questioning children: interactional evidence of implicit bias in medical interviews', *Social Psychology Quarterly*, 70 (4): 424–41.

Voutilainen, L., Peräkylä, A. and Ruusuvuori, J. (2010) 'Recognition and interpretation: responding to emotional experience in psychotherapy', *Research on Language and Social Interaction*, 44 (1): 85–107.

Weiste, E. and Peräkylä, A. (2013) 'A comparative conversation analytic study of formulations in psychoanalysis and cognitive psychotherapy', *Research on Language and Social Interaction*, 46 (4): 299–321.

TWENTY SIX

Writing Qualitative Research: Practice, Genre, and Audience

Amir Marvasti

About this chapter

Focusing on writing as both a process and the outcome of qualitative research, this chapter offers novice researchers a framework for assessing their work. In particular, writing qualitative research is presented as a three-facet enterprise that involves practice, genre and audiences. Practice refers to the ongoing, fluid dimensions as well as the basic skills or craft of writing. The discussion of genre deals with the various stylistic choices available to social scientists, particularly to qualitative researchers. Finally, audience selection addresses the strategic choices authors have to consider as they try to publish their work and make it accessible to various audiences. The three constituent elements of writing are applied to the case of online publishing. It is argued that a 'perfect paper' is one that strikes a balance between these three dimensions regardless of the particular medium of representation.

Keywords

writing, genre, audience, researcher roles, peer review, online publishing

INTRODUCTION

The field of qualitative research is rich with analytical options, representational styles and publication outlets. Questions about how much data, how to analyse the data, how to write it all down and what to include in the final manuscript become progressively more difficult as one learns about the variety of qualitative paradigms. Many of these issues have been addressed elsewhere in this book and are beyond the focus of this chapter. Here I focus on writing qualitative research.

I think it is possible to locate points of common interest across the diverse landscape of qualitative research. For example, while there are many styles of interviewing (structured, open ended, ethnographic, etc.), we would all agree that, at a minimum, an interview requires questions and respondents. Similarly, while representational choices may seem infinite, the practice and logic of writing itself is not entirely without boundaries. In this chapter, I borrow from the insights of reader response (Iser, 1978), genre (Freedman and Medway, 1994), and writing process (Park, 2005) theories to offer a vision of 'good writing' in qualitative research based on three interrelated themes: (1) the ongoing practice and craft of writing, (2) writing genres, and (3) external evaluation of writing. I end the chapter by applying these three concepts to the case of online publishing.

In keeping with my own emphasis on audience expectations and purposeful writing, I should begin by noting that the intended audience for this chapter is novice qualitative researchers and graduate students. Therefore, my examples and citations were chosen to serve the interests of this specific group. I should also note that although I have avoided reifying a strict qualitative–quantitative distinction, the material presented here does vary in its relevance to conventional methodological camps. In particular, the discussion of genre goes furthest in addressing the specific needs of qualitative researchers whereas other sections may be useful to novice writers, in general.

THE CRAFT AND PRACTICE OF WRITING

Writing is typically thought of as a unique, creative form of self-expression, and that myth may be a large part of the problem. Even in its most self-consciously creative manifestations, writing is a craft that involves endless practice and the mastery of techniques. Creativity and technical know-how are not mutually exclusive dimensions of writing; great ideas, no matter how profound, cannot be expressed without the basic skills of writing. Fortunately, for social scientists interested in the technical conventions of writing, there is no shortage of instructional books. For qualitative researchers, in particular, there is a growing market of how-to texts that include at least a chapter on writing theses and dissertations, with some entirely devoted to the basics of writing qualitative research (see, for example, Wolcott, 2009).

However, technical know-how develops in tandem with actual, ongoing practice. Specifically, writing could be envisioned and taught as a fluid process of organizing and articulating loosely connected observations. In this context, the researcher/writer (embedded in time and place and in interaction with others) has to constantly re-evaluate initial ideas. Let me illustrate this point using an example from my own research. At the beginning of my ethnography of a homeless shelter, I wanted to organize my dissertation around the notion that the homeless are 'the postmodern heroes of our time'. The idea was inspired by interviews with homeless men who had said things like 'It sucks to be a citizen' or 'I feel sorry for the poor bastards who're enslaved by their work. I'm free to sleep where I want and go where I want'. I interpreted such statements as clear rejections of the modern, capitalist premise of productive labour. Chatting in coffee shops with fellow students, I championed the cause of the homeless by quoting their anti-work statements, translating my field notes into political slogans. However, when it came to writing the dissertation, aside from a few broad declarations like 'It appears that some homeless people reject conventional notions of work', I had little else to write on the topic.

Fortunately, as my writing and analysis progressed, with the help of my peers and dissertation director, I focused on another idea that seemed more in synch with the empirical evidence and my sociological training. In particular, my data seemed to show that the very notion of 'the homeless' was problematic. The men and women on the streets and in shelters viewed their circumstances from many different standpoints. Some thought of their situation as a type of personal freedom whereas others said they were 'miserable'. This way of analysing and writing about my fieldwork became the foundation of my research and was further polished as the writing went on.

This example is illustrative of 'writing process theory', or the idea that writing is an on-going activity that embodies the author, his or her audience(s), and a larger cultural and institutional context. According to this approach:

> Writing always has a bidirectional movement, both inner and outer, and contains both personal and social elements. The act of writing has an inner movement, which results in nothing less than the construction of self, as well as an outer movement, because the writing as text exists as a cultural artifact that is meant for others to read. (Park, 2005: 142)

In this chapter I follow this paradigm by emphasizing that one practices writing over time, in association with others (e.g. mentors, peers and reviewers) and in specific settings. Qualitative research texts, in particular, are not written overnight and 'independently', but they emerge in a context and in collaboration with others, much like any other social practice. Thinking about writing as an ongoing practice in this way balances the emphasis on technical know-how (e.g. spelling and grammar) with the fluid and varied contexts, which, as shown in the next two sections, further expand and limit the author's choices.

Key points

- Become familiar with the basics of writing research papers through how-to books.
- Be both flexible and self-critical about your writing.
- Learn to focus your writing by curbing and directing your inspirations.
- Remember that writing is a skill that can be improved with practice over time.

ORGANIZATION AND GENRE

There are many ways to write social science research. As Howard Becker puts it:

> Scholarly writers have to ... express an argument clearly enough that readers can follow the reasoning and accept the conclusions. They make this job harder than it need be when they think there is only One Right Way to do it ... They simplify their work, on the other hand, when they recognize that there are many effective ways to say something and that their job is only to choose one and execute it so that readers will know what they are doing. (1986: 43)

In this section, I consider the range of writing choices, alluded to by Becker, in two ways. I begin by discussing how a research manuscript can be organized in terms of varying emphasis on method, theory and findings. I then turn to variations in genre as another way of mapping the landscape of writing qualitative research.

Organization

The most widely used mode of writing a research paper, whether qualitative or quantitative, organizes the text into four elements: *introduction*, *methods*, *analysis* and *conclusion*. Think of each section as answering a different set of questions, as outlined below.

> *Introduction:* What is the topic of your paper? Have there been previous studies on this topic?
>
> *Methods:* What was the size of the sample for the study? How and where was the sample collected? How is the data to be analysed? Or 'Why should the readers believe the study?' (James Holstein, personal correspondence, 20 July 2015).
>
> *Analysis:* What is the empirical evidence for this study? What social processes are revealed by the data? How does it support the researcher's claims about a particular sociological topic or process?
>
> *Conclusion:* How is the study of interest to ordinary people or policy-makers? In what ways could it be improved or expanded (i.e. the proverbial call for 'further research')?

Most other styles of writing research papers are variations of this standard theme. What changes is the degree of emphasis placed on each of the four components (i.e. introduction, methods, analysis and conclusion).

Genre and the alternative ways of writing

In the social sciences, there is a growing awareness of the rhetorical dimensions of writing and representing facts, particularly among ethnographic researchers (see, for example, Alasuutari, 1995; Gubrium and Holstein, 1997). Perhaps the work that is mostly widely cited in this context is James Clifford and George Marcus's *Writing Culture: The Poetics and Politics of Ethnography* (1986), which states in its introduction: 'the making of ethnography is artisanal, tied to the worldly work of writing' (1986: 6). John Van Maanen's *Tales of the Field* is another important analysis of the stylistic features of qualitative writing. Through secondary analysis, Van Maanen (1988) identifies different genres of ethnographic texts (e.g. realist, confessional and impressionist). He argues that rather than describing a single social reality seen from multiple perspectives, variations in writing construct realities of their own. Similarly, in *Writing Strategies: Reaching Diverse Audiences*, Laurel Richardson emphasizes the significance of 'frame, tone, narrative stance, metaphors, and audience' (1990: 49) and reminds qualitative researchers that:

> they can write up the same material in different ways. The material is malleable … How we shape the material depends upon how far along we are in our research, and who we want to read it, for what reasons. The same material can be shaped into a realist article, a postmodernist one, or some admixture of the two. (1990: 49)

While some have dismissed the textual shift as a passing fad, others (see, for example, Ellis and Bochner, 1996; Richardson 1997; Richardson and St. Pierre, 2005) have embraced it as the new logic of social science and have proposed alternative writing strategies that go beyond the traditional organization of a research paper outlined earlier. In the remainder of this section, I offer a brief survey of these alternative writing practices by focusing on the following three genres: (1) writing with pictures, (2) writing the story, and (3) writing the author. I end the section with a critical assessment of these genres.

Writing with pictures

While the visual has always had a place in the social sciences, its use and analysis have fluctuated over the history of various disciplines (see Emmison in this volume). For example, more than a hundred years ago, the *American Journal of Sociology*, the flagship journal of the discipline, published a number of articles that used photos as data (see Stasz, 1979). According to Elizabeth Chaplin (1994: 201), the first manuscript of this type was F. Blackmar's *The Smoky Pilgrims* published in 1897. The study depicted poverty in rural Kansas using posed photographs. Yet, this earlier interest in the visual waned as the written word accompanied with numerical analysis became the dominant mode of analysis. In a way, statistical figures, charts and tables became the visual centrepieces of professional sociological publications.

In the broad context of writing in the social sciences, one can think of the visual in two ways: (1) writing about pictures and (2) writing with pictures. Writing about pictures involves the analysis of existing images, often for the purpose of cultural critique. For example, in his landmark sociological study *Gender Advertisements* (1979), Erving Goffman analysed how gender roles and expectations are reflected in magazine ads. Using over 500 photos, he critiqued the taken-for-granted nature of gender relations in Western societies. Specifically, Goffman showed that magazine ads in the late 1970s depicted men in active roles (doing things like helping patients or playing in sports) and the women as mere spectators, passively watching the men's activities.

By contrast, writing with pictures involves creating first-hand visual material for the purpose of illustrating, complementing or even transcending the written text. In the social sciences, anthropology is a leader of the use of pictorial and filmic materials for illustrative purposes. For example, Gregory Bateson and Margaret Mead's *Balinese Character: A Photographic Analysis* (1942) juxtaposes text and the visual in a complementary way so that one would enhance the meaning of the other.

As Douglas Harper (2005) notes, emerging computer technologies have facilitated the use of visual material in social research. Particularly, multimedia texts can now easily combine pictures and written material in the same context. Additionally, multimedia texts can be posted on internet websites accessible to users virtually from any location in the world. A key feature of internet-posted multimedia text (e.g. 'hypertext') is that the material does not have to be read or viewed linearly like a bound book. So-called 'hot links' or 'hyperlinks' allow the readers to jump from one passage to another. For example, while reading a hypertext ethnography, the reader can click on pictures from the field, see an image of a respondent, and click on his name to see excerpts from an interview with that respondent.

Writing the story

Some qualitative researchers approach writing as a type of storytelling. In this genre of writing, the researchers narrate the characters and the 'scenes' in which the data was collected. Additionally, the author's reflections and the roles he or she assumed in the study can become part of the story. For example, Carolyn Ellis and Arthur Bochner's (1992) personal experience with abortion is told using the following familiar narrative headings:

The Story

Scene 1: The Pregnancy Test and the Test of Pregnancy

Scene 2: Making the Decision

Scene 3: Dealing with the Decision

Scene 4: The Preabortion Procedure

Scene 5: The Abortion

Epilogue

(adapted from Ellis and Bochner, 1992: 79-101)

The decision to write in a narrative style tends to hinge on the data and data collection method. For example, ethnographic methods are better suited for storied writing as the research procedures readily lend themselves to the mainstays of storytelling (e.g. characters and settings). Conceivably, any ethnography can be written as the story of someone entering a site and reporting their experiences. For example, William Whyte's classic ethnography *Street Corner Society* (1949) can be reduced to the story of a white man living with Italian immigrants in the inner city.

Writing the author

Writing the author into the field notes, or autoethnography, is another genre of representing qualitative research. A thorough survey of this type of writing can be found in the introductory chapter of Deborah Reed-Danahay's *Auto/Ethnography* (1997), which presents autoethnographic writing as essentially a self-reflexive account of social experience. Accordingly, autoethnographic texts explicitly aim to include the author and embed his or her experiences in a broader social context, or as Reed-Danahay puts it: autoethnography is a 'self-narrative that places the self within a social context' (1997: 9).

However, how this is achieved and for what purposes is the subject of considerable debate and contention. In Reed-Danahay's chapter there seems to be a continuum of representational strategies for autoethnographers. On the one hand, there is the minimally self-referential text that simply adds the author's own subjective voice to the many voices and observations from the field. On the other hand, there is 'pure', 'native' experience represented with little or no intervention from academic sources.

In the field of autoethnography, Carol Ronai is exemplary because of her ability to combine the best analytical innovations of this genre with superior aesthetic sensibility. Her story, 'My mother is mentally retarded' (Ronai, 1996), is a classic example of what she calls a 'multi-layered account'. In this particular form of autoethnography, the author's experiential account is juxtaposed with academic and popular discourses. The descriptions are layered and deliberately disjointed using a set of asterisks.

Words of caution on genre and the aesthetics of writing

The status of 'alternative' does not exempt these texts from critical assessment. For example, some critics point out that some representational experiments simply result in bad writing. For example, in her review of Ellis's *The Ethnographic I: A Methodological Novel about Autoethnography*, Pamela Moro writes:

> The real question is, perhaps, whether Ellis is a good enough writer to pull off this heartfelt endeavor. Writing good fiction is hard; writing compelling dialogue is extremely hard. I am not entirely sure if what Ellis has written is a 'novel' ... It is as though she has taken the shell of a novel and poured into it the material of textbook. (2006: 266)

Others question whether alternative writing forms are effective in achieving their emancipatory goals. For example, Paul Atkinson and Sara Delamont caution that some writing experimentations inadvertently (1) re-centre the social scientist as the all-knowing author and (2) promote an individualized rather than an interactive view of social experience:

> we warn against the wholesale acceptance of aesthetic criteria in the reconstruction of social life. In many contexts, there is a danger of collapsing the various forms of social action into one aesthetic mode – that is, implicitly revalorizing the authorial voice of the social scientist – and of transforming socially shared and culturally shaped phenomena into the subject matter of an undifferentiated but esoteric literary genre. (2005: 823)

Similarly, Norm Denzin stresses that an interest in the aesthetics of writing should not exclude its political content and implications: 'Ethics, aesthetics, political praxis, and epistemology are joined' (2000: 258).

On the other hand, some wonder, what exactly is being represented. For example, Jay Gubrium warns against 'self-referential writing' that 'eclipses' or loses sight of the subject matter of research. In his words:

> I know that the subject matter can be the experience of the researcher, but what I'm concerned with here is the emphasis this can take in the final written product. If you do aim to feature your place in a project in writing, in particular yourself and your relation with others, then write about how that relates to broader issues of personal and interpersonal experience in the circumstances. (2009)

David Silverman (2007: 119) advances this critique by suggesting that alternative writing and related genres are trendy tropes that lack substance:

* Contemporary qualitative research has been infiltrated by two elements: the experience game of Romanticism and ... the pastiche of Post-Modernism.
* Both these elements derive from an unthinking adoption of certain features of contemporary culture. [Silverman suggests that following this path is dangerous and reminds us of the perverted versions of science in the twentieth century when Soviet science and Nazi science flourished.]
* Under these auspices, qualitative research can amount to 'bullshit' conceived, not in its pejorative and vernacular sense, but as overly kitsch, overly-jargonized and over-theorized.

Key points

* Research manuscripts generally include the following: introduction, methods, results and conclusion.
* Different writing genres allow you to orient readers towards particular features of your research project, such as the author, the visual dimensions or the story.
* An aesthetic orientation towards writing is not a licence to ignore the analytics and politics of representation.

AUDIENCES: PUBLICATION OUTLETS AND REVIEWERS

Research texts are not intended for researchers' own consumption but for external audiences. To illustrate this point, let's begin with a form of writing that is largely intended for self-use (i.e. personal diaries). What goes into such documents is traditionally considered self-directed and private, so much so that the unauthorized reading of them is considered taboo in Western cultures. In a diary the words can appear in any order and have many meanings, and no external authority is expected to proofread it or demand clarification.

Of course, the 'private diary' as an ideal type is fast changing (web-based forums such as Twitter and text-messaging now make it possible for the personal to become public, and diaries of famous people have always been of interest to the public and publishers). Nonetheless, if we were to think of writing on a continuum of audiences, private diaries would fall on the extreme where the audience is essentially reduced to the self. On the other hand, we would find research reports that are explicitly tailored to the needs of an external audience, which could vary from small committees overseeing a dissertation to editors and reviewers evaluating a manuscript for publication. The next section offers some how-to, as well as analytical, guidance for navigating the world of audiences for qualitative research with an emphasis on journal publications.

Strategic choices

The two common choices for publishing social science research are books and journal articles. As you consider the two choices, it is important to keep in mind that book and journal publications are given different weights in the tenure process, and for one's professional career in general. For example, in 'Books vs. articles: two ways of publishing sociology' Alan Wolf (1990) shows that the balance between book and article production fluctuates considerably across academic institutions, at least in the United States. As Wolf notes, that pluralism in scholarly publications is useful and necessary; books and articles allow for different treatments of topics under analysis and they allow sociologists to reach different audiences. However, it is unlikely that a qualitative researcher will pass the tenure requirements at major academic institutions without journal publications. With that in mind, the remainder of this section considers the basic requirements of journal publishing.

Responding to editors' and reviewers' comments

Most journal articles are rejected or returned with a request for substantial revision from the reviewers whose comments are returned to the author along with a letter from the editor. If the editor's letter contains the phrase 'revise-and-resubmit', especially when preceded by 'strongly encourage you to', that is very good news. In revising the paper, authors are advised to give special attention to the reviewers' comments that were echoed by the editor. In other words, one may ignore some of the reviewers' comments, but it would be a huge mistake to set aside the editor's suggestions.

After submitting several papers, it is possible to see a pattern among the reviewers. Some are undoubtedly more helpful than others. It is important to keep in mind that reviewers provide their services to editors free of charge, often spending hours reading and commenting on a paper. Indeed, it might be empowering for writers to think of their reviewers as people with diverse motivations and interests. To this end, here is a loose categorization scheme of reviewers to help further contextualize the writing and publication process for novices:

- *Editor impressers*: their comments tend to be directed more at the journal editor than the authors. These reviewers write detailed (sometimes irrelevant) reviews with the hope of being invited to contribute their own manuscript to the journal.
- *Ego bruisers*: these reviewers seem to receive pleasure from attacking the competition in their field. They have elevated their insulting and backhanded comments to an art form (one can almost hear them giggling at their own handywork in between the lines).
- *Ego bruised*: these reviewers are primarily concerned with the critique of their own work or that someone neglected to cite them. Their comments sometimes include direct references to their own articles.
- *Shoddy reviewers*: these folks (usually well-established scholars in their field) do not really read the papers they are asked to comment on. Their reviews contain comments so brief and perfunctory as if to suggest to the editor, 'Don't bother me with this kind of submission again'.
- *Helpful reviewers*: these are the ideal reviewers. They actually read the papers carefully and provide specific suggestions for improving them.

James Holstein offers two additional types of reviewers: 1) 'generous reviewer – willing to let everyone have his/her say, and let the reader decide' and 2) 'the gatekeeper or the guardian of the discipline, who doesn't want anything to enter the canon unless it is first rate' (personal correspondence, 20 July 2015).

Research roles and audiences

Envisioning reviewers as audiences with different roles and expectations of their own puts the qualitative researcher in the position of an actor, and the writing itself becomes a type of interaction, initially with an audience of reviewers and editors and eventually the readership of the journal as a whole. The next logical question then is: what role should the researcher assume in the course of this interaction? For example, should researchers allow personal or political values to enter their writing as a method of persuasion? As in the case of genre, and perhaps as an extension of it, here too qualitative researchers have many choices.

David Silverman (2006: 351–9) suggests that researchers can assume one of three roles in this context. First, there is the position of the 'scholar'. In this capacity, the researcher is interested in science for the sake of science. The second research role is that of a 'state counsellor'. Here, the goal is to work closely with interested policy-makers. In this role, sociologists might be viewed as social engineers who assist state bureaucrats in a joint effort to create a 'better' society. Finally, there is the 'partisan' role, where the sociologist sides with a particular group. In Silverman's words, 'the partisan seeks to provide the theoretical and factual resources for a political struggle aimed at transforming the assumptions through which both political and administrative games are played' (2006: 265). The partisan role is best captured in an often quoted statement by Howard Becker in which he asks sociologists, 'Whose side are we on?' (1967: 239). Table 26.1 summarizes Silverman's three research roles.

Along with reflecting on their specific research roles, writers should also be responsive to the demands of their audience(s). As Anselm Strauss and Juliet Corbin put it, researchers should ask, 'What style can I use to reach each audience [i.e. academics, practitioners and laymen]?' and be aware that 'the style and shape of presentation should be sensitive to and reflect the targeted audience(s)' (1998: 256). Indeed, it is the absence of such awareness that characterizes novice technical writers. In her review of *Interacting with Audiences* (Blakeslee, 2001), Janet Zepernick offers this useful list of audience-related problems that plague novice writers:

- insufficient understanding of the audience's expectations,
- inability to predict the kinds of claims the audience will be prepared to accept, and
- unwillingness (or inability) to subordinate aspects of the work that the writer personally finds most interesting or most difficult to the interests and informational requirements of the audience. (2003: 245)

Table 26.1 Silverman's three research roles

Role	Politics	Commitment
Scholar	Liberal	Knowledge for knowledge's sake, protected by scholar's conscience
State counsellor	Bureaucratic	Social engineering or enlightenment for policy-makers
Partisan	Leftwing Rightwing	Knowledge to support both a political theory and political practice

Source: adapted from Silverman (2006: 353)

Having considered the central themes of writing in general, let us now turn our attention to their implications one of the latest innovations in the social sciences, online publishing.

ONLINE PUBLISHING

The web has become an exciting venue for writing and publishing academic research. Indeed, the web collapses the distance between writing and publishing so that what is typed on a computer keyboard is instantly posted online and thus available to a global audience. The material published online could range from blogs, to open access journals to traditional books and articles digitalized for the purpose of consumption and dissemination on the web. Astonishingly, as of 2010 Google Books (an online service) had digitally scanned about 10 million books (Jackson, 2010). Exceedingly recognized as a legitimate way of disseminating scholarly research, online or e-publishing presents both familiar and new challenges. Below I discuss some of these issues in the context of this chapter's three central themes: practice, genre and audience.

Practice

A unique feature of e-publishing is that it allows for readers/users to participate in the writing process. In this sense, online writing practices can be communal to the degree that they encourage an ongoing conversation between readers and authors. The online encyclopedia Wikipedia is often referenced as an example of this type cooperative authorship. As E. Johanna Hartelius puts it:

> The notion of dialogic expertise reflects Wikipedians' [Wikipedia contributors'] assumption that knowledge production is a constantly evolving social negotiation. Truth on Wikipedia rises from multiple interactions between utterances within the discourse community ... For Wikipedia, knowledge is a process of collaborative invention rather than the property of a single person. (2010: 514)

Relatedly, writing and publishing online allows greater flexibility for editing and revising the text. In the words of Thomas Thurston, with online writing, 'The paint never dries. The medium invites one to tinker endlessly' (1999: 251).

Genre

In terms of representational practices, online publishing offers the widest range of possibilities. Photographs, videos and audio-clips can all be included in the context of online publishing (see Vannini, 2012). For example, a researcher can post videotape images of an interview online along with the transcripts and analysis, thus allowing readers to both observe and read the interview. However, a word of caution is in order. Multimedia content should not be used as 'frivolous bells and whistles ... for some pointlessly futuristic style of publishing' (Cooper, 2013: 332).

Audience

Theoretically, the audience for an online publication is anyone in the world with access to the internet. In reality, access to online publications (scholarly ones in particular) is constrained by many factors. For example, certain databases are proprietary and are only available to registered users. At the same time, it is likely that 'the websites you are browsing automatically suggest articles for you based on a sophisticated content taxonomy, your user profile, past browsing behaviour, and the browsing behaviour of similar users' (Cooper, 2013: 329). Other intervening factors include government censorship and lack of internet access in impoverished communities and nations. So users' access to material posted online is less immediate and direct than it would seem at first glance.

One way to fulfil the internet's promise of universal access is through 'open access' publishing, which ideally would provide free access to any reader from anywhere in the world. In the United Kingdom, for example, it is hoped that under a government initiative, 'research papers that describe work paid for by the British taxpayer will be free online for universities, companies and individuals to use for any purpose, wherever they are in the world' (Sample, 2012). However, making scientific knowledge accessible on the scale of the World Wide Web creates many complications and questions. In the context of scholarly publications, the most important issues are 'the ways online sources of knowledge are judged, and the question of who deserves to be called authority' (Leitch, 2014: 1). Consider, for example, the case of *PloS One*, a prominent open access publisher of research manuscripts in the natural sciences, which operates on the principle of 'publish first, judge later' (Giles, 2007: 9). Specifically, after an initial review, which could be limited to a single editor, a manuscript is published if it is 'methodologically sound'. Subsequently:

> Visitors to the *PLoS One* website can, for example, attach comments to specific parts of a paper and rate the paper as a whole. Data from those systems, as well as download and citation statistics, will then allow *PLoS One*'s editors to identify and promote the papers that researchers are talking about. 'We're trying to make a journal where papers are not the end point, they are the start of a discussion', says *PLoS One* managing editor Chris Surridge, based in Cambridge, UK. (Giles, 2007: 9)

While this innovative approach is not without its merits (e.g. a faster review process and ongoing discussion about the quality of a published paper), the fact that it appears to circumvent the rigour of the traditional peer-review raises eyebrows among some academics. Indeed, for some, academic publications that are exclusively available online are deemed less prestigious and less credible, especially if a journal has a high acceptance rate and requires a sizeable fee from its authors. Therefore, it is prudent to carefully examine an online journal's review process before submitting one's research. At a minimum, it is important to recognize that a journal's 'review process reflects a view of what research should look like. It encourages some kinds of work and discourages others' (Davis, 2014: 199).

That said, it may be that the effect of the 'digital revolution' on writing, publishing and reading is less dramatic than some have speculated. For example, Liam Cooper reminds us of the stability in the format and the criteria for judging the quality scholarly publications:

> Peer review, articles and books, and citation are still very much the currency of academic life, and that is overwhelmingly likely to remain the case for the foreseeable future ... the success of an article is always going to be dependent on whether or not it is well articulated, original, and rigorous. It is hard to imagine a future for the academy where this isn't the case. (2013: 333-4)

Similarly, much has been made of the 'hypertext' capacity of online publications, which means that instead of following the text in a linear fashion, readers can move from one part of the text to another by clicking on a word or an image. Yet, as Thomas Thurston notes:

> We have had more practice with hypertext than many of us might care to let on. With one finger anchored in the index, another in the footnotes, a pen or pencil close at hand to mark a passage or record a note, our use of the book belies whatever formal linearity it may claim. (1999: 252)

Key points

- Online publishing is a growing trend.
- Online publishing could encourage collaboration with and feedback from readers.
- Multimedia content is especially suited for online publishing.
- Online publications have the potential of reaching a global audience.
- Online publications challenge the conventional views of authorship and peer-review.

CHAPTER SUMMARY AND FUTURE PROSPECTS

It can be argued that the ideal type of qualitative writing is a text that incorporates the following three elements into a well-balanced report:

- *Practice and craft of writing:* conveying research ideas coherently.
- *Organization and genre:* structuring the manuscript and presenting findings in line with one's chosen writing conventions and style.
- *Audience expectations and researcher role:* being aware of and accountable to the demands of intended publication outlet and its consumers.

Attending to these criteria simultaneously amounts to understanding writing as rhetorical practice aimed at persuading a particular audience. In this context, writing is an ongoing and socially embedded practice (Van Maanen, 2006: 14). More than just a means to convey ideas, writing becomes what Pertti Alasuutari calls a 'literary process' that:

> resembles riding a bicycle. Not in that once you have learned it you'll master it, but because riding a bike is based on consecutive repairments of balance. The staggerings or whole detours of the text have to be repaired over and over again so that they do not lead the story line in the wrong direction; and the rambling of the first draft cannot be seen in the final product. (1995: 178)

At the same time, it is worth considering that the 'perfect paper' is in some ways a fiction. In the words of Howard Becker: 'No report in any medium or genre, following no-matter-how-strict rule, will solve all problems, answer all questions, or avoid all potential troubles' (2007: 131). Thus, the best advice for writing good social science may be to keep writing and always be prepared to make compromises and adapt your text to suit the needs of your audience.

There are, of course, numerous theoretical issues in the context of writing that demand further attention and point to the very philosophy of science. For example, we can ask: to what extent should researchers try to change audience expectations by experimenting with new genres and, in a sense, reinvent their field? This question relates to the larger issue of writing as an instrument of disciplinary change. One answer would be that the progress of science is one gradual accumulation of knowledge. Or as Karl Popper (1963) would put it, science follows a process of 'conjectures and refutations' whereby new knowledge tests and replaces old knowledge. In this context, writing is viewed as a medium for conveying facts. By contrast, if we adopt Thomas Kuhn's notion of 'paradigm shifts' (1996), writing social science becomes more politicized. Kuhn departs from Popperian philosophy by approaching scientific knowledge as a human activity that is conditioned by particular socio-historical forces. Therefore, to the extent that alternative writing challenges mainstream tropes, it should be encouraged as the fuel for change, or scientific progress. Whether the landscape of writing practices and expectations should be expanded or curbed will likely remain a matter of contention in the field of qualitative research.

Study questions

1. What are the different ways in which a qualitative research manuscript could be organized?
2. What are the different genres of writing qualitative research?
3. What are some criticisms against so-called alternative methods of writing qualitative research?
4. What is the relationship between researcher role and audience expectations?
5. What are the unique features of online publishing?

Recommended reading

Becker, H. (1981) *Exploring Society Photographically*. Evanston, IL: Mary and Leigh Block Gallery, Northwestern University Press.
A groundbreaking and readable book on the use of photography in social research.

Billig. M. (2013) *Learn to Write Badly: How to Succeed in the Social Sciences*. New York: Cambridge University Press.
Suggests that academic institutions inadvertently teach and reward poor writing skills.

Vannini, P. (ed.) (2012) *Popularizing Research: Engaging New Media, Genre, and Audiences*. New York: Peter Lang.
Lists the many ways in which one can bring social science research to larger audiences.

Van Maanen, J. (2011) *Tales of the Field: On Writing Ethnography* (2nd edn). Chicago and London: University of Chicago Press.
Examines ethnographic genres and shows how writing is both analytical and aesthetic.

Rose, G. (2012) *Visual Methodologies* (3rd edn). London: Sage.
Offers a complete survey of the field of visual analysis.

Behar, R. and Gordon, D. (1995) *Women Writing Culture*. Berkeley, CA: University of California Press.
An important contribution to alternative ways of writing ethnographies, particularly from a feminist perspective.

Wolcott, H. F. (2009) *Writing Up Qualitative Research* (3rd edn). Thousand Oaks, CA: Sage.
Details the process of writing a qualitative research manuscript from start to finish.

Recommended online resources

The companion website for Phillip Vannini's Popularizing Research:
www.popularizingresearch.net

Durham University's 'Writing Across Boundaries':
www.dur.ac.uk/writingacrossboundaries/

Durham University's 'Writing on Writing':
www.dur.ac.uk/writingacrossboundaries/writingonwriting/

The University of Queensland's PhD Writing Tips:
www.uq.edu.au/student-services/phdwriting/

References

Alasuutari, P. (1995) *Researching Culture: Qualitative Method and Cultural Studies*. London: Sage.
Atkinson, P. and Delamont, S. (2005) 'Analytic perspectives', in N. Denzin and Y. S. Lincoln (eds), *The Handbook of Qualitative Research* (3rd edn). Thousand Oaks, CA: Sage, pp. 821–40.
Bateson, G. and Mead, M. (1942) *The Balinese Character: A Photographic Analysis*. New York: New York Academy of Sciences.
Becker, H. (1967) 'Whose side are we on?', *Social Problems*, 14: 239–47.
Becker, H. (1986) *Writing for Social Scientists: How to Start and Finish Your Thesis, Book, or Article*. Chicago: University of Chicago Press.
Becker, H. (2007) *Telling about Society*. Chicago, IL: University of Chicago Press.
Blakeslee, A. M. (2001) *Interacting with Audiences: Social Influences on the Production of Scientific Writing*. Mahwah, NJ: Lawrence Erlbaum.
Chaplin, E. (1994) *Sociology and Visual Representation*. London: Routledge.
Clifford, J. and Marcus, G. (eds) (1986) *Writing Culture: The Poetics and Politics of Ethnography*. Berkeley, CA: University of California Press.
Cooper, L. (2013) 'Trends in online academic publishing', *Metaphilosophy*, 44 (3): 327–34. doi:10.1111/meta.12025.

Davis, G. F. (2014) 'Editorial essay: why do we still have journals?', *Administrative Science Quarterly*, 59 (2): 193–201. doi:10.1177/0001839214534186.

Denzin, N. (2000) 'Aesthetics and the practices of qualitative inquiry', *Qualitative Inquiry* 6: 256–65.

Ellis, C. and Bochner, A. (1992) 'Telling and performing personal stories: the constraints of choice in abortion', in C. Ellis and A. Bochner (eds), *Investigating Subjectivity*. Newbury Park, CA: Sage, pp. 79–101.

Ellis, C. and Bochner, A. P. (1996) *Composing Ethnography: Alternative Forms of Qualitative Writing*. Walnut Creek, California: AltaMira Press.

Freedman, A, and Medway, P. (eds) (1994) *Genre and the New Rhetoric*. London: Taylor & Francis.

Giles, J. (2007) 'Open-access journal will publish first, judge later', *Nature*, 445: 9.

Goffman, E. (1979) *Gender Advertisements*. Cambridge, MA: Harvard University Press.

Gubrium, J. (2009) 'Curbing self-referential writing', Durham University. www.dur.ac.uk/writingacrossboundaries/writingonwriting/jaygubrium/ (accessed 10 December 2015).

Gubrium, J. and Holstein, J. (1997) *The New Language of Qualitative Method*. New York: Oxford University Press.

Harper, D. (2005) 'What's new visually?', in N. Denzin and Y. S. Lincoln (eds), *The Handbook of Qualitative Research* (3rd edn). Thousand Oaks, CA: Sage, pp. 176–98.

Hartelius, E. J. (2010) 'Wikipedia and the emergence of dialogic expertise', *Southern Communication Journal*, 75 (5): 505–26. doi:10.1080/10417940903377169.

Iser, W. (1978). *The Implied Reader: Patterns of Communication in Prose Fiction from Bunyan to Beckett*. Baltimore, MD: Johns Hopkins University Press

Jackson, J. (2010) 'Google: 129 million different books have been published', *PC World*, 6 August. www.pcworld.com/article/202803/google_129_million_different_books_have_been_published.html (accessed 10 December 2015).

Kuhn, T. (1996) *The Structure of Scientific Revolutions*. Chicago, IL: University of Chicago Press.

Leitch, T. M. (2014). *Wikipedia U: Knowledge, Authority, and Liberal Education in the Digital Age*. Baltimore, MD: Johns Hopkins University Press.

Moro, P. (2006) 'It takes a darn good writer: a review of ethnographic I', *Symbolic Interaction*, 29 (2): 265–9.

Park, J. (2005). *Writing at the Edge: Narrative and Writing Process Theory*. New York: Peter Lang.

Popper, K. (1963) *Conjectures and Refutations: The Growth of Scientific Knowledge*. London: Routledge.

Ronai, C. (1996) 'My mother is mentally retarded', in C. Ellis and A. Bochner (eds), *Composing Ethnography: Alternative Forms of Qualitative Writing*. Walnut Creek, CA: Altamira Press, pp. 109–31.

Reed-Danahay, D. (1997) *Auto/Ethnography: Rewriting the Self and the Social*. Oxford: Berg.

Richardson, L. (1990) *Writing Strategies: Reaching Diverse Audiences*. Newbury Park, CA: Sage.

Richardson, L. (1997) *Fields of Play: Constructing an Academic Life*. New Brunswick, NJ: Rutgers University Press.

Richardson, L. and St. Pierre, E. A. (2005) 'Writing: a method of inquiry', in N. Denzin and Y. S. Lincoln (eds), *The Handbook of Qualitative Research* (3rd edn). Thousand Oaks, CA: Sage, pp. 959–78.

Sample, I. (2012) 'Free access to British scientific research within two years', *The Guardian*, 15 July. www.theguardian.com/science/2012/jul/15/free-access-british-scientific-research (accessed 10 December 2015).

Silverman, D. (2006) *Interpreting Qualitative Data* (3rd edn). London: Sage.

Silverman, D. (2007) *A Very Short, Fairly Interesting and Reasonably Cheap Book about Qualitative Research*. London: Sage.

Stasz, C. (1979) 'The early history of visual sociology', in J. Wagner (ed.) *Images of Information: Still Photography in the Social Sciences*. Beverly Hills, CA: Sage, pp. 119–36.

Strauss, A. and Corbin, J. (1998) *Basics of Qualitative Research: Techniques and Procedures for Developing Grounded Theory* (2nd edn). Thousand Oaks, CA: Sage.

Thurston, T. (1999) 'New questions for new media: scholarly writing and online publishing', *American Quarterly*, 51 (2): 250–3. doi:10.1353/aq.1999.0031.

Van Maanen, J. (1988) *Tales of the Field*. Chicago, IL: University of Chicago Press.

Van Maanen, J. (2006) 'Ethnography then and now', *Qualitative Research in Organizations and Management*, 1 (1): 13–21.

Vannini, P. (ed.) (2012) *Popularizing Research: Engaging New Media, Genre, and Audiences*. New York: Peter Lang.

Whyte, W. F. (1949) *Street Corner Society*. Chicago, IL: University of Chicago Press.

Wolcott, H. F. (2009) *Writing Up Qualitative Research* (3rd edn). Thousand Oaks, CA: Sage.

Wolf, A. (1990) 'Books vs. articles: two ways of publishing sociology', *Sociological Forum*, 5 (3): 477–89.

Zepernick, J. S. (2003) 'Review of the book *Interacting with Audiences: Social Influences on the Production of Scientific Writing* by A. Blakeslee, 2001', *Journal of Business and Technical Communication*, 17 (2): 243–7.

APPENDIX
Transcription Conventions

[	C2: quite a [while Mo: [yea	Left brackets indicate the point at which a current speaker's talk is overlapped by another's talk.
=	W: that I'm aware of = C: =Yes. Would you confirm that?	Equal signs, one at the end of a line and one at the beginning, indicate no gap between the two lines.
(-4)	Yes (.2) yeah	Numbers in parentheses indicate elapsed time in silence in tenths of a second.
(.)	to get (.) treatment	A dot in parentheses indicates a tiny gap probably no more than one-tenth of a second.
_____	What's *up?*	Underscoring indicates some form of stress, via pitch and/or amplitude.
::	O:*kay?*	Colons indicate prolongation of the immediately prior sound. The length of the row of colons indicates the length of the prolongation.
WORD	I've got ENOUGH TO WORRY ABOUT	Capitals, except at the beginnings of lines, indicate especially loud sounds relative to the surrounding talk.
.hhhh	I feel that (.2) .hhh	A row of h's prefixed by a dot indicates an inbreath; without a dot, an outbreath. The length of the row of h's indicates the length of the in- or outbreath.

( )	future risks and ( ) and life ( )	Empty parentheses indicate the transcriber's inability to hear what was said.
(word)	Would you see (there) anything positive	Parenthesized words are possible hearings.
(( ))	confirm that ((continues))	Double parentheses contain author's descriptions rather than transcriptions.
.,?	What do you think?	Indicate speaker's intonation (. = falling intonation; = flat or slightly rising intonation)
>	> What do you think?	Indicates data later discussed

Author Index

Subject Index